THE FRANKLIN REPORT®

The Insider's Guide to Home Services

www.franklinreport.com

NEW YORK CITY

FIFTH EDITION

Allgood Press

New York

AN ALLGOOD PRESS PUBLICATION

EDITOR IN CHIEF
Elizabeth Franklin

MAIN CONTRIBUTORS
Emily Max Bodine, Liza Bulos, Beverly Hevron, Fred Nicolaus

TECHNOLOGY TEAM
Michael Brennan, Charles "Skip" Schloss

GRAPHIC DESIGNER
Jason Paul Guzman

PROJECT EDITOR
Joy Goodwin

COPY EDITOR
Charles Kotsonis

COVER CONCEPT AND ILLUSTRATION
J.C. Suares, Chesley McLaren

INTERIOR DESIGN ON FRONT COVER
Eric Cohler Inc.

SPECIAL THANKS TO
Pete Mueller, Jeffrey Sechrest, Josie Domo

Allgood Press
New York

Table of Contents

THE FRANKLIN REPORT®
The Insider's Guide to Home Services

INTRODUCTION

Welcome to the fifth edition of *The Franklin Report* (New York City), the regional edition of a national series of guides. *The Franklin Report* is a comprehensive survey of the city's top home service providers, based on client and peer reviews. Some of these companies and individuals have been profiled in national magazines, and others are well-kept secrets or rising stars, but all reportedly excel in their fields. Since the firms are the "best of class," the quality ratings are consistently high. Remember, a "3" rating in quality is still "very strong," and for most people is all that is necessary for most jobs.

In this book, you will find factual information and opinions about service providers from architects and interior designers to electricians and millworkers. We invite you to use this guide and participate in our project. To submit reports on providers you have used, please visit our website at www.franklinreport.com or use the postcard or reference forms provided at the end of this book. We are committed to keeping all reviews absolutely anonymous.

Our mission is to simplify the task of choosing a home service provider by codifying the "word-of-mouth" approach. We do the homework for you with detailed fact checking, research, and extensive interviews of both service providers and their clients. We then give you and the community a chance to contribute to this ongoing dialogue. We hope you will join us.

The evaluations and reports on the service providers in *The Franklin Report* are based on factual information from the providers themselves, publicly available information, commentary from industry experts, and thousands of in-depth customer interviews and surveys submitted through our website and by e-mail, fax, telephone, and in person. The Summary, Specific Comments, and Ratings that make up each entry are based on these sources and do not reflect the opinion of *The Franklin Report*. You can always visit www.franklinreport.com for the latest information on these service providers.

We have gone to great lengths to ensure that our information originates from verifiable and reliable sources, and have conducted follow-up interviews when any questions arose. In addition, it is our policy to disregard any unsubstantiated information or surveys that differ markedly from the consensus view.

Each service category opens with a brief, informative introduction to the specific home service industry. These summaries provide facts and valuable insights on how to choose a service provider, including realistic expectations and cost considerations. Armed with this information, you'll be well prepared to speak to service providers listed in *The Franklin Report* and make your best choice. In addition, the following section, "What You Should Know About Hiring a Service Provider," covers general issues that apply to all the home service categories, from interior design to air conditioning.

Each listing contains the following components:

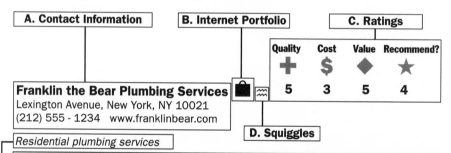

	Quality	Cost	Value	Recommend?
	+	$	◆	★
Franklin the Bear Plumbing Services	5	3	5	4

A. Contact Information

B. Internet Portfolio

C. Ratings

Franklin the Bear Plumbing Services
Lexington Avenue, New York, NY 10021
(212) 555 - 1234 www.franklinbear.com

D. Squiggles

Residential plumbing services

References roar with praise for Franklin the Bear. We hear that principal Franklin and his band of service "cubs" ably attend to the plumbing needs at some of New York's top tree houses. Available 24 hours for emergencies, clients tell us that Franklin and his crew actually work better at night, especially in the summer months. One note of caution, however—getting service in the dead of winter seems to be quite difficult, and clients note that Franklin's cheerfulness fades a bit as the days grow shorter.

Franklin the Bear has been a family-owned and -operated business for generations. The firm undertakes full plumbing renovations as well as maintenance work.

"Frankly, my dear, the Bear is the best!" "Great service. Just try to avoid January."

E. Services and Specialties

F. Summary and Specific Comments

A. Contact Information: Service providers are listed alphabetically by the first word in the name of the company (Alexander Zed Designs comes before Elizabeth Anderson Designs). Some vendors provide multiple home services and are listed in more than one category.

B. Internet Portfolio: The Vendors with portfolios are listed at the front of their respective sections. Visit our website at www.franklinreport.com to see a portfolio of online images of this company's work and a description of their philosophy and latest projects.

C. Ratings: Providers are rated in four columns—Quality, Cost, Value, and Recommend?—on a 5-point scale, with 5 as the highest rating. **Keep in mind that because we only include the firms that received the most positive reviews, a 3 in Quality is still an excellent score: the ratings differentiate the top providers.**

Note also that while a high rating is generally better, a higher Cost rating means that the company is more expensive. Reading the introductory section of each home service category will help you understand the specific pricing structure in each profession. Value is determined by the relationship between Quality and Cost. Recommend? indicates whether the customer would use the provider again or recommend the firm to a friend.

Quality
    5 – Highest Imaginable
    4 – Outstanding
    3 – Strong
    2 – Moderate
    1 – Adequate

Cost
    5 – Over the Top
    4 – Expensive
    3 – Reasonable
    2 – Moderate
    1 – Inexpensive

Value
    5 – Extraordinary Value,
        Worth Every Penny
    4 – Good Value
    3 – Mediocre Value
    2 – Poor Value
    1 – Horrible Value

Recommend?
    5 – My First and Only Choice
    4 – On My Short List, Would
        Recommend to a Friend
    3 – Very Satisfied, Might Hire Again
    2 – Have Reservations
    1 – Not Pleased, Would Not Hire Again

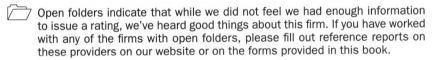 Open folders indicate that while we did not feel we had enough information to issue a rating, we've heard good things about this firm. If you have worked with any of the firms with open folders, please fill out reference reports on these providers on our website or on the forms provided in this book.

D. Squiggles: The graphic of two squiggly lines indicates a significant number of mixed reviews about a provider.

E. Services and Specialties: This describes the main services the company provides.

F. Summary and Specific Comments: *The Franklin Report* editors distilled information from all sources to write a summary profiling each service provider that reflects the consensus view. In select categories, where appropriate, we use several abbreviations to indicate certain special recognitions the firm has received:

> AD 100: listed in *Architectural Digest's* top 100
> HB Top Designers: listed in *House Beautiful's* annual compendium
> ID Hall of Fame: Interior Design's Hall of Fame Award
> AIA Fellow: The American Institute of Architects Award
> KB: Participation in the Kips Bay Decorator Show House

A number of schools are mentioned throughout this section, with the indicated abbreviations: Fashion Institute of Technology (FIT), New York School of Interior Design (NYSID), Parsons School of Design (Parsons), and Rhode Island School of Design (RISD).

In Specific Comments, clients, peers, and industry experts describe the process of working with the service provider—and the end results—in their own words.

What You Should Know About
Hiring a Service Provider

Hiring a service provider to work in your home is not a task to be undertaken lightly. In addition to issues of quality, cost, and scheduling, keep in mind that these professionals (and their employees) may become an integral, albeit temporary, part of your life. The following eight-step process will help you make the best choice.

1. Determine Your Needs

First, you need to think about the nature and scope of your project. The service provider that may be perfect for a full-scale renovation may be unresponsive and unnecessarily costly for repair or maintenance work. Are you looking for simple built-in bookcases or an integrated, elaborate library? Next, weigh your priorities. Is it crucial that the project is done by the holidays? Or is it more important to get a particular style? Is budget a driving factor? Evaluating your requirements will make it easier to decide upon a vendor, because you will know where you can compromise and where you can't. Your requirements may evolve as you learn more about what is in the marketplace, but it's a good idea not to stray too far from your original intent.

2. Identify Possible Candidates

To find the best professional for the job, start by asking for recommendations from friends, colleagues, neighbors, your building superintendent, and related service providers you trust. *The Franklin Report* will help you evaluate those candidates and identify others by offering insight into their competitive strengths and weaknesses.

3. Check Public Records

To make most efficient use of your time, first do quick background checks of the candidates to eliminate those with questionable records. For each specific category, city or state licenses may be required or professional associations may offer additional information (check *The Franklin Report* overviews for specifics on each category). If you are investigating *The Franklin Report* service providers, you will be informed of past client satisfaction in this book and on our regularly updated website, www.franklinreport.com.

4. Interview Service Providers

While it may not be necessary to conduct a face-to-face interview with a provider who is only going to do a one- or two-day project, phone interviews are recommended before they show up. For larger projects, it is wise to meet with the potential providers to learn all you possibly can about process, expectations, quality, and price and to judge your potential compatibility. Don't be shy. Personality and style "fit" are extremely important for long-term projects that will involve design decisions and complicated ongoing dialogues, but are less critical when seeking a professional steam cleaner.

5

The following are general interview questions that will help you make the most of discussions with potential vendors. More specific questions that apply to each specific profession may be found in the category overviews.

- ✧ How long have you been in the business?

- ✧ What are your areas of expertise?

- ✧ Have you recently completed similar jobs? Can I speak with these clients for a reference?

- ✧ Who will be my primary day-to-day contact? What percentage of time will they spend on-site?

- ✧ What sections of the job will be done by your employees and what sections will be subcontracted?

- ✧ Are you licensed, registered, and insured? What about the subcontractors? (It is crucial to verify that all workers are covered by workman's compensation—otherwise, you may be liable for any job-site injuries.)

- ✧ How long will the project take to complete? Any concerns or qualifications?

- ✧ Do you offer warranties? Do you provide written contracts? Will the contract have an arbitration clause?

- ✧ Are you a member of any national or local professional associations? (While not essential, this can show dedication to the profession.)

- ✧ How will we communicate with each other? Will we have regular meetings?

Other things to consider:

- ✧ How long it took them to return your initial phone call.

- ✧ Whether or not the firm's principal attended the initial meeting.

- ✧ How receptive they were to your ideas.

- ✧ How thoughtful and flexible they were in pricing, budgeting, and scheduling.

- ✧ Personality/fit and how interested they were in your project.

Licenses, registrations, insurance, bonding, and permits are key parts of the equation, but are category dependent (again, check the overviews). Any suspicious activity on this front, like a contractor who asks you to get the permits yourself or can't seem to find his proof of insurance, is a red-flag event. Similarly, anyone who refuses to give you references, asks for all the money up front, or who tells you what a great deal you can have if you sign today should be eliminated from your list.

5. SPEAK WITH PAST CLIENTS

In discussions with references provided by the potential candidates, be aware that these clients are probably their greatest fans. For a more balanced view, review their *Franklin Report* write-up.

Suggested questions for client references:

- ✧ What was the scope of your project?

- ✧ Were you happy with both the process and quality of the result?

- ✧ How involved were you in the process?

- ✧ Were they responsive to your concerns?

- ✧ Were work crews timely and courteous, and did they leave the job site clean?
- ✧ Did they stick to schedule and budget?
- ✧ Were they worth the cost?
- ✧ Were they communicative and professional about any issues or changes?
- ✧ Were they available for any necessary follow-up?
- ✧ Would you use this firm again?

6. ASK ABOUT COST

Each service category works differently in terms of pricing structure. Projects may be priced on a flat fee, estimated or actual time, a percentage over materials, a percent of the total job (if other contractors are involved), or a host of other variations. What appears difficult and costly to some providers may be routine for others. Many providers will be responsive to working with you on price (and it is always worth a try). However, under strong economic conditions, the service provider may only be pushed so far—they may actually be interviewing you during your call. For more specific details and recommendations, see the pricing discussions in each of *The Franklin Report* category overviews.

7. EVALUATE THE BIDS AND MAKE YOUR CHOICE

Narrow your list and ask for at least three bids for substantial jobs. Describe your project clearly and thoroughly, including any timing constraints. Once received, do your best to compare the bids on an "apples to apples" basis. Ask each provider to break down their bids so you can see whether some include more services or higher quality specifications (processes and materials) than others. Don't be afraid to keep asking questions until you fully understand the differences between the bids.

Cheaper is not always better, as a bid might be lower because the workers are less skilled or the materials are of lower quality. Compare samples where possible. If speed is important, you may be willing to pay more for the person who can start next week instead of six months from now and who shows more reliability on timing issues.

8. NEGOTIATE A CONTRACT

Just as with pricing, you will need to understand what the acceptable business practices are within each industry and negotiate a contract, if appropriate. Most service professionals have standard contracts that they prefer.

SMALLER JOBS: For one-time-only situations that you will be supervising (rug cleaning, window washing, etc.), a full-blown contract approved by your lawyer is generally not necessary. Just ask for a written estimate after you thoroughly discuss the job with the provider.

Larger jobs: For larger projects, such as a general contracting job that will cost thousands of dollars and will involve many people and lots of materials, a detailed contract is essential. Don't be afraid to ask about anything that is unclear to you. This is all part of the communication process, and you don't want to be working with a service provider who intimidates you into accepting anything that you don't understand.

The contract should clearly spell out, in plain English, the following:

⋄ The scope of the project in specific, sequential stages.

⋄ A detailed list of all required building materials, including quality specifications. They should meet minimum code standards, unless otherwise specified.

⋄ Completion schedule. Don't be too harsh here, since much may be contingent upon building conditions or supply deliveries. Some, but very few, providers are open to a bonus/penalty system in meeting specific timing deadlines.

⋄ A payment schedule.

⋄ Permit issues and responsibilities if applicable.

⋄ A description of how any scope changes ("change orders") will be processed and priced.

⋄ The specific tasks and accountability of the service provider, noting exactly what they will and will not do.

Once the contract is written, you may want an attorney to review and identify any potential issues. While most homeowners do not take this step, it could save you from costly and frustrating complications further down the road.

9. Overseeing the Job

No matter how professional your team of service providers may be, they need your input and direction to satisfactorily complete the job. Be specific as to who will supervise on-site and who will be the overall project manager (responsible for the interaction between service providers and, ultimately, the dreaded punch lists). This task will fall to you unless you assign it away.

On larger projects, generally the architect (usually within their standard fee contract) or the interior designer (usually for an additional fee) will fulfill the project manager role. You should be available and encourage periodic meetings to ensure that there are no surprises in design, timing, or budget. Whether or not you have a project manager, stay on top of the process (but do not get in the way), as this will be your home long after the dust settles and these professionals move on to the next project.

The *Franklin Report* website—a virtual companion to this reference book—is updated regularly with new vendor commentaries and other helpful material about home repairs, maintenance, and renovations, at www.franklinreport.com. With expert, accessible information guiding you through the process and dedicated professionals on the job, every stage of your home project will move smoothly toward completion. Knowledge is power, regardless of whether you're engaging a plumber for a contained upgrade or a general contractor for a new custom home. *The Franklin Report* is your companion in this process, with current, insightful home service information.

Hiring an Air Conditioning & Heating Service Provider

Known in the trades as Heating, Ventilation, and Air Conditioning (HVAC), this home service industry keeps your climate controlled and your family comfortable. HVAC professionals are also often responsible for custom sheet-metal work, such as kitchen hoods and copper window dressing. An HVAC system means central air, central heat, and central convenience, and when it's expertly installed and maintained, you can pretend it's May all year.

An HVAC Primer

All air conditioning (AC) systems operate on the same principle: a fan sucks in your home's warm air, sends it across coils that contain a refrigerant chemical, then blows the cooled air into the room. Central AC operates with two principle components: a condensing unit and an evaporator coil. The condenser pressurizes the refrigerant to cool it. Heat is released in the process, so the condenser must be located outside the home or with an opening to the outside. The cooled refrigerant is then pushed to the evaporator coil, where it cools and dehumidifies the warm air collected from your plenum (the dead space above the ceiling). Finally, this cool air is directed via ductwork back into the rooms. If that doesn't sound science fiction-y enough, newer (more expensive) systems use ultraviolet light to clean dirty coils, and complicated chemical processes to recycle some of the energy lost in the process.

Heating is supplied in one of three ways: forced air, hydronic, or steam. In the forced-air system, air is heated by your furnace or a heat pump, and a blower pushes it through the heat source, then into your home. While a furnace heats the air by burning natural gas, oil, wood, or coal, a heat pump functions like an air conditioner with the refrigerant cycle reversed. Chill is captured by the condenser and warm air is produced with the evaporator coil. The air is further heated through electric heating coils at the blower. In the hydronic system, water is heated via gas or electricity in a boiler and distributed to radiators. The steam system works similarly to the hydronic with steam, rather than water, distributed directly to radiators.

How Much Do You Need?

Like any technical industry, the HVAC world is chock full of confusing jargon and complicated acronyms. Don't get sucked in, just understand three simple things and you can make it through an HVAC conversation without your eyes glazing over.

1. **The BTU** (British Thermal Unit) is used to measure the capacities of furnaces, boilers, heat pumps, and air conditioners. Essentially, the amount of BTUs a system can process is how much air it can either heat or cool. Air conditioning systems are often measured in "tons," with one ton equaling 12,000 BTUs. The standard for an 800 square foot space is 30,000 BTUs of heat and one ton of air-conditioning. Obviously, the bigger the space, the more capacity you will need.

2. **The SEER,** or Seasonal Energy Efficiency Rating, measures the relationship between space and the energy needed to properly condition its climate. Equipment with higher SEERs will condition more space with less capacity. The higher the SEER, the higher the quality (and

cost) of the equipment and the lower your energy bills. The minimum SEER in New York is thirteen, though premier systems can go as high as eighteen.

3. **The CFM** (Cubic Feet per Minute) is the measurement of airflow through your ductwork. Essentially, it's how quickly your system can properly condition a space. Ducts are a significant aspect of HVAC system efficiency. Obviously, you want to have as direct a path as possible between the heat/cool source and the space it's meant to condition. If the ductwork is too small, the distance from the source too far, or if there are too many bends, the airflow will suffer. Designers specify the amount of CFMs necessary for a system to be efficient. If this target isn't met, the efficiency of your system is compromised because your equipment has to work harder than it should for a given space.

On Cost and Contracts

As in any other trade, you'll be charged for labor, materials, and a 10 to 20% markup for overhead, profit, and tax. Demand a flat fee for equipment and installation of new systems. Make sure the estimate specifies any other associated work—electrical, plumbing, plaster—that may be necessary for the installation. All makes and models of equipment should be spelled out on the bid proposal. It's okay to sign off on the bid proposal to execute the work, but it should refer to drawings (best generated by an engineer as opposed to a sketch on the back of a napkin) and they should be attached. Clean up, transportation, commencement and completion dates, payment schedule, change-order procedure, licensing, and insurance information should all be included in the contract—if not on the bid proposal. The technician should be responsible for the cost and time of obtaining permits. If your HVAC professional is fishing for a service agreement to cover the gaps in the warranty, see if you can get him to discount his price.

On Service

There are a lot of variables in HVAC, so warranties count. One year for parts and labor is typical. You should get your mechanical contractor to do a checkup once a year. Many offer early-bird spring maintenance specials before the busy AC season of summer begins, when pinning down a date with a technician is about as easy as hailing a cab in a downpour. Travel or truck fees are often charged with the diagnostic, with average hourly rates in the city running from $100 to $150. A higher rate usually means that a team will be coming, so make sure that your job justifies multiple technicians. Also keep in mind that given insurance, parking fines, and gas prices, it's expensive for an HVAC company to come to your home, so minimum charges are standard.

Treat HVAC like oral hygiene—you wouldn't neglect to brush your teeth between check-ups, and you shouldn't neglect your filters between visits from the

HVAC guy. Change them once a month in the summer—dirty filters will degrade the system's efficiency. It's easy to do—just get a lesson before the installer leaves. Also know where the gauges and valves are and learn how to read them. And try to maintain a good relationship with your mechanical man after the job. You don't want to have to pay someone else to become familiar with your custom-designed, intricate home system.

WHAT SHOULD I LOOK FOR IN AN HVAC PROFESSIONAL?

Your HVAC service provider is essentially putting the lungs into your house, and you don't pick your surgeon based on a nudge and a wink. Talk to general contractors and ask who they recommend. Know that HVAC invariably involves plumbing and electrical work. You want to know whether the person you hire can handle the work necessary to make the system function, or if you'll have to bring in other trades to assist. If there is going to be work in and around your existing space, find out how clean and careful he is.

Choose the service provider and system best suited to your project. For renovations in tight spaces like condos or historic bungalows, where ceiling height is precious, high-pressure air-conditioning systems that utilize small-diameter ducts permit retrofitting with little disruption to the surrounding structure. Large townhouses often demand computerized multiple-zoning systems, which allow for regulating different temperatures in different parts of the house. When renovating around steam, many HVAC professionals will recommend switching to hydronic. For the green-minded, ozone-friendly refrigerant, while a little more expensive, should be an option given by every high-end mechanical pro. Your research into a good HVAC person will be more effective if you learn a few things about how these systems work.

CREDENTIALS, PLEASE

HVAC is a complicated field. With all the inter-trade coordination, mechanical-speak, and math involved, your mechanical contractor should be backed up with the required licensing and insurance. This includes coverage for general liability, workman's comp, and property damage. Manufacturers and distributors are a great source for recommending mechanical contractors, and often distinguish the best with awards. The EPA requires anyone working with refrigerant to be licensed. For more information, check out the Air Conditioning Contractors of America website at www.acca.org.

QUESTIONS YOUR HVAC CONTRACTOR WILL ASK

✧ Where is the interior unit going to go? Large utility room? A closet?

✧ Do you have permission to place a condenser outside? From the co-op? The city?

✧ Is there enough ceiling height to add ductwork?

✧ Where do you want the controls? How many zones?

AIR CONDITIONING & HEATING

💼 FIRMS WITH ONLINE PORTFOLIOS* 💼

Cool Air Inc. 💼
348 East 76th Street, New York, NY 10021
(212) 744 - 4224 www.coolairnyc.com

	Quality	Cost	Value	Recommend?
Cool Air Inc.	4	3.5	4	3.5

Window and thru-wall HVAC sales, installation, service, and storage

With a straightforward name, over 70 years in the biz, and a solid staff of 25, Cool Air is well equipped to make summers in Manhattan more bearable. The firm provides sales, installation, service, and cleaning of window and thru-wall air-conditioning units. Recently they've been focusing more attention on duct-less systems and small central units for high-end homes.

We hear Cool Air tries to be forthright about how long it will take to make a service call. The technicians will make service calls year round, and Cool Air offers winter storage and spring cleaning specials. Customers also appreciate the reasonable diagnostic rate.

"They do the thru-wall stuff the bigger guys won't touch." *"A reliable service for the everyday HVAC stuff."*

FIRMS WITHOUT ONLINE PORTFOLIOS

Airtronics Air Conditioning
63 West 38th Street, New York, NY 10018
(212) 302 - 2020 airtronicscorp@aol.com

	Quality	Cost	Value	Recommend?
Airtronics Air Conditioning	4.5	4	4.5	4.5

Central and incremental HVAC design, installation, and service

Twenty-five years ago, a photographer came to Airtronics with a special request: He'd bought an old bank building and wanted to convert the vault into storage space for his slides. Airtronics designed that system and is still servicing it today. With a reputation founded on reliability and longevity, this good-value firm specializes in designing central air systems and incremental heating and cooling units. The company also furnishes whisper-quiet systems to recording studios and editing suites. References find the firm's staff of eight and its outside support team to be "thoroughly professional" and "inventive." Savvy architects, manufacturers and homeowners often call Airtronics to correct the errors made by other mechanical contractors.

We hear second-generation HVAC man Mike Novack not only designs Airtronics' installations himself—he also finds workable solutions to complex problems with older systems. Sources report that the work looks good, functions well, and stays within its engineering limits. Response time is said to be quick and the crews are attentive. The firm even has a special division to cut holes, patch, and paint. Warranties include one year parts and labor; the firm recommends additional preventative maintenance service contracts that cover labor.

"Reliable, knowledgeable, accessible. One of the best companies I have contracted." *"A very reliable and responsible company doing quality work."* *"They did what they said they would do, on time and for the cost quoted."*

*We invite you to visit www.franklinreport.com to view images of their work.

12

All Aire Conditioning Co. Inc.

4	4	4	4

41 East 29th Street, New York, NY 10016
(718) 991 - 0055

Central HVAC design, installation, and service; cogeneration

We hear this HVAC company gives every job its all, working with supers and general contractors to beat even the most humid summers. All Aire services existing central AC systems in Park Avenue penthouses, performs brownstone retrofits, and offers full design/build services. To maintain a premium level of quality, All Aire fabricates all its own custom sheet metal and piping in-house. Its technicians also stay on top of the latest technological wizardry, including a process called cogeneration, by which by-products of power generation are used to heat buildings, thus trimming utility costs. The company is familiar with duct-less and split systems and can service such high-pressure AC systems as Space Pak or Unico, but it will not work on window or thru-wall AC units.

All Aire boasts CAD engineering services and employs fifteen service vehicles on the road. To get a service technician to your door, a one-time charge is assessed that includes two hours of free labor. The firm's top-notch quality comes at prices that make All Aire a solid high-end value.

"Solid. Full of integrity. Safe. It's a great, great company." "Truly unique. We've worked with them for years." "I could go on and on about how great they were." "Very professional. Not all their mechanics are as good as [principal] Cory Glick, but if you've got him, you've got the best."

AMHAC

4	3.5	4.5	4

365 White Plains Road, Eastchester, NY 10709
(914) 337 - 5555   www.amhac.com

HVAC design, installation, and service

With a 75-person staff of design engineers, licensed electricians, field technicians, and an in-house team for sheet metal and piping, AMHAC is truly "full service." After more than 40 years of specializing in challenging high-end residential projects, we're told AMHAC has a roster of over 15,000 residential and commercial clients in Manhattan, the Bronx, and Fairfield and Westchester counties. Clients are impressed by the company's "professional, polite" staff, who are said to tackle the most complex installations—and the most mundane maintenance chores—with equal dedication. The firm works hard to keep its customer service top-notch, holding training seminars every other month to keep employees well-versed in the latest technology.

The firm's 30,000 square foot Eastchester facility hosts a showroom displaying heating and air-conditioning units as well as zoning controls, lighting controls, and more. AMHAC's sizable resources, which include a fleet of service vehicles, enable it to offer 24-hour heating and 48-hour AC response times. Response can be even quicker if you have an ongoing maintenance contract. AMHAC also offers Saturday office hours and a 24/7 phone service. All these services don't come cheap, but thanks to the firm's high quality, clients say AMHAC is still a good value.

"They perform when others can't or won't." "Excels in customer service." "They came through with flying colors." "Worth paying more for." "Good follow-up, but their planning could have been better." "Their proposal was the most professional." "The only contractor we felt was reliable, honest, and full-service."

	Quality +	Cost $	Value ◆	Recommend? ★

Amrus Mechanical Company Inc.

	Quality	Cost	Value	Recommend?
Amrus Mechanical Company Inc.	4.5	4	4.5	4.5

26-12 4th Street, Astoria, NY 11102
(718) 932 - 2444   amrus932@aol.com

Central HVAC design, installation, and service

Amrus principal Ken Ellert has been working in HVAC since the Beatles came to America. He and his twenty-person staff bring a formidable amount of experience to Manhattan's finer brownstones and lofts. Amrus offers design, installation, and service, collaborating with a second Ellert-owned company for sheet metal and plumbing. Amrus delivers the kind of quality its high-end Manhattan clients demand, especially on repair jobs.

Amrus works on all makes and models, from ductless climate control systems to pool dehumidification systems. We're told the company's "remarkable" employees strive to preserve the architectural integrity of the apartment.

Amrus also offers a wide option of preventive maintenance programs, each tailored to meet a client's specific needs. Though the company sometimes has trouble meeting demand during the summer rush, they triage their calls carefully to make sure the appropriate team is sent to each job. That means that Amrus typically sends two technicians rather than one, a strategy that is effective, if not cheap. Given the firm's overall mid-range costs and superior quality, clients stand by Amrus.

"Honest and capable." "Great follow-up." "Works well with architect to address field conditions." "Unable to find a whistling noise in my system." "Ken has worked for us for fourteen years." "Nice to do business with." "Always come quickly when called."

Arista

	Quality	Cost	Value	Recommend?
Arista	4	4.5	3.5	4

38-26 10th Street, Long Island City, NY 11101
(718) 937 - 1400   www.aristair.com

HVAC design, installation, and service

An HVAC company with an impressive pedigree, Arista has been in the business since 1949. Nowadays, the firm's focus is on residential service. Construction professionals often recommend the company, noting its knowledge of the complicated high-tech systems (like the Mitsubishi City Multi system) that are so prevalent in high-end residential work. In fact, the company has even designed a sound attenuation unit (with the aid of an acoustical engineer) to run as quiet as a breeze.

Clients tell us president Scott Berger and the rest of the staff are enjoyable to work with, though they wish the same mechanic would be sent to each job consistently. We're also told Arista's post-construction maintenance program is among the best in the city. There are some who feel that Arista's prices are at the top, but no one doubts that the quality is high.

"The best in the city, hands down." "They are so dedicated to service." "Great service, but a confusing bill." "Very helpful and informative. Will lay it out for you in plain language."

Blackstone HVAC

	Quality	Cost	Value	Recommend?
Blackstone HVAC	4	3.5	4.5	4

14 Chauncey Avenue, New Rochelle, NY 10801
(914) 235 - 0809   blackstonecompanies@msn.com

Custom HVAC design, installation, and service

We hear this small company is a rock-solid choice for heating and cooling installation and service. Established eight years ago, the majority of Blackstone's work is in Manhattan and Westchester County. Owner Jim Black will take on most mechanical systems, including air balancing, but tends to stick with high-end gear like geo-thermal systems. We're told Blackstone excels in design, coming up with innovative and conscientious solutions. As an added bonus, the company also works on pneumatic control systems.

Clients say Blackstone personnel do immaculate work, making sure installations run quietly and have fail-safe measures. If something does go wrong, past clients are serviced on a 24-hour emergency basis. The rates—standard for some services and high-end for others—are said to be justified in light of the extra effort put into every small detail. It's this reputation for excellence that can sometimes get Blackstone overbooked.

"Fabulous at solving problems and making things fit." "Don't wait until summer to reach him!"

Charles W. Beers Inc.   4.5   4   4.5   5

45-33 Davis Street, Long Island City, NY 11101
(718) 361 - 7322

Custom HVAC sales, design, and installation to the trade

In the late 1970s, Charles Beers designed and installed a state-of-the-art HVAC system for a wealthy Manhattan financier. Two weeks later he received a call. Everything was working fine, except the candles on the dining room table, which were burning at uneven speeds. Beers handled this HVAC emergency and, 30 years later, his son John carries on the tradition of fanatical attention to detail. Clients say the company knows how to deal with co-ops, building codes, and time restrictions, and is especially familiar with the exacting quality and customer service standards demanded by New York's high-end customers. Even the competition gives rave reviews to Beers' appreciation for aesthetics.

The firm's focus is design and installation, carried out by a small and experienced staff. While clients admit that long-term service isn't the company's strong point, they say that the system will be installed correctly to begin with, so you'll seldom need service. Beers is known for helping architects and interior designers realize their designs, using custom work to hide the guts of any HVAC installation and making the unsightly disappear into the architectural integrity of the home. Clients say that the very expensive price tag reflects the very significant quality of the workmanship.

"Head and shoulders above the rest." "Old-line guys. Their reputation is great. Maybe even too good to be true." "Probably the best." "They make the system vanish into the walls."

Comfort Air Conditioning and Heating   4.5   4.5   4   4.5

162 West Park Avenue, Long Beach, NY 11561
(516) 889 - 1540

Central HVAC design and installation to the trade

Comfort Air is on the shortlist of many of Manhattan's top residential contractors. In recent years, the company has nearly doubled its staff and has taken on significant projects in the Dakota, Trump Towers, and the Richard Meier buildings on Perry Street—as well as many townhouses, Comfort's original specialty.

Comfort Air usually works directly under architects and builders in a design/ build capacity, and existing homeowner clients can reap the rewards of the firm's conscientious service program. The company also boasts its own plumbers, and will do "innovative design" and control work. In fact, Comfort's technicians were recently certified to install and maintain the uber-advanced Mitsubishi City Multi system, which is capable of extreme levels of remote control, should you ever want to cool down your Park Avenue apartment from an internet cafe in Venice.

References say principal David Kliers, who started Comfort Air in 1989, is a "hands-on" manager who knows the job. He anticipates needs and resolves potential problems in advance—much more than many of his competitors, industry sources report. The caliber of Comfort's work is not for those on a tight budget, but for those clients who can afford it, contractors say, "What a difference!"

	Quality	Cost	Value	Recommend?
	✚	$	◆	★

"I've seen David correct engineers on very technical points." "He's more concerned about the client than the architect and the engineer combined." "As a GC, I can always get information from Kliers that I can't get from other mechanical subcontractors." "One of the most professional companies I've worked with."

Ely Cooling Corp.   3.5   3.5   4   4
459 Columbus Avenue, Suite 118, New York, NY 10024
(212) 534 - 6610
Central HVAC installation and service

After over 25 years of selling, installing, and servicing central air-conditioning systems for Manhattan residences and completing a broad array of commercial jobs, Ely Cooling has a loyal following. Founder Ely Franco still lends hands-on expertise to projects, which range from museum-type spaces to the most upscale of addresses.

Full-time emergency service is available for clients both old and new, and Ely has a large supply of parts for immediate service. Fees for a diagnostic service call are deducted from the final tab if the client goes with Ely for the job. Some report that the smaller repair jobs can feel rushed. However there is no charge for estimates on the installation of new equipment, and Ely provides solid maintenance contracts, especially on larger jobs.

"Not only is his understanding of air-conditioning systems outstanding, but he is reliable, trustworthy, and impeccable in his work." "He has always accommodated everything we have needed and been very fair with his pricing."

Figlia & Sons Inc.   4   3.5   4.5   4
746 East 9th Street, New York, NY 10009
(212) 686 - 0094 www.figlia-sons.com
Incremental HVAC sales, installation, and service

Figlia & Sons has been in the HVAC biz for over 45 years—long enough to have been around the block a few times, but not over the hill. This family-owned company focuses on installation and service of incremental heating and cooling units for residential customers. Clients, contractors, and management companies call on Figlia for what we're told is prompt, professional service in Manhattan.

Figlia's unique leg up on the competition is a large downtown warehouse, stocked with Icecap, WeatherTwin, Zoneaire, Traine, Friedrich, Climatemaster, McQuay, and more recently, Islandaire and Retroaire units. It allows for a quick response time, and we're told that other HVAC companies will sometimes buy from Figlia, rather than the manufacturer. The company does not service central systems with ductwork, and will only do window-unit installation if you buy the unit direct from Figlia. A typical service contract includes labor and some small parts. References report that prices are competitive.

"When manufacturers can't come through, we call them." "One of the few companies in Manhattan that does what it says and charges reasonable prices." "Their office may officially close at 5, but you can often get the owner on the phone until 7."

Hamilton Air   4   3.5   4   4.5
262 West 38th Street, New York, NY 10036
(212) 682 - 2710 www.hamiltonair.com
Full-service HVAC sales, installation, and service

In a field where many firms split their time between residential and commercial work, Hamilton stands out as a company focused on working with homeowners. We hear Hamilton has the resources and know-how to pull off complex installations others won't touch, taking on everything from ducted central systems to ductless split systems to through-the-wall and window units. Residential clients say Hamilton delivers the goods quickly and effectively.

Hamilton boasts an engineering department that oversees the design, application, and installation of central AC systems. Its service arm handles equipment repairs, warranty work, and maintenance for over 10,000 Manhattanites (which we hear can occasionally lead to slower response times). Both departments are backed by a factory in New Jersey that handles warranty work, service, cleaning, and overhauling of equipment and manufacture of custom sheet metal. Hamilton's office staff will even assist with landmark applications and prewar buildings. Veteran clients recommend getting your system checked during the winter to avoid the summer rush.

"Very responsive to client's needs, with excellent delivery and timing. I use no one else." "I hear they are the best, but they've never returned my phone calls." "As a decorator I wouldn't let anyone else in my client's apartment." "Worth it for the tough installations." "They give you alternatives for cost. Not just one way to do anything."

Nu-Way Air Conditioning   4   3.5   4.5   4
52-15 35th Street, Long Island City, NY 11101
(718) 472 - 9890
Custom HVAC design, installation, and repair

For its many satisfied clients, Nu-Way is the only way. Sources tell us the principal of this experienced firm, Thomas Queenan, is a thoughtful, knowledgeable problem solver who is familiar with working in the city's most prestigious residences, doing design, installation, or service. Customers, contractors, and building supervisors all admire Nu-Way's excellent customer service and top-quality work. Nu-Way's design acumen is often tapped by the city's finest architects. Clients say Queenan "is a master" and "delivers outstanding quality."

The company employs its own sheet metal mechanics and AC technicians for custom installations. Headquartered not far from Midtown, we hear the firm's friendly service personnel usually arrive in a flash, but can get backlogged during the busy summer season. Work on thru-wall or window units is limited to past customers. The firm is highly recommended as a good value.

"A delight to work with." "Seemed great but were more expensive than the guy I chose instead. I'm sorry now I didn't choose them; my guy took an extra month." "When Tom comes, he's amazing, but they need another guy at the top—he can only answer so many calls." "They always work through a problem until it is resolved, and always with a smile."

Polar Mechanical Corp.   4.5   4.5   4   4
221 51st Street, Brooklyn, NY 11220
(212) 431 - 4449
Custom HVAC design and installation

A high-end firm for those who prefer arctic breezes to tropical humidity, Polar Mechanical has recently risen to the forefront of the market. The folks at Polar have been keeping things cool for fifteen years, but their addition of an in-house sheet metal division in 2003 garnered them additional praise from insiders and clients alike—as well as an appearance on Bob Villa's "This Old House."

We hear principal Joe Yannaco is adept at "fitting ten pounds of equipment into a five-pound space," an important consideration in an industry that's "all about aesthetics." Yannaco's technicians don't work on PTAC units, but they are certified to install and maintain Mitsubishi's City Multi system, the latest and greatest in integrated HVAC. Polar doesn't really do day-to-day service, but they have a special unlisted phone line for established clients who need emergency help. Polar's elite services come at a premium, but many are happy to pay for the superior quality of the work.

"Good guys, good work." "They love making the client happy, and they'll go out of their way to make it happen."

17

	Quality 	Cost $	Value ◆	Recommend? ★

Power Cooling Inc.   3   3   4   4
43-43 Vernon Boulevard, Long Island City, NY 11101
(718) 784 - 1300

HVAC installation and service

Power Cooling has used its considerable muscle in all five boroughs of New York since Ed Koch was mayor. References say the company, with its staff of 90, has evolved into a well-resourced, efficient, and reliable establishment. The firm takes on both residential and commercial HVAC projects: installing, cleaning, repairing, and selling a wide variety of air-conditioning systems. For no-frills installation and service, Power is a cost-effective choice.

"I've worked with them on a few jobs—they've never let me down."

Pro-Tech Heating & Plumbing Corp.
1112 Clinton Street, Whitestone, NY 11357
(718) 767 - 9067

Plumbing and heating services

See Pro-Tech Heating & Plumbing Corp.'s full report under the heading Plumbers

Winds Service   3.5   3.5   4   4
1401 Blondell Avenue, Bronx, NY 10461
(718) 824 - 6700 www.windsservice.com

HVAC design, installation, and service

From design and installation of top-of-the-line central AC systems to setting window AC units, from brand-new construction to retrofitting existing buildings, we hear this versatile firm can handle the call. The company recently merged with its sister organization, allowing the new-and-improved Winds to cover both installation and maintenance. Sources say that its generalist approach can sometimes hurt the details, but overall the firm does solid work. Winds' service trucks are equipped with two-way radio and the necessary parts to keep systems in operation. While the majority of its work is in Manhattan, more significant projects can lure the company up to Westchester County. Established general contractors and leading manufacturers like SpacePak recommend Winds, while clients appreciate its mid-range costs.

"Very flexible, they had no problem altering their designs as the apartment was being built." "Could have been better on clean-up, but they managed to fit huge equipment into a small space." "They have the manpower to get big jobs done."

Hiring an Appraiser

Do you need to know the value of a necklace so you can sell it, or do you suspect that the IRS has overvalued and overbilled you? Or have you been watching the *Antiques Road Show* and suspect that the antique clock you just inherited could finance your child's college education? Appraisals are customized to meet the needs of a property owner, so examine your motives before seeking an appraisal. You may realize that you do not need a professional appraisal at all. For instance, if you're simply curious about the value of your grandparents' silverware or your aunt's antique hairpin, an informal estimate from a knowledgeable professional—also known as a verbal appraisal—will probably suffice. If, however, your property needs to be valued for a specific transactional purpose such as an insurance policy, taxation, a prenuptial agreement, sale, donation, or equitable distribution, you probably need a signed and binding appraisal from a professional.

What Kind of Appraiser Do I Need?

Once you have determined that you need a professional appraiser, assess the size, nature, and scope of the property that needs appraising. If an entire estate needs to be evaluated for insurance, probate, or taxation purposes, your best option is probably either a generalist or a large appraisal firm with various specialists, who together have the expertise needed to evaluate the diverse contents of the estate. On the other hand, if you need an appraisal for a single item or homogenous collection of like items—such as a manuscript or set of manuscripts that you would like to donate to a museum—a specialist would be ideal.

The purpose of the appraisal usually dictates the kind of appraisal you should seek. Property can be evaluated for its fair market value (FMV), replacement value, income value, etc. There's no such thing as intrinsic value, and sentimental value is in your eyes alone. Note that each kind of valuation will probably yield a different dollar figure and serve a different purpose. For instance, while replacement value is appropriate for an insurance policy, fair market value is a more useful valuation if you want to sell an item. The former can sometimes be several thousands of dollars more than the latter. Discuss your requirements with the professional appraiser to ensure that he or she performs the right kind of evaluation.

Keeping It Official

Contrary to popular belief, professionals cannot produce appraisals upon a glance. While informal estimates may certainly be had in this fashion (as evidenced by the *Antiques Road Show*), accredited professionals usually require extensive research to do a thorough, official job. They must produce a signed and binding report presenting the appraiser's objectivity, an account of the valuation process, the source of the data used, the methodology adopted, and the limitations of the appraisal in relation to the item. Valuations for legal transactions must be conducted by qualified, accredited appraisers who have no conflicting interest in the property, such as wanting to purchase it or to act as an agent for a potential sale. If appraisers seem to have an interest in the property they are appraising, the integrity of their appraisal may later be questioned and the property subsequently valued at a different rate. You then could become involved in lengthy negotiations and costly litigation in order to collect the money you expected.

So if you're looking to have a painting evaluated for insurance purposes, having an auction house conduct the appraisal would not be appropriate. If an item is to be auctioned, however, the auction house usually appraises it. This is because any potential conflict of the appraiser's interest in the property is entirely transparent and can only work to the advantage of the property owner.

PRICING SYSTEMS

Appraisers usually charge either by the hour—sometimes stipulating to a minimum number of hours per project—or by the day, plus travel expenses. Daily rates average from $1,500 to $2,000. Typically, hourly rates range from $150 to $500, depending on the reputation of the appraiser and the kind of valuation required. Informal estimates are considerably cheaper than formal appraisals. In fact, they are often free, and sometimes don't even require an appointment— many auction houses have walk-in days. Auction houses often offer a discount on their appraisal rates if the property is to be consigned to them for sale.

THE APPRAISING PROFESSION

There are a variety of professional organizations that give appraisers accreditation, but two of the most well-known and respected are the American Society of Appraisers (ASA) and the Appraisers Association of America (AAA). To receive accreditation from the ASA, appraisers must pass rigorous written and oral exams totaling a minimum of eight hours and submit sample appraisal reports for review. They are subject to local credit and background investigations and are screened by an ethics committee. Each appraiser earns a professional designation in one or more specialized areas, such as jewelry, fine art, manuscripts, or antique silver. The AAA has a less formalized review process, but members must be reviewed by a panel of experts before they are admitted. While many expert appraisers choose not to become accredited, hiring a certified appraiser ensures high standards of knowledge, professionalism, and experience. In other words, don't dismiss an appraiser just because he or she is not accredited, but it certainly can't hurt. Owners seeking professional appraisals should contact their local ASA or AAA chapter to perform a preliminary background check—they can also file grievances about appraisers with these organizations. The ASA can be reached at (703) 478-2228 or www.appraisers.org and the AAA at (212) 889-5404 or www.appraisersassoc.org.

UNDERSTANDING APPRAISAL VALUE JARGON

✧ Fair market value (FMV), also called fair value, is the price that an interested (but not desperate) party would be willing to pay for an item on the open market. The FMV method is generally used for appraising art, antiques, and other valuables for the purpose of sale or equitable distribution.

✧ Replacement value is the estimated cost of replacing an item. It includes the premium over FMV that an individual might be willing to pay in order to obtain a lost or destroyed item. Replacement value is used most frequently for insurance purposes.

✧ Income value is the estimated value of income that an item will yield over time. Generally used with real estate, income value is also used to assess the value of items that are being loaned or rented, such as jewelry and works of art. Income value appraisals show up in New York divorce court, too. The income value of a professional degree earned during a marriage is assessed so that both parties may benefit equally from the income it will yield in the future.

APPRAISERS—ART & ANTIQUES

💼 FIRMS WITH ONLINE PORTFOLIOS* 💼

Consolidated Appraisal Company Inc. 💼   4.5   4   4.5   5
60 East 42nd Street, Suite 1464, New York, NY 10165
(212) 682 - 1650 www.consolidatedappraisal.com
Distinguished residential, estate, industrial, and commercial appraisal services

This large firm claims to perform more appraisals of residential contents for insurance purposes than any other firm in the country. In business for almost 85 years, Consolidated Appraisal Company is a full-service independent appraisal company with specialists on hand to appraise general furnishings and fine arts, including paintings, sculpture, graphics, ceramics, rugs, jewelry, rare books, and coins. Clients use Consolidated to appraise the entire contents of their home or a collection of items—the company is not geared to appraise single items. Fees are calculated hourly with a minimum charge.

The company believes in teaching the client about appraisals by dedicating some of its effort toward community education. Consolidated puts out a newsletter, *The Consolidated Appraisal Report*, which keeps the firm in touch with its client base and provides up-to-date information on the industry and the importance of appraisals for financial purposes.

"We have used Consolidated for over 30 years. Always professional." "Wouldn't use anyone else." "If they don't know something, they won't try to make it up. They'll tell you up front, do the research, and get back to you quickly."

Michael Capo Appraisals 💼   5   4.5   4.5   5
43 Greenwich Avenue, New York, NY 10014
(212) 242 - 7179
Fine art and antiques consulting and appraisal services

We hear third-generation antiques dealer Michael Capo belongs to that rare breed of appraiser, the consummate professional who knows everything but is incapable of condescension. Backed by more than 35 years of experience, Capo appraises antique furniture, paintings, silver, and decorative art for clients as prestigious as the White House and the Brooklyn Museum. He has also testified as an expert witness in both high- and low-profile cases.

Clients have the highest regard for Capo's work. Many customers have maintained a professional working relationship with him for decades—and several of the top auction houses have him on their "recommend" list. Capo charges a substantial per-hour fee with a minimum, plus traveling expenses. He is a former board member of the Appraisers Association of America and has been an adjunct professor at both New York University and the New School for Social Research.

"We always refer our clients to Mr. Capo." "His work is impeccable." "Worked with him for over twenty years—that's how much we respect him."

*We invite you to visit www.franklinreport.com to view images of their work.

21

	Quality	Cost	Value	Recommend?
	✚	$	◆	★

FIRMS WITHOUT ONLINE PORTFOLIOS

Alex Rosenberg Fine Art   5   5   4   5
3 East 69th Street, Suite 11B, New York, NY 10021
(212) 628 - 0606   www.alexrosenbergfineart.com

Elite fine art appraisal services

Not the man to call if you just want Aunt Millie's antique thimble evaluated, Alex Rosenberg, Dr. Sc. is a master appraiser with over 35 years' experience. He performs top-tier fine art appraisals for auction or donation purposes and will act as an expert witness in court, but these days he mostly passes on smaller insurance jobs. Sources roundly praise his sound judgment and unshakeable integrity. Both the AAA and ASA list Mr. Rosenberg as a certified senior member. He is also active in the academic community of appraisers, teaching at the Instituto Superior de Arte in Havana and NYU. His hourly fee is one of the highest in the business, but clients who've used other appraisers say no one else has matched the standard set by Rosenberg.

"Very knowledgeable and accurate with his appraisals." "Excellent research and great judgment." "He's been around forever and has seen it all." "At the top of his game. An elder statesman."

Antiquorum   4   3.5   4.5   4
609 Fifth Avenue, Suite 503, New York, NY 10017
(212) 750 - 1103   www.antiquorum.com

Auction house services for valuable timepieces

With offices all over the world, a comprehensive online database and over 30 years of experience, this Swiss auction house specializing in valuable timepieces runs effectively as...well, a Swiss watch. We hear that Antiquorum is the place to go to have your antique watch or clock evaluated, but keep in mind that they only provide formal appraisals for auctioning, not for insurance purposes. Antiquorum's auctioneers have a good reputation, both for breaking sales records and for charging a modest fee. In fact, we're told that if you send in a brief description and photo, the company will provide you with a prompt, informal evaluation of your timepiece via e-mail, free of charge.

Appraisal Resource Associates Inc.   3.5   3   4.5   4
133 Pacific Street, Brooklyn, NY 11201
(718) 852 - 4961   www.appraisalresources.com

Personal property appraisal services

Appraisal Resource Associates has three qualified experts on hand to evaluate anything from an entire estate to an antique napkin ring, mostly for insurance purposes. Principal Frances Zeman, "a pleasure to work with," has been in the business for over 25 years, during which time she has earned high marks from both her clients and the American Society of Appraisers. She also works tirelessly to promote the value of appraisals through teaching, writings, and appearances in popular venues like NBC's "Today" show. Because the staff is small, sometimes the firm will subcontract out an expert, but the unshakeably upbeat Zeman is well connected. Depending on the job, the fee can be an hourly charge, a per diem, or a flat rate. All fall at the affordable end of the spectrum.

"Frances treats my clients wonderfully." "Their professionalism and cheerfulness go a long way."

Appraisal Services Associates   4   3   4.5   4
232 Madison Avenue, Suite 600, New York, NY 10016
(212) 679 - 3400   www.appraisalserv.com
Litigation support and fine art appraisal services

Helmed by cheerful expert Charles Rosoff, this independent company provides appraisal services for fine arts, antiques, decorative arts, office content, and personal property. Rosoff, a senior member of the American Society of Appraisers, is a general expert in 19th and 20th century Western art and antiques and does appraisals in all areas. We hear Rosoff and his staff are particularly adept at dealing with legal issues and untying knots in the tax code, a specialty helpful for those in the midst of an equal distribution or charitable donation situation. The small size of the company means that an unusual piece of artwork will necessitate outside experts. The company also offers curatorial services.

"Not only did he assess the value of my library, but of my desk too." "They had the job of appraising every item in a $60 million estate for tax purposes, and everything we presented sailed right through the IRS. Can't see how they could have done better." "Amiable and more than pleasant to work with."

Beverlee N. Friedman   3   3   4   3.5
245 East 93rd Street, Suite 4K, New York, NY 10128
(212) 348 - 1335
Personal property, antiques, and decorative art appraisal services

Sole proprietor Beverlee N. Friedman is an expert in antiques and decorative art, but we're told she's also a competent generalist who can give solid estimates on "mixed bag estates." A board member of the Appraisers Association of America and a senior appraiser with the American Society of Appraisers, Friedman works with the residential and corporate communities alike and will travel to meet a client's needs. References report that her fees (usually charged on a per diem basis) are modest and reasonable.

Christie's   4   4   4   4
20 Rockefeller Plaza, New York, NY 10020
(212) 636 - 2000   www.christies.com
Auction appraisal services

As much an institution as an auction house, Christie's is widely recognized as a powerful global force in the art and antiques world. The North American office has been headquartered in Rockefeller Center since 1999, but the history of the organization extends back almost two and a half centuries. In fact, Christie's longevity is key to its reputability, and a central reason why it—along with Sotheby's—dominates the high-end auction market.

Christie's primary business is auctions. Its appraisal services are geared to that activity and are tailored to represent the seller's interests. Christie's large and knowledgeable staff covers a wide range of specialty areas, including American furniture and decorative art, American paintings, antiquities, books and manuscripts, Chinese ceramics and works of art, Chinese paintings, contemporary art, European ceramics and glass, European furniture, and European works of art, among others. The company's authority and size carry a lot of weight in the art world, but its scale can lead to inconsistent service—some sources report diligent and authoritative appraisers, others felt the experience was rushed and incomplete. Drop-in, informal estimates are free. For a formal appraisal, slightly

Quality	Cost	Value	Recommend?
✚	$	◆	★

upscale hourly fees are added on to a base cost. The charge is then rebated if the client chooses to auction the item within one year of the appraisal, which most find to be an excellent value.

"A great experience—very polite and professional." "Wouldn't use them for insurance appraisals, but they have the auction process down cold." "They give a much higher priority to more valuable items. If you come in with something small, they speed you through it." "Came within days for the appraisal and they were well-versed and very knowledgeable."

Cynthia S.H. Bowers   3   3   4   3
145 East 74th Street, New York, NY 10021
(212) 288 - 2860

Estate and insurance appraisal services

Cynthia Bowers' boutique firm specializes in decorative art and antiques, specifically appraising Continental and American furniture for insurance value. However, as a 25-year veteran of the business, Bowers can appraise a variety of styles and eras, for all purposes. Residential clients make up a large part of her business, especially those needing formal insurance valuations prior to a large move. Bowers charges an hourly fee, which varies from very reasonable to somewhat expensive depending on the service performed.

"I recommend people to her whenever antique furniture comes into the picture."

Doyle New York   4   3.5   4.5   4.5
175 East 87th Street, New York, NY 10128
(212) 427 - 2730   www.doylenewyork.com

Auction appraisal services

Doyle New York is one of Manhattan's best-known boutique auction houses, a more intimate alternative to Christie's and Sotheby's. Under the stewardship of Kathleen Doyle, this privately held, 40-year-old company has become known for its specialty auctions of paintings, jewelry, furniture, and haute couture clothing. Walk-in appraisals—frequently performed by regulars on PBS's Antiques Roadshow—are available every Monday morning, though rugs require an appointment. Verbal appraisals are provided at no charge, while a written version prepared for insurance or estate planning purposes requires a fee. In case you can't drop by, the company has a growing network of regional representatives throughout the East Coast and beyond. Depending on the item, Doyle will sometimes offer to buy from clients directly, a convenient option for those who wish to bypass the auction process.

"More personal than bigger auction houses." "They work harder on the small stuff."

	Quality	Cost	Value	Recommend?
	+	**$**	**◆**	**★**

Eli Wilner & Company

4.5   4.5   4   4.5

1525 York Avenue, New York, NY 10028
(212) 744 - 6521   www.eliwilner.com

Exceptional frame restoration and frame appraisal services

Affectionately known in the industry as "Mr. Frame," Eli Wilner is considered the ultimate authority on antique American and European frames. Since 1983, Wilner and his professional staff of twenty have carved a niche for themselves as specialists in period framing. Wilner is a leading frame dealer, restorer, appraiser, and collector's authority with an A-list clientele that includes the White House, the Metropolitan Museum of Art, and Sotheby's. We're told that clients appreciate his sensitivity and discerning eye. Appraisals are provided based on client photographs or in-house consultations, with Wilner (of course) preferring the latter. Both verbal and written appraisals are available, with the former at a considerably lesser cost.

"Extremely well-known in the business, everyone respects him." "Great, personal service."

Lauren Stanley

4   4   4   4

300 East 51st Street, New York, NY 10022
(212) 888 - 6732   www.laurenstanley.com

Appraiser of fine American silver

Sources say Lauren Stanley knows everything there is to know about 19th and 20th century American silver. His eponymous boutique company is chiefly a retail operation, with the largest inventory of its kind in the country. However, Stanley will appraise silver for insurance or resale purposes. The firm's distinguished client base includes museums and collectors from around the world. Stanley charges a standard (if steep) hourly fee, and will only appraise by appointment.

Masterson Gurr Johns

5   4   5   5

122 East 55th Street, 2nd Floor, New York, NY 10022
(212) 486 - 7373   www.gurrjohns.com

First-rate fine and decorative art appraisal services

An independent appraisal and art consulting firm with its finger on the pulse of the global market, Masterson Gurr Johns has offices in New York, London, and Germany. For more than 60 years, the New York headquarters has focused on providing appraisal services to high-profile companies and well-heeled individual clients. The firm is known for its high-level expertise in the fine arts market and offers art consultation services to collectors as well. Clients praise the company's ability to provide appraisals for a wide variety of jobs—from a single item to a large collection. Fees are billed at a (significant) fixed rate on an hourly basis.

Masterson Gurr Johns prides itself on the high level of expertise it brings to each job. With a staff of four generalists and twenty-eight specialists, experience is paramount to the firm's success. Each general appraiser has over ten years' experience, and all are current or pending members of the Appraisers Association of America. All independent consultants are chosen based on expertise and complete objectivity. Sources say the firm is particularly adept at dealing with the complications of appraising an entire estate.

"One of the best." "They provide the highest level of expertise, and we would definitely refer their firm to future clients." "Cream of the crop. Having international offices can make a big difference for a big, messy collection."

	Quality	Cost	Value	Recommend?
	✚	$	◆	★

New York Fine Art Appraisers Inc.   4.5   3.5   4.5   5
410 Park Avenue, Suite 1530, New York, NY 10022
(212) 772 - 0319   www.nyfaa.com
Fine art and estate appraisal services

Though the name is new (it used to be Jason Rahm & Associates), this firm has been providing independent appraisal services—primarily for insurance purposes—to New York City's elite for over 25 years. The company's areas of expertise include paintings, sculpture, silver, decorative art, furniture, and porcelain. Clients include private collectors, insurance companies, attorneys, movers, and estate planners.

Principal Jason Rahm, an accredited senior member of the American Society of Appraisers, personally visits the client's home or office to photograph and examine each article to be appraised. Within a matter of weeks, a report, including color photographs, is personally presented to the client. NYFAA is strictly an appraisal company; it won't assist in the buying or selling of art works. The firm is roundly praised for its level of experience and the personal attention it gives to clients.

"A gentleman." "We have enjoyed a long-term relationship with this firm—they provide excellent service." "A fun and interesting experience."

O'Toole-Ewald Art Associates Inc.   4.5   4   4.5   5
1133 Broadway, Suite 1107, New York, NY 10010
(212) 989 - 5151   www.otoole-ewald.com
Quality fine art appraisal and expert witness services

With eleven on-staff appraisers and a library of over 11,000 volumes, O'Toole-Ewald brings the intellectual muscle of a university to the evaluation process. Fittingly, much of the firm's work is on large-scale jobs: major litigation, expert witness cases, damage evaluations, fraud investigations, whole-estate appraisals, corporate art collections, and the like. However, principal Elin Lake Ewald—an accredited senior member of the American Society of Appraisers—has been known to take on smaller projects, especially if they engage her curiosity. The specialists on staff cover a wide range of expertise—paintings, textiles and rugs, silver, glass, ceramics, books, photography, and gems. Because so many areas are covered, O'Toole-Ewald rarely has to go out of house to appraise an item, an important factor in maintaining strict confidentiality. The firm charges a relatively low hourly rate, which allows them to book enough time for solid research. High-profile sources report that O'Toole-Ewald is a pleasure to work with, and that its appraisals are always enlightening.

"Their intellectual curiosity is impressive." "A positive experience for over ten years." "They have given us speedy appraisals and enabled us to make appropriate business decisions."

Phillips de Pury & Company   4   3.5   4.5   4
450 West 15th Street, New York, NY 10011
(212) 940 - 1200   www.phillipsdepury.com
Fine and decorative art auction services

Strangely enough for a bicentenarian auction house, Phillips has a distinctly contemporary focus. A leading international auction firm (number three behind Sotheby's and Christie's) with offices around the world, it holds regular auctions in modern and contemporary art, 20th century design, photography, and rare jewels. The firm's appraisal specialists will provide private and corporate clients with formal written valuations on anything from a single item to full-house contents for insurance, probate, trusts, and estates. Phillips' New York office conducts free walk-in appraisals and valuations, and each department offers an informal on-line evaluation service to give the customer an idea of the likely auction value of an item. We hear the only thing this firm undervalues is its own time—prices are said to be a great deal.

"A little more specialized than Sotheby's and Christie's, Phillips corners niche markets and dotes on them more." "You won't get a big marketing campaign, but the staff works hard to make up the difference." "Good service, good prices, good people."

Sotheby's   4   3.5   4.5   5

1334 York Avenue, New York, NY 10021
(212) 606 - 7000 www.sothebys.com

Auction appraisal services

As the oldest major fine art and antiques auction house in the world (in that respect, it beats Christie's by 22 years), Sotheby's has the authority of an institution. However, it is still first and foremost a business (the company is publicly traded), with 100 offices around the world, hundreds of employees, and a grand headquarters on the Upper East Side.

Sotheby's appraisal staff comprises 200 specialists representing over 70 collecting categories, including jewelry, furniture and decorative arts, porcelain, silver, antique rugs, prints, and paintings, among many others. Though auctioning is Sotheby's primary function, its appraisal staff can prepare documents to suit the client's needs—whether they be estate planning, insurance, charitable contributions, or fair market value.

The firm's moderate fees are based on the volume and nature of the property, as well as the time and the number of specialists involved in the appraisal. If the appraised property is consigned to Sotheby's for sale within one year of the appraisal, a prorated portion of the fee is refunded. For larger estates and collections, fees for written evaluations are negotiable and are generally very competitive. Though the auction-driven nature of Sotheby's means you might be "shuffled off to Buffalo" if you're not bringing in an expensive collection, the firm's "professionalism" and "expertise" are appreciated by many satisfied clients.

"Wonderful specialists. I learned so much from my appraisal experience." "Unless you're in the $10,000 range, you'll probably have to deal with a junior associate. Still, they were quite professional." "The appraisal process was quite clear."

Swann Galleries Inc.   4   4   4   4

104 East 25th Street, New York, NY 10010
(212) 254 - 4710 www.swanngalleries.com

Auction appraisal services

This mid-sized auction house enjoys the double distinction of being a third-generation family-owned business and the largest rare book auctioneer in the world. The Swann Galleries began in 1941, specializing in rare books, maps, atlases, and manuscripts. Today, the company also sells posters, photographs, prints, and drawings.

Appraisal services are usually undertaken only for large collections, in connection with items to be auctioned by Swann Galleries. However, if they have time, the staff of fifteen experts will take a look at whatever you can show them, for any purpose. The hourly fee is expensive, so think twice before bringing in all your stoop sale "treasures," but we hear that the smaller size of this firm often leads to more focused expertise and personal attention. A low buyer's premium is also considered a major plus.

"Interesting, innovative auctioning." "They really bring in the niche collectors. That can be good or bad, depending on what you're selling." "They have a very professional staff, but they won't turn their noses up at you."

	Quality 	Cost $	Value ◆	Recommend? ★

Tepper Galleries

	4	4	4	4

110 East 25th Street, New York, NY 10010
(212) 677 - 5300   www.teppergalleries.com

Auction appraisal services; estate specialists

Tepper Galleries is a small, pedigreed auction house that specializes in the assessment and sale of entire estates. As such, the staff is equipped to handle a wide range of items, including antique and reproduction furniture, jewelry, art, silver, carpets, and decorative objects, dating as far back as the 18th century.

A truly "full service" firm, Tepper Galleries will evaluate, pack, ship, and sell the contents of an entire estate, leaving the property "broom clean." Tepper also offers weekly walk-in appraisals on Monday, Tuesday, and Thursday. For items too large to transport, Tepper's staff will appraise on-site, but only by appointment. Verbal estimates are offered free of charge. Written appraisals, which contain a complete description of the item including its provenance and fair market value, require a minimum fee plus an hourly rate that's on the expensive side.

Timothy Tetlow Appraisal Co.

	4	4	4	4.5

176 East 77th Street, New York, NY 10021
(212) 535 - 2406

General appraisal services

Accomplished generalist Timothy Tetlow has the breadth of knowledge to assess a complete collection, from cameos to Caravaggios. Though he does have some academic experience, this 30-year veteran of the appraisal business has primarily honed his skills on the job, first at Sotheby's and then as an independent consultant. Past projects include assessment of large, high-profile estates for insurance purposes and fair market value assessment of smaller fine art collections. Those who have worked with him appreciate Tetlow's expertise, immaculate professionalism, and charming accent. A member of the Appraisers Association of America, Tetlow charges an upper-end hourly rate.

"I'd use him for anything." "Sophisticated and wise." "This may be an oxymoron, but Tim is a specialized generalist. He knows a lot about a great deal."

William Edgerton

	4	3	5	4

PO Box 1007, Darien, CT 06820
(203) 655 - 0566   wedgerton@aol.com

Wine appraisal

Formerly a real estate appraiser, William Edgerton has focused on only one room in the house since 1987: the cellar. Edgerton evaluates wine collections for property division, damage evaluation, and insurance purposes prior to a move. Also, although it's somewhat rare, Edgerton is called in from time to time as a wine gumshoe: he identifies fradulent bottles.

As the lone accredited member of the American Society of Appraisers with a specialty in wine, and as the creator of the first comprehensive guide to wine prices, his expertise is in high demand, but Edgerton nevertheless charges a reasonable rate. He will also evaluate cheaper bottles for a drastically reduced fee, if not for free. Sources report that Edgerton is pleasant to work with, a master of his trade, and more than able to recommend a good wine to go with dinner.

"Wrote the book on wine appraisal, literally."

Hiring an Architect

Creating a home will be one of the largest investments of your lifetime. An excellent architect can make your dreams come true and, just as important, help you avoid construction nightmares. He is the protector of your investment and your ally in ensuring that the subcontractors deliver exactly what you have envisioned.

An architect's work lives on indefinitely, leaving an indelible mark on people's lives and on the community. Famous architects have made history with their brilliant work as well as their eccentricities: Frank Lloyd Wright demanded control over every inch of a house's design, right down to the table settings; Stanford White brought as much drama to his life (and death) as he did to the stunning spaces he created. But don't get your heart set on achieving fame through an architect who brings celebrity to your address. The best matches are usually made with talented, hard-working, experienced professionals who are able to commit themselves fully to your project because they are not household names.

The architect is your guide through the entire building process—from refining your vision and defining your needs to documenting them in plans and specifications; from suggesting contractors to counseling on budget; from monitoring the progress and quality of construction to certifying payment to the contractor; and from answering questions to settling disputes. The architect is the point person working on behalf of your interests. The clarity and thoroughness of his drawings and the extensiveness of your architect's involvement in the design and building process are the keystones to a successful project. If the architect forgets a beam, the whole job could come crashing down—and most likely you'll have to pay a little extra to get that beam retrofitted.

Where Do I Start?

Choosing an architect isn't easy. Each professional has his or her own design philosophy, style, and way of doing business. Talk to friends, realtors, and contractors. You should interview three to five firms to get a sense of what you're looking for.

Make sure to meet with the individual who will be designing the project, not just a principal selling you on the firm. If you and the architect don't click, move on. The most important thing to look for is stylistic understanding and good chemistry. You're going to be working closely for a long time, bouncing ideas and problems off each other with a lot at stake. You want somebody with whom you'll enjoy the ride. Not surprisingly, architects consider the same thing when choosing which clients to take on.

Get a sense of the quality of the architect's past designs. Ask to see not only his portfolio, but the blueprints of those past jobs. The architect's clarity and thoroughness will be evident in the detailing and the notes. Not all blueprints are created equal, and the same goes for the people who draft them. Another important step is to get feedback from past clients. You want to know if a prospect was accessible and collaborative, if he was expedient in turning drawings around and responsive to questions and revisions, and if he visited the site and met with the contractor regularly.

If an architect makes his living doing leading-edge homes and you have a French Tudor house, it's clear that this collaboration isn't going to work. Go with somebody who is well-versed in the style you're looking for. Also keep in mind that the specific structure to be designed is as important as the style. An architect who has never designed a rooftop addition in Manhattan is bound to be ignorant of certain details and codes that will inevitably become major factors in the job. This may also be the case if you are renovating an old townhouse in Gramercy Park and are subject to historic preservation restrictions. Your architect should relate to your personality, preferences, vision, logistical constraints, and lifestyle.

SPECIFIC CONSIDERATIONS

It's very important to have a realistic sense of the possibilities and limitations regarding budget and building codes. It's the architect's job to define these things for you. Identify how familiar a candidate is with the local codes, and whether he is sensitive to cost. He needs to be able to help you navigate the permitting and inspection process and massage the budget by substituting materials and methods or modifying the design. Also, you should be vocal about any special stylistic interests and timing specifications you have from the outset. If using a particular contractor or building an environmentally considerate and efficient home is important to you, speak up. Remember, certain architects only dip their toes in certain ponds.

ON COST AND CONTRACTS

If you think you've found a partner, it's time to start thinking about the fee. There are no set fees for architectural services. The scope of the job, the level of quality and detail, the pace and length of schedule, and the number of other clients the firm has already taken on will all factor into how an architect calculates his service.

An architect will typically charge either an hourly rate or a percentage of construction, but some do a combination of the two. For example, some architects may charge hourly through the schematics stage, then charge a percentage of construction cost for the remainder of the project. Alternatively, there may be a fixed fee based on hourly rates, or an hourly rate that is not to exceed a certain percentage of construction.

Regardless of the method of calculation, standard fees for New York will typically range from eighteen to twenty percent of the total construction cost. Larger projects generally have smaller fee percentages. For example, an architect might only charge twelve percent to design a mega-mansion in Greenwich. At some of the most established and high-profile firms, the percentage might be elevated (but never should be over twenty-five percent), based on the architect's status and reputation in the industry. Interestingly, these rates have consolidated and decreased slightly over the last few years—as of the last publishing of The Franklin Report, standard architecture fees ranged from eighteen to twenty-two percent. Also, keep in mind that fees vary from region to region. For example, in Palm Beach, the best local architects in town are only charging ten to fifteen percent.

The fee, the responsibilities associated with it (revisions through permitting, frequency of on-site visits, payment certifications, and punch list review), and the compensation procedure for any extra work should be spelled out in a contract. This can be an Architect's Letter of Agreement, or a standard contract issued by the American Institute of Architects (AIA) (which is highly recommended).

LICENSES AND PERMITS

To earn his title and to receive the official stamp necessary for a building permit, an architect must have a state license. However, he does not have to be a member of the AIA (Frank Lloyd Wright never joined). The typical qualifications for licensing are: 1) a degree from an accredited school of architecture, requiring three or more years of study, 2) three years of apprenticeship under the supervision of a licensed architect, and 3) passage of a five-day exam. Exact requirements vary from state to state. Cities require that drawings submitted for permit review be certified by a state-licensed professional.

It is also essential that your architect be very familiar with local building code requirements and regulations. Local codes vary widely, and a small misunderstanding can lead to a big inflation of budget and schedule after everyone has committed to a particular plan. In New York, as in most places, any alteration that does not fit the building code's definition of a minor repair requires an architect's application and certification of plans for approval and issuance of a building permit. The city building department also requires the architect to certify completion of the construction before anyone can occupy the space. If you live in a landmark building, you will also have to consider the approval of your plans by the Landmarks Commission. Your architect should be responsible for filing all the appropriate paperwork and addressing any code concerns during the permitting process.

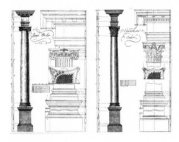

THE ARCHITECTURAL DESIGN PROCESS

Whether you're courting your architect or have already made the plunge, communication is critical. You are choosing someone to translate an epic fantasy that only you have imagined into three-dimensional reality. For an architect to develop an idea, you need to be able to convey in detail what it is you are looking for. Bring sketches, pictures, notes, clippings, Rorschach tests—anything that will tune him in to your frequency. And take your turn to listen. Your architect will invariably come up with design ideas, offering inventive solutions and innovative alternatives to your rough-hewn proposal. Also, you want an architect who can deliver options.

Once you've made your architect the designer of record, your first big discussion should involve fleshing out your nebulous dreams into cold hard details. The number of rooms, how and when you will use them, and the flow of space are questions he will need answered in order to come up with a first round of schematic designs. Don't panic if these are incomplete. These rough sketches and drawings will be revised and refined as you review them until you are satisfied. The architect may produce a model to help you visualize the layout of your future residence.

HOW LONG WILL IT TAKE TO DRAW UP A PLAN?

The easy answer is: until you can make your mind up. But even when you are finally satisfied, you'd be astounded by the number of people who get to throw in their two cents before construction begins. After you and your architect have agreed on the drawings, they may pass through the hands of various historical, design, or landmark review boards; planning and zoning boards; structural, mechanical, electrical, and plumbing engineers; fire, life/safety, and Americans with Disabilities Act (ADA) reviewers; and your kids. After the experience, you'll know how a writer feels when he tries to get his screenplay through the Hollywood system unscathed. Depending on the complexity of the job and profile of the location, expect the process to take from two to six months.

Once the basic layout is approved, the architect can move forward and prepare more detailed drawings to define the scale and scope of the project. It's never truer than in construction that the devil is in the details. You must communicate absolutely everything your heart desires. Finishes, brands, models, installation methods, notations on code, fixture selection, materials to be used—they all need to be documented in plans and specs by the architect. At this point, the cost estimate gets a whole lot clearer.

THE ARCHITECT THROUGH THE PROCESS

Most people approach contractor candidates with thorough and clear documents in hand. However, it is recommended that you include a contractor at the outset of the design process in order to get a realistic assessment of construction costs—otherwise, you may be disappointed by budget-busting bids that the architect has spent hours designing (often at large hourly rates). Your architect will manage (or assist you in) the process of hiring a contractor to coordinate construction. Your architect should be able to recommend several candidates from a stable of reliable and friendly contractors. Or, you may have your own ideas. It is typical for several contractors to bid a job. Your architect can help you sift through the proposals to make sure that everything necessary is included and that you are comparing apples to apples. Ultimately, however, the decision to hire the contractor is yours.

Throughout construction, the architect is responsible for making frequent appearances on-site to monitor job progress, troubleshoot, answer questions, and verify that all details and code requirements are being met per his plans and specs. It is becoming increasingly common for banks to require the architect of record to certify pay applications in order to release funding to the contractor. Again, this requires the architect to visit the site to assess whether or not the work completed is commensurate with the request for payment. As construction draws to a close, the architect must lead the "punch list process" of those missing, incomplete, unpolished, and mishandled loose ends.

Working with an architect who matches your personality, ideas, and particular project will make this one of the most memorable adventures of your life. You may enjoy building your house so much that, like Thomas Jefferson, you'll immediately make a habit of it. "Architecture is my delight," wrote Jefferson, "and putting up and pulling down one of my favorite amusements."

DRAWING IS JUST THE BEGINNING. YOU ALSO HIRE AN ARCHITECT TO:

✧ Interpret code.

✧ Estimate budget and schedule.

✧ Offer options for materials and methods.

✧ Recommend contractors and review bids.

✧ Document contractual obligations.

✧ Sign and seal plans for permitting.

✧ Review and certify pay applications.

✧ Monitor progress and quality.

ARCHITECTS

🛍 FIRMS WITH ONLINE PORTFOLIOS* 🛍

1100 Architect PC 🛍   4.5   4.5   4   4.5
475 Tenth Avenue, 10th Floor, New York, NY 10018
(212) 645 - 1011 www.1100architect.com
Earnest, modern, restrained architecture

David Piscuskas and Juergen Riehm are recognized for their distinctive and refined modernistic yet humanistic approach. With an open yet disciplined richness of texture, color, and light, they often incorporate humble and rugged materials (such as wood, stone, and resin) to counterbalance contemporary lines. Their signature "modern contemporary expression" has garnered much praise in the press and among peers. Clients call the firm's handsome interiors inviting and elegant.

About half of 1100 Architect's twenty to twenty-five yearly projects are residential, which are evenly split between gut renovations and new construction. Clients applaud the firm for acknowledging the fact that real people must live and work comfortably, and that the designs "belong to the owners, not to the architects." 1100 Architect generally takes on substantial projects in Manhattan, but also works in the Hamptons, Westchester, and Fairfield County. Clients include noted retail establishments and institutions like TSE Cashmere, J. Crew, Rene Lezard, Shiseido, the Robert Mapplethorpe Foundation, and the Little Red Schoolhouse. Celebrity clients include Jasper Johns, April Gornik, Liam Neeson, Willem Dafoe, and Christy Turlington.

David Piscuskas received a B.A. from Brown, studied at RISD, and received an M.Arch from the University of California. Juergen Riehm received a degree in architecture from Fachhochschule Rheinland-Pfalz and was recently named an AIA Fellow. The two worked together with Walter Chatham from 1983 to 1986 before launching their own venture. Sources say they appreciate the duo's constant architectural exploration in every project, which renders each space unique and forward-thinking. The firm does its own innovative interior design with coordinating cabinetry and accessories and has also collaborated with interior designers quite successfully. A standard percentage of total construction costs is charged, with smaller projects commanding a slightly higher percentage.

"Remarkable vision." "Creative, original solutions to the issues of the Manhattan apartment dweller." "An exceptional firm that I have worked with for years...they get my highest recommendation." "Incredibly good at adapting to the client's program and ideas." "Their ability to innovate and create spaces of functional elegance is uncanny." "While ornament-free, they are leading a new wave of modernistic architecture that is disciplined, yet has warmth and soul." "Despite their expertise and obvious talent, an overabundance of ego was never a problem." "They could not have been nicer or more professional."

*We invite you to visit www.franklinreport.com to view images of their work.

	Quality	Cost	Value	Recommend?
	+	$	◆	★

Ageloff & Associates

4	3	5	5

57 East 11th Street, Suite 8B, New York, NY 10003
(212) 375 - 0678   www.ageloff.com

Warm, engaging, classical residential architecture

Clients say Scott Ageloff "won't accept anything less than the best," and as a result, they won't accept anyone other than Ageloff & Associates. Ageloff, the dean of the New York School of Interior Design, with both an undergraduate and an M.Arch from Yale, is extremely well versed (some say "brilliant") in combining interior design and architecture. He also wins accolades for collaborating with clients to make their style resonate with his own.

Ageloff is said to have a good sense of relational elements, mixing old details of a structure with a modern, livable look. We hear clients' favorite element about working with Ageloff is his ability to suggest creative, unexpected touches that end up being the most beloved aspects of the home. He is also commended for his wide range of sources and his "inherent understanding" of the appropriate price point for a given client.

Organization is another Ageloff strength, as is his kind and pleasant demeanor. Clients add his follow-up is "terrific" and "when he says one week, he means one week." There are ten people in the highly effective office and about twenty projects at a time, but Ageloff "is always there to hold your hand." He has worked in some of the most prominent Manhattan spaces (four apartments in the Dakota), and is also happy to undertake smaller spaces, starting at about $150,000. Adept at bringing people with different points of view together to find a happy solution, he is often recommended by high-end contractors.

References cite Ageloff's ability to work within a budget, and his sensitivity to the situation at hand. He works on a reasonable hourly rate with a small mark-up over net on products. All clients say that his fees are absolutely worth the price and he saved them from potentially costly errors. His ability to do interior design as well as architectural work further controls costs. ASID.

"Scott is smart, savvy, very calm, organized, responsive, honest, creative, and fun to work with." "He was sensitive to my terror about the whole project, and thanks to Scott, what I began with dread, I finished with fun." "Never dictatorial." "I am really not 'into' the whole designing, shopping thing, so for me to say it was painless is really saying something." "Very decent and correct gentleman." "Never missed a deadline." "I still call him years after our renovation to ask his opinion about subsequent purchases." "My husband originally chose Scott, and I wanted to be cheap, holding the budget to $150,000. Scott was honest enough to say that was impossible. There were no surprises with Ageloff & Associates." "Scott helped us sharpen the pencil and intelligently cut down the contractor's estimate." "The finished product was beyond my original hopes and even my wildest dreams!"

Alan Wanzenberg Architect, PC

4.5	4.5	4	4.5

333 West 52nd Street, New York, NY 10019
(212) 489 - 7980   www.alanwanzenberg.com

Restrained, thoughtful, luxurious residential architecture

Alan Wanzenberg is one of a handful of New York architects to be informally knighted by "those that know." With an understanding of the history of his craft, Wanzenberg's classical style also reveals his appreciation for proportion and scale, without ever looking formulaic. Adept at developing "wonderfully understated" craftsman detailing that is driven by the client's taste and the context of the project, there is always a special twist. The architect is also receptive to more modern projects, which he has done with success. Known to have "a personal connection" to his work, Wanzenberg is driven by "intellectual pursuits in design."

After graduating Berkeley and Harvard (M.Arch) and working for three years with I.M. Pei, Wanzenberg started Johnson & Wanzenberg with his longtime collaborator, the late Jed Johnson. Several years later, the architecture side became an independent entity, and now Wanzenberg and his sixteen-person staff also offer interior design, which range from updated traditional to more contemporary. The firm's commissions tend to be large-scale projects, for which budgets average $1.5 million to $3 million, but Wanzenberg has been known to do much smaller jobs. Residential is the sole focus with commissions mainly in New York City and the regional area. The firm takes on equal numbers of city renovations, historic restorations, and new single-family homes. Insiders say Wanzenberg takes great interest in the detailing of libraries, kitchens, and bathrooms, where his design skill truly shines.

Sources tell us Wanzenberg is a man of integrity, up front about costs and budgets so that money doesn't become an issue in the design process. Described as a "big time client advocate," Wanzenberg has been known to meet with a potential client four times before taking on a job in order to fully understand the client's needs. The firm charges standard fees based on an hourly rate with a percentage cap. AD 100, 2000, 2002.

"Alan very much enjoys engaging his clients in the intellectual process." "Charming." "He is the psychological leader of the substantial interiors group with a strong interest in that area." "There is a distinct penchant for American and English Arts & Crafts." "Alan is clearly involved in the overall, but not really the details." "The net price of all product is shown on the bills, which gives me great comfort." "Alan and the team are on your side." "Alan took the longest time viewing the site and developing the plans to make sure he got it right." "There was an audible sigh of relief from the locals when the house was built, as Alan was respectful of the neighborhood." "Alan is so thoughtful, and a softspoken gentleman. But he absolutely gets it done."

Alexander Gorlin Architects

4.5   4.5   4   5

137 Varick Street, 5th Floor, New York, NY 10013
(212) 229 - 1199 www.gorlinarchitect.com

Modern, sinuous architecture with warmth

While many others talk a good game about modern with warmth, Alexander Gorlin really means it. Gorlin is praised for his deft creation of "modern, sensual spaces" that maximize the use of space and natural light. There are saturated warm woods, deep shades of luxurious color, and sinuous lines throughout. Think Le Corbusier or Frank Lloyd Wright with depth and modern comforts. Described as highly intellectual, Gorlin established this firm of nine in 1987. While clearly intrigued by the lure of institutional legacy, he has a fondness for residential work, taking on a handful of residential projects each year, including the apartment of Daniel Libeskind, named master planner of The Freedom Tower.

Gorlin holds degrees from Cooper Union and Yale and trained with I.M. Pei. He has taught at the Yale School of Architecture and has long been sought by clients in the media and fashion industries. His wide-ranging portfolio includes designs for apartments, houses, office buildings, affordable housing, high-rise complexes, synagogues, museums, city parks, and household items. Clients say that Gorlin is committed to creating a work of art every time, though some caution that he can be a bit rigid in his thinking about style. Potential clients should familiarize themselves with the look and be prepared to enjoy experimentation. Clients praise Gorlin for his "impeccable taste" and inherent design sense. To that end, Rizzoli has published a monograph of his work featuring 28 projects.

Much of the firm's work takes place in New York City, Westchester, and Fairfield counties, and there have also been projects from Spain to Nova Scotia to California. The firm charges a higher percentage of construction costs. AD 100, 2000, 2002, 2004. AIA Fellow 2005.

"He has a great sense of design, style, and integrity." "Not only do you get an amazing home, you get a thorough education in the craft and process of architecture." "I love the simple elegance of the design." "Nothing extraneous, linear yet textural." "We never even talked to another architect, we picked him straight away." "The plans are very detailed. In fact, the contractor said they are the most complete and explicit plans he's ever seen." "He was very quick to pick up on exactly what we wanted. And I love his tremendous artistic expertise."

Allan Greenberg, Architect, LLC 🛍   5   4.5   4.5   5

45 East Putnam Avenue, Suite 101, Greenwich, CT 06830
(203) 661 - 0447   www.allangreenberg.com

Resplendent, substantial, classical residential and institutional architecture

Known in architectural circles as a pioneer in the current wave of rediscovered Classicism, Allan Greenberg was building grand shingle-style homes well before they became the must-have 80s accessory in the Hamptons. An ardent defender of all things classical, Greenberg's firm is often hired by government agencies to build statuesque structures that will stand the test of time. Recent projects include a Connecticut Superior Courthouse, the Luxembourg Embassy in DC, and the Treaty Ceremony Room at the US State Department. Prestigious commercial institutions also value the illustrious look that Greenberg achieves. Commissions include Turnbull & Asser's US headquarters, Tommy Hilfiger's Beverly Hills flagship, Bergdorf Goodman's facade renovation, and the D&D Building's snazzy new neo-classical lobby.

This strong proclivity for the eminent and classical translates very well to the residential market—assuming the client is of the mindset to fund the very best. About eight residential projects are taken on at a time, and are evenly split between large-scale renovations and new-home construction. In addition to substantial apartments and sprawling classical estates, Greenberg enjoys working on traditional farms, stables, greenhouses, and barns. Greenberg and his staff will take on projects with budgets ranging from $500,000 to $20 million, all of which are richly detailed.

A South African native, Greenberg received his M.Arch from Yale and has taught at Yale, U. Penn, and Columbia. He established the firm of 25 in 1960 and remains the sole principal. There are offices in Washington DC, New York, and Greenwich. Forty-plus years in the business put his discriminating clients at ease; we hear he has a rational and very thorough process "that's as tight as a drum." The firm charges a higher fee based on hourly costs or a percentage of overall construction costs.

"The most serious Classical architect of our generation." "He understands exactly why the greatest architecture of Greece and Rome has stood the test of time." "Brought Classicism back to respectability with dignity—and he was doing this 30 years ago." "His designs lift the spirit." "They not only get the architecture perfectly,

but also manage the entire process so well: interior design, construction management, post-construction services." "We were a very small client for Allan. He clearly was not there for the day-to-day, but was involved enough to know what was going on to a detail level. And the overall professionalism of the firm was excellent."

Austin Patterson Disston Architects, LLC ▣

5	4.5	4.5	5

376 Pequot Avenue, Southport, CT 06890
(203) 255 - 4031 www.apdarchitects.com

Highly detailed, versatile custom residential architecture

Acclaimed for their innovative designs for difficult sites—waterfront in particular—the architects of Austin Patterson Disston are well versed in the historical roots of Revival and Shingle styles and the streamlined simplicity of contemporary homes. They are said to maintain a sensitivity to scale and detail no matter what the language. Insiders say the "quirky and really clever" David Austin has a wealth of knowledge and a refreshing sense of humor. Not to be found relaxing in a posh corner office, sources tell us the partners are in the "design trenches" with the rest of this 30-person staff, constantly exchanging ideas in a fluid environment. Clients say the genuine enthusiasm of this firm's collaborative approach makes it one of the most sought-after firms in the area.

After training with Philip Johnson, Austin started the firm in 1963, later partnering with McKee Patterson (1982) and Stuart Disston (1994). Austin Patterson Disston's three partners are all heavily involved in every design process while each oversees one-third of the projects. Clients say the firm's impeccable attention to detail is second only to its superior client relations. "You don't buy a product with them," we're told, "what you buy is a solution to a unique design challenge."

In 2000, the firm opened a second office in Quogue, serving the Hamptons. Handling about 30 projects at a time, with budgets ranging from $400,000 to $10 million, Austin Patterson Disston designs mostly large residential projects in Connecticut, Eastern Long Island, and in and around the city. The firm bills on standard hourly, fixed, or percentage-based fees.

"In about an hour and a half, McKee came up with some drawings. Four weeks later, they were still the perfect concept. We never changed a single thing." "They're definitely creative, but they don't put you into something that's too far out." "A great outfit to deal with, and no attitudes either, thank God." "They could have built some dopey ranch for me, but they came up with a beautiful carriage house." "It was expensive, but we knew that going in and there were no surprises."

Belsey & Mahla Architects ▣

4.5	4.5	4	4.5

41 Union Square, Suite 836, New York, NY 10003
(212) 924 - 7948 www.belseyandmahla.com

Tailored, individualistic, residential architecture

Hailed by clients as "immaculate professionals," Erika Belsey and Philip Mahla approach each project with the natural enthusiasm of people who do what they love. Luckily for their clients, what they love is thoughtful, full-service, sleeves-rolled-up residential architecture. Though Belsey cut her teeth on Milanese Modernism, and Mahla his on Texan ranch houses, both shy away from stylistic proclamations, preferring to focus on developing a home that fits the needs of its inhabitants. Known as relentless editors, Belsey and Mahla continually add and subtract in all phases of a project, from hand-drawn schematics to installation. They are also sticklers for detail: if it makes sense to widen a hallway by six inches, they'll find a way to do it.

Belsey received her M.Arch at Yale and worked at various international firms before a stint at Skidmore, Owings and Merrill. There, she met Mahla, who earned his degree at Rice University. The two quickly discovered a kinship that ran from a mutual respect for Rosario Candela to a childhood obsession with the World Book encyclopedia sets. Conveniently, Belsey and Mahla also shared a dissatisfaction with the impersonality of large-scale architectural firms. Hence, the formation of this boutique company in 1994. Though there have been opportunities to grow, Belsey & Mahla Architects remains a two-person operation. Says Belsey, "There's no part of the process we don't enjoy, so we never saw the need to pass it off to anyone else."

The firm charges a standard markup on construction and usually spaces payments out on a monthly plan. Clients often ask for interior design advice, and while the pair is happy to oblige, their official responsibilities are limited to "everything that's not soft." Though Belsey and Mahla prefer to take on large residential projects, they have been known to make an exception if the creative challenge is unique. To ensure that each job receives its due, the firm will only take on a small number of projects at a time (around five). This can make Belsey and Mahla difficult to book, but devoted clients say it's worth the wait.

"Erika and Philip don't stop listening to you throughout the process, and they don't stop improving on the original design." "They took what I had in mind and made it better." "Their attention to detail reaches a near-neurotic level. They even shopped for shoe and tie racks." "We have weekly meetings with them, and they keep minutes, which allows us to track the progress of the job." "Very present on the job site. They breathe down the contractor's neck." "They gave us the most thorough bid proposal I've ever seen." "They wanted to use pear and I wanted walnut. Rather than trying to argue with me, they worked out a compromise." "Their attention to detail—from the doorstops to the moldings—was impeccable." "Expert at taking seemingly insoluble problems and creating showstoppers." "They were worried the process was slowing down, so they scheduled emergency meetings and we got back on track." "People ask me how I can run an office, practice law, raise three kids, and renovate my home. 'Erika and Phil,' I say. They worry so I don't have to."

BKSK Architects 📖   4   4   4   5
28 West 25th Street, 4th Floor, New York, NY 10010
(212) 807 - 9600 www.bkskarch.com
Modern-with-soul to traditional-with-attitude residential and commercial architecture

BKSK is adept at creating engaging, livable spaces and effectively incorporating its clients' interests. This established firm is not committed to a particular style, instead taking pride in its versatility: from calming, warm, clean, earthy modern spaces to traditional paneled walls with transparent glass interspersed. For projects that have a historic component, BKSK infuses the classic with a "fresh approach." And the modern is intelligent, with movable partitions offering a flexible utilitarian arrangement. Sources remark that all BKSK designs are "beautiful and coherent." The firm generally takes on substantially sized projects that can range up to $45 million for multi-family projects.

Principals of the firm are Stephen F. Byrns, Harry Kendall, George Schieferdecker, and Joan Krevlin. The firm was launched in 1985 as BKS, but added another "K" when the firm combined forces with Krevlin in 1992. Of the firm's annual commissions, about 50% are residential projects. There are about 30 in the firm, and we understand that junior architects may sometimes take on more of the workload than anticipated. Roughly half of the company's projects occur in Manhattan, but BKSK also takes on projects in the Hamptons, Westchester, and New Jersey. The firm recently worked on several residential communities in the midwest.

Recent local projects include a penthouse in Tribeca, a fifteen-story loft-style apartment building (also in Tribeca), a new 15,000 square foot visitor's center for the Queens Botanical Garden, a high-profile interim visitors' center adjacent to the WTC site, and a new town center for the Village of Plainsboro, New Jersey.

BKSK charges an hourly fee with a maximum not to exceed a standard percentage of total construction costs. Given its excellent commercial track record, the firm has an excellent reputation for coming in on time and on budget.

"They started from the ground up—asking us tons of questions about our lifestyle." "Highly innovative. By switching the layout of the rooms, our Central Park view filled the apartment with light." "Their follow-up was excellent and they really knew the coding issues well." "They get the highest rating in regard to articulating our ideas into the plan." "Very complete drawings. In fact, they were recommended by the builder." "Always available to meet, and really went the extra mile." "They are of great integrity—doing everything they said they'd do." "Slightly understaffed on the support side." "You name it—they figured it out. Even selected most of the furniture." "We now think of our architect as a friend—how often does that happen after a multi-million dollar project?"

Bromley Caldari Architects   4   4   4   4.5
242 West 27th Street, New York, NY 10001
(212) 620 - 4250   www.bromleycaldari.com
Modern, warm, playful residential and commercial architecture

Equally adept at designing beach houses in the Hamptons, renovating apartments in Manhattan, or constructing a freestanding new home on the roof of a Madison Avenue building, Bromley Caldari awakens spaces with becoming modern lines. The two principals are known for their easygoing natures, enthusiasm for their work, and commitment to personal service—as well as for resolving challenges and creating excitement in every project. Shrubs growing wild in your living room? A bathroom on a fire escape? We hear they can solve it all. By employing its distinctive modern style with clean, handsome original lines, Bromley Caldari "makes new out of the old," with industrial materials often adding wit and whimsy.

This firm currently employs ten, evenly split between architects and interior decorators (Bromley Caldari often oversees both functions for its clients). About 60% of annual commissions are residential, the majority of which are in Manhattan. The firm, originally known as Bromley/Jacobsen, was founded in 1974 by Scott Bromley and evolved into a partnership with Jerry Caldari in 1991. Bromley holds a degree from McGill University, Caldari from Clemson. Recent New York City projects have included a substantial townhouse combination, a chic pied-a-terre, the gut renovation of a duplex penthouse overlooking Central Park, and the restoration of the B'nai Jeshurun Synagogue (seen in "Sex and the City"). Responsible for the design of the infamous Studio 54 in the 1970s, the firm has also completed work in the Hamptons, Fire Island, Westchester and Nassau counties, as well as California, Florida, Brazil, and Russia.

Bromley Caldari boasts a steady roster of return clients and also does a fair share of pro-bono work for non-profits. The firm charges an hourly rate with a maximum not to exceed a higher-than-standard percentage of total construction costs. ID Hall of Fame.

"We gave them absolute freedom to create a one-of-a-kind residence with very few restrictions and the result is a breathtaking jewel with perfect, luxurious craftsmanship in every corner, surrounded by fluid lines and shadows." "Scott's strength is his spatial relations—he really knows how to create an inviting openness." "Scott's work is beyond creative." "Jerry is so collaborative. He brings out the best in you and the project was a dream fulfilled." "You have to like details, as they will leave no corner untouched." "They took the bargain of the century and turned it into something remarkable." "Such incredibly likable characters." "The end product is truly miraculous, and all accomplished with a minimum stress brought about by a maximum of good humor."

	Quality	Cost	Value	Recommend?
	+	**$**	**◆**	**★**

Cha & Innerhofer Architecture + Design   4   3.5   4.5   5

611 Broadway, Suite 540, New York, NY 10012
(212) 477 - 6957   www.cha-innerhofer.com

Versatile, worldly residential architecture and interior design

Paul Cha and Margaret Innerhofer bring a cerebral amalgamation of Far Eastern and Classical European influences to a diverse practice that is equally at ease working in Modernist, budget-conscious, downtown lofts and 18th-century English inspired Park Avenue residences. We hear Cha & Innerhofer "like working with enthusiastic and involved clients" that share a love for the design process. In turn, clients wax poetic about this husband and wife team, saying that they "give 110%" and are an "incredible combination of Zen-like intellectual creativity and Teutonic construction precision."

Cha, a native of Taiwan with architecture degrees from Virginia and Harvard, trained with the very best: Richard Meier, Ferguson Shamamian & Rattner, and Gwathmey & Siegel. Innerhofer, who grew up and studied in Italy, focuses on interior design and makes sure all the pieces fall into place properly. The firm takes on projects with modest budgets ranging from $250,000 to $1.5 million, the vast majority of which are gut renovations, with an occasional ground-up home in the suburbs. Nearly all of Cha & Innerhofer's commissions are residential and take place in Manhattan, although the firm has also completed projects in the Hamptons and Rhinebeck, as well as Italy and China.

We're told Cha & Innerhofer appreciate buildings "with good bones" and treat each project with sensitivity to budget and a strong interest in the client's lifestyle. Only a few major projects are taken on at a time so they can stay on top of all details. Cha & Innerhofer charges a standard fee based on a percentage of overall construction costs.

"After floundering in the abyss of designer hell, we called on Cha & Innerhofer and to say that we are pleased is an understatement." "Incorporated our ideas and didn't fall into the trap of using clichéd or stale design ideas." "Despite our unsightly and decrepit townhouse, Paul astutely transformed it into a luminous and exquisite home." "Both Paul and Margaret are delightful to work with." "Obsessive, mostly to the good." "We gave them a budget that was quite modest, and they delivered the work as if we were Park Avenue super-elite." "Meticulous, reliable, imaginative, and always accessible, no matter how small the issue."

Coburn Architecture ■   4   4   4   4.5

45 Main Street, Studio 1210, Brooklyn, NY 11201
(718) 624 - 1700   www.coburnarch.com

Pragmatic, modern, transitional residential architecture; row house specialists

Given carte blanche, principal Brendan Coburn most enjoys designing tailored, modern spaces. However, on more than one occasion he has successfully played preservationist, convincing dubious homeowners that their original moldings are worth holding on to. In all cases, Coburn takes a straightforward, pragmatic approach to residential architecture. Rather than imposing a grand point of view on his clients' homes, he listens to their concerns and looks for the simplest and most elegant solution to each. The result is always layered and eclectic, yet completely logical—impressive and unique, but not brash or flamboyant.

Recent Coburn projects have included country houses in Connecticut and the Hamptons; the occasional Upper West Side or Upper East Side apartment, and a large number of row houses in Brooklyn and the West Village. The last-mentioned is a particular specialty, as Coburn grew up in a row house and has been affectionately tinkering with them all his life. Sources highlight this aspect of the firm, saying "I wouldn't recommend anyone else for that kind of work."

Coburn studied architecture at the University of Virginia, then went on to earn his M.Arch at Yale. Not one to sit quietly in the library, he had built a house and received a large Hamptons commission before graduation. Those two jobs were the seeds of today's firm, which has since grown to a sturdy staff of sixteen. Collectively, the team takes on around twenty projects at a time, with Coburn or a partner (Ward Welch, a former classmate of Coburn's at UVA, earns special praise from clients for his work on country houses; Jason Boutin handles commercial jobs) helming the design and the staff implementing the details. Depending on the project, the planning and permit stage ranges from four to eight months, with landmark clearance (another specialty of the firm) factored in. Clients say the staff is pleasantly informal, very creative, and fun to work with.

"I've worked with a lot of architects. Coburn really represented my best interests, and I couldn't say that of everyone." "Ward really takes delight in his job. The contractor was tearing down the walls on my house in Columbia County and Ward drove up just to see what would be underneath." "Their addition to my house in Amagansett is seamless." "Brendan was available to help me choose an apartment, his advice was invaluable." "Ward always kept his cool, even if I lost mine." "They maintained the integrity of my pre-war apartment." "I was in Texas while the house was being renovated, and Ward was great about staying in touch. He was very reassuring." "Sometimes I worry, because they take on so many jobs, but I never felt ignored." "They did go over the schedule, but it was worth it; the house was perfect." "A very collaborative process." "A lot of my friends have used architects who drew up these beautiful plans, but when they were built, nothing worked. I never felt that way with Coburn. Both Brendan and Ward grew up working on houses as teenagers, and they have a real feel for the way things are put together." "I had to rein them in on budget a bit." "They gave me different options in terms of budget. Even when I chose the cheapest option, it turned out beautiful." "Ward has a house out in the Hamptons, so when he was there, he wouldn't charge me travel time to work on my project." "Won't look down their noses at small jobs." "They made a mistake in billing that I didn't notice. A week later, I got a call from their accounting department, pointing out the mistake and giving me a refund." "Modest, decent, smart, real people."

Craig Nealy Architects 🏢   4.5   4.5   4   4
49 West 38th Street, Suite 12A, New York, NY 10018
(917) 342 - 0060   www.craignealy.com

Modern, engaging, innovative architecture and interior design

Clients describe this firm's style as glamorous, soft and accessible modern, incorporating a high-style feel into contemporary settings that are "progressive without being alienating." His high-profile commercial work clearly informs his residential designs which often feature clean, unembellished walls and surfaces, neutral-honed materials, and cantilevered bookshelves. The firm not only does the interior decorating for most of its architectural projects, but will also do interior design independently. Clients generally praise the firm's professionalism and commitment to the project, and say the staff is attentive at meetings, the follow-up is excellent, and the overall product is of high quality.

Principal Craig Nealy, a graduate of Cornell who has taught architecture at Yale, founded the predecessor firm in 1998. Nealy currently heads an office of ten. About a third of the firm's commissions are residential, and cover a wide range of services—from bathroom renovations to multi-million-dollar apartment rehabilitation projects to the design of ashtrays. On the retail side, Nealy has completed eight projects for Vera Wang (flagship, showrooms at Bloomingdale's and Bergdorf's), the S.T. Dupont Paris showroom, and sixteen stores for Louis Vuitton. Other commercial ventures include Sotheby's new "Bid" restaurant, a lobby for the World Bank in Washington, and a substantial prototype hotel in India. Nealy's star is clearly rising with multiple jobs from prestigious clients.

The firm charges a standard percentage of construction costs and standard markups over net for interiors, and handles each service with a separate contract. The company's Romantic Modern retail boutique has moved to its offices where engaged clients can find luxurious and comfortable furniture and rare and compelling accessories.

"Craig uses materials in creative, imaginative ways and skillfully introduces unique design features." *"Outstanding quality of design and construction administration."* *"They understood our taste and pre-selected appropriate choices, sparing us from being overwhelmed by dozens of design and fabric possibilities."* *"Not the most organized."* *"They have strong opinions about certain things."* *"Craig himself can sometimes be hard to reach, but there are good project managers."* *"Results are what count, and Craig's designs are both beautiful and functional."*

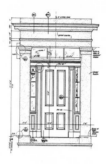

Curtis + Ginsberg Architects LLP 🏠   4   3.5   4.5   4.5

180 Varick Street, 5th Floor, New York, NY 10014
(212) 929 - 4417 www.cplusga.com

Residential and institutional architecture with a modern focus

Sought out as one of the rare firms that is highly sympathetic to the client's needs, fears, and overall input, Curtis + Ginsberg has earned a reputation for being "the kind of architect that most people want, but can't find." Described as "easygoing" and "grounded," Darby Curtis and Mark Ginsberg are said to create spaces that closely follow their clients' vision. About 25% of the work is residential, including additions, renovations, and combinations of Manhattan apartments. The style is usually more modern and often done on the Upper West Side and Tribeca. The firm also specializes in multi-family residences, recently receiving kudos from the press for designing the first apartment building to use photovoltaic power on the roof.

Clients say that the firm creates design solutions that are extremely pleasing to the eye, yet practical for modern living. The company is also described as flexible, practical, and respectful of budget limitations and time constraints. Curtis + Ginsberg is equally willing to do interiors or architecture. Generally taking on larger projects, the firm will not hesitate to take on those of smaller scale ($300K+), which are of exceptional design interest. Known for taking the time to "walk" clients through the entire process, much repeat business is developed from the high level of customer service.

This firm of thirteen has been in business for over a decade, with principals Curtis and Ginsberg personally overseeing each project. Curtis holds a degree from Columbia and Ginsberg one from Penn. Current projects include a townhouse renovation and addition for music production studios, a penthouse apartment, and a classic Upper West Side apartment. The firm charges an hourly fee not to exceed a standard percentage of total construction costs. Ginsberg AIA Fellow 2006.

"They are absolutely delightful and get the job done." "A rare case of high-quality and integrity." "They came up with extremely creative solutions for our office renovations that met our rather tight budget constraints." "I do not have a ton of discretionary income, and they really held the cost down." "At my request, they worked with a builder of less quality than they would normally deal with, and did that with grace and ease." "Incredibly hassle free." "Never a cluttered or fussy result." "Darby came to the old apartment and we spent lots of time discussing what we liked and did not." "Available whenever needed." "I wouldn't think twice about hiring the firm again." "Darby's recommendations were great. She led the team and was very responsive and patient with us."

David Bergman Architect ▮   3.5   3.5   4   4.5

241 Eldridge Street, Suite 3R, New York, NY 10002
(212) 475 - 3106 www.cyberg.com

Modern-edged residential and commercial architecture

Praised as much for his trustworthy nature as his excellent architecture skills, David Bergman has earned the respect of his loyal clientele. Clients refer Bergman to friends and family for projects that range from one-room renovations to sprawling single-family homes. We hear Bergman's style is fairly contemporary—warm modern—with one-of-a-kind craftsman touches and interesting materials and textures. Working in a close collaborative environment with clients, it is reported that he takes their ideas very seriously.

A small shop of two to three people, Bergman established his firm in 1985. We are told Bergman is quick to solve problems that may arise throughout the course of a project and is a meticulous manager of any endeavor he undertakes. The firm works in Manhattan, the Hamptons, and Westchester and Fairfield counties. There is an effort to weave in green design—including recycled, sustainable, and energy-conserving products—without sacrificing the look. Clients say they trust Bergman to the point of leaving large projects in his hands unsupervised for long periods of time, with the confidence that he will deliver on time and on budget.

Bergman received a B.A. from Yale in architecture and economics and an M.Arch from Princeton. He has taught at Parsons for over ten years. Clients and colleagues alike have lauded him for his technical and aesthetic skills, and his ability to combine the two seamlessly. The architect also designs his own line of "Fire & Water" lighting and furniture. The firm charges an hourly rate not to exceed a percentage of construction, which can slightly exceed standard percentages on smaller projects.

"A talented architect, but also a good person." "He's almost too easy to work with." "His teaching skills clearly came through in my experience as I asked him many questions that probably drove him crazy." "Has a tremendous amount of patience." "A progressive style, with lots of unique touches that reflected my interests." "His inspiration with lighting is particularly wonderful, and was well integrated into the design."

David Howell Design Inc. ▮   4   4   4   4

200 Park Avenue South, Suite 1518, New York, NY 10003
(212) 477 - 7700 www.davidhowell.net

Creative, contemporary, unique residential architecture

David Howell designs lively, contemporary homes that tickle the imagination. Many of his projects are downtown and undeniably urban. Interestingly, Howell's use of large windows, raw stone, and unpainted wood gives his work an open, rustic quality even in the urban canyons of New York. In this and in a certain "elemental optimism," the warmth of his native country—New Zealand—shines through.

	Quality	Cost	Value	Recommend?
	✚	$	◆	★

An active collaborator who likes strong ideas, Howell works best with clients who view the architectural process as a chance to exercise creative muscle, not a chore. He returns the favor with extreme focus and attention to detail. In the early nineties, Howell came to New York on a research grant to study the relationship between artisans and architects. Among other findings, he discovered that he wanted to stay. After working for Clodagh Design International for three years, he founded his own firm in 1995. Currently, Howell fields a staff of twelve, taking on between 20 and 25 projects in various stages at a time. Sources report that Howell is most involved at the front and back ends; he guides the design phase carefully, allows associates to handle planning details, then returns to make sure construction goes smoothly. He considers the surrounding environment paramount and will turn down commissions (say, a Park Avenue style lobby in Tribeca) that don't match his aesthetic.

Though Howell himself has a relaxed professional style, the firm's process is designed to satisfy obsessives. The staff sets up individual websites for each project, so clients can download schematics and track progress. Weekly meetings keep things moving, and references report that budgets are followed closely. Howell generally takes on jobs in the $250,000 vicinity, though a unique creative challenge can lower that bar considerably. Fees are also flexible, ranging from an hourly charge to a slightly-higher-than-standard percentage over construction. Clients, many of whom have worked with Howell multiple times, report that he is the best of both worlds: a true talent without the accompanying artistic temperament. They recommend him wholeheartedly for unique, design-oriented architecture.

"He's a Modernist, but he gives things warmth by really listening to what the client wants. It always feels like a home, not a gallery." "DHD recently helped me renovate my new apartment. Attention to detail was excellent, and the quality of service was first-class." "Very contemporary designs, but they were also able to adapt to my own preferences." "When I had found my new office it was a blank canvas. Of the six designers I brought in, only David Howell 'got it'." "He's almost too nice!" "There were some mistakes, as there always are. The difference is that David knew how to deal with them." "He continued to be a great support to me even after the offices were finished." "He's neither the most expensive, nor the cheapest." "David turned what would have been a stressful and difficult process into an exciting and fun one." "I had to rein him in due to budgetary constraints, and he dealt with this in the same calm, responsible manner that he displayed throughout the project." "I'm a real estate professional, and I've been involved in 25 projects with David over the past decade. He's the only person I'd hire." "I have recommended David to three different clients—all to rave reviews!"

David McMahon 🏠   4.5   4.5   4   5

155 East 56th Street, New York, NY 10022
(212) 755 - 2551

Pedigreed, transitional residential architecture and interior design

David McMahon is appreciated for his extensive experience, excellent communication skills, keen wit, and pleasant demeanor. While there is no signature style, McMahon clearly has a modern approach to his work, melding classic elements with a fresh outlook for timeless, slightly eclectic compositions. After sixteen years at Parish-Hadley, it is not surprising that McMahon also has an exemplary grasp of the traditional aesthetic (having successfully completed a number of period Georgian and French interiors) and can gracefully combine that classical framework with the more modern. Regardless of the genre, all McMahon spaces are heralded for their warmth and elegance.

McMahon, who studied at RISD, started the firm in 1997. Following Mrs. Parish's belief that "all things beautiful go together," the firm also does interior design and has several interior designers on staff. McMahon, the primary client contact, is involved with all details, including the purchasing of artwork (often in Paris). With just three in staff, McMahon may be spread a bit thin given the high demand for his talents, but clients are happy to get his firsthand advice. Nearly all of the work is residential; mostly million-dollar-plus Upper East Side apartment gut renovations. In addition to his New York area clientele, McMahon has completed projects in Miami, Georgia, California, the Hamptons, and Bermuda.

The firm charges an hourly rate or a standard percentage of construction costs that increases for smaller projects. For interiors, McMahon charges a low markup over net on design products, which is clearly shown on all bills. Some say McMahon could be somewhat more cost-conscious, but all are very happy with the end result.

"He cares very much about what he does and is passionate without an overbearing ego." "David's architectural sophistication keeps my zealous eye under control." "He respected the age and quirkiness of the original house, but made it better and infinitely more livable." "I would not think of beginning any new project or concept without David's consultation." "His ease of manner, patience, and knowledge of trade sourcing are things I always count on." "He is just tons of fun." "I think hiring an architect can often be an exercise in futility, but I wholeheartedly recommend David." "He aims for the highest architectural goals, not one to cut corners."

David Nahon Architects   3.5   3   4.5   4
340 West 89th Street, New York, NY 10024
(212) 580 - 0773

Classical residential architecture with a modern focus

While well-versed in many styles of design, David Nahon leans towards neutral tones and clean lines, most often creating handsome, modern spaces. He earns accolades from clients for a winning combination of high quality and prices that won't break the bank. Clients also appreciate the personalized service they receive from Nahon, which allows them to play an active role in the entire process—from design to construction. Sources cite excellent client relations, Nahon's helpful hand-drawn plans, and his easygoing manner as additional pluses to work with the firm.

This firm has been in business for more than 30 years, and sole principal Nahon holds two degrees from Columbia. All of Nahon's work is residential and takes place in the New York metro area. He takes on projects of all sizes—from one-room renovations to large brownstone gut rehabs (he has a special fondness for brownstones as he lives in one himself). The firm charges an hourly rate or a lower percentage of total construction costs.

"There is very little pressure in working with David—when I need to speak to him, he's always available." "Old school attitude which can be a bit relaxed." "It's so pleasantly different from what you'd think working with a high-end architect would be. Going to visit him is like going to a relative's house—it's so laid back." "A one man show that works out of his brownstone to keep the costs down." "David does everything methodically. No computer, no e-mail. All the plans are by hand. Always available by phone so not a problem for us, but might frustrate others." "The quality of the spaces he creates is great and I didn't have to dip into the kids' college funds." "David goes out of his way to make it work for the client. He uses the vertical space to carve out more closet space, and uses high-style—instead of high-cost—items." "Will work in stages as the budget allows." "David found the contractor for us, who was also terrific." "Does have a preference for the modern. I really wanted a dark library and he wanted a white library. He eventually came around." "He puts in the extra hours and develops really nice relationships with clients." "Smooth sailing. No complaints at all."

Dineen Architecture + Design PC

56 East 81st Street, New York, NY 10028
(212) 249 - 2575 www.dineenarchitecture.com

Quality	Cost	Value	Recommend?
4	4	4	4.5

Modern, romantic, comfortable residential architecture

Joan Dineen is appreciated for her ability to integrate architecture and interior design seamlessly. The rooms are "calm and unassuming," yet fresh and becoming in their modern simplicity and use of natural materials. The lines are lean and the palette monochromatic. Clients feel that she creates rooms that are a pleasure to live in, and that have longevity. Moreover, supporters say she is involved in every detail and makes the process fun.

The firm is a small operation of two architects and two interior designers plus support staff. Principal Joan Dineen, a graduate of Cornell and Columbia Universities, has been doing residential projects for over fifteen years. Most of the firms work is done in Manhattan, although they have done work in Miami, Cape Cod, Seattle, and the Hamptons. Most projects include a mix of architectural and interior design work, although the firm is happy to coordinate with third parties.

Current work includes residences at the Time Warner Center, the Dakota, and other projects in Manhattan and the Hamptons. The firm bills architecture and interior design services under separate contracts, with standard percentages of construction or purchases charged for fees.

"Exceeded our expectations. Innovative use of materials: stone, marble, all in a rugged yet polished manner." "It is so rare to find someone with such great talent and no ego." "Excellent construction management as well." "End product is beautiful, livable, and timeless. And Joan is a very nice person." "The work looks fresh but not too trendy." "Serene space of timeless elegance, a dream come true." "The style is bold without being intimidating. A curved balcony, a soaring wall of bookcases create a dramatic effect." "She has the touch, knowing how to create magical spaces." "Very positive experience in every way. We would definitely use her again."

Edward Ira Schachner, Architect

Quality	Cost	Value	Recommend?
4	3.5	4.5	4.5

555 Eighth Avenue, Suite 1810, New York, NY 10018
(212) 967 - 0220 eischach@verizon.net

Updated traditional architecture and interior design

With an attentive, full-service, smaller firm, Edward Ira Schachner very much enjoys working with clients to create contemporary yet traditional spaces that are typically "painterly" and "European" in nature. Rooms look like they have evolved over time, and are usually muted in color, with "nothing being too perfect."

The firm is one-shop architecture and interior design shop that listens to its clients and delivers an individual product, right down to "choosing the bedding and deciding where to hang the pictures." Canadian born and educated, Schachner moved to New York in 1980. He worked with industry icons Peter Marino, Shelton Mindel, and Thierry Despont before founding his firm in 1991. There are just three in staff and the firm limits its workload to about eight new projects each year, most of which are high-end renovations in Manhattan. The firm concentrates solely on residential work and budgets starting at $250,000 and topping out at $2 million. In addition to working in the city, Schachner also works in the Hamptons, and has finished projects in France, Israel, and Canada. The firm charges standard fees based on a percentage of overall construction costs.

"Ira is very easy to work with. Very thoughtful with solutions to spatial and design problems." "We had already been through a renovation that did not work for us. Almost sold the townhouse, but Ira created a good flow and definition." "Ira was a wonderful collaborator with our decorator and landscape designer." "Each room is unique, but it all hangs together beautifully." "There are strong proportions and a neutral tonality." "Ira is extremely patient and willing to look at a problem through

your eyes to solve it." "Good attention to clients with regular visits, but as things wind down, it may be necessary to keep on top of him if he is really busy at the time. Not a major issue given how harmonious a partner he is overall." "Higher standards than warranted for the kids' rooms. But we worked it out very well." "We went sheet shopping at ABC and browsed the Restoration Hardware catalog together—all with no markup." "I now have the most beautiful home, and feel uplifted every time I walk through the front door." "Working with Ira was a delightful experience, and the end result exceeded my expectations."

Elskop*Scholz   4   4   4   4

350 Fifth Avenue, Suite 7518, New York, NY 10118
(212) 244 - 1307   www.elskopscholz.com

Contextually sensitive residential architecture and interior design

Christopher Scholz and Ines Elskop have established a reputation for "out of the box creative design thinking" and giving clients a unique product that is a direct and personal reflection of the clients' lifestyles. Elskop and Scholz are said to be excellent at helping to guide clients through the design process, engaging them in every phase with "good, strong, professional opinions." This husband and wife team like complex issues and are known for coming up with elegant solutions. The firm is best known for its modern design, which consists mainly of sizeable gut renovations and additions.

The firm was created in 1992 by principals Scholz, who holds a graduate architecture degree from Columbia, and Elskop, who studied at Princeton. In this small shop of five, the principals do all the design details themselves. They take on about six projects at a time, half of which are residential projects in Manhattan. The firm also works in Westchester and Dutchess counties, as well as parts of New Jersey. Elskop*Scholz's commissions carry construction budgets ranging from $250,000 to $1.5 million.

Recent projects include the gut renovation of an apartment with modern elements in a restored classic prewar building on Park Avenue, as well as a guesthouse, garage, and studio in Dutchess County whose exteriors are rendered completely of copper. The firm also does the interior design of nearly all of its projects, and rarely works with an outside decorator. Elskop*Scholz charges a standard percentage of overall construction costs, with bills that are "transparent and clear, without any hidden costs."

"There is real thinking time devoted to the creative process. They are always trying to come up with a novel yet reasonable approach, without being absurd or cutting edge." "You can't be too rigid in your thinking as a client because with them, there is a lot of give and take." "They took our boring Upper West Side 950 square feet and completely changed it, making it a jewel." "Chris immediately saw the possibilities—he moved and pocketed doors, and the light fell a completely different way." "Chris is very engaged in the concept of architecture." "Ines is focused on the process and the details. She also understands what is appropriate for the space and for the client. They make a great team." "Extremely sensitive to context." "You do need to check in every few days to make sure it's still on track." "Very respectful of cost." "I am an architecture junkie and I think their design was perfect."

Erica Broberg Architect   4   4   4   4

605 East 82nd Street, Suite 14A, New York, NY 10028
(212) 787 - 7976   www.ericabrobergarchitect.com

Versatile residential architecture sensitive to city and country living

Described by many as "young, bright, and talented" Erica Broberg has expanded her practice from working on Shingle-style homes in the Hamptons to include overseeing townhouse and apartment renovations in Manhattan. Broberg has a refreshing design approach, with clean, crisp, classic lines that represent the historic view but are never overbearing. Known for her traditional projects,

Broberg has recently taken on more commissions in the modern aesthetic, tempered by "moderate and classical" lines. Clients say they particularly appreciate Broberg's tasteful use of materials that look "wholesome and right for the setting." While the designs are roundly applauded, the process has been known to bog down in the change order phase.

Broberg is the sole principal of the small firm of five she established in 1998 after working for other New York-area firms for eight years. She holds a B.A. in architecture from Catholic University and also studied in Versailles. All of Broberg's commissions are residential, with about one-third of her 30 annual projects taking place in Manhattan and the remainder in the Hamptons. The firm's design expertise is in historically accurate home renovations, which make up nearly half of Broberg's practice.

We are told Broberg enthusiastically takes on projects with a wide range of budgets and scopes, doing anything from a high-end kitchen renovation to a $5 million estate on the ocean. The firm recently purchased an upper-end kitchen cabinet company, Smith River Kitchens (also in FR). The firm charges an hourly fee with a cap. Some clients say that the hours can be more than they anticipated upfront.

"She designs with enthusiasm, professionalism, and creativity." "You will get the best out of Erica if you work closely with her." "She is patient and resourceful." "I was taken by her hands-on style and willingness to roll up her sleeves." "Erica is savvy, quick, and accurate and has a lot of great ideas at every step." "Erica was always interested in drawing up another version, even after I said enough, enough." "Her sensitivity to scale and the environs—and thorough knowledge of local code—helped us get rapid town approval." "She was the only architect who listened to me." "She knows how to create the 'right look'—especially important in my neighborhood."

Eric J. Smith Architects, PC 📷   5   4.5   4.5   5
72 Spring Street, 7th Floor, New York, NY 10012
(212) 334 - 3993   lprocida@ejsarchitects.com

Decorous, historically classical residential architecture

Steeped in the glorious historic past yet completely relevant in modern times, clients describe Eric Smith's work as "stunning perfection." It is said that he has a passion for classical design and Old World craftsmanship, with no detail overlooked. Not surprisingly, most say Smith's forte is in historic preservation or new designs that look as if they have been built over generations. Clients say they very much enjoy the process, especially given Smith's accommodating nature.

Smith graduated from the University of Illinois in architecture, spending his last year at Versailles in an honors program. After doing architecture in Chicago for a few years, Smith met David Anthony Easton in 1983 on a Lake Forest estate, and a great collaboration commenced. Smith moved to New York the next year to run Easton's drafting department, which became the core of Eric J. Smith Architects, formed in 1987. Currently there are 25 employees with Smith, and about half his commissions continue to be in conjunction with Easton. The firm is devoted to a residential practice, with about a third of the work in Manhattan, a third in the regional area, and a third elsewhere. Clients say Smith continues to be their primary contact.

With a large and efficient staff, the firm can take on projects as small as a one bedroom (penthouse) and as large as the imagination. There is an excellent budgeting process, but materials, costs, and fees are in the upper end of the range.

"Extreme classical detailing with modern elegance." "Can also do 'Greenwich-Relaxed' in a genteel manner that is of extraordinary quality, but looks like you are not trying too hard." "Eric restores my faith in men. He is just such a wonderful human being." "Every detail is perfect." "People say it takes them a few visits to take it all

in." "The most amazing service. He is so patient if there are any questions." "Bills are all clear and detailed." "Eric has a very positive attitude. He can solve all problems." "We were sent digital pictures each day as the house was built." "Such a pleasure."

Ethelind Coblin Architect (ECAPC)   3.5 3.5 4 4.5

505 Eighth Avenue, Suite 2202, New York, NY 10018
(212) 967 - 2490 www.newyork-architects.com/ecoblin
Custom residential architecture

Known mostly for her traditional-style gut renovations in the city, Ethelind Coblin is said to take a highly collaborative approach with her clients. Clients commend Coblin's soothing and charming personality, and say working with her firm is low-key and relaxed in a very professional way. We are told Coblin and her associates are willing to take on every aspect of a project, from interior decorating to down to the cabinetwork and paint color selection.

This firm of ten has been in business since 1989 with Coblin as the sole principal. She holds undergraduate degrees from both the University of Kentucky and Vanderbilt. Most of the firm's projects are fairly small in nature—it is happy to take on a bathroom or a kitchen—and we are told Coblin enjoys challenging small renovations. However, projects can also go past the million-dollar mark. The firm typically takes on six to eight projects each year, in addition to consulting jobs.

Nearly all of the firm's work is Manhattan residential, although Coblin will take on the occasional project in the Hamptons or Westchester/Fairfield County. While most of the firm's work is in renovations, Coblin also works with co-op apartment buildings designing lobbies and other common areas, and will also do small additions to existing structures. Recent projects include a duplex apartment combination on Park Avenue and several lobby/hall renovations. The firm charges a standard hourly fee.

"Ethelind was very responsive and willing to work within our limited budget." "She was very responsive to my concerns and made every effort to address them." "Ethelind really respects the client, and in turn, we really trusted her." "Our managing agent described the architectural plans as the best he had ever seen in his many years in that capacity." "I found her very imaginative and creative in the brainstorming and design process." "Extremely innovative thinking. And she really stayed with the project." "They could use more back office help, perhaps." "She's very clear—communications were excellent." "Very professional and businesslike."

Fairfax & Sammons Architects, PC   5 4.5 4.5 4.5

67 Gansevoort Street, 2nd Floor, New York, NY 10014
(212) 255 - 0704 www.fairfaxandsammons.com
Traditional, warm residential architecture

Best known for its period classical work, Fairfax & Sammons is strongly attuned to historical precedent and inherently trusted by clients to achieve the highest design standards. Favorite projects include a Corinthian-columned, fieldstone-clad, American Federal country house in Virginia and an Italian Renaissance palazzo called "Il Palmetto" in Palm Beach. Most homes reflect the Jeffersonian ideals of classical proportion inspired by 16th century architect Palladio; even a recent Anglo-Caribbean commission has Chippendale railings and round oculus windows. The firm's strength is in "vernacular traditions," and they are said to bring a very sensible and functional approach while ensuring that the finished product is warm, inviting, and "beautifully crafted."

Principals of this eighteen-person firm, founded in 1992, are Anne Fairfax and Richard Sammons, a husband-and-wife team who both earned architecture degrees from the University of Virginia, where they met. Sammons previously worked for the ebullient classicist David Easton, and sits on the boards of Classical America and The Historic House Trust, in addition to helping to organize a salon dedicated to classical music, poetry, art, and architecture. *The New York Times* includes Sammons on its short list of antediluvian "Young Turk New Classicists" and Rizzoli is doing a monograph.

Fairfax & Sammons takes on about ten new projects each year, all of which are residential and half of which are in the Manhattan area. Budgets for such projects start as small as $100,000 with the sky as the limit, ranging from studios to mega-mansions. About half of the firm's projects are new homes, with the rest split between renovations and historical preservation work. The firm charges a standard percentage of construction costs, and there is a strong commitment to budget and schedule without sacrificing aesthetics.

"Anne and Richard are both lovely to work with." "Strong commitment to quality and architectural integrity, but are more than willing to take the ultimate decision from the client." "Richard is the design genius and Anne does everything else." "Richard has an unerring eye for proportion." "You learn so much in the process." "They transformed my tiny West Village apartment by installing old French doors to the garden, making the space look 400 years old. It is magical." "I would not recommend for modern work (and I do not think they would take it on)." "They don't give any credit to their regional partners or subs, and thus the relationships can be strained there." "Very good management process—timing, budget, collaboration with contractor." "They stay three steps ahead of the contractor to avoid issues." "Very involved in the interior design as well." "I feel comfortable calling with a small question and they will quickly follow up." "Hire for an ultimate design experience."

Ferguson & Shamamian Architects, LLP 🛍 | 5 | 4.5 | 4 | 5

270 Lafayette Street, Suite 300, New York, NY 10012
(212) 941 - 8088 www.fergusonshamamian.com

Classical, vernacular, inspired residential and estate architecture

Ferguson & Shamamian has achieved iconic stature in architectural and rarified social circles for its intellectual approach toward classicism as the basis of all great design. New homes are the firm's forte, and these are massive undertakings, usually entailing years of specific wainscoting and doorknob detailing. The results are nothing short of breathtaking—uplifting, spirited, livable masterpieces born of rich provenance. Clients may be involved in every excruciating detail or may be provided with turn-key resolution, but in either case, we hear the partners prefer to work with clients who share their architectural philosophy.

Partners Mark Ferguson, who holds an M.Arch from Princeton, and Oscar Shamamian, who holds an M.Arch from Columbia, created the firm in 1988 after working together at Parish-Hadley. The large shop currently employs 60, with about 20 to 25 projects ongoing and eight to ten new projects annually. Insiders tell us the firm is efficient in its design process and extremely attentive—a principal is involved in every project. Nearly all the work is done for the residential market, about a quarter of it in Manhattan, a quarter in the regional area, and the balance coast to coast, including the Hamptons, Nantucket, Martha's Vineyard, Florida, and California.

While more than half the firm's docket is taken up with new home construction, it regularly takes on gut renovations and alterations/additions of apartments, townhouses, and homes. Ferguson & Shamamian also offers master planning and design of resort communities. Though it takes on many large Park and Fifth Avenue projects for celebrity clients, the firm remains grounded and will accept a few projects with mid-level budgets for select clients. Not surprisingly, all this excellence comes at a high cost, mostly due to higher caliber materials. The firm charges an hourly rate, which generally falls within the standard percentage of total construction costs.

"Their design sensibility is unparalleled." "The spirit of their work is like the craftsman of generations past." "Even at Yale, Mark was recognized to be one of the most talented." "They are artful in their restorations, staying true to the historic period.

This may involve bringing in reclaimed chestnut floors, but it is a remarkable result." "They will have thoughtful moldings even within their more modern forays." "Much more comfortable working in the traditional genre." "Great for people for whom money is not an issue." "A bit confident in their ways." "The budgets are prodigious, but realistic." "Going for quality, not volume." "They cater ultimately to the client, despite being a big, influential firm." "Instant pedigree. The best traditional architecture being created today."

FORM Architecture + Interiors   4   3.5   4.5   4.5
88 East 10th Street, New York, NY 10003
(212) 206 - 6430   www.formarch.com
Strikingly clean, modern architecture

FORM Architecture has been on the receiving end of praise from clients and the media alike for its becoming, modern aesthetic. Clients report that the firm can get just as excited about doing an historic Italianate renovation, as long as there is an eye towards expanding the light and flow. Its many supporters praise the firm for being sympathetic to their needs and answering questions with thoughtful, not rehearsed answers. We're also told the firm is quick with follow-ups and approaches each project with enthusiasm.

Brent Leonard and Sean Webb are the principals of the eight-person firm, which has been in business since 1999 and in practice for much longer under different names. Leonard holds a degree from Parsons College and Webb holds an M.Arch. from the University of Texas. Approximately 90% of the firm's work is residential, with much of it taking place in Manhattan and the Hamptons. FORM has also worked in Westchester and Fairfield counties, Boston, Wyoming, California, and Canada.

Recent projects speak to the firm's versatility, including a classic 57th Street triplex, a historic Brooklyn townhouse, a Calgary prairie house, an East Hampton Zen hideaway, and a Fire Island beach house. The firm works on either an hourly rate or a standard percentage of total construction costs, and is priced under market. HB Top Designers, 2000.

"Brent and Sean always work together as a team, so you get two excellent minds thinking over the issues." "They make the process fun." "You get the principals." "They really believe in Modern, but are happy to take that sensibility and apply the intellectual concept to historic motifs." "Not the best at getting started, but once they are on your case, they are completely there for you." "They are happy for you to pick up the pencil and tracing paper to see what you are thinking." "No surprises." "We were so happy with how it was turning out, that we upped the budget."

Gleicher Design Group   4   4   4   4.5
135 Fifth Avenue, 2nd Floor, New York, NY 10010
(212) 462 - 2789   www.gleicherdesign.com
Handsome modern residential architecture

A "simplicity of detail" coupled with the "versatility to design both handsome modern and elegant traditional spaces" are the keys to Gleicher Design Group's success, references report. They tell us the firm excels in gut renovations of apartments and townhouses on the Upper East and Upper West sides, but also takes on new homes and additions. Principal Paul Gleicher's "honest," "thoughtful," and "involved" approach to design is just one of many reasons clients have returned for other projects. Additionally, sources speak of Gleicher's soothing personality and how he is able to take the stress out of any situation with his positive outlook.

This firm of six was created in 1989 by sole principal Paul Gleicher after he spent time at Davis Brody & Associates and Haverson-Rockwell Architects. He holds an M.Arch. from Columbia. Gleicher and his associates' average about fifteen new projects each year, most of which are in and around the city. There is an in-house expertise in zoning issues and environmentally friendly design. He has recently partnered with *House Beautiful* on issues surrounding the topic, "How to Renovate Responsibly" featuring a house with a grass roof.

Gleicher Design Group has worked with numerous celebrity clients and also does interior decorating with two full-time design associates. The firm charges a standard percentage of overall construction costs. Clients appreciate the fact that Gleitcher "works really hard to make intelligent economic choices."

"He's just got an extraordinary gift for a brand of modern design that is warm and rich without being austere." "Their modern style often has a clean, Japanese flair to it which makes it so interesting." "Paul is very reasonable, easygoing, and wants to please." "Could have been a bit more coordination and planning on the integration of the surfaces and appliances." "His judgment and taste are terrific, and his integrity is of the highest order." "The weekly meetings were run professionally." "He gave us great economic options, although we usually went for the more expensive version, you always felt he was happy to go either way." "Moving from Manhattan to Westchester was daunting, but they understood what we wanted even when we couldn't articulate it." "Got what we wanted and more." "I would use him again in a heartbeat."

Hottenroth & Joseph Architects 🛍 4 3 5 5
1181 Broadway, 5th Floor, New York, NY 10001
(212) 941 - 1900   info@hjnyc.com
Traditional residential architecture specializing in renovations

Clients laud David Hottenroth and Jim Joseph for their tireless devotion to each project, their respect for the integrity of existing structures, and their delightful perspective. Highly recommended by some of the top marquee decorators in town, the demand for their services is growing every year. Best known for their empathy for traditional forms, they do "impeccable work" while maintaining and building upon the character of each commission. It is also noted that they have a keen ability to solve problems on the fly.

This firm of thirteen has been in business for over a decade and is led by principals Hottenroth, a graduate of the University of Cincinnati, and Joseph, who holds degrees from Cincinnati and Columbia. More than 80% of the firm's work is residential, with a particular strength in townhouses and home additions. The firm takes on projects with modest six-figure budgets (such as kitchens and smaller renovations) but also skillfully handles large, multi-million-dollar renovations and homes.

More than half of the firm's work takes place within Manhattan, with happy clients often recommending the firm to friends in the Hamptons and beyond—Westchester County, Montclair, Sun Valley, Center Island, and Palm Beach. Recent projects include a West Village townhouse penthouse addition and an Upper East Side gut renovation and elevator addition. The firm charges a lower than standard percentage of overall construction costs.

"Very thorough and conscientious, with impeccable taste." "Able to turn my vague longings into concrete plans that captured my vision perfectly." "An unerring eye." "Their distinct talents and characteristics complement each other, forming the ideal team." "David is clear, straightforward, and charming, and so good at interpreting

the client's desires." "Jim has the aesthetic fire." "Remarkably, they finished our Italianate brownstone in Brooklyn in five months. So accommodating." "While we would absolutely use them again, they are not the best at strictly sticking to a budget because they want it to be perfect. That was the right answer in the long run." "They actually came in right on schedule and a little under budget with us." "They get along remarkably well with some of the more demanding decorators in town. So likable, empathetic, did not impose views." "They are gifted architects who combine the qualities of ingenuity, taste, and professionalism." "So incredibly patient with us as we changed our minds continually." "It has been a joy."

James D'Auria Associates PC Architects 🏛   4.5   4.5   4   4.5
20 West 36th Street, 12th Floor, New York, NY 10018
(212) 268 - 1142 www.jda-architect.com

Mostly modern, comprehensive residential architecture

With a broad understanding of multiple styles, clients say they trust James D'Auria for projects ranging from cutting-edge modern design to traditional. More recently, the firm has received accolades from the press and clients for its modern, but not minimalist design. Clients say they appreciate D'Auria's keen ability to create environments that reflect clients' tastes. The firm's typical residential projects are gut renovations in Manhattan or new-home construction in the suburbs. The firm offers interior design services on projects that it acts as the architect for, and typically takes on both roles.

D'Auria, the sole principal of the firm, received a B. Arch from Pratt and studied in Florence for a year. The firm has been in business since 1974 and has grown to a staff of eight, with two interior designers, nine architects, and an administrative staff of three. D'Auria typically takes on twenty to thirty projects each year. About 50% of D'Auria's projects are in Manhattan, with the other half in the regional area, usually the Hamptons. The firm will not shy away from smaller projects. From small lofts to multi-million-dollar homes on the residential side and from small boutiques (Lacoste, Judith Ripka) to restaurants and showrooms (Skechers, Carolina Herrera) on the commercial side, D'Auria has a diversified practice.

Some recent projects include a large traditional apartment for Bryant Gumbel that was converted from three adjoining apartments. The firm also recently completed a 4,000 square foot loft on Duane Street and a traditional new home in Amagansett. The firm generally charges a higher percentage of total construction costs for its architectural services and standard hourly rates for its interior decorating services.

"James was knowledgeable, open, and honest about what he could and couldn't do." "Despite his considerable expertise, he was always open to new ideas and willing to alter his plans and views." "On occasion, he pressed his view without being argumentative or condescending." "Ever aware that it's the client's project—not his, and that it's about the client's satisfaction—not his ego." "James and his team embraced our project and completed it to his standards—which, quite simply, are the highest and best." "I have worked with a variety of decorators and architects, and James was the first one that really worked for us." "When friends come over the first question they ask is 'Who was the architect?'" "He not only completed the project on time and on budget, but he became a dear friend."

John B. Murray Architect, LLC 🏛   4.5   4.5   4   4.5
36 West 25th Street, 9th Floor, New York, NY 10010
(212) 242 - 8600 www.jbmarchitect.com

Quintessentially classical residential architecture

John Murray is among a small handful of exceptional New York residential architects that inherently understand the meaning of Park Avenue vernacular. Murray is an adamant traditionalist whose projects range from formal, classical Palladian to a more relaxed well-heeled look. Sources praise Murray for his architectural skill and experience and his dedication to historic design and form. Though "extremely busy," Murray reportedly makes himself very accessible, with thorough follow-up.

A graduate of Carnegie Mellon, Murray was a founding partner of Ferguson, Murray, and Shamamian before starting his own firm in 1998. While generally embarking on large-scale gut renovations, the firm will take on smaller projects with an interesting twist or an intriguing challenge. While some say Murray's taste for the highest form of design occasionally leads him to suggest more changes than are perhaps strictly necessary, he is known to be receptive to clients' suggestions and sympathetic to their design and budgetary interests.

The majority of Murray's work is in New York City and Connecticut, although he takes on projects across the country. Sources say that while his fine work still suits high-end tastes, he is considerably more affordable now that he is on his own. The firm generally charges a slightly higher percentage of overall construction costs but will occasionally work on an hourly rate.

"A magnificent sense of classical design." "Carriage trade masterpieces." "The weekly meeting minutes ensure that the project remains on track." "Not only is John courteous, but he is eager to teach and discuss ideas." "Could be a bit more assertive, because he absolutely knows what is right for the space." "The team is the essence of quality, sensitivity, and obsessiveness. In short, the best." "Very good client skills—kept us calm throughout." "Wish there was more support staff, to leverage John's time." "He upholds the very top standards of quality, at all times." "If you want the best, be prepared to pay." "He isn't a bargain, but he's a great value." "Our job was on budget, on time, and perfect."

J.P. Franzen Associates Architects 📖   4.5   3.5   5   4.5
95 Harbor Road, Southport, CT 06890
(203) 259 - 0529   jfranzen@franzenarchitects.com

Adaptive, carefully tailored custom residential, commercial, and institutional architecture

Citing that "people treasure the unique flavor of each little New England town," Jack Franzen has made it a point to be a student of those subtle changes from place to place. Clients say he "gets it right" and "gives you something that also feels wonderful." Most clients look to Franzen's staff for its traditional work, although the firm is said to be just as coherent in a contemporary design language. Sources say Franzen has "fantastic sources" and is said to be a master at choosing rich natural woods. With a landscape architect on staff, J.P. Franzen Associates also designs gardens, pools, and hardscape. References tell us that Franzen has become a magnet for clients with difficult sites—particularly those with waterfront property or those with tricky zoning rules.

Franzen created the firm in 1986 and stands at ten strong—with no plans on growing any bigger. He holds two architecture degrees from Cornell and is a Fellow of the AIA. We're told Franzen works mostly in the suburbs, preferring to "draw instead of drive too far." Of the company's fifteen annual residential projects, about five are ground-up projects. The rest are large-scale renovations, with many taking place in historic districts, which Franzen knows all too well as a member of the historic district commission in Fairfield. Franzen is reportedly involved in each project.

Insiders say Franzen has a knack for turning those difficult sites into beautiful homes that fit into the landscape and take advantage of views. The firm's commissions carry budgets of $250,000 to $8 million. The firm charges a slightly lower fee based on a percentage of overall construction costs. AIA Fellow, 2001.

"I couldn't be more delighted with Jack. He's just a pleasure to work with." "As long as you keep the lines of communication open, everything will go smoothly." "No hidden fees or change-order costs."

Kathryn McGraw Berry   3.5   3   4.5   4.5

8 East 96th Street, New York, NY 10128
(212) 426 - 7407   kmcgberry@aol.com
Contemporary/transitional residential architecture

Kathryn McGraw Berry creates high-end contemporary designs that have been described as "transitional modern with an eclectic twist." Working as a sole practitioner for over fifteen years, she has developed a strong following as a residential and commercial architect for clients on Park Avenue and downtown, working in new buildings and on renovations. She also offers interior design services, and clients praise the clean lines and contemporary flair of her spaces.

An award-winning architect, Berry is selective about her work, taking on only a few jobs per year. Clients appreciate her delightful nature and natural grace. Berry received a B.A. in literature from Berkeley and a B.Arch from Cooper Union. She recently completed a model apartment for the Trump Park Avenue and offices for music legend Keith Richards. The firm charges a standard fee based on a combination of hourly rates or percentage of construction costs.

"Kathryn is charming and very talented." "She develops excellent client relationships." "Understands what is appropriate in each setting."

Kenne Shepherd Interior Design
Architecture PLLC ▪   3.5   3.5   4   4

54 West 21st Street, New York, NY 10010
(212) 206 - 6336   www.kenneshepherd.com
Clean, modern residential and commercial architecture

Well-honed materials, a sophisticated use of lighting and a clean contemporary aesthetic are consistent factors in the works of Kenne Shepherd. Most interiors also feature more neutral whites and beiges, strong clean lines, and restrained geometric luxe offering "a retreat from the chaos of daily life." Shepherd believes in a strong collaborative process to "bring out the best" of the client's identity and personal style.

On all projects, the company distinguishes itself with its professionalism, attention to detail, and a strong analytical approach. Founded in 1993, the firm has a staff of five, which handles about five residential renovation projects annually. Shepherd grew up in Idaho and graduated from Idaho's architecture school. While the firm often works for high-profile luxury fashion designers and retailers, they have been doing more residential work as of late. Shepherd uses her insights and skills in developing trademark showroom branding to the home. Commercial clients have included Lancôme, Wolford America, Nicole Miller, Nars, Bergdorf's Men's Shops, Calvin Klein's Madison Avenue flagship store, and Salvatore Ferragamo's six year US market expansion. The back office is notably strong, reflecting its ability to deal with multinational corporations.

Residential projects generally start with budgets of $200,000 and go up to $2 million. Shepherd often works on a standard hourly rate or may charge a slightly lower fee as a percentage of construction. Clients say she is creative in her use of less expensive, alternative yet luxurious materials that have been used in commercial applications.

"Light and simplicity of line are used to create a mood." "Shepherd's designs invigorate and uplift the spirit." "Our taste runs to the modern so it was a perfect fit." "Very easy to work with." "There is nothing extraneous—reminds us of a commercial look in its drama and fun energy." "Kenne was very innovative. Used materials that were less known in the residential marketplace." "The monochromatic whites would not be highly practical for kids, but this was our pied-a-terre." "A show piece." "She was quite available and very down to earth."

Koko Architecture + Design ▣   4   4   4   4.5

799 Greenwich Street, Suite 1N, New York, NY 10014
(212) 206 - 3638   www.kokoarch.com

Modern Asian-inspired residential architecture with a twist

Thoughtful about function and sensitive to budget, the "young and dynamic" team of Adam Weintraub and Mishi Hosono create modern designs that are "never stark or cold." Said to be honest, hardworking, and kind, this husband-wife team use muted colors "that are in between the colors that people think exist." Making use of "interesting, but not necessarily expensive" materials including concrete panels and other texture-rich elements, the results are sophisticated yet practical. They are said to be "architects first and foremost, but also experts on furniture and textiles."

Weintraub and Hosono are principals of this firm of four, created in 2000. Weintraub holds architecture degrees from Harvard and Penn, while Hosono holds both undergraduate and graduate architecture degrees from Penn. Hosono brings a stellar resume to her practice, having worked and trained with Peter Marino and Tsao & McKown. The firm takes on roughly a dozen projects annually, 60% of which are residential. The vast majority of these deal with apartment renovations, although the firm is said to be "equally capable" of taking on ground-up single-family homes. The firm will consider projects of nearly any size and scope, given that they make a "connection" with the overall program or the client.

Projects may have fairly modest budgets, ranging from $150,000 to $1.5 million, averaging around $600,000. Approximately 80% of the firm's work takes place in Manhattan, with a sizeable following in Chicago. The firm charges a standard percentage of overall construction costs.

"Incredibly pleasant, bright, and articulate." "Very open-minded." "Mishi's uncanny color sensibility and Adam's space design turned another postwar cookie-cutter into something special." "Extremely personable, with an accommodating style, but not shy about getting the point across when you're going the wrong way." "Excellent working relationship with our contractor." "Highlights include lighting that perfectly fit the space and color suggestions that really made the house." "Ours was a tricky job with limited time and budget, and they couldn't have been easier to work with." "You enjoy their company as you would your friends' and thoroughly respect and admire them as architectural professionals."

Larson and Paul Architects ▣   4   4.5   4   4

118 Chambers Street, 4th Floor, New York, NY 10007
(212) 587 - 1900   www.larsonandpaul.com

Residential, commercial, and retail architecture

Douglas Larson recently joined forces with Rodman Paul merging the strong interests of both parties in high-end integrated residential architecture. Together and separately, they have designed many new homes and gut renovations with strong, clean lines that are referential but not beholden to historical precedent. Both architects are comfortable with a range of historical styles as well as modern idioms, using this knowledge as best applied to the context of the situation. Most of the projects are substantial in size and scope, and include the interior and landscape design. It's this excellent full service that distinguishes the firm.

"Tad" Paul grew up in California and received a degree in urban studies from Harvard and a M.Arch from Columbia. Doug Larson holds degrees in environmental and structural engineering from U. Penn and a M. Arch from U. Michigan. Larson apprenticed with Peter Marino. In 2004, Paul, most recently at Ashkar & Paul, and Larson, most recently at Bell. Larson Architects, combined their individual practices. There are 14 people total at the firm and about 60% of the work is residential, with the remainder mostly in boutique retail. Larson has been instrumental in the strategic design of the classic J. McLaughlin retail stores throughout the area.

The principals are "personally thrifty and careful with budgets," which can start as low as $200,000. A range of economic alternatives is given for all situations. We hear they do appreciate quality, though, and "don't believe in cutting corners." The firm charges a combination of percentage of construction and hourly rates.

"Incredible dedication." "Clean, traditional, upper-end. Can handle Park Ave." "Tad asked us about our lifestyle—right down to how many suits I had and how I hung them, so that the closet would be designed with the hangers at the right heights." "Tad takes himself very seriously can be quite intense in pursuit of quality and top workmanship." "When you find someone with the skill and focus of Doug you do not give them up. We have used him for many projects for the last seven years." "They are very deep into the detail and have all the requisite knowledge." "A scholarly approach. We learned so much." "Not the best support team. Often running on empty." "They knew precisely what kinds of furniture finishes would stand the moisture in the air of the house on Long Island and directed us to think about styles that would work with that." "Very responsible." "They make it right if there's ever an issue."

Lichten Craig Architects, LLP ▪   4.5   4   4.5   4.5

6 West 18th Street, 9th Floor, New York, NY 10011
(212) 229 - 0200   www.lichtencraig.com

Distinguished, classical residential architecture and interior design

Classic style, strong standards, and a personable approach are the qualities most often used to describe Lichten Craig Architects. Headed by Kevin Lichten and Joan Craig, the firm creates designs known for distinct and comely traditional detail, and regularly handles Park Avenue apartments, historic townhouses, and suburban country homes. Lichten Craig is highly recommended by clients for a cohesive design vision that combines comfort, function, and elegance. References describe the team as willing and able to accommodate clients' interests and style preferences, although the architects have been known to strongly advocate design integrity. In 2004, Lichten Craig opened a second office in Chicago, headed by Craig. Both offices successfully offer interior design services, but also collaborate well with top decorators.

The principals previously practiced separately for over a decade, joining forces in 1995. Lichten holds a B.A. from Brown and a M.Arch from Yale, and practiced with both Edward Larrabee Barnes and Fox & Fowle. Craig holds a B.A. from Wesleyan and a M.Arch. from Princeton. She practiced with Skidmore, Owings & Merrill as well as Buttrick, White, & Burtis. The leading interior designer is Joel Woodard, who pursued fashion design for almost a decade (successfully producing his own line for Bergdorf's and others), graduated from NYSID, and worked with Noel Jeffrey before joining Lichten Craig. The firm has worked at many of the best addresses in the city and also at several of their corresponding second-home outposts: Cape Cod, Onteora, and the Dominican Republic.

Lichten Craig's projects usually entail substantial renovations and new construction, but the firm is also willing to undertake smaller projects. References say that the principals are readily available once the project gets going and that the support staff is helpful. The firm also receives high marks for understanding family living and working well with contractors. The practice charges standard architectural percentage rates or a fixed fee. Interior design is done on a standard hourly basis with net pricing, or on cost-plus.

"They inherently understand a classic updated vision, with a sense of fun balanced with a sense of propriety." "There will be dignified moldings and a historical perspective." "Kevin has a truly educated architectural point of view." "Raised the standards of the contractors and represented our interests well." "Developed a cohesive vision for our international-style townhouse." "They are very precise and very meticulous, but sometimes need encouragement to move onto the next issue." "The interior design side is equally professional and skillful." "They were more disciplined on budget than we were." "Quite focused and polished."

Louis Mackall, Architect 🖼   4   3.5   4.5   5
135 Leetes Island Road, Guilford, CT 06437
(203) 415 - 6988   mackall@mac.com
Collaborative architecture, millwork specialist

Clients rave about Louis Mackall, who is said to be brilliant, kind, and keenly attuned to the client's needs. Winning fans from the Dakota in Manhattan to Connecticut, Westchester, and Long Island, this "consistently creative" architect and "Renaissance man" is lauded for both his historic restoration work and his innovative new design concepts. Clients say he "constantly outdoes himself," making each rendition more exciting and developing the maximum impact—all for a reasonable fee.

A graduate of Yale and Yale Architecture School, Mackall has been practicing architecture since 1968 and also co-helms Breakfast Woodworks, one of the region's most prestigious millwork outfits. Clients are not only impressed with the results of this one-man-show, but also amazed by the process. The architect will walk into a new project, listen to the client's objectives, then immediately jump up and take measurements with a Leica Laser integrated with a computer produced from his backpack. Within days, you will have "accurate, incredible CAD plans that are accurate to three millimeters." This unusual methodology keeps costs down and allows for almost automatic change orders.

Mackall is known to be gentle with clients and tough with subs in the same calm, measured manner that both respect. Said to be almost "too fair" when it comes to pricing, the firm typically charges on an hourly basis. We hear Mackall takes on only a few jobs at a time and is completely dedicated to making each one a success.

"A whirlwind genius." "Louis took a napkin sketch and turned it into a collective dream." "I had two ratty apartments. He turned it all into a $5 million spread." "He is incredible to work with from a decorator's point of view." "Louis came in, took kitchen measurements, and e-mailed the sketches to the client seven minutes later." "Mechanically the plans work perfectly to 1/16 of an inch." "The designs can be a bit esoteric, lots of curved walls." "Once he designed a preppy lighthouse concept for a beach house that the client just did not get. But he made revisions quickly and it all worked out fabulously in the end." "We had a leak in our new roof. He came down and stood there to make sure every nail was pounded in correctly." "Excellent negotiator. Was always there to fight on our behalf." "Flexible, caring, and creative." "Finished within the budget." "Can take longer than you would like, because sometimes he gets carried away with the creative process." "A well-timed sense of humor combined with his skill and flexibility made it easy and fun to work with him." "Likes the iterative process." "An intriguing country gentleman that understands NYC sophistication." "A no-brainier-type of recommendation."

		Quality	Cost	Value	Recommend?
		+	$	◆	★

M (Group) LLC

152 West 88th Street, New York, NY 10024
(212) 874 - 0773 www.mgrouponline.com

Chic, urban, classic interior design and architecture

See M (Group) LLC's full report under the heading Interior Designers & Decorators

May Architects P.C. 📷 3.5 3 4.5 4

1449 Lexington Avenue, New York, NY 10128
(212) 534 - 2850 www.mayarchitects.com

Restrained traditional architecture

Manhattan apartment and loft owners look to Penny May and her small firm for large-scale gut renovations. Usually working on traditional apartments, May is said to take cues from the classic architectural bones while incorporating modern twists to "avoid predictability." We hear May is highly involved in every project and puts clients at ease with her pleasant demeanor and commitment to personal attention.

This firm of four was created in 1991 by May, a graduate of Barnard College and the Columbia University School of Architecture. Typically, only three to four major residential projects are done at a time, keeping May accessible to clients. Most of the firm's work is on prewar apartments on the Upper East Side, in the 2,200 to 2,500 square foot range. May has also completed residential projects in the Hamptons, Westchester County, Connecticut, and New Jersey.

The firm charges a somewhat less than standard percentage of overall construction costs. Willing to go in stages at the behest of the client, the architect is said to present realistic estimates upfront.

"Transformed our apartment from an ugly duckling to a lovely swan." "There are virtually no unknowns when we get a set of drawings from Penny." "Penny is very pleasant and clear; a straight shooter." "She designed the whole thing and then found a cabinet maker which was much better than Smallbone at much less cost." "All handpainted, and she found the crew." "Great also at organizing and implementation." "Very easygoing, but professional." "Tried to resolve any conflicts to the benefit of the client." "Can also do contemporary." "Not grandiose ideas. Practical." "Virtually everything in the apartment was changed, with an effect nothing short of spectacular."

Michael Davis Architects & Interiors   4 4 4 4.5

435 Hudson Street, 8th Floor, New York, NY 10014
(212) 645 - 6066 www.michaeldavisarchitects.com

Vernacular, personalized architecture

Michael Davis creates homes that are utterly unique to the client—whether it's a bohemian-feeling rooftop addition in the Village, a historically accurate English fieldstone cottage in the suburbs, or a loft gallery on lower Fifth. He is said to be sensible, creative, charismatic, and flexible in both his architectural abilities and his personality. Clients say the personable Davis works very closely with them to understand their lifestyles, tastes, and needs, creating a comfortable and beautiful "portraiture of their lifestyle."

Born and raised in New York City, Davis studied art history and comparative literature at Brown and earned an M.Arch from Harvard. He established the firm in 1993 and currently heads a team of six. The firm takes on projects around the country, from Boston to San Francisco, but most of its endeavors are in New York City and Westchester. Interiors are usually also done in house. Davis meticulously chooses the finest (although not necessarily the most expensive) materials himself, even if it means a buying trip to Europe for furniture or Indonesia for architectural artifacts. He also appreciates the historical elements of his craft and uses a variety of salvaged materials such as doors, floors, and light fixtures in order to give his work a character of "patina and permanence."

About half of Davis' ten annual projects are large apartment renovations, but he also does smaller projects, ground-up homes, and historical preservation. Projects carry a wide range of budgets: from $200,000 to $4 million (new construction). Davis takes pride in being able to work either on the economic side or in no-holds-barred luxury. The firm charges a standard percentage of construction costs.

"Michael totally maintained the spirit of the place. The perfect guy if you are trying to obtain a specific look or feel." "During the interview process he stood out of the pack as the only architect who understood interior design as well as architecture." "The details are amazing; he put trim on the overhead beams to soften the edges." "Fairly responsive." "The contractor, painters, and carpenter he brought in were also terrific." "No budget is ever met, but we spent the money wisely." "The back office is not the best, especially at keeping the billing organized." "As an accountant, I can vouch that he is always upfront and honest." "Michael is an outstanding architect and one of the more decent human beings on the planet." "We have already recommended Michael to two friends." "I can't imagine using anyone else."

MR Architecture + Decor 🛍   3.5   3.5   4   4
150 West 28th Street, Suite 1102, New York, NY 10001
(212) 989 - 9300 www.mrarch.com
Modern, stylized architecture and interior design

With distinct Mies-inspired modern minimalist style, MR Architecture has designed numerous residential, commercial, and retail spaces in Manhattan. Residential projects make up the majority of the firm's portfolio, though its designers have also developed the smart, chic look of such illustrious commercial clients as J. Mendel, Takashimaya, and Origins. Neutral colors, artfully shaped upholstery, and brushed stainless often factor into the picture. The firm is noted by clients to have a strong interest in the functionality and the creative aesthetic of a project, without grandstanding on the architecture.

Created in 1995 by sole principal David Mann, a graduate of Pratt, MR Architecture currently employs sixteen (reflecting significant recent growth). Sources tell us Mann is a very hands-on principal "with no attitude" and that the staff is usually very responsive. The firm takes on about ten residences each year, a third of which for whom it also does the interior design. MR Architecture generally works on gut renovations of residences, nearly all of which are in the city.

The firm charges a slightly less than standard percentage of overall construction costs. They are noted to be good about working with highly involved clients, but if the client prefers they can also "take the ball and run with it." HB Top Designers, 2000.

"David worked with us down to the details of the lamps and the picture frames." "So flexible, nice to work with." "Inventive. If you do not want to invest in an original mid-century piece, David will come up with great alternatives." "There was a typed

list at every meeting." "Not hugely focused on solving architectural issues." "I would bid out the job to contractors beyond the firm's short list." "Everyone at the office is smart and together." "Underperformed when it came to the final stages, but I think that's typical of the industry." "They are so concerned about keeping to the param-eters of initial budgets that they took the overage off the final bill." "I had a baby shower and four people wanted to hire David." "A specific look that is winsome."

Murphy Burnham & Buttrick Architects ▪ 4.5 4.5 4 4.5
48 West 37th Street, 14th Floor, New York, NY 10018
(212) 768 - 7676 www.mbbarch.com

Tailored, modern residential and classical/historical institutional architecture

Murphy, Burnham & Buttrick is distinguished by its commitment to excellence and its strong knowledge base, whether the project be an internationally modern style or focused on historical preservation. The residential work tends to be quite modern: spare, monochromatic, and simple in its refinement. There may be striking stainless steel-clad millwork, translucent glass partitions, and a balance of neutral textures resulting in a light-filled, layered respite. The architects also bridge modern and more traditional quite successfully, with strong references to historic precedent taken in an innovative direction, such as a wall of classic mul-lioned glass for light diffusion between rooms. In all cases, the firm is noted for its professionalism and focus on client service.

Partners Harry Buttrick, Mary Burnham, and Jeffrey Murphy each bring exten-sive knowledge to the party. Buttrick has worked as an architect in New York for more than 40 years—he previously founded Buttrick, White, & Burtis, and has reshaped some of New York's most treasured institutions (Trinity School, Convent of Sacred Heart, St. Bartholomew's Church, St. Thomas's Choir School). Buttrick is an AIA Fellow (1994) and holds B.A. and M.Arch degrees from Har-vard. Burnham (Buttrick's daughter) holds degrees from Penn (summa) and Yale (M.Arch), worked with Richard Meier and Hardy Holtzman, and ran her own firm for six years. Murphy holds degrees from U. Virginia and Harvard (M.Arch), worked with I.M. Pei and Gwathmey Siegel, and practiced at his own firm for seven years. Their 25-person firm takes on about twenty new projects a year, half residential and half institutional. The principals offer a complete range of architectural, planning, and interior design services.

The firm's residential work varies in scale, from 1,200 to upwards of 8,000 square feet, and includes townhouses and loft renovations downtown, apart-ments uptown, and large single-family new home construction. Most of the firm's work is in New York, Connecticut, and Florida, including a five-story town-house in Greenwich Village, a 4,000 square foot loft on lower Fifth, and a 7,000 square foot new waterfront home in Westport. The firm charges a higher hourly rate or percentage of total construction costs, and structures proposals to meet the needs of its clients.

"Extremely thorough in their attention to quality and detail." "Sensitive to existing architecture, yet able to introduce a fresh, modern design." "Great relationship with the contractors and consultants which made the entire process seamless." "Excel-lent depth—you get a senior designer when you need one and access to a strong second line to get the project done." "They brought our pre-war apartment into the 21st century." "Over the past summer, they completed a project for us on time and on budget, and were absolutely fabulous throughout the process."

Naiztat and Ham Architects ▪ 4.5 3.5 5 5
430 West 14th Street, Suite 302, New York, NY 10014
(212) 675 - 2932 www.naiztatandham.com

Residential architecture

Clients find this experienced husband-and-wife firm "truly a gem," while peers tell us they "keep getting better with each job." Diane Naiztat and Alex Ham are equally comfortable designing in modernist or traditional styles, creating interiors that are "at once innovative and classic." The two met while studying at Cornell. Their firm, founded in 1988, commands a high volume of work, both residential and commercial (usually one big job at a time), mostly within New York City. A residential gut renovation or sub-renovation is the norm, running from $400,000 to $2 million. For new clients it needs to be a full project, but for old clients we're told the firm will do anything that is interesting. It has also undertaken work in Westchester and Connecticut.

References describe this small shop of five as creative and reliable and its partners as very approachable and "amazingly responsive," noting the team is "always on the spot" during unexpected problems, devising solutions with care, empathy, and efficiency. Some consider Naiztat one of the most "visionary" designers they have had the opportunity to work with, noting that she is thorough, meticulous, and "full of great ideas" when it comes to color and space.

Ham is known for his technical capabilities. Contractors love these two for their very complete drawings, and clients are thrilled that there is very little room for contractor error/delay, given the excellent detail. The firm is commended for its ability to listen to ideas while remaining honest to the integrity of the structure. They are said to be "soup to nuts" architects, dealing with all issues to the end.

Sources agree that "they know their business well and are fun and easy to work with, saying they will return for future projects. The practice charges a flat fee for a scope of work, and hourly for anything above and beyond that established scope.

"Diane and Alex swooped in and saved the day after we had a bad experience with another architect. No problem is insurmountable for this pair." "They have set themselves apart from their contemporaries." "As a general contractor, I am always ecstatic to work with them—they make our job easier." "Diane and Alex have a fabulous sense of space." "What was so important was their attention to detail from our first discussion to the last paint stroke on the wall." "Get them while you can! Or at least get on their waiting list." "Made the mind-boggling prospect of shopping for materials a breeze." "The duo was absolutely tenacious, working through the problems inherent with the existing structure until they created something that far exceeded our wildest dreams." "Their aim is to make clients happy."

Page Goolrick Architect PC 🛍   4   4   4   4

20 West 22nd Street, Suite 1505, New York, NY 10010
(212) 219 - 3666 www.goolrick.com

Streamlined, functional, modern residential architecture

Architect and accomplished sailor Page Goolrick designs with the utility, simplicity, and elegance of a streamlined yacht. Her clients speak of homes where everything is shipshape: appliances fit perfectly into their cupboards, clothes fold neatly into drawers, and keys are never lost. Wherever possible, spaces serve double (if not triple) functions, making the most out of New York's close quarters. While the look—unbroken lines, wood with a natural finish, neutral tones—is certainly modern, Goolrick's designs are not cold or uninviting. Clients say she teases charm out of simple shapes, warmth out of natural light, and color out of open vistas. Many hire her to do an apartment, then, admiring the graceful efficiency she achieves, bring her to the office, or vice versa. In either setting, clients appreciate Goolrick's aggressive pursuit of perfection, from schematics to screws.

Goolrick opened her boutique firm in 1989, drawing on eight years of experience at various companies on both coasts. With a staff of three, she focuses on three to four projects at a time, most in New York and Connecticut, though Goolrick is also licensed in New Jersey and California. For new clients, budgets are generally in the vicinity of $500,000, with a standard markup on construction. Clients note that Goolrick's efficient designs usually have efficient budgets; prices are high, but nothing is wasted. They also praise her involvement on the job site, citing her rapport with subcontractors as the factor that makes everything go smoothly. Those seeking frills and excess ornamentation should go elsewhere, but even traditional interior designers like to bring Goolrick in as a space consultant, saying her mantra of "clean, clean, clean" is refreshing.

"Page approaches architecture logically and rationally and is obsessed with the way things work and fit." "I appreciate her refined eye and disdain for ornamentation and excess fluff." "Page provided an original and creative solution to awkward layout problems. As a result, I was able to sell the apartment for $50,000 over the asking price." "She's very focused, she hones in on what needs to be done and does it. Not for the wishy-washy." "Hire her for your interior design as well. Her architectural ideas are so specific, it's important to have her go all the way." "I am a designer and usually exhaust clients with exacting attention to all aspects of a job. Page does a thing I thought not possible: when working with me, she almost wore me out with the amount of care and attention she gave to the details." "A dinstinct look—not for everyone." "Very strict about sticking to the budget." "After designing and managing the construction of my apartment she went on to do the same for my office, my in-laws' offices, their city apartment, their country home, my brother-in-law's home, and the Manhattan and London homes of a close friend of mine. Everyone has good words to say about her."

Patrick Gerard Carmody 🛍️   4   3   5   5

175 Fifth Avenue, Suite 811, New York, NY 10010
(212) 206 - 3620   pg.carmody@verizon.net
Traditional, impeccable residential architecture

Patrick Carmody's classical approach to architecture extends beyond style to execution. He tends to work in a traditional vein with a light touch. Clients say Carmody has particular gifts with space design and the relationship of functional elements. In his methodical management of details and patient attention to client preferences throughout many rounds of revisions, this young architect has come to produce what one contractor calls "the best work by a sole practitioner I have ever seen."

A Louisiana native, Carmody studied architecture at Rice University and then worked at Saunders and Walsh. Founded in 1999, the firm's focus is on high-end residential projects in New York City, many of them 3,000 to 4,000 square foot gut renovations on Park and Fifth avenues. Projects outside Manhattan have included a shingle-style house in Westchester and a clean-lined Art Deco-style home in Miami's South Beach.

Carmody is described as highly professional, efficient, and a perfectionist by both clients and contractors. He is known to always have the client's best interests at heart. In turn, sources find this Shreveport native a "lovely man" and tell us he is strong on managing the small and large details of the project, which makes clients feel that nothing is getting lost between the cracks. Carmody's work is described as "top-notch" and well worth the comparatively modest fee based upon cost of construction.

"We knew Patrick was the right architect for the project the first time he walked through the house." "We interviewed many architects and Patrick stood head and shoulders above the rest." "He inherently gets the Upper East Side thing." "Patrick is passionate about his work and his work quality is impeccable." "He is more demanding of the workmen than I am, and I am extremely demanding." "His quick mind and lively imagination mix winningly with his quaint Louisiana charm." "We quickly learned to read his silences." "I emailed him fifteen times today, and he is incredibly responsive." "His design was graceful, simple, and precise, deceptively so." "I learned to defer to his judgment. He was right every time." "The most amazing work ethic." "He respected our budget and the concept of return on investment." "He exceeded our expectations from day one."

Peter Pennoyer Architects   4.5   4.5   4   4
432 Park Avenue South, 11th Floor, New York, NY 10016
(212) 779 - 9765 www.ppapc.com
Residential and landmark architecture

Peter Pennoyer is especially well suited to execute challenging assignments involving historic, classical structures. And if the inspired moldings, cornices, and resonant details are not in place, you can count on Pennoyer to incorporate them seamlessly. The firm approaches its work with an "imaginative historicism," channeling Edith Wharton and Warren & Wetmore (in fact, Pennoyer recently went to press with a W&W compilation, an early 1900's architectural choice of Old New York). Pennoyer specializes in major landmark residential work in New York and will only do very high-end smaller jobs for past clients. Projects include several Upper East Side townhouses and apartments, a horse farm in Virginia, a home in Southampton, a lodge in the Adirondacks and a ski house in Utah, and several of New York's most prestigious private clubs.

Pennoyer received an M.Arch from Columbia, and has worked with Robert Stern, The Smithsonian Institution, and the NYC Landmarks Preservation Commission. For over twenty years he has directed his own firm which is now about 25 people strong. We hear he is very selective about his jobs, taking great care and attention with each one. Clients are also selective with Pennoyer, hiring the firm only for more complicated situations, given the high cost of construction. The office is said to have a highly competent staff. Pennoyer himself is known for a "responsible and cooperative" business attitude, however, we're told his sensitivity to cost and budget can be tempered by his determination to deliver the highest possible quality for the client, be it through design or materials. Fee structure depends on the scope of the project.

"One of the very few on the short list of the best architects for American Classicism on Park Avenue." "He gets the look of the finest right away which is helpful, because he is hard to persuade to your point of view." "Really wants to get it right, all the details, sometimes to the point beyond where I understand." "He turned a hellhole of a wrecked townhouse into the most beautiful space imaginable." "He lives and breathes the style of the nineteenth century gentleman architects." "Skilled at delivering extraordinary work at a comparably high cost structure." "Can really stress out the contractor." "Would not be appropriate for mid-sized jobs." "He is to architecture what Tiffany is to jewelry." "Well known by the carriage trade of New York."

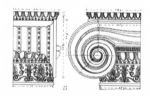

Reed Rubey Architect   3.5   3.5   4   4
200 Park Avenue South, Suite 1515, New York, NY 10003
(212) 505 - 9982 reedrubey@aol.com
Conservative, elegant, precise residential architecture

Clients tell us "there cannot be a more sincere architect in New York" than Reed Rubey, who has earned his reputation as a precise, intelligent, and creative practitioner. Clients are just as impressed with his honesty, integrity, and warmth. Rubey's designs consist of conservative, elegant lines that are classically inspired, yet can just as well frame contemporary spaces based upon the clients' preferences. He is known to always produce enforceable, well-thought-out design documents. Clients tell us Rubey's meticulous preparation ensures their projects are executed on budget, but timing may sometimes slip.

Rubey studied at Stanford for his B.A. and received his M.Arch from Harvard. Clients appreciate that Rubey's small practice—opened in 1984 and currently totaling two—allows their project to be the direct focus of the principal. They tell us Rubey's great care extends beyond excellent plans and specs to the handling of clients.

The majority of Rubey's work consists of Manhattan residences, with projects starting around $200,000 and averaging about $500,000. The firm also works in Greenwich and Long Island. This firm typically bills by the hour, equaling a somewhat below standard fee structure (given the low overhead).

"He became part of our family." "Very efficient. Excellent drawings. Answers problems straight away." "Good with clients. Give him a schedule and he will meet the time limits." "His clients are very happy. He is extremely careful—he takes his time. Don't use him for something you want done in a hurry." "Reed came up with plans to my exact specifications. I loved them. Then he asked if I'd like to see what he would do with the space. When I saw his ideas, I pushed the others aside and we started the project immediately." "The condo board loved his ideas, and he worked really well with them." "Really a nice guy."

Robert Rich 🛍️   4.5   4.5   4   4.5

160 Fifth Avenue, Suite 903, New York, NY 10010
(212) 645 - 4631 www.robertrichassociates.com
Comely, stately, traditional residential architectural design

This admitted traditionalist strives for clear and well-defined architecture that clients admire as both unique and standing the test of time. The stated concept is to create spaces that are true to the client, in tune with the site, and that exhibit fresh life with brush-strokes of cutting-edge, ever-evolving design. The results truly stand out of the pack in their achievement of a rarified look. While Rich doesn't specialize in restoration, many feel that his attention to detail is well suited to renovation and period work.

The firm chiefly has its hand in the remodeling of prewar apartments in Manhattan and usually in conjunction with one of the most upscale (read: highest cost) decorators in town. Rich has also done projects with larger-scale historic homes in Aspen, Bedford, and Aiken. Projects range upwards from $250,000 to well beyond.

This Mississippi native graduated Tulane with a B.Arch and a master's in urban development. While he has the degrees, Rich never sat for the exam, so he is not licensed. He established his practice twenty years ago and has remained small—only himself and an associate. Customers mark this as a positive, noting that Rich personally spends a great deal of time and energy supervising each stage of construction, ensuring that the entire team of contractors and subcontractors follow through at every phase of the project. A high volume of repeat business speaks to the confidence that Rich and his work inspire in clients. We hear most projects are assessed a fixed fee for Rich's design efforts, while smaller ones are charged on an above-average hourly basis.

"A true traditionalist." "Not overdone—understands the country club set look. But does it with panache." "He evaluated our needs and desires and translated them into an ideal home." "A bit over-the-top in personality, but this works in your favor when he is on your team." "Fastidious." "Extraordinarily nice to work with." "Oversees contractors very directly, so much so it probably drives them nuts." "A delightful experience working with him—so much so that we never considering shopping elsewhere for subsequent projects."

Roger Ferris + Partners 🛍️   4.5   4.5   4   5
285 Riverside Avenue, Westport, CT 06880
(203) 222 - 4848   www.ferrisarch.com

Intelligent, highly-detailed, custom residential and commercial architecture

From its stark minimalist creations to classic Shingle-style homes to environmentally green idioms, Roger Ferris and his team are recognized for their excellence in design—and they have seventeen AIA awards to prove it. Better known for striking, modern composures, the firm espouses a philosophy of innovation and collaboration that is at the core of the business. Insiders say regardless of the style, the firm "really crosses all the t's and dots all the i's," and is widely known for producing some of the best construction documents in the industry. References say the 50-person office works and "feels" like a small one.

Founded in 1986, Principal Roger Ferris (M.Arch. Harvard), Partner David Beem (RPI), and Partner Robert Marx (Yale, M.Arch Texas) win accolades from clients for their thoroughness and focus. Beem has been with the enterprise for eighteen years and Marx for ten. The residential studio has twenty employees, yet takes on only eight to ten select projects each year, devoting the time and attention needed to uphold high standards of detail and design diligence. Thus, those with smaller budgets should probably shop elsewhere, as residential projects start at about $500,000 and top out well above that. Half renovation and half new construction, most jobs are in Manhattan, Westchester, and Fairfield, though Ferris has also completed multiple projects in Palm Beach, LA, and the Bahamas.

Beyond residential work, the firm also has a 30-person commercial design studio, handling high-end retail and office spaces as well as country clubs. The firm charges a flat fee, which is equivalent to a standard percentage of overall construction costs (which are generally high due to the clients' refined taste levels in materials). There is a substantial set of repeat clients.

"Roger really wants his work to matter." "He is not interested in leaving his fingerprint on the project, yet definitely leads the way with regard to exciting designs." "Roger is very exacting, definitive, and up front." "You couldn't get me to move out of this house for all the tea in China." "The columns seem to be floating right out of the yard." "His designs are bold without being overpowering. Subtle and sophisticated at the same time." "Works for the carriage trade of New York. Those in the know." "Creates amazing designs, yet they are also functional and pragmatic." "Roger is a wonderful, warm, engaging, special man." "I wouldn't even talk to another architect."

Ronnette Riley Architect 🛍️   3.5   3.5   4   4
350 Fifth Avenue, Suite 8001, New York, NY 10118
(212) 594 - 4015   www.ronnetteriley.com

Unified, functional, modern residential, commercial, and retail architecture

Ronnette Riley has been called "one the most successful woman in architecture today," and she is one of only a handful of women to head her own firm. The firm is known for inventive and hip retail, corporate, and residential spaces around New York, which are described as "contemporary with warm touches." There is a clean, tailored, unified, monochromatic look, distinctly modern without forgetting function. Strength of character is seen in the work, which has a clarity of position. Clients say Riley's "can-do attitude" assures that the project will cross the finish line.

Riley received an M.Arch from Harvard and was associated with Philip Johnson for eight years. Clients find her staff of eight "kind and understanding," and compliment the firm's quality and creativity. Riley takes on the interior design as well as the architecture, helped by an excellent understanding of the latest architectural terrain through her exposure to the retail world. The team is given kudos for managing projects and budgets effectively and maintaining excellent communication with the clients and the contractors.

Branching out with recent award-winning projects like the Apple Store in Soho, the firm is located significantly atop the Empire State Building. Recent work has included commercial spaces for New World Coffee, John Barrett's at Bergdorf's, and Restoration Hardware. Open to doing smaller institutional and residential work, the firm has completed over 500 residential projects in Manhattan since its inception in 1987. All in all, Riley is known as a well-diversified, highly competent force in architecture. AIA Fellow 1998.

"Very talented, very driven, very busy." "Ronnette and her staff were responsive and helpful." "Ronnette makes it her business to know new materials, new solutions." "Very good at what they do." "Absolutely gets it done." "Highly confident." "Can be very set in their design vision, with less sensitivity to alternatives." "Will reply to e-mails within 15 minutes and help you from the pillars (space design) to the pillows (decor)."

S. Russell Groves 🛍   4.5   3.5   5   4.5
210 11th Avenue, Suite 502, New York, NY 10001
(212) 929 - 5221 www.srussellgroves.com

Restrained, elegant modern residential and retail architecture and interior design

It is difficult to accomplish that perfect balance between restraint and elegance, but Russell Groves does just that. His clean modern spaces offer luxury and tranquility with an open flow, sensuous materials on geometric forms, and a maze of hidden closets. There is a strong predilection for a harmony of warm creams and beiges, furnishings of the Modernist movement, and detailing in natural travertine and custom woods. Clients find the spaces "serene and clean," with no clutter and plenty of storage. In Groves' multifunctional universe, walls don't just look alluring, they work. The simplicity of the look belies the functionality of the designs, which make sense for clients' busy, urban lifestyles.

Groves founded his firm in 1995 after graduating from RISD and working with Peter Marino. The medium-sized office of about ten has a high-profile retail client base (Coach's Madison Avenue flagship, Emporio Armani, LeSportsac's flagship, the new Frederic Fekkai salon at Bendel's), but also a strong commitment to the residential market. Clients say Groves is a "very sweet person" who fields a great team. It is said he's so in tune with clients' needs and expectations that Groves' first suggestion often hits the mark. Some report that his attention to perfection can complicate the process, but all agree that the quality of his work is impeccable.

Mindful of budget and timeline constraints (given the retail successes), references say Groves provides great options concerning both aesthetics and economics. The firm charges a set fee on percentage of construction, and clients tell us "value is key with Russell." HB Top Designers, 1999, 2000.

"Terrific appreciation of existing architecture but with a totally fresh and thoroughly modern eye." "Design that fits the times and stands the test of time." "So worth it. Russell never short changes you." "Russell listened to our entire family. Even our two-year-old daughter." "Only negative is that some of the custom furniture may not be easy to maintain." "The expertise of the interior design matches that of the architecture." "I liked the firm so much I wish I could become a partner." "At the heels of the masters."

Selldorf Architects 🛍   4   4   4   4.5
62 White Street, 5th Floor, New York, NY 10013
(212) 219 - 9571 www.selldorf.com

Minimalistic, modern residential architecture and interior design

Heralded for her renovation of the Neue Galerie, Annabelle Selldorf is recognized for her skill in "designing for art." Her minimalist-modern designs get maximum exposure in loft-like downtown galleries and modern residential spaces. We're told Selldorf focuses on simplicity and function. Sleek and uncluttered spaces gain levity from the proportion, warmth of materials, and openness she considers to be the core of each design. Clients comment on her careful use of white and muted colors, her respect for detail and the intelligence of her work. Her straightforward, no-frills, unpretentious manner is as evident in her designs as her approach. She also can successfully mix modern and traditional elements.

Born in Germany to a family of architects, Selldorf continues to work in Venice, Zurich, and London, as well as in New York. The architect attended Pratt and gained valuable on-the-job experience working for a general contractor. The office of 25, including 19 architects, is said to quite helpful. While most projects are quite high end, often with excellent art integrally involved, smaller apartments of 2,000 square feet are also taken on regularly. We hear this inspired architect makes the completion of complex projects timely and efficient. Not known for the tightest drawings in the city, references report that she is nonetheless "quick to solve a problem." The firm charges a standard percentage of the construction cost. Selldorf recently introduced a line of furniture with tailored proportions, Vica, which is manufactured in the factory founded by her grandmother in Cologne. AD 100, 2000, 2002, 2004.

"While Annabelle is best known for her more neutral palette, she happily incorporated our interest in bright florals and opulent touches on a selective basis. Created fun, yet sophisticated spaces." "Tends toward the elegant, not the everyday." "She made the ugliest sofa amazing with an extraordinary giraffe print." "Annabelle is the only architect I know who has a perfect sense of volume, harmony of scale, and light, as well as the compatibility of architecture and art." "Can be quite innovative and ambitious in a good way." "Thought of the most incredible Indian soapstone floor, which was also very economical." "Annabelle was there for weekly meetings during the construction phase, and then kept up to speed, but she travels a lot." "Billing and timing on target." "She helped me through the stressful times with her ability to remain calm and with her sense of humor." "We developed such a nice relationship."

Shelton, Mindel & Associates 📷   5   5   4   5
56 West 22nd Street, Suite 12, New York, NY 10010
(212) 243 - 3939   smaconnect@aol.com
Sensuous, carefully edited, modern residential architecture

Still forward thinking and adventurous after 25 years in the business, Peter Shelton and Lee Mindel are icons of the "simplicity through rigor" mantra. The pair is lauded for its ability to lure clients into the spell of contemporary clarity with refined, controlled spaces that are minimal yet rich in detail. The firm is characterized by a signature style best described as Beguiling Modern, with an underlying Blue Chip mentality. The architects are also intimately involved in the interior design of their spaces, often creating custom furniture and lighting schemes that are said to be "brushstrokes of the larger plan."

Clients report partners Shelton and Mindel are "smart, likeable, conscientious" architects who "exhibit zero attitude." The firm is also highly respected throughout the building and design professions. While we hear the focus with which the firm pursues the realization of its design vision sometimes leaves less regard for creature comforts, clients say there's no question they feel at home in Shelton and Mindel's highly original, deft architecture. The company has worked in many of Manhattan's best buildings, with 6,000 square feet being the norm.

Both began their studies at the University of Pennsylvania. Shelton graduated from Pratt in 1975 and then joined Edward Durell Stone and later Emery Roth & Sons. Mindel graduated from Harvard in 1976, and worked for Skidmore, Owings & Merill and then Rogers, Butler, Burgun. The firm was founded in 1978 and currently employs about fifteen people. There is an intellectual, collegial atmosphere at the office and many of the staff have been there for over fifteen years. The team has received many tributes, including sixteen AIA awards and a place in the Interior Design Hall of Fame. The company also designs products for Waterworks, Knoll, Nessen Lighting, and V'Soske. A flat percentage of the overall construction is charged to cover both architecture and design fees. Mindel AIA Fellow 2000. AD 100, 2000, 2002, 2004. HB Top Designers, 1999, 2000, 2001, 2003, 2004, 2005. ID Hall of Fame.

"Transcending architecture, culminating in art." "I highly recommend them for their high standards, impeccable designs and strong professionalism." "A warm and unpretentious manner that belies fairly strict adherence to the Modern view." "Supremely disciplined in their focus to trim away all excess." "They can also do traditional, but not the chintz thing." "You must do it their way." "Always trying to create more space or, at least a sense of space, especially in Manhattan apartments." "Lee and Peter live their projects 24/7." "The back office is fabulous." "Big personality and a special approach." "An extraordinary ability to see the end game." "Costs are high but in line with the estimates." "They work and work until they create something magical."

Siris/Coombs Architects   4   3.5   4.5   4.5
211 West 19th Street, New York, NY 10011
(212) 580 - 2220 www.siriscoombs.com

Handsome, practical, residential architecture, rooftop additions

Clients speak highly of the integrity of this "honest" firm's work, which we hear combines value with "imagination—a rare commodity these days." The Siris/Coombs vision is a "livable modernism" with an emphasis on clarity of plan, appropriate materials, and attentiveness to detail. Rooms are said to be practical and functional with minimal excess, highlighted by restrained, handsome natural wood surfaces. Noted for a commitment to the residential market, the company's resume includes private homes, townhouses, lofts, and apartments in New York City and Connecticut. In addition, rooftop additions have become a unique specialty for which the firm is recognized.

Founded in 1982, the firm established its reputation with a triplex penthouse the principals built for themselves atop a twelve-story building. Jane Siris graduated Barnard College with a B.A. and Columbia with an M.Arch. Husband Peter Coombs received his B.A. from Amherst and his M.Arch from Columbia. Clients say the firm distinguishes itself with excellent service that includes collaborative up front presentations, regular meetings, and strong/timely execution. This flexible duo reportedly offers a variety of workable options concerning both aesthetics and budget. References were equally impressed with Siris' and Coombs' knowledge of "nuts and bolts" when dealing with contractors and city agencies.

We're told both Siris and Coombs have "top-notch" people skills, and do everything possible to make clients' homes beautiful without bankrupting them. A gentle consistency of form throughout their projects ensures no budgetary or design surprises. The fee is typically a standard percentage of total construction cost.

"Jane and Peter made suggestions to our apartment that we could not have envisioned, adding economic value and improving our style of living." "Peter is a gentle man and a gentleman with a twinkle in his eye, creative solutions, and impeccable taste." "I am full of admiration for Peter's ability to take a complex project and break it into its many pieces, and then respond to the challenges." "They have always understood easy simplicity—even before it was fashionable." "Jane has no foibles. None! She is truly an intellectual. I loved working with her." "Creative, highly professional, and well organized." "They bring a sophisticated and well-integrated aesthetic vision to their work."

SPG Architects 🛍 4 3.5 4.5 4.5

136 West 21st Street, 6th Floor, New York, NY 10011
(212) 366 - 5500 www.spgarchitects.com

Refined, thoroughly modern residential and commercial architecture with panache

With strong modern clarity, the designs of SPG resonate warmth and spirit. The look is highly unified and highly edited. But a generous use of natural materials in clean, flush planes enriches the space and adds thoughtful complexity. To SPG, traditional means maintaining the moldings and interfusing sleek linear cabinetry throughout. The result is a consistent "spatial experience" with a polished and joyful demeanor.

Caroline "Coty" Sidnam, who founded the firm over twenty years ago, was joined by Eric Gartner as partner in 1993. Sidnam was an undergraduate at Kenyon and Sarah Lawrence, then received her architecture degree from Cooper Union. Gartner received both his B.S. and M.Arch from the University of Virginia. The practice employs twelve architects who collectively draw inspiration from the rapport they develop with clients. Clients speak of an easy manner and strong creativity at both the staff and principal level. Residential projects make up about a third of the firm's "state-of-the-art" work, which includes the renovation and construction of many co-op and condominium apartments, urban townhouses, and second homes.

The firm has also cultivated an impressive commercial and retail roster which includes AOL's Manhattan corporate offices, Polo Sport's prototype Madison Avenue flagship, and the Hartmann luggage store among others. This new-wave commercial/retail work clearly informs the firm's residential compositions and offers a strong level of budgeting and timeliness. Fees are slightly under the standard range.

"The best architectural team—they ensured a truly fun and successful experience." "The whole crew is professional, smart, fresh, creative, talented, sensible, thoughtful, thorough, honest, and just a group of solid citizens—people we really liked." "Attention to us and the project was unwavering." "Very complete drawings with no surprises. Thus, the contractor stayed on target." "Strong personalities that you would have to click with." "They kept us on budget, even when we thought about straying." "Their contractor contacts were excellent—we rave them as much as we do the architect." "The end result looked just like the drawings." "Like working with good friends." "We'll never have to search for an architecture team again—they're keepers."

Stephen Wang + Associates
Architects PLLC 🛍 4.5 4 4.5 5

135 East 55th Street, New York, NY 10022
(212) 829 - 9494 stephen@swarchitect.com

Personalized, detailed, responsive residential architecture

Sought out by movie stars and star decorators, Stephen Wang is loyal to his clients, and they respond with praise and loyalty. With capabilities in a wide variety of design genres, Wang's greatest strength is his ability to listen and deliver. Whether it is traditional mahogany paneling, Continental chic, or Industrial-tinged modern with panache, Wang understands what people want and works extremely hard to please. He is said to be very detail oriented, attending all client meetings and usually managing the overall process. Furthermore, clients cite Wang's even-keeled temperament as a major factor contributing to a "pleasant, successful experience."

Of Norwegian heritage and born and raised in Australia, Wang wanted to be an architect from the age of twelve. After working in architecture for a time in Australia and Europe, he won a scholarship to study sustainable design in the US in 1988. Soon after, he started his own practice in New York. The firm remains small, with eight on staff usually handling about ten major gut renovations at a time in the upper end of the market. Wang has capable project managers (with the firm six to fourteen years) on every job, but is known as a bit of a "control freak," staying on top of every aspect, much to the clients' delight.

At this point in his career, most of the projects tend to be quite large, with a minimum of about $800,000, but Wang will take on a door if he thinks the project will be interesting (as he did for Madonna). For normal mortals, Wang is open to doing a few rooms. Wang's fee is on the lower side, but he encourages the use of higher-end materials since most of the cost is in labor. Reportedly, the firm is very focused on time and money, with excellent cost analysis programming and communications.

"Clients LOVE them, they keep things running smoothly." "Traditional. Creative. They do different things." "Highest quality; does all Park Avenue." "Distinguished, easy to work with." "Impeccable taste, innovative design." "Very able to take the client's intent and enhance beautifully." "Not at all a formulaic approach. They take pride in providing outstanding service." "Very hands-on in every aspect. Managed the entire construction process." "Entrenched in the process." "Stephen enjoys the process down to the furniture level." "Among the most charming in the business." "Pleasure to be with." "One of the only businesses that actually believe that the client is right." "Responsive, detail-oriented, even-tempered." "In a word: user-friendly."

Steven Harris Architects LLP   4.5 4.5 4 4
50 Warren Street, New York, NY 10007
(212) 587 - 1108 www.stevenharrisarchitects.com
Innovative, intellectual residential architecture

Clients admire Steven Harris, a "walking dictionary of architecture" who can execute projects in a "timely, diligent, and responsible" manner. We're told this Yale professor is an intellectual and inventive problem solver who can often see solutions where others cannot. While Harris takes his client's tastes and the project's setting into account, he is said to have a distinct point of view that is "highly theoretical." This may evolve into many different forms: a modern uptown townhouse, an edgy downtown space, an historic 18th century farmhouse, or a colorful Florida beach house—but all are distinct and intellectually compelling. References advise a review of Harris' paradigmatic portfolio before embarking on a project, but past clients wouldn't consider anyone else for future projects. Several have insisted that Harris see a new piece of property before purchase.

Sources say Harris is witty, down-to-earth, and fun. He is reportedly respectful of budgets, and if necessary can turn his creativity to finding less expensive design solutions. With a reputation for flawless execution and project management, the firm cares for every conceivable detail, shields the client from the more arduous parts of the construction process, and keeps the builders focused. Clients love the fact Harris can't help but share his "extraordinary depth and breadth of knowledge." The office is 25 people strong, and usually undertakes the interior design as well. In all projects, Harris is intimately involved in the design phase.

Harris earned a B.A. from New College, a B.F.A. from RISD and a M.Arch from Princeton. He holds a professorship at Yale's architecture school and has also taught at Princeton and Harvard. He is co-author with Deborah Berke of *Architecture of the Everyday*. Before starting his own firm in 1985, he worked with such architecture greats as Michael Graves and Charles Gwathmey.

Harris either charges a standard percentage of construction costs or a combination of this and an hourly fee. For his interior design services, he typically charges an hourly fee, passing discounts on to clients. In the last ten years, Harris has done thirty-five townhouses, numerous large apartment renovations, and several homes around the world in various vernaculars.

"Steven and his associates are incredibly talented and imaginative." "He has an uncanny ability to solve difficult problems very quickly." "It took him ten minutes to understand the space and see what could be done with it." "Highly innovative." "They designed a five-floor interior that was consistent and integrated—color, interior design, scale—everything." "Can get lost on an unrealistic tangent. Unfortunately, we did not figure this out until many billing hours later. "Great teacher—extraordinary depth and breadth of knowledge." "Must specifically like what he does." "Idiosyncratic." "The approach is research-oriented." "Very prominent in the profession." "The senior project managers run the whole project end-to-end." "Harris gets the 'pick of the litter' from the graduating class at Yale—he has some of the best and the brightest of the last ten years." "It is a dynamic office that is run like a studio." "We are embarking upon our third project with Steven."

Timothy Bryant Architect    4.5   4   4.5   4
66 West Broadway, New York, NY 10007
(212) 571 - 6885 www.timothybryant.com

Classical, tailored, detail-oriented residential architecture

Timothy Bryant designs mature, classically influenced homes for clients who put authenticity and couture detailing at the top of their lists. Though traditional in nature, projects are never overwhelmed by extraneous flourishes: rooms often end up painted white, since the lines speak for themselves. Bryant, who makes his initial drawings in pencil, values historical accuracy and a proper sense of context. References report that Bryant's homes are classically constructed down to the shingles, and praise his affinity for designing and supervising both apartment renovations and ground-up projects (which he has executed throughout the Northeast, California, and Idaho). Bryant has collaborated with some of the top talents in interior design, including Glen Gissler and Victoria Hagan, all of whom admire the "dressmaker's details" that characterize his work.

Bryant, who is British, grew up accompanying his builder father to job sites. In England he studied both interior design and architecture, but never finished the latter degree and instead emigrated to America. Once here, he worked for Thierry Despont for four years. Hez went on to stints for a variety of disparate companies, everything from a small lighting design firm to architectural icon Ferguson & Shamamian. In 1997 he founded this namesake firm, which now has a staff of ten, taking on fifteen to twenty projects at a time. References report that Bryant's multifaceted education makes him something of a polyglot: "he speaks decorator-ese, contractor-ese, lighting designer-ese, and everything you could think of. That comes in handy on the big, serious jobs."

References report that Bryant is in the top tier of the market, but that his rates (charged hourly, not to exceed a certain percentage) are a notch below most competitors. He typically won't take on whole projects with construction budgets of less than $500,000, but will work on a consultancy basis or provide drawings on smaller-scale jobs. A certifiable workaholic, clients say that Bryant keeps long hours and turns around drawings lightning-quick. Pleasant and professional, Bryant is said to be happiest when discussing his work.

"My contractor, who got up at four in the morning, said sometimes Tim would still be up working, delighted to talk to him about moldings in the middle of the night." "Tim takes a big idea and then details it up and down. He thinks about things other architects skim over." "His houses are classically done, from top to bottom. He doesn't tweak or invent things." "The book of drawings he gave us was enormous. There were seven pages detailing the birdhouse alone." "We had ebony detailing on our doors, and Tim insisted on finding us ebony doorknobs to match. They're beautiful!" "For classical spaces, he's the best I've ever seen." "He solved any problems onsite."

"Friendly and outgoing. He came to my birthday party." "Always knows how to keep the client happy, but then again, he's very good at finding clients who appreciate his vision." "This is his life's work, and he takes it seriously." "He has a great sense of appropriateness." "I'm an interior designer, and he collaborated with me on my own apartment very fluidly. There was no attitude or ego." "Tim works really well with subcontractors." "Expensive, but absolutely worth it." "Timothy is a well-kept, and well-worth-it, secret." "A fine residential architect, in the best sense."

Turett Collaborative Architects   4   4   4   4.5

86 Franklin Street, 3rd Floor, New York, NY 10013
(212) 965 - 1244   www.turettarch.com

Cutting-edge, creative residential architecture

Wayne Turett, principal of his namesake firm, designs with an agile mind and an inventive spirit. Turett first made his mark on New York in the mid-eighties, redesigning a classic urban icon, the newsstand (making him one of the city's only architects whose influence can be seen on almost every street). Following that, he worked on a number of commercial products, including the invention and management of the NewsBar chain. Turett brings that same entrepreneurial spark to his current focus: residential architecture. His projects tend to be large, often in scale and always in ambition. They blend a crisp contemporary style with unique flourishes, livening up everything from country retreats to townhouses (the latter being a particular specialty). Clients emphasize Turett's creativity, but also praise his patience and integrity, saying he will only take those commissions on which he can do his best work.

Turett received architectural degrees from the University of Illinois and Pratt, then worked for a small New York architect before founding this firm in 1984. He currently fields a staff of six, with about ten projects in various stages going on at once. Clients say he is the most animated during the design phase, where his problem-solving skills and attention to detail are roundly praised. Once construction begins, a project manager steps up to bat, handling the follow-through, while Turett remains available if issues arise. Weekly meetings are standard, though for more involved projects, the firm is often in daily contact with clients. The firm has an interior designer on staff, and can supervise the building process as well, making it a true full-service operation.

Budgets are rarely below $150,000 and are more often twice that. Clients note that Turett's experience in commercial architecture means that the paperwork is always tidy and organized. They also stress that Turett is brilliant with creative challenges, saying that while all architects solve problems, Turett "solves them in ways that nobody has ever thought of."

"We had a tough project due to lack of interior light, out-of-date plumbing, and a 'divided' narrow area. Wayne + Co brought our long, narrow dark loft into the light by raising a loft and creating a new and fabulous open connected interior design." "Does his best work on complete projects." "Wayne was able to deal with a sometimes difficult contractor with skills of a diplomat." "Listened to me, but insisted on some points. There was some friction, but he was right, so I'm glad he stuck to his guns." "Wayne is both classic and avant-garde." "A good listener." "Wayne will find a way to make your home more interesting." "The architecture was very high end—it included a floor fish pond in the living room, an elevator, custom stairs, a custom kitchen, and much more." "Don't try to make him do anything too traditional, let him do what he does best: clean, contemporary, brilliant work." "Wayne has a straightforward, unpretentious style of explanation that is disarming. Mutual respect and calmness (as well as lightheartedness) seems to be the most fitting description of his office." "For Wayne, design is not produced in a vacuum but responds to unique conditions established by the client and site."

	Quality 	Cost $	Value ◆	Recommend? ★

Turino Kalberer Architects   4   3   5   5
462 Broadway, 3rd Floor, New York, NY 10013
(212) 219 - 3007

Classic, becoming, traditional residential architecture

Known for her understated, upscale "Park Avenue look," Julie Kalberer is lauded for her managerial skills as well as her architectural talents. "If anyone could help you enjoy the process of home renovation, it would be Julie," says an enthusiastic client. Sources suggest that homeowners looking for clean, traditional, classic elegance couldn't do better than to hire this architecture firm. The four-person practice is known for skilled execution and excellent attention to detail, and for its cost-effective and budget-conscious designs. Focusing exclusively on the residential market, half of the work is Manhattan-based apartments and the rest is on homes across the country (Watch Hill, Millbrook, Charleston, Seattle).

This widely published architect received her M.Arch from Columbia University. She then trained with Peter Pennoyer before creating her own firm in 1990. Clients laud Kalberer for her lively, energetic, and outgoing personality as well as her strong background in preservation. Both contractors and prominent local architects praise her "flawless drawings" and recognize her work as being of the highest caliber.

Fees are somewhat lower than the standard range, and clients report that she is excellent about offering a wide range of aesthetic and budget choices. Projects range from mid-sized to large residences. Clients deem the firm to be very reasonably priced, with a few wondering if the firm actually charges enough.

"Julie has a wonderful eye and gives practical advice, while always being professional, diligent, and reliable." "Julie was able to keep the spirit of the turn-of-the-century building in bringing my apartment up to the year 2000." "Came up with an innovative layout that both optimized the space and addressed the expense and timing constraints." "They know how to produce complete and accurate drawings." "Always responsive to the questions, needs, and anxieties any project in New York entails." "Very reliable and predictable." "Has a realistic budget and sticks to it." "Great project management. Julie knows how to get things expedited." "Conscientious and honest."

Vail Associates Architects   4   4   4   5
53 West 72nd Street, Suite 1, New York, NY 10023
(212) 877 - 0094 www.vailassociatesarchitects.com

Classic, user-friendly, high-end residential architecture

This "superb" designer has clients calling him their "architect for life." Thomas Vail tenders his design services to a primarily uptown residential clientele, who find him to be creative, helpful, and responsive. Projects are mostly gut renovations of apartments and townhouses, as well as new construction in the city, Westchester, and out on the Cape. When not overwhelmed with clients wanting to conscript him for life, we hear Vail's small firm will entertain small projects.

Before venturing out on his own in 1990, Vail worked at Skidmore, Owings & Merrill. Clients compliment the affable Vail for his thoughtful attention to detail and the amount of time he dedicates to addressing all their ideas and issues. He respects and encourages a client's taste, finding it critical to the realization of the project, which more often than not can be framed as traditional. While Vail's style changes with the customer climate, his service is as solid as a ski mountain. Designers and contractors are as quick to recommend Vail Associates to clients in search of an architect.

The firm generally charges a percentage of construction, which falls within standard industry rates, depending on the scope of the project.

	Quality	Cost	Value	Recommend?
	✚	$	◆	★

"Excellent design, extremely professional, and totally committed to service and follow-up to the very end." "As the decorator, I feel that Tom made the project seamless and delighted the client with the results." "Listens to the client, none of the usual architect 'if I didn't think of it, it must be bad' stuff." "Honest, direct, and classically trained." "He is quite in demand and needs to hire a bigger administrative staff now." "So incredibly personable, but not quite as efficient." "Great creativity, smart work, terrific value, nice people, and a pleasure to work with." "Comprehensive construction documents—as a repeat client, I feel confident using and recommending him again and again."

Victoria Benatar Architect PLLC   3.5   4   4   4

220 East 57th Street, Suite 2K, New York, NY 10022
(212) 755 - 0525 www.victoriabenatar.com
Effective residential architecture and consulting

Victoria Benatar is sought after for deftly incorporating sleek, linear forms into her "wired" designs that feature the latest in home automation and networking. Her style has been described as "comfortable and practical" with a penchant for the neutral tones and clean lines of the modern aesthetic (although she has also taken on a number of more traditional projects). Clients applaud her "careful use of every inch of space" and her collaborative approach. She is said to improve the client's quality of life by closely analyzing their lifestyle patterns and preferences.

Benatar has been a sole practitioner since establishing her firm in 1983. She studied in her native Venezuela for her undergraduate degree and received a M.S. from Columbia University in architecture and urban design. Approximately 80% of her projects are residential commissions, including complete apartment and home renovations, or serving as a consultant. The majority of Benatar's work takes place in Manhattan, though she has also completed projects in Florida, Spain, and Venezuela. Part-time assistants may be brought in on an as-needed basis.

Benatar takes on projects of modest budgets ranging from single-room renovations to large-scale gut renovations topping $5 million. She charges slightly higher fees based on an hourly rate, but clients say her efficiency more than makes up for the differential.

"Extremely imaginative with superlative taste." "She has been able to comply with all of our needs without breaking the harmony of the space." "She asked all the right questions up front." "Victoria was able to include all of the comfort of our old 5,000 square foot penthouse into our newer, smaller-sized apartment." "Did an excellent job with great efficiency, always doing her best to supply superior quality at reasonable costs." "She turned a standard apartment into a more luxurious and larger-feeling space." "Every nook and cranny was utilized." "Made me feel like I was her only client." "Very mindful of our needs, collaborative and helpful." "Victoria made the process very easy. I would work with her again." "I am very satisfied."

Victoria Blau Architect, PLLC   3.5   3.5   4   4

200 Park Avenue South, Suite 1310, New York, NY 10003
(212) 529 - 2050 www.vblau.com
Contemporary, unique, tailored residential architecture

Victoria Blau, principal of this young Manhattan firm, carves out unique habitats in an urban environment. The open spaces and clean lines of contemporary architecture dominate, with raw natural materials used for warmth and color. Clients enjoy urbane and sophisticated homes, without sacrificing "the relaxed factor." Sources also commend her ability to take an idea and creatively develop it. For example, one client wanted a room devoted entirely to his wine collection, but Blau suggested they instead extend racks along a long wall. The result was attractive, functional, and ultimately one of the client's favorite features.

In 1987, the teenaged Blau gave up swimming and horseback riding in favor of a Harvard summer camp for aspiring architects. The first in a long chain of educational credentials, she then studied architecture and fine art at Columbia, earned her M.Arch at Penn, then went back for a degree in real estate development at Columbia. In between, she put in four years as a project architect at Gwathmey Siegel & Associates. Blau has been helming her own projects since 1998, but the firm officially opened its doors in 2003. With a staff of four, Blau likes to limit the number of projects to four or five. Clients—generally bachelors and young families—speak warmly of working with Blau, whose passion and "spark of irreverence" make the process fun.

Depending on the size of the job, Blau's fee ranges from below market to above, but typically it comes in at a standard percentage of construction. She prefers to take on complete jobs, though a substantial build-out won't necessarily be sniffed at (especially if it provides a creative challenge). Most projects have been lofts and apartments downtown, with the occasional Upper East Side exception. Blau will also design interiors, including custom furniture. She has also been called on to accompany clients to scout potential properties. For creative, calming safe havens from the hustle and bustle of the city, clients recommend Blau unequivocally.

"Contemporary work with an emphasis on materials." "She managed to get a lot of warmth out of woods and stone." "I thought her aesthetic was fine, but what really stuck out was her project management. She was on top of every phase of the process, especially the proposal." "Very clever solutions to all the hundreds of little problems I laid out." "It was hard to imagine the finished project, but Victoria's vision turned out to be stunning." "I wouldn't recommend her for a Georgian mansion out in the Hamptons, but the city apartments I've seen are wonderful." "She's very open to using budget-friendly materials." "Great at creative budget solutions." "Treats her work like an artistic pursuit." "She approached the project with the presumption that it was going to be fun, and it was." "I'm going to use her for all my future projects."

Weil Friedman Architects   3.5   3.5   4   5
30 East 92nd Street, New York, NY 10128
(212) 534 - 1240 wfa@bellatlantic.net
Classic, tailored architecture and interior design

Greta Weil and Barbara Friedman devote their practice entirely to residential design, creating a "classic, fresh look" that clients say is never overdone. We hear Weil Friedman studies every aspect of living in a space from the perspective of the client and integrates these discoveries into architecture. Not surprisingly, sources find the firm very practical about and responsive to "real-life" issues. Clients also appreciate the low-key style these architects use to guide them through the design process, while industry professionals acknowledge the excellence of the firm's drawings and project management. All these attributes contribute to keeping the jobs running smoothly.

This firm is appreciated for its accommodating perspective. We hear the principals are "articulate" and share "a great sense of humor," making the process "fun." After gaining experience at Kohn Pederson Fox Associates, these two joined forces to tackle mainly complete renovations of city residences and significant additions and renovations of clients' second houses outside the city. Balancing their own families with work, the principals have an "excellent view of the realities of family life." Projects on which these two talented women are currently working include the combination of two apartments to create a duplex on the Upper East Side and a "significant" addition for a client in Southampton.

Weil and Friedman currently have as much work as they can reasonably handle, so supporters encourage new prospective clients to be patient. While dependent upon the scope of a project, Weil Friedman typically charges a standard percentage of construction for its services, which often includes doing the interiors as well.

"They really get that clean, rich, comfortable look." "Very creative design solutions." "Before they started it was not a nice old house, but now it is." "Thorough, conscientious, and hardworking above and beyond the call of duty." "Preserved the original lines of the saltbox in our Hamptons house while still achieving the objective." "Contractors have commented how they don't leave anything out of their plans." "Attentive project management and oversight, and also budget-conscious." "Equally talented with interior design and architecture—great to work with one team." "They manage projects well, even from a distance, and are very proactive about problem solving when things do crop up." "We thank the day they were recommended to us."

William T. Georgis Architect   4.5   4.5   4   5

233 East 72nd Street, New York, NY 10021
(212) 288 - 6280   lindsley@wtgarch.com

Residential architecture and interior design with luxurious, modern restraint

Architect and interior designer William T. Georgis is said to reinterpret modernism, combining clean lines with sumptuous materials. The designs are often a sequence of fluid spaces—unadorned, yet highly stylish. Park Avenue is reconfigured into a series of modern open rooms, glamorously retrofitted with linear yet comely surfaces such as marble, slate, onyx, and plate glass. References report that Georgis takes pride in tending to every facet of his projects himself, including the furniture and the hardware. We hear he is creative, witty, and refined, and that these qualities translate clearly in his work.

Georgis received a B.A. from Stanford and an M.Arch from Princeton, trained with architect/guru Robert Venturi, and was an associate of Robert A.M. Stern's for eight years. Among recent projects are the design of a new townhouse in Manhattan, Chinatown Restaurant, a new house in Amagansett, and the renovation and interiors of two Upper East Side apartments. He also is known for the lobby renovation at Lever House, and examples of his decorative work are in the permanent collection at the Metropolitan Museum, the Art Institute of Chicago, and the Denver Art Museum. He leads four full-time architects and four interior designers to create his "extremely high-end, extremely creative interiors." KB 1996. AD 100, 2000.

"Bill does very high-end work, and he's a very hands-on guy." "Fabulous designs and highly dependable." "Funny sensibility. Great guy." "Museum world. Gets a lot of art collectors." "Even the kids' rooms have Miesian undertones with workable and fresh, yet sleek and modern built-ins." "Uptown apartments with a downtown feel."

William Green & Associates ▪   4   4   4   4.5

6 West 18th Street, 7th Floor, New York, NY 10011
(212) 924 - 2828   www.wgaarchitects.net

Classical, detailed, residential architecture and interiors

This boutique operation achieves "an elevated level of service" as a result of principal William Green's full-tilt management style. Sources say Green is adept at creating classically-oriented designs that are timeless and have a distinct respect for proportion and scale. He even approaches the actual drawing in a classic way, with everything being done by hand, right down to the tiniest molding or hardware detail. The details, especially the moldings, are unusually thoughtful and precise. The architect is also said to design in a modern context with success. He has continued to follow his vision of building homes that project "a sense of place" in the community, as well as creating designs that are sensitive to budgetary constraints without compromising quality.

Green heads a team of four and projects are typically gut renovations, split between residential and commercial clients. The firm continues to take on more and more new-home construction outside the City, in places like Greenwich, Bedford, Westport, and the Hamptons—and as far away as Japan and France. The firm takes on approximately fifteen residential projects each year of varying scopes. Green is known to control all aspects of a project, be it the design of architecture, landscape, interiors, or furniture, and we hear he pursues his vision through to the end.

Green received his B.F.A. from Tufts and a M.Arch from the University of Colorado. Before starting the firm in 1986, Green worked with design giants Skidmore Owings & Merrill and Davis, Brody. He is described as a gentle, dedicated man, who tries to bring a serious artistic component to every project. The aptly named Green is also known to be committed to ecological issues. The firm has also served the commercial/institutional market including Fendi, Bellevue Hospital, and the Guggenheim and Louvre Museums. Charging a standard fee based on hourly or a percentage of construction costs, clients say Green and his team are consistently on time and on budget.

"Bill has such a calming demeanor, nothing rattles him and that quality tends to create a really pleasant atmosphere." "Helpful, bright, innovative, polite, and demure." "He truly believes in what he is doing and his ideas are rock solid." "Takes the time to listen to the client." "Bill has an enormous sense of humor and an even larger concern for our world." "Have had a ten-year relationship with Bill working on both small and multimillion-dollar projects, and I've never been disappointed." "Does beautiful work and has great taste." "A clear and meticulous thinker." "Completely dependable and on target." "We hired Bill again and recommend him to others." "Offers visionary and perfect service."

workshop/apd, LLC 🛍   **4**   **3**   **5**   **4.5**
555 Eighth Avenue, Suite 1509, New York, NY 10018
(212) 273 - 9712 www.workshopapd.com
Graceful, modern residential architecture with historic character

This small, rising star has gained a spot in the Manhattan design cosmos for its becoming, warm, modern designs that reflect a sense of historical perspective, particularly in pre-war spaces. The furnishings may be mostly contrasting, linear, mid-century neutrals, but there may also be a graceful turn-of-century chair leg reminiscent of Hepplewhite, antique French rugs, and "architecture that makes sense in these historic apartments." Moldings, herringbone floors, wainscoting (albeit pared down), and traditional plaster fireplace mantles (albeit painted ambient white) all find a natural home here. The result is a graceful synthesis of contemporary and classic.

Clients tell us partners Andrew Kotchen and Matthew Berman are "charming and delightful," and that the firm's dedication and enthusiasm make the process enjoyable. Kotchen and Berman are also acknowledged for maintaining high-quality standards, as they guide a team of fourteen. References state that they are pleased with the principals' attentive and responsive personal service, remarking that they are full of exciting ideas. As a result, most clients "can't wait to work with" the firm again.

Kotchen received his B.A. from Lehigh and his M.Arch from the U. of Michigan in 1996. A year later, he established his own practice in Nantucket, relocating to NYC several years later. Berman also received his B.A. from Lehigh, and received his M.Arch from Columbia, joining Kotchen in 1999. The vast majority of the firm's work is residential apartments, usually 1,400 to 3,500 square feet. The practice maintains a second office in Nantucket, which comprises about 40% of the docket. There are surprisingly low fees, with a flat fee or hourlies based on the scope of the project not to exceed a very low percentage of construction.

"Completely dedicated to fulfilling their clients' wishes." "Incredibly hard-working." "Excellent at coming up with dynamic design solutions." "Gave us what we wanted and more." "A little young and inexperienced in terms of organization and contractor/sub coordination, but totally worth it." "Great relationship with all the contractors and subs." "At times function was sacrificed for form." "Transformed two rooms into a beautiful mass of space." "Really smart, savvy, talented, and personable." "Simply all-around great guys. My dog loves them, too!" "As for all good things, patience, patience." "We are starting another project with them and trust them completely." "My best friend is also using at my recommendation."

FIRMS WITHOUT ONLINE PORTFOLIOS

Anderson Architects P.C.   4   3.5   4.5   4
555 West 25th Street, 6th Floor, New York, NY 10001
(212) 620 - 0996 www.andersonarch.com
Individualistic, modern, handsome commercial and residential architecture

Ross Anderson is recognized for his inventive, forward-thinking modern designs outfitted in streamlined walls of natural wood and glass, highly customized to the vernacular. For his own Vermont home, that means wide pine siding evocative of a nearby covered bridge; for a New York loft, it may mean wide open spaces, blond wood floors, minimal furniture, and as many skylights as possible. From the time he founded the *Harvard Architectural Review*, Anderson has believed in the power of the site and the use of appropriate materials. His unique search for "authentic architecture" has won him much critical acclaim as a "serious architect."

This firm of seventeen has existed under its current name for the past nine years, and as Anderson Schwartz Architects before that. Principals of the firm are Anderson, who holds degrees from Stanford and Harvard, and M.J. Sagan, who studied at Penn State. About a third of the firm's work is residential, and about a third takes place in Manhattan. Most are substantial new home construction and renovation projects that start as small as two bedrooms and can reach seven figures under the direction of the client.

The firm has worked on a number of downtown residential projects, particularly in Tribeca. Recent commercial/institutional jobs include art galleries, offices for bn.com a one-million-square-foot office campus for Abercrombie and Fitch in Ohio, and the refurbishment of Manhattan's Friends Seminary. They are currently doing a residential master plan for one of the largest landowners in Florida. The firm charges a lower hourly rate or percentage of total construction costs that increases for smaller projects. Anderson AIA Fellow 2002.

"Most anybody can be trained to design a space, but what Ross did was understand our intentions, live our lifestyle, and feel what we felt." "Ross has become a valued colleague and dear friend." "From the beginning, the challenge was huge, but Ross' work consistently exceeded our expectations." "He understands the DNA of our company and translated that into a magnificent space." "Very in tune with current modern architecture trends, but more institutional. Picking out icemakers is not his thing." "A major thinker, but organization is not his strong point." "It is wonderful to deal with someone so smart and talented." "An absolute joy to work with, and a creative and responsive staff."

	Quality +	Cost $	Value ◆	Recommend? ★

Atkin Kramer Architects   3.5   3   4.5   4.5

490 West End Avenue, Suite 1B, New York, NY 10024
(212) 877 - 7994   atkinkramer@aol.com

Updated traditional residential architecture

Terry Atkin has a supportive group of clients who appreciate her architectural expertise and her hands-on management style. Though she leans toward the traditional, Atkin is adept at personalizing each project with a vernacular feel. Best known for her detailed work on Manhattan's prewar buildings, Atkin can successfully combine the bones of these older edifices with the clients' more modern interests and cleaner surfaces.

Atkin is a sole practitioner of this twenty-year-old firm and holds architecture degrees from the Universities of Virginia and Pennsylvania. The vast majority of Atkin's work is residential and most projects take place in Manhattan. Atkin has extensive experience with duplex renovations in some of the city's most exclusive neighborhoods. In addition to her work in New York City, Atkin's aptitude for new home design and renovation takes her to Long Island and upstate New York. Project minimums are usually in the "reasonable" range, though some caution that budgets should be firmly established early to ensure that costs stay in line.

Clients tell us Atkin's competency and client focus is the hallmark of her style, actively incorporating clients' preferences into her work. The firm enjoys numerous return clients who recruit Atkin's services for multiple projects. Atkin is known as a hands-on manager who charges a fair hourly rate without compromising quality.

"She 'cracks the whip' with the contractors!" "Really puts herself out for the client." "We have already recommended her to others in our building and our neighborhood." "She encouraged us to save the moldings, but add a sleek teak kitchen which works beautifully." "She transformed an utterly soul-less 80s interior into an Arts and Crafts home with enormous charm and substance." "She is practical and available, and she warranted my complete trust." "Terry chooses her projects very deliberately, careful not to overcommit herself." "She competently resolved all issues." "Anyone lucky enough to work with Terry will be very pleased with the experience and the result."

Boris Baranovich Architects   4   4   4   5

28 West 25th Street, 5th Floor, New York, NY 10010
(212) 627 - 1150   www.borisbaranovicharchitects.com

Traditional residential architecture

Clients and peers recognize Boris Baranovich mostly for his traditional, classical style of architectural design with an emphasis on French, English, and American Shingle styles. Baranovich is also known for being a "finisher"—always tying up loose ends. While some say his style can be a bit heavy, all appreciate his attention to detail and high-quality work. Clients also praise Baranovich for his accommodating nature and ability to execute their wishes. They describe him as thoughtful, polite, honest, and a strong communicator.

Baranovich holds a degree from Pratt and is the sole principal of this eighteen-person firm, which has been in business since 1984. Early in his career he trained with David Easton. The firm takes on six to eight new projects each year. Large projects start at about half a million and go up to the tens of millions. Beyond Manhattan, his work can be seen from New Jersey to Greenwich and the Hamptons. The firm charges an hourly rate that is comparable to a standard percentage of total construction costs.

"A very literal and detailed translation of the glorious past." "The pool house looks as if it has been there since 1904 when the house was built." "While the costs are not small, Boris is very sensitive to keeping to budget." "Office organization not a strong point; a bit slow in pushing our production, but well worth the wait." "Was happy to

speak to us on Sunday evenings at 10pm." "Boris always tries to please. He never says 'this is the way it should be.'" "He is always ready to make a trip to the site within minutes." "He can turn new construction into a dazzling showpiece of grandeur and elegance." "Totally trustworthy."

Campion A. Platt Architects   4.5   4.5   4   5
152 Madison Avenue, Suite 900, New York, NY 10016
(212) 779 - 3835 www.campionplatt.com
Characteristic, modern-edged residential architecture and interiors

With a holistic approach and an appreciation for a wide variety of worldly architectural styles, Campion Platt strives to create chic, comprehensive creations. All are poignantly stylistic with a modern edge, and an earnest nod to former days of glory within the appropriate context. High-rise apartments often get a personality of cosmopolitan dash, while an 1850s Sag Harbor home retained its period sea theme while incorporating modern twists. Sources are quick to praise Platt's outgoing personality, thoroughness in providing weekly budget reports, and close supervision of contractors.

Platt grew up in Switzerland and knew as a teenager that he wanted to pursue architecture. After graduating from the U. Michigan and Columbia, he created the firm in 1984. For about twenty years, the firm remained small with about six employees and six to ten major projects a year, but its recent success has allowed for growth and it is now expanding to about sixteen people and thirty projects a year. The staff includes many with interior design expertise, which is integral to the design plans. Platt frequently travels to Europe and the Far East to purchase art and furniture for his clients, and to stay current and gain insight, resulting in the exotic influences and distinct personalities of his work.

Some clients say Platt can be overly structured about his visions, but that the end product is always superior, although quite pricey. Most of the residential projects are gut renovations that generally hover around the half million-dollar mark. Typical of his work is the recent 4,800 square foot gut renovation of a modern townhouse in Manhattan, featuring a garden, new finishes, and custom furniture. He also designed Soho's MercBar—an amalgamation of Adirondack chic, Wild West ruggedness, and New York hip. Platt's architectural fees and product markups are in the standard range, with standard oversight fees, but the materials costs can fall at the higher end of the range . AD 100, 2000, 2002, 2004.

"Campion is a delight to work with. There is always a fantastic image in his head of the concept theme and the end result." "He has a good balance between creative design and functionality." "Extremely talented—with a good, creative eye." "Could be a bit better with compromise." "The team is very much involved with the contractors and the subs." "He should work with high-end customers who appreciate the highest quality." "Immediately reacts and responds to my ideas." "He is more than just an architect. He is a style-maker."

Centerbrook Architects and Planners LLC   4.5   4   4.5   4.5
67 Main Sreet, PO Box 955, Centerbrook, CT 06409
(860) 767 - 0175 www.centerbrook.com
Historically interpretive, regionally influenced architecture

This large, national firm has earned praise from clients, peers, and the media for its regionally specific, uplifting, and restrained designs. Innovative in their approach but clearly harkening back to a simpler time, the firm's commissions cover a wide scope—from family homes, law schools, and art museums to entire communities. With an approach that is distinctly American, sources are enthusiastic about the firm's meticulous attention to detail while keeping clients' visions at the forefront. Others commend Centerbrook for the ability to deliver within estimated timetables and for its extremely professional design plans.

Centerbrook was established in 1975 and is located in a renovated factory on the Falls River in Centerbrook, Connecticut. This firm of 70 architects takes on dozens of projects each year, of which about 15% are residential. Partners of the firm are William H. Grover, Jefferson Riley, Mark Simon, Chad Floyd, and James C. Childress; James A. Coan and Charles G. Mueller serve as principals. The legacy of the late Charles W. Moore, a founding partner, continues to inspire.

The firm's "exhilarating and creative" work and stylistic versatility has won many awards—as well as many happy return clients. Residential projects include new construction, renovations, and additions, and range from $500,000 to $15 million. The firm charges a lower than standard percentage of overall construction costs and is noted by clients to be highly sensitive to their budgets. AIA Firm Award 1988.

"The architects designed a work of art that is also a wonderfully comfortable home to live in." "They translated our dreams into a startling unique interpretation of a traditional home." "The designs are classic, basic, yet playful." "Superb interpretive skill, bring a staid historic concept alive with a modern wash." "There are exquisite details in moldings, cabinetry, natural and artificial light." "Can't imagine that they would know what do with a traditional Park Avenue apartment—not their forte." "Very well organized back office. If the principal is not available, then the message gets through." "Flexible and swift in examining value engineering concepts." "A modest budget was not a deterrent for them, though it was with others I interviewed." "The entire experience was wonderful. The result brought us untold happiness."

Cicognani Kalla Architects   4.5   4   4.5   4.5
6 East 46th Street, New York, NY 10017
(212) 308 - 4811   pc@cicognanikalla.com

Warm, vernacular residential and institutional architecture

An internationally renowned firm, Cicognani Kalla is a mid-size practice known for high quality work and a highly collaborative attitude. Working both in rural and urban settings, the firm is versatile in its range of abilities, seeking client input. From a new, jewel-like country home in the Hamptons to a classical gut renovation on Park Avenue, sources tell us Cicognani Kalla will take on projects of all sizes—providing they prove to be an interesting challenge. In all cases, clients tell us the end results are successful and "rich, yet comfortable."

We hear the firm likes to have a hand in the creation of all aspects of a particular space—including the design of pools, gardens, and interiors. In addition to residential projects, the firm has designed art galleries, offices, and restaurants. In 1994, they completed the Heinz Architectural Center at the Carnegie Museum of Art in Pittsburgh. Described by references as enthusiastic and intelligent, Ann Kalla was educated at Carnegie Mellon and Columbia University. Awarded an AIA medal in 1980, Kalla held an assistant professorship at Columbia for three years and worked on several invitational international competition projects. In 1985, Kalla and Pietro Cicognani, also educated at Columbia, then spent several years after graduation on commercial and institutional projects around the globe.

The firm's clients are some of the most discriminating business people and philanthropists in New York. About 85% of the work is residential. Recent projects have been completed on Park, Fifth, and Central Park West, as well as in

Southampton, Millbrook, Hobe Sound, Beaverkill, and Italy. Pricing is at the level one should expect for outstanding work, with standard percentages of construction or hourly fees.

"A combination of visionary work and practicality." "Each project has its own attitude, its own merit." "There is a sincerity to the work." "One has a sense that the home has always been there and belongs there." "Incredibly classy, not overdone." "The rooms have a generational warmth, never glitzy." "Came up with a tangible, thought provoking concept." "Great at bridging cultural gaps when working with international firms and projects." "They're both as much educators as they are architects." "Real architects with a great back office."

Cooper, Robertson & Partners   5   5   4   5
311 West 43rd Street, 13th Floor, New York, NY 10036
(212) 247 - 1717 www.cooperrobertson.com
August residential and institutional architecture

While very few of the firm's commissions are residential, the stature of its impressive homes more than makes up for the limited quantity. Regularly featured in *Architectural Digest*, these visionary structures are usually built in highly prestigious locations such as Casa de Campo, Martha's Vineyard, Wassabuc and, most often, the Hamptons. Not to be undertaken lightly, each home has an exalted theme and no expense is spared. The grounds, outbuildings, and gardens are also planned by the firm for a fully realized state. Clients heartily recommend Jaquelin Robertson, who usually oversees the building process, to their well-heeled friends, both for the "joy of the process" and for the "stunning results."

But Robertson and his associates, Alexander Cooper and David McGregor, are also staunch believers in excellence in urban planning, and the firm is primarily involved to that end. The company was instrumental in the planning and design of Battery Park City, the development of the MoMA Art Center, Disney's Celebration, and campus master plans for Yale University, Trinity College, Duke University, and Colgate University. Several years back, Robertson worked with such luminaries as Mayor John Lindsay and the Shah of Iran in urban design.

Founded in 1979 by Robertson and Cooper, there are 85 employees and 18 partners, many of whom have worked together for decades. Robertson grew up in Virginia, and received his B.A. and M.Arch from Yale and his B.A. from Oxford, where he was a Rhodes Scholar. He was formerly the Dean of the U. Va. Architecture School. Cooper also received his B.A. and M.Arch. from Yale, and founded the Columbia University Urban Design School. McGregor received his B.A. from Harvard and Ph.D. from Columbia and is the firm's managing director. While costs are equal to the level of the extraordinary quality, clients say the longevity of the result makes it a good value. Cooper AIA Fellow 1986, and Robertson AIA Fellow 1979. AD 100, 2000, 2002, 2004.

"One of the best there is." "Mr. Robertson is such a gentleman." "Will only consider $10 million homes in the Hamptons at this point." "Doing an 18,000 square foot new home with a massive gambrel roof is routine for Jaque." "Huge personality in the finished result and the process is so professional." "The firm is very large but extremely effective, down to the last detail." "For the top end residential projects, you absolutely get the attention of the partners."

Daniel Romualdez Architects   5   4.5   4.5   4.5
119 West 23rd Street, Suite 909, New York, NY 10011
(212) 989 - 8429 daniel@danielromualdezarchitecture.com
Glamorous, yet unpretentious residential architecture

With more than a nod to the mid-century masters, Daniel Romualdez is creating an outstanding reputation of his own among New York's architectural, social, and fashion glitterati. Romualdez has that special "je ne sais quoi" that strikes a perfect balance between the high and the humble. While most pieces have a special provenance, it can be Louis XV, Edwin Lutyens, or Crate & Barrel (specially reupholstered, of course). While clearly modern, the open spaces have clear historical references. The results are stunning, comfortable, and inviting. Romualdez is regarded as a charming, polished man who takes a calm and thoughtful approach to his work.

Romualdez, the son of a Filipino diplomat, was born in Manila and raised to become a banker. After graduating from Yale and Columbia (M.Arch), he worked for the renowned Thierry Despont, and then for Robert Stern for five years before founding his own practice in 1993. One of his first projects was the quick transformation of a bleak ranch house in eastern Long Island into a dream getaway, which was picked up by all the shelter mags and launched his career. There is a staff of twelve that works mainly on very high-end residential projects. The firm recently added an interior design arm to fully integrate the look, and they are said to be particularly adept at enhancing clients' art collections with an appropriate setting.

Clients have included Matt and Annette Lauder, Marina Rust, Tory Burch, Diane von Furstenberg, fantasy jeweler James de Givenchy, and the *NYT*'s architecture critic, Paul Goldberger. All this expertise comes at an equally lofty cost, but is said to be well worth it. HB Top Designers, 1999, 2000, 2001, 2002, 2003, 2004, 2005.

"Daniel is a connoisseur of all historical periods, and can incorporate it exquisitely into a modern framework." "A chic viewpoint hearkening to a classical past." "Amazing attention to detail." "From a dealer's viewpoint, I think that he has an exquisite eye and taste." "I am a fashion designer, and I think Daniel is one of the most creative, talented people I have ever met." "A nice guy who knows everyone in the universe." "Daniel absolutely understands the client's perspective, he creates something beautifully modern yet highly livable." "His designs are just like a perfect French hand rub polish—elegant, beautiful, and immaculate."

Daniel Rowen Architects   4.5   4.5   4   4.5
555 West 25th Street, 6th Floor, New York, NY 10001
(212) 947 - 9109   djrowen@aol.com
Modern, innovative high-end residential, commercial and retail architecture

Known for the simplicity, elegance, and intelligence of the modern spaces he creates, Daniel Rowen is in demand. His close-valued palette, restrained interiors, and polished facades are highly valued by Manhattan's hip residential crowd and by his innovative commercial clients. The vast majority of the firm's projects are gut renovations of large apartments, townhouses, and offices in exclusive Manhattan locations. Rowen places a strong emphasis on client relationships, and is said to be quite selective about his clientele, favoring those who share his lofty vision. Described as engaging and worldly, he is said to approach every project as though he is creating a unique and special work of art.

Rowen, the sole principal of this small firm of five, holds degrees from Brown and Yale. Trained under Charles Gwathmey, Rowen has had his own practice since 1985. He did all of Martha Stewart's commercial spaces, including her 150,000 square foot offices. He is also the architect for Michael Kors, having designed the offices, the showrooms, and the Soho and flagship stores. Recent residential work includes a 5,500 square foot apartment in the Majestic (a collaboration with Philippe Starck), an apartment combination in the Beresford, and participation in the Houses at Sagaponac. Beyond Manhattan, Rowen has worked in London, Tokyo, San Francisco, and the Hamptons—where he maintains a second office location.

Clients say Rowen is an extremely talented architect who also happens to be "the perfect lunch partner." The firm works on a percentage of construction somewhat higher than the standard rate.

	Quality	Cost	Value	Recommend?
	+	$	◆	★

"Modern, cool, and elegant." "He has been able to listen to and accept my suggestions as well as be appropriately persistent when he had something he wanted." "He provided me a design within ten days, which was an exact rendering of everything I wanted." "Second to none in regards to accommodating the timelines, budgets, and overall needs of clients." "If your personality and design style click with him, it can be great." "He's as fun to have around as a friend as he is as an architect." "He doesn't miss a single detail." "The only architect my husband and I ever fully respected, admired, and thoroughly enjoyed (five others before him!)." "It has been nothing but an honor to work with him."

Deborah Berke & Partners Architects LLP   4.5   4.5   4   4.5
220 Fifth Avenue, 7th Floor, New York, NY 10001
(212) 229 - 9211   www.dberke.com

Understated, informed, modern institutional and residential architecture

Deborah Berke, an associate professor of architecture at Yale University, has gained an international following for her subtle yet thoughtful spaces designed in a distinctive, minimalist style. These are showpieces of refined simplicity, luxurious yet humble. Modern materials are used in a creative manner: steel and cherry wood cabinets, sliding partitions of aluminum and translucent acrylic. Berke and her "exceptional staff" have been described as "very talented" and "totally professional," producing beautiful, elegant, functional designs. Clients who have retained Berke for residential work commend her as "an artist" and praise her work for its "ease of living."

Berke received a B.F.A. and a B.Arch from RISD, and a master's in urban planning from City University. She founded her firm in 1982. While not much residential work is taken on, the firm receives praise from its private clients. Recent projects have included several downtown lofts, an apartment in the Trump Hotel, and a relatively modest, yet superbly crafted home in Greenwich. A co-editor of the 1997 book, *Architecture of the Everyday*, Berke recognizes and emphasizes the allure of simple, serviceable materials in her designs.

Her work's "easy elegance" has earned Berke a number of distinguished jobs, including homes and stores in the planned community of Seaside, Florida, as well as CK Calvin Klein boutiques and the new Yale University School of Art. Berke works extensively in New York City, Westchester, Fairfield, and Litchfield counties. ID Hall of Fame.

"The minute I met Deborah I knew she was the one for the project." "We feel privileged to work with her." "So smart, nice, and candid. And, with children of her own, she understands the family perspective." "A major player." "Your aesthetics must be very compatible with Deborah's because there is a distinct point of view." "Too hip for some." "Works really well with artists and musicians." "There is a real affection for ordinary materials: galvanized steel over polished marble." "Quite expensive, but totally worth it for a work of art." "Completely professional on all fronts." "The only problem with the project is that it is going to end soon." "On a scale of one to five for quality, I give her a ten."

Desai/Chia Studio   4   3.5   4.5   4.5
54 West 21st Street, Suite 703, New York, NY 10010
(212) 366 - 9630   www.desaichia.com

Innovatively progressive, sculptural residential architecture

Clients say they are drawn to this firm's simplistic, minimalist spaces and modern aesthetic. The firm maximizes existing natural light and open space while incorporating innovative materials such as plastics, resin, concrete, metals, and bamboo. Clients say they appreciate the clean flow of Desai/Chia spaces and the controlled manner in which the cutting-edge materials are presented. The firm takes on a variety of project types, but is probably best known for its elegant loft renovations with a maximum of reflected light with Eastern influences. Desai/Chia also does apartment renovations, additions, and smaller new construction projects. The firm generally handles mid-sized renovations, but has also completed larger multi-million-dollar projects.

This small firm of three opened its doors in 1994. Principals are Arjun Desai, who holds degrees from MIT and Bennington College, and Katherine Chia, who has degrees from Amherst College and MIT and previously worked with Maya Lin. The firm designs between ten and fifteen projects each year, the vast majority of which are in Manhattan and are residential in nature. The firm charges an hourly rate not to exceed the standard percentage of overall construction costs. HB Top Designers, 2000.

"The team provided a maximum amount of service with a minimum amount of attitude." "Their creativity and ability to create an incredible feeling of space astounded me." "They took a boxy 35-year-old rent-controlled apartment and turned it into something that takes people's breath away." "While all architects are meticulous, they are extra meticulous. While that can be a bit frustrating from a timing perspective, everything was so well thought out that it was clearly worth it." "Almost everything was custom, which did take time." "They not only were engaged in the aesthetics, but also the mechanics of the apartment. So now everything works so well." "Every project is like an immaculate conception for them. If you are not very dedicated as well, they might not be the people for you." "Jumped on top of any issues." "All their subs were wonderful too." "They were always here to talk to the subs." "Worth every penny." "All deadlines, budgets, and promises were kept, and their kindness in dealing with me and all of my questions will always bring me back to them."

Gabellini Sheppard Associates, LLP 4 4 4 4.5
665 Broadway, Suite 706, New York, NY 10012
(212) 388 - 1700 www.gabellinisheppard.com
Modern, ethereal, artistic high-end commercial and residential architecture

Having designed the Giorgio Armani Center in Milan, the Nicole Farhi flagship store in New York, and Jil Sander boutiques worldwide, Michael Gabellini is known for his links to the fashion world, art galleries, and museums. Highly respected and admired for its modern, minimalist style of design, this firm is lauded by clients for finding new ways to interpret the modern aesthetic. Sources tell us the firm approaches each project with meticulous planning in order to create spacious, elegant designs that implement the importance of natural light through simple means. New Yorkers (and tourists worldwide) have seen his work in the redesign of Rockefeller Center's Fifth Avenue facade.

Created in 1991, the firm employs a staff of 31, led by principals Michael Gabellini, Daniel Garbowit, and Kimberly Sheppard, all graduates of RISD. The group takes on anywhere from twelve to twenty-four projects each year. Insiders describe Gabellini as an artist who works in architectural materials—in fact, he initially enrolled at RISD to become a sculptor, and segued to architecture. The firm focuses primarily on large, high-end jobs, accepting few smaller projects. The residential practice constitutes only 10 to 20% of its portfolio, mostly gut apartment renovations featuring unique forms: abundant glass shoji screens, sliding and pivoting walls, edgy metal, and concrete moldings. Most are monochromatic, and many are for fashion insiders.

Much of the residential work is in Manhattan: Chelsea, Midtown, and the Upper East Side. The firm generally works on a fixed fee, comparable to a slightly higher than standard percentage of total construction costs. Gabellini AIA Fellow 2004. ID Hall of Fame.

"Michael and his team are extreme professionals and perfectionists, leaving no detail outstanding." "He is an artist who works with space and light with the use of only the very best materials." "If one could put apartments into museums, you would find Michael's work in the MoMA." "The walls float like magic." "Exquisite minimalist work."

	Quality	Cost	Value	Recommend?
	✚	$	◆	★

GF55 Architects   3.5   3.5   4   5

19 West 21st Street, Suite 1201, New York, NY 10010
(212) 352 - 3099 www.gf55.com

Modern residential, commercial, and institutional architecture

GF55 is known for its tailored modern geometric designs with linear interior panache. Clients praise the firm for its detailed drawings, swift execution, and "New York quality without the New York attitude." We hear the firm's architects are consummate professionals who listen and respond to clients' needs, while suggesting inventive, refreshing new ideas.

This firm of eighteen has been in business since 1984 and is headed up by principals Leonard Fusco and David E. Gross. Fusco holds degrees from Columbia and Penn, while Gross has two degrees from Penn. About one-third of GF55's annual projects are residential, with the remainder being a mix of commercial and institutional. In addition to its architectural services, GF55 will also decorate the interiors of projects it designs. The body of work includes high-end custom homes, affordable housing developments, senior centers, and retail concepts. Given their diverse client base, they are said to be very proficient at cost management with detailed estimates and alternative design concepts.

Approximately 40% of the firm's work takes place in Manhattan, with the rest in the metro area, Ohio and Florida. Recent Manhattan projects include the gut rehab of an 8,000 square foot Upper East Side traditional townhouse and the renovation of a 22,500 square foot triplex at Trump International. The firm is also known outside of the US for its extensive design of commercial space across Central America. GF55 charges a standard percentage of total construction costs.

"While they can also do more traditional work, they really have their heart and soul into the more modern and mid-century modern genres." "They successfully put a contemporary addition on to a traditional Colonial, and it worked surprisingly well." "An excellent New York firm without New York snobbery." "Very practical, and they get the job done."

Gwathmey Siegel & Associates Architects   4.5   5   4   4.5

475 Tenth Avenue, 3rd Floor, New York, NY 10018
(212) 947 - 1240 www.gwathmey-siegel.com

Curvilinear and dramatic institutional, commercial, and residential architecture

With their indelible signature of curvilinear planes and sculpted hierarchy, Charles Gwathmey and Robert Siegel have earned a devoted following and more than 100 awards. While better known for their institutional projects such as the celebrated addition to the Guggenheim Museum and buildings for Harvard, Princeton, and Cornell, the firm also takes on residential works—usually voluminous new homes for high profile clients. In Manhattan, they have done gut renovations for Jerry Seinfeld, Steven Spielberg, and various other creative souls. Adapted to city life, Gwathmey's forms become sloping and curving walls, multifarious ceiling heights, and inventive geometries of light producing an articulated flow. Clients feel as if they collaborate with the firm to create a work of art.

Gwathmey, a Fulbright scholar, graduated from Yale in 1962 with a M.Arch and became an AIA Fellow in 1981. Siegel, a graduate of Pratt and Harvard, is president of Pratt's board of trustees and became an AIA Fellow in 1991. Both architects have taught at some of the country's most prestigious universities. Their high-powered firm of 80 was founded in 1967. We're told these architects believe that complete architectural solution includes interior design—and that their distinct look is usually considered most hospitable to mid-century furnishings.

Not surprisingly, the firm's few residential projects command exceptional budgets and receive incredible, yet understated detailing. The working documents are said to be exceptional. The firm charges a significantly higher percentage of total construction costs. AD 100, 2000, 2002, 2004. ID Hall of Fame. AIA Fellow, 1981.

"We were able to get an architectural masterpiece without sacrificing practical living comfort." "It's been exhilarating, exciting, and an education in the modern aesthetic." "The most amazing part about it was watching Charlie's ideas come to fruition. I would do it all again." "We were a relatively small client, and did not receive the attention we would have liked." "Incredibly beautiful but no longer really inventive." "Quite faithful to their own tradition." "The execution right down to the last detail was absolutely flawless." "Absolutely everything is custom." "It was a perfect collaboration of our ideas and enlightenment by them." "Totally worth it if you buy into the dream." "Like living in a jewel."

James Bodnar Architect   4   4   4   4.5
110 East 78th Street, New York, NY 10021
(212) 794 - 0744 www.jbodnar.com
Contextual, residential architecture

Ranging from contemporary high-rise apartments to traditional fieldstone cottages, James Bodnar has earned a reputation for staying true to each project's appropriate style. Modern spaces receive steel fittings and geometric patterning, while the more traditional get a mix of custom millwork and updated trims. We are told Bodnar can go to great lengths to achieve aesthetic consistency and refinement. Best known for his high-quality additions to existing homes and renovations of landmark historical buildings, clients say he does an excellent job of communicating and developing seamless plans.

Bodnar studied at Catholic University, Yale, and the American Academy in Rome. He is the sole principal of the seven-person firm that he started in 1990. Clients praise Bodnar for providing them with personalized up-to-date information about projects with a password-protected area of his website—where clients can review a complete archive of sketches and photographs. Approximately half of the firm's commissions are residential. The firm takes on projects of all sizes, from small one-room renovations up to large multimillion-dollar homes.

Much of Bodnar's residential work takes place in Manhattan, with other jobs spanning the country, from Santa Barbara to Nantucket, Westchester, and Vermont. Some notable recent projects include the renovation of a 12,000 square foot landmark midtown building for a not-for-profit company, the reconstruction of a 17,000 square foot East Side townhouse into a private investment bank, and a 2,000 square foot, seven-room addition to a suburban farmhouse. The firm charges an hourly fee up to a maximum (standard) percentage of total cost of construction.

"We found Jim to be extremely thoughtful, creative, diligent, and pragmatic in his approach." "He never panics, and has a very calming influence when things out of his control seem to be coming unraveled." "Never pretentious, though he's a perfectionist." "A really decent human being, and a delight to work with." "He was looking for a level of quality above our level of interest." "A very good listener who tries to get everything just right for the client."

Karen L. Jacobson Architects Studio   4   3   5   5
103 Reade Street, New York, NY 10013
(212) 571 - 1116 www.kljarch.com
Modern architecture with a soft hand

Karen Jacobson has impressed many clients with her modern designs imbued with warmth, her excellent project management skills, and her contextual outreach to clients. This Gwathmey-trained architect has a strong roster of famous clients who say they are devoted to her talent and unpretentious personality. Jacobson is also respected for her ability to work effectively with idiosyncratic

spaces such as carriage houses, apartment combinations, and brownstone additions. For Jacobson, we hear, "No detail is too small to take seriously." The results have been roundly praised as successful.

Founded twenty years ago, this small firm employs three, including Jacobson, a graduate of Princeton. Clients say that the small size is a big asset, in that they get to work with Jacobson directly. Half of the firm's work is in Manhattan—but it also takes on numerous projects in the Hamptons, Westchester, and Fairfield. A fair amount of the firm's work is the design of new houses, primarily in upstate New York and Connecticut. Jacobson also does a considerable amount of work within the medical field, often working on plastic surgeons' offices, in addition to offering interior design services.

The firm tends to accept projects with mid-range budgets of $300,000 to over a million. Clients with limited budgets applaud Jacobson's clever use of materials and space, saying that they saved money by hiring her and certainly ended up with a better result. The firm charges an hourly rate not to exceed the standard to a lower percentage of overall construction costs.

"We were overjoyed to work with Karen. She is a terrific listener with an excellent sense of style." "Lovely, quick, charming, forthcoming. Excellent fit for the profession." "Invariably came up with creative solutions to the many roadblocks we encountered along the way." "Highly efficient and absolutely lets nothing slip." "The bid package was so complete that the contractors had no room for questions." "Amazing materials selection, which adds such warmth." "Karen can distinguish between the 800 shades of white, and used the one just perfect for our photography collection." "She steers you to the highest quality that is practical for your budget but never pressures you." "As a competitor of Karen's, we have only heard good things." "She created a fabulous space from almost nothing." "We recommended her to my brother, best friend, and my neighbor." "Came in on time and amazed my friends."

KSA Architects/Alfred Wen   4   3.5   4.5   4

45 West 34th Street, Suite 1209, New York, NY 10001
(212) 643 - 2655   ayw.ksa@gmail.com
Traditional residential architecture

Clients say Alfred Wen of KSA is an excellent architect, a careful listener, and a person who develops each project as a reflection of the client's customized vision. We are told this small firm pays close attention to detail—both in regard to the physical project and the notion of personalized client relations. KSA generally takes on traditional-style projects but remains flexible. Like his keen eye for proportion, Wen's creative, collaborative approach is a valued asset of the firm.

Alfred Wen, a graduate of Princeton and Columbia, is the sole principal of this two-architect firm created in 1981. Approximately 60% of the firm's work is residential, the vast majority of which takes place in Manhattan—particularly on the Upper East Side. KSA also works in the Hamptons and in Westchester and Fairfield counties. The firm's scope of projects ranges from small five-figure projects up to $1 million. KSA charges a standard percentage of total construction costs.

"Very tasteful, clean, classic." "Not overdone." "Extremely thorough. So thorough, it can drive me nuts as a subcontractor, but it is great for the client." "Listens well, great attitude." "I respect him very much." "Patient, master of his craft." "Creative and practical approach to design." "Not at all greedy." "Since he is on his own, basically, he can take a day or so to get back to you." "Not at all a prima donna." "My husband is a really tough client. Alfred did nine different versions of the kitchen without blinking." "Easy to work with—a gem." "I love going to my apartment every night."

	Quality +	Cost $	Value ◆	Recommend? ★

Michael Middleton Dwyer, Architect

	4.5	4.5	4	5

30 Gansevoort Street, New York, NY 10014
(212) 242 - 6767

Full-tilt, traditional, preservationist residential architecture

Michael Dwyer is celebrated for his commitment to historically classical architecture and preservationist traditions. Insiders tell us this firm is extremely sensitive about maintaining the strict integrity of its projects—to the point of being dubbed "fastidious preservationists." We hear Dwyer has a strong command of historical reference and is adept at renovating prewar building interiors. Sources praise Dwyer's impressive intellect and charming nature while noting that the firm's "confidence in its skills" may come across as rigid to the unsuspecting clients. Insiders tell us this firm works closely—and well—with some of the area's better-known interior decorators.

Formed in 1995, the company currently employs a staff of six. Dwyer, a graduate of Penn, previously worked with the renowned firm Buttrick, White, and Burtis. Half of the firm's work takes place in Manhattan, with the remainder mostly in the Hamptons and Westchester. Around 65% of the firm's yearly workload is residential, including high-end gut renovations and new-home construction and alterations. In 1995, Middleton was dubbed one of the "Young Old Fogies" of architecture by the *New York Times* for his devotion to the classical past.

The firm generally takes on mid-sized projects but continues to take on smaller projects as well as large multimillion-dollar endeavors (including epic yachts and the renovation of Rudolph Nureyev's former apartment in the Dakota). He recently edited the book, *Great Houses of the Hudson River*, highlighting the architecture and decorative arts of the period. Dwyer charges an hourly rate or standard percentage of overall construction costs.

"He understates rather than overstates." "He is an absolutely wonderful neoclassical designer." "Scrupulously honest." "I really appreciate their intellectual approach to the architectural challenge." "Draws like an angel." "Unparalleled as a historic preservationist."

Ogawa/Depardon Architects

	4	4	4	5

69 Mercer Street, 2nd Floor, New York, NY 10012
(212) 627 - 7390   www.oda-ny.com

Modern, stylistic architecture

The partnership of Kathryn Ogawa and Gilles Depardon creates clean modern architecture and interior design with what clients call "unlimited imagination and creativity." What differentiates Ogawa/Depardon from the pack, we're told, is a marked sensitivity to clients' needs. Described as attentive and talented, the principals are considered true advocates for their patrons. Aesthetically, there is usually an outline of traditional wood and/or stone against which poignant walls of glass and modern interior surfaces are poignantly juxtaposed. Their goal is simple yet refined architecture that is easily understood.

The partnership was formed in 1987. Ogawa was raised in LA, educated at USC, and previously practiced in LA, Rome, and at I.M. Pei in New York. Depardon was born in France, educated at Harvard, and practiced in Paris, Rome, and at Skidmore, Owings in New York. We hear both are extremely thorough at preparing drawings and dedicated to high-quality materials and construction without cutting any corners. The partners are also known for having "really good people" working for them. The firm concentrates much of its energy on townhouses (twenty in the New York area), apartments, and single-family houses across Manhattan and Brooklyn. It also does international and area second homes, and is respected for its commercial work. Fees are based hourly with a cap percentage of construction, which accrues to a figure within the standard range.

"There were tears in my eyes when I saw how beautiful the apartment was upon completion." "Gilles has fabulous structural insights." "Kathy is extremely sensitive to every detail. And she is willing to move anything around—even after the drawings are done." "They are parents; normal people. They get it." "Such a pleasure, especially compared to the other architects I've used over the years." "They turned a depressing, dark townhouse into a masterpiece by pushing out the back and filling it with light." "My good friend walked in and hired them on the spot." "Elegant modern, but definitely modern. That is their strength—don't think I'd hire them otherwise." "Goes beyond what the architect is required to do. The firm's clients are extraordinarily lucky." "Won't compromise on quality. Their loyalty is to their clients."

Peter L. Gluck and Partners   4.5   3.5   5   4.5
646 West 131st Street, New York, NY 10027
(212) 690 - 4950   www.gluckpartners.com
Modern, integrated institutional, commercial, and residential architecture

No one embarks upon a project with Peter Gluck lightly. To do so is to make a clear commitment to building a unique Modern edifice to be admired and noticed. Museum groups will visit. Gluck brings an unflinchingly crystalline view to each project, making it an intellectual pursuit of the highest caliber. Stylistically, the forms are sculptural, sleek, and geometric, with Japanese influences. Interestingly, there is also a strong commitment to affordability—in the use of materials and in the relatively low architectural fees—which is fundamental to the firm's mission.

A graduate of the Yale School of Architecture, Gluck spent a few years in Japan before opening his firm in 1972. The main focus is in institutional work (a day care center in East Harlem, a charter school in the South Bronx) and affordable housing ($160/square foot housing in Aspen). But Gluck will work with a lucky few each year on new residential properties. A holistic approach is taken, with the firm handling all aspects of design, from interior decor to landscape planning.

Clients and peers alike are extremely taken by Gluck's style and highly recommend his services; however, they suggest that potential clients familiarize themselves with his distinctive work before embarking upon a project. AD 100, 2000, 2002, 2004.

"Extraordinarily interesting work." "So cool, so calm, but on a mission to save the world from mundane architecture." "Peter is unique. A serious architect that can absolutely deal with function at reasonable costs." "Peter spent a lot of time understanding how we lived and how the sun played on the land before he went to the boards." "Primarily a scholar and secondly an architect." "There are certain things he will not compromise on." "Peter was always available; when I called he was the one that picked up the phone." "There is a fantastic back office that is also passionate about architecture." "Unwavering in his sincerity." "He let in light in every way possible." "Lots of quirks purposely built into the design with amazing details." "I think 10,000 people have seen the house in three years." "We enjoyed every second of the relationship." "I used to be an adamant traditionalist, but Peter turned me into an ardent Modernist."

Peter Marino & Associates   4.5   5   3.5   4

150 East 58th Street, 36th Floor, New York, NY 10022
(212) 752 - 5444 www.petermarinoarchitect.com

Polished, glamorous retail, hospitality, and residential architecture

This "architect to the rich and famous" designs and decorates retail and residential spaces for some of the most prestigious names in New York and the world, including Chanel, Fendi, Louis Vuitton, Giorgio Armani, Barneys, and Christian Dior. There is a very consistent look which positively proclaims the pinnacle of opulent luxury, generally featuring ecru furnishings and walls, extravagant polished marble, and touches of charismatic black and white (often in the form of multi-million dollar modern art).

Peter Marino's comprehensive approach encompasses designing furniture, lamps, and rugs for interiors, as well as advising on art collections for residential clients. Reductive in style and taste, Marino's work is described as "handsome yet provocative," but not too modernist. Over-the-top products and materials are an integral part of his design approach. He designed one recent apartment around a developing art collection; works by Willem de Kooning and Andy Warhol peacefully coexist with 18th century chairs and Coromandel screens.

With 80 architects and 25 interior designers (140+ total) on staff and offices in New York, East Hampton, Philadelphia, and Santa Barbara, Marino's is certainly one of the larger firms. Marino graduated Cornell and worked for Skidmore Owings & Merrill and I.M. Pei before founding his firm in 1978. Recent residential projects have included a suite at the Pierre and designs for Armani, Yves Saint Laurent, Bernard Arnault, and the Aga Khan. His first client was Andy Warhol, whom Marino sites as a major influence, along with Jean-Michel Frank. Clients like the cutting-edge feel of the firm's design work, and though some believe Marino's reputation may outstrip his achievements by just a notch, the majority feels that the elegant classicism of his work is "as good as it gets." AIA Fellow 2006. AD 100, 2000, 2002, 2004. HB Top Designers, 1999, 2000, 2001, 2002, 2003, 2004, 2005. ID Hall of Fame.

"Like eating out at a top restaurant—you pay a lot, but you get the highest quality." "Look at the website before you consider—there is a certain look and Peter is quite forceful in that agenda." "It is way more about the surfaces than the architecture." "Peter is a world traveler, with a very heavily staffed office." "A difficult back office environment." "Doing more now for the ladies who lunch, who really enjoy his company." "Be prepared with an open checkbook." "The finished rooms are like sparkling jewels." "The epitome of New York glamour." "The work is all polished flair and charm, just like Peter."

Pierce Allen

80 Eight Avenue, Suite 1602, New York, NY 10011
(212) 627 - 5440 www.pierceallen.com

Eclectic, fun, colorful interior design

See Pierce Allen's full report under the heading Interior Designers & Decorators

Richard Meier and Partners   5   4.5   5   5

475 Tenth Avenue, 6th Floor, New York, NY 10018
(212) 967 - 6060 www.richardmeier.com

Modern, forward-thinking institutional and residential architecture

Since he's an architectural deity himself, it's fitting that the Vatican is one of Richard Meier's clients. While museums, high-tech medical facilities, commercial buildings, and major civic commissions exemplify Meier's work, he still blesses a limited number of residential clients with his renowned talent. We hear the Cornell-educated Meier only selects serious projects with doubly serious budgets.

Recognized worldwide for his emphasis on light, geometric precision, and extensive use of glass, Richard Meier's modern work exemplifies the architect's own definition of his profession: "Architecture is the thoughtful making of space." His work shows the influence of Le Corbusier in the balance, mathematical rhythm, and cubic forms it employs, but focuses on creating volumes of space within a building. Meier's predominantly white palette highlights vertical and horizontal elements and shifting grids, and porcelain panels often lend luminosity to otherwise monochromatic surfaces. A winner of the prestigious Pritzker Award in 1984, Meier is famous for many buildings, but arguably his most acclaimed work is the Getty Center in Los Angeles.

Meier oversees a large staff, with several high-ranking associates assisting in the execution of his designs. Recent projects include two glass-curtained apartment buildings on Perry Street, a redesign of Avery Fisher Hall at Lincoln Center, and a twelve-story glass condominium in Miami with the most understated title in modern architecture: "Beach House." AIA Fellow 1976. AD 100, 2000, 2002, 2004. ID Hall of Fame.

"As good as it gets." "The Itzhak Perlman of architecture." "On the Perry Street project the design was gorgeous, but some of the practical details fell through the cracks." "The most serious architect working today." "Probably the most well-known architect of our time."

Robert A. M. Stern Architects   5   5   4.5   5
460 West 34th Street, 18th Floor, New York, NY 10001
(212) 967 - 5100 www.ramsa.com

Classically opulent institutional, commercial, and residential architecture

Robert Stern's influence in the architectural community is strong and deep. Stern is known as a passionate architect who views architecture as the embodiment of social values and culture. While about two-thirds of his projects are for institutions, he made his name designing large homes and continues to always have more than a few on the docket. Stern will embark on a project only after he has familiarized himself with the local building traditions as well as the wishes and styles of the individual clients. He will usually combine styles and materials to uniquely suit each project. Past designs include sprawling, gabled, shingle-style houses on Long Island (a specialty), a Regency home in Bel Air, a Jeffersonian construct at the University of Virginia, a simple clapboard museum in Massachusetts, and an 85-foot version of Mickey's conical hat for Disney's new building in Burbank. He believes in the dream, and delivers.

Stern's namesake firm employs 140 professionals, 32 of them registered architects. Remarkably, Stern reportedly is involved with the design of all projects and reviews them at every stage. The firm usually does interior design work to complement the architecture, including the manufacture of custom furniture. Manhattan clients say that Stern tends to focus his design on one or more centers of the house, which "always look phenomenal." Given his huge and loyal following, it is unsurprising that he is a bit less sensitive to the needs of the "mere mortal in need of good closet space," but still he is said to deliver something extraordinary every time.

Currently the dean of his alma mater, the Yale School of Architecture, he has written and edited over twenty books on design, taught thousands of students at Columbia and Yale, and hosted a PBS series. As a practitioner, he was influenced early on by Le Corbusier, Frank Lloyd Wright, and Robert Venturi. Through the years, however, he began incorporating classical elements (such as extensive arches and moldings) into his tailored designs. Today, he describes himself as a modern traditionalist, and his works relate more closely to their historical prototypes. Very little is started for under $2 million. But you can purchase an apartment in a chic Stern designed building, of which there are seven-and-counting in New York City—covering many neighborhoods, from Battery Park to Tribeca, and the Upper East and West Sides. Stern AIA Fellow 1984. AD 100, 2000, 2002, 2004. ID Hall of Fame.

"When you sign on to the Stern program, you get a masterpiece." "The furnishings always look fabulous, but sometimes form takes precedence over function." "When you work with Bob you know he has an incredible vision, but you do not always know what that vision is. Nevertheless, you are comfortable it will turn out magnificently, and it does." "He interviews you." "Despite the large office, Bob really makes an effort to have every project be original and be involved in the creation of that dream." "He has to have the leeway to make one or two rooms an over-the-top fantasy, and the rest of the rooms can stay within budget." "As an architect, myself, I can state that lots of people emulate Bob's designs, but he still does it best." "Working with Bob is an experience I would not have traded for anything." "A living legend."

Studio for Civil Architecture   5   4.5   4.5   4.5
462 Broadway, 3rd Floor, New York, NY 10013
(212) 625 - 3336 www.thecivilstudio.com

Distinguished, exceptional, traditional residential architecture

Donald Rattner is undeniably one of the great masters of the traditional classical form practicing today. Stepping into his rooms, one steps into the spatial dignity of years gone by, generous symmetric proportions, generations of hand-polished marble and limestone, lovingly worn fieldstone and clapboard. The moldings are strong and handsome, the details intricate and thoughtful. Rattner seeks to resurrect a knowledge of traditional building through his extensive teaching, writing, and lecturing. Insiders say his extensive experience and commitment to classical design make this newly created firm one of the highest integrity.

Rattner holds a B.A. in art history from Columbia and an M.Arch from Princeton. After working with famed classicist Allan Greenberg, he joined Ferguson and Murray in 1988, rose to partner, and then established his own firm in 2002. Insiders say Rattner created this smaller firm of about eight to personally devote more attention to each project, and to pursue academic interests and high-end property development. He partners with Andrew Friedman, who holds a degree from Cooper Union.

The majority of projects are residential in nature (including private communities and clubs), focusing on large-scale gut renovations and ground-up homes up and down the eastern seaboard. About a quarter of the work is in Manhattan. Most residential projects carry significant budgets ranging from $500,000 to $3.5 million, but the firm will take on smaller projects such as a kitchen or bathroom renovations for select clients. The firm charges standard fees based on a combination of hourly rates and/or a percentage of overall construction costs.

"He has a reputation and a body of work that speaks for itself." "Clearly has a carefully honed understanding for fine design and the classical elements that make it so." "Don has a great collaborative approach, balanced with a natural ability to lead and teach." "The spaces look at least a hundred years old, but the team is also excellent about knowing all the latest technologies for modern convenience." "They offer the full package and really understand the New York luxury market—can deal with soundproofing and finding the ultimate silver-plated door knobs from France." "Don magically creates homes and apartments that have instant credibility and inherent gentility."

	Quality	Cost	Value	Recommend?
	+	$	◆	★

Tsao & McKown Architects 4.5 4.5 4 4

20 Vandam Street, 10th Floor, New York, NY 10013
(212) 337 - 2617 www.tsao-mckown.com

High-end commercial and residential architecture

There is a refined, sophisticated, fluidity in the original work of Calvin Tsao and Zack McKown, known for their "masculine modernism." Since 1985, these partners have enhanced the subtleties of surfaces, textures, and light, often with oblique 70s lines of worldliness and form. They are as much about the color (usually neutrals tending toward earthiness) and the furnishings as the architecture, with a holistic view. What appears stylish about the firm's work actually evolves from an earnest and arduous study of the subject and context.

The partnership's first major commissions were commercial enterprises in Singapore and Shanghai. Currently, most of the firm's work is nearby, including hotel interiors (the Tribeca Grand), museum interiors and exhibitions (Geoffrey Beene Retrospective), high-fashion boutiques (Nautica), restaurants (the Metrazur at Grand Central), and of course, apartment and townhouse interiors. Beyond merely designing furniture, the duo ventures into the creation of gas fireplaces, sinks, bathtubs, dinnerware, candlesticks, and picture frames.

The firm's diversity of projects builds on the duo's expertise creating technologically advanced spaces, while showing off its excellent attention to detail. Sources say the partners readily bring that same excellence to its residential work, including commissions for clients Ian Schrager and Josie Natori. HB Top Designers, 1999, 2000, 2001, 2002, 2003, 2004. ID Hall of Fame.

"I cannot say enough about the wonderful job provided by Tsao & McKown. The team was extremely professional, always organized and thorough." "The design talent of their creative staff is unmatched." "Can be quirky and iconoclastic." "They lyrically layered a modernistic view in my prewar apartment, sensitively and appropriately."

Hiring an Audio/Visual Design & Installation Service Provider

These days, one doesn't have to crave global domination to enjoy a room that can, at the push of a button, transform itself into a ground control headquarters that rivals any James Bond villain setup. Home theaters, multi-zone entertainment systems, home-automation and lighting controls, online capability—if you can dream it, they can hook it up. Just make sure you ask for the remote, or you may never be able to use what you paid for. Audio/visual (A/V) home service providers can seamlessly integrate almost anything—media walls, touch screen panels, speakers, structured cabling—into your existing components or into the architectural integrity of any room. If this isn't possible, they will build new cabinets to accommodate the equipment. Custom installation is the name of the game.

What to Expect From an A/V Specialist

A/V providers can be contracted through general contractors, designers, or directly by you. Whomever they bill, communication with the homeowner is essential. When courting your A/V guru, remember that they may specialize in only a few of the following areas: audio, video, telephone, Internet, security, and lighting and climate control. A service provider who excels in home theater installation may not be as well versed in, or even deal with, security. You should also know whether the service provider can connect all your various electronic systems together, a process known as integration. Determine your needs, get references, and ask questions. Will the A/V specialist both design and engineer your project, or will he or she be coordinating with other trades?

Even when working through a designer, a good A/V contractor will want to meet with you one-on-one to assess your needs. Make the time. You don't want your system to outreach your ability or desire to operate it. These days, most A/V companies will want to sell you a complete package with MP3 libraries, motorized blinds, plasma screens, and HVAC all connected and controlled by a central panel. Those systems are tempting, but don't get swept up in your tech-happy A/V provider's enthusiasm for all the cool things available to you. Stand fast. Are you really looking for a movie palace complete with stadium seating, and does it really need to be tied into the landscape lighting and the air conditioner in the kitchen? Remember, the latest may not be the greatest if the newest innovation hasn't been around long enough to be time-tested. Some A/V contractors prefer a lag time of six months after the introduction of a product so that they can follow its performance before recommending it to their customers. If you're the first one in on a new gizmo, know that you may be the first one out of luck if it breaks. The means of customization and the materials used differ widely from shop to shop. Some contractors only work in certain brands. Others will install anything you want. Request that the bid proposal be itemized and a sketch attached if you want the finished product to perfectly match your dreams.

Who Will Install My New System?

Although you'll first talk with either a principal or a representative of the A/V firm, traditionally a crew of field techs will be dispatched to perform the installation and service. Don't fret—this crew is likely to be as well informed and passionate about its business as any front man. Just keep in mind that it's invaluable to be able to speak to the same person from the beginning to the end of the project, whether it's the principal or the project manager.

Though all systems need electricity to run, miscommunication on the subject of power is common during A/V installations. Usually, the problem is one of responsibility: who is going to do what? Some A/V providers want your electrician to pull the low-voltage cable if he's already onsite and already holds a permit, eliminating a coordination headache. Many prefer to do it themselves, knowing that some electricians treat delicate cables with all the care of baggage handlers at JFK. Just check that someone's on it before the walls close up. Also, know that A/V contractors are not going to install or relocate the electrical receptacles that will power up your system and provide the jolt for the sub-woofers. That's still your electrician's job.

PRICING AND SERVICE WARRANTIES

The cost of your A/V project will be a reflection of the design work involved, the degree of customization, the type and number of devices and pieces of equipment to be installed, the length of cable to be pulled, and the anticipated man hours, plus overhead and profit. Many jobs require a deposit of up to 50%, with progress payments to be made when materials and equipment arrive on-site, and again upon job completion. The warranty should appear on the bid proposal. A year of free service is standard. As is a detailed explanation of what button on the remote turns the thing on.

LICENSE CONSIDERATIONS

Because this is a relatively new field, there is currently no licensing requirement for A/V services in New York City. Fortunately, this also means that no permit is required. Check your municipality, however, because where it's mandated, these service providers should be licensed and insured. If you're still confused, the Custom Electronic Design and Installation Association (CEDIA at www.cedia. org) is an excellent resource.

TRENDS

When it comes to home theater, DVD players have replaced videotapes and laserdiscs as the standard format, but don't throw your VCR out the window—it's good to keep one on hand so you can still watch those old home movies. Format is very important, but the quality of the TV itself is also key, and new advances are made every year. The advent of High Definition Television (HDTV) ensures a crisp, clear picture, and wafer-thin Plasma TVs can be hung on any wall in the house. If a theater-like experience is what you're after, digital projectors, an increasingly common option, replicate it nicely.

Of course, your A/V system isn't limited to movies alone. Cutting-edge, multi-zone entertainment systems allow you to play CDs or MP3s jukebox-style or listen to the radio in any room of the house. It's not at all unheard of to program a system to play your favorite song when you get home. And these systems are rarely limited to music and videos, they include home automation as well. Things like wireless lighting controls, climate controls, motorized blinds, sprinklers, and security can all be wired together and accessed over the Internet. Not all of those options are necessary, of course. But tell that to the late-working Manhattanite who has just come home to a nicely cooled, well-lit apartment with Mozart coming from the kitchen and *Seinfeld* reruns coming from the den.

HOW TO GET THE MOST OUT OF YOUR SYSTEM

✧ Sit down with the installer to discuss your wants and needs in detail.

✧ Don't rush for the newest technology.

✧ Only install gear you'll actually use.

✧ Don't fall asleep during the technician's instructions on how to program each device.

AUDIO/VISUAL DESIGN & INSTALLATION

🛍 FIRMS WITH ONLINE PORTFOLIOS* 🛍

Electronic Interiors Inc. 🛍　　　　4.5　4.5　4　4.5
40 West Elm Street, Greenwich, CT 06830
(203) 629 - 5622   jillkent@aol.com
Highly customized A/V system design and installation; home automation

Industry star Jill Kent of Electronic Interiors has been designing cutting-edge home theater systems for over two decades. Her client roster—packed with Hollywood A-listers, sports stars, and financial giants—speaks for itself. Most of Kent's referrals come from the trade, but she does a fair amount of work directly with homeowners.

Using Crestron integration and Lutron lighting equipment, Kent creates highly customized systems based on the client's needs. From elaborate projection systems to simple plasma setups, insiders say Electronic Interiors provides a top-notch listening and viewing experience—and can help even the least techno-savvy operate their new toys.

Kent's services also include home integration of everything from lighting controls to HVAC. Kent offers a one-year parts and labor warranty and honors all manufacturers' warranties. We hear her small staff is "flexible" and "professional." She is a founding member and four-year board member of the CEDIA trade association, and was the first woman to act as chair of their annual expo in 2005. Having been featured in *Architectural Digest*, *Fortune*, and *New York* magazine, Electronic Interiors' services do not come cheap, but we understand the quality is of the highest imaginable caliber.

"Very detail-oriented and very concerned with aesthetics." "Her forethought and planning make the process and the end product better." "Works well with other subcontractors."

InnerSpace Electronics Inc. 🛍　　　　4.5　4.5　4　5
74 Fox Island Road, Port Chester, NY 10573
(914) 937 - 9700   www.innerspaceelectronics.com
Top-notch A/V design and installation; home automation specialists

Andrea and Barry Reiner started InnerSpace with a little money and a whole lot of dedication. Today their clients still benefit from that can-do spirit, though InnerSpace could hardly be described as "little" anymore. Boasting a list of services that includes design and installation of home theater systems, lighting control equipment, home automation systems, electronic window treatments, soundproofing, intercom systems, and boardrooms, InnerSpace delivers the goods both locally and nationally. With a staff of 26, the firm can offer competitive service rates, and can handle projects ranging from $12,000 to $750,000.

Clients praise the "sophisticated, yet simple to use" systems, and references say InnerSpace is the place to go for those interested in home management systems. Sources say the staff comes with a wealth of knowledge, and InnerSpace receives high marks for remaining available to clients long after the project is

*We invite you to visit www.franklinreport.com to view images of their work.

99

finished. With high-end product lines such as Runco, Sonance, Audio Request, and Crestron combined with a good one-year parts and service warranty, clients say the company is worth its considerable price tag.

"Will stay late until the job is done right." "Responded right away when I messed things up." "Not only really good at what they do, but Barry and Andrea are just genuinely nice people." "We're thinking of flying them to California to wire our home out there, because we can't find anyone else as good."

Lyric Hi-Fi Inc. 💼   4   4   4   4
1221 Lexington Avenue, New York, NY 10028
(212) 535 - 5710 www.lyricusa.com

A/V system design, installation, sales, and service; home automation

Launched in 1959, Lyric is still doing what it did from the beginning—identifying sonic trends early and staying on the cutting edge. A pioneer of custom installation as well as the creator of some of the nation's first remote-controlled audio installations, founder Michael Kay earns respect and approval from references and peers alike. His two go-to guys, Leonard Bellezza and Dan Mondoro, took over the operation in 2004, but Kay, a grandfatherly figure, still hangs around the Lexington Avenue store, dispensing sage audio advice.

The firm's staff of nearly two dozen includes project managers who act as A/V liaisons between customers and their designers or architects. Because Lyric has bases in Manhattan and White Plains, it can often provide same-day service for clients experiencing problems. The company, which offers a one-year warranty on parts and labor, handles a wide range of projects, from entry level component music and A/V systems to cinema and home automation systems in the much-coveted six-figure bracket. Some references say getting in touch with a principal can be difficult, but most leave happy.

"The granddaddy of high-end audio/video stores." "Work was well thought out and included extra capacity wiring to allow for future capabilities." "Staff is well trained and experienced." "Responded immediately whenever renovation contractor was ready for his work or had a question." "They were accommodating when I asked to use my old equipment to keep cost down."

FIRMS WITHOUT ONLINE PORTFOLIOS

Aaron's Media Inc.   4   3   4.5   4.5
107 Harper Terrace, Cedar Grove, NJ 07009
(973) 477 - 3544 aaronsmedia@msn.com

A/V system installation and service

Aaron's Media Inc. is an ideal firm for those who demand the boss's attention, since clients always deal directly with principal Aaron Brown. Former customers praise Brown for being effective, attentive, and up-to-date on the latest technology. We're told his small, three-person company works closely with architects and designers to build and install the system that best suits the customer's needs. References also note that when it comes time to install, they feel safe leaving their keys with the trustworthy Brown.

Aaron's works mainly on big jobs, such as whole home audio/video installation, but the firm will also take on smaller projects for select clients. This good-value, respected company serves large swaths of New York and New Jersey for installations, but do note that if you're looking for integration work, it's not Aaron's forte.

"Service is his middle name." "No surprises." "Focuses on making sure the customer is happy." "Aaron made even my mother happy, which is not easy to do." "Friendly and easy to communicate with."

Audio by James Inc.   3.5   3   4.5   4.5
571 Knollwood Road, Ridgewood, NJ 07450
(201) 493 - 7282   abyj@msn.com
A/V and telephone system installation and service; audio specialist

Principal James Taylor isn't who you think he is, but he does know good sound. From mid-fi to hi-fi, we hear there are few better. Audio by James' client base is mainly residential and mostly in New York City and New Jersey, but the company will travel farther afield if need be. Taylor has deliberately kept his business small (only three employees), preferring to maintain a personal involvement with each job. Clients appreciate the close-knit team's focus on aesthetics, with particular attention directed to wire hiding and equipment placement. Some sources wish Taylor were more available, but most appreciate the individualized attention he gives to each job.

In addition to home theater, multi-room, and surround-sound installations, the firm also installs telephone systems, keypads, and outdoor speakers. Taylor is said to be a perfectionist, a trait that we hear shows up in the outstanding quality of his systems. In business since 1987, Audio by James has enjoyed its success through word-of-mouth from customers and peers and is truly an insider's find.

"He set up an amazing system for my home." "Very reliable—we can call him whenever we need him." "Gets the job done perfectly." "Punctual and extremely neat."

Audio Command Systems   5   4.5   4.5   4.5
694 Main Street, Westbury, NY 11590
(516) 997 - 5800   www.audiocommand.com
Elite A/V system design, installation, and service; home automation

This expert firm consistently delivers cutting-edge technology—and is frequently called upon to give a command performance in a celebrity's home. Industry professionals and clients both agree that Audio Command Systems is one of the premier designers and installers in the country. With offices in New York, Los Angeles, and Southern Florida, Audio Command Systems has 28 years of experience in high-end markets.

Audio Command is in demand. According to *CE Pro* (a trade journal), the firm has been one of the top five revenue-producing AV firms in the country for five years in a row. Audio Command handles projects with budgets starting at $100,000, going up to $1.5 million. To serve clients, the firm has a staff of 75 "knowledgeable and reliable" employees, with one project manager assigned to each client. While we have heard that this firm is quick to respond to architects, contractors, and clients with large installations, some say smaller projects can get lost in the shuffle. The company maintains no inventory and orders components and materials on a project-by-project basis. Clients say the lack of pressure to move stock contributes to its emphasis on customer service. Clients also report favorably on the firm's techno-savvy, saying Audio Command is fully in command of the latest developments in the field.

"The best technology available, and extremely competent." "They know what to do and how to get it done." "Recommending these guys is the best favor I could do for any audiophile." "Always does a sound job for me." "Big firm with large pool of resources. They carry a lot of weight in the business."

	Quality	Cost	Value	Recommend?
	✚	$	◆	★

Audio Den

| | 4 | 4 | 4 | 4 |

2845 Middle Country Road, Lake Grove, NY 11755
(631) 585 - 5600 www.audioden.com

A/V and home automation system installation and service; home theater specialists

Audio Den deals primarily with the home theater market, but we hear it's branching out into lighting control, thermostat, and music server integration as well. Audio Den works directly with homeowners in New York City and the Hamptons, and clients tell us the firm delivers the correct systems on time and provides service long after a job is complete. The company takes on a high number of jobs—sometimes up to twelve during any given week, a pace that leaves some clients wishing the service was a bit more personal. Few, however, can find fault with Audio Den's technicians, who we hear are expert in accommodating the needs of decorators and clients alike. The firm also boasts a full-time staff of programmers to satisfy the high-tech side of the business.

References report that Audio Den may not always be gung-ho on the latest advancements in the field, sometimes preferring to use proven technologies. But these techies are praised for taking a homeowner's vision and bringing it to fruition.

"Conscientious, careful, and efficient." "Pleasant people designing outstanding systems." "Not afraid to take on any request, no matter how wild it is." "Exceedingly neat and easy to get in touch with at all times. They work for my clients in the Hamptons, and my clients invariably end up hiring them to do their other homes."

Audio Video Crafts

| | 4.5 | 4.5 | 4 | 4 |

9-09 44th Avenue, Long Island City, NY 11101
(212) 996 - 8300 info@avcrafts.com

A/V systems, lighting design, intercom systems, home automation; home theater specialists

Audio Video Crafts' territory is superior home theaters, audio/video systems, lighting, and intercoms, mostly in Manhattan. Regularly named one of the top 50 dealers in the nation by the industry magazine *CE Pro*, this efficient 22-person firm is adept at tackling design challenges, like outfitting a major TV star's multi-story garage with a state-of-the-art entertainment system. But like other NYC A/V firms, AVC has broadened its focus in recent years to include more integration and home automation, especially with Crestron equipment.

The firm's technicians do all work (even software programming) in-house, which helps things move quickly and cuts costs. If the job is a big one (and we hear many of AVC's projects are), the design, which is computer-aided, is free, as the firm charges retail for the components and installation services. Large and small clients alike rave about the company's expertise, but smaller-scale clients express some concerns about customer service. Upper-end prices reinforce the company's image as a place for people who are serious about their A/V systems.

"They did a fantastic job designing my apartment-wide system, but it was tough to get them to come back to finish up." "Initial installation and response was great." "These guys are serious professionals. I respect their love of the business and desire to design to the highest quality standards."

Audio Video Systems Inc.

| | 5 | 4.5 | 5 | 5 |

275 Hillside Avenue, Williston Park, NY 11596
(516) 739 - 1010 www.audiovideosystems.com

Expert A/V system design and installation; home automation

For over 24 years, Audio Video Systems has been called upon not only to design and install high-end entertainment and integration systems, but to fix mistakes made by others. Acclaimed by manufacturers and industry publications alike, this 45-person firm delivers top-quality service to the greater New York area with its talented and extremely accessible technicians.

Designers and contractors recommend the firm for its eye for detail and ability to coordinate, while clients are repeatedly impressed by follow-through and willingness to please after the job is finished. Audio Video Systems' prices are not cheap, but clients agree that the quality could not be higher, especially in the area of training. The staff will both install a top-notch system and teach you how to use it, a key factor for those who have been left high and dry with eight remotes. The firm has also established itself as one of the "best and brightest" in the industry, regularly rated by *CE Pro* as one of the top five revenue-producing firms in the United States.

"Head and shoulders above the rest." "They wire for future problems." "Technicians were courteous and professional, and their response time was quick." "These are my guys. I wouldn't go with anyone else." "They make things idiot-proof." "Came back to teach my child about the system after he wasn't initially around to learn it." "They treated my project with the utmost respect and didn't make me feel like my job was too small for them. Customer service was great, too—friendly and informative." "I can call them on the weekend and get help."

Audio/Video Excellence LLC   3.5   3.5   4   4
343 Manville Road, Pleasantville, NY 10570
(914) 747 - 1411

A/V systems; home theater and home automation specialists

When it comes to home theaters and A/V integration, sources tell us that Audio/Video Excellence delivers...well, excellence. For twenty years, this firm has been specializing in whole-house audio and video distribution, custom media rooms, and home theater designs. Additionally, the company handles home automation by linking lighting, heating, ventilation, security, and telephone systems to operate in total harmony. It can even tackle unique jobs, like linking twenty pinball machines and a home theater to run from the same automation panel. References are generally pleased with Audio/Video Excellence's ability to refine their lifestyles by bringing 21st century technology smoothly into the home.

"They come in neat and leave neat: no stomping around in muddy boots or leaving wires hanging out of the walls." "Installation is perfect and always on schedule. Sometimes servicing broken equipment can take a while." "Very professional, a rarity in the A/V business."

Audiodesign   3.5   3.5   4   4
1955 Black Rock Turnpike, Fairfield, CT 06432
(203) 336 - 4401   www.audiodesign.com

A/V systems design and installation; retail sales

Clients say Audiodesign's comprehensive one- and two-year warranties are one huge reason why this firm boasts a dedicated clientele and a busy schedule. In business since the 1980s, Audiodesign was bought by current owner Ira Fagan in 1999. The firm serves all of Westchester and Fairfield counties, as well as New York City and beyond. With a burgeoning business in designing dedicated media rooms, residential cinemas, and multiroom A/V systems, Audiodesign handles upwards of 150 projects each year that range from small $5,000 retail jobs to massive $500,000 custom systems. Though Fagan is primarily a techie, we hear his aesthetic sense has developed nicely.

Audiodesign has a staff of eleven, five of whom are installers. The company also installs telephone networks, lighting and climate-control systems, and motorized blinds, but does not do computer networking. Some clients say that

Fagan has pushed back deadlines, but many vouch for Audiodesign's service, noting that the company really helps the end user feel comfortable with the system.

"Hey, with a two-year warranty that includes service and in-home maintenance, I certainly wouldn't roll the dice and go somewhere else."

Cerami & Associates Inc.   4   4   4   5
404 Fifth Avenue, New York, NY 10018
(212) 370 - 1776 www.ceramiassociates.com
Acoustical consulting

For those who take sound seriously, the respected acoustical engineering firm of Cerami & Associates will consult on the acoustics of anything from an audio/ video system to an apartment gym. Though the company does not actually sell or install systems, clients say Cerami makes excellent recommendations about appropriate materials and design to meet clients' needs. Sources tell us the staff is extremely helpful and resourceful in tackling and solving even the most complicated problems. Cerami is used by the best high-end contractors and architects in the city on jobs that require a careful consideration of the acoustic environment—and are willing to pay upper-range prices for very sound advice.

"The only game in town for high-quality acoustical engineering." "They preserved my neighbor's sanity and our relationship due to the sound of my gym over their bedroom." "Great problem solvers."

Curt A. Barad Audio Video Inc.   4.5   4   4.5   4.5
3585 Lawson Boulevard, Oceanside, NY 11572
(516) 763 - 4144 www.baradav.com

Exceptional A/V system design, installation, and service; home automation

Barad Audio's policy of having roving technicians both on the Upper East Side and in the Hamptons ensures that you'll get quick service at both your winter and summer abodes. This company's game is high-end residential systems, and clients say they play it well, giving Barad high marks for technological audio/visual expertise, excellent designs, and quick custom work. Barad is also lauded for offering a range of economic alternatives. We hear the firm can deliver the highest quality the client requests, but "won't sell you expensive speakers that you can't tell the difference between the next model down."

Recently, the company added lighting control to its list of services, and that, along with sophisticated integration, has become a significant part of its business. Barad technicians (fifteen of whom are always on the road, in case of an "audio/video emergency") are well-versed in the popular Crestron and AMX systems. We hear the company is willing and able to assemble the ultimate setup from scratch, customize a new system around your existing components, or happily design a basic system. The firm also wins points for thoroughness and follow-through. Principal Curt Barad is praised for his honesty, straightforwardness and relatively reasonable costs, given the high quality of service. Barad and his staff are said to be neat and unobtrusive; what's even better, they "understand aesthetics too."

"My kids were desperate to watch a movie on the projector screen for a sleepover party and Curt came over that afternoon to fix it." "They are helpful, intelligent, focused guys with the best information, but they are not pushy or audio snobs. They will do what is right for the client and the job." "As a high-end decorator, I love these guys. They listen to the client and deliver the goods." "Sunny, easy to get in touch with, and great problem solvers."

Design Installations

	Quality	Cost	Value	Recommend?
	4	4	4	4

464 Westport Avenue, Norwalk, CT 06851
(203) 847 - 2777   www.designinstallations.com

A/V system design and installation; telephone and home automation systems; computer networking

In the competetive world of high-end residential A/V and automation, Design Installations has earned a stellar reputation among both clients and competitors. Typical projects, including large-scale home theater systems, telephone systems, computer networking, and lighting controls, come in at about $50,000. Specialty projects—such as a 22,000 square foot home in Greenwich, or a special video and DVR rig for an internet poker champ—can run up to $300,000.

More than half of the company's projects come directly from client referrals, but Design Installations also works very closely with architects, designers, and contractors. In business since 1984, this firm of eight is headed by partners Dean Smith and Rick Samuels. They are said to provide excellent service and up-to-the-minute knowledge at upper-end prices.

"Rick and the rest of the staff are serious about what they do and know the ins and outs better than most." "Nice guys." "It's really great that these guys can do it all and I don't have to call seven different companies." "You may have to wait to get an installation date, because they are swamped with work. It's worth the wait." "During the installation my house was struck by lightning and a portion of the system was destroyed. These guys worked quickly and efficiently and had my system up and running fast."

Electronic Environments

	Quality	Cost	Value	Recommend?
	3.5	3.5	4	4.5

247 West 37th Street, Suite 704, New York, NY 10018
(212) 997 - 1110

A/V and telephone system installation and service

We hear that accessibility, great ideas, and an engaging personality are just a few of the things Kim Michels, principal of Electronic Environments, has to offer. The firm handles high-end audio/video design and installation work, and its services come with an installation warranty that matches the duration of the warranty from the component manufacturer. Electronic Environments also installs telephone systems and will consider projects of all sizes. Sources appreciate the firm's excellent on-site training and reasonable prices.

"Terrific ideas, terrific service." "Honest and skilled." "A pleasure to work with, couldn't be happier with results." "Classy, professional, and efficient." "I've worked with Electronic Environments for over fifteen years, and I've always been delighted with their conscientiousness and reliability."

Electronics Design Group Inc.

	Quality	Cost	Value	Recommend?
	4.5	4.5	4	4

60 Ethel Road West, Suite 4, Piscataway, NJ 08854
(732) 650 - 9800   www.edgonline.com

Top-of-the-line A/V, lighting, and telephone system design and installation; home automation

For nearly two decades this Garden State firm has been providing top-notch A/V gear to the metro area. Recognized as a force to be reckoned with even by its competitors, EDG recently won "Dealer of the Year" from CEDIA, a trade organization. The company specializes in the custom design, integration, and installation of sophisticated home theater, multi-room audio, lighting, structured wiring, motorized blinds, and telephone/intercom systems. EDG does take on commercial projects, but its specialty is high-end residential jobs. The firm can be found in Park Avenue duplexes and 30,000 square foot homes, sometimes working directly with home-owners. Clients praise the smooth interaction between Electronics Design Group and their architects, builders, and interior designers, judging the upper-end prices to be worth every penny.

"Bob, Ed, and Co. run an excellent business with high-quality specialists." "They are honest, and they understand the critical nature of their systems and stand by their work." "An A+ rating from me."

Innovative Audio Video Showrooms   4   4   4   4
150 East 58th Street, New York, NY 10155
(212) 634 - 4444 www.innovativeaudiovideo.com

A/V system design, installation, and sales; home automation

Recently expanding from Brooklyn to Manhattan, Innovative Audio Video has made a name for itself in the Big Apple, earning a spot in *New York* magazine's 2005 "Best Of" edition. The showroom may be A/V techie heaven, but we hear the staff is good at putting things into plain English. The company sells and installs complete audio/video systems, home theaters, lighting control, and home automation equipment, and will help you figure out how to use it, too.

Clients tell us principal Elliot Fishkin and his team are flexible and attentive to individual needs, but are also skilled at working with a large design team. Innovative will also work with telephones and security, but not as stand-alone systems. Satisfied customers especially praise the "low-pressure, stress-free environment" and are content to pay elevated prices for elevated quality.

"Designers of top-of-the-line, stealth systems." "No pushy salespeople." "Best products with the best service!"

Metro A.V.   4   3.5   4.5   4.5
128 Musgnug Avenue, Mineola, NY 11501
(516) 294 - 2949 metroav@optonline.net

A/V system design and installation; home automation specialists

Metro's not just in the metro area anymore. On the rise in recent years, this firm has increased its staff and taken on jobs as far away as California. The firm installs home theaters, audio systems, CCTV, and—increasingly—home integration packages with Crestron and Lutron systems.

The programming staff is said to be top-notch, and will personalize audio set-ups to accommodate the listening tastes of casual head-boppers and obsessive audiophiles alike. We hear the technicians' attention and responsiveness earn them a warm welcome wherever they go, from Westchester to Manhattan to the Hamptons—and beyond. Metro is known to work in concert with the client's architect and designer to get exactly what is needed both visually and technologically. Clients describe the firm's services as professional, honest, dependable, personable—and a very good deal.

	Quality	Cost	Value	Recommend?
	✚	$	◆	★

"Well worth the money because they provide a value-added service that you can't get elsewhere." "Wiring up all the rooms of my penthouse was certainly a challenge, but Tom Dolciotta and his staff did an excellent job."

Park Avenue Audio   4   3.5   4.5   4.5
425 Park Avenue South, New York, NY 10016
(212) 685 - 8101   www.parkavenueaudio.com

Innovative A/V system design and installation; home automation

For over 35 years, Park Avenue Audio has been delivering A/V solutions as classy as its namesake. Led by "on the ball" principal Dennis Yetikyel, the firm receives high marks for satisfying the high-tech requirements of private homeowners, architects, builders, and designers.

This fourteen-person team offers audio and video distribution, custom home theaters, and complete systems integration. Clients say they are happy to come back time and again to Park Avenue Audio for what they say are creative, elegant, and upscale A/V designs. Over and over, we hear that this outfit delivers cutting-edge systems. Past projects include a renovated YMCA building-cum-experimental design space and a gleaming Park Avenue (where else?) penthouse. Park Avenue will also handle mid-range projects. The firm's polite, attentive service and just-north-of-reasonable prices are said to be definite assets.

"Complete gentlemen." "Attentive to my audiophile needs." "Work done exactly as promised." "Absolutely up to speed."

Performance Imaging   4   4   4   3.5
115 East Putnam Avenue, Greenwich, CT 06830
(203) 504 - 5200   www.performanceimaging.net

A/V system design and installation; home automation

With only six years in business, Performance Imaging is a relative youngster, but already this upstart has established itself as an industry leader, recognized by *CE Pro* as one of the top ten dealers (based on volume) nationwide. Located in Greenwich, Performance receives enthusiastic applause from clients for its design and installation of residential and commercial systems for audio and video, lighting, home automation, and security.

Recently the company has switched CEOs a few times, but architects and designers haven't stopped praising Performance Imaging's ability to create systems that are virtually invisible until activated. Homeowners agree, noting the staff's exceptional attention to detail and willingness to explain technical points. While the company's services don't come cheap, sources say excellent maintenance services and diligent follow-ups make it all worthwhile.

"No doubt, they're one of the big dogs in town. They handle some serious projects." "Accommodating, resourceful, and sensitive to my budget concerns." "They were able to use my old equipment to keep costs down." "Dependable." "I am a lifelong audiophile, and I couldn't be happier or more impressed with the system they designed."

Scott Trusty   4   3   5   4.5
127 Joffre Avenue, Stamford, CT 06905
(917) 459 - 8901   bok22@optonline.net

A/V consulting

Clients rely on Scott Trusty to help them navigate what he calls "the minefield of electronics." Trusty has been working in the city (as well as Westchester and Fairfield counties) for well over 30 years, earning his stripes designing and installing high-end residential home theaters and automation systems. Recently, he's turned his attention to consultation, focusing on designing systems and training clients to use them, but not actually installing the equipment himself. For the installation work, Trusty relies on his (ahem) trusty shortlist of solid A/V companies.

We hear that Trusty "knows everything about sound." Sources say he's just as attentive on small jobs as he is on larger projects, and his fees are a great value on either. Clients especially like how Trusty sweats the details, right down to working with the contractor on the appropriate type of plasterboard to be used for the ultimate acoustics or doing research on the perfect TV to meet a client's specific space and budget needs. For those thinking of going the consultant route, references confirm you can rely on Trusty.

"He's a straight-shooter—you won't get any BS from him." "He's been around long enough to tell the difference between a gadget and a meaningful piece of equipment." "Passionate about what he does, great with people, and he delivers." "Absolutely fantastic." "He's the only contractor my wife feels comfortable leaving alone in the house."

Sound by Singer   4   3.5   4.5   4.5

18 East 16th Street, New York, NY 10003
(212) 924 - 8600 www.soundbysinger.com
A/V system design and installation; home automation

In business since the days of the eight-track tape, Sound by Singer has built up an international reputation for high-end audio and video installation. Based in Manhattan with a 15,000 square foot A/V demonstration showroom, this twenty-person firm serves as a consultant to many of its peers and boasts design and installation teams that serve clients around the world.

Sound by Singer can handle anything from home integration and control to home theaters and complex multi-room audio systems. For principal Andrew Singer, high-end doesn't just mean expensive. Singer looks for equipment that really performs. We hear the wide range of parts he carries is a gift to clients on a decent budget. Clients say Singer and his crew share a passion for providing sleek, deluxe entertainment systems in the most cost-effective way.

"Sound by Singer is like staying at the Four Seasons—first-class service." "These guys really know their business." "Very accommodating to clients." "Andy isn't merely a vendor but a trusted advisor both to me and to the countless others I have recommended him to."

Sound Sight Technologies   4   3.5   4.5   4.5

124 West 30th Street, Suite 208, New York, NY 10001
(212) 760 - 0892 www.soundsightonline.com
A/V and home automation system design, installation, and service; lighting design

We hear this respected firm is great at keeping all that sound out of sight. Led by principal Robert Friedland, Sound Sight Technologies is dedicated not only to high-end audio/video but also to full system integration. The firm offers design, installation, and instruction services for such projects as brownstone renovations and corporate makeovers, without forgetting the smaller projects.

We're told that architects recommend Sound Sight repeatedly to clients, probably because of the highly detailed drawings and careful project organization. We also hear that Friedland is "extremely dedicated" to his work. Sources say he'll go the extra mile to keep his clients satisfied, even calling to check up long after he's off the payroll. If anything, clients report, he almost tries to do too much. Still, healthy repeat business suggests that past customers appreciate Sound Sight's services—and the relatively reasonable tab.

"He's the most professional A/V installer I've ever worked with." "When our temporary satellite dish went down in a snowstorm, the president of the company climbed

up onto the roof to clear off the snow at 9 PM." "Excellent people." "The absolute best. I live all the way out in New Canaan, but one of his technicians completely retuned my system, and didn't even charge me."

Stereo Exchange   3   3   4   3.5
627 Broadway, New York, NY 10012
(212) 505 - 1111 www.stereoexchange.com
A/V system design, installation, and sales

Stereo Exchange began life as a place for Manhattanites to trade in their eight-tracks. Today, it's primarily a high-end retailer, though the firm's installation division will integrate high-end audio, video, and automation systems into new construction and existing homes and businesses. Working closely with architects, designers, builders, and homeowners, Stereo Exchange's 30-person staff understands the latest technologies and provides honest, knowledgeable information, without the techno-babble. The well-priced firm's reputation for what clients call "excellent systems" is the hard-earned result of more than fifteen years spent integrating state-of-the-art equipment.

Theo Kalomirakis Theaters   5   5   4   5
35 West 36th Street, 10th Floor East, New York, NY 10018
(212) 244 - 2404 www.tktheaters.com
Superior home theater design

As the legend goes, "father of home theater" Theo Kalomirakis unwittingly invented home theater in his Brooklyn basement. Kalomirakis, a magazine art director and right-hand man for Malcolm Forbes at the time, began inviting fellow magazine-types to his home to watch movies on A/V systems he had cleverly rigged to get the maximum theater-like experience. When the writers who attended started writing about Kalomirakis's home theater in various publications, he was inundated with requests from film buffs, begging him to do the same thing in their basements.

Twenty years later, Kalomirakis is still at the forefront of home theater design, taking on projects worldwide for entertainment, business, political figures, and royalty (literally). Eddie Murphy, The Rock, and Cal Ripken, Jr. all have Kalomirakis-designed home theaters. A guru in his field, Kalomirakis has even written two books on the subject.

Kalomirakis and his team of eleven design ultra-high-end theaters in three phases: schematic design, design development, and construction documentation. While the firm will design the space (he has registered architects on staff) and handle the interior design, it will not recommend electronics. That's left up to the carefully selected A/V installation subcontractors. Kalomirakis and company generally do not build theaters from the ground up or deal with structural elements, preferring to incorporate their own designs harmoniously into the existing design of the house.

The firm takes on about 40 theaters each year, ranging from just 300 square feet all the way up to 19,000 square foot A/V "villages" in people's homes. The villages can include a flabbergasting array of dance clubs, theaters, and mini-multi-media theme parks. But if you want a Kalomirakis theater in your home, be prepared to shell out about $350 per square foot—and that's not including electronics. Using that formula, projects range from $45,000 up to a whopping $2 million.

"He's got the best reputation in the business." "His designs are spectacular, they'll take your breath away." "Highest price tag out there." "I'm a huge fan, but if my wife knew what it cost, she would kill me."

	Quality +	Cost $	Value ◆	Recommend? ★

Ultimate Sound & Installation Inc.

Quality 3.5 | Cost 3 | Value 4.5 | Recommend? 4

36-16 29th Street, Long Island City, NY 11106
(718) 729 - 2111 www.ultimateinstallations.com

A/V, automation, and lighting system design and installation

We're told this firm really strives for the ultimate in new technology, keeping its technicians up-to-the-minute with regular training sessions. From what we hear, it's the technicians' commitment to their work that really backs up Ultimate's good name.

The firm offers a wide variety of services to NYC-area clients (and, in fact, to some as far afield as Wyoming), including high-end telephone, audio, video, home theater, security, computer networking, motorized blinds, and lighting control systems. One of the company's specialties is integrating multiple systems and providing remote access—so you can switch on your air-conditioning on the commute home, or check on your pooch from your computer at work. Clients recommend Jack Borenstein and Ultimate to their friends because of the high level of service and good follow-up. Ultimate will deal with clients directly, but also works with many of the top architects, designers, and contractors in the city.

"A pleasure to work with from beginning to end." "Their insight and design ideas resulted in a system that truly exceeded by expectations." "Met all demands with a smile." "Never any complaints from him, he just makes it work."

Video Installations Plus Inc.

Quality 4 | Cost 3.5 | Value 4.5 | Recommend? 5

45 East Hartsdale Avenue, Hartsdale, NY 10530
(914) 328 - 1771 www.avtelecom.com

A/V system design and installation; home automation

Principal Alan Poltrack's philosophy is that "people need help on all levels and at all budgets." This client-friendly approach makes his company popular with its customers. We hear that whether a client wants a $200,000 home cinema or a $15,000 hi-fi audio system, the Video Installations Plus staff listens carefully.

The company is best known for integrating audio, video, satellite, telephone, and lighting systems for clients from Westchester to Connecticut to Long Island (the firm will even outfit your boat). Poltrack, the consummate techie, used to build robots at the University of Massachusetts, and we're told his designs are quite innovative. The vast majority of the company's 45 annual projects are residential and come from client referrals—however, Video Installations Plus has been known to work very closely with architects and contractors. This small company of six earns glowing reviews from customers for designing user-friendly systems with a solid one-year warranty covering parts and labor on all its craftsmanship.

"A small company that really takes the time to work with you individually." "Very willing to explain and teach how to use the equipment." "Responsive to our needs at all times." "Has more than twenty years' experience in the business and it shows."

Hiring a Closet Designer

Aahh…the all-important closet. If you are a true New Yorker, you know that closet space is one of the most treasured assets of a Manhattan apartment. Are you embarrassed to take your guest's coats, because you're not sure what's going to come crashing down as soon as you open the closet door? Do you arrive late to dinner because you can't remember into which dark corner you last crammed that elegant pair of heels?

If you want to get maximum use out of minimum space, it's time to call a closet professional. These wizards can sometimes double or triple your existing storage, without moving a single wall. The result? Tidier closets—and tidier rooms.

Where Do I Start?

In a time when some homeowners view closet design just as important as kitchen and bath design, you have an endless choice of styles—from traditional to contemporary, casual to formal—and a large assortment of accessories.

There are many options to consider in designing custom closets. For a bedroom closet, you can choose to have more hanging space and fewer shelves—or vice versa, depending on your particular wardrobe. Hanging double rods (one above another) for short items such as jackets and shirts will maximize the hanging space. You can also incorporate drawers, shoe cubbies, sectioned jewelry drawers, and slide-out tie and belt racks. The numerous "extras" include fireproof walls, a fold-out ironing board and steamer, a safe for valuables, cedar-lined walls and floors, a folding table, hydraulic lifts, valets, mirrored walls and doors, task lighting, a separate heating and air-conditioning system, and designer hardware.

Remember: custom closets are just that—customized for your particular needs and space. Familiarize yourself with the options and consider your own habits. Which items do you access most often? Which closets are the most cluttered? Are you happy with your organization scheme, or do you need to re-allocate your closet space to reflect new priorities (like strollers and toys)?

Some closet professionals specialize in design and rethinking of storage, while others expect to take their cues from you. If you are considering working with a design professional, seek out someone who listens well, and with whom you have a natural chemistry. The designer's work will have an intimate influence on your family's day-to-day life, so you should feel comfortable with him or her. Ideally, the designer should listen closely to your needs, then provide creative, thoughtful solutions that will serve you well for years.

If you can't visualize what you want or just need some ideas, start by visiting the closet companies. Many stores have showrooms that display their work. Some companies will come to your home to give a free consultation and estimate. Closet professionals can help you determine the exact configuration of shelving, hanging space, and accessories to best organize your closets.

Material Choices

Most closet professionals use similar materials. One of the most popular is pressed wood covered with either a wood veneer or melamine (also called laminate). Wood veneer is a thin layer of wood; melamine is a thin layer of vinyl.

Some companies offer more than 30 colors to choose from. Pressed wood with a wood veneer gives the appearance of being solid wood. Melamine is durable and comes in numerous color choices, making it a favorite among customers.

Another popular material is vinyl-covered steel wire, which produces a clean and contemporary look. Because this surface is a wire grid and not a solid mass, it allows good air circulation throughout the closet. However, the grids can leave an imprint on soft clothing, so a piece of cardboard or Plexiglas may be needed to cover shelves or the bottoms of baskets. Vinyl-covered steel wire sliding baskets allows you to see what is in the drawers without opening them, which can be a great benefit in the case of unreachable or hard-to-access spots.

It is generally difficult to find closet companies that use solid wood, because it is so expensive and can warp and change over time. However solid wood is very attractive, and is generally used in the highest quality applications.

In many cases your closet professional will be able to provide choices of materials that will match existing millwork and cabinetry already in your home. This is a cost-efficient way to create a consistent look throughout the various rooms of your apartment.

ON COST

The cost of custom closets depends on the size and scope of the specific job. There may be a retainer fee and/or a minimum installation fee. After the size of the job, the most important influence on the price is the choice of material. Other details such as the condition of the existing walls will also drive costs. The more prep work a company has to do, the more expensive the job will be.

By far the most expensive material is solid wood. However, if it is important to you that your closet looks like a room in a mansion, with architectural details, inset panels and artistic moldings, you might consider taking your job to a millworker instead of a closet company (see our section on Millworkers).

Pressed wood is much more stable and much less expensive than solid wood. The cost of pressed wood with a veneer depends on what kind of wood veneer you choose. Cherry is more expensive than maple, for example. A wood veneer finish will be two to three times the price of melamine. Vinyl-covered steel wire is the cheapest closet system in terms of materials—and also the easiest to install, saving you money on labor.

A completely customized closet could be as much as $4,000, with an entire renovation of all closet and storage systems reaching beyond $500,000. But as mentioned above, there are many factors that affect this price, so be sure to discuss all options with your closet professional. You should confirm that all accessories and options are included in the final specifications and estimate of your project.

WHAT SHOULD I EXPECT FROM A CLOSET DESIGNER?

Do not underestimate the professionalism needed for maximizing and organizing your home's storage spaces. Closet companies should have liability insurance and, if doing installations that require electrical work, a home improvement license. You should also inquire about each company's warranty, which can range in duration anywhere from one year to a lifetime.

While some companies do everything themselves, from design to installation, others consult and design and then subcontract the actual installation to someone else. Ask exactly how much of the project is kept in house. You also want to find out how long the process takes. For example, if the company has to order your favorite brass doorknobs from Italy, it is going to take longer than using materials that are readily available. Consider your time constraints—are you willing to wait months for the perfect fittings? Also, note that a company might not be able to immediately install your closet due to demand, and it could take a few weeks to begin the job.

BE A CLOSET MAVEN

- ✧ For the kids, install adjustable shelves that can accommodate a wardrobe that grows with them. If space allows, consider pullout bins for toys.

- ✧ Wire shelves (vinyl-covered or bare) and louvered doors offer better ventilation than pressed wood shelves. Towels or damp items will dry faster and the air will stay fresher. Consider using wire shelves for mudroom and bathroom closets, attics, and basements.

- ✧ A cedar closet helps to protect off-season clothes from moths.

- ✧ Adding a drop-down ironing board in your walk-in closet allows you to quickly press out wrinkles.

- ✧ Install a light in your closet so you may see all of your items. You can even wire it so that the light goes on and off automatically when you open and close the door.

- ✧ Your choice of hangers not only effects the overall appearance of your closet, but can also effect the space used. Be sure to take this into consideration when planning the use of space.

- ✧ Decide whether you will rotate seasonal clothing before you design your closet.

CLOSET DESIGNERS

🛍 FIRMS WITH ONLINE PORTFOLIOS* 🛍

The Closet Lady Manhattan	**4.5**	**4**	**4.5**	**4.5**

Murphy Bed Inc. 🛍
1 Lincoln Plaza, Suite 23P, New York, NY 10023
(212) 362 - 0428 www.closetlady.com
Comprehensive home and office organization

Labeling Doreen Tuman the Closet Lady is an understated way of describing this self-proclaimed perfectionist—she not only designs closets, but organizes entire homes and offices as well. We hear that Tuman's more than eighteen years of experience in the business is reflected in her quite specific designs and her ability to understand the exact needs of clients. All of her work is subcontracted, however, she only uses the finest of professionals. Although initial consultation and design fees may seem high, clients say the overall cost is "quite respectable." Her infectious enthusiasm and quality of service have won high praise among customers. Tuman will work with architects, interior designers, and contractors.

"Doreen finds space where none existed." "Her solutions are creative and practical." "In my brand new apartment, her closets are the 'wow' factor." "She organized my life, that's what I needed." "She sees it through to the end." "Can call her at any time." "Thorough, honest, personable. Would hire again in a heartbeat." "Her work is supreme."

FIRMS WITHOUT ONLINE PORTFOLIOS

California Closets	**3.5**	**3.5**	**4**	**4**

1625 York Avenue, New York, NY 10028
(212) 517 - 7877 www.calclosets.com
Closet consultation, design, and installation

If the closet industry could have a pop icon, California Closets would probably be it. A household name all over the country, the firm has been consulting, designing, and installing home organizational units since 1978. Using modern computerized production methods, this company creates specific measurements according to the needs of the customer, mostly to match their standardized closet components. A variety of materials are available, ranging from wire to laminates to solid wood. California Closets will customize the interior of any closet, entertainment center, office, or even a laundry room at what we hear are "upper-end-but-not-outrageous" prices. This "one-stop" closet haven also offers individual components for sale, should the client want to do the installations themselves. Although clients say the size of the firm may seem overwhelming at first, many were impressed with the company's efficiency from beginning to end.

"Very knowledgeable and professional." "For your basic closet, they know just what to do. However, I would not recommend them for top millwork." "Adequate, if somewhat 'cookie cutter' approach to design." "Excellent for utilizing closet space." "Serve

*We invite you to visit www.franklinreport.com to view images of their work.

114

basic needs but not the place to go for recessed panelled mahogany." "Reasonable prices for efficient service." "Dictated, but definitely interesting designs."

Clos-ette   4.5   4.5   4   4.5

41 Union Square West, Suite 820, New York, NY 10003
(212) 337 - 9771   www.clos-ette.com

Holistic organizational design

Carving a niche for itself, Clos-ette performs not only regular fabrications and installations but provides specialized "holistic organizational" services. Founder Melanie Charlton first sends in a team to take an inventory of the client's possessions, then tailors the closet design to the individual. With a small in-house staff of architects, editors, and stylists, Charlton orchestrates the organizational process—from inventory to design to installation. The firm prides itself on installing only custom-made closets—"no prefabricated stuff."

For its primarily residential clientele, Clos-ette's projects range from an "inexpensive" $15,000 closet to an extensive $1.5 million project. The detail-oriented Charlton works with textile and fabric specialists, a metallurgist, and craftsmen who can handle all species of wood. The company has been featured in *Vogue*, *The New York Times*, *InStyle Magazine*, *Gotham Magazine*, and *The London Times*, to name a few. From elegant, traditional designs to high-tech security closets with ocular recognition capability, Clos-ette promises to make the whole installation and organizational process a "painless experience"—and for those who can afford it, the final results are "extraordinary."

"Great taste and design skills." "Did not waste any space and made all of it organized and pretty." "Melanie is my closet and storage therapist." "Was creative with space —invaluable in a Manhattan apartment." "Customer service is phenomenal when trying to land a contract but subsequent encounters are less than professional." "Melanie has great style and a keen eye." "The only choice in closets." "The architect/design team does excellent work—at quite high prices." "The staff creates unimaginable synergy in that 'forgotten space'—the closet." "Her installations are so amazing. She made me, a gay man, enjoy being in the closet!"

Closet Systems Group   3.5   3.5   4   3.5

810 Homboldt Street, Brooklyn, NY 11222
(212) 627 - 1717   www.robertscottinc.com

Closet consultation, design, and installation

Modern machinery and well-trained craftsmen are the watchwords of the Closet Systems Group. Founded in 1980, this custom-closet firm (helmed by Robert Scott) consists of twenty employees, including both designers and installers. Each project is started and completed within the company, creating a truly customized closet system, yet insiders say Closet Systems is willing to work with the client's architect, interior designer, or contractor as well. Clients say that the firm's small size creates a sense of intimacy and high quality that is difficult to find among larger firms—although some references had trouble contacting the company when modifications were needed.

The firm does around 200 projects per year in collaboration with its in-house installers and consultants. Projects average around $1,500, with some going up to $150,000. Most tell us that Closet Systems Group is flexible about design schemes and is prompt at fixing problems when they arise.

"The closet is designed with you in mind; what you want is what you get." "All of their shelving is adjustable with the ability for it to move with you." "Not amazingly creative, but perfect for high-end cookie-cutter work." "Decent quality work." "Works with all types of materials." "Fast turnaround."

Closets by Design
4   3.5   4.5   4.5

606 Franklin Avenue, Mt. Vernon, NY 10550
(914) 665 - 6800 www.closetsbydesign.com
Closet design and installation

Although a part of a bigger, national franchise, the Closets by Design local office receives high marks for its ability to provide both the personalized service of a small company and the resources of a larger one. Headquartered in California, Closets by Design has franchises all over the country. The New York office, which opened in September 2005, is headed by Joe Stanley and Peter Shah. Most of the firm's clientele consists of individual homeowners in Manhattan, Westchester, and the Bronx. The team at Closets by Design also works with architects, designers, and contractors.

Closets by Design not only provides customized closets—it also builds home entertainment centers, offices, work areas, and libraries. With nine designers, four production people, and four installers on staff, the company is "on top of things," from the design process to the cutting and production to the actual installation of the finished product. With around fifteen installations a month, average prices per project are in the $3,500 range. Clients comment favorably on the firm's ability to create designs that are accessible to a wide range of budgets, with materials from melamine to solid wood.

"One of the high points of our renovation process." "Did a fantastic job." "Delightful." "Personable and always cordial and professional."

Creative Closets
3.5   3   4.5   4

364 Amsterdam Avenue, New York, NY 10024
(212) 496 - 2473 www.creativeclosets.info
Closet consultation, design, and installation

Creative Closets was established in 1984 and continues to satisfy discriminating clients in Manhattan, as well as parts of the Hamptons and Westchester. The firm's two principals, Curt Bohlen and Agostino Rocchi, met while working for another company and felt they could produce "better results at reasonable prices." With six installers and three designers on board, the firm designs and installs open wire and solid melamine systems. Creative Closets can outfit every closet in a newly renovated Manhattan apartment or just install one or two smaller closet systems. Prices range from a reasonable $350 closet to a $15,000 installation. This busy, mid-sized firm takes on around 1,400 projects per year. Clients are mostly residential, though the firm has outfitted some commercial spaces as well. Creative Closets has a showroom in Manhattan and another one in Elmsford, New York.

"Work was done within the time frame and exactly at cost." "Great maintenance on their work—will come back for work that was installed years ago." "Hard to get through but will always call back." "Solid, durable, mid-market quality."

European Closet & Cabinet   3.5   3.5   4   4
214 49th Street, Brooklyn, NY 11220
(718) 567 - 7121   www.europeancloset.com
Closet consultation, design, and installation

Established in 1982, this ten-person firm mainly uses laminate and high-density particleboard to create customized closet units and provides consulting, design, and installation. Clients say that European Closet & Cabinet offers modular closets, yet modifications can be made when needed. This method of design provides customers with solid quality at more reasonable fees.

"Even knew how the dry cleaners folded clothes." "No space wasted." "Good for mid-market to upper-end projects." "Very sophisticated." "The most professional people I've worked with."

Linda London Ltd.   5   5   4   4.5
200 East 62nd Street, New York, NY 10021
(212) 751 - 5011   linda@lindalondonltd.com
Comprehensive home and office organization

Sources tell us Linda London is more than a closet organizer—she can organize your entire home as well. Known to many designers and people in the trade as the "closet lady to the stars," London has been taming clutter for more than thirteen years. London provides the design and then uses only high-end craftsmen to build her intricate creations. Customers say they are amazed at her ability to maximize functionality without compromising style and tastefulness. Though she's not cheap, fans say "You get what you pay for—Linda is first rate."

"Overcame adversity." "Very funny." "Quality was great." "Great attention to detail and access to suppliers." "She is in another world versus your typical high-volume closet company." "She understands the interests, needs, and desires of the rich and famous and designs to get it right the first time."

Poliform USA   4.5   4.5   4   4.5
150 East 58th Street, 9th Floor, New York, NY 10155
(212) 421 - 1220   www.poliformusa.com
Closet design and installation, kitchen and door sales and installation

Founded 52 years ago in Italy, Poliform commands a prominent position among clients and design professionals around the world. This very high-end firm is called upon for kitchen design, closets, wall-to-wall storage solutions, and wardrobe systems, most of which are described as sleek, contemporary, and modern.

The firm offers complete renovations of kitchens (but not baths), providing design expertise and a wide selection of cabinetry, countertops, sophisticated closet components, and Miele appliances. Each piece is customized to suit the client's needs and is offered in a variety of natural wood finishes and colors. Specializing in Italian-based product lines of doors, closets, and furniture, Poliform works with clients and their designers to create unique kitchens, closets, and living spaces.

Hiring a Computer Installation & Maintenance Service Provider

Maybe you'd like to connect the computer in your home office to the one in your teenager's room to share Internet access. You're worried, however, that if you do it yourself, your "network" will turn on the ceiling fans and trip the security system. Fortunately, there are plenty of computer service providers who install networks and software, set up new computer systems, and perform other tasks that may require more technical expertise than you possess. Today's world requires a new approach to home computer needs, and computer technicians have up-to-the-minute knowledge. Home networks are fast becoming essential in a high-speed world of connectivity. Your computer setup needs to be as custom fit as a tailored suit for you to get the full benefit. While common sense dictates that you should leave the nitty-gritty details to a skilled technician, knowing what to expect will streamline the process.

Do I Need a Computer Network?

What is a network, exactly? A cable modem? DSL? A wireless network? A firewall? And, most importantly, are any of these relevant to your needs or current system?

The most basic network is two connected computers that can share files, Internet access, and printers. If you have to save something to a disk, then put that disk into another computer to open a file on the second machine, you are not on a network. Network size is almost limitless, and the largest corporations and government offices have a mind-boggling number of computers exchanging information. A common home network consists of three computers: the home office machine, the kids' computer, and maybe a laptop. In a network, computers are linked to an Ethernet hub, which is then linked to a printer and a modem. This usually requires running wire throughout the house and coordinating phone/cable jacks.

Why should you consider a home network? Quite simply, convenience. With a home network files can be transferred easily, printers and Internet access shared, and phone lines freed up for that important incoming call from your mother-in-law. While this may seem like a sophisticated setup for a home, times are changing. Many kids now do their homework on the computer, more people work from home, and everyone wants to be on the Internet—all at the same time. Home networks can save money because they avoid the added expense of multiple printers and Internet hookups. You'll need to buy a hub, the connection point for all elements of a network, which starts at about $50. Though most new computers (and all Macintoshes) already have network adapters installed, older computers may require purchase of a network card, which costs from $15 to $50. And the addition of wireless capabilities to most computers will require an additional adapter purchase.

High-Speed Internet Connections

Internet access through a conventional phone line severely limits your online speed and efficiency. Both a Digital Subscriber Line (DSL) and a cable modem are as much as 100 times faster than a standard analog (telephone) hook-up. A DSL line uses the same cabling as regular telephone lines, but it operates on a higher, idle frequency, allowing the user to be on the Internet and the telephone at the same time. Also, DSL service is always connected, so the user never has to dial up and wait for a connection. Cable is a broadband connection, which means that lots of information can travel simultaneously. (That's how all those cable channels can be available at the same time.) A cable modem is also always "on," but it runs on TV cable lines. The speed is comparable to DSL, with one difference: cable modems use a shared bandwidth. This means that speed depends on how many subscribers in the neighborhood are using that cable service: the more users, the more traffic, and the slower the connection. Because DSL runs on single telephone lines, this isn't an issue. In both cases, find out whether the telephone lines and cable connections in your area are equipped with this service. There are various providers, and promotions offering free installation are common. Computer technician companies will install the DSL connection, but generally are not themselves providers of Internet connectivity. Monthly service for your connection will cost between $35 and $90.

Most broadband service packages and home network packages come with a firewall installed. This indispensable part of any Internet-ready computer protects the system from hackers and includes options, such as a parental control feature that allows parents to block inappropriate sites.

THE WIRELESS ALTERNATIVE

Wireless networking is now commonly available and can be a practical choice for home networks. Wireless saves having to drill holes through walls or floors and makes the layout of a home office or computer network more flexible. If the network needs to be expanded, wireless networking makes the change easy and inexpensive. A wireless network consists of an Ethernet hub and receiver cards inserted into the computers (though all new Macs and most newer PCs have internal receiver cards already installed). These cards extend slightly from the machine and each has a small antenna which sends and receives information. Wireless networks can operate as quickly as a standard network, though steel beams and thick walls can slow down or break up a connection. A wireless access point or router can cost anywhere from $50 to $300. Have a computer technician advise you on whether or not a wireless system is best for you. He'll likely do so based on actual tests, the results of which will vary depending on the distance between machines, home construction type, and the location of steel beams and ductwork.

BUYING A NEW COMPUTER: WHERE DO I START?

If your experience lies specifically with PCs (IBM compatible) or Macintoshes, you may want to stick with the type of computer already familiar to you. (Some technicians focus on one type or the other, which can narrow your search for a good techie, too.) If there are children in the house, consider what machines their schools use. One computer technician suggests starting with an issue of *PC Magazine* or *Macworld* to see what's available and use it as a reference when you speak to someone about models, memory sizes, and accessories. This way you can get a clear idea of what appeals to you and have a more productive conversation with your computer consultant. It's usually not a wise idea to buy the cheapest model available. There is, after all, a reason they are cheap.

ON COST

Computer technicians generally charge an hourly service fee, which can range from $60 to almost $200 per hour. In *The Franklin Report*, standard costs fall in the range of $90 to $110 per hour. However, please remember there are other factors that may affect the final cost. Before you hire a technician, ask whether the fee is calculated only in hourly increments. If you go fifteen minutes into the next hour, are you charged for a full additional hour? Will there be a charge for travel? You will be charged extra for whatever hardware or software you purchase. Discuss exactly what will be installed to avoid hidden costs.

The key to any home service is the quality of the time spent, not the quantity. A good service provider will not squander the hours for which they are billing you, but will arrive prepared to solve your problem as quickly as possible. Ask whether the technician charges for support on the phone after he's made a house call. Often he won't if you just need clarification on the service he recently provided. Once you're a customer, some technicians will even respond to a new question if it doesn't take too long, but others will want the clock to start running again. Find out your techie's policy and how flexible he is. Some consultants offer a package containing a given number of help hours, which can be a combination of an initial house call, follow-up visits at home, and time on the phone. This might be a good option for someone just starting out.

INSURANCE AND CONTRACTS

Most computer maintenance technicians carry some sort of business insurance that protects them from the repercussions of damaging your computer or network. This insurance is for everyone's benefit, and any service that handles office networks will carry it. If you choose a smaller operation, find out if and how they are covered. Computer service providers may have contracts with business accounts, but this is rare with home service. Ask your technician about the firm's policy.

WHAT TO EXPECT FROM A TECHIE

Depending on the scope of the service, the principal of the company may perform the work personally or send out technicians. The key is finding someone who responds quickly and who is well-versed in the equipment to be serviced. Also, since the computer industry moves at such a fast pace, it's infinitely helpful to work with someone who has a sense of the future of the industry, both in terms of hardware and software.

Steer clear of computer service professionals who act as if everyone should have been born with a computer gene. In truth, a lot of people just nod when they are told they need an updated USB port to handle the increased amount of EDI coming in over the DSL lines. You want someone who will listen to you, set up exactly what you need, and ensure that you fully understand it. Quickly try to get a sense of whether the techie helping you only speaks in techno-babble. Believe it or not, there are technicians out there who can make computers understandable, and you shouldn't have to put up with someone who does not patiently explain things in plain English.

INTERNET JARGON

(At least you can sound like you know what you're talking about.)

◇ **bandwidth:** Measured in bits per second (bps), bandwidth is the amount of data that can be both sent and received through a connection.

◇ **cookie:** A message a Web server sends to your browser when certain Web pages are visited. The cookie is stored and a message is sent back every time the user requests that page. This allows the page to be customized. For example, after you purchase something on Amazon.com, your user name will appear to welcome you every time you log on from the same computer.

◆ **cyberspace:** The interconnected, non-physical space created by the Internet and the World Wide Web, where information is transferred and people communicate electronically through computer networks.

◆ **DSL** (Digital Subscriber Line): A method for sending data over regular phone lines. A DSL circuit is much faster than a regular phone connection. It uses the same wires already in place for regular phone service, but since it uses an unused frequency you can talk on the phone while connected to the Internet.

◆ **ISP** (Internet Service Provider): A company that provides access to the Internet, usually for a monthly fee. Most homes use an ISP, such as AOL or Compuserve, to connect to the Internet.

◆ **LAN** (Local Area Network): A computer network limited to the immediate area, for example, a private residence. Ethernet is the most common type of connection used for LANs.

◆ **modem:** A communication device that allows a computer to talk to other computers. Modems vary in speed from slower telephone modems to significantly faster DSL and cable modems.

◆ **network:** Any two or more computers connected together to share resources, such as files, a printer, or Internet access.

◆ **newbie:** Term for someone who is new to computers or the Internet. It is not an insult, just a description. If you are reading this, you could be a newbie.

◆ **snail mail:** Regular paper mail delivered by the US Postal Service. Why use the Postal Service when you can shoot a letter over in seconds via e-mail?

◆ **spam:** Junk mail over your e-mail, which wastes your time and the network's bandwidth. Ways of combating spam include filters or private service providers, such as AOL.

◆ **URL** (Uniform Resource Locator): Represents the address used to locate a certain file, directory, or page on the World Wide Web (www.franklinreport.com is a URL).

◆ **T-1:** A wide bandwidth Internet connection that can carry data at 1.544 megabits per second (that's fast).

◆ **web browser:** Software such as Safari or Internet Explorer that allows the user to access the World Wide Web by translating the language used to build web pages. Short term: "browser."

COMPUTER INSTALLATION & MAINTENANCE

🖼 FIRMS WITH ONLINE PORTFOLIOS* 🖼

Computer Guys 🖼   4   3   5   4

18 East 16th Street, 2nd Floor, New York, NY 10003
(212) 414-0321 www.computerguysny.com

Computer installation, networking, training, and support

The guys (and gals) of Computer Guys are happy to assist in choosing the right system for your home or office (be it Mac or PC), install your new computer, set up your home or business network, repair your broken machine (they are Microsoft certified), train you to use your software more effectively, help you get connected to the internet, and troubleshoot when things go wrong. About the only thing this eight-year-old firm won't do is sell you hardware or software, but they will guide you in the right direction. The company works mainly in Manhattan, providing phone help or hourly billed home support. Clients are consistently pleased with the results, and the moderate fees.

"They solve complex problems in record time and show you how to avoid similar disasters in the future." "I always call them in a panic and they take care of whatever computer glitch there is." "Extremely savvy, but they did try to work too fast." "Very professional staff. I'm an extremely demanding and difficult client—they came up with some very simple but creative solutions that enhanced my business."

FIRMS WITHOUT ONLINE PORTFOLIOS

Amnet PC Solution   3.5   3.5   3.5   4

229 East 53rd Street, New York, NY 10022
(212) 593-2425 www.amnetsolution.com

PC installation, networking, and support; data recovery specialists

A small firm specializing in data recovery, they're the guys to call when you spill that Frappuccino on your hard drive. Since 1988, Amnet PC Solution has provided individuals and small to mid-sized Manhattan (and only Manhattan) companies with networking, installation, consulting, training, maintenance, and repair services for PC systems (for Macs, the company will only recover data). We hear the staff of three offers good service at standard prices.

"Very reliable and trustworthy. We've used them for five years, and have found no reason to switch to another company." "No major complaints—a nice and responsive company." "Can get files back once you've already given up on them."

Braveline Technology   4   4   4   4.5

136 West 21st Street, 8th Floor, New York, NY 10011
(212) 376-4000 www.braveline.com

Business-focused computer installation, networking, and support; web/database design

We hear the best thing about the commercial-minded Braveline is that they'll bring the same professional team to your home as they will to a corporate headquarters. Formerly "Brave New Consultants," the name change reflects the

*We invite you to visit www.franklinreport.com to view images of their work.

fact that this mid-sized firm is no longer a new kid on the tech block. Because its primary customers are businesses, the range of services the company offers is wide: everything from simple troubleshooting to web and database design. Their expertise, however, carries a business price: the minimum charge for a service call is not cheap (bring your machine into the shop, and the cost is reduced). Clients who don't mind the prices are quite happy with the results, saying that Braveline systems are "rock solid." The firm operates almost solely in Manhattan, where it is "happy to work with anyone."

"Did everything they promised and more." "It did cost more than we would have liked, but everything they did was excellent." "Techs were brilliant."

CBI Connect   4.5   4.5   4   5
821 Broadway, 4th Floor, New York, NY 10003
(212) 777 - 0700 www.cbi-connect.com

Business-oriented computer networking and support; security specialists

Dedicated to keeping New York City hooked up, CBI Connect offers local and wide-area networking solutions and internet connectivity for both residential and business clients on both PCs and Macs. Principal Craig Bueker, who was profiled in both *GQ's* "Man of the Month" column and *New York* magazine, comes very highly recommended by those who appreciate his personal yet professional service. Not the company to call if you just want a CD burned, CBI will only take on very large projects (think a home business, or a huge private network), where their business-level expertise will translate. Prices are among the highest in the industry, but we're told that CBI's technicians are among the industry's most skilled.

"They have a broad range of information and always treat our needs with prompt, personal attention." "You never have to wait on hold, listening to bad Muzak." "Getting bigger and bigger, but haven't lost the personal touch." "CBI personnel are extremely efficient, courteous, and always ready to help with any computer-related problems." "Phone calls are returned immediately, which I genuinely appreciate."

Compushine   3.5   3.5   4   4.5
30 East 60th Street, New York, NY 10021
(212) 371 - 1525 www.compushine.com

Computer networking and support, A/V systems, and telephone systems

Living up to its name, Compushine comes brilliantly recommended by clients for the range of services offered by its staff. That includes help with computers, telephones, satellite dishes, and audio/video systems. Ten-year veterans of Manhattan's private techie industry, Compushine employs a staff of twenty, including some Microsoft-certified technicians. The company works with both residential and commercial clients, most of whom report prompt service. Help over the phone is not standard, since technicians are usually in the field and would rather come to your door. Never fear if you just need a quick solution—Compushine has no minimum charge.

Computer services offered by Compushine include installation, networking, emergency troubleshooting, and maintenance of systems, as well as consultation regarding hardware and software purchases and training. The company installs wireless networks and clients tell us the work is done skillfully. Telephone services offered include installation, wiring, and maintenance for homeowners and businesses. Bottom line, the company shines at a variety of tasks, and will perform them all for an industry-standard hourly fee.

"Frank and speedy—very helpful. They spent almost twenty minutes on the phone with me, just answering my questions." "Upfront about costs and very honest. They let me know what they could and couldn't do." "Always works within my demands, and always does superior work."

Computer ER   3.5   3   4.5   4.5

350 Fifth Avenue, Suite 6711, New York, NY 10118
(212) 317 - 9233 www.computerer.com

PC installation, networking, and support; emergency specialists

When it comes to healing Manhattan's PC injuries, this ER will do everything short of sending George Clooney to your home. This small firm installs computer hardware—including home networks—and also provides on-site technical service (as well as phone help), consultation, training, sales, and maintenance for PC systems. Primarily, the company works with small businesses, either out of the home or an office. You can have technicians make house calls for repair work—service is guaranteed within an hour if it's an emergency—but we're told the company offers a price break if you bring in your malfunctioning hardware to their Fifth Avenue hospital. Computer ER is considered to be efficient and reasonably priced.

"Never had a problem in six years of service." "We've worked with them for a couple of years and have been very happy." "They're like members of the family to our small business. They're very patient and they give us lots of hands-on attention and support." "They've rescued us from a ton of near-disaster situations."

Computer Guru of New York   4   3   5   4.5

31 Union Square West, Suite 15E, New York, NY 10003
(646) 483 - 5713 david@silberman.org

Computer training, installation, networking, and support

Like a true Guru should be, David Silberman is available seven days a week for computer counseling of either the practical or philosophical variety. Primarily, he does training and troubleshooting for both Macs and PCs, but we're told he also provides installation, networking, and consulting services to both businesses and individuals, and backs it all up with phone support. Silberman does not sell hardware or software—nor does he do repairs—but he does offer consultation for clients looking for purchasing or repair advice.

Most of Silberman's clientele is in Manhattan, although he will trek farther afield if his travel expenses are compensated. Clients report that he is generous with his time, and are happy to recommend this fair and friendly company.

"Top-notch in every regard—and a bargain." "Can be hard to get in touch with, but once you do, he's very helpful." "I consider it a plus that he calls to alert me if he'll be late." "He's an extremely honorable guy."

CTSI Consulting/Computer Tutor   4   3.5   4.5   4.5

118 West 79th Street, New York, NY 10024
(212) 787 - 6636 ctsi@nyc.rr.com

Computer consulting, training, networking, and support; web/database design

Bruce Stark, principal of CTSI Consulting/Computer Tutor, has lent his distinct blend of techie virtuosity and thorough service to individuals and small businesses for over twenty years. CTSI will help you research and purchase a system, train you to use it, set up and support a small cable or wireless network, and save you if the whole thing falls apart. It will also set up a custom database to suit your needs. While initially Stark ran the business himself, riding around town on a scooter, the firm now has three Mac and three PC technicians, whom sources describe as competent and reliable. The majority of CTSI's customers are in Manhattan, but we are told the staff will venture outside of the city—including Westchester—for an added travel fee. Personalized phone help for existing clients is available.

"Courteous, thorough consultants." "They have so much knowledge about the systems they use that telephone support is usually all that is needed." "Emergencies handled speedily." "He's extremely trustworthy—I give him the keys to my house." "They're there when we need them."

De Castro Computer Services   3   3   4   4
By appointment only, New York, NY 10011
(212) 206 - 8330   sdc14@mac.com
Computer training and web design training; graphics specialist

A full-time professor of computer science at Touro College, Susan De Castro moonlights as a consultant who will school you in the ways of web design and graphics software support like Photoshop and ImageReady. Clients tell us that De Castro is a patient and easygoing teacher, offering training, troubleshooting, and internet support for both the computer literate and the techno-impaired, on both Macintosh and PC computers. Whether she's providing computer support for a child trying to catch up with schoolwork or parents trying to catch up with their child, clients appreciate De Castro's reasonable rates and down-to-earth service.

"Susan is very patient with me and gladly answers all of my questions, no matter how rudimentary." "Her schedule can be tight, but she's always helpful, especially with training."

Domino Computing Inc.   4.5   4.5   4   5
183 Madison Avenue, Suite 519, New York, NY 10016
(212) 583 - 9987   www.dominocomputing.com
Computer consulting, installation, networking, support, and sales

We hear Domino lines up tech problems and knocks them down, one by one. This full-service company works with all brands of computers and handles projects for homeowners and small businesses alike. In addition to installation, diagnostic support, networking, e-mail hosting, web design, disaster recovery, consultation, security, server, and internet services, the company also sells both hardware and software at a reasonable markup. We hear Domino excels at setting up and troubleshooting home networks. It's fairly young, as tech companies go, but the dedicated staff has already won a loyal and satisfied following among individual clients, especially those on the Upper East and Upper West Side.

"They feel like members of our company." "I had one tech experience before this which was very frustrating. The other company was very hard to track down. Domino is the opposite—they are very reliable, accessible, and responsive." "Domino has been a crucial part of our success."

EastEndTech   4   4   4   5
PO Box 1593, New York, NY 10028
(212) 772 - 1758   www.eastendtech.net
PC sales, installation, consulting, networking, and support

In business since computers took up entire rooms, principal Don Klein brings a wide range of experience to EastEndTech. He's been at all levels of the business, and his company offers comprehensive computer help to single-PC households and large corporations alike. That includes installation, design, service, and most networking or internet needs. In recent years, remote access programs have allowed Klein and Co. to fix computers over the internet, which we hear is a popular way to save time and costs. Servicing every item the company sells (and many they don't sell), EastEndTech has earned a superior reputation for prompt and courteous service calls.

The firm is knowledgeable in all things PC, but will only service and install a Mac if it's part of a larger network. The firm serves Westchester, southern Connecticut, and other suburban New York locales in addition to Manhattan and Long Island. EastEnd only carries enough inventory to honor its service contracts, so if you're looking to purchase a large system, don't expect it on the spot. However, once you're an established customer, hardware is supplied at cost. Phone service does come with a fee, but established clients—who generally receive a reduced rate—don't mind. For them, EastEnd is the only place to call.

"Understands your needs, assuages your fears, and makes a match with the right products." "He's available for meltdowns and quick-fixes too!" "Unfailingly patient with me, a complete computer idiot." "Like a bulldog—he doesn't let go of a problem until it's solved." "Don Klein is the anchor in the storm. When the computer system misbehaves, he not only provides fast, effective technical help, but invaluable hand holding."

Geek Squad

3.5 3 4.5 4.5

At various Best Buy stores, or by appointment
(800) 433 - 5778 www.geeksquad.com

Computer installation, networking, support, and sales

The eponymous squad drives around in black-and-white faux police cruisers; and yes, they come to your door in full uniform, brandishing computer badges. Clients say the company lives up to its nerdy name, offering soup-to-nuts computer services—they will install anything from a wireless home network to a 150-machine corporate system. These officers also track down adware, spyware, and viruses.

Geek Squad has a deal with Best Buy, it maintains service centers in many of the chain's stores, and will sell Best Buy products (as well as their own brands) on house calls. The Squad's prices are fairly cheap, and since they charge by flat rate for specific tasks, you'll always know what you're paying for. You can also get a reduced rate by bringing your machine in to them, and clients praise the free phone service for existing customers. The large size of the company may lead to the occasional bureaucratic tangle, but overall the good citizens of New York appreciate their expertise and advice, even if "the novelty act can get a little tired."

"Only issue is that you're not always dealing with the same person." "Good price, good service."

MacMechanix

4 3.5 4.5 4.5

928 Broadway, Suite 1105, New York, NY 10010
(212) 473 - 6613 www.macmechanix.com

Macintosh training, installation, networking, and support; graphics specialists

While taking pride in their depth of knowledge, principal John Greenleaf and his "band of merry techsters" focus more on good communication than technical jargon. To that end, all of his technicians have performing arts experience and can put the most complex problems into "idiot-proof language." We hear MacMechanix is well regarded by a wide range of customers who call on them for help when installing, troubleshooting, repairing, and networking their Macs. The company even has a PC guy, in case there's a rebel in the family. Greenleaf and his staff of six don't sell hardware or software, but they do offer affordable training, in OSX, Dot.Mac, and other Apple-centric areas. Clients cite the firm's quick response time as a plus, noting they usually get help the same day or the next. The firm also gets high praise from its graphics clients.

"I've learned a lot from John—he is an extremely patient teacher, even when I ask very naive questions." "He's particularly good with graphics software, and is constantly updating his knowledge and skills." "I can't run my business without John."

MacTechnologies Consulting   4   3.5   4.5   4.5

545 Eighth Avenue, Suite 401, New York, NY 10018
(212) 201 - 1465 www.mactechnologies.com

Macintosh training, installation, networking, and support

Given the name, it's no surprise that MacTechnologies provides full-service consultation for all Macintosh systems. We hear the company, run by Kem Tekinay, is small and dedicated, and that it establishes long-term relationships based on "honesty and personalized service." In addition to consulting, the firm provides custom programming, networking, troubleshooting, maintenance, and on-site training including e-mail, internet, and software support.

MacTechnologies consults mainly in Manhattan (a one-hour minimum is required), although technicians will travel farther afield for a higher hourly rate and a two-hour minimum. Phone service is billed at the normal rate, in half-hour increments, but we hear Tekinay doesn't charge for quick fixes. MacTechnologies does not sell Macs, but can address most other customer requests.

"Kem is our in-house mechanic." "He keeps our computers running, period." "Not cheap, but quick to respond to all issues, so you get your money's worth." "Kem is patient with us, a real rarity among computer guys."

NuLogic Inc.   4.5   4   4.5   4.5

360 East 88th Street, Suite 21C, New York, NY 10128
(212) 427 - 7408 www.nulogic.net

Computer installation, networking, and support; security specialists

Whether building wireless networks or Linux firewalls, NuLogic gets New Yorkers' computer systems up and keeps them running. NuLogic specializes in internet technologies and security, but also offers installation, upgrades, maintenance, and consultation on all platforms.

Lars Larsen comes highly recommended by his many repeat clients, who describe him as a master of his trade—and extremely responsible and pleasant. Larsen doesn't sell hardware or software, but clients tell us he can help sort out the good from the bad and recommend a system for you. Though NuLogic works with small, medium, and large businesses, we hear that many individuals also call on the company for help with their home or home office needs. Larsen and his staff of consultants also do work in surrounding areas, including Westchester County, New Jersey, and Connecticut.

"Lars has never ever let us down. He is always there, fixing our problems and keeping our business running smoothly." "Lars is reliable, dependable, brilliant." "Always asks the right questions." "Timely, responsive, and, above all, a nice guy. I couldn't wish for a better computer guy." "Lars is a valuable, irreplaceable part of my work life." "Stays late to get the job done."

Personal Technology Solutions   4   3.5   4.5   5

6 West 18th Street, 2nd Floor, New York, NY 10011
(212) 206 - 9619 www.ptsolutions.com
Computer installation, service, and tutoring

Personal Technology Solutions, a straight-talking, no-frills IT firm, delivers what the name promises—individually tailored guidance through the ever-knottier technology universe. Services performed include networking, installation, tutoring, and round-the-clock rescues in the event of a digital emergency.

Co-founders Josh Feder and Rafi Kronzon are said to net the best techie employees by offering them a chance at partnership in their company. The end result, sources say, is a friendly firm that strives to answer every question you have and maybe a few you didn't know you had. Hourly fees aren't the cheapest, but, when asked about service, clients offer a bevy of flattering adjectives: "responsive, competent, and patient."

"Finally, technical people who speak plain English!" "Solved an extremely thorny internet problem for me and I haven't used anyone else since." "I trust them. I know very little about technology, but they never take advantage of that." "They interpret future needs and save me money in the long run."

Progressive Computing Inc.   4   4   4   5

60 East 42nd Street, Suite 1310, New York, NY 10165
(212) 681 - 1212 www.pro-comp.com
Computer training, installation, networking, and support; security specialists

Originally formed by two computer experts in 1992, Progressive Computing recently merged with another computer company owned by a former Broadway stagehand. This unique parnership services showbiz moguls, businesses, and private individuals, mostly in Manhattan. One of its number-one services is dealing with data protection issues (viruses, spam, internet breaches, and proper backups) but the team will assist with all computer needs—from local- and wide-area networking to troubleshooting and repair.

Progressive works with both business and residential customers, with some clients happily fitting into both categories. It does not, however, work with Macintosh systems. We hear the firm and its five technicians offer 24-hour service in emergency situations, although in general, two-day advance notice is preferred. Phone service is billed at the normal hourly rate. Clients laud Progressive for its top-notch service and professional one-on-one instruction. Its diagnostic services also receive high praise. Clients note that Progressive's consultants are good at identifying issues beforehand to avoid costly manufacturers' service visits—and won't try to sell you something new if you don't need it.

"They come on time, fix both the simple stuff and the complicated stuff, and even dress well. I've used them for 15 years." "Never condescending in any way, even when I ask very basic questions." "The staff is very knowledgeable and really listens well." "Extremely professional, and a joy to work with." "Can't say anything negative, only kudos."

RCS Computer Experience   3   3   4   3.5

575 Madison Avenue, New York, NY 10022
(212) 949 - 6935 www.rcsnet.com
Computer sales and support

A large, Willy Wonka-esque showroom of integrated computer technology is the draw at RCS. Their bread and butter is selling new equipment, but the company also offers service, installation, and networking for both Macintoshes and PCs. If you bring your machine in to them, their hourly rate is one of the cheapest in the business, but we hear the technicians have a limited range of knowledge.

Home help is also available, with rates nearly doubled. Customers report the sales staff is friendly and helpful, and that, despite its size, the company offers personal service.

"I called to get information on networking and found the staff to be very helpful." *"Sales is obviously number one here, but they were very up front with their prices."* *"Some of their guys are better than others."*

| Reality Works Consulting | 4 | 3 | 4.5 | 4.5 |

49 Hop Brook Road, Brookfield, CT 06804
(203) 740 - 7082   tristerk@aol.com
Computer installation, networking, and support; internet specialist

Clients say Reality Works principal Chris Doherty is a "diligent and thorough" computer wizard who goes to great lengths to find solutions to even the most baffling hardware, software, and network issues. The company provides large, corporate-level information technologies to small businesses and individuals in Manhattan and the metro area.

Reality Works offers installation, troubleshooting, repair, networking, and consultation services for both Macintosh and PC systems. Doherty is reputed to be particularly skilled at addressing connectivity solutions for high-speed internet access. Rates are quite affordable, and if a problem can be fixed easily over the phone, Doherty will often do it for free. References describe Doherty as patient and efficient, and they appreciate his down-to-earth approach of explaining complicated problems in terms they can easily understand.

"He might take a while, but he always figures out the problem in the end—even if the manufacturer can't figure it out." *"There have been many nights when I've gone to bed and he's still working on the problem. And then he turns out the lights when he's done."* *"I keep telling him he should charge for phone support for existing clients."* *"We would be lost without Chris. You could not find a nicer guy and he is always there in an emergency."*

| Rivera Technics | 4 | 4 | 4 | 4 |

By appointment only, (212) 460 - 8862   rivtech@inch.com
Macintosh installation, networking, and support

This dynamic husband-and-wife duo has been in business since 1990, working mainly with Macintosh computers for businesses and some long-standing residential clients in Manhattan. The couple offers a full package: consulting, tech support, networking, and installation services, but does not sell hardware or software. Rates are above standard, but if a client is on retainer, phone help is offered free of charge. Sources praise the affable, reliable service, saying Rivera Technics will respond to emergencies day or night.

"They'll stick around until the problem is fixed."

| Techknowledge/G | 3.5 | 3 | 4.5 | 5 |

130 East 18th Street, New York, NY 10003
(212) 254 - 8731   www.techknowledgeg.com
Computer consulting, training, networking, and support

We hear clients call principal Gail Heimberg when they want to get more out of their Mac or PC. For over fifteen years, Techknowledge/G has been giving advice on buying hardware and software, assisting with networking the family jumble of computers, optimizing existing systems, and teaching Manhattanites how to do that thing in Microsoft Excel that they should have written down but didn't. Heimberg's focus is on home systems and individuals—from novices to more technically adept users, but she also works with small businesses, setting up networks and providing other consulting services.

Customers tell us Heimberg is a patient, competent, and responsible teacher who keeps her clients' interests in mind at all times. Additional services include computer installation, troubleshooting, technical support, and assistance with internet access issues. Past customers and computer retailers often recommend Techknowledge/G for excellent service at mid-range prices.

"When you are wandering through the wilderness, it is great to have someone show you the way." "Very reliable, never late, responsive. I think her rates are very fair."

Technology Management Resources   3.5   3.5   4   3.5
By appointment only, New York, NY 10010
(212) 243 - 3553

Business-focused computer installation, networking, and support

Though primarily dedicated to setting up computer systems for commercial establishments, Technology Management Resources will also consult with residential clients. We hear TMR keeps its client list short, as it is dedicated to customer-driven, high-quality work. TMR offers ongoing tech support, maintenance, troubleshooting, and crash rescues, and works with both PC and Macintosh systems. The consultants at this firm operate on either a retainer or a per-hour fee, and although we hear that TMR is not inexpensive, we're told the cost-conscious technicians are honest and fair.

"Quality work, they set it up so you don't have to keep calling." "Difficult to get on the phone sometimes." "More focus on the commercial side of things."

Tekserve   4.5   3   4.5   5
119 West 23rd Street, New York, NY 10011
(212) 929 - 3645   www.tekserve.com

Macintosh repairs, support, and upgrades

Something of a clubhouse for Mac geeks, working with Tekserve is reportedly as enjoyable an experience as fixing a broken computer can be. The company will tackle hardware and software problems, upgrade systems, and recover data (you pay only if their technicians are successful). The only catch is, you have to bring your machine to them for service on a first-come, first-served basis.

The average turnaround time on repairs is seven to ten days, but the average hourly cost is moderate and estimates are free. Clients report that Tekserve's smart technicians know Macs (and only Macs) inside and out, and that it's one of the best places in the city to get your Apple fully checked out. The company also sells and configures systems, but its real bread-and-butter strength is its service. Those who absolutely can't drop by the store will benefit from the company's (more expensive) house call program, but will miss out on the full Tekserve experience.

"I can't say enough. They were unbelievably fast, reliable, and competent." "A hip, downtown vibe." "They really love tinkering with Macs, so all the Mac geeks love them." "A factory, but a really good one." "Avoid rush times." "Incredible service for the price. The only catch is the line, which can be really long."

Wonderplay Inc.   3.5   3.5   4   4
235 West 76th Street, Suite 12E, New York, NY 10023
(212) 595 - 7894   stangold@earthlink.net

Computer training, installation, and support; digital photography specialists

Stan Goldberg works well with kids, grandparents, moms, dads, and professionals all. He's been in the computer business for ages (he even taught Jackie O. how to work a desktop) and he performs a range of services, including in-home installation, advice on system set-up and purchases, support, and training.

A professional photographer himself, Goldberg will also help you figure out your new digital camera. Most clients appreciate this patient, focused, responsive Southern gentleman who is always accessible via phone or by e-mail. Goldberg is said to be a good teacher who is organized, considerate, and talented at explaining technology clearly and simply. His firm serves both individuals and small businesses, charging a standard hourly rate. Although most are happy with the results, some say Goldberg's better at solving routine problems than complex ones.

"With Stan Goldberg doing your computer work, you won't have any more worries." "Wouldn't call him for complicated technical stuff, but he trains very well." "He works well with busy executives, harried housewives, and kids, too." "If he buys equipment, he always looks for the best prices." "He installed all this extra software that killed my operating system, and took forever to remove it."

Hiring a Contractor, Builder, or Construction Manager

Undertaking a big repair or renovation can be intimidating, especially the selection of your commander-in-chief—the contractor. An excellent contractor is vital to any major household work. This professional, like a general, takes in the big picture as well as the details, is seasoned through experience, knows his troops and the system, gets the job done well and on time, and wins your admiration in the process. Here's a field guide to enlisting a five-star contractor:

Job Description

A traditional general contractor (GC) bids and builds from an architect's or designer's plans and specifications (the contract documents). The GC's duties are to interpret the drawings, execute the contracts, secure the permits, supervise the trades, manage the budget, make the schedule, deliver the quality—and call it a day. There are design/build contracting firms that will draw up the contract documents, eliminating the need for an architect. Be aware, however, that many firms which call themselves design/build really only offer conceptual assistance. They do not have practicing architects in-house, and must farm out design services to certified professionals.

Some warn that this one-stop shop approach more often than not results in uninspired design and cookie-cutter "McMansions," while others believe that nobody is more qualified to see a set of plans realized than its designer. It really depends on the aesthetic acumen of your builder. While the design/build route often appears less costly than hiring an outside architect, the architect serves as a critical check on the GC. Construction management offers an alternative to hiring the traditional GC. Clients themselves contract with individual trades and the construction manager handles all payments and project administration for a fee based on total job cost. Some clients laud this "open book" approach, while others say it lacks an incentive to save and adds another layer of costs.

We've often found the best GCs want to be involved early in the project and work closely with the architect or designer, even at the conceptual stage. It is at this point they can lend their experience to head off potential problems with the execution of certain designs, and help formulate a more precise picture of the project budget. Often homeowners will have the architect design the apartment or townhouse of their dreams, and then keel over when the bids come in 30 percent over budget. Using a GC in preconstruction gives homeowners the option of tailoring their dreams to their budget without losing sleep.

What to Look for in a Contractor

Picking the right general contractor is all about communication. A homeowner needs to know as much about the GC's capabilities as the GC needs to know about a homeowner's expectations. With stakes this high—mortgages, reputations, living another day at your in-laws—it's essential for everyone to feel completely secure in the GC's leadership on the job and the direction of the project. You should feel comfortable stating your wishes to the contractor and have confidence in his ability to listen, explain, cooperate, and delegate. Is this someone you can work with?

If you take the traditional bid and build route, make sure your contract documents are clear and thorough before you approach any GC. If you choose to go design/build, look for a firm that is sympathetic and attuned to your sense of style, and make sure the company does indeed produce quality detailed drawings. Sign-ing up for preconstruction services gives you an opportunity to vet your GC without committing to the whole job. Your candidate should be experienced in jobs of a similar type: restoration, renovation, or new construction. Do you want a versatile GC or one that specializes? The GC should be well versed in your project's architectural features, building applications, specialty installations, customizations—and in delivering the overall level of quality you expect. Consider the scale of the GC's past jobs, including cost and total square footage. You don't want to be the job stuck below the radar screen of a commercial-minded contractor, or hook your wagon to a little guy who can't muster the horsepower.

You want the GC to be fluent in the code requirements and logistical considerations of your locale. Negotiating the elevators and summer scheduling restrictions of a Park Avenue pre-war is a very different task than outfitting an industrial space in the Meatpacking District for residential habitation. The city and state permitting and inspection processes, guard-gate community boards, and building management companies are notorious instruments of delay. Also, nail down your GC's availability. If he can't commit to a target start date, you cannot depend on his ability to stick to a completion date, and chances are you'll be living in a construction battle zone for an indefinite time.

Finally, you wouldn't let a stranger in your door, so before you invite a platoon of workers brandishing power tools and sack lunches, get references. The GCs listed in this section are certainly among the most reputable we've found, but talk to clients and inspect jobs in progress yourself to get a feel for a GC's abilities and current slate of jobs. Also talk to those clients with jobs completed to get a reading on how a GC maintains his word and work. Though more than 30 states now require licensing or registration for GCs, New York is not one of them.

On Cost

Typically, three bids should suffice for a clear and fair comparison of estimates of project cost. But in a hot market it still may mean approaching twice that number just to get a telephone call returned. The more established GCs may bid only for architects with whom they have a relationship, or referrals, or on particularly plum projects. The most sought-after work on a negotiated fee, and are hired not for the bottom line, but for the fact that a client feels 110% secure with his choice.

Cost is a reflection of material and labor (as provided directly or through subcontractors), bonding and insurance, the general conditions (overhead to keep the job running), and the fee. General conditions and the fee are calculated as percentages of the total hard-construction costs, approximately 18 to 25% in New York these days (20% is the norm), though the percentage will vary depending on the cost, size, complexity, and location of the job. Bonding offers insurance against a GC's failure to perform or pay subcontractors. It's a protection against negligence and against liens—claims of debt that can be attached to the title of your property and prevent it from being sold until all liens are settled. Insurance covers full liability and workman's compensation. Any and all associated permit fees (calculated by the city as a percentage of total job cost), deposits, or taxes also figure into the cost. For the most part, bids should fall within several thousand dollars of each other, and the degree to which prices vary will depend on the quality and cost of their subcontractors, their internal resources and overhead, their ability to interpret plans accurately and honestly, their ability to meet the schedule, how conservatively they wish to estimate, and of course, you. At the end of the day your choice of materials and methods of construction, as well as the number of change orders (see below), determine where the chips are likely to fall.

In *The Franklin Report* a 3 Cost reflects a contractor typically charging 20% profit and overhead on $50,000 to $250,000 projects that involve standard high-end technical or decorative work.

NEGOTIATING THE BIDS

Jumping on the low bid may be tempting, but don't take the bait. If a bid is enticingly low, it almost assuredly signals that the GC doesn't fully grasp the scope or has value-engineered without your consent. If a major cost discrepancy in the bidding process does arise, chances are either the GC caught an unnoticed problem and accounted for it (in which case hire them), the GC did not thoroughly read the plans (in which case don't hire them), or the architectural documents themselves are too vague (in which case get on your architect).

A good GC doesn't lowball, he negotiates. Don't be shy about requesting a thorough cost breakdown. If the GC's numbers come from subcontractors, you may ask for the subs' bid sheets. Remember, the more subcontractors are employed, the more overhead and fee markups will inflate the bottom line. In-house carpenters, for example, are a plus, giving the GC direct control over the trade many consider to be the engine that drives the job. Any top GC draws from a small, consistent stable of subcontractors. These prices tend to be higher due to lack of competition and constant demand for the subs' services. While loyalty speaks for standards of quality, it's always your prerogative to ask the GC for an alternative sub. Just don't be surprised if he refuses.

COMMISSIONING YOUR GENERAL

Cost is always a factor, but at the end of the day personality is at least as important. Again, can you work together? Don't settle for anything less than a principal of a contracting firm who expresses interest in the status of your job both at the outset and throughout. The tone is set from the top. You should feel like you can not only trust your GC with the keys to your house, but also enjoy having him around. Goodness knows he'll be spending enough time there.

Once the job begins, he should dispatch an on-site supervisor and assign a project manager. In some cases a working foreman will super on-site, in others it may be the company owner. In any case, these on-site managers will be the ones coordinating with your architect or designer. Weekly site meetings are a must. As with picking the right GC, running a smooth and successful job is all about communication.

GET IT IN WRITING

About the only thing that doesn't need to be detailed in your contract documents are the middle names of the contractor's children. Otherwise every detail should be recorded on paper. The plans and specs furnished by your designer provide the fundamental outline of the job. This means noting every raw material and product—including brand, model number, color, and installation method. Be meticulous. If it's not on the drawings, it's not going to show up in your home, unless of course you're willing to sign the change order.

The change order, you ask? If you make a request that deviates from the pro-ject's scope as defined by the contract documents, expect to pay. Some changes may be inevitable, if you are unfortunate enough not to have x-ray vision or if you fall prey to your own whimsical inclinations halfway through the job. But be sure that any charges passed under your nose weren't already in the original contract. Ask your architect or construction manager to investigate each submission to make sure everything's on the level—otherwise, it's up to you. Spell out in the contract how change orders will be handled. A smart idea is to fix the unit costs for labor and material that were established with the original contract so there are no surprises about the price of extras.

Be warned, a GC's obligation to meet code does not shield you from a city's permitting and inspection mania. Your contract documents must refer to the applicable codes. Because many are open to interpretation, a city official on a bad day can be a major source of change orders. The rub: if it's not on the drawings, the GC will not claim responsibility. Remember, however, that the GC should be absolutely responsible for obtaining the necessary permits for the job. This includes filing your plans and specs with the city for review and approval.

DECIDE UPON A PAYMENT SCHEDULE

If your partnership with a GC is a waltz, and contract documents the choreography, then payment provides the music. Your contract should specify the schedule of payment. Nothing will undermine a job more than misunderstandings about money. If payment is expected on a certain date, don't expect workers to show up if you miss it. Commit to what you can do. The most desirable arrangement is progressive payment on a phase-completion basis. Use benchmarks, like pouring the foundation or rocking up the walls, to close the end of a phase. Agree on the amount of each payment beforehand. It's a great incentive to push the GC through each phase.

Monthly payments are an alternative, but this set-up requires more attention to accounting and is less of an incentive. A request for bi-weekly payments does not bode well—it may indicate that the GC doesn't have the capital to run the job properly. In any case, if you don't want to be dropped, keep the music going. Be sure to hold on to retention—10% of the money owed on the job—until all punch list items have been completed and all warranties, manuals, etc. have been handed over.

With many mortgage agreements mandating higher interest charges during construction, penalties charged for not making move-in deadlines and the cost of renting space elsewhere, you might find a busted schedule more painful than a busted budget. Use incentives to motivate the GC to keep costs low and to make schedule. Bonuses go over much better than "damages clauses" that threaten penalties for blowing a deadline. Most GCs won't go for them and they're almost impossible to enforce.

TIE UP LOOSE ENDS

Punch-list items are loose ends such as missing fixtures, polishing finishes, and fine-tuning systems. Left hanging, the punch list and warranties are things that will keep your GC in your life much longer than either of you care for. Spell out the procedure and schedule for generating, attacking, and revisiting punch list issues. A good GC doesn't need to be handheld through the process, but it should be clear from the outset who's doing what. And give him a break if everything is not perfect at first. Be patient.

Most of the warranties passed on by the GC are from the subs and manufacturers. Many GCs will offer an umbrella warranty. Ideally you want to have one contact person if things go wrong. Some firms have a computerized database for tracking customer warranties. Warranties can range from one year on parts and labor for equipment to ten years on workmanship items. Any decent GC will be attentive to past clients long into the future. No warranty should kick in until the day the certificate of occupation or completion is issued by the city or municipality.

COVER YOUR BACK

Remember, success is as much about being thorough in your research and preparation as it is about personal chemistry and communication. All this can be wrapped up in a tidy little standard AIA (American Institute of Architects) contract with the usual qualifications attached: plans and specs, the GC's bid proposal, terms and conditions, gated community regulations, and anything else you want to include.

TIPS FOR A PAINLESS JOB

✧ Make contract documents as detailed, clear, and complete as possible.

✧ Establish good chemistry and communication between yourself, the GC, and the architect.

✧ Have the GC hold weekly site meetings with subcontractors.

✧ Make payments on schedule.

✧ Trust the contractor and keep a sense of humor.

CONTRACTORS & BUILDERS

🛍 FIRMS WITH ONLINE PORTFOLIOS* 🛍

3-D Laboratory Inc. 🛍   5   4   4.5   4.5
268 Water Street, New York, NY 10038
(212) 791 - 7070   www.3-dlaboratory.com

Superb renovations and construction management

3-D Laboratory accomplishes "extreme" results under challenging time re-straints. Clients say "It can't be done" is not part of the 3-D vocabulary. For old-fashioned craftsmanship on a fast-track schedule in prime Manhattan neighbor-hoods, the firm provides a level of service "yet to be matched." Residential and commercial customers are "floored" by 3-D's artfully realized renovations. We hear the staffers' "grasp of technology and creative problem-solving skills" give them an edge among their competitors. In addition to custom design services, the firm offers pre-planning project assistance in site selection, lease negotia-tion, cost estimation, and value engineering.

3-D's can-do attitude is forged by owner Randy Polumbo. A graduate of Coo-per Union, Polumbo's entrepreneurial spirit inspired him to open first an archi-tectural mill workshop, then a general contracting business in 1986. We hear 3-D's upbeat personnel are "organized" and "true to their word." Counted among the firm's large pool of in-house craftspeople are architectural millwork, tile, and metalwork specialists, along with 25 project managers. As if that weren't enough, 3-D also offers a product line that includes medicine chests, stylized radiators, and Forster Swiss-fabricated metal kitchens. Most say quality sur-passes the significant cost of a million-plus for gut renovations.

"By far the best contractor in NYC." "Managers from the firm are polite—nobody ever screams." "I use 3-D for all my big jobs—their on-staff skilled craftsmen are exceptional." "We had a heating problem—they came up with the right solution." "They can do anything you imagine. Randy Polumbo and all his staff make you feel like you're their only (and best) client." "Personable, well-educated, and exacting artisans." "Great pride in their work—outstanding accomplishments—only negative was completion time." "They have a very positive, can-do attitude, but are quite ex-pensive." "I can't take my eyes off my apartment." "Their in-house technical problem solving is truly amazing."

A. Robeson Inc. 🛍   4   3.5   4.5   4
80 Broad Street, 5th Floor, New York, NY 10004
(212) 925 - 1095   www.arobeson.com

Contemporary interior construction, carpentry, and millwork

Anthony Robeson is said to be "proactive" and "patient" when dealing with high-profile and demanding clients. This relatively new firm is already receiving accolades from industry experts, who appreciate Robeson's "personal involve-ment" and the fact that "he returns again and again to meet all expectations." At the firm's lofty woodworking shop, Di Legno produces custom pieces to the delight of Robeson's Upper East Side, Upper West Side, and Tribeca clients.

Robeson gets high marks from homeowners with high standards. Launching the company in 2002, Robeson previously led projects as a vice president at

We invite you to visit www.franklinreport.com to view images of their work.

the renowned 3-D Laboratory. The firm's foremen, crew of eleven, and subs are a "dedicated, talented, and respectful team." Most assignments are residential gut renovations, with budgets in character with the "excellent" quality—$500,000 to $1.3 million.

"Anthony and the crew are true professionals." "Extremely knowledgeable. They execute high-quality work." "Anthony was a pleasure to work with. His honesty, attention to detail, and quality are a rare combination." "Robeson is incredible, very clear when dealing with clients." "All aspects of the job were complete and met our expectations." "Maintained a high level of focus and commitment throughout the job." "Provides robust solutions to any issue that may arise." "Beautiful end results."

Bauhaus Construction Corp.   4.5   4   4.5   4.5
347 Fifth Avenue, Suite 1304, New York, NY 10016
(212) 779 - 3450   www.bauhausny.com
Large contemporary and traditional renovations

The "well-orchestrated operation" of Bauhaus Construction is prized by internationally acclaimed architects, blue chip private clients, and high-profile retailers. The New York-based firm takes on projects in Manhattan and throughout the country, collaborating on residential projects that tend to be large and require expert knowledge of commercial applications.

Principal Max Zeitler left the Old World for the New over 25 years ago. Arriving in New York with a business and engineering degree, he went to work for a buddy in the construction business. He launched Bauhaus in 1989 with a commercial bent. (The firm recently completed a 35,000 square foot H&M store in midtown Manhattan.) However,ttt private clients report they don't feel shortchanged by the "efficient staff," who respond very well to their specific residential needs, and know tricks of the trade from the commercial side to keep costs down. Customers tell us the work is carried out by strong and dependable project mangers and subcontractors with strict precision. If something goes wrong, "the boys at Bauhaus" fix it. The best news is that Bauhaus delivers exceptional quality on time and within budget. For striking results, expect to pay anywhere from $500,000 to $3 million for total guts.

"No muss and no fuss with Bauhaus." "Delivers pain-free renovation." "Museum-quality work. Pure class!" "Top of the heap." "Great, Bauhaus talks the talk and walks the walk." "Honest and honorable. One of the best." "Completed work close to schedule and paid attention to the details." "Able to accomplish big tasks with complex details." "Definitely follows through from beginning to end on project." "Very nice to work with and very accommodating."

Bernsohn & Fetner   5   4.5   4.5   5
625 West 51st Street, New York, NY 10019
(212) 315 - 4330   www.bfbuilding.com
First-rate gut renovations and construction management

When you need "extremely high-quality work" and time is of the essence, "look no further" than Bernsohn & Fetner. Fans tell us "they move heaven and earth to meet your deadline." The bulk of the company's projects are large, extremely high-end custom residential jobs for an A-list roster of corporate and celebrity clients in New York City, Westchester, and Fairfield. But B&F also performs swank corporate and retail build-outs and ongoing maintenance at Manhattan's most distinguished addresses. The firm received rave reviews for its work on Jean Georges' latest chic restaurant, Perry Street.

References report that B&F heads projects with "go-get-'em" efficient supervision, and that the firm's affable, easygoing principals offer hands-on assistance in all undertakings. Established in 1983, partners Randall Bernsohn and Steven Fetner "do what they say they will do." This "very team-oriented" management outfit subs out its trades and sees all projects through to the end, leaving no detail unaddressed. The results, clients say, are "amazing," while the pricing is "decent, considering they are the absolute best." Numbers start at $300 plus per square foot, but we hear the firm does consider projects at $500,000 depending upon the client, and the task at hand.

"We work all over the country, and B&F is one of the very best contractors we have had the privilege to work with. They are simply awesome." "Magnificent team." "Almost too precise—very much a perfectionist." "Honest and professional. Beyond any expectation." "The management is second to none." "Handles subs very well—has a tight control." "Randy is wonderful, he sees the positive side to everything." "This is the very best at top, top prices." "They deliver museum quality." "We can give them the work and not have to worry about them getting it done, and done right." "Randy is a straight shooter and honest." "Very blunt about cost." "Very nice. Randy is low-key." "They have to do good work. Their clients demand it."

C&A Custom Builders Inc. 🏠   3.5   3   4.5   4.5
101 West 23rd Street, Suite 2218, New York, NY 10011
(212) 445 - 0400   www.cacustombuilders.com
Modern and classic interior renovation

Known for taking both an "artistic" and a "professional" approach to each construction project, Christopher Anna of C&A Custom Builders produces a "pleasant experience" for his clients—and "admirable" results. We hear Anna brings a sensitive eye for design to his work, thanks to his Arts and Crafts and photography background. C&A works closely with industry professionals, consulting on materials, presenting competitive budgets, and managing to coordinate plans and specs for smaller renovation jobs without an architect attached. In business since 1999, C&A operates a satellite office in Woodstock, New York that serves many New York City expatriates and weekenders.

Anna grew up in the Garden State and graduated from the School of Visual Arts. After mastering the crafts of custom furniture-making and cabinetry, he moved into the field of contracting, where he now caters to residential and commercial clients. We hear his "highly skilled" in-house team of fourteen handle most of the work, but the company crews up for larger jobs. Typical operations run the gamut from custom kitchens in Brooklyn Heights at $25,000 to overhauls in Manhattan with budgets for guts starting at $500,000 plus.

"I turned to C&A to tackle a high-concept retail space in NYC's meatpacking district. Chris and his New York crew worked without an architect, taking my ideas and drawings, and often times improvising on-site to get a desired result." "Most importantly Chris recognizes the stress that can be caused by a large-scale construction project and he works hard to minimize this disruption." "C&A was quite generous in doing touch-up work after we moved in—work necessitated not by them but by movers, handymen, and others who helped set up our apartment." "Work was spec'd quickly, done rapidly but well, and delivered at a finish date that had been very aggressive. These guys were great!" "Despite the occasional hitch, we always felt that C&A would deal with us with honesty and integrity. This is a rare and valuable characteristic in a contractor." "Their men have treated the building and our neighborhood with the utmost care and respect."

Cayley Barrett Associates   4   3.5   4.5   4.5

238 East Grand Street, Fleetwood, NY 10552
(914) 667 - 4527   cba1993@aol.com
General contracting and project management

"Delightful" to work with and "marvelous" at coming up with practical solutions, principal Joy Licht is a "real pro," according to clients. Licht's "hard working," thoughtful construction management firm specializes in interior renovation, architectural restoration, kitchens, and baths on the Upper East Side and Upper West Side, as well as Brooklyn Heights and Westchester. Licht is known to be very personable and to get along well with building management.

Licht, who started out as a decorator, was kept waiting one day by a construction crew, and decided she could add excellent value on that side of the equation. She formed Cayley Barrett in 1992. Clients commend Licht's "cheerful attitude" and her excellent hand-holding, whether it's a weekend check-up or a call before bed to put a customer's mind at ease. Her crews of in-house carpenters and decorative finishers are determined to make each project a success. Cayley teams with architects or works in a design/build capacity on projects ballparking between $100,000 for a small kitchen to $2 million for gut renovations. There are no absolute minimums, but if the budget is unrealistic for Cayley quality, Licht will tell you.

"Great personal integrity. Joy is always in touch, hardworking, and very trustworthy." "Joy is one person I cannot live without." "Reliable, professional, and highly qualified." "If Joy gave you a price it was all-encompassing." "Whatever it took, she did it." "Really vets the issues beforehand. Made good suggestions." "Absolutely would use again."

Certified of NY Inc.    4   4   4   4.5

623 West 51st Street, New York, NY 10019
(212) 397 - 1945   www.certifiedconstruction.com
Diverse renovations

In collaboration with architects, principal Michael Borrico of Certified of NY brings "great ideas and design concepts" to building solutions. This "confident" and "extremely meticulous" firm, in business for over nineteen years, focuses its general contracting efforts on upscale residential properties and restaurants, often on Manhattan's Upper East Side.

After gaining experience with a large construction firm, Borrico launched the business in 1986. Clients find Certified's staff of 50 "courteous" and "reliable," commenting that the firm's self-performed architectural millwork, finishes, carpentry, drywall, painting, and demolition make it an all-around efficient, full-service contractor. We hear the project managers cover many operations with "extreme professionalism." Certified completes small tasks at $350,000, but gut renovations are the bulk of its business, with budgets of $2 million to $4 million for prewar penthouses and townhouses.

"I am looking to buy the apartment next door and would use Certified again." "Overall very capable and among the best in the industry." "Staff was responsive to control-freak client with professionalism and humor." "Problems not anticipated (or missed) by architect were solved swiftly and with minimal disruption." "A difficult landlord was a chronic problem but Certified shielded me well."

Chilmark Builders Inc.   4.5   4   4.5   5

One Vanderbilt Avenue, Pleasantville, NY 10570
(914) 769 - 3416   www.chilmarkbuilders.com
Distinguished renovations and construction management

Ranked high for its "sharp performance" and praised as a "finisher" by clients, Chilmark Builders has garnered accolades as a high-end residential general contractor of large-scale renovations and new construction in New York City, Westchester County, and Greenwich, Connecticut since 1996. At its specialty millwork shop, the firm demonstrates skillful replication and Old World craftsmanship. Chilmark also offers construction management and consulting services.

Coming from a long line of architects, Westchester local John Ginsbern is stamped by the industry as "a stand-up guy," while clients come away impressed by his intelligent, reliable, and efficient management team. Partner Wayne Walter of Birmingham, England wins high points for his expert carpentry knowledge and his leadership as a construction manager. We're told the firm's recommendations improve the quality of the job both before and during the process. A preferred builder for many prominent Gotham architects, Chilmark and its staff of twenty promise an experience that is nothing less than "absolutely fantastic." This kind of service and expertise comes with a high sticker price: $2 million to $6 million on notable residences, with the occasional small (but choice) job at $500,000.

"They are so good, they make it look easy." "High levels of professionalism, efficiency, expertise, courtesy, and timeliness." "The firm stands out among general contractors with whom we have had much experience over the years." "Chilmark goes the extra mile." "Top of the line." "Got the sense that no matter what the cost, I was getting big quality." "Contributed a lot of ideas that enhanced the value of my house and the look I was going for."

D.H.E. Company Inc.   4   4   4   4

37 Canal Street, New York, NY 10002
(212) 228 - 8005   www.dhecompany.com
General contracting and substantial restoration

A list of blissful clients dish that this "cool-headed, warm-hearted" contractor "consistently" delivers the goods. D.H.E. specializes in renovating luxury apartments in historic Manhattan buildings and substantial restorations of city townhouses. A diverse roster of hotel, designer, and celeb clients find D.H.E. remains enthusiastic and attentive to every detail.

Principal Douglas Cohen comes recommended as a "calm," creative problem solver who communicates well with his collaborators. After proving successful as a cabinetmaker, Cohen opened the general contracting firm in 1986. We're told his crews are "well-managed," unerringly professional, and always "courteous" and "personable" toward the client. D.H.E. will sometimes do a project for $500,000, but the average gut is $1 million to $2 million.

"My project was under a considerable time constraint. Doug and his foreman Bill worked with their heads, hands, and hearts to make sure the work was done on time and done beautifully." "No matter how crazy it gets—and it can get really crazy—they come through." "Cohen is a very organized, thorough, nice person." "We have completed eight projects together and I have found their workmanship, professionalism, and ability to be of the highest quality." "They completed the job within the promised time period and basically within our budget." "They have always made me feel that the client's and my needs are of paramount importance."

Davenport Contracting Inc. ▉   4.5   4.5   4   5

78 Harvard Street, Stamford, CT 06902
(203) 324 - 6308   www.davenportcontracting.com
Detailed large-scale renovations and new construction

Endorsed by both architects and clients, Davenport Contracting accomplishes "exceptional results" and "builds lasting relationships." Most past clients enjoy an "extremely positive experience" with the firm. Davenport takes on tear-downs, showpiece restorations, and high-end apartment renovations on Manhattan's Upper East Side and in the surrounding Connecticut and Westchester suburbs. The

	Quality	Cost	Value	Recommend?
	✚	$	◆	★

firm's satellite mill shop, DCI, contributes casework and cabinets with efficiency and expediency while its property management company keeps everything buttoned up for past clients.

Since meeting on the job in 1983, principals Brian MacDonald and Richard J. Koch have been building together. "Reliable and attentive," Davenport professionals are "open and constructive in dealing with changes and issues" as they pop up, and pride themselves on keeping everyone well informed. With 50 on staff and up to 200 subs who have been with the team forever, Davenport is equipped to handle the big jobs. Dispatching their own seasoned carpenters, we hear MacDonald and Koch stay visible throughout the process. An average of six to eight large-scale projects are undertaken at the same time, with budgets from $700,000 to $7 million.

"We had an amazing, exciting, fulfilling experience with Davenport. We would build another house with them in a minute!" "They worked so well with the architect and welcomed our involvement in any and all details." "Notwithstanding the magnitude and complexity of the job, they performed admirably and in a friendly, spirited way." "The subcontractors they hired did superb jobs—millwork, trim work, tiled stone, painters, everyone!" "They are very fair, reasonable people to deal with and very organized in terms of paperwork and process." "They provided real value in getting appropriate specialists involved." "We were so happy to move into our home ON TIME and WITHIN BUDGET!!"

Designer's Home Improvement Inc. 🏠   4   3   5   4.5

160 East 84th Street, Suite 3E, New York, NY 10028
(212) 249 - 5696   cjg160@aol.com
Well-managed renovations and kitchen and bath design

A "quite proficient" contracting company, Designer's Home Improvement combines "exemplary" building know-how with "excellent design and color sense." This small firm renovates kitchens, baths, and entire apartments in Manhattan and the Hamptons with courteous crews who stay on the job until the client is satisfied.

Since founding the company in 1993, principal Charles Guarino has been personally supervising from concept through completion. Guarino is known to be smart, patient, and capable of "managing complexity extremely well." Moreover, Guarino's "creative and pragmatic ideas" are often tapped for kitchen and bath designs. Clients say the firm of twenty delivers a unique job on time and on budget, with very good quality. Several soup-to-nuts assignments are taken at one time with budgets of $100,000 to $500,000.

"Charles is an excellent contractor. He always sought out good solutions." "If I ever have any work there will only be one name on the list, Charles Guarino." "What impressed me the most was anything that popped up these guys took care of in orderly fashion." "Charles is very hardworking and always responsive when problems arise." "He is organized, says what he is going to do exactly, and executes the plan. He has saved me several times because of the inadequacies of my designer." "Charles will not begin a project until the crew slated for your job has completed their previous task. Therefore, you never have to worry about having half a crew to complete your job!"

DiSalvo Contracting Company Inc. 🏠   4.5   4   4.5   5

4214 Third Avenue, Brooklyn, NY 11232
(718) 832 - 9400   www.disalvocontracting.com
Complete renovations, carpentry, and millwork

Gotham designers tell us "no one delivers quality" like Vincent DiSalvo and his family operation. Since 1977, the firm has focused on six- and seven-figure renovations and restorations of luxury residences in the New York area, often in prewar Manhattan buildings. Company craftsmen perform all the carpentry, marble, painting, faux finish, and Venetian stucco work.

DiSalvo's clients describe him as a "true gentleman" who is "above board" about any issue and "probably fussier about finishes than most designers." We hear his polite, thorough, and responsive team of 52 craftsmen works on five to eight projects simultaneously, impressing building supers and neighbors alike. Partial remodels have budgets starting at $300,000, but the bulk of business is mid- to large-scale renovations that reach from $2 million up to $5 million.

"Vinnie was amazing to work with—always a professional of the HIGHEST caliber." "The work was fabulous, on time, and not one penny over contract. I would never work with anyone else." "One year later, when I had troubles with my Viking Range, he took care of it for me at no extra cost." "When we put it out to bid, Vinnie picked up drawings from the architect himself. He was the only one who sat down with our architect, and asked questions to make sure he understood everything and gave a good bid." "Very eager to do things at his cost if he thinks it's the right thing to do. And Vinnie is not an aggressive biller." "My super never had to pester him." "A year later he'll still get a guy here in twenty minutes."

Drew Construction 💼   3.5   2.5   4.5   4.5

888 Eighth Avenue, Suite 20P, New York, NY 10019
(212) 489 - 1715 aferris@nyc.rr.com

Small to mid-size renovations

Drew Construction wins kudos for its "excellent client communication." A go-to contractor for small to mid-size projects throughout the metro area—from full apartment renovations, kitchens, and showrooms in Manhattan to additions in Westchester—the firm even takes on maintenance and repair jobs. We hear Drew sustains an elevated level of service whether it's a one-day job or an eight-month project. Those who remain in the house during renovation find this firm adept at tiptoeing (albeit with power tools) around their lives.

Principal Andrew Ferris has been working in the high-end residential building field since he was fourteen. He built the business in 2000. "Articulate and patient," Ferris is said to be "really good at explaining things to befuddled clients." Sources also compliment the firm's "good clear billing," praising the handling of changes and add-ons. Ferris likes to service everyone's budget; we hear you can get a kitchen or bathroom remodel for $20,000, with total guts (according to the apartment size) from $250,000 to $500,000.

"His price is right for good work." "As long as Andrew's in business, I won't bother calling any other contractor." "His customer service skills are great." "I have done three renovations with different contractors. Andrew and Drew Construction are definitely the best." "Good crew, good work." "Out of everyone in the crew, the electricians were great." "This man is knowledgeable, honest, and utterly reliable. I would recommend him to anyone without hesitation or reservation." "Andrew is an honest contractor and very nice guy."

Duce Construction 💼   4.5   4   4.5   5

412 West 127th Street, New York, NY 10027
(212) 316 - 2400 www.duceconstructioncorp.com

Solid renovations and construction management

Considered a leader, Duce Construction "prevails" when matching existing antique materials and Old World craftsmanship is required. The firm performs pricy residential rehabs and expansions in New York City, Westchester, and the Hamptons, as well as soup-to-nuts design/build services. Clients are "impressed from the start" with this contractor's troubleshooting and cost-taming abilities.

Principal Rory McCreesh hails from the Emerald Isle and started the firm in 1989. He "lavishes generous attention" on each project and works hard to get to know the client and the home. We're told his large group of skilled and diligent staff and subs also delight. Sources say the firm turns around a "bid that is by far the most detailed" they have seen. Kitchen and bathroom remodels generally price out at $200,000, with the average budget for guts falling at $500,000 to $2 million plus.

"Highly recommended—superb staff." "Courteous, finished before schedule, first-class work from start to finish." "Worked for us previously on townhouse renovation—did an amazing job." "Lighting work was very difficult and they were meticulous so as to avoid damaging work of great delicacy." "Duce truly cares about and takes pride in the quality of its work. Rory McCreesh is top-rate." "The effort he puts into doing the littlest thing is incredible." "Before Rory even had the job he came in with an armada of all the trades. We met everyone and heard what they had to offer. No one knew our 1928 stone Tudor better. Including us!" "We are almost one year post construction, and they are terrific about coming back to fix minor (and I mean minor) issues shortly after I call them."

Edmund Lewis Ltd.   4   3.5   4.5   4.5

346 West 121st Street, New York, NY 10027
(212) 665 - 9999 www.edmundlewis.com
Comprehensive restorations and gut renovations

Edmund Lewis's expertise in reconstructing details in 19th century residences is "vast and refined." The firm keeps busy with cosmetic fix-ups, gut renovations, and restorations from Harlem brownstones to Central Park West kitchens to Brooklyn Heights landmark homes. The likable Lewis is said to be a "down-to-earth contractor with a jolly sense of humor" who makes projects enjoyable for all. We hear the firm is as attentive to its clients as it is to the bottom line.

Lewis began his career as a professional painter over twenty years ago in London. After a stint as the renovation project supervisor for the Museum of the Moving Image in Queens, Lewis opened his firm in 1998. Today he personally oversees the day-to-day building process with a staff of twenty and a group of subs who work "hard and fast." Sources praise the crew (from Lewis to the guy carrying garbage) for being "very respectful." Per square foot prices go from $350 to $750 with total guts starting at $500,000 plus. Busy clients are A-OK with the cost, remarking they appreciate Lewis answering e-mails via BlackBerry.

"Very professional at all levels." "Ed took responsibility for my previous mistakes." "We moved into a new apartment and we hired Ed's company to paint—the work was very neat and professional and the crew was courteous to us and our neighbors." "Ed even consulted on our audio system and installed it quickly with excellent results." "His subs are skilled ladies and gentlemen." "Worked very well with the decorator I hired." "I cannot speak highly enough about Eddie and his company. I was in dire straits and they did an amazing, sophisticated, beautiful, ON TIME job involving a whole new bathroom! Not to mention Eddie's constant humor, warmth, and human understanding." "Edmund and his skilled team of painters and plasterers made my kitchen look new—the work was superb and came on time and on budget."

Fanuka Contracting   4.5   4   4.5   5

59-49 56th Avenue, Maspeth, NY 11378
(718) 353 - 4518 www.fanuka.com
Distinctive gut renovations and fine custom millwork

Since we last caught up with this second-generation master cabinetmaker-turned-contractor, Steve Fanuka has become a rising star in the high-end construction community. Servicing top designers, music celebrities, and moguls from all industries, clients say "Fanuka rocks!" Performing a variety of contracting duties on interior renovation all over the established and trendy parts of town, the shop also designs, builds, and installs interior millwork in the Hamptons, Westchester, and Connecticut. Even though the firm has completed work for the White House, its labor is available to John Q. Public.

The enthusiastic and young principal Fanuka apprenticed with the same craftsman in Croatia who taught his father, spending summers pulling nails out of cabinets, straightening them, and re-setting them in order to learn how to respect the wood. In 1994 Fanuka took over the firm his father Rod established in 1967 and its staff of 22. Fanuka and his project managers oversee remodels and installations with an average of 100 subs, while his father keeps the mill shop running masterfully. Clients find this friendly firm "busy, but reliable," noting Fanuka is "honest about details and risks." Although mainstream projects range in size from 2,000 to 5,000 square feet with budgets of under $250,000 to $1.5 million, we hear Fanuka will build a radiator cover just because he likes you.

"A very responsible and knowledgeable team with all-around superb workmanship— beautiful cabinetry as well." "They always go above and beyond the call of duty and they are available any time of day or night." "Fanuka works until their clients are happy. Our customers always remember their dedication, and we designers really appreciate it." "With three young kids, the project had to be on time—just twelve weeks to gut—Steve finished on the last day with a very short punch list." "Honest, caring follow-through, intelligent, great ideas, punctual, good subcontractors, and personable team." "Actually returns phone calls, has a project manager, which makes life easier for all." "His crew provided timely updates and told me where we were in the process." "Will come back for any complaint, anytime in the future and will throw in extras on the job." "Fanuka makes some of the most beautiful cabinetry around."

Fort Hill Construction   5   5   4   5
200 Riverside Drive, Suite 1C, New York, NY 10025
(212) 665 - 1583   www.forthill.com

Supreme renovations and construction management

A-list clientele and acclaimed design professionals are awed by the museum-quality work, ceaseless attention to detail, and "take it or leave it bids" delivered by this construction management and general contracting firm. Fort Hill, started in 1971, selects only a handful of big-ticket residential projects, from multi-story penthouse guts to country estates. The firm also maintains a drafting/minor design division to accommodate smaller projects and a service unit to care for existing customers. Headquartered in LA with offices in New York and Boston, Fort Hill has the luxury of rotating its considerable manpower between cities when necessary.

George Peper, Jim Kweskin, Mark Spector, and the other original partners have cultivated a family business into a "factory of perfectionism." The Fort Hill family extends to the ranks of craftsmen, supervisors, and managers that run generations deep. Clients report that the firm's famously unflappable staff does very well to get even the biggest egos through a home's front door. In order to experience Fort Hill's exquisite style, be prepared to pay upwards from $250,000 to $6 million.

"Great people to work with: honest, great craftsmanship, management, and integrity. Excellent and diverse project experience with excellent subcontractor resources and team approach." "Fort Hill's work is superb and they have a great team approach to providing renovation services. I have used them on a few projects and all have come out with top-quality results in a timely manner." "Jim is a nice guy, never gets excited." "If you had a separate ranking for honesty these guys would be the highest of all the contractors." "They are expensive, but totally worth it." "Top-top notch. Among top four in New York history." "We liked Fort Hill so much that we are doing phase two of our project with them."

Godwin Inc. 🖿

4.5   3.5   5   5

215 East 58th Street, Suite 503, New York, NY 10022
(212) 308 - 0558   www.godwin-inc.com

Upscale renovations, kitchen and bath design

The word is that Godwin Inc. is "sterling" to work with and "extremely sharp and insightful." At the conclusion of projects, neighbors have even thanked the company's well-heeled clients for making their street or building more beautiful. Specializing in kitchens, baths, and gut renovations, Godwin is known to be capable and skillful in a wide variety of areas, and has served customers all over town. The firm partners with McIver-Morgan Interior Design to offer interior decorating services.

Partner Steve Godwin handles construction and has been serving clients since 1985, while Rod Pleasants joined twelve years ago and oversees the interior design firm. Customers are pleased with the intelligence and initiative they bring to a job. They tell us Godwin's suggestions lead to a better overall product, and his explanations invite them into the process. We're also told the solid, on-site project management brings cost in "exactly as projected." Construction on a 2,500 square foot space ranges from $500,000 to $1 million, depending on the level of details and materials. Sources remark those prices are "excellent" considering the "exceptional quality work" the firm accomplishes.

"Steve gets it! More than any other contractor I have used, he has a great eye." "They look at themselves as problem solvers." "Steve gives constant attention to detail and has enough vision to make his perfectionism cost-effective." "The results made me realize that other work I had experienced was inferior." "The job he did altered the course of my life. Wouldn't have embarked on the home if it weren't for the success of the apartment project." "With any job there are always delays, but they work hard to come in right on time." "Middle to high prices but at the end of the day, I don't get nickel-and-dimed." "The quality difference is so outstanding that friends who came to visit after the renovation thought I had moved."

Grand Renovation Inc. 🖿

4   3   5   4.5

85 Wythe Avenue, Brooklyn, NY 11211
(718) 599 - 7070   www.grandrenovation.com

Brownstone restorations, traditional apartment renovations, and construction management

The guys over at Grand Renovation will "confidently" restore your brownstone with all the quintessential features of the past—or renovate an Upper East Side apartment in the modern vernacular. Brothers John and Brian Buchbinder realize distinctive urban residential environments with "knowledgeable" professionalism and "good humor." This general contracting and construction management firm works on Manhattan and Brooklyn renovations and restoration projects. Clients tell us the company takes both an educated and collaborative approach.

John Buchbinder received an MFA from Pratt and fell into the construction business in 1985 after the darkroom he built impressed friends. We hear he is "patient," "imaginative," and "listens to clients' wishes," and corrals together a crew of "excellent craftsmen" who toe to Grand's "high standards." Brian Buchbinder, who has a law degree from NYU, came on board to tend to the daily operations.

We hear the firm specializes in working on occupied premises. Customers commend the firm for its "genuine" respect for their home. Noted as a "fairly" priced firm, Grand Renovation is said to squeeze the best quality out of every grand you spend. Conversions start at $80,000, and budget on a 3,000 square foot apartment goes up to $500,000. Cosmetic work ranges from $100 to $300 per square foot with an average project at $100,000.

"Neighbors are very impressed with the deck Grand built—especially the iron work." "When an issue came up on the architect's drawings, John came to the rescue." "Quality work and I trust them." "John has great ideas and listens. He will work within your price range and effectively minimize surprises." "Timetable ran a little longer than expected but John stayed on top of it." "What they did was exactly what we asked for and often better. They had great solutions to problems both aesthetic and practical." "John Buchbinder himself is very professional and knowledgeable, honest and personable."

Graphic Builders Inc. 📷   4   3.5   4.5   5
45 West Fort Lee Road, Bogota, NJ 07603
(201) 488 - 8638 www.graphicbuildersinc.com
Boutique contracting and custom cabinetry

"A dream team" is how clients of Graphic Builders describe owners Martin and Mary McElroy. This boutique general contractor "thrills" Upper East Side customers with its dedication and attentiveness. We hear the firm is as comfortable and diligent at taking care of the odds and ends of jobs as it is at overseeing major renovations, showing superior skill in woodworking. Patrons say, "Martin doesn't go for the quick and easy—he's a perfectionist."

Many are consistently impressed by the way Martin and Mary "don't just listen, but hear" their wishes. A carpenter by trade, Martin relocated from Ireland in the 1980s and by 1997 had opened a contracting business. Mary added her background in project management and technology. From the office to the painters, everyone is reportedly friendly and eager to help. We hear this firm "keeps good track of everything" and "is excellent on the final punch list." Graphic Builders also works hard to make its pricing agreeable, which really pays off for the client. Most of the firm's projects fall between 3,000 and 5,000 square feet, with per square foot costs at $250 to $400.

"Graphic Builders did an outstanding job on the renovation of our ten-room Upper East Side apartment." "Mary and Martin are the most devoted and sincere contractors I have ever met." "He consistently under-promises and over-delivers. To me this is the most important aspect of choosing a contractor." "Graphic solves problems through creativity and works hand-in-glove with the architect and cabinetmakers to come up with the best designs." "They deliver service one would usually get with larger and more expensive firms." "They are fair, honest, and good." "Fixed things out of the contract just because he knew they should be done." "Graphic is one of the most thorough firms we have ever had the pleasure of working with."

Gryphon Construction 📷   4   3.5   4.5   5
20 West 20th Street, Suite 407, New York, NY 10011
(212) 633 - 9586 gryphoncon@verizon.net
Major renovations with Old World craftsmanship

Regulars say Gryphon is a "gem" they want to keep all to themselves, remarking that owner Jerry Leiken is "like one of the family." Clients say this "multifaceted" contractor "gets it," combining a customer-focused, straightforward approach with an eye for detail. Customers turn to Gryphon Construction for Manhattan interior renovation projects of all sizes, saying they love the firm's "all-around great-guy way of working." We hear the firm is "very respectful" of the top buildings they work in on the Upper East Side, Central Park South, and Central Park West.

Since the operation started in 1988, Leiken (who comes from a long line of mason contractors) takes only a selective number of larger jobs a year to ensure they get his full personal attention. Fans say he is "amazingly helpful" in terms of ideas and problem solving. Every job site has a foreman and is worked on by a consistent group of subcontractors, who we're told possess a one-on-one, old-time craftsmanship appeal in which "they want you to love their work as much as they loved making it." Budgets for small projects (for repeat customers only) start at $37,000 and the typical ultra job is $2 million.

"I have used Gryphon for three renovations and the work is superb!" "They are reliable, precise, clean, and extremely personable." "Jerry just seems to make things happen in a gentlemanly way." "Great eye for detail. He's more finicky than our designer." "Great project managers." "The best way to describe them is to say they make a situation inherently fraught with anxiety a pleasure." "I almost don't want them to leave. I feel like I'm going to mess up their great work."

Homecrest 🛍   3.5   3.5   4   4
231 West 29th Street, New York, NY 10001
(212) 868 - 3860

High-end renovation, restoration, and cabinetry

Architects solicit Homecrest for its "notable" accomplishments and principal Michael Fishelson's agreeable personality. Trumpeted for its fine finishes, Homecrest has been indulging the renovation and restoration whims of Gotham clients on townhouses and apartments since it opened in 1982. The firm controls its own cabinetry shop and offers customized maintenance programs.

Fishelson sets the tone and stays connected via weekly sit-downs with Homecrest clients. We hear the firm uses technology to be more responsive and give more personalized service: The BlackBerry-toting principal will instantly respond to any issues while an internal tracking system stays on top of issues through their resolution. With a minimum of $100,000 for new clients, functions range from painting a room (for an existing client only) for $20,000, up to $3 million for guts.

"Michael is a very charming and likeable person." "So many of his craftsmen are devoted to him." "It's so beautiful, it's like Christmas in every room." "Realized work is very good." "They may come with a high price tag, but it's a competitive one." "Michael makes sure everything is perfect before anyone leaves the job site. He is much more interested in making the client happy than in his own bottom line."

ICI Construction Corp.   4   3.5   4.5   4.5

58-24 64th Street, Maspeth, NY 11378
(718) 326 - 4373   stevenmoy_ici@yahoo.com
Skillful interior renovation

Characterized by designers as a "construction god," owner Steven Moy of ICI Construction has a loyal following. This "unflappable" and "extremely generous" contractor gets the highest marks "in every regard." ICI shoulders interior renovation work on everything from Park Avenue graystones to upscale townhouses. Clients delight in the experience, and tell us "you would trust Steven Moy with your children."

An interior designer by trade, Moy received an Industrial Design degree from Pratt and started his construction firm in 1995. Defined as a well-equipped company, the shop has 40 employees and a "masterful" cabinetry shop. Moy is described as "hyper-responsible" and "exceedingly pleasant." Sources report he swarms the job with divisions of neat, hardworking craftsmen who meet deadlines and exceed expectations, all at a palatable price. With three to eight projects going at one time, the firm builds small jobs with budgets of $250,000 and big jobs of up to $2.5 million.

"My client loved the work so much, she held a dinner party in his honor." "ICI's quality is the finest." "Prices are very fair for extremely high-quality work." "Hands down, the best ever!" "Their standards are as high as ours. We never had to worry." "If he doesn't know how to do it, he'll figure it out soon thereafter, and do it well." "Steve has high integrity, is very responsive, and took care of later little problems." "Easy to deal with." "I have been using ICI for many projects over the years and Steve is very loyal." "Works hard to give customer fair price." "Over the years Steve has become a member of the family." "There is nobody like ICI."

Integkral Design & Construction LLC   3.5   3.5   4   4.5

24 Sodom Lane, Derby, CT 06418
(203) 735 - 2798   www.integkral.com
General contracting and design/build services

Delighted clients praise Integkral Design & Construction for delivering their vision—a product of principal George Kral's careful planning, strong management, and exacting standards. This interior renovation specialist's projects span bathroom remodels, monster guts, and apartment merges in Manhattan, Westchester, and Connecticut. We hear clients often implement Kral's creative suggestions throughout the job. While in the midst of construction, clients often store their belongings at Integkral's new 1,500 square foot storage facility.

Kral grew up in the contracting business and received his M.Arch from the Parsons School of Design. After working for several architecture firms, the agreeable Kral opened his own company in 1993. We hear the firm is dependable and responds to calls "instantaneously." Kral and his staff are described as professional and pleasant by clients and their neighbors. Depending upon materials and finishes, guts usually start at $2 million. Apartment conversions start at $200 per square foot and go up to $600 per square foot.

"George and project manager David are a great team. They are very organized, detail oriented, fair, careful. Timely." "We are on track to design and renovate a ten-family apartment building into a single family brownstone in ten months. The conversion required approval by NYC Landmarks." "Integkral estimates were very good and change order very fair." "They are constantly coming up with good improvements that will make the finished project better—often at their own cost." "Nice beyond description—I loved working with George." "Very reliable." "Start to finish, I had a purely pleasant experience." "We have found Integkral to be very responsive, on time, and accurate in estimating costs." "Very careful planners. Super quality." "It's George's attentiveness that keeps things on track."

	Quality	Cost	Value	Recommend?
	✚	$	◆	★

Interior Management Inc.

| 5 | 5 | 4 | 5 |

403 East 62nd Street, New York, NY 10021
(212) 750 - 3700 www.interiormanagement.com
Extraordinary interior renovation

A "shining star" in the contracting business, Interior Management works with the hottest architects and decorators in town. Patrons praise its artisanship "beyond any other." The firm specializes in renovating traditionally appointed Manhattan residences with high budgets, achieving first-rate results even when time is short. Clients are "wowed" by the company's positive attitude, "amazing" follow-through, and friendly management.

Mark Martinez, who picked up the reins from his well-liked father Al, displays the elder Martinez' knowledge and professionalism. He heads up a staff of 40, with the crew being carefully screened. Clients (who are greeted with flowers and champagne in their new home) recall the experience as one they "will always treasure." Interior Management is also known to consult on decorating and even move in furniture and make beds, and dispatches a maintenance staff for follow-up tasks. Although clients can expect to pay $400 to $1,200 per square foot with complete costs hovering around $4 million, they say they don't mind since the work is "truly a cut above the rest."

"The only contractor who even comes close to doing what he says he will do." "The job site was always clean enough to eat off the floor." "I can't say enough to express the wonderful experience I had." "We call him 'Mr. No Problem.' Whenever there is an issue, he says no problem." "Finished the work in record-breaking time. I was so impressed with every aspect of the company and staff." "He even took care of our change of address for the utility companies." "Interior does so many extras—they put hooks on all the doors." "Our building was so impressed with Mark's professionalism." "If I have a problem with the audio, the craftsman who installed it will call cable for me." "I would never move forward with a project without Mark." "People love my apartment and I feel very indebted to them."

Izzo Construction Corp.

| 3.5 | 2.5 | 5 | 4.5 |

80 Morningside Drive, New York, NY 10027
(212) 662 - 5695 www.izzoconstruction.com
General contacting and custom carpentry

Jean Esposito heads up this third-generation general contracting company, founded in 1932 by her grandfather, a European craftsman. We hear Esposito continues the firm's "commendable work" with an accommodating, can-do attitude. Izzo Construction is known to take on everything from a simple door-hanging project to gutting a large New York City apartment, accomplishing excellent work in good time.

Certified this year with the Empire State development association for female-owned businesses, Esposito coordinates a crew of over 40 Izzo tradespeople, including custom cabinetmakers and woodworkers, tile and masonry layers, and painters and wallpaperers. With an emphasis on high-end interior renovations, the firm's efforts focus mostly on residential and institutional jobs on the Upper West Side of Manhattan. However the firm will take on choice jobs in Westchester and Long Island. With the average budget for a project way under a million, clients tell us this "fabulous contractor" comes at a good price.

"I was truly satisfied beyond my expectations with the level of service and quality of work performed by this company." "I have dealt with contractors before, but have never received such help and consideration as I did from Izzo Construction." "Very responsive, never hesitates to send a worker over for small jobs." "They renewed my faith in general contractors." "I have recommended Izzo Construction to all friends and neighbors."

	Quality	Cost	Value	Recommend?
	✚	$	◆	★

John Petrocelli Construction   4.5   3.5   4.5   5
7E Abbott Avenue, Palisades Park, NJ 07650
(201) 945 - 5600   info@jpetrocelli.com
Choice renovations and cosmetic makeovers

John Petrocelli is known to be "imaginative" and "quick to find economical solutions" for his clients. Petrocelli's firm, which splits its work between Manhattan and New Jersey, offers "meticulous" general contracting services ranging from small jobs to gut renovations. In-house specialties include tile work, millwork, painting, and carpentry. Renovators tell us this firm exhibits a "work ethic rarely seen today" on projects both large and small, and ensures everything comes in on time and within budget.

Petrocelli has worked hard to build his reputation since he started the firm in 1980. References find "everyone in the company, from John on down, to be totally professional and a pleasure to work with." Clients like Petrocelli so much we hear they have never even felt the need to consider other contractors, noting he is "scrupulous in providing detailed, honest financial estimates in advance—and he stands by them." Though costly, guts and cosmetic makeovers are said to be a good value for the quality at between $750,000 to $1 million.

"John and I have a great working relationship." "John is always efficient, reliable, and true to his word." "When Petrocelli is the contractor all is taken care of." "We lived in the apartment during the project and the crew did everything possible to make us comfortable and to respect our privacy." "I have worked with John Petrocelli Construction on two major gut renovations of prewar apartments in New York City in the last five years. Suffice it to say, I am one of the few people in the city who enjoyed this process and that is in large part to John and his crew." "They all take pride in what they do. John was extremely responsive and reliable. We highly recommend him." "I never thought I could speak enthusiastically about the work of a contractor working in New York City."

Knockout Renovation Services Inc. ▮   4   2.5   5   5
300 East 95th Street, New York, NY 10128
(212) 599 - 5060   www.knockoutrenovation.com
Complete residential interior remodeling; kitchen and bath specialists

This "very professional" and convenient firm has fans knocking on its door for its residential interior renovations of complete apartments and houses (as well as one-off kitchens and bathrooms) in Manhattan, Brooklyn, and Staten Island. Knockout offers design/build services, performs all trades in-house, and is a dealer for major manufacturers, and will also collaborate with outside designers. The firm's "one-stop-shopping" is praised for simplifying an otherwise complicated process for the homeowner.

Knockout has developed a solid reputation since opening in 1992. Customers describe principal Keith Steier as "knowledgeable" and "attentive," reporting that Steier's project management system moves quickly to handle any problems efficiently. Prices are extremely reasonable considering the excellent quality. A typical 1,500 square foot gut ranges anywhere from $60,000 to $250,000, depending upon materials and finishes, with kitchen and bath remodels averaging $50,000.

"They helped me with design and supplied all the materials." "A fantastic job. I would recommend them highly." "Single source for all necessary materials." "Very professional." "There was a high level of communication between myself and the Knockout group." "There were no surprises and the finished work far exceeded my expectations." "Creative in finding solutions to inevitable unforeseen problems." "Went the extra mile to assure work was done on time. Outstanding."

	Quality	Cost	Value	Recommend?
	+	$	◆	★

MCCS Group/Jordan Dry Wall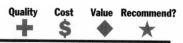

3.5   3   4.5   4.5

29 Cypress Street, Yonkers, NY 10704
(646) 879 - 5731   rcarthy@optonline.net

General contracting and carpentry

The family-run MCCS Group/Jordan Dry Wall performs seamless gut renovations and kitchen and bath remodels on Manhattan's Upper East and Upper West Sides. Principal Mark Carthy, a charming "straight shooter," has caught the eye of New York designers, who have him on their speed dial.

An Irish lad, the "honest and extremely hard working" Carthy has come a long way since he opened his shop in 1998. A carpenter by trade, Carthy still keeps a small woodwork shop, but focuses on leading his crew of 64 on a bevy of large and small projects, with wife Rosheen handling the administrative side of the business. Experts are impressed with his talent for management and his seemingly limitless ability to come up with solutions. The more-than-fair prices per square foot range from $110 to $200.

"I do not have enough positive adjectives to describe Mark and his colleagues." "Smart and always available." "Can handle any problem. Finishes everything AHEAD of schedule." "Have recommended him to many friends who feel the same as I do." "Mark always puts his customers first."

Miller and Raved

4.5   4.5   4   4

2 Hamilton Avenue, Suite 207, New Rochelle, NY 10801
(914) 632 - 3555

Substantial renovation and restoration

The "top-notch" and "well-established" team of Miller and Raved has celebrated names in the design world turning to it for "meticulously detailed projects" of exceptional quality. With over 40 years of exquisite work behind them, we hear these two never fail to impress. Active in Manhattan and around the globe, we hear the principals will go wherever the job takes them, and are as happy to work on a kid's room as on an estate.

Partners Charles Miller, who tends to the details, and Roy Raved, who massages the clients, were high school buddies before starting the business in 1963. Industry insiders tell us Miller and Raved show intense dedication to each project. Heading up a staff of 40 and some "truly amazing" subs, M&R weave knowledge, staunch professionalism, and planning expertise into a tapestry of overall outstanding project management. The firm is more expensive than most, with average budgets into the multi-millions.

"Very loyal to their clients." "If 100 is the highest quality, then they are 101!" "Really exceptional." "High-end, great guys. Very reliable." "Their timing is terrific." "They are smart and know exactly what to do and how to put it together."

MyHome

4.5   3.5   4.5   4.5

353 West 48th Street, New York, NY 10036
(212) 666 - 2888   www.myhomeus.com

Comprehensive design/build services

Offering a single solution to interior renovation, MyHome "relieves stress" for customers contemplating gut renovations or kitchen and bathroom remodels. MyHome eliminates the need to gather several resources to complete a job. Its showrooms around town showcase flooring, cabinets, tiles, lighting fixtures, and much more. The firm's in-house architects, decorators, and seasoned craftsmen deliver excellent quality and one-stop shopping. Several top real estate professionals note that clients are "overjoyed with the end results."

Partners Mayan Metzler and Yoel Piotraut formed a friendship and a business in 2000 after meeting on a job site. In five years the company's reputation has grown by leaps and bounds. It recently opened two new showrooms this year—one in midtown, and another on the Upper East Side. Clients are quick to say they are "especially impressed" with the dynamic and astute staff of professionals. Whether you have a pied-a-terre downtown or a Fifth Avenue townhouse, My-Home will service your budget, with projects from $40,000 (for a simple kitchen remodel) to $2 million (for a high-end gut).

"The work was meticulous. Often the workers chose to do things in a difficult or tedious way for the sake of a better finished product." "When I recommend MyHome for a job, there are never any complaints, only good news." "Their project manger Osh is incredibly detailed, efficient, courteous—and knows his business." "I called for a proposal last night and this morning they delivered—no waiting around—very efficient." "One thing I will say, nobody has an attitude." "Very cooperative, congenial, and thorough." "The supervisors are very knowledgeable, skilled, and creative." "Very responsive. High energy." "Outstanding service by the whole team." "I have renovated before at other residences. MyHome surpassed them all—the designer, contractor, and foreman could not have been more responsive and helpful."

Myriad Construction 💼   4   3.5   4.5   4.5
790 Madison Avenue, Suite 601, New York, NY 10021
(212) 472-0004   www.myriadconstruction.net
Construction management, general contracting, and residential support

Among the myriad skills of this construction manager and general contractor is the execution of high-end, large-scale residential work for well-heeled Manhattanites. Customers say Myriad's familiarity with coordinating complex design details proves a major asset when it comes to more ambitious residential projects.

Clients are particularly impressed by principal Erich Schoenherr's ability to solve somewhat knotty technical and mechanical issues while still demonstrating an aesthetic sensibility. In business since 1987, Schoenherr has twenty employees, and we are told the firm and its subcontractors are dedicated to doing excellent work. On average, four to seven projects run at one time, and may range in size from 2,000 to 5,000 square feet. Myriad can do a simple conversion for $500,000, but keep in mind typical jobs are in the million-dollar range.

"You can tell Erich has many years of experience, and he works well with designers." "We have hired them to do several projects and are impressed with their team." "They always have an experienced on-site manager for each job." "Myriad especially shines in difficult situations. They are used to doing very high-end stuff."

Peter Di Natale & Associates 💼   3.5   3.5   4   4.5
37 Main Street, Cold Spring, NY 10516
(845) 265 - 3101   pdnainc@aol.com
General contracting and kitchen/bathroom remodels

Patrons enthuse about Peter Di Natale & Associates' work on high-end residential interiors, from kitchen remodels to slab-to-slab gut rebuilds in the New York City area. We hear this contractor is a natural for self-described "more difficult" clients, as it is scrupulously responsive to their input and questions.

Owner Peter Di Natale values the personal touch that has made this a "one-of-a-kind contractor" since 1990. Di Natale, who has a civil engineering degree, credits his father, a professional estimator, with teaching him the business. Clients speak highly of his personal patience and determination, as well as the "good core group" of twelve that works with him. We hear the Di Natale team makes the process "fun." Budgets range from $300,000 for conversions to $1.3 million for total guts.

"Peter is a gentleman who gets the job done right." "They have highly skilled job foremen." "Peter is dedicated to client service and is backed by a personable, very

competent office staff." "I am the one person I know who actually enjoyed my relationship with my contractor." "Doesn't have his fingers in too many fires." "Not the lowest bid, but came in on budget and timeframe with work of the highest caliber and no unfair and unexpected add-ons." "Very responsive and honest—rare qualities in a contractor."

Pier Head Associates Limited 🛍 4 3.5 4.5 4
35 West 36th Street, 7th Floor, New York, NY 10018
(212) 966 - 2234 www.pierhead.com
General contracting and construction management

A vast number of "quality projects" and a reputation for good management have many heads turning toward Pier Head Associates. We hear partners Peter Daw and Sheri Best run a "well-orchestrated" outfit that consistently pleases its clients. Together with their team they perform contracting and construction management duties on residential renovations, restorations, additions, and extensions. The shop welcomes projects in Manhattan from the Battery to Harlem, as well as jobs in Brooklyn and Jersey City. When a gap in the schedule permits, the firm will accept smaller jobs, as well as commercial work.

Daw, who has a background in historical restoration, and Best, who started out as an artist, formed the firm back in 1993, but have been working together for more than twenty years. We hear they take care to dispatch the crew members best suited to the client's personality. With fabulous in-house tile guys and a newly expanded mill shop, the company maintains firm control on cost, quality, and schedule. The shop also shares an office with an architect, adding to the Pier Head brain trust. Depending upon size, a gut renovation goes from $1 million to $4 million, with some budgets at $300,000 and $400,000.

"Pier Head did an outstanding job in a timely fashion." "The employees are friendly, responsible, and trustworthy. I never saw a sullen face and they returned for punchlist." "Peter Daw is experienced, personable, and easy to work with. He quickly tells you if something you are proposing is off the wall, even if it means less work for the crew." "I did use a designer who uses Pier Head frequently, so this may have affected the timeliness of the work." "A delight. Absolutely meticulous." "They get a good read on the client." "A pleasure to work with." "His staff is top-notch." "Always strives to satisfy his clients." "We've been using them for years."

Pizzo Brothers Inc. 🛍 4 3.5 4.5 4.5
628 West 131st Street, New York, NY 10027
(212) 491 - 8499 www.pizzobrothers.com

Brownstone and apartment renovations and window restoration

The Pizzos have had their professional hard hats on for three generations. The family-run firm, based out of a 9,000 square foot upper Manhattan space, specializes in the renovation of luxury apartments and brownstones, turn of the century lobbies, and historically relevant windows. We hear no matter what the task, the work is "outstanding" and the Pizzos and their staff "never fail to go the extra mile."

	Quality	Cost	Value	Recommend?
	+	$	◆	★

Brothers Frank and Ed Pizzo run the company their grandfather started back in the 1940s. Clients say the duo act as advisors, coming up with good solutions that put quality first. Pizzo's crew of 50 includes exceptional craftsmen who have been with the firm "forever." Well worth the going-rate prices, the firm splits projects between kitchen and bath, guts, and window restoration, with budgets of $200,000 to $1 million.

"The Pizzos were so nice to have around, I was depressed when they finished." "Frank and Ed run a very clean site, making sure at the end of the day nothing is left out." "You never feel duped with these guys." "The Pizzo brothers are first-rate professionals." "Everyone to whom we have recommended them has been as happy with the results as we have been."

RD Rice Construction Inc.   5   4.5   4.5   4.5
532 West 30th Street, New York, NY 10001
(212) 268 - 1414   www.rdrice.com

Superior renovations and construction management

Top architects single out RD Rice for its team approach from the start of the design phase through completion. This widely published, well-connected contractor takes on prime high-end residential renovation projects in Manhattan. Its talented workforce and adept managers accommodate some of the most demanding, high-profile clients in the city. The firm's millwork, produced in its own 25,000 square foot shop, is considered an in-house specialty.

Clients describe principal Doug Rice (who got his start buying and refurbishing old Victorian homes in San Francisco) as delightful, quick-witted, and a wonder to work with. Since 1995, Rice has been building a stellar reputation on his commitment to "service, service, service." Rice plays an active role in each job with his staff of 40 following in his footsteps. He can even be found assisting a client in selecting marble from a quarry in Italy. Homeowners looking for an RD masterpiece can expect to spend $400 to $500 plus per square foot, with complete costs of $2.5 million plus for a 5,000 square foot apartment gut.

"Their management and organizational skills keep the project on track, especially under tight deadlines." "Maintenance department provided skilled follow-up service after we moved in with their 'handyman' service." "There is no detail overlooked—they were back in a second to deal with problems and issues that came up, even when it wasn't related to the job." "All levels of workers are smart, personable, and dependable—easy to have in your home." "Excellent service, always available for emergencies and non-emergencies. Good stuff."

RD Wright Inc.   4   4   4   4.5
527 West 29th Street, New York, NY 10001
(212) 971 - 7501   douglas.reetz@verizon.net

General contracting

Sources tell us this intelligent, down-to-earth, and "civilized" contractor performs high-end residential renovations with good workmanship and a good attitude. References only half-jest that the "pleasantness" and "timeliness" of working with RD Wright "will help keep your marriage together" during a stressful renovation. The firm is also diplomatic with sensitive neighbors and co-op boards.

After working his way from the South of France to Greece as a skilled laborer, principal Doug Reetz came home and started his firm in 1986. Clients find Reetz to be a "charming" character who will volunteer ideas for managing costs and improving efficiency. Sources tell us he does not cut corners and is a hands-on leader for his strong staff of fifteen. Gut renovations generally start at $400 per square foot and end up costing $2 million. For his many repeat customers, Reetz will also work on small tasks with budgets of $150,000.

"We were blessed to have a contractor with energy and commitment to completing our renovation." "Under-promised and over-delivered." "Highest quality craftsmanship from all their trades." "Easy to talk to and patiently explains every detail." "He gets the job done, and you will like him when the job is over." "Folksy style, but extremely professional and responsive." "I never have to chase him." "He can communicate well with the client and the architect." "Despite setbacks and debate with the co-op's architect, the project was delivered on schedule and with detail and beauty we did not originally expect." "A year later we still get timely response to requests for adjustments." "You will probably want to be his friend and will love living in your apartment." "Doug's humor and calm problem-solving lowered my blood pressure."

Rusk Renovations Inc.    4   3.5   4.5   4.5

583 West 215th Street, Suite A5, New York, NY 10034
(212) 544 - 0986 www.ruskrenovations.com
General contracting and kitchen and bath remodels

John Rusk of Rusk Renovations excels in customer service, "consulting with clients every step of the way." Architects note that Rusk is the kind of dedicated contractor who they can depend on. Skilled in both traditional and modern interiors, the company does its core business in guts and kitchen and bathroom remodels. With assignments all over town, Rusk is pleased to be one of the in-house contractors for famed El Dorado. In 2000, the firm won the Lucy G. Moses Award from the New York Landmarks Conservancy for its work.

After teaching himself carpentry, Rusk opened the firm in 1986. Rusk has written about his experiences in the book *On Time and On Budget,* and he and his ten "professional craftsmen" practice what he preaches, delivering three to four major projects simultaneously and efficiently. Rusk's clientele, primarily young families, appreciate rational budgets from $200,000 to $600,000.

"The man is a mensch, one of the best. I give a copy of his book to everyone of my kitchen clients. I suggest they read it before they hire him." "John works well with both architects and clients. He is honest and determined to meet both budget and schedule." "Rusk is willing to take on medium jobs which are just as difficult as large jobs, but not as desirable to larger firms." "The firm provided me with an excellent experience. The crew was reliable, professional, trustworthy, and extremely competent." "If you value your peace of mind, you can't do better than Rusk Renovations. John has high standards, exceptional integrity, and he is a pleasure to work with." "He inspired confidence at our first meeting, it stayed on budget, and we were very happy with the results. Since then we've recommended Rusk to everyone we know who was planning a renovation, and everyone has thanked us."

SilverLining Interiors   4.5   4.5   4   5

2091 Broadway, 3rd Floor, New York, NY 10023
(212) 496 - 7800 www.silverlininginteriors.com
Considerable interior renovation and decorative finish specialists

This "honest, reliable, and energetic" organization has evolved from a painting and decorative finish guru into one of the best and brightest total interior renovation contractors in Manhattan. From refined Art Deco prewars to striking minimalist architecture in Soho, SilverLining projects reach from $500,000 into the multimillions. True to its beginnings, the firm maintains in-house finishing crews that include painters, tile installers, carpenters, plasterers, stainers, paperhangers, and glazers. (Custom plasterwork is also a specialty.)

We hear principal Joshua Wiener proves both a tireless client champion and a man in tune with good taste. Not surprisingly, his wife is interior designer Eve Robinson, with whom he occasionally teams. Though the staff numbers 168, sources say each tradesperson and manager working for the company is helpful and proud of his or her contribution to the elegant and original finished product. In the end, SilverLining prices as it plays, in the upper echelon, with the firm's integrated painting division reportedly a big scheduling advantage.

"Josh delivers what he promises. The work done was spectacular. It felt like boot camp around here." "Both the project manager and the foreman were incredible; I can't say enough good things about the entire crew." "Expensive, but they are by no means the highest bidders on the job." "I'd like these contractors to move in with us. Everyone who works at SilverLining is a dream." "One of the best of the best—beautiful craftsmanship, terrific level of service and professionalism." "I believe the strong work ethic, the pride in doing quality work, and the desire to give the customer the best renovation possible comes right from the top—from Josh Wiener." "SilverLining is the only contractor we will ever use on a job and the only one we will recommend to others."

Sweeney + Conroy Inc.   4.5   4.5   4   5

31 Great Jones Street, New York, NY 10012
(212) 995 - 5099   www.sweeneyandconroy.com
Major penthouse and townhouse renovations

"Nothing is left to chance" with this "very frank" contractor who "doesn't just build a design—he gets involved and cares about what it is they are building." Sweeney + Conroy specializes in gut townhouse and penthouse renovations and structural work in Manhattan. The firm also takes on smaller projects of inspired design, plus minor service items for past customers.

Principals Sean Sweeney and Jim Conroy, who started the firm in 1995, possess decades of construction experience between them. Described as "hard-working guys" with "zero pretentiousness," they are "totally active" in every job. Clients applaud SCI's staff of 100, telling us the firm's "foreman made it all happen" and the "wonderful office girls" were "right there" for calls and questions. SCI budgets tip the scales with gut renovations at $2 million plus.

"Best contractor I ever saw. Five stars." "Over a two-year project, never one day of argument." "Almost perfect. And I was a contractor." "Very precise. Asks a lot of questions about minute details." "A lot of integration. Exceptional coordination. Headed things off before they were a problem." "I had two huge notebooks of backup materials." "My other contracting experience was a joke compared to this one."

Taconic Builders Inc.   5   4.5   4.5   5

136 West 21st Street, 12th Floor, New York, NY 10011
(212) 929 - 7811   www.taconicbuilders.com
Deluxe renovations and new construction

Considered "rock solid," Taconic Builders has established a supreme reputation for being "first rate in every way." Architects, decorators, and homeowners all praise both the amazing workmanship and the ease of teaming with Taconic, which keeps its job sites plugged in with internet-ready field terminals. Between gut renovations in premier Manhattan buildings and new construction in the Hamptons and Westchester, the firm's accomplishments are second to none.

Supporters say co-owners Gerry Holbrook and James Hanley "hire the most competent people for the job, then demand perfection." We hear Taconic's large group of "top-notch" craftsmen, design professionals, and project managers are a pleasure to have around. In business since 1986, the outfit works equally well with clients who want to get into the minutiae of their project as it does with those who are away in Paris for the duration. They tell us Taconic also deals "really well" with the "persnickety co-op," and that the firm's service staff keeps projects fine-tuned long after completion.

Budgets fall squarely at the $2 million to $3 million mark—with $250,000 the minimum for new clients. However, regular patrons can count on Taconic for something as small as a kitchen tune-up.

"Excellent project managers and job superintendents. Truly care about their jobs, clients and architects." "A very professional organization from the top to the on-site management." "Everything they did for us was fabulous." "We were delighted and surprised that our relationship with a New York contractor could be so positive." "The job has been a pleasure from beginning to end. Excellent suggestions and advice throughout the project." "Definitely the place to go to if you can afford it." "I give Taconic my unconditional recommendation." "Easy to work with, love them!"

Taocon Inc.

4.5	4	4.5	5

244 5th Avenue, 3rd Floor, New York, NY 10001
(212) 689 - 7799 www.taocon.com

Skilled renovations and construction management

"Craftsmen, businessmen, and gentlemen," the team at Taocon has been tapped for Manhattan gut renovations at high-end residences and at businesses like *Time Out New York* magazine and Shiseido. Some top-notch architects report they look to this firm to drive a job, especially on tricky projects when layouts, schedules, and budgets are a challenge.

We're told partners David Schlachet and Steven Lamazor, who started the firm in 1988, "have their finger on the pulse," maintaining a sterling reputation with "plenty of creativity," "total integrity," and "dependable personnel." They field over 60 employees, including drywall, framing, and carpentry crews who keep jobsites tidy. Projects run the gamut, with budgets from $200 to $800 per square foot and average costs falling between $500,000 to $5 million.

"Steve is delightful, cool, calm, and collected." "The firm is highly organized with excellent project managers." "Great subs, superb cabinetmaker." "A dream contractor." "Great team. Delivered a difficult project on time and on budget, a first for me!" "Finished a six-month project in seven months, and that's good timing in our world." "The ultimate professional." "Flexible and realistic on contract issues." "Absolutely use them if they will take your job."

The I. Grace Company Inc.

5	5	4	4.5

403 East 91st Street, New York, NY 10128
(212) 987 - 1900 www.igrace.com

Commissioned private residences, service, and maintenance; special projects

This nationally renowned residential construction company possesses both finesse and firepower. Clients are drawn to the personal and intimate service combined with proven manpower to take on projects of any size and scope. Services include new construction, historic restorations, construction management, and architectural interiors, for spaces ranging from New England country estates to New York City lofts. In addition to the large-scale, museum-quality projects for which the company is best known, I. Grace maintains ongoing relationships with clients by completing small projects through its service arm. Its impressive roster of patrons includes Wall Street executives, celebrities, and other power players.

Founded in 1988 by David Cohen, I. Grace engages the construction management process with six divisions, including the flagship headquarters in New York City. The same business philosophy of quality and integrity extends to its New England, West Coast, and Long Island entities and its Special Projects and Service/Maintenance divisions. We hear the firm's 100-plus team "consistently demonstrates a responsiveness to the needs, concerns, and ambitions of the customer." From the CEO to the project manager to the large staff of field employees, the company's employees exemplify "old school" values by building lasting relationships. For those who can afford it, I. Grace promises white-glove treatment with white-collar acumen, with major renovations in NYC starting at $5 million and up.

"I. Grace is the Rolls-Royce of contractors." "The only choice for clients with high expectations." "The I. Grace Company excels in management of a construction project, and brings to the table a dedicated team of skilled personnel to get the job done with the utmost care." "They are a pleasure to work with. That's difficult to say when it comes to contractors!" "Fabulous. Did whatever they had to do to get the job done." "The firm is great about working under summer work rules." "I. Grace exemplifies superior quality, professionalism, and total dedication to each and every step in the process."

The Renovated Home   4   3   5   5

1477 3rd Avenue, Suite 2, New York, NY 10028
(212) 517 - 7020 www.therenovatedhome.com

High-end custom design/build services

Industry professionals say this upper-end design/build firm takes a "common sense approach" to gut renovations and kitchen and bath overhauls. A fixture in Manhattan since 1985, The Renovated Home's resume has a long list of satisfied customers, who laud the company's respectful and responsive personnel, and clients tell us its craftspeople are "exceptional." Owner Lee Stahl is known to be in the office on Sunday, and available to clients via two cell phones and a BlackBerry. We are also told the big-hearted Stahl donates 1% of gross sales of projects to various charities.

Four to six large commissions are taken simultaneously and typically run between $400,000 to 1.6 million on the high-end. With a 3,000 square foot Upper East Side showroom displaying a variety of quality tiles, cabinets, and flooring and with all services and trades provided in-house, clients can't get enough of the "one-stop" convenience.

"Everyone of my clients rave about Lee's work." "In a world where things invariably go awry, it's nice to know that you can trust the service promised by my contractor." "Very honest, he won't waste your time. If he thinks it won't work he tells you." "Renovating in Manhattan is scary. Lee and Toby made things easy." "Swift, reliable, within budget, and on schedule—what else is there?" He did one project for us, and we were counting on him to renovate our new apartment. Unfortunately he decided not to take the job." "The punch list can take some time but they completed everything." "Lee takes pride in his work and wanted to do a quality job. Their workmen are still coming back a year later if anything needs adjusting or fixing." "I give them my highest recommendation." "Experts at what they do."

Tom Law and Associates

202 West 78th Street, Suite B, New York, NY 10024
(212) 362-5227 tlaltd@nyc.rr.com

Complete apartment renovations, kitchen plus bathroom renovations

See Tom Law and Associates full report under the heading Kitchen & Bath Designers

Traditional Line Ltd.   5   4   5   4

143 West 21st Street, New York, NY 10011
(212) 627 - 3555 traditionalline@earthlink.net

Exacting, refined restorations and renovations

A master of nearly forgotten techniques, Jim Boorstein of Traditional Line is "top-drawer" in restoration and preservation. Admirers say he "creates magic" while resuscitating private residences, museums, and public buildings in Manhattan. Boorstein's astonishing talents include the refinish and restoration of complex woodworking details as well as reproduction of panels, mantelpieces, stairways, and period hardware. The firm even does furniture restoration. Traditional's extensive knowledge and skill is best applied to landmark houses and apartments dating from 1760 to 1950.

Originally a sculptor, Boorstein shaped the firm in 1984 after completing the restoration of the New American period rooms at the Metropolitan Museum of Art. Clients remark that Traditional's twenty craftsmen are "truly artisans" and are always mindful of the client's space. Customers praise the firm's work, but note that if there's work to be done that's not attached to restoration, you might want to resolve it first. At any one time, Boorstein will take on two sizeable restoration projects and numerous smaller tasks. Small projects start at $25,000, while large residential spaces come with multi-million-dollar price tags.

"I'm thrilled with the results and recommended them to three friends. They are the only people that can do work in my apartment." "Brilliant—and in addition, extremely nice people to work with." "The de-installation of the Spanish Mudjar ceiling in the Islamic Galleries at the Metropolitan Museum of Art was a challenging project and Traditional Line carried out all aspects of it in the most responsible and professional manner." "Their expertise and qualifications for handling historic interiors are unparalleled." "All restoration work was satisfactory if expensive." "Project took longer than necessary." "If it is not their issue or in their contract, they will not help you solve the problem." "Top of the heap for what they do." "Nobody at Traditional Line I wouldn't work with again. The best thing out there. I recommend them to everybody!" "Honest, hardworking, and dedicated to what they do." "We went through four contractors before we found Traditional Line, and will look no further."

Watters Construction Inc. 🛍️   3.5   3   4.5   4.5

127 Pennsylvania Avenue, Tuckahoe, NY 10707
(646) 302 - 0984   mwatters@verizon.net
General contracting and cabinetry and millwork

In the rough seas of residential renovations, we hear this firm keeps a client's head above water. Watters Construction has been performing smaller and mid-sized high-end residential contracting jobs in Manhattan and Westchester since 1986. The firm works closely with renowned architects and also produces its own millwork.

Clients applaud principal Martin Watters—who they find friendly and flexible. The company's smallish size means Watters wades knee-deep in every project. We're told he is quite the professional with his crew of ten, laying everything out in advance and sharing cost-saving tips with his clients. References report that Watters' gut renovation price of $500,000 won't sink your budget, and is worth every penny.

"One of my rare experiences with a contractor, knows what he's doing and gets it done." "The prior contractor screwed up, Watters redid everything and it took eight working days." "Honestly, I adore Martin." "Not only did Martin or the firm respond to our phone calls and keep appointments, we found that there were no hidden costs whatsoever." "He is an excellent communicator and is always there when you need him." "A door fell off a cabinet two days before Christmas and Martin came right over to fix it."

Wise Construction LLC. 🛍️   4   4   4   4.5

81 Barrow Street, New York, NY 10014
(212) 929 - 6181   www.wiseconstructionllc.com
High-end contemporary renovations

The "insightful" contractor Richard Wise is considered an excellent communicator and creative problem solver by the many designers who appreciate him. Wise Construction takes on high-end contemporary residential and commercial renovations all over town, often in Manhattan's hip downtown neighborhoods and on the Upper West Side. Clients tell us Wise makes the process educational, informing them every step of the way.

A hometown boy with initiative, Wise nailed a construction job in his teens and started his company in 1980 at the age of twenty. We hear the shop is more about quality than about quantity: "doing the job right the first time" is this firm's motto. A medium-sized staff of experienced craftsmen and subs has stayed loyal to Wise since the beginning, and these workers prove to be both "talented and reliable." Industry professionals note the company provides "realistic budgets and meets deadlines without sacrificing on the details." Two to three projects are simultaneously undertaken with sizeable price tags of $1 million to $4 million each.

"The best builders are the ones who have zero limitations. Any new design, any new concept, not only can Wise Construction build it to perfection—they set the high standard for how it's done!" "Even now three years later, we can call on Wise if there is an issue." "Richard is great. I didn't know him before we started to build and now he's my friend." "Wise accomplished everything I dreamed." "I was thrilled he completed the punch-list so fast and effectively." "Wise outlasted my last three architects." "They solved problems and improved upon our details." "Highest quality of handiwork and finishes." "Excellent communication and accessibility throughout the project." "Wise delivered a fantastic product."

ZMK Group Inc.   4   3.5   4.5   5

192 Lexington Avenue, Suite 501, New York, NY 10016
(212) 252 - 1400 www.zmkgroup.com

Complete residential renovation

Fluent in the urban lifestyle, ZMK Group offers a "wealth of good information, endless options, and distinctive quality" for clients in Gramercy Park, Soho, Tribeca, the West Village, and the Upper East Side. ZMK takes on full-scale renovations of prewar and postwar apartments, conversions of lofts, and complete structural overhaul of brownstone townhouses, as well as commercial work. Sources tell us the firm also works on building lasting relationships.

Principal Zachary M. Kaplan, who launched the firm in 1992, is known to be "very cooperative" with a "sharp eye for details" and to truly understand life in the big city. The native New Yorker's hometown advantage is evident in his knowledge and contacts. Kaplan's reportedly competent and courteous managerial staff and "spectacularly" skilled tradesmen work on nine jobs simultaneously, with budgets of $400,000 to $2 million. The majority of work prices out at $900,000 for comprehensive gut renovations.

"Zack and his staff were always available, friendly, and responsive. The end product was flawless." "I thought Zack was kidding when he described his attention to details, but you should see the gorgeous custom work on the crown and base moldings, doors, stone fireplace, and cherry cabinets! Well worth it!" "ZMK brought thoughtful order and clarity to the renovation of our loft." "Zack could often sense when my wife or I were concerned about an issue and would bring it up before we would even mention it." "Provided invaluable suggestions and input on cost- and time-effective solutions to our complicated design."

Zoric Construction Corp.   4   3.5   4.5   5

21-44 Harman Street, Ridgewood, NY 11385
(718) 386 - 7141 zoricconstruction@aol.com

Classical renovation

Elite designers dub the energetic John Zoric "a contractor with really good taste" and "a perfectionist with a big heart." Zoric Construction specializes in apartment and brownstone rehabs and renovations where traditional woodwork, plaster, and ornamental painting are most prominently on display—typically in New York's tonier neighborhoods. The firm's triple threat of diligence, courteousness, and artistic touch especially delights its clients.

The man on the marquee, Zoric, earned an engineering degree in Europe before spending over twenty years in the building profession. Homeowners confess that they "relied on him more than on our architect for design ideas." The small operation, in business since 1987, boasts its own woodworking shop. There are eight on staff, with subs called in according to the job. Clients are particularly impressed by the fact that Zoric performs much of the trades work himself. In fact, customers are so smitten with Zoric, they're "afraid to tell him how inexpensive he really is." A broad range of prices for guts go from $200 to $400 per square foot, with complete costs at $250,000 to $2 million.

"John is an excellent contractor—we cannot speak highly enough about the quality of his work." "His execution is terrific." "John delivered on everything he promised. He didn't finish until we were happy with every detail. I would recommend him without reservation." "John is a terrific problem solver and comes up with creative solutions. Those who work with him are well-trained, hardworking, and respectful." "Enormous attention to detail. As a perfectionist, his only weakness is he's sometimes slow—but no slower than average and definitely worth the wait." "I've used John's company through the years and he's completed four home renovations, two office build-outs, and numerous changes in both throughout the years." "I've never checked a bill of John's because he's as honest as my mother." "With Zoric you get quality craftsmanship at the most reasonable prices possible."

FIRMS WITHOUT ONLINE PORTFOLIOS

A.E. Greyson and Company   4   4   4   3.5
55 Washington Street, Suite 824, Brooklyn, NY 11201
(212) 337 - 0929
General contracting

This widely published, accomplished general contractor is on the shortlist of Manhattan architectural firms that are familiar with significant seven- and eight-figure residential commissions. A.E. Greyson's high-end savvy is also engaged for commercial jobs. Whoever the client, A.E. Greyson is reputed to pull off complex projects "without a hitch." Principal Joseph Kusnick, an architect by training, started the business in 1995. We're told Kusnick brings a passionate interest to his work—qualities that clients find comforting and architects find refreshing. While sources find the firm's managers diligent, some are "deluged by paperwork." Even so, A.E. Greyson is "very upfront regarding time frames" and we hear there are "no surprises," especially in costs. Kitchen and bathroom remodels typically start at $100,000 and complete overhauls go up to $2 million. Clients are "amazed" by the firm's willingness to return years later for tasks of any size.

"It was worth every penny." "SO complex and they handled it without a problem." "I would use him again in a minute." "He was dependable, honest, and sincere in his predictions of how long things would take to complete." "On occasion Joseph would fly off the handle." "A good contractor but a hothead sometimes." "Things were always under control." "Took over where the other guy didn't finish and was happy to fix whatever wasn't correct. Very detail-oriented."

Alliance Builders Corp.   4.5   3.5   5   4.5
236 West 26th Street, Suite 605, New York, NY 10001
(212) 463 - 9229   www.alliancebuilders.com
Artisanal gut renovations and construction management

Alliance Builders' meticulous follow-through reportedly results in a "first-rate" fit and finish. Collaborating with design professionals, the artisans of this gen-

eral contracting firm execute high-end commercial and residential apartments, townhouses, and brownstones all over Manhattan. We're told the shop's impressive in-house engineering capabilities and pre-construction services complement its construction management.

Larry Kahn's fine arts background and partner Robert Cook's engineering experience, combined with 30 years' expertise in the industry, set a low-key, forward-thinking tone at Alliance. In business since 1993, the company has 40 employees on staff and a network of loyal "top-notch" subs. The firm works to clarify the architect's intent and identify potential holes that inevitably arise between concept and execution. Drafting approximately five projects at a time, the shop works on gut renovations along with expanding spaces and floor additions. Although a typical Alliance job prices out at $2 million, with some as high as $5 million, the firm has been known to take on smaller projects with budgets in the $500,000 range.

"Dependable, reliable, and ethical." "They're renovating our house in Martha's Vineyard and we would use them again...." "Very good quality. Detail-oriented. Cares about what he does and does a good job." "No surprises or questions." "Copper skylights that they didn't install were starting to crack and they took it upon themselves to fix them." "They even covered for our unorganized decorator." "Handled relationship with the neighborhood very well. One old lady had nothing to do but complain every day so to satisfy her, they built a birdbath." "No part of the job where I thought there was something else they could have done."

ARC Interiors

	3.5	3	4.5	5

PO Box 870, New York, NY 10002
(212) 226 - 9209   arcinteriors@aol.com
General contracting, millwork, and cabinetry

Specializing in custom millwork, this general contractor produces "precisely and beautifully" realized work for a prominent clientele. ARC Interiors restores and renovates homes in Manhattan and select Brooklyn neighborhoods. With 23 years of experience under his utility belt, principal Garry Wishart is a "genuine personality" who guides projects in an "organized, upfront manner."

An Englishman with old-school sensibilities, Wishart apprenticed as a carpenter and sharpened his skills working as a project supervisor. He formed ARC in 1995. With its own carpentry shop, a staff of ten, and good subs who are described as "caring craftsmen," ARC accomplishes both traditional and modern tasks. Wishart's ability to tap into and refine what his clients are looking for results in "ecstatic" reactions to work "so much nicer than I had imagined." Prices are described as a "good deal" for the high-quality work. Individual carpentry items are priced at $15,000 with small kitchen and bathroom overhauls averaging $80,000. Total guts price out at $300,000 to $1 million.

"Garry is always prepared and impressed me with his follow-through." "First-quality professionalism." "Nice guys, extremely conscientious. I miss them coming in the morning." "Garry has an excellent eye for detail, good taste, and a good personality." "I really trust Garry. When he says it's going to look good, it'll look good." "The price is right."

Axios Construction Corp.

4   3   5   4.5

25-94 38th Street, Astoria, NY 11103
(718) 278 - 5908

Detailed renovations and conversions

Manhattanites tell us Axios Construction's "skillful" and "careful" staff can maneuver through an occupied apartment without a hitch. Axios specializes in spearheading high-end Manhattan renovations large or small, from downtown loft conversions to total guts on CPW. Sources tell us the firm has been renovating apartments at the San Remo for the past twelve years with excellent results.

Brooklyn-born principal Frank Koumantaris, who holds a master's degree in architecture from Yale, established the firm with partner Nick Georgiadis in 1993. Highly competent in project management, the outfit's design-savvy team of eleven can also facilitate full-design/build services. In the end, we're told, references "couldn't be happier" with the experience; past clients say they recommend Axios "to anyone and everyone" doing construction in the New York area. We hear the firm proves as accommodating and responsible to a client stationed in France as to an active participant. Further noted is Axios's ability to complete a nine-month project in as little as six months. Prices range from $100,000 to $1.5 million, with $800,000 the average.

"Small, tightly run company. Every employee is dedicated and the quality of the work reflects this." "It's very beneficial that one of the partners has an architectural education, because it really shows in the details." "Axios consistently chooses the best construction method as opposed to the most expedient." "Finishes are great—known for superb paint jobs." "Frank is very personable and excellent with business operations." "Axios lived up to my high expectations." "Called them in to fix another contractor's work." "Our apartment was beautifully and ultra-carefully renovated under the complete and personal supervision of Frank and Nick." "Nick is an Old World guy—a real perfectionist. He came back several times after the work was done to fix things that he thought were not up to his high standards." "The superintendent and staff of my building—as well as my neighbors—consistently commented on this firm's courteousness and cleanliness." "We lived in the apartment while the work was being done, and they worked around our schedule and accommodated all our needs."

Barrett Campbell LLC

4   3   5   4.5

325 Degraw Street, Brooklyn, NY 11231
(718) 802 - 1105 www.barrettcampbell.com

Innovative interior renovation

Architects appreciate Tom Barrett's "good eye for details and sense of color." The New York native also gets kudos for his "innovative" interior renovation projects. He teams with wife Robin Campbell, a former TV commercial producer who keeps projects running "efficiently without complications." We hear the couple makes a "good combo" and that "dealing with them is a pleasure." Projects range from Upper West Side and Chelsea co-op conversions to bathroom remodels in Brooklyn brownstones.

Barrett brings a background in the arts to the firm he started in 1989. While we're told Barrett is creatively "strong-willed" and "you have to be assertive," in the end clients say this "dream contractor" delivers everything "entirely to expectations" and "honors the budget." Work performed on a 2,000 square foot apartment averages $500,000 with customers realizing "real-world prices for unreal quality."

"Although this was a relatively small project, I feel we had Tom's complete attention. In a very diplomatic way, he talked us out of our original plan and into a MUCH better one." "Tom has incredible taste and can make everything work efficiently even in small spaces." "On-time delivery of finished apartment, creative design services." "Robin and Tom are very easy to work with, extremely flexible. They contributed good

ideas that ultimately improved the project." "We got what we wanted, plus his ideas, all for a very reasonable price." "Very honest and upfront." "Workers were all efficient and polite."

Burr Graal Glass   4   3.5   4.5   4
54 Leonard Street, New York, NY 10013
(212) 925 - 1016 howardburr@nyc.rr.com

Classical and contemporary gut renovations

Howard Burr of Burr Graal Glass assembles building elements "creatively" and "smoothly," impressing even the most jaded New Yorker. Customers tell us the firm "rises to the challenge" of Manhattan residential construction. Flexible and accommodating, the forthright Burr "clicks with even the most demanding personalities."

Burr, who grew up in Connecticut, had mastered cabinetry by his early teens. He holds both an MFA in sculpture from the Maryland Institute and an MBA from NYU. Clients, who include artists and Wall Streeters, find Burr to be an "on-the-job impresario" who is nevertheless "always reachable." They tell us Burr asks questions and does "scrupulous research" in order to meet the detailed requirements of each project on its stated budget. Renovations of raw downtown lofts and refined uptown penthouses come with budgets between $500,000 and $2 million.

"Howard takes pride in his work—has great subs—sticks to the time frame." "As an architect, I will say he knows his stuff and often pushes us—but we're OK with it." "Howard's word is bond." "Aims the budget for you." "I was so impressed with quality, price, and professionalism that I recommended Howard to many of my architect and contractor friends who have now used him for more than six projects—all with great success, including some of their own residences." "Opinionated but always has good suggestions." "He communicated effectively with my architect and brought matters to our attention that needed further detailing so that the project could stay on schedule." "No shortcuts with this firm—good craftsmanship."

Clark Construction Corp.   5   5   4   5
117 Hudson Street, Suite 2, New York, NY 10013
(212) 219 - 1783 clarkco117@aol.com

Deluxe large-scale renovations

"Premier" contractor Clark Construction has big projects, big budgets, big personality, and big recommendations for what we are told is "truly top-of-the-line, museum-quality work." The firm, helmed by Chris Clark, has grown rapidly in reputation and scope since its start in 1983, doing high-profile residential and commercial work for clients in New York City. We hear Clark, a committed professional, is armed with a stable of A-list subcontractors and worth every nickel he charges (though, we understand, the nickels add up quickly).

While some find Clark's personality charming, others say he "shouldn't believe all his press," especially architects, who aren't heartbroken to find out this company prefers to work directly with clients. Clark's loyal customers often go to this "classy operation" first when a complicated project demands unsurpassed finish work. Patrons tell us the firm excels in customer service, staying in touch and remaining available long after the project is completed.

The firm takes on ten jobs at a time, mostly gut renovations with some bathroom and kitchen remodels for repeat clients. An average residential overhaul of 5,000 to 7,000 square feet has a big price tag of $600 per square foot, ending up in the $3 million to $5 million range.

"Shines at traditional." "Clark's timing is so good. We had to complete a ballroom for a wedding in an impossible time frame and they did an amazing job so quickly and efficiently." "Chris is a gentleman compared to other contractors." "We were shocked at the honesty and integrity of all the people in the organization." "Chris and staff are

forceful in letting the architect know exactly what they need." "My kitchen designer was a nightmare and Chris saved the day!" "Chris took a year of what I thought would be heartburn and turned it into a pleasurable experience." "Extremely expensive but five years later I still stay in contact with Rhonda in the office—she is terrific—without her it wouldn't work." "Not the only guy who does exceptionally high-quality work. Never came back to finish the punch list!" "Chris doesn't hide the fact he knows he's good." "Really helps the client and architect with detailed budgets." "This is an extraordinary operation; peak projects—it can handle anything." "Top of the heap." "Clark is the second coming of Donald Trump."

DeBono Brothers   4   4   4   4.5
101-21 101st Street, Ozone Park, NY 11416
(718) 821 - 6830
General contracting and design/build services

This "exceptionally reliable" contractor is "fully equipped" to do any kind of work with a "distinctive Old World flavor." In business in New York for 27 years, the family-run firm specializes in classically styled, detail-laden renovations of prewar apartments and townhouses in Manhattan. "Better in their details than most graphic artists," DeBono Brothers also offers design/build services.

The four brothers—Anthony, Lenny, Larry, and Chris—were trained in their native Malta and opened the business in 1984. We hear every member of the DeBono family, blood or otherwise, "takes pride in their work." Clients say guests "literally come in and lose their breath" upon seeing DeBono's impressive work; budgets run from $1 million to $2 million.

"DeBono is very detail-oriented. The work is excellent, the best." "At this point, I consider Anthony a personal friend. I just adore him and go to him for everything. I don't even bid out anymore, and that's a testament to his integrity." "He's a honey." "They're not the lowest-priced for sure, but they're on time, within budget, and they get it right." "They would call and say, 'Are you sure you want this? Because I don't think it will work.' Instead of just doing it."

DSA Builders Inc.   4   4   4   4.5
231 West 29th Street, Suite 1407, New York, NY 10001
(212) 684 - 4307   www.dsabuilders.com
General contracting and construction management

We hear this specialist in substantial renovation has sophistication and style. DSA's "meticulous" attention to detail, "yummy" design, and excellent crafts-manship (especially on cabinetry) has won them a decidedly uptown clientele. Established in 1998, the firm continues to draw bigger and more complex projects, as evidenced by its installation of a 1,500 square foot showhouse in Grand Central Terminal during rush hour.

We're told that partners Mitchell Dennis and Carrie Salter make an extremely effective and balanced team. While Dennis orchestrates the field, Salter keeps the clients and architects in tune. Her experience as a designer and senior project manager makes relations painless, and in the case of younger architects, even instructive. With a group of ten accomplished craftsmen, DSA performs cosmetic makeovers starting at $100,000 to high-end finish renovations of $3 million.

"Incredible detail, which architects like." "Co-op board loved them, they clean up and got along well with building staff." "Outstanding contractor, everyone works well together." "Mitchell was always available, he is very intense when it comes to work, but a very calm person." "They are rare. True to both designer and client." "Made me feel like I was their only client. Cared for my apartment as if it were their own." "I highly recommend them. I may be the only person in New York City who has redone an apartment and still loves to say nice things about her contractor!"

	Quality	Cost	Value	Recommend?
	✚	$	◆	★

Hanjo Contractors

| | 4.5 | 4 | 4.5 | 5 |

104-31 Jamaica Avenue, Richmond Hill, NY 11418
(718) 805 - 4731   hanjo@nyc.rr.com

Considerable renovations, kitchen and bath remodels, and specialty millwork

Clients can't stop saying nice things about Hanjo Contracting owner Hanjo Mariacher and his excellent craftsmen. Word is this "honorable" contracting professional delivers an "elegant," "superior product." Hanjo helms complete Manhattan apartment renovations and kitchen and bath remodels, specializing in custom millwork and cabinetry. Residents, designers, and building managers all praise the firm's "impressive attitude." Even a co-op board president who lived down the hall from construction was happy to see they kept things "neat as a pin."

Mariacher, a gifted woodworker who hails from a small farm near Salzburg, Austria, keeps jobs running like glockenspiels. He opened the New York shop in 1982. Now, with a team of 30 and over 100 subcontractors, son Adrian and daughter Christine take leading roles, facilitating twenty projects at one time. Reports say Mariacher asks thoughtful questions and gives good advice, and that working with his helpful, likable crew "is a blast." John, the foreman, is said to be proud of his work and have a great sense of humor. Considered "very flexible" on price with size and materials the deciding factor, Hanjo charges from $200 to $500 per square foot, with complete gut renovations going up to $2 million.

"Fast, quality workmanship, lots of attention to details, excellent follow-up, clean-up, and order." "No complaints—many good ideas as project progressed." "Firm has the technical skills to handle the most difficult problems. The owner, Hanjo Mariacher takes a personal interest in each job." "All workers were pleasant, cooperative, efficient, and took pride in their work." "On time and on budget. This was our third project with Hanjo and they do very good work for very good value." "A terrific, well-organized company with a dedicated group of specialists." "Very honest, highly competent team that can work under severe time constraints and maintain quality." "Has better design ideas than the typical architect and more practical and cost efficient." "Fabulous in all respects, especially with last-minute end-of-project changes."

Horacio Mercado Associates

| | 4 | 3 | 5 | 4 |

345 West 22nd Street, New York, NY 10011
(212) 541 - 5034   www.hmercado.com

General contracting and restorations

A "champion" to the many grateful architects who depend on him, Horacio Mercado's integrity, ideas, and "mind-blowing quality" have clients clamoring for an encore. Mercado's firm undertakes apartment guts and landmark restorations for private clients, as well as public space renovations, in notable New York apartment buildings. Mercado also takes on smaller jobs, often on the Upper West Side, for repeat clients. We hear he even has his own office in the renowned Ansonia, where his firm has done over 300 renovations. Mercado also maintains his own millwork shop that specializes in reproducing windows, doors, and architectural features for prewar buildings.

Born in Argentina, Mercado earned an architecture degree from Columbia University before starting his business in 1991. We're told he brings a developed design sense that offers practical solutions to his projects. Clients remark on the "not only cheerful, but talented" group of craftsmen he employs. Many feel that Mercado could easily charge more for his "incredible work," comforting personality, and dedication. Gut renovations measure in size from 1,500 to 6,000 square feet with budgets of $200,000 to $700,000.

"As an architect I really appreciate the fact he understands what I do." "I hire Mercado for lots of projects, and it has made my life so easy." "If he says it'll take six months, I know my client will be able to move in right on time, even if there are odds

and ends to finish." "No one ever complains about the price because they know he's worth more." "For those who don't feel the need for a Park Avenue stalwart, Mercado's firm proves a winning choice." "I spent every waking moment with Horacio. If it wasn't for him I would have had a nervous breakdown." "It was like Fantasia. He had magic coming out of his fingers." "Brilliant, just brilliant. My husband comes from an interior design background and thinks he's a genius." "Horacio seamlessly takes care of everything." "I bought two more apartments just to work with him." "He has great respect for you and your money."

Innovative Concepts/Diane Slovak   4   3   5   5

PO Box 138, Georgetown, CT 06829
(203) 222 - 1319 dianeslovak@hotmail.com
Remodels, additions, and new construction

Diane Slovak's clients appreciate her "approachable personality" and the "intelligent thought process" she brings to a project. Her firm, Innovative Concepts, will take on a small bathroom remodel with the same enthusiasm as a high-profile penthouse, and the workmanship "speaks for itself." Catering primarily to a Connecticut and Westchester clientele, Innovative Concepts also works from Manhattan to Rockland County.

A former research scientist in bio-medical engineering, Slovak took off her white coat to become a member of ASID. While working as an in-house designer for a large construction company she was drawn to the contracting side of the business. Since opening her own firm in 1985, she has applied her detail-oriented approach to the homebuilding industry. Sources say Slovak's technical and aesthetic suggestions "never lead you down the wrong road." The firm manufactures uniquely detailed cabinetry out of its Redding, Connecticut shop and employs its own stable of painters and masons. New York prices start at $250 per square foot, and go up to $600. Projects range from $10,000 to $1 million with $150,000 to $300,000 the norm.

"Diane always knows what to do to tackle any problem." "Her subs are all first-rate. I wouldn't take a project without her." "A superb professional." "A very detailed and thorough contractor. No details are overlooked." "Our cottage looks magnificent— and was a major selling point when our house went on the market." "Diane was highly professional. Her work was done on time and she demanded quality workmanship."

Larson Construction Corp.   5   5   4.5   5

36 Cooper Square, Suite 4R, New York, NY 10003
(212) 420 - 1544
Impressive renovation and design/build services

Considered a major player in industry circles, this gentleman contractor is a "true partner" in the building process. In its third decade of New York residential, gallery, corporate, and retail construction, Larson can hand-pick a few prime projects per year, and will also act in a design/build capacity. Larson's choice clientele includes marquee decorators who commission the company for their own private homes.

Principal Alfred Larson, whose background is in design and fine art, opened the firm in 1980. Larson collaborates closely with homeowners and architects, personally maintaining a presence onsite. We're told the firm "works with discretion and flexibility" to accommodate its clients' every need. A small staff of "excellent" foremen and "marvelous" subcontractors add to the firm's allure. High-quality accomplishments come with equally high price tags of between $1 million and $4 million.

"Couldn't imagine a builder this amazing." "The Leonardo of builders." "Very good guy, everybody loves him. Does museum-quality work." "Specialized where high finishes are required." "He was very involved. Went shopping with me for hardware

and marble. Even designed a closet space for me." "Subs very neat and tidy. The craftsmanship was excellent." "Fred is choosy about picking his clients—he likes to work in a happy environment."

Lico Contracting Inc.   5   4.5   4.5   4.5

29-10 20th Avenue, Astoria, NY 11105
(718) 932 - 8300   www.licocontracting.com
Premium renovations and restorations

In its fifth decade of building, this family-owned firm's reputation is nearly as "impeccable" as its museum-quality work. Lico performs mainly large gut renovation projects in Manhattan, Long Island, Westchester, and Connecticut for a roster of blue-chip clients in a diplomatic and timely manner. A "very helpful" staff of upwards of 85 performs carpentry and millwork services in-house and produces "beautiful" shop drawings. Industry sources say Lico has entrenched relationships with the best subcontractors in NYC.

Clients say president Rich Bruno, "the Daniel Boulud of contractors," orchestrates a fine experience, along with his professional on-site managers. The firm's workers take great care with details and communicate well about all aspects of a project. Like any elite player in the field, Lico's expertise comes at a premium, with renovation budgets between $2 million and $10 million.

"Richard is very responsive to design projects." "Lico's project managers are direct and are experts." "You can call Richard day or night and he will know every detail regarding your project." "An older company with great experience." "Mindful of everything that involves the clients and their home comfort." "Richard knows how to delegate and understands what each job requires." "Strives for strong customer service." "We have had them work on two of our apartments, and they have always been extremely professional, conscientious, fair, and, most important, very proud of what they do."

Matilda Construction Inc.   4   4   4   5

522 West 37th Street, New York, NY 10018
(212) 586 - 5794   mckennanyc@mac.com
General contracting

This "very enthusiastic" contractor leaves no stone unturned on residential projects large and small. Matilda has been around since 1988, and we hear its dedicated crew of thirteen take great pride in their work and in sticking to the schedule. Clients all over Manhattan and Hoboken tell us that when it comes to quality, Matilda is "more demanding than the architect."

Principal Tim McKenna comes recommended as a straightforward businessman who doesn't waste time or money. Clients tell us his keen eye for design and insightful recommendations, coupled with precision execution, make for "a superb value." Matilda's average job prices between $600,000 to $2 million, and we're told customers who can afford Matilda are as happy with the bill as with the end results.

"I took a chance on Tim after reading about him. It was a shot in the dark that turned out great!" "Very honest and his price was fair." "On a scale of 1 to 10, he's a 12!" "Tim has an answer for everything." "Project took longer than I expected but that was the co-op's fault—he worked diligently." "Tim always picked up the phone." "He has an incredible workshop where he keeps everything for old jobs." "I was glad to have him on my team." "Exactly the same great service, whether it's a $5,000 job or a $100,000 job." "Not only did he do great work, but I would be happy to have him as my dinner partner."

MZM Construction Corp.

4   3.5   4.5   4.5

3 Elyse Drive, New City, NY 10956
(845) 638 - 2694   www.mzmcorp.com

General contracting and construction management

Whether outfitting slick corporate HQs or remodeling high-tech city kitchens, this straight-arrow general contractor hits the mark. Established in 1992, MZM works in Manhattan, Westchester, and Fairfield on a diverse slate of jobs. MZM's broad background allows it to execute technically challenging projects with no room for error, featuring special forms, shoring, and structural elements.

Principal Mike Hirsch's 27-plus years in the construction industry have taken him from project engineer on the French and Japanese Pavilions at Disney's EP-COT Center to rehabbing a seven-story Tribeca residence. His partner, Robert Winnicki, brings 27 years of experience of his own in running the firm's field operations, while project manager "Magic" oversees all New York tasks. Together they manage a staff of fifteen and a crew of "on the ball" subs. Considered "easier to get in touch with and more reliable" than the competition, MZM is also an exceedingly good value. Budgets for NYC apartments range between $200,000 for kitchen and bath to $1 million plus for gutting a 3,000 square foot apartment.

"Mike is a calming influence, very rational." "They've come in to fix the little tiny things after the job." "He has a great supervisor on-site, but I can always call Mike." "They hand-filed all the cornices to make them fit perfectly."

New York Craftsmen's Collective

4   3.5   4.5   4

80 East 2nd Street, New York, NY 10003
(212) 477 - 4477   nycraftsmen@hotmail.com

Artisanal renovation, millwork, and cabinetry

Clients describe New York Craftsmen's Collective as "an army of sensitive soldiers who come equipped with skills and drills," as adept performing smaller apartment remodels as serious upstate restoration work. Many contractors count on these artisans for their millwork and cabinetry talents. Sources say principal Norman Sukkar is "funny and charming" and gives any construction hiccups immediate treatment. The workers do as promised "with only minimal disruption of the household" and "clean up at the end of every day." We also hear Sukkar is the kind of guy a customer "can call back five years after a job and he will come and fix or touch up gladly." Architects appreciate the Collective's sensitivity to design while understanding "the big picture."

Sukkar's workers are more like artists with construction tools, not surprising for a guy with an MFA degree from Pratt. We hear the group of expert craftsmen in a variety of home services fields work together to produce "thrilling" results for residential clients in Manhattan, Long Island, Westchester, and the Hamptons. Since its beginnings in 1980, the firm has been known to deliver a caliber of quality as high as any budget demands. But it can also make a budget go farther than most, with prices ranging from $100,000 up to $2 million.

"Been there, done that—these guys blow all other contractors out of the water with their attention to detail and design sense." "Guys who can take old walls and turn them into mirrors." "We were confused at times as to whether they were architects

or builders—they solved some pretty sticky issues and at a reasonable cost to boot!" "At the start of the job, they were our second-lowest bid. They were fair on any changes, they did some things gratis, and their work was outstanding." "Norman Sukkar runs a tight ship." "They were well-mannered, highly skilled, and solved several design issues." "GREAT finishers, details, details, details." "Not only WOULD I use them again...I AM using them again. And will continue to do so until I run out of projects or out of money."

Nordic Custom Builders Inc.   4.5   4   4.5   4.5
125 Greenwich Avenue, 3rd Floor, Greenwich, CT 06830
(203) 629 - 0430   thor@nordiccustom.com
Tailor-made renovations and construction management

Nordic receives a flurry of four-star reviews from the coolest names in the industry. A general contractor and construction management firm specializing in custom residential construction in Manhattan, the Hamptons, Westchester, and Greenwich, Nordic is known for "well-organized, accurate scheduling" and a "commitment to the work equal to that of the designer and architect." Nordic's impressive 15,000 square foot millwork facility, a tremendous woodworking resource, is located in Mount Vernon, New York.

Principals Thor Magnus and Eamonn Ryan have been working together since 1992. Reports indicate that Magnus and Ryan "adopt the client's perspective" and show "outstanding judgment" throughout the process. We hear "attention to detail is unsurpassed" and paperwork is "prepared like clockwork," all at a cost below that of comparable builders. Sources tell us the subs have been with Nordic since the beginning and are "extremely proud of the work they achieve." Catering only to a residential clientele, Nordic handles six to eight major projects per year, with prices at $350 to $600 per square foot and totals averaging $1 million to $2 million.

"When you work with Nordic you feel like you are working with a first-rate team. Personalities and big egos are left at home." "Nordic is my first choice for every project in Manhattan and Fairfield. Among the best I've worked with anywhere in the country." "They did everything right. Fast, professional, and accurate." "The principals at Nordic are gentlemen. Client-oriented problem solvers." "A building experience we would definitely repeat." "They insist on the highest-quality work but are also flexible." "I would hire Nordic in a flash."

Profile Group   3.5   3.5   4   4
433 West 260th Street, Riverdale, NY 10471
(718) 796 - 5770
Large and small interior renovations

Insiders regard Profile Group principal Patrick Corr as a "gallant" man with "lots of integrity." Overseeing gut renovations, and kitchen and bathroom projects all over Manhattan, Corr and his team of skilled crew never overextend themselves and are considered a steal by designers. Decorators note their clients find him so "pleasant" they feel free to call Corr directly for new tasks, while many repeat customers tell us Profile cares for everything they throw at it, without knocking their budgets out of the ballpark.

Corr studied construction economics in his homeland Ireland, opening Profile in 1992. The small team of craftsmen is described as very diligent and delivering fine work quickly. Profile tackles both large and small jobs, focusing on interior renovations that start at $250 per square foot with large jobs at $500,000 to $1 million.

"He is the KING of maintenance and follow-through." "A group of pleasant whistling Irishmen." "He is a real asset and always comes through." "After the project was finished we didn't know how to use the circuit breakers—Patrick happily came over and showed us." "Patrick is a gentleman and very approachable." "Great guys to

work with—very responsible, responsive, and always pleasant." "They work REALLY HARD and have rewarded us time and time again." "Always see the same guys on a job—not who they picked up at Janovic that day!" "Patrick wears his heart on his sleeve." "Price was just right—not the most expensive—a bargain for Manhattan." "They aim to please."

R.C. Metell Construction Inc.   4.5   4.5   4   5
198 West Haviland Lane, Stamford, CT 06903
(203) 968 - 1777
Substantial renovations

Architects and interior designers alike recognize R.C. Metell's "consummate dedication to details and quality." The firm takes on very high-end residential interior jobs on the Upper East Side and Upper West Side and new construction in Connecticut. Principal Ron Metell is described as a committed team player who works well with industry insiders and is able to navigate his clients' restrictive schedules.

Metell has a great sense of humor, but he's serious about the quality of his work and the integrity of his business. Metell, who's been around construction all his life, started his own firm in 1985. Today he manages a staff of twelve with up to fifty subs. Clients who have worked with Metell on multiple projects (including one whose project he rescued after another contractor dropped it) appreciate his dedication to their interests. Customers also appreciate Metell's accurate and timely billing. Sources tell us Metell will take small projects from regular clients, but the bulk of his business is large $2 million to $5 million jobs.

"Ron is extremely personable and proactive." "No corners are cut, but they will offer alternatives to the architectural details if they seem unreasonable." "Extremely high attention to detail and follow-up." "Works well with our interior design firm." "Ron was very considerate of summer hours and got the job done before school started."

Ridgeway Interiors   4   3.5   4.5   4.5
11714 Union Turnpike, Kew Gardens, NY 11415
(914) 843 - 0832   lawrence@ridgewayinteriors.com
Interior renovation and maintenance

Be it buttoning up a single bedroom or gutting a whole brownstone, Ridgeway's efforts garner good reviews every time. References in Manhattan rely on this "completely agreeable" contractor for everything from small upkeep tasks to $1 million interior build-outs. Clients appreciate that the firm does whatever is necessary to cultivate a healthy long-term relationship. Principal Lawrence Mullane, who started the company in 1989, and partner Glen Miller, who climbed aboard in 1995, personally steer every job, every day. A small crew of fifteen "exceptional" carpenters and painters contribute to what clients characterize as "a great and unique experience."

"The built-ins are beautiful—exceptional craftsmanship." "Ridgeway's team is very creative in terms of coming up with good solutions." "They had expertise in all areas and gave detailed and knowledgeable input in every regard." "They were not only competent and highly professional, but also pleasant and helpful." "I have renovated three times in NYC. This experience was outstanding." "For people who want quality, I am very happy to recommend Ridgeway Interiors."

SMI Construction Management   5   5   4   5
43-15 Dutch Kills Street, Long Island City, NY 11101
(718) 937 - 1090   steve@smiconst.com
Ultimate renovations and construction management

Hot with Manhattan's smart set, this busy contractor is a professional's professional. Having evolved from high-caliber millworker to top-gun GC over the course of 27 years, Steve Mark of SMI specializes in significant townhouse re-habs and apartment renovations. The firm also offers construction management services and does its own tiling, plastering, and general carpentry, all of which adds to the efficient big picture.

Mark, a "rare talent," has produced superb service since 1977. Clients admire Mark as a "straight shooter" who's dedicated to getting every detail perfectly right. They say he and his crew and "exceptional" subs deliver a level of finished product above expectations, even given the high price. Ten jobs are undertaken at one time, primarily on the Upper East and Upper West Sides, with budgets from $1 million to $10 million.

"In a league of his own." "Only if you want the top—Steve is a cut above the rest." "By far they are the best contractors—no one like them." "Steve is a finisher. He never leaves anything halfway." "We sent out six bid packages. Only two contractors bothered to respond in any detail. Steve Mark was at the apartment the next morning with six subcontractors to make sure the numbers in his bid would be accurate."

Strasser & Associates Inc.   5   4.5   4.5   5

35 Hillside Avenue, Airmont, NY 10952
(845) 425 - 0650   peterstrasser@mac.com

Historical restoration

"No detail is too small" for this "preservation-minded" contractor whose his-torical landmark expertise is "miles beyond" the competition. Strasser & Asso-ciates Inc. specializes in the restoration of turn-of-the-century townhouses and other historically significant architecture in the metropolitan area. Whatever the work, the company requires collaboration at the outset with the design profes-sional.

Peter Strasser has 30 years of experience behind him. A former sculptor whose restoration skills have been tapped by the Met, Strasser brings a "low key" demeanor and "outstanding judgment" to his firm. S&A started business in 1990, and employs fifteen of the most talented craftsmen in NYC. We hear Strasser "knows all the right people to go to," turning to "starving artist types" that "deliver" the firm's notable high-end finishes. Always conscious of budget, Strasser will meet with the client, often before the architect makes suggestions. S&A projects run from $300,000 to $5 million, but the firm doesn't have to be enlisted to do an entire home; it will take on kitchens and bathrooms with chal-lenging and fascinating restoration elements.

"Strasser performed extensive renovation of my fireplaces and brought them back to original form. An amazing job. I can see the intricate details now." "A rare find—Peter is bordering on artist." "Skillful team of workmen and very respectful of our apart-ment." "Who knew you could ever want to end a home renovation job with a cham-pagne toast to your contractors?" "Expensive but the quality was worth it." "Very accommodating and I never felt misled." "Stands behind his work and re-visits to make sure everything is A-OK." "Real pros who are uniformly nice people." "Based on their extensive experience they really knew what was important, where to spend my budget, and how to make the job come out better than planned."

Temple Contracting Inc.   4   4   4   4.5

20 West 20th Street, Suite 1001, New York, NY 10011
(212) 691 - 8032   jrtribe@rcn.com

General contracting

Temple Contracting calms clients' construction fears by making each one feel like the center of its attention. Homeowners who sign on with this small firm brag of their "stunning" experiences. Dependable and attentive, the company "meets deadlines" and comes "close to the highest-possible quality."

Owner Jim Tribe brings over 30 years' experience to the shop he opened in 1992. Given his cadre of talented, multi-disciplined craftsmen, customers claim there's "no monkeying around" with Temple on the clock. We are told the crew members, who resemble "a team of professors," are smart and considerate. Presiding over three projects at a time, Temple performs high-end residential guts and multi-room renovations with budgets of $1.5 million to $2 million.

"As an architect, I appreciate Temple's need to make the end result truly beautiful." "They looked neat and academic and blasted classical music while they worked. They're absolutely wonderful." "1/2 step down from museum quality but close to highest quality." "Not an extra cost added to the contract every time you turn around."

The Residential Interiors Corporation   4   4   4   4.5
227 West 29th Street, New York, NY 10001
(212) 239 - 6860   office@resintcorp.com
Substantial apartment and townhouse renovations

With over 25 years in business, owner Arthur Jussel of The Residential Interiors Corportation is highly respected by industry insiders and private patrons for his integrity, ability, and exemplary work. Intimidating gut renovations on the Upper East Side and Central Park West are the firm's specialty. Customers remark that the team at The Residential plans, prepares, and executes all projects with the highest quality, precision, and timeliness. We hear Jussel "runs a tight ship," captaining a crew of sixteen field workers who prove "professional and caring" in their attitude toward the client and the tasks they perform. Jussel himself, who launched the firm in 1980, is noted for his good eye for detail, not surprising coming from "the son of a society decorator." Architects find Jussel just "makes life easy" by asking the right questions and addressing issues before they walk on-site, while designers trust him with their own apartment renovations.

Townhouse and apartment overhauls run into the millions of dollars, retaining a focus on quality regardless of scope. Typically, prices go from $300 to $500 per square foot with the average gut costing $2 million. However, if Jussel feels a connection to a particular idea, he will take on a job for less—especially if it's a repeat client.

"As an architect I have worked with him for nine years and if it was up to me, I would use Arthur for every job—he makes me look that good." "Board president of an Upper East Side building called to say how thrilled they were with The Residential Interiors." "With Arthur on the job there is never friction—the same subs have been with him for years." "Jussel sets the tone for his managers who are well educated and intelligent." "Prices aren't cheap but the firm always comes in on budget—some guys might bid lower but they end up coming in higher." "Their architects love them, their clients love them, their subcontractors love them." "Always honest and forthright and up-front."

Thomas J. Connolly   4   3   5   5
100 West 92nd Street, Suite 27D, New York, NY 10025
(212) 787 - 2017   www.tcnyc.com
General contracting and kitchen and baths

Clients call this "straight ahead" contractor a thorough and hands-on partner in renovation. The "no fuss" Thomas Connolly has been working in New York City since 1972. His firm excels in "impeccable" and fairly priced kitchens, baths, and whole apartment renovations, typically on Central Park West and the Upper East Side.

A sole proprietor, Connolly is on the job himself, guiding the progress each day. We hear "his ability to work within the gist of the client's desires while hewing to practicality" satisfies both the design and the pocketbook. References report he assembles crews that are not only extremely capable at their work, but intelligent and even "interesting to talk to." In addition, Connolly takes only one job at a time, focusing all his efforts to get the job complete on schedule. Projects range from under $25,000 to over $100,000, with $50,000 the average.

"Tom demonstrates an unusual breadth of expertise in a variety of building trades. He takes the initiative to troubleshoot problems unforeseen by the layperson, for example, pointing out code violations that need to be addressed." "Connolly requires an owner who is available for consultation throughout the project; I was quite willing to play this role, and we developed a good collaborative relationship." "Excellent problem solving very much in the 'consider it done' style." "Tom is very creative about fulfilling a client's wishes." "Our building manager loved his clean-up ethic." "After a three-year search we found no one willing to take our job at a price we could afford. Then Tom found us a crackerjack carpenter."

Uberto Construction   5   5   4   4.5
129 West 86th Street, New York, NY 10024
(212) 874 - 4100

Top-shelf interior renovation

The depth of this organization's resources, especially its savvy management, terrific foremen, and experienced staff put Uberto at the top of most designers' wish lists. The firm of 63, which opened in 1982, expertly executes tricky and extremely detailed high-end residential renovations in Manhattan. First-rate cabinetry is produced in a 9,000 square foot shop located on the historic Red Hook piers in Brooklyn and overseen by a graduate of the Lycée Professionnel des métiers du bâtiment, considered the finest woodworking school in France.

Principal Pierre Crosby, a graduate of the University of Virginia School of Architecture, is known as an intelligent, soft-spoken man who pays extraordinary attention to detail and brings a measured manner to his work. Clients boast that Crosby works to remedy any situation and still meets deadlines. Crosby's elite clients can expect to pay top dollar for his stellar finishes and consummate perfectionism.

"They were fantastic and the owner was very responsible." "The millworkers were especially amazing." "Quality is unparalleled." "Good political and management skills." "Pierre Crosby is a gentleman. A real man of his word." "His French craftsmen are a goldmine—an undiscovered treasure trove." "Get a price from Pierre first!" "The company reflects its people, trustworthy." "Pierre and his crew are obsessed with getting it perfectly right."

William Paster Inc.   4   4   4   4.5
153 West 27th Street, Suite 1001, New York, NY 10001
(212) 242 - 3403   williampasterinc@yahoo.com

General contracting

"Always deferential to the client," this contractor " redeems the profession" for anyone who has ever had a negative building experience. William Paster will take on complete renovations or just a few rooms, as well as ground-up residences anywhere in Manhattan. The firm often works closely with architects, who praise its skill in executing finely detailed, complex projects.

We hear the "calm, patient, considerate" Paster, who started the business in 1997, is admirably "good at negotiating the relationship triangle of architect, client, and contractor." A carpenter by trade, Paster started building theater scenery off-Broadway, which ultimatley led to his role of general contractor. Paster assembles a group of thirty "amiable, trustworthy and polite" crew members, and manages the project personally on-site. His firm also fields a woodworking studio for ultra-custom architectural millwork. Sources tell us there is no layer of bureaucracy—Paster is happy to give out his personal cell phone number.

The firm will take on a smattering of small tasks for repeat clients with budgets for kitchen and bath at $50,000, but the bulk of business is guts at around $2 million.

"Reliable, flexible, honest, good-humored. Diligent with punch list!" *"Wouldn't use anybody else."* *"On time, on budget, dependable, friendly people, always left house clean, really good people and beautiful work."* *"We were expecting a baby, so timing was key. Baby was born on September 17th, expected job completion was September 15th and actual completion was September 5th!"* *"He can even resolve any issues with the apartment building staff."* *"We would not think of using anyone else!"*

Hiring a Decorative Painter or Colorist

A wall-sized mural that recreates a Pompeiian gallery . . . majestic Greek columns beside the swimming pool . . . famous storybook characters dancing along the walls of a child's room . . . these enchanting effects are the work of decorative painters.

Decorative Painting: A Master Tradition

Decorative painting is an art form that uses techniques that have been passed down through the centuries from one artisan to the next. Today's decorative painters come from a variety of backgrounds—some have fine art degrees, many have studied the techniques of the Old Masters in Europe, and some have been schooled specifically in decorative painting.

These professionals carry the legacy of a tradition that was once passed from master to apprentice. Both artists and craftsmen, superior decorative painters have a thorough knowledge of specific historical and decorative styles, and the ability to translate their knowledge into a historically accurate work of art. Others, however, are clearly unqualified to attempt this painstaking work.

There are many forms of decorative painting. Some of the most popular include fresco, murals, and *trompe l'oeil painting*, which is so photographically accurate that it "tricks" the eye into believing in the painted object's three-dimensional reality. Over time, these techniques, materials, and conservation methods have been enhanced and improved, allowing artists and artisans to produce works that have lasted—and will last—for centuries.

When you are considering any decorative painting style, ask to see a portfolio of the artist's work and, if possible, to visit a home that has work of a similar nature. Decorative showhouses are also an excellent venue in which to witness the artistry of decorative painting. Many decorative painters use these showcases to demonstrate their talents. If working with an interior designer, consult with him or her on the project and how it will enhance your overall room design. If the designer finds the artist for you, ask how the referral will affect fees. Artists should also provide you with advance renderings of the work to be produced.

Decorative painting can be a major investment, but certainly one with the potential for exquisite results.

Decorative Finishes: The Art of Imitation

Decorative finishes, often called "faux finishes," are used by painters to add depth or to imitate materials such as marble, wood, paper, stone, metal, and fabric. These finishes can be elegant, whimsical, or dramatic, depending upon the artist and the paint technique utilized. Current trends today include fake wood ("faux bois") paneled libraries, limestone facades, and "washed" finishes. When done by a gifted artist, a faux finish can cost more than the material being imitated. Decorative finishes customize a space with color and texture, often serving as a dramatic reflection of the owner's style.

Pricing Systems

Fees vary widely for decorative painting and are based on many factors, including the scope and scale of the project, the degree of difficulty, and the expertise of the painter. Ask your contractor to provide you with a sample board of the paint technique you desire. Some charge for this service while others include it in the total cost of the project. Decorative finishes can be charged on a per person or on a per day basis, and sometimes a square foot basis, but are usually priced per job.

In the case of murals or decorative finishes, the final product is often considered "art," and is much more subjective price-wise. As with acquiring any work of art, the process of commissioning these works is an involved one. There are meetings with the homeowner, decorator, and painter to determine a style or theme and to incorporate the decorative work into the overall design plan. Time frames for completing a job are usually longer compared with ordinary decorative painting jobs, and costs are considerably higher.

Colorists:

Picking the right colors for your home is a daunting task. Even the most attractive room can be ruined by an improper shade, and paints are notorious for looking different on the walls than they did on the color chart.

Colorists are creative professionals who usually have a background and education in the decorative arts. Both highly skilled and knowledgeable, many are referred to as architectural colorists. These professionals create site-specific custom palettes that can improve the interior and exterior of your house or apartment. If done right, the end result is beautiful—and may even increase the value of your home.

A colorist can be hired directly by a homeowner or brought into the project by a decorator or architect. He or she may be asked to develop a color scheme from the ground up, or after the furniture and trimmings are in place. If your home has historical relevance, a colorist can bring it back to its original splendor. Prices are high for this kind of expertise, but in the long run choosing the right colors will give you many years of pleasure. *The Franklin Report* offers a range of client-tested colorists for your consideration.

Tips when Picking a Decorative Painter or Colorist:

✦ This is a major undertaking, so take the time to interview more than one candidate.

✦ Ask for credentials and images of completed projects.

✦ The decorative professional should provide you with a small sample of what the finished project will look like.

✦ Get price estimates and specifications in writing.

DECORATIVE PAINTERS & COLORISTS

A Trompe L'oeil Inc. 💼   4.5   3.5   5   4.5
255 Huguenot Street, Suite 2501, New Rochelle, NY 10801
(646) 785 - 3587 www.atrompeloeil.com

Singular decorative painting, murals, and Italian plaster

Fresh on the American scene (but certainly no stranger to the faux finish world) is Patrick Bancel, a low-key, understated, and modest artisan whom clients describe as "a master." Originally from France, Bancel studied and worked alongside icons of the decorative painting world for eighteen years before bringing his company, A Trompe L'oeil, to the United States. Bancel's natural ability has been refined by practical experience like a fine wine, and patrons toast him all over the world. A true artist, Bancel has also put his brush to fine art canvases, some of which hang in galleries across Europe and the US.

Bancel studied the Dutch masters and honed his Old World technique working as Assistant Director of the famed Van Der Kelen Institute of Painting in Brussels. Today, he works for himself, taking on projects in and around New York and Los Angeles in every imaginable decorative discipline: faux finishes, trompe l'oeil, paintings on canvas, aging, glazing, murals, gold leaf, and on and on. Bancel is said to possess the kind of dedication to his craft that is rare in this country, and clients say they are "thrilled" to have found him. The excellent prices seem very reasonable for these "works of art."

"His knowledge of Old World techniques is not often seen anymore. It is a breath of fresh air to see this dedication." "Patrick not only has the pure talent needed for top projects, but his personality and demeanor make you want to work with him again and again." "A real can-do attitude." "Clearly a master at his craft, with great vision and superior skill. He is a pleasure to work with." "My living room has been transformed and enriched beyond my highest expectations." "Patrick is extremely likable, modest, and reliable. A real find."

Andrea & Timothy Biggs Painting 💼   4.5   4   4.5   5
279 Sterling Place, Brooklyn, NY 11238
(718) 857 - 9034 amtgbiggs@earthlink.net

Exquisite faux finishes and murals

"There isn't anything these two better halves can't do" say fans of this creative combo. Andrea and Tim Biggs teamed up in 1985, and offer a wide variety of decorative work for both residential and commercial clients. Together they have developed an expansive portfolio. Trompe l'oeil murals are sometimes combined with landscape painting to create architectural illusions. The team also does large-scale murals with a focus on floral, organic or fantasy imagery, and faux finishes—including glazing and marbleizing for ornamental pieces, walls, and ceilings.

Andrea, who holds an MFA from Bard College, and Tim, who studied design at Parsons, often produce their own creations, but they also reproduce traditional artworks, and create pieces that bring the clients' visions to fruition. Sources

*We invite you to visit www.franklinreport.com to view images of their work.

179

say they collaborate closely with designers and architects to integrate their work into the overall design. One architect "can't imagine anyone not being pleased," and clients concur, praising work that is "easy on the eye, easy on the budget."

"Andrea and Tim are both extraordinarily talented." "I love working with them—they're honest, businesslike, and reliable." "Their faux-marble work has held up beautifully for ten years and counting." "They always do what they commit to—flexible, professional, and client-oriented." "They listened well to what we wanted, and came up with a selection of suitable samples." "Prices are extremely fair, and they've never gone over budget. They could charge more, but don't." "Such a delight, they even played lovely classical music while working." "Head and shoulders above the rest." "In a word—beautiful."

Andrew Tedesco Studios Inc. 　　5　4.5　4.5　5
122 West 26th Street, New York, NY 10001
(212) 924 - 8438　www.andrewtedesco.com
Timeless decorative painting and murals

Clients say Andrew Tedesco is a "versatile and brilliant artist," praising his quality and creativity—from high-end glazing and gold-leaf ceilings to murals, trompe l'oeil, and fine art. Tedesco has done residential and commercial work, both on-site and in his studio, since 1990. Impressed with his ability to take their ideas to another level, clients note Tedesco adapts the work to fit the space while balancing their taste with his style of painting. He is known to work with the city's top decorators, and is routinely seen at Kips Bay and at the French Design Showcase. In addition to Manhattan's Upper East Side and Upper West Side, Tedesco's work takes him around the country on projects in Miami, Chicago, and Boston.

A fourth-generation artist, Tedesco was educated at Parsons School of Design, and also spent time working with Broadway scenic artists. He has drawn on these experiences to create a unique personal style, often using the palettes of Old Masters. With three artists on staff, Tedesco "delivers the sort of top quality work that only true artisans can take credit for." We're told his impressive results may come at a premium, but are well worth it. KB 1998, 2000, 2002, 2004.

"'Savant' decribes Andrew perfectly." "He is especially good with ceiling murals, and jobs that require a lot of classical detailing and historical research." "All our clients love his work—he tries his best to satisfy the most outrageous requests from our clients." "Adheres to deadlines, and provides advance technical drawings that help our clients visualize the final outcome." "An extremely high-quality painter." "He is not only creative and inventive in his concepts, but his execution is outstanding." "Andrew's talent is complemented by his charming and engaging personality." "He always keeps up with the latest techniques, and new presentation methods." "A truly talented artist."

Applied Aesthetics 　　4　3.5　4.5　5
90 Valentine Avenue, Glen Cove, NY 11542
(516) 759 - 2188　aapaintstudio@netscape.net
Decorative painting, gilding, and plaster finishes

Sought after by some of the most reputable decorators and architects in New York, Jennifer Hakker and the team at Applied Aesthetics perform all kinds of decorative and specialty painting. Specializing in plaster finishes, gilding, and wood graining, Hakker also handles trompe l'oeil, painted furniture, and fabrics. References say she is a marked creative talent who shows a real interest in the ideas her clients bring to the table. Loyal fans appreciate the "consistently superior results," so much so that Applied Aesthetics is often called upon to work on their second residences and vacation homes.

A Long Island native, Hakker studied at the Fashion Institute of Technology, and finished up at the American College in London. She began stunning audiences with her decorative painting talent in 1985. We hear clients are so in awe of her finishes, they don't give her bill a second glance. KB 2001

"Takes decorative painting to new heights." "A magician with paint!" "Applied Aesthetics are modern-day masters." "The final project is always more brilliant than I imagined." "Jennifer and her crew are the most reliable, focused, and talented decorative painters I have ever worked with." "Her work is consistently superior, and she is extremely professional." "I would never have anyone else touch my walls." "Impeccable attention to detail."

Audra Frank Painting 📷
1118-A North Avenue, Plainfield, NJ 07062
(800) 293 - 2212   www.audrafrankpainting.com

Exceptional straight and decorative painting, wallpapering, and color and product consulting

See Audra Frank Painting's full report under the heading Painters & Wallpapers

Carol Cannon 📷   3.5   3   4.5   5
32-45 37th Street, Astoria, NY 11103
(718) 956 - 9334   www.carolcannon.com

Decorative painting, murals, and color consultation

Clients are equally impressed by Carol Cannon's dedication to her craft and by her decorative painting, which includes all types of special effect treatments for walls, ceilings, floors, and furniture, and murals in both classical and abstract motifs. We hear the "charming Cannon" is unsatisfied until she can capture exactly the right color. References describe her as reliable, fair, and very honest. Known for her trellis mural at Nicholas Antiques in the D&D building, Cannon works throughout New York City and the Hamptons. In addition, she has been known to travel the country, or the world, to handle projects in the vacation homes of her clients.

With a fine arts degree from the School of Visual Arts, and a degree in art therapy from the New School, Cannon started her own business in 1990. She also performs interior renovation for the Frick Collection on the Upper East Side. Fees depend on the commission, but are typically "a very good deal."

"Carol is a softspoken woman with amazing talent." "The work speaks for itself." "Delivers that dreamy look." "Can get you exactly the right texture, color, and mood." "Carol's abilities have thus far been without limit, her skills without peers." "She can create free-hand drawings of anything." "Very accommodating—works hard to get it right." "She should be charging more but doesn't." "Very consistent and very professional."

Chuck Hettinger 📷   4.5   3.5   5   4.5
208 East 13th Street, New York, NY 10003
(212) 614 - 9848   chettinger@nyc.rr.com

Notable decorative painting and color consultations

Self-taught artist Chuck Hettinger merges the skills and sensibilities of mixed media and decorative painting with great success. Since 1980, he has focused on decorative surface work, including special glazes, stripes, faux bois, and marbling. A notable specialty is his stenciling, which is often custom-designed and site-specific, and has been described as "modern and practical." Hettinger's mixed media work is shown in New York galleries, and sold to patrons both locally and around the world. In addition to his other projects, he will do color consultations.

A number of distinguished clients and top decorators recommended Hettinger, labeling him "a true artist" who also has "a sense of humor." They say working with this witty, friendly, and easygoing artisan is a treat. Hettinger hires extras as he needs them, still coming in with final totals in the middle of the range.

"Chuck likes to stay on the cutting edge, always comes up with unique ideas." "An uncommon person—you can sense he loves the work." "Knows what to do and how to do it—beautifully." "Not the most expensive but if you're looking for the lowest bid, don't bother." "The stencil work is really fantastic."

DeersTooth Hand Painted Murals	4.5	3.5	5	5
& Furniture				

10 Cedar Street, Dobbs Ferry, NY 10522
(914) 674 - 6413 www.deerstooth.com

Whimsical murals and decorative painting; hand-painted furniture

From their first visit to this small company's "storefront headquarters"—a virtual portfolio of their work complete with painted rugs, windows, and shelves—clients are enamored with DeersTooth. Founded in 1998 by artist Lisa Samalin, this firm specializes in murals, decorative painting, and hand-painted furniture, and is known to paint on almost any surface. Samalin, who studied fine art at the School of Visual Arts, corrals her small stable of artists to create projects that are described as thoughtful, inspired, and magical. Whether transforming an Upper East Side restaurant into Portofino, Italy or turning a residential dining room into a 1920s speakeasy, clients say Samalin uses her taste and talent to "really connect" with their vision.

Sources report that Samalin thoroughly researches each project, and spends hours consulting with the customer prior to putting brush to wall (or anything else they let her paint). Throughout the process the team is said to be detail-oriented, showing a genuine concern for the client's needs—and all at a reasonable price.

"Her talent is a gift. A pleasure to be around." "The only way to describe the magnificence of Lisa's work is to say that she is divinely inspired." "She is generous with her time, her creativity is boundless—and she is really nice." "Lisa is no ordinary painter, she is an enchantress." "I was pregnant and knew I was having a girl. We found Lisa to paint a garden theme in the nursery, but I was scheduled to have the baby delivered before I could see the finished room. When I came home from the hospital, I was greeted by the most magical nursery I could have ever imagined."

Donald Kaufman Color	5	3.5	5	5

336 West 37th Street, Suite 801, New York, NY 10018
(212) 594 - 2608 www.donaldkaufmancolor.com

First-class architectural color consulting

Donald Kaufman and his partner and wife, Taffy Dahl, are recognized as America's foremost architectural color consultants. Using their own proprietary pigment-saturated paint, the duo mixes custom paint colors to uniquely suit the site location, the intensity of the light, the interior fabrics and trim hues, and the personality of the client. Both trained in the fine arts, Kaufman and Dahl have developed a devoted clientele of color aficionados including Richard Meier, Mariette Himes Gomez, and Philip Johnson (who gave them "color carte blanche" for his New York apartment). About half their work is done for architects and decorators and the other half directly for homeowners.

In business since 1975, Kaufman and Dahl arrive with a rather large rolling suitcase of thousands of brushed samples, and go to work considering each room rather like a doctor approaching a patient. They bring to this specialized craft a wealth of experience and specific, discrete analysis. While clearly masters, there is a "yin-yang" to their views, with Kaufman more focused on the technical, and Dahl more sensitive to the ambiance. Between them they get it exactly right, and are never miffed if the client asks for a "whiter shade of pale."

The firm has created custom color palettes for innumerable residences across the country, and also for galleries and museums including the Frick, the Metropolitan Museum of Art, and the J. Paul Getty Fine Arts Center. Commercial endeavors include the Delano Hotel in Miami and the Calvin Klein flagship store in New York. There is a minimum consultation cost of $7,500. The pair has also written two books on color, which display and outline their philosophy. Eighty-four standard shades of their specialty-mixed paint may be purchased directly by calling 201-568-2226 with gallons at $66 to $85.

"Genius, they understand color better than anyone." "I was skeptical that their paint colors could make a difference, but the depth and luminosity of the paint is magical." "All of the finest decorators and painters in New York know and respect Don and Taffy." "The millwork glows as it never did before." "I would highly recommend them to anyone. While not cheap, they clearly can make more of an impact than a decorator if you are on a tight budget." "They make an otherwise agonizing process fun—with a glorious result."

Ira Smolin Painting

1435 Lexington Avenue, New York, NY 10128
(212) 831 - 0205   www.smolinpainting.com
Straight and decorative painting, wallpapering, and color consultation

See Ira Smolin Painting's full report under the heading Painters & Wallpapers

James Alan Smith 🏠   5   4.5   4.5   5

PO Box 2580, Southampton, NY 11969
(631) 457-9561   jamesalan56@hotmail.com
Stunning decorative painting and murals

Boosters attribute James Alan Smith's "breathtaking" accomplishments to the wide range of superior skills he brings to his decorative painting. Smith, who holds a master's degree in dance from Ohio State University, is known for the lyrical style of his work, which includes complex trompe l'oeil and murals on both canvas and walls. Smith's parquet patterned floors, hand-painted in Japan oils, round out his skills in all areas of a room.

Smith's education in the decorative arts came from his mentor, the late master Richard Lowell Neas, and time spent learning and teaching at the Isabel O'Neil Studio in New York. Enchanting clients since 1983, Smith's work is described as phenomenal; moreover, his personable and trustworthy disposition "make the entire process a pleasant experience." Sources say Smith is "the anointed one" in the world of high-end interior design—and fans say, deservedly so. Expect to pay a pretty price for beautiful work. KB 1987, 1990, 1991, 1995, 1998, 2000, 2005.

"It's hard to get better than James." "My relationship with James began with the installation of a magnificent mural in my dining room. He has since continued to work his magic on two more homes." "The team working with James has a rhythm and hand that is remarkably consistent with his own." "Fabulous. A real gentleman." "James gets the picture and then paints it flawlessly!" "Goes out of his way to make sure that everything is always more than perfect." "The top and only choice for those that can afford him." "James has been doing projects for twenty years for me. His work is superb, he's extremely talented, and easy to work with."

	Quality	Cost	Value	Recommend?
	✚	$	◆	★

Joe Stallone

	5	4	5	5

75 Riverside Drive, Suite 2R, New York, NY 10024
(212) 787 - 2011

Impressive decorative painting and finishing

Joe Stallone's renowned talents are in high demand among New York's top decorators and glitterati. A specialist in high-end wall glazing, architectural gilding, faux semi-precious stones, and pattern painting on floors and furniture, Stallone is also known for using rare faux woods in painted marquetry. Adding to this impressive repertoire, we're told he does "super-realistic" faux wood graining, and a wide range of different faux marbles.

Stallone and his work have been featured on Martha Stewart's Home Show, and in numerous publications, including *The New York Times, Architectural Digest,* and *Town & Country*. He is said to be efficient, organized, neat, and courteous, and maintains the highest quality of craftsmanship on projects large and small by working on every job himself—one at a time.

In business since 1987, Stallone has developed and refined his skills in decorative painting and finishing. He graduated from the world's oldest and most prestigious decorative painting school, the Van Der Kelen School in Brussels, studied at the Leonard Pardon Decorative Painting School in New York City, and received both a bachelor's and a master's degree in art. He has taught at the college level, and conducts workshops in decorative painting. All this experience doesn't come cheap, but then again, his peers sometimes charge even more.

"A true professional." "He is a genius—absolutely fabulous." "I will use him forever." "Joe is always in demand." "Clients know they are getting an amazing artist, and his work will be admired for many years to come." "A one-man show with impressive results." "Joe treats each client and project with TLC." "My clients are blown away by his talent."

Karin Linder

	4.5	3.5	5	5

629 East 6th Street, Suite 5, New York, NY 10009
(212) 598 - 0559 www.karinlinder.com

Remarkable frescoes, trompe l'oeil, and decorative painting

Known for her faded and romantic style, trompe l'oeil, frescoes, and decorative finishes, artist Karin Linder has officially been in business since 1983, but has had a brush in her hand since childhood. Clients come back to her project after project not only for her "extraordinary" painting skills, but for her expert design sense. We're told Linder is efficient, getting in and out of a project in record time, and that having her in your home is a "real treat." Examples of her extensive portfolio have appeared in design publications like *Architectural Digest, Town & Country,* and *House Beautiful*. For this "lifelike," "exquisite" work, expect to pay significant prices.

"She is a treasure." "The designs she created were not only gorgeous in and of themselves, but also incorporated elements that made them blend with the color schemes and patterns of other elements in the rooms." "Karin is an encyclopedia in her knowledge of interior design." "Not only did she make my apartment into a canvas with her spectacular painting skills, she also had great design ideas." "Very unique and special." "Karin gave my kitchen European country charm." "Everything flows together which was my hope—her imaginative artistic ability made it a reality for me."

	Quality	Cost	Value	Recommend?
	+	$	♦	★

Lillian Heard Studio 🛍   3.5   3.5   4   4.5
790 President Street, Suite 3R, Brooklyn, NY 11215
(718) 230 - 8693 www.lillianheardstudio.com
Murals, Venetian plaster, stenciling, and painted floors

Lillian Heard specializes in decorative plaster techniques, including Venetian plaster and traditional lime putty plaster, producing walls that resemble polished marble, stone, or fresco. In addition to her skills in specialty plasters, Heard is known for the spare style of her "atmospheric landscape" murals. She and her small team also do painted floors, stenciling, and glazes.

Trained at the Art Institute of Chicago, Heard has been attending to clients in New York City since 1994. (Heard's first job was the Dakota Jackson showroom wall at the D&D building.) She does some work internationally. Prices are in line with the going rates, but fans say their chief reason for choosing Heard is her "elegant, but durable" work.

"Lillian's work is lovely." "Everyone that walks into my apartment comments on the beautiful walls and ceilings she executed." "Her work has lasted for four years in absolute pristine condition." "Heard is a sensitive and dedicated artist, but expensive." "Very pleasant to work with." "Accommodating with scheduling, and has a great attitude." "Exceeds expectations on every project—my first choice for any job."

Miro Art Inc. 🛍   5   4.5   4.5   5
20 Bronxville Gen Drive, Bronxville, NY 10708
(914) 237 - 6306 www.miroart.org
Majestic decorative painting and frescoes; restoration of paintings and furniture

"Majestic" is the best way to characterize the singular achievements of Polish-born artist Roman Kujawa of Miro Art. Whenever Miro Art is on the case, you can be sure that the quality of the work is "breathtaking" and the projects very high-end (for example, the Blue Room in the White House). The team is in high demand by some of the most prestigious decorators and architects in New York City—and in the country. Specializing in decorative painting finishes like gilding and imitation limestone, these artists are also well known for their frescoes and trompe l'oeil work, along with their meticulous restorations of paintings and furniture, which are said to be "expensive, but so worth it."

"A 21st century master!" "Roman is not just talented, he is a true artist, and worked miracles in some very difficult situations." "He is very Creative with a capital C!" "A treasure—nobody does it like him." "A very accommodating man and a pleasure to have in my home." "Not just good but great." "Their work is exquisite."

Osmundo Echevarria & Associates 🛍   4   4   4   4.5
129 West 29th Street, 11th Floor, New York, NY 10001
(212) 868 - 3029 oeche@aol.com
Hand-painted furniture, floors, and murals

Manhattan's swank decorators have only the finest things to say about decorative painter Osmundo Echevarria. We're told that whether he's painting an intricate marquetry design or revamping a beloved piece of furniture, Echevarria and his studio artists "have a masterful grasp of all kinds of painting techniques." Old and neglected furniture is transformed with antiquing; gilding, distressing, and marbleizing. The firm's reproductions of chinoiserie scenes are especially notable. If that's not enough, we hear the life-like murals and painted floors are also splendid.

The Cuban expatriate Echevarria fled his homeland in the 1960s, and went on to receive his degree from the School of Visual Arts. He opened his own firm in

1991, and today leads ten craftsmen. Sources tell us a "visit to his studio is a must." Clients also say Echevarria stands by his work and meets tight deadlines. Costs are upper-end.

"Always easy to work with, Osmundo has the patience of a saint, and the aesthetic appreciation and artistic ability of an Old World master." "Mundy has worked on nearly every one of our projects in some manner or another over the last fourteen years. And for this I am grateful. He has played no small part in making our projects as successful as they have been." "Honest, timely, amazing artistic talent. Goes the extra step to do a perfect job."

Pigments of the Imagination 　　　　4.5　4　4.5　4.5
43-01 21st Street, Suite 232A, Long Island City, NY 11011
(718) 392 - 5780　www.diannewarner.com
Magnificent murals and painted floors

Pigments of the Imagination performs "beyond the figments of your imagination," a praise often uttered by its Park and Fifth Avenue clients. The inlaid floors, magnificent murals, glazing, and gold leaf finishes are said to be unmatched. We're told that Pigments' decorative painting is so good, decorators make a point of selecting the firm for those impossible-to-please clients.

The team may be high on clients' lists, but their feet are planted firmly on the ground. Dianne Warner and Robert Graey have many years of experience between them. The duo formed the company together in 2003. Customers say the firm's work "is never compromised," and that the duo lives up to high expectations generated by its upper-end prices and estimable reputation. KB 1996, 2004.

"We worked with Dianne for fifteen years prior to Pigments, and her work is the finest in the industry." "Pigments comes up with the most imaginative original solutions that are perfect for every client." "The quality of decorative painting surpasses anyone else, and if there is a problem such as a leak that affects the mural, they return immediately to repair it." "Our room was transformed from an empty box into a sophisticated and beautiful boys nursery with an airplane mural on the ceiling." "Dianne and her partner Robert are lovely and extremely talented, and in terms of professionalism and likeability, they are tops." "We think the two are great!"

Red Branch Painting Studio 　　　4.5　4.5　4　4.5
42-50 Richards Street, Brooklyn, NY 11231
(917) 804 - 9961　www.redbranchstudio.com
Detailed murals, stencil floors, and decorative painting

Surpassing clients' expectations, Alan Carroll of Red Branch Painting Studio creates spectacular murals, stencil floors, and decorative finishes (wood graining, faux bois, and marbling) for some of New York's prominent citizens and celebrities. Prestigious decorators remark that Carroll's outstanding trompe l'oeil "comes alive with imagery."

An Irish import, Carroll carries on his family's 80-year tradition of decorative painting. Stepping onto these shores in 1994, Carroll first tested the waters with a top decorative firm, and then sailed out on his own. Recently the company has been developing sophisticated digital printing techniques, allowing them to achieve "stunning" effects at a reasonable cost. Reviews are first-rate, and no one quibbles over his "well deserved" steep prices. KB 2003, 2006.

"Alan's work should be in museums!" "He painted an extraordinary landscape." "Created three artistic masterpieces that are breathtaking. Each piece of art brings the room to life and is always the center of conversation when we entertain." "Alan's ability to color match is remarkable. His faux wood is the best I have seen." "I had him paint my library in mahogany to match some paneled doors, and you can't tell the difference no matter how close you get."

Renaissance Decorative Artistry 💼   4   3   5   5
111 East 14th Street, Suite 202, New York, NY 10003
(212) 252 - 2273 www.deanbarger.com
Murals, custom stenciling, and faux finishes

Impressing celebrities and top designers since 1987, Dean Barger and the small team at Renaissance Decorative Artistry have developed quite a following for their sophisticated murals, multilayered stenciling, and high-end faux finishes. (In fact, some say they are reluctant to share him with the public.) Dividing his time between New York City and Maine, Barger, who has a fine arts background and studied in Europe, is described as pleasant, low-key, and an absolute delight to work with. We hear his work is inspired, and his rates more than fair. KB 2002, 2005.

"Not only an excellent artist, a really nice guy." "Dean's murals are conversational, and excite everyone who sees them." "Extraordinary work." "Stencil work so fine." "I don't want to give him up." "Dean is wonderful, his work outstanding."

Skinner Interiors 💼
71 First Place, Brooklyn, NY 11231
(718) 243 - 1378 www.skinnerinteriors.com
Straight and decorative painting, wallpapering, and plasterwork

See Skinner Interiors' full report under the heading Painters & Wallpaperers

Studio Unique Inc. 💼   5   3   5   5
40 Norman Place, Tenafly, NJ 07670
(201) 894 - 8912 studiounique@yahoo.com
Spectacular faux finishes, decorative textures, murals, and high-end straight painting

Those who discover this rising star are treated to a truly "unique" approach to decorative painting and finishing. With endless ideas, exquisite taste, and the passion to consistently come up with something new, owner Andrei Kievsky is at the helm of Studio Unique. Well-traveled and multitalented (his resume includes Cultural Attache for the Russian Ministry of Foreign Affairs), Kievsky has always been drawn to art. After immigrating to the US in 1989, he followed his heart, and fine-tuned his natural artistic abilities by studying at The Isabel O'Neil Studio in New York City and The Finishing School in Long Island.

Since 1994, Kievsky and his small team of artisans have been thrilling decorators and homeowners with projects ranging from the truly traditional to the innovative and cutting-edge. We hear that if a finish "doesn't exist," he will invent it—much of his spare time is spent in his studio experimenting and developing new techniques. Creatively, sources say, Kievsky effortlessly adapts to any style and scenario. His business side is equally impressive, resulting in excellent prices for his customers. Citing the prompt, professional, and trustworthy way Kievsky runs his operation, clients recommend Studio Unique with wholehearted enthusiasm.

"An inspiration, anyone working on his team should be honored." "Andrei's work is spectacular." "Honest, dependable, hard-working, and extremely talented." "We use

him for all of our decorative finishing and consider him to be a great find." "Committed to excellence." "If you are looking for something completely different and beautiful, Andrei is the man." "In addition to the exceptional work, Andrei returns every call, is prompt, attentive, and genuine."

Woerth Street Studio

3.5   3.5   4   4

1382 Third Avenue, Suite 364, New York, NY 10021
(212) 472 - 3356   www.woerthstreetstudio.com
Decorative painting

Monica Tatjana Götz can trace her painting roots to three generations of Götz gilders on Woerth Street in Hof, Germany. In 1999, she founded Woerth Street Studios in Manhattan after a formal education in fine art and graphic design. Nicknamed "Ms. Restless" by her friends and clients, painting is not just an occupation, but an obsession for Götz. She specializes in "classic glazing, dramatic textures and patterns, marbling, woodgraining, trompe l'oeil, and gilding, applying them to walls, ceilings, floors, trim, and furniture." We hear that Götz's ability to match colors to her clients' desire is "almost uncanny." Her interests also extend to photography and hand-crafting accessories to match from lampshades to objets d'art.

Modest to a fault, Götz insists "I just like making cool stuff." From roots in custom decorative and residential work, her firm has expanded to commercial work and larger jobs. Götz prefers to "crew-up" from New York's deep bench of hungry painters, schooled in the fine arts. Her clients describe her as a "problem solver" who seems to be "everywhere at once." Woerth Street's practical and "hands-on" work relationships ensure that the only surprises are happy ones.

"Her trompe l'oeil is truly a site to see." "Extremely flexible. Open to suggestions and will implement them on the spot if possible." "Very nice to work with. I would not hesitate to either use again or recommend to a client or friend."

Yona Verwer Studio ▪

4   3   5   5

336 East 13th Street, Suite C5, New York, NY 10003
(212) 674 - 5015   www.yvstudio.com
Decorative painting and murals

Lauded as a true artist, Yona Verwer has been doing decorative painting and murals for New Yorkers since 1986. While the firm does all kinds of specialty finishes including glazes, gilding, stenciling, plaster effects, and faux finishes, it's her murals that especially charm clients. These pieces, described as whimsical, fanciful, and inspiring, are applied on canvas and on walls.

Verwer, who is from Holland, holds an MFA from the Royal Academy of Fine Art at the Hague. She creates contemporary pieces of her own design or will execute any style a client prefers, including classical and trompe l'oeil. References report she has an extensive planning process designed to keep the customer involved at every stage of the project, and is a patient and understanding collaborator. Sources tell us that Verwer is extremely ethical, citing her fair prices and the exceptional quality this company delivers.

"Yona did a beautiful mural for our twins' bedroom, and worked wonderfully with us to achieve a room our kids will enjoy for years." "She is very talented and a pleasure to work with." "Yona is an excellent artist—her work is truly valuable." "Yona is patient, understanding, and will work through anything to make sure the designer and end user are happy." "Not only do I feel I got more than I paid for, but visitors have uniformly remarked that the piece 'makes the room' and upgrades the overall value of the apartment."

FIRMS WITHOUT ONLINE PORTFOLIOS

Alton Inc.   4   3.5   4.5   4.5
40-19 35th Avenue, Long Island City, NY 11101
(718) 784 - 4230   tom@altonpainting.com
Straight and decorative painting and wallpapering

The painter of choice for a number of high-end building professionals who cater to Upper East Side clients, Alton offers competent straight and decorative painting and wallpapering. We hear Alton excels in faux finishes, trompe l'oeil, graining, gilding, Venetian plaster, and stucco. Unlike many other practitioners of decorative work, this firm does all of its own prep work, which we're told is exemplary.

A native of Croatia, Tom Buric set up shop in 1996. Buric juggles seven projects simultaneously, with excellent results clients peg to the example Buric sets for his team of guys. Achieving its goal every time, the firm scores high points for quality and price.

"Tom has made many of my clients happy!" "I was so impressed with Tom's workmanship and incredible reliability that I have continued to use him for every project." "Very responsive, agreeable, and takes his work to heart." "Great prep work." "They did a fantastic job—well worth the money." "Their Venetian stucco is extremely beautiful." "You won't be disappointed—ever."

Bill Gibbons Studio   4   4   4   4
3080 Hull Avenue, Suite 5E, Bronx, NY 10467
(212) 227 - 0039   www.billgibbons.com
Murals on canvas

Bill Gibbons creates traditional murals on canvas in his New York City studio; once painted, they are installed like wallpaper in the client's residence—and can be removed and reinstalled as needed. His work includes classical pieces, architectural renderings, landscapes, and trompe l'oeil paintings. In business for over fifteen years, he works frequently with New York City interior designers, as well as with private clients.

Gibbons developed a clientele in 1988, after earning a BFA from the School of Visual Arts and an MFA from the New York Academy of Art. A one-man show, we understand his prices may be bolder than some others, but then so, fans say, is his art.

"Bill is capable of many different styles of painting, but I especially admire his classical murals." "I consider him a complex artist with a big range." "Bill's murals are mysterious and magical." "My clients thank me over and over for bringing him into the project."

Decorative Art & Design   5   4   5   5
418 Lakeside Drive, Stamford, CT 06903
(203) 968 - 8445   www.decartdesign.com
Extraordinary plasters and decorative painting

Mile' Djuric of Decorative Art & Design has created a fan base that is a virtual who's who of New York—yet we hear he remains down to earth and wonderful to work with. The designers and architects that Djuric collaborates with often hire him to work in their own homes in addition to those of their clients. In the design community, this is the highest compliment.

The Yugoslavian-born, and largely self-taught Djuric constantly strives for excellence. Djuric is said to pick apart common problems in the industry, so he can make sure they do not happen on his projects. In business since 1990, Djuric focuses his small business on the artful application of decorative plasters

in every imaginable form. We hear this master of color uses rare techniques, and is continually experimenting to come up with new ideas. From twenty different plasters to satin, flat, mica, and glossy finishes, clients are thrilled with the results. While he's not the cheapest guy on the block, Djuric's work leaves customers in awe.

"An innovator, and he is always pushing to be the best." "Mile's style is not only beautiful but extremely inventive, it's not your average wall finish, this is art." "He is my favorite craftsman to work with—insightful, professional, and above all—talented." "Mile' is a true gem." "He is great with clients, and stands behind every job he does. I'm fortunate to know him." "A wonderful artist and businessman." "Djuric is such an interesting person—he is so talented, and when you get to know him, you immediately have a friend." "Not only is Mile' wonderful, he assembled a staff of artisans who are equally nice to have on any project." "I wish all of my contractors were just like Mile'."

Edward Micca Decorative Painting   4.5   3.5   5   4.5
312 Bayport Avenue, Bayport, NY 11705
(631) 472 - 3559 edmicca@yahoo.com
Distinctive decorative and straight painting and wallpapering

A one-man operation, Edward Micca keeps tight control of his projects from start to finish, making it a priority to do all of his own prep work. Micca will do any paintable surface, creating interesting "leather" walls, tinted and colored plasters, wood graining and glazes, and pearlized finishes. He has also been known to tackle trompe l'oeil projects with finesse.

A favorite among professionals, the "charming" and low-key Micca has been creating his decorative finishes in New York and farther afield (in the United States and Europe) for more than 25 years. Micca's grandfather worked with a brush, so it was natural that he picked up painting. Clients tell us his work rivals some of the best in the field. We are told Micca is "extremely popular" and only takes on two projects at once, hiring assistants as he needs them. Given the high-quality work he produces, clients are pleasantly surprised by the modest costs.

"Edward is extremely capable of making interesting suggestions concerning color and technique application." "The quality of his work exceeds the cost." "He wallpapered a bedroom with a cathedral ceiling in my home. A carpenter accidentally broke through, and Mr. Micca was able to repair this with what very little leftover wallpaper remained. I have yet to find the horizontal cut and joining the repair necessitated." "His glazing is absolutely amazing!"

EverGreene Painting Studios   4   4.5   3.5   4
450 West 31st Street, 7th Floor, New York, NY 10001
(212) 244 - 2800 www.evergreene.com
Trade only—Decorative painting, murals, plaster, and restoration

A large New York City decorative arts studio with a national presence, EverGreene has both the manpower and the experience to handle large commercial projects or finely finished residences. Working exclusively through decorators and architects, the 27-year-old business employs experts who are fluent in every aspect of decorative painting, murals, plaster, and restoration work. While Ever-Greene fields over 125 employees on projects nationwide, and provides literally thousands of samples to peruse and inspire, we hear the firm's dedicated and diverse staff still make personalized service a priority. Though upper-end, prices have been described as generally worth it for the body of knowledge the Ever-Greene team brings to a project.

In 2001 EverGreene added a hand-painted wallpaper division to its repertoire, named Studio E Inc. Located at the EverGreene office, Studio E creates hand-painted couture wallpapers for sale through Niermann Weeks Inc. in New York.

"Extreme—very thorough and excellent team." "Although big, each project is per-formed with amazing artistic results." "Sweeping images in large scale." "Huge ca-pabilities—they can do just about anything." "I call on them regularly for their talent, professionalism, and creativity."

Grand Illusion Decorative Painting Inc. 5   5   4   5
20 West 20th Street, Suite 1009, New York, NY 10011
(212) 675 - 2286   pfinkel@earthlink.net
Outstanding decorative painting, special finishing, and murals

Fans rave that Pierre Finkelstein of Grand Illusion produces "extraordinarily realistic" finishes using original 18th- and 19th-century techniques. In business since 1986, his small firm focuses on very high-end residential and museum decorative painting and finishes, and also creates murals.

Finkelstein comes to the decorative painting world with an impressive back-ground, including training at the Van Der Kelen Painting Institute in Brussels. He has authored two books on the subject of decorative painting and finishes and teaches classes in his studio. Working with some of the top decorators and designers in New York, the firm's private client list has its share of instantly rec-ognizable names. Patrons consider Finkelstein's work outstanding, and while we hear it can cost a pretty penny, there's no doubt about its remarkable quality.

"Brilliant—all the masters rolled into one!" "The best painter of faux bois in the world!" "Best of the best." "The only issue is how to get on his dance card." "No at-titude and a joy to be around." "Don't expect to get by on the cheap." "Inspiring to be around his work. It brings back the past." "Charming and wonderful to work with."

Lauren J. Chisholm   4   3   5   4.5
20 West 72nd Street, Suite 707B, New York, NY 10023
(917) 538 - 7684
Decorative finishes, murals, and hand-painted tiles

Approaching each project with a positive attitude and sincere interest in pleas-ing her clients, Lauren Chisholm does decorative painting, murals, and glazing in New York City and on Long Island. We are told that she does extensive research and planning for her trompe l'oeil and mural projects, making the end result all the more spectacular. Chisholm also hand-paints silk pillows with botanical de-signs, and will hand-paint kitchen tiles, bath tiles, and sinks.

Chisholm started taking on clients in 1993, and has since developed a long list of repeat customers. Impressed with the quality of the work she turns out, Chisholm's patrons often comment on her masterful trompe l'oeil and lovely brushstrokes. Clients are pleased with the rich work and appreciate the moder-ate prices.

"Lauren is a phenomenal artist." "A very talented woman who can design and paint almost anything." "Lauren painted in seven rooms in my house over the past year. She has painted everything from curtains on the dining room wall to court jesters in my den. Her work is outstanding and her imagination and ideas are endless." "She is a delight to work with and deserves only the highest praise." "Magnificent skills."

	Quality	Cost	Value	Recommend?
	✚	$	◆	★

Natasha Bergreen & Liza Cousins

4 4 4 4

40 East 94th Street, New York, NY 10128
(212) 427 - 2655 ncbnyc@aol.com

Admirable decorative painting and finishing; color consulting

For over nineteen years, the partnership between sisters Natasha Bergreen and Liza Cousins has benefited from their complementary talents. Bergreen and Cousins provide an abundance of services, including painting stripes, gilding, glazing, marbleizing, and other classic and contemporary finishes—plus color consulting. Although their specialty is decorative painting and finishes, the sisters have begun to accept some design projects as well.

Bergreen studied with Leonard Pardon after attending art school and both she and Cousins studied decorative painting in London. We are told their talents are in demand by many top designers who have worked with the duo for years. Given the superior quality of the artistic finishes, the firm's high prices are expected. KB 2001, 2002.

"Natasha and Liza have been my primary decorative painters for the last nine years. They are wonderful. Five Star." "Not your average decorative painter—most original and creative. A pleasure to work with—no prima donnas!" "We have been working with them since 1995. They are always enthusiastic and provide a great deal of creative input. My clients have always been impressed with their work and the style they inject into a project."

Optical Grays Inc.

4 3.5 4.5 5

300 East 93rd Street, Suite 40A, New York, NY 10128
(212) 686 - 7371 opticalgrays@yahoo.com

Trade only—Decorative painting for floors, walls, and ceilings

Reserving his firm's services exclusively for top-trade professionals, Andy Holland of Optical Grays brings a background in art and theatrical scenic painting to the decorative painting business. Holland, who opened the company in 1984, has had work published in top design magazines, including his noteworthy custom-designed ceilings, stenciled walls and floors, and unique floor marquetry design technique. Holland and his team have also been known to create hand-painted silk panels. We're told this firm works well as part of a team of architects, contractors, and decorators, and contributes "buoyant personalities as well as skills." The high-quality work Optical Grays helps produce leaves clients bubbling over with appreciation for both the awesome finish and excellent prices.

"Andy is full of life." "Exquisite floor painting." "Excellent problem solver and good listener." "Works for the best of the best."

Painting by Picker

219 East 85th Street, New York, NY 10028
(212) 535 - 6380

Straight and decorative painting and wallpapering

See Painting by Picker's full report under the heading Painters & Wallpaperers

Paulin Paris

5 5 4 5

409 East 64th Street, Suite 6H, New York, NY 10022
(212) 472 - 2485 www.paulin-paris.com

Superb high-end decorative painting, sculpture, and murals

The spectacular creations of Paulin Paris grace the fashion houses of Dior and Valentino, the Zuber fabric and wallpaper studio, and elite homes around the world. Trained at the Ecole des Beaux Arts, this master takes his inspiration from the gilded past—but creates murals, paintings, and sculptures that exude modern allure. But lest you think of Paris as a temperamental "artiste," references applaud his willingness to tailor his vision to the client's desires. In fact, insiders roundly praise Paris' ability to approach a project as an artist, while also working alongside the architect and designer.

For over sixteen years, Paris has traveled from his native France to exclusive homes around the globe. Paris divides his time between his studios in New York, Paris, and Los Angeles, where he works on murals, paintings, and sculptures and handles five to six big projects per year. An average project takes roughly two months and a hefty investment, but no one's complaining. In fact, Paris' fellow artists at the most elite levels of fashion of design are clamoring for his time—a sure indicator of the brilliance of his work.

"I have never seen such beautiful work!" "If you can afford him, you will spend the rest of your life admiring his work." "Paris is extraordinarily talented, and a wonderful person as well."

Penna Inc.

405 East 51st Street, Suite 6F, New York, NY 10022
(212) 935 - 5747   www.pennainc.com

Straight and decorative painting, custom glazes, wallcovering, and leather installation

See Penna Inc.'s full report under the heading Painters & Wallpaperers

Pennington Painting & Restoration LLC

800 Hoydens Hill Road, Fairfield, CT 06824
(203) 319 - 1800   fpball@yahoo.com

High-end interior and exterior painting, decorative finishing, cabinet glazing, and wall-papering

See Pennington Painting & Restoration LLC's full report under the heading Painters & Wallpaperers

Richard Pellicci Decorative Painting   4.5   3   4.5   5

65 Radnor Avenue, Croton-on-Hudson, NY 10520
(914) 271 - 6710   yofaux@earthlink.net

Decorative painting and murals

"Low-key," "charming," and "talented" are just three of the adjectives clients have used to describe Richard Pellicci. This former book illustrator, who studied at The New York Phoenix School of Design (now the Manhattan outpost of Pratt) was inspired to take up his brush after seeing exquisite decorative finishes on trips to Europe.

A one-man show since 1985, Pellicci is a "secret source" for customers who adore his "beautiful" work and original ideas. Pellicci also matches fabrics and can contribute to the entire design process. His repertoire includes wall glazing, faux bois, strie, marbleizing, and murals, all well worth their affordable prices. His work has been featured in major design publications.

"It is a rare combination when you find a faux finisher who is both brilliant, creative, and incredibly diligent." "Old school and richly executed accomplishments." "I only allow great artisans to work on my home, and Richard is at the top of my list." "Richard is talented, warm, funny, considerate—and when he leaves, his work is a lovely reminder of him." "His color choices literally make the project." "The grape leaves he did in my powder room are so good that people think it's wallpaper." "Richard has painted a variety of finishes—his plaid is our favorite, but his traditional work is also wonderful." "Impeccable design sense."

	Quality	Cost	Value	Recommend?
	+	$	◆	★

Teles & Adams

| | 4 | 4 | 4 | 4.5 |

PO Box 682, Palisades, NY 10694
(845) 365 - 2917   telesadams@optonline.net
Decorative painting

Uptown clients absolutely adore this duo for both their "professional approach" and "incredible talent." Coming from unique backgrounds (James Adams went to Yale and studied forestry, biology, and art history; Brazilian-born Rubens Teles is a member of the faculty of The American Folk Art Museum and Marymount College in New York City), they bring a wealth of ideas and inspirations to their decorative painting business, launched in 1992.

Teles and Adams work frequently with decorators and are praised for their ability to handle a wide array of finishes and techniques. But industry insiders say their American- and English-inspired designs really put them on the map. (In 1994, the partners wrote a book entitled *Folk Finishes*.) In addition to painting walls and floors, Teles and Adams are involved in customizing a line of accessories for the home; clients love the fact that they can take a swatch of fabric or carpet, and have their trays, waste baskets, and other items painted to match.

"Perfectionists, and more—impossible to get better than this." "I love working with Rubens and James—they are polite, professional, and fun." "Sometimes hard to get because of their busy schedule, but worth the wait." "They have such a complete range of skills in addition to their folk art specialty." "You have to see their work to know how happy I was to write the check." "My clients love having them in their homes—so respectful and so talented." "Their strength is Americana faux painting and stenciling." "They came up with the perfect color within minutes." "The price was completely appropriate for the work."

The Finished Wall

| | 4 | 3.5 | 4.5 | 4.5 |

325 Smith Street, 2nd Floor, Brooklyn, NY 11231
(718) 855 - 5426   thefinishedwall@yahoo.com
Gilding and fine decorative wall finishes

Described by clients as "energetic," "creative," and "professional," Angela Caban of The Finished Wall has been both a Broadway actress and a serious student of fine art and restoration. We hear her unique background gives Caban a unique perspective on decorating a home or business with paint and plaster. Making her debut as a decorative painter in 1996, Caban really connected with her customers, who say she does something "magical" for each individual project. Recently, she reproduced all the Tiffany tile and decorative finishes in the newly restored Hudson Theatre.

Sources say Caban is an expert at wall finishes. In addition to working in clients' homes, she can be found in her studio creating pieces for future installation, such as gilded panels or murals. Prices are described as surprisingly moderate for the level of skill, quality, and customer service Caban and her small staff provide.

"Angela is a real person—somebody you can shoot the breeze with." "Her work has exceeded our expectations." "Angela's enthusiasm, knowledge, and professionalism are what truly set her apart from her competition." "Really fun to work with." "It is a treat to find a fine craftsman who is also bright, personable, witty, and willing to make that extra effort." "It is very obvious that Angela loves what she does and it shows—her work is exceptional."

	Quality	Cost	Value	Recommend?
	✚	$	◆	★

True-Faux Murals, Inc.

4 4 4 4.5

103 West 70th, 4C, New York, NY 10023
(917) 385 - 5462   www.true-fauxmurals.com

Murals and decorative finishes

City designers are awestruck by father-and-son duo Glenn and Austin Palmer-Smith. Forming True-Faux Murals in 2001, the team combines its talents with pretty impressive results. True-Faux paints everything from animal themes to elaborate landscapes, executing murals with "great beauty." Fans say the Palmer-Smiths thoroughly enjoy working with each other. Clients note their trompe l'oeil "is the real deal."

Glenn spent years working in the photography industry before switching gears, while son Austin (who always knew he would be an artist) chased his dream and studied fine art in college. For their services, expect to wait in the queue: Only ten commissions are completed per year, and we hear True-Faux's fashionable clientele are happy to pay its designer prices.

"Outstanding talent." "It's lovely to work with a father-and-son team who are so sensitive, creative, and willing to please." "Glenn and Austin are wonderful and easy to work with. They are not temperamental, and have always met deadlines, sometimes unveiling the work earlier." "There is usually something witty in their work, which my clients adore, and they are utterly professional, which my staff adores."

Hiring an Electrician or Lighting Designer

Birds of a different feather, these two professions still flock together, both peddling a little Thomas Edison magic. An electrician's main concerns are practicing safety and delivering convenience. A lighting designer's interest is in conjuring atmospheres that at once massage a client's mood, amplify architectural elements, and provide late-night safety. While the true measure of a successful lighting design job is its inspiration to the eye, a good electrician's work is invisible.

How to Choose an Excellent Electrician

Dealing with electricity and wiring is intimidating, and for good reason—you are placing your family and home at risk if it is not handled properly. This is not the area for cutting costs by doing it yourself (or by hiring the lowest-priced service provider). Think of Chevy Chase putting his Christmas light cords into one giant, sagging cluster of adapters in *National Lampoon's Christmas Vacation*. Hilarious, but maybe a little close to home.

The first thing you should consider is safety. Companies that don't take the time to meticulously lay out projects should be avoided, as should firms that perform hit-and-run installations or pass off cheap product. Talk to contractor and homeowner references to get the inside scoop on what firms do inside the walls. Make sure to ask safety-related questions, and if your prospective electrician seems unsure, move on immediately.

You'll also need to identify the right electrician for your scope of work. Some do only large installations while others concentrate on service and repairs. A company that specializes exclusively in "designer" electrical work (such as the lighting of artwork and retrofitting museum-quality finishes) may not be geared for a large gut renovation. In addition to providing the high-voltage infrastructure that supports the myriad outlets, switches, fixtures, and appliances in your home, many electricians also install the low-voltage cabling that supports audio/visual, telecommunication, computer, and lighting systems. For these low-voltage systems, they will typically not install the hardware or do the programming, but should coordinate with the specialists who do.

How to Choose an Excellent Lighting Designer

With the exception of its role in nighttime security, lighting design is an aesthetic enterprise. Whether bathing interiors in a soothing glow, dramatically highlighting the architectural features of your home's facade, illuminating artwork, or bringing a magical feel to landscapes, a lighting designer tries to capture a mood. These professionals work as consultants, sitting down with the client and walking through the space to come up with a lighting scheme that best reflects one's lifestyle. As such, expect them to ask a lot of questions to pinpoint what presses your buttons. And speaking of buttons, don't be pressured into buying lighting schemes, fixtures, or systems just because they're deemed the best technology out there. What's best for you is what counts.

A lighting design professional integrates fixtures (both industrial and custom-created) with high-tech lighting control systems such as Lutron HomeWorks, Vantage and Lighttouch, to achieve their vision. In some instances, especially when only low-voltage wiring is involved, they can install their own work without the help of an outside electrician. Though for the most part, these designers will produce lighting layouts and the electrician will perform the installation and interface with the control systems. Whoever is responsible for programming these systems should walk the homeowner through the control operations.

Important Pre- and Post-Project Considerations

Electrical and lighting work often requires cutting into a wall to gain access to wires. There are two issues to think about here—cleanup and repair. Sheetrock debris and plaster dust are very difficult to clean up, so the electrician should put up protective plastic sheeting to keep dust from infiltrating your entire house. Some will repair the wall with plaster, but it is unlikely that they will sand and repaint it. Be sure to discuss this beforehand, clearly identifying the extent of the electrician's responsibility—and get it in writing. When doing renovation or installation work, your electrician may suggest adding additional wiring for future use. This may sound like he's just trying to charge you more, but it's actually a very good idea. It is easier to add wiring and setups in the beginning for that dreamed-of central air-conditioning system, six-line phone system, or computer network you envision in your future. This avoids the headache of having to tear up walls and floors several years down the road, and saves a great deal of money, too. Also, before your electrician or lighting consultant leaves, make sure you know which switch controls do what and that all circuit breakers are labeled properly. Do not let him disappear without doing this, because he is the only one who knows. Wandering around in the dark in search of a phantom blown fuse, or being tormented nightly by landscape lights that snap on at 3 AM can be quite annoying.

On Cost

For smaller jobs and service calls, which include repair and maintenance, most companies charge an hourly rate. Hourlies for electricians in New York these days range anywhere from $60 to $160. Some companies charge a set fee for a visit, or a higher rate the first hour, then have flat-rate charges for each task performed, such as per outlet relocated or fixture installed. Others insist on doing a consultation to provide you with an estimate before any work is started.

On new, large-scale electrical installations and renovations, the electrical contractor will submit a total bid for the work. The price should be broken down by each task performed so you can compare apples to apples with other bids. A company's standards in relation to product and safety, the depth of its resources and the demand it's in can all affect cost. Fees for contract renovation work are typically higher per hour and per square foot than those for new construction.

Lighting designers may also charge hourly rates—anywhere from $100 to $160 an hour—for design and oversight of installation. For larger projects they may charge a fee based upon the total budget or square footage of the project.

With a little preparation, you will be able to save money by saving the service provider's time. In most cases, an electrician will need to cut into walls to gain access to wires or to replace fixtures. This is something you should think about before the workmen arrive. You may want to move or cover up that priceless antique sideboard rather than leaving it to the electrical crew. By taking care of the little things in advance, you allow your electrical professional to get right to work, you won't have to fret about your antiques, and your billable time will be shorter. In the end, consider the company with the best reputation for quality and service, not just the low bidder.

Licensing, Insurance and Permits

You should only consider a full-time licensed professional for your electrical needs. A license from the Department of Labor is required for any electrical work, and all work must be filed with the city. This includes any installation related to light, heat, and power. As always, ask for the contractor's license number and proof of workman's compensation and liability insurance. In contrast, lighting designers require no license to operate. However, if they're going to program lighting control systems, they should be certified by the manufacturers to do so. And in either case, your electrical contractor should always be responsible for obtaining all permits necessary for your job.

Guarantees and Service Agreements

Your service provider should always stand behind all of his or her work. Be sure to ask about service agreements. Many electrical professionals provide regular "check-ups" and inspections. It may seem like wasted money at first, but over time these measures can prevent an emergency. Lighting designers may offer focusing sessions to re-adjust and fine-tune your lighting scheme according to season.

ELECTRICIANS & LIGHTING DESIGNERS

📁 FIRMS WITH ONLINE PORTFOLIOS* 📁

Christopher Jon Electrical 💼 📁 📁 📁 📁
159 Northern Boulevard, Suite 202, Great Neck, NY 11021
(718) 389 - 9898 www.christjon.com
Residential electrical installation and service

Greg Yale Associates Illumination 💼   **4.5**   **4.5**   **4**   **5**
27 Henry Road, Southampton, NY 11968
(631) 287 - 2132 www.gregyalelighting.com
Subtle, elegant landscape lighting design

Greg Yale's landscape lighting designs are at their best when you barely notice them; his palette consists of glows and auras, not spotlights or glares. A nationally recognized expert in the field, Yale has been working to inform and reshape the landscape design world through sophisticated, artistic lighting. We hear clients appreciate both the aesthetic and the practical side of his work, as Yale's designs increase security and allow homeowners to enjoy their gardens any time of night. In recent years, Yale has been moving his signature low-voltage approach inside the home, taking on large indoor residential projects. Given the national scope of the company, the staff is relatively small: ten people. However, that figure includes both a master electrician and an expert tree climber. In other words, you may have to wait to get Yale to work on your property, but once he's on the job, all the angles are covered. The company also offers long-term maintenance contracts. Fees are at the top of the market, but Yale's Ivy League-caliber designs make clients light up.

"A master." "His lighting reshaped our property. At night, looking out, we can still enjoy our garden. It's just beautiful." "Maintains a very subtle effect." "Lets you enjoy your garden whenever you want to."

Levy Lighting 💼   **4**   **4**   **4**   **4**
214 West 29th Street, Suite 1006, New York NY, 10001
(212) 925 - 4640 www.levylighting.com
Commercial and residential electrical installation and service

Should you desire, Ira Levy can tap into his theatrical lighting experience to bring some pizazz into your home, but those with more subdued tastes applaud him as well. His five-person company is noted more for its versatility than a particular style, and to that end it takes on residential jobs, commercial projects, product launches, fashion shows, and everything in between. Clients report favorably on Levy's process, which includes a walkthrough followed by a proposal, both free. Once hired, Levy provides detailed plans, including specifications for the necessary fixtures, which you can purchase through him. He does not, however, install the lights himself (though the company does have a division for on-site adjustment). With design fees from $2,500 on up, Levy's expertise is not

*We invite you to visit www.franklinreport.com to view images of their work.

199

for those on a tight budget, but clients appreciate the variety of effects he can produce, from clean white illumination to whirling stars, projected on a child's bedroom wall.

"They take the initiative to go above and beyond."

Studio 87 🛍	**4**	**4**	**4**	**5**

301 East 21st Street #3-M
New York NY 10010
(917) 582 - 7822 www.studio87.com
Commercial and residential electrical installation and service

Well-connected principal Staci Solomon-Ruiz, an eighteen-year veteran of the business, works with New York City homeowners to design a lighting system that best suits the unique character of their space. Ruiz, who started her career with a fixture-hunting trip through Europe, is expert in both traditional and modern styles from around the world. Clients say she is talented, aggressive about problem solving, confident, and rock solid on deadlines.

We hear that Ruiz's relationships with lighting manufacturers allow her clients to get good prices, a key element in an aspect of decoration that—by her own admission—is never at the top of anyone's budget. Ruiz herself charges a flat consultation fee based on the square footage of the home she's working in. Her services—which don't include installation—are just north of cheap, but those who utilize her talents end up seeing the light.

"Willing and able to work within budget constraints." "Talkative, lively, assertive, and professional. She was always accessible and knew exactly what we wanted." "Moves quickly and gets it done on a budget." "She can quickly survey a space and determine the best way to light it in terms of design and functionality." "Always keeps the client in mind, even when she doesn't have to."

FIRMS WITHOUT ONLINE PORTFOLIOS

A.S.M. Electric	**3.5**	**3.5**	**4**	**4**

353 West 39th Street, New York, NY 10018
(212) 695 - 0498
Commercial and residential electrical installation and service

A.S.M.'s small size (two people: father and son) gives the company both flexibility and freedom, their strongest assets. Neil and Barry Korman, who value their non-union independence, tackle both large electrical installation jobs and tiny service calls. We hear clients appreciate the firm's expertise and efficiency—and the fact that it brooks no nonsense from even the most prestigious GCs, whether working on a brownstone or a brownout. The small size of the company does have its disadvantages: A.S.M. won't take on new construction projects and there's often a wait for service. However, references report that the Kormans show up when they say they will and don't charge any more than they have to.

"Won't let you get stuck in a corner and then shrug his shoulders. He'll speak up, even if it means less money for him." "Outspoken and on the ball."

AC Morgan	**4**	**3.5**	**4.5**	**4**

80 Brook Avenue, Bayshore, NY 11706
(917) 257 - 2768 morales81@aol.com
Commercial and residential electrical installation and service

AC Morgan is run by Ray Morales, a veteran electrician who puts client satisfaction above all else—he's used to taking off his shoes while working. Morales' eight-person company takes on large residential projects but prides itself on taking small repair and installation work as seriously as complete gut renovations.

Clients concur, telling us AC Morgan is a problem-solving firm that searches for the long-term solution rather than the quick fix. Customers also enjoy Morales' sense of humor. Morales is also said to be very fair in making contract adjustments if necessary. Though some say "his crew is not quite as good as he is," the same sources point out that everyone on the team is impeccably neat, friendly, and more than willing to fix any mistakes. A low hourly rate seals the deal.

"Especially good at problem solving. He took a lot of initiative with regard to the overall picture." "Make sure to get Ray or his second-in-command involved. Sometimes the troops need straightening out, and they're both excellent at it." "Gets right to work and does a great job." "Will redo their work if there's a mistake, however small." "Very, very fair when it comes to prices." "Extremely diligent and competent."

Altman Electric   3.5   3.5   4   4
283 West 11th Street, New York, NY 10014
(212) 924 - 0400   www.altmanelectric.com
Residential and commercial electrical installation and service

Clients praise Altman Electric for straddling the fence between resourceful large company and personable family operation; it has the muscle for big projects, but you can always get the owner—Richard Altman—on the phone. This second-generation, family-run electrical contractor delivers what we hear is high-quality work in a courteous, efficient manner, on renovations and simple fixes alike. Manhattan and Westchester County residential work has been Altman's bread and butter for over 50 years, and the firm has earned a number of repeat clients (who generally receive priority on service calls). The company's minimum fee and hourly rate are said to be mid-range and "completely fair."

"Mr. Altman came on time, efficiently evaluated the problem, and solved it when he promised." "Neat and clean." "I use him for the trickier stuff." "Office staff could be better, but Richard Altman is everything you could ask for in an electrician." "Top-notch service and quality workmanship. Richard Altman is personable, knowledgeable and a true testament to the company's success."

Barth-Gross Electric Co. Inc.   4.5   4.5   4   4.5
110 West 26th Street, New York, NY 10001
(212) 929 - 0446
Top-tier large-scale residential electrical work

In business since 1919, we hear this 35-person firm performs "textbook" electrical work for some of the pickiest locations (fancy hotels, commercial buildings, Fifth and Park Avenue residences) in the city. It's true that Barth-Gross concentrates on commercial assignments, but this firm will still take on large top-tier residential projects—just don't call them to change a lightbulb. One of only a handful of companies endorsed by Lutron for installation, Barth-Gross often gets the first call for complex projects that require sophisticated engineering and coordination.

Owner Roy Barth is an electrical engineer himself, and since he's always involved at the outset of each job, clients report that the estimate is always accurate and expert. We hear any changes in cost, a rarity, are communicated to the client immediately. Barth is widely respected and liked in the industry, not only for the depth of his knowledge and character but for his hands-on involvement. While no one hedges around the fact that this firm is expensive, they all say the cost is warranted.

"One of the best in the business." "There was never a person from this company that wasn't good. And that's pretty much because of Roy. I can't think of a better man." "Perfect work, but expensive."

Cammarata Electric Co. 3.5 3.5 4 4
1673 Unionport Road, Bronx, NY 10462
(718) 409 - 0743

Commercial and residential electrical installation and service

Cammarata Electric recently celebrated its 20th birthday, but unlike most 20-year-olds, it hasn't grown bigger over time. Preferring to maintain a tight-knit family feel to the business, principal Anthony Cammarata has kept the staff size to five and the focus on close relationships with established clients. That includes work for non-profits throughout the city, as well as residential jobs in Manhattan and the Bronx. While sources agree they might not use the firm for massive complicated work, they wholeheartedly recommend Cammarata for standard renovations, installations, and fixes. Existing clients also praise Cammarata and Co.'s response times, saying you can expect service "within 24 hours on a high side of standard."

"Surprisingly good response time for a small company." "99 out of 100 jobs require no additional work. And they'll come quickly for that one job." "Friendly, accessible people."

Coachmen Electric 3.5 3 4.5 4.5
256 West 38th Street, New York, NY 10018
(888) 398 - 3635 coachmen2@aol.com

High-end residential electrical installation

We're told this nine-person company stakes its reputation on customer service, caring for clients on the Upper East Side and in other select Manhattan neighborhoods. Though Coachmen will take small service calls from anyone, it gives priority to current customers, a policy clients appreciate.

Coachmen's stable doors have been open nearly twenty years, and owner Stephen Tate's electrical expertise spans three decades. The bulk of the firm's muscle is put to high-end residential projects, with restoration (think 19th century brownstones) being a particular specialty. Sources occasionally report tardy technicians, but they're quick to add that Tate is conscientious about calling ahead if he'll be late, and fans pardon him in light of his industry-low hourly rate.

"Not a sheep, he'll speak up if something is wrong." "I value his design advice." "When I need something fixed down the line, he remembers the ins and the outs of the building."

Gabe's Works 4.5 3.5 5 4.5
94-49 50th Avenue, Elmhurst, NY 11373
(718) 699 - 6333

Masterful installation and repair of specialty lighting fixtures

Gabe is Gabriel Velasquez, and his works are specialized lighting fixtures, which he repairs. Valasquez has been practicing his trade for close to twenty years, preferring direct relationships with decorators, designers, and architects. Clients tell us he performs assembly, installation, and repair work on elaborate chandeliers, antique fixtures, and custom sconces. The spotlight is on one-of-a-kind high-end fixtures here, handled with exceptional care. Some clients declare they wouldn't let anyone else near their priceless fixtures. Customers also appreciate Valasquez's practice of charging on a per-project basis, giving an estimate before the work begins.

"Calm, helpful, and informative." "He won't take on smaller jobs unless you've already worked with him." "A gentleman and a veteran." "Very high-end and specialized. A true craftsman."

Gunzer Electric   4   4   4   5
36-36 34th Street, Long Island City, NY 11106
(718) 392 - 2219   www.gunzerelectric.com
Commercial, industrial, institutional, and residential electrical work

With almost 30 years in the business, 30 employees, and a guaranteed 30-minute response time in Manhattan, Gunzer Electric's magic number conjures up a great deal of customer satisfaction. While the company works with a handful of high-end contractors on large-scale renovations or restorations—both residential and commercial—we hear the team most enjoys working directly with homeowners, often on smaller jobs. Clients applaud Gunzer's excellent customer service, and say this family-owned and -operated firm treats even the little tasks with a high degree of importance.

Gunzer's expertise extends into all areas of industry troubleshooting and maintenance, as well as specialties like fire-alarm installation, structured cabling for audio/video systems and computers, lighting control design and installation, and—more recently—clean air systems and energy conservation. The firm is also licensed in New York State for fire-alarm installation. While Gunzer's price quotes might cause some clients to cringe, even the cringers admit that the quality is top-notch.

"They are fabulous!" "Everything went exactly according to plan. I am recommending the company to everyone."

K&G Electric Co. Inc.   3.5   3   4.5   4
3925 Broadway, New York, NY 10001
(212) 923 - 2550   www.kgelectric.com
Residential electrical installation and service

K&G Electric is a large, 70-year-old firm run by four brothers who spend the bulk of their time in the field, not in the office. Because of its size and longevity, the company has the expertise and manpower to take on both tiny and immense jobs in any of the five boroughs. Whether it's installing a fixture, doing maintenance work for some of the most prestigious buildings in Manhattan, or conducting an electrical overhaul on a major renovation, this company comes highly recommended. Its rates—charged by the hour for small jobs, fixed prices for large jobs—are standard. While we hear the crews are all business, most clients say they are more than willing to forgo the pleasantries in exchange for rock-solid, high-end service.

"They have been around a long time, know what they are doing and can do it all." "Not the most polite people in the city, but they do the job right and leave it spotless." "Absolutely dependable, highly skilled employees who know what they are doing."

Lamp Surgeon
4 3.5 4.5 5

By appointment only
(917) 414 - 0426 lampsurgeon@aol.com

On-site lamp repair and rewiring

This surgeon makes house calls, and clients are "overjoyed" at such "a unique service"—rewiring lamps right on the premises. Be it a chandelier, a mini-halogen, a temperamental three-way, or a European fixture converted to US voltage, this electrician is on call. Making his rounds in Westchester and New York City, he is even available to assess antique finds before purchase, or to provide a custom lamp shade if necessary. However, Lamp Surgeon will not do new installation work. The surgeon is Roy Schneit, a 30-year veteran of the lighting business and the former owner of a light shop in Manhattan. He works alongside "Nurse" (and wife) Lois, who handles the office. Clients shower the pair with flattering adjectives, including "prompt," "professional," "knowledgeable" and "obliging." Prices—ranging from "fantastic bargain" to "fair deal"—are always quoted over the phone.

"Neat and careful, great with antiques." "His professional competence is matched by his unfailing courtesy and punctuality." "The cost was exactly as he quoted beforehand on the phone." "It would have been such a nuisance to schlep these lamps to a repair shop. And a 'regular' electrician would have charged substantially more." "He gives accurate estimates and works efficiently."

LLE Electric Inc.
4 3.5 4.5 4.5

236 West 26th Street, Suite 605, New York, NY 10001
(212) 924 - 6787

Residential electrical installation and service

This reliable shop specializing in residential work is "definitely one of the better ones" in the city, according to references. We hear clients appreciate the advantage of calling on the same expertise and "nice" crew members that bring in LLE's larger, high-end gut renovation projects for their smaller jobs. Run by Vince Lalomia, who has over twenty years of lighting design experience, LLE also provides lighting design and consultation services to architects, as well as installation of complex Lutron lighting control systems. Peers compliment Lalomia on his professionalism and dedication to the job and to his customers. His clients tell us Lalomia's thoroughness and dependability keep them confident and assured that the job will be done right. Sources say Lalomia's crews are punctual and "very affable." These active problem solvers reportedly get the work done quickly—and always pick up after themselves.

"Vince is a great guy who does really good work." "Incredible. Came out at a last-minute situation and fixed everything." "If left to my own devices, I'm always on-time, so I appreciate LLE's guys showing up when they said they would." "It's difficult to get a great electrician for a smaller job. Thank goodness for LLE."

Madison Electric Company Inc.
4.5 4 4.5 4.5

208-05 35th Avenue, Bayside, NY 11361
(718) 229 - 5520

High-end residential electrical installation and service

Clients tell us over and over that this full-service electrical contractor is one of the most reliable outfits in New York. Madison has been serving both residential and commercial customers in the high-end market here in Manhattan for over five decades. Contractors, architects, and designers all agree that Madison's staff is made up of consummate professionals. We hear the firm turns around estimates quickly, completes jobs on or before schedule, and is great in emergencies. Client's also find Madison's crew courteous, clean and "very knowledgeable in every aspect of our electrical installation needs." References mention that one of the three partners—John Van Blerkom, Pete

Danielsson, or Larry Zassman—will always show up on the job. Clients say all three strive to make Madison a "leader in luxury residential contracting" by providing personal attention and a high standard of quality workmanship at a lower price than you'd expect.

"Top-notch problem solvers. Great attitude. Very can-do efficient and pragmatic." "Highly reliable. I only use Madison." "They do excellent work!" "Really excellent service at decent pricing." "Working with Madison Electric was a great experience. They were always responsive and professional." "The job was completed on time, looked good and every detail attended to. I would highly recommend them."

Manteo Electric Inc.   3.5   3.5   4   4
11 Ocean Avenue, Staten Island, NY 10305
(718) 981 - 6500   manteoelectric@si.rr.com
Large-scale electrical installation and service

With over four generations in business, this modest-sized, multi-talented electrical contractor designs and installs large-scale, top-of-the-market penthouse and brownstone lighting and power renovations, while also taking regular service calls. We hear the firm's lighting design and engineering capabilities are often called upon by industry professionals. References say Agrippino "Pino" Manteo, grandson of the original Manteo, keeps himself, his son, Michael, and the rest of the staff on top of cutting-edge technologies. In addition to structured cabling, "smart houses," and home theater systems, the company is also familiar with fiber-optic lighting and remote lighting control systems that require no wires or cutting into walls during a renovation. We're told Manteo fields a dedicated, knowledgeable, and conscientious crew reflecting the best of the company. Customers confirm Manteo does everything he can to retain their business. It's even printed on the back of their shirts: "Whatever Lola wants, Lola gets." The firm's service is so consistent, landmark buildings use it for general maintenance. But be warned that a consistently semi-high price goes along with the consistently dedicated service.

"He'd rather send one great electrician than four average guys. It usually saves you money."

Michael J. Dotzel & Sons   4   4   4   3.5
402 East 63rd Street, New York, NY 10021
(212) 838 - 2890   mdotzel@aol.com
Light fixture restoration, antique restoration, and art metal work

As befits a company that keeps antique lighting fixtures alive and well, Dotzel has been going strong since 1943. This family-run business repairs and restores chandeliers, sconces, and lamps by reproducing old hardware, recasting metal parts, and restoring finishes. It also reproduces particularly rare items and sells them in a small Upper East Side showroom. While expert antiques dealers and auction houses recommend Mike Dotzel for his skills and service, some customers find Dotzel's prices and persona over the top.

"He's eccentric, but you can't knock his expertise."

Midland Electrical   4   3.5   4.5   4
37-36 61st Street, Woodside, NY 11377
(718) 894 - 4300   midlandele@aol.com
High-end residential electrical installation, upgrades, and service

This mid-sized electrical installation firm has references from high up; it does work for building managers, general contractors, and the Catholic church. Since 1993, principal Fintan Murray has been helming jobs in Manhattan and New Jersey. He prefers large commercial installations. However, we hear that if the company does take on a residential job, a team plucked from the veteran crew of sixteen will get the job done quickly, quietly, and with precision. Clients also report that Murray is good at staying on budget and won't surprise you with "horrible hidden extras."

"A pleasure to have in your home." "Quality work done as promised and completed on time." "Fintan is a fun guy who only gets impatient if people slow him down." "Good quality, great price." "I've used them for seven years and never had a problem."

Mistretta Electric   3.5   3.5   4   3.5
35-07 Riverdale Avenue, Bronx, NY 10463
(718) 548 - 1649
Residential electrical installation and service

This father-son shop takes on anything electric that deals with light, heat, or power. At work for more than twenty years, Mistretta's services range from small repair jobs to complete electric rehabs in gut renovations. We hear the firm can even rewire antique fixtures and will install structured cabling for computers, A/V, and control systems. References recommend Mistretta Electric because the company can be counted on to get the job done. We are told that all at Mistretta are pleasant to work with and produce a solid product for a fair price.

"Very nice man, with good abilities." "Gets the job done in a reasonable manner."

Polyphase Electric Inc.   3.5   3.5   4   4.5
41-20 38th Street, Long Island City, NY 11101
(718) 392 - 0885
Electrical installation and service

The most customer-conscious contractors and discriminating building managers call on Polyphase for residential work throughout Manhattan, from downtown lofts to uptown brownstones. We hear the firm's professionals work on projects varying in size and cost, from maintenance calls to major renovations. References tell us they do good-quality work and are very personable and accommodating. These features, along with very reasonable prices, may be why many clients have asked Polyphase to work on their second homes outside the city as well.

"Great team. A real family feel."

Pro Electric Corp.   3.5   3   4.5   4
137 King Street, Brooklyn, NY 11231
(718) 625 - 1995
Residential and commercial electrical work

References say Pro Electric is a straightforward firm that delivers exactly what it promises: safe, solid electrical installations. The company works throughout the five boroughs, preferring to tackle renovations and restorations. However, principal Vito Liotine—a twenty-year veteran of the business with a no-frills attitude regarding electric work—will pick up smaller projects and maintenance work, especially for repeat clients. We hear his rates are mid-range for the high end.

"Good work and good value." "Owner is deeply involved in all the work."

	Quality	Cost	Value	Recommend?
	+	$	◆	★

Ral-Bar Electricians

3	3	4	3.5

34-09 45th Street, Long Island City, NY 11101
(718) 786 - 9430 ralbarelec@aol.com
Residential electric installation and service

Whether it's creating an entire electrical system in an old building, lighting up the city's public parks, or installing a ceiling fan in your bedroom, Ral-Bar gets the job done for a moderate price. While the company's client list includes the National Parks Department and all of the city's public pools, half their work is residential and according to satisfied customers, Ral-Bar's "terrific" workers do "tremendous work" on jobs small and large.

"Can be a pain to get in touch with, but good on the job."

RHR Electric Co. Inc.

4.5	4	4.5	4.5

135 West 29th Street, Suite 1202, New York, NY 10001
(212) 564 - 8520 joe@rhrelectric.com
Residential electrical work

Though down-to-earth principal Joe Leonard insists that the acronym RHR is "just letters," references say it could easily stand for "reliable, handy, and reasonable." This 20-person, union electric firm has honed its skill on large, high-profile commercial installations for the past 20 years. Because most new buildings in the city are apartments, RHR has wisely shifted its focus to high-end residential and has been doing very well in that world. We hear Leonard and Co. approach their work with a simple and straightforward attitude: they do it right the first time and leave the space clean. We also hear they're great "forensic electricians," meaning that they can figure out what prior electricians did wrong. Because of its commercial past, references report that RHR is not set up to do small-scale work, but they laud the firm's surgical precision on large tasks. For a company that has outfitted several operation rooms, that's expected.

"I've done every single high-end residential project with them for over thirteen years, and they've never disappointed." "They really understand a decorator's needs." "On one installation, they figured out how to run a wiring system up through a velvet-covered bookshelf without damaging anything. You can't get much better than that."

Hiring a Fine Arts Services Provider

Assembling a collection of fine art can be an enlightening and rewarding pastime, not to mention a sound investment. Caring for that same collection can be a royal headache. What seems simple—buying paintings and hanging them on the wall—actually involves a number of steps: transportation, handling, framing, hanging, insurance, cataloguing, restoration...the list goes on. And if any phase of the process is handled improperly, either a single piece or the whole collection can be jeopardized. Luckily, there is no shortage of talented professionals available to care for your pieces at every stage of ownership. And if your collection grows from hobby to serious interest, there are art advisors who expertly oversee the whole process.

Art Advisors

Think of an advisor (sometimes called a "consultant") as the producer of Your Collection, the movie. He or she should make things run smoothly, but never take creative control away from you, the director. A good advisor will know what you have (by keeping a detailed catalog and researching provenance), what you want (by listening well and taking the time to explore your aesthetic), and how to get it (by keeping an eye on the galleries and auction houses). He or she will also handle the details, like framing, handling, and insurance. All of this should be done in an atmosphere of complete confidentiality.

Art advisors sometimes charge by the hour and sometimes on a flat fee, depending on the type of work being done. Because the position demands a high level of expertise, don't expect low rates (around $150 per hour, or its flat fee equivalent, is minimal). However, do expect your advisor to be financially disinterested. All advisors have relationships with galleries and dealers—it's part of the job—but none of these relationships should involve money. In other words, if an advisor is pushing you towards a particular dealer or gallery even if you're not interested, then it's time to find a new advisor.

Going it Alone

A good advisor is a boon to a small collection and almost a necessity for a large, ambitious one, but you don't need one for every little task. To that end, we've included a list of companies in this section that will provide individual services like installation, storage, and restoration. An advisor would normally help you choose these firms, but, with a little research, you can certainly make the choice yourself. Because these professionals are experts, their services are rarely cheap (most charge a high hourly rate). However, hiring a subpar provider can result in damage that fair outweighs the money you might save.

Tips

Here are a few tips on caring for your own collection:

✧ Document your pieces carefully, with photographs and notes on provenance. Even if you're not going to insure an item, this information will help you get organized.

✧ Insist on an appropriate professional. If you need a Japanese ceramic repaired, make sure to find an expert that can do just that. Even a related expert, such as a master of South American pottery, might make a costly mistake.

✧ When transporting a piece from place to place, keep in mind that a standard moving company will not be prepared to properly handle or hang valuable art works. Some companies even refuse to handle fine art, because their insurance doesn't cover loss or damage. Hire a professional.

✧ A frame can make or break a piece, literally. Some frames trap moisture, leading to mold. Others contain damaging chemicals that are released over time. Museum-quality archival frames, while expensive, extend the longevity of your pieces.

✧ Take a holistic approach to displaying your collection. Keep in mind what looks good, what fits together, and what will last. That watercolor may be perfect in the living room, but prolonged exposure to sunlight can quickly fade it to obscurity. Remember: Hanging anything over a source of heat or moisture is dangerous.

FINE ARTS SERVICES

🛍 FIRMS WITH ONLINE PORTFOLIOS* 🛍

Amiel & Phillips 🛍   4   4   4   4.5

PO Box 595, Lenox Hill Station, New York, NY 10025
(917) 863 - 9819 www.amiel-phillips.com
Elite art advisors; interior design specialists

Over the span of their 25-year careers, art advisors Karen Amiel and Ann Phillips frequently saw their peers butt heads with clients' decorators over what paintings to buy. Should the works match the wallpaper, or should they satisfy a grand academic conceit? To neatly sidestep these territorial battles, the pair started a business to advise decorators, architects, and their clients on savvy ways to incorporate fine art into their work. Amiel and Phillips' process is simple: going from a designer's plan, they research the market and produce a variety of options, which the designer and the client choose from. The firm then purchases the chosen works and attends to their storage, transportation, and installation. Amiel and Phillips charge a standard markup on whatever they buy, but sources report that they never try to push overpriced pieces, and can work on any budget. The research is academic and multilayered, but we hear the firm is adept at bringing the client into the process, with regular updates and guided gallery outings.

"They have a thorough knowledge of the art community and were a great help." "They beat all their deadlines and gave a great presentation." "At first, they gave me too many options, but as we kept working together, they learned my aesthetic and now they give me exactly what I need." "They can bring a project in for a lot of money or very little."

Miro Art Inc. 🛍

20 Bronxville Gen Drive, Bronxville, NY 10708
(914) 237 - 6306 www.miroart.org
Majestic decorative painting and frescoes; restoration of paintings and furniture

See Miro Art Inc.'s full report under the heading Decorative Painters & Colorists

FIRMS WITHOUT ONLINE PORTFOLIOS

Alvarez Fine Art Services Inc   4   4   4   4.5

29 West 36th Street, New York, NY 10018
(212) 244 - 5255 www.alvarezfas.com
Restoration, conservation, and framing of works on paper

Alvarez Fine Art Services runs a brisk business in the restoration and conservation of artworks on paper, typically the most vulnerable of artistic media. The seven-person company also operates a museum-quality frame shop, enabling it to offer a complete service package to the top galleries, premier auction houses, and individual collectors who frequent this popular firm. When performed in-house, evaluations (which include a suggested course of action, ranging from a

*We invite you to visit www.franklinreport.com to view images of their work.

simple cleaning to a complete restoration) are free. After that, prices range from the standard to the stratospheric, but high-profile references report that you'll find few better firms.

"I recommend them wholeheartedly." "The kings of paper." "Might not necessarily use them for framing, but their conservation work is really great." "Very responsive."

ARP Art Installations   3.5   3.5   4   4.5
8320 98th Street, Suite 3B, Woodhaven, NY 11421
(718) 577 - 0610   arpartinstall@aol.com
Fine art installation and hanging

Though Allen R. Piper's job—handling and installing fine art—entails hands-on contact with the work of the world's best artists, he maintains a modest, down-to-earth attitude. Since starting off as an assistant at a frame shop, Piper has been making pictures hang straight since 1981, though he's never seen the need to expand the business beyond himself. References report favorably on his efficiency and expertise. Though ARP does not carry liability insurance, we hear Piper is extremely cautious and will stand by the quality of his work. All in all, ARP is an affordable, well-kept secret that we hear is "good at installing pictures but terrible at marketing."

"I've used him for over twenty years." "Knows what he's talking about. I value his design input." "A real human being, very personable."

Cary Cornell Design   4.5   4.5   4   5
1804 Third Avenue, Suite 6, New York, NY 10029
(212) 348 - 1225   www.illhangforyou.com
Top-tier art installation and hanging

Raised by prominent art dealers, Cary Cornell's pool of art biz knowledge is deeper than most—his experience goes back to age twelve, when he would stretch canvasses to earn pocket money. Though he's been working with paintings in various capacities ever since, his art design and installation business began in 1998. The process is simple: First, Cornell and a two-man team come to an apartment and work with the owner to decide on an arrangement. Design, safety, and conservation factors are all taken into consideration. The team then carefully positions each frame and affixes it to the wall by the least intrusive method possible. Cornell reports that he has never damaged a piece, though his exhaustive insurance policy would cover it if he did. High-profile clients (including some of the top decorators in New York) report that he is knowledgeable, careful, thorough, and professional. You can also have Cornell's team do light contracting and renovation work. His rates are certainly high end, but we hear that you only have to hire Cornell once.

"Once he hangs a painting or a mirror, it's never crooked again." "Takes his job extremely seriously." "Not particularly cheap, but he takes the time to make sure it's perfect."

Cirker's   4   4   4   4
444 West 55th Street, New York, NY 10019
(212) 484 - 0200   www.cirkers.com
Fine art storage

Of all the art storage firms in New York, Cirker's probably has the most humble origins—it started as a single horse-drawn wagon in 1873. Five generations

	Quality	Cost	Value	Recommend?
	✚	$	◆	★

later, the company is now a large organization with a solid reputation among art world professionals for safe, secure storage and transportation. Notable features include climate control, computerized inventory, and centrally monitored burglar and fire alarms. References cite the firm's all-purpose, "Swiss-army-knife approach" to storage as a plus: Cirker's has the staff and resources on hand to install, de-install, transport, store, and display pieces of art at a moment's notice. The fees involved are pricey but not unreasonable, given the quality of service and the convenience of Cirker's midtown location.

"They're very accommodating." "Because they offer a good range of services, you don't have to go running around trying to find a million different people to do all the things that need to be done."

Cranmer Art Conservation   4   4   4   4
21 Mercer Street, New York, NY 10013
(212) 966 - 9167 www.cranmerartconservation.com
Fine art conservation and restoration

Art professionals turn to this Guggenheim-trained conservationist for a mix of "science and artistry," an important blend of talents in a field where restoring too much can be as damaging as not restoring at all. Dana Cranmer has been in the business for over 35 years and has worked on thousands of artworks of all stripes (including over 1,200 by Mark Rothko—she was the house conservationist for his organization for six years). Because much of her experience has been on 20th century pieces, clients don't routinely bring Cranmer older works, but she relies on a dedicated staff of four experienced professionals to cover a variety of genres and periods. References report that the firm is small and casual, yet extremely professional. Sources also cite Cranmer's accessible Soho location as a plus. Prices are said to be standard for her level of expertise.

"Recommend her wholeheartedly." "Specializes in 20th century stuff, the weirder and more complicated jobs." "Once I brought her a painting with a quarter-inch hole in a part that was just canvas. Somehow she rewove the canvas and you couldn't see a thing."

Elizabeth Levine Associates   4   4   4   4
565 West End Avenue, New York, NY 10024
(212) 874 - 5334 elassociates@nyc.rr.com
Fine art consultation

Sources applaud Elizabeth Levine's polite manner, dedication to clients, and fiercely independent spirit. Indeed, Levine carved her own path through the wilds of the art market, starting as a painter herself, then teaching at the MoMA until she found her true calling: consultation. She and her three associates help clients with every aspect of their collections, including research, purchase, conservation, sale, and even pure aesthetics; a recent project found her collaborating with a decorator on outfitting a new apartment. Levine's focus is generally on handling contemporary art for newer collectors, but, like anyone who has been in the business for 28 years, she has many long-running clients, private and corporate alike. Sources describe her fees as standard.

"A very sweet woman who has been in the business for a long time." "She really takes care of her clients. Won't just sign you up then forget about you."

ILevel   5   4   5   5
37 East 7th Street, New York, NY 10003
(212) 477 - 4319 www.ilevel.biz
Premier art installation and hanging

We hear that David Kassel and Co. have the manpower to hang your collection and the brainpower to chat about it over tea. Each member of ILevel's ten-person team has a fine arts background, giving the company a leg up in the design phase of the process; while assisting a client in the arrangement of pictures, the staff takes well-researched principles of color, light, art history, and conservation into consideration. As soon as a particular combination is agreed upon, the pieces are carefully hung, with the entire process backed by hefty liability insurance.

ILevel's list of clients includes celebrities, large corporations, A-list decorators, and major galleries, but those with more modest collections need not fear: though it has been in business over twenty years, Kassel insists that the company isn't snobbish about the kinds of pictures it will hang. Rates—charged by the hour—are not cheap, but not super-expensive either. Top references say, "I wouldn't hang a thing without him."

"Extremely professional and understanding of the client's needs." "They actually know the significance of what they're handling, which makes a huge difference." "They keep me sane." "They bring a military-style precision to the job."

Ruth Catone   4.5   4.5   4   4
302 West 13th Street, New York, NY 10014
(212) 367 - 8067   office@ruthcatone.com
Fine art consultation

This art consultancy firm is the brainchild of gallery veteran Andrew Ruth and British press expert Gabriel Catone. The pair joined forces with the mutual goal of developing close relationships with clients and building intelligent, respectable collections for them. To that end, they've kept their pool of clients small (from twelve to fifteen) and close, with regular communication a priority. We hear that helping clients develop a personal aesthetic is a large part of the business, and whether that entails historical fact-finding or guided gallery tours, Ruth and Catone are up for the job.

Though their customers range from experienced collectors to first-timers, the academic bent of the firm and the "high-powered professionalism" of its principals is a better fit for the serious art aficionado than the casual museum-goer. Ruth and Catone focus on the 20th and 21st centuries, and sources say the pair can handle anything in that period. References also praise the firm's policy of strict confidentiality and economic disinterestedness; it works for the client and the client only.

"Serious and academic but not uptight. They are true professionals." "They don't play games—you ask them a question, they give you an exact answer." "Not cheap, but completely worth it. They fix complicated problems with ease."

The Fortress   4   4   4   3.5
49-20 5th Street, Long Island City, NY 11101
(718) 937 - 5500   www.thefortress.com
Art storage

The Fortress is just that, a high-security building designed to safeguard its contents. Only, in lieu of moats and dragons, this storage facility has electronic key cards and around-the-clock video surveillance. Though anything can be kept

	Quality	Cost	Value	Recommend?
	+	$	◆	★

in this Queens safehouse, it is especially designed to protect and preserve fine art and antiques. Notable features include climate control, monitored access, inventory management services, a viewing gallery, and an in-house transportation staff. Clients include top museums and auction houses, as well as private collectors. Prices are certainly on the high end of the scale, but references report that there's plenty of wiggle room, and that The Fortress will open its gates to those on a smaller budget.

"Serious security." "Not necessary for rinky-dink items, but essential for high-end stuff."

Timothy Sammons Fine Art Agents   4.5   4.5   4   4
19 East 66th Street, New York, NY 10021
(212) 288 - 6806 www.timothy-sammons.com
Fine art consultation

This well-connected firm has a direct, no-nonsense approach to fine art transactions. References say the team at Timothy Sammons examines what the client wants to buy or sell, takes the pulse of the market, then puts two and two together. The method is simple, but the expertise is deep. Sammons himself worked at Sotheby's for fourteen years, where he ran the Chinese Art Department then subsequently worked to establish a Trust and Estates Department. A perfect reflection of his interest in both aesthetics and economics, the firm is said to focus on both factors when helping a client with a collection. It also attends to conservation, insurance, and evaluation. No one-man show, Sammons has six senior partners and offices in both London and New York.

"Very professional and very high level." "Not for weekend collectors. This is serious art, bought and sold at the top of the market."

Vara Global Fine Arts   4   3.5   4   4.5
141 Wooster Street, Suite 4D, New York, NY 10012
(212) 475 - 4404 www.varaart.com
Fine art appraisal and curatorial services

Formerly the National Fine Arts Specialist in the appraisal department at the Chubb insurance group, principal Renee Vara uses her insider's advantage when evaluating a collection for replacement value. However, Vara's services go beyond simple appraisal. A senior member of the Appraisers Association of America and a veteran handholder, Vara will follow a collection "from purchase to sale," helping her clients buy wisely, choose a proper frame, catalog accurately, store safely, and sell for the right price, all in an environment of high confidentiality.

Vara herself, an expert in modern and contemporary art, knows how to preserve works in such unlikely mediums as magic marker and day-glo paint. The company will handle older pieces and antiques as well, but those with a collection of pre-Colombian statuary might consider another specialist. Vara is quite active in the art world, staging exhibits and speaking on the subject of appraisal and preservation. Sources say she is well connected, an important factor in a business that depends on relentless networking. Costs are more than reasonable, considering Vara's dual expertise in collecting and insuring.

"Watching her catalog a collection is something else. She's very thorough." "Vara takes confidentiality very seriously." "She has her hand in a bunch of different pots at once, she's very very busy. People in the art world love working with her." "Renee really puts the insurance company at ease. She knows how to work with them and speaks their language."

HIRING A FLOORING SERVICE PROVIDER

From classic brownstones to modern, cutting-edge buildings, New York's architectural diversity and its inhabitants' eclectic tastes result in a virtual flooring free-for-all. Be it carpet, vinyl, wood, tile, stone, cork, rubber, or concrete, flooring creates the basic ambience of a room—and must be as durable as it is attractive.

WHAT ARE MY CHOICES?

Flooring options fall into five basic categories: wood, laminate, vinyl, carpet, and hard tile (see section introduction to Tile, Marble, and Stone).

To get ideas, look through home furnishing magazines, but be sure to pay a visit to a flooring showroom or two as well—flooring is very tactile. Internet sites that will help you learn more about flooring options and the best way to care for them include Floorfacts, a consumer site filled with links and information (www.floorfacts.com) the Carpet & Rug Institute (www.carpet-rug.com) and the National Wood Flooring Association's site (www.woodfloors.org).

After considering the following descriptions of basic floor types, you should be able to choose flooring that best meets your specific demands for style and maintenance.

WOOD

A real wood floor never goes out of style—and probably has the best resale value. It complements every decor, from minimalist to Louis XIV, and generally ages gracefully. The most popular woods used in flooring are oak and maple, which can be stained or color-washed to your exact specifications. Wood flooring can be designed in numerous patterns, limited only by your imagination (and budget). Some of the most popular are parquet, plank, strip, and herringbone. When choosing a stain color, have your contractor apply a few samples and look at them in different kinds of light. Think of the ambience you are trying to create in the room—traditional or modern, casual or formal, spacious or cozy. Wood floors can be bleached—for a light and airy look—or painted. Hardwood floors can be customized to satisfy every taste and personality and installed in any room, regardless of what type of flooring—concrete, existing boards, or particleboard subflooring—is already there.

Aesthetically, a wood floor is stunning. But consider a few issues before you make this your final choice. How much traffic does the room get every day? Hardwood floors can be dented and scratched, especially by high-heeled shoes, and they may not be the best choice for beachfront properties where sand and salt water are traipsed around. Although a variety of urethane finishes provide excellent protection (and shine), they do not completely prevent dents and scratches. These same finishes, however, make today's wood floors much easier to clean and maintain than those of previous generations. Humidity is another factor to consider. If the humidity in your area varies from season to season, a wood floor will expand and contract with the rise and fall of moisture in the air. Storing the wood on-site for a period of time before installing will allow it to acclimatize to the specific humidity level in the home. The service provider should consider whether the floor is being installed in a particularly humid or dry time of the year, and make his measurements accordingly.

LAMINATES

If you love the look of real wood but have an active household, laminate flooring may be the perfect choice for you. Laminates are plastic- or wood-based products that look like hardwood. They come in various textures and are durable and easy to maintain. A wood-patterned laminate floor has some significant advantages over the real thing—for example, it will not be discolored by sunlight and is very scratch-resistant. Laminate floors wear well and usually come with a guarantee of ten years or more, however, they cannot be refinished like wood. Laminates can also imitate the look of stone, marble, or tile, offering a wide variety of creative styles you may not have imag-ined.

Cleanups are also a breeze with laminate flooring. Laminates repel liquid and do not allow stains to set in. This point alone saves your floor, your time, and your peace of mind. Design snobs will, however, look down their noses at laminate as an imitation product.

Both hardwood floors and laminates, while possessing the great qualities of longevity and beauty, are expensive. If you are looking to invest less money, you may want to explore vinyl or carpet floor coverings.

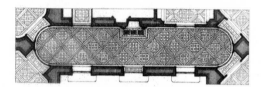

VINYL/LINOLEUM

The retro chic of vinyl or linoleum is often the least expensive choice, and offers more options than any other type of flooring: an eye-popping palette of colors, marbling, prints, and patterns. Linoleum is primarily made from all-natural products such as flax, wood powder, and resin. The backing is made from a natural grass called jute, while vinyl's backing is made from polyester. Both are durable and easy to maintain.

Although it resists moisture, vinyl can stain, so spills need to be handled quickly and carefully, following the manufacturer's directions. The material is vulnerable to scuffing and can also tear—from furniture that may be moved across it or sharp objects that fall to the floor.

CARPETING

A cozy, lush floor covering, carpeting adds warmth, soundproofing, texture, color, and insulation to a room. When considering carpeting, think about whether you'll need a light-, medium-, or heavy-duty type. Industry experts suggest light-duty for occasionally trafficked areas, medium-duty for the bedroom or office, and heavy-duty for hallways, stairs, and other high-traffic areas. Carpeting requires extra maintenance, as stains are more difficult to remove and general cleaning is more work. Wool is much easier to deep-steam clean than nylon, but is more expensive. A protective sealant may be applied to fend off future spills and stains. However, if you or someone in your home is allergy-prone, carpeting is not a good option, since it retains dirt, dust, and other particles.

HARD TILE

Ceramic, quarry (stone, including marble) and terra cotta make up this premium category of floor covering. The look and feel of a hard-tiled floor is unlike any other, with grooves and textures that can be felt underfoot. Often used in kitchens and baths, and an ideal choice for indoor/outdoor rooms, tile flooring can give a distinct look and originality to any room in your home. In light colors, these materials do take on stains, so keep this in mind when choosing hard tile for particular rooms. Tile may be one of the most expensive kinds of flooring, but its remarkable beauty and longevity make it a good investment.

SPECIALTY OPTIONS

Cork floors, made from the ground-up bark of an oak tree, are a hot option these days. A natural material, each tile shows variations in shades and tones, and the final product is finished like a hardwood floor. While comparable to wood in price, cork has a more buoyant feel under the feet. Cork's ability to weather spills receives mixed reviews.

A contemporary, cool option is polished or stamped concrete. Stamped concrete is concrete patterned to resemble brick, slate, flagstone, stone, tile and even wood. Colors and patterns for stamped concrete are often chosen to blend with other stone, tile, or wood. Polished concrete is achieved by grinding concrete floor surfaces to a high-gloss finish that never needs waxings or coatings. Installation can be quite involved and comes at a higher price.

ON COST

Some floor installers charge by the square foot and others by the job. Most providers charge by the hour for cleaning and repairing. If your service provider charges by the hour, confirm whether this fee is per person per hour, or an hourly rate for the whole team. Inquire about whether there is a charge for moving furniture around. And make sure your order includes extra quantities of flooring in your dye lot to replace broken, worn, or stained sections in the future. This is especially crucial with hard tile, which can crack if something heavy is dropped on it, and with any other material which stains easily.

KNOW YOUR FLOOR

Insist upon receiving written information about the care and maintenance of your new flooring. What cleaning products should you use and what should you definitely avoid? Is there a standard timetable for cleaning your hardwood floor or carpeting? Does your carpet warranty come with a consumer hotline for stain emergencies? Who can you call for advice about stains and/or damage?

SERVICE AND WARRANTIES

Before you sign a work agreement, find out exactly who will be installing your floor. Will your contact from the firm be doing the job himself, or bringing in a different crew? Make sure that the firm will supply nails, glue, and other installation accessories. Does the company have its own workshop or warehouse? If so, it will have more control over the product than one that purchases its materials from another supplier.

Finally, ask the company if it does repairs as well as installation. It's always a good idea to have the installer supply the material, so he can't point fingers at the product manufacturer if there is a problem. Both the flooring company and the flooring material manufacturers should have warranties for your new floor coverings. Remember, whatever material you choose, it's only as good as its installation.

FLOORING COMPARISON CHART

RATINGS: Very Poor * Poor ** Average *** Good **** Excellent *****

BASIC FLOOR TYPES:	VINYL	WOOD	LAMINATE	HARDTILE	CARPET
Ease of Maintenance	****	***	****	****	***
Damage Resistance	**	***	****	*****	***
Moisture Resistance	*****	*	***	*****	*
Stain Resistance	***	**	*****	*****	**
Fade Resistance	***	**	*****	*****	***
Scratch Resistance	**	***	****	****	N/A
Ease of Repair	*	***	**	**	*
Softness Under Foot	**	*	*	*	*****
Design/Color Selection	*****	**	**	***	****
◇Price Range (sq. ft.)	$.50 - $4.50	$2.50 - $6.00	$2.50 - $5.00	$2.50 $8.00	$.50- $5.00

◇ The price range is for material only and is to be used as a general guideline.
Prices will vary from supplier to supplier.

FLOORING INSTALLATION & REPAIR

🛍 FIRMS WITH ONLINE PORTFOLIOS* 🛍

800 Rug Wash 🛍
20 Enterprise Avenue, Secaucus, NJ 07094
(800) 784 - 9274   rugwash@aol.com
Rug, carpet, upholstery cleaning and repair; flooring installation and maintenance

See 800 Rug Wash's full report under the heading Rugs—Cleaning & Repair

Architectural Flooring Resource Inc. 🛍   4.5   3   4.5   5
135 West 27th Street, 6th Floor, New York, NY 10001
(212) 242 - 2705
Comprehensive flooring installation, refinishing, and maintenance

"An architect's dream resource for flooring," is what people are saying about Architectural Flooring Resource. The firm supplies, installs, cleans, and maintains wood, tile, cork, rubber, vinyl, laminates, and wall-to-wall carpet. Although the majority of the firm's work is commercial, Architectural Flooring also works on residential projects with architects, designers, and contractors. Owner Cathy Leidersdorff and her team will also work directly with homeowners.

Established in 1993, the company serves all of New York, New Jersey, Philadelphia, the Hamptons, and Westchester. Now with an expanded workforce, the team at AFR have worked on commissions at JP Morgan Chase, AIG, Sony Pictures, and the Museum of Modern Art, to name a few. Enthusiastic clients tell us this company has a great work ethic, is extremely responsive, and can accommodate almost any budget with the vast resources available to it. Pricing is said to be reasonable, especially considering the efficient service and quality product.

"One of the few I really trust." "Excellent installation team." "Open to ideas and suggestions." "Wide selection of floors." "My flooring contractor for the last ten years." "Working with them means the job will be taken seriously."

Chelsea Floor Covering 🛍   4   3.5   4.5   5
139 West 19th Street, New York, NY 10011
(212) 243 - 0375   www.chelseafloors.com
Flooring retail, installation, refinishing, waxing, and cleaning

Clients rave about the personalized service at this family-owned Manhattan flooring business, which has served the area for more than 50 years. Chelsea installs, repairs, and sells carpet, linoleum, vinyl, laminates, pre-finished wood, cork, and rubber flooring. In keeping abreast of the latest in flooring, the company recently added plynyl (a woven vinyl floor covering) to its inventory. Chelsea is also capable of pouring self-leveling concrete floors and refinishing many types of surfaces.

Managed by Bosco brothers Kenny and Dennis Junior, Chelsea Floor Covering delivers fine floors to both residential and commercial clients in all areas of Manhattan, many of whom have come back time and time again. The company works mostly with architects, designers, contractors, and building management

*We invite you to visit www.franklinreport.com to view images of their work.

219

	Quality	Cost	Value	Recommend?
	✚	$	◆	★

firms, but will occasionally work directly with homeowners. The twenty-man firm includes in-house installers and refinishers, as well as account executives that oversee all projects from start to finish.

References describe Chelsea's workers as neat, punctual, and organized. They also appreciate the fact that the company adheres to its moderate budgets and meets the scheduled deadlines.

"Experts in their field." "Delivered floors the day before and installation was done right on schedule." "They were on time. They stayed on budget. They were perfect." "Flexible with scheduling. Responsive." "Haven't raised prices in years! One of the most reliable sources for flooring needs."

Elite Floor Service Inc.   3.5   3   4.5   4.5
12 Saratoga Avenue, Yonkers, NY 10705
(212) 228 - 1050
Wood flooring installation and refinishing

Since opening its doors in 1991, Elite Floor Service has been an established fixture in the Manhattan flooring business. Sources praise the politeness and workmanship of Elite's craftsmen and staff. Customers applaud the conscientious follow-up and reasonable prices. Though some references express minor concerns about tidiness, most say they'd readily recommend the company to friends.

Elite generally works in Manhattan, the surrounding boroughs, and some parts of Westchester. From traditional oak to new age bamboo to dark exotics, this firm works with all types of wood flooring. The company installs, refinishes, sands, repairs, creates custom designs and inlays, and does a lot of staining and pickling.

Helmed by founder Robert Rutledge, a carpenter by trade, the company works with designers, architects, and contractors, and directly with homeowners on mostly residential projects. Elite has a large number of clients who need standard floor installations and refinishing services, and are happy to get them at moderate prices.

"Unbelievably polite, considerate. They do a great job." "I was very pleased. There were no surprises." "Fabulous work ethic." "Have used them for several projects and could not praise them enough." "Never had a problem getting service or correcting something I was not completely satisfied with."

Haywood Berk Floor Company Inc.   5   4.5   4.5   4.5
414 West Broadway, New York, NY 10012
(212) 242 - 0047   hayberk180@aol.com
Expert wood flooring installation, refinishing, custom designs, and repair

As one of the oldest flooring companies in New York, Haywood Berk is now in its third generation of Berks. Otto Berk established the company in 1921. Today grandson Roger, described by sources as a knowledgeable craftsman, is said to run the family firm with dedication and professionalism. Indeed, references are quick to say good things about Haywood Berk's attention to detail and commitment to high-quality service. We also hear that a Haywood Berk floor "holds up for a very long time" and that the craftsmanship is "absolutely superb" with "exquisite" detailing. Many top-tier designers will not consider anyone else for their discriminating clients.

The firm deals only with wood, and performs services such as installation, restoration, custom design, staining, pickling, refinishing, and repair. This residential and commercial firm takes on almost 200 jobs per year in Manhattan, the Hamptons, Westchester, Connecticut, and Los Angeles. Recently, Berk finished projects for Carnegie Hall, the South Street Seaport Museum, Bergdorf Goodman's Jazz at Lincoln Center, The Bloomberg Building, and the newly renovated MOMA. While some wish the customer service was slightly more responsive, most agree these veterans' top-of-the-line product justifies their upper-tier prices.

"Good job. Do it until they get it right." "Hard to get through to them as they often did not return phone calls, but I know that their work quality will always be excellent." "As a decorator, I can schedule their work within two weeks on a consistent basis." "Roger understands his products, but more important he understands his high-end client base." "Clearly not cheap, but an absolute bargain given the quality." "I didn't even know they came in to sand my floors—they protected the furniture so well and didn't leave any mess behind." "Great with matching old and new floors." "Another contractor said the only hope my floors had was to completely take out everything; but Roger came in, fixed the problem areas, and literally saved me thousands of dollars."

Janos P. Spitzer Flooring 🛍 ✓   5   4.5   4.5   4.5

131 West 24th Street, New York, NY 10010
(212) 627 - 1818   www.janosspitzerflooring.com

Elite wood flooring installation, custom design, repair, and restoration

Serving high-end clients and satisfying their discriminating tastes is not an easy task, but clients say Janos Spitzer does both flawlessly—the same way that he creates his beautiful wood floors. Established in 1962, Spitzer installs, restores, repairs, sands, and finishes wood floors for mostly residential and some commercial interiors. From modernists whose cutting-edge designs require floors with low-grain definition so they look like "shields of glass" to traditionalists who prefer classical borders, intricate medallions, or antique finishes, we hear Spitzer "can deliver" with "exquisite" workmanship.

Spitzer works with some of the best designers, architects, and homeowners in Manhattan, the Hamptons, Westchester, and California. His impressive roster of clients includes Mark Hampton Inc., The Four Seasons, David Anthony Easton, McMillen Inc., John B. Murray, and Philip Johnson, to name a few. Known as one of the best in the country by clients and industry insiders alike for his custom designs and inlays, Spitzer works with local, imported, and exotic woods. Everything is crafted and fabricated in his own workshop.

The company has been featured in such prominent publications as *The New York Times* and *Architectural Digest*. This firm is also a member of The National Wood Flooring Association. In the Spring of 2002, Spitzer was licensed by the American Institute of Architects to hold seminars on wood flooring. Always keeping abreast with the latest, Spitzer is an advocate of using Huber Wood and other sustainable products as sub-floors instead of plywood. Recent commissions include replication of an intricate 1895 floor for the Convent of The Sacred Heart and as design consultant for the massive Bloomberg Building. Samples of Spitzer's work can be viewed at his 2,400 square foot showroom, which is regarded by insiders as a "must-see" in the city.

We hear that the Spitzer team is prompt, attentive, accommodating, and very professional. References say that Spitzer himself is honorable, honest, a "hands-on dedicated businessman," and generally, "just terrific to work with." Although some say that his talent is coupled with an artist's temperament, the majority agree that the firm's extensive knowledge, commitment to excellence, elegant designs, and attention to detail are top-of-the-line—just like its prices.

"The top man in the business." "No one can quite match his ability." "He really understands how to make the perfect wood floor." "Excellent work ethic." "Very, very good. Not the cheapest in the world, but worth every penny." "Great people." "A genius with an artist's temperament." "A wonderful Old World craftsman." "In a league of its own."

	Quality	Cost	Value	Recommend?
	+	$	◆	★

New York Flooring    4   3.5   4.5   4

129 East 124th Street, New York, NY 10035
(212) 427 - 6262   www.newyorkflooring.com

Wood flooring installation, refinishing, maintenance, and repair

Residential clients and experts in the home services trade describe their experiences with New York Flooring as "delightful." Some swear by this company, vowing that they will use no other. We're told the firm is prompt, attentive, respectful of clients' wishes, and extremely dependable. According to clients, the quality of the work is some of the best in Manhattan.

Along with its sister company, Eastside Floor Services, New York Flooring works solely on wood floors and performs a wide range of services such as installation, refinishing, maintenance, creation of custom designs and inlays, and repair. This family-owned firm will also do custom work in its in-house workshop. In business for over 60 years, the company works with many well-known architects, contractors, and designers as well as residential clients. New York Flooring has done projects at the White House and Gracie Mansion and for a number of celebrities.

New York Flooring's workers are craftsmen who take "great care and pride" in their work, use only the best materials and "consistently exceed expectations." While most clients feel the floors are worth every penny, others say the company is a bit pricey for standard jobs.

"I recommend them highly." "They're a good value, given the high quality." "Accommodating. Can handle any job." "Good quality. Adequate customer service."

New Wood    4.5   3.5   5   4.5

382 Canal Place, Bronx, NY 10451
(718) 665 - 5400   www.newwoodco.com

Wood floor installation, finishing, sanding, restoration, and repair

Don't let the name fool you—New Wood will bring in a brand new floor, but it will also make your old floor look new again. Since its founding in 1982, the company has been installing, repairing, restoring, sanding, and finishing—plus creating custom designs, inlays, and borders for—wood floors. Owner and founder Peter Downs also does full service consultations for both domestic and exotic woods. The firm serves a predominantly high-end residential clientele, rarely working on commercial projects. Most of the company's projects are on the Upper East Side of Manhattan and in some areas of Westchester and Connecticut. New Wood is a member of the National Wood Flooring Association and the National Trust for Historic Preservation. In 2005, the company opened its showroom on the Upper West Side, which boasts a wide variety of exotics. The showroom is by appointment only.

We hear that these craftsmen are very professional, have an excellent work ethic, and are considerate of the client's home and belongings. New Wood gets high marks for being well organized and responsible. Happy customers delight in the beautiful floors and efficient service, and prices are said to be reasonable for the high-end market.

"Personalized service." "Works well with other tradesmen in the business." "Excellent at mixing stains and matching floors." "Wonderful administrative support and very good at keeping appointments." "A real expert in a difficult trade." "Understands the level of quality my clients demand and knows how to meet a schedule." "I can always depend upon them for consistent, responsive, top quality work."

Pat Pellegrini Floors 🛍   4.5   3.5   4.5   5

29-12 39th Avenue, Long Island City, NY 11101
(212) 533 - 2600   www.pellegrinifloorscorp.com
Wood flooring installation and refinishing

In business since 1960, Pat Pellegrini works exclusively on wood floors, doing installations, repairs, sanding, bleaching, staining and refinishing, and producing standard inlays and designs. His firm works with decorators, architects, and home owners mostly in Manhattan, Queens, Long Island, and the Hamptons. Pellegrini boasts an extensive background in flooring having been raised in the business—his father and grandfather were both flooring craftsmen in his hometown: Bari, Italy. Today, Pellegrini has sixteen workmen, ten trucks, and a 25,000 square foot workroom.

Pellegrini is lauded as a "wonderful man and a great floorer." Clients say he and his workmen are polite, prompt, and committed to doing a good job. If there is a problem, references report, Pellegrini will be more than happy to come back and fix it. The work is said to be of high quality and very reasonably priced. Satisfied customers have used him more than once and recommended him to friends and family, secure in the knowledge that Pellegrini will stand behind his work 100%.

"He laid a beautiful floor—hire him." "Prompt, professional, neat." "Beautiful job, I highly recommend Pat." "Very positive experience. He comes when he says he will." "The floor looks better than what I expected." "It's been three years and the floors are holding up well."

Scerri Quality Wood Floors 🛍   4.5   4   4.5   5

426 East 73rd Street, New York, NY 10021
(212) 472 - 0671   www.gonefinishing.com
Superior hardwood retail, installation, refinishing, custom design, and repair

"Top-notch" is the consensus among patrons of Scerri Quality Wood Floors, who report that they enjoy working both with the management and with the professional, neat, and courteous workmen. Clients note the firm's willingness to listen to customers' ideas and its accommodating approach to projects—a winning combination that brings many customers back year after year.

In business for more than 25 years, the firm focuses on wood flooring, particularly installation, restoration, retail, and repair. Scerri will design, manufacture, and install all of its work. A large part of the firm's business is working with medallions, borders, and inlays. The firm also produces wooden stairways and handcrafted barnyard furniture.

Sources tell us the company serves trade architects and designers as well as high-end residential clients at upper-range prices. While most of its work is on the Upper East Side and in second homes in the country, Scerri also does some smaller projects for more budget-conscious clients.

"There are almost no contractors I've used that I can recommend, but I recommend Scerri highly." "Very efficient—superb work." "Can do any finish you want." "Meticulous. Incredible attention to detail."

	Quality	Cost	Value	Recommend?
	✚	$	◆	★

FIRMS WITHOUT ONLINE PORTFOLIOS

All Boro Floor Service   3   3   4   4
135 East 233rd Street, Bronx, NY 10470
(718) 231 - 6911   allboroflooring@verizon.net
Wood flooring installation, refinishing, and waxing

For years, satisfied clients and well-known contractors have used All Boro repeatedly. Besides installing hardwood floors, All Boro does scraping, refinishing, waxing, and staining. Its workmen also do custom floor projects, specializing in white pickled floors. In business for eleven years, this residential and commercial firm works mostly in Manhattan and some parts of Westchester and New Jersey. It will only supply the floors it installs.

"Hardworking," "skilled," and "honest" are some of the terms clients use to describe this seasoned firm. All Boro gives free estimates that are described as moderate to reasonable.

"Honest. They get the job done under difficult circumstances." "Above what I expected." "Excellent value for the price."

American Custom Wood Flooring   3   3   4   4
3615 Greystone Avenue, Bronx, NY 10463
(718) 548 - 9275

Wood floor installation, cleaning, repair, custom design, and inlays

American Custom Wood Flooring focuses exclusively on the installation, repair, cleaning, and maintenance of wood floors—including custom designs and inlays. The firm generally takes on commercial projects in Manhattan, working with contractors and architects, but will also work directly with homeowners on residential projects. In business for fifteen years, American usually charges by the job and will work on new construction as well as existing structures. This five-man company will move furniture upon request for an additional charge. Clients attest that the firm is professional, prompt, and neat, and adheres to budgets and deadlines.

"They understand their business." "The job is performed professionally." "Have used them for several years. No complaints."

Aronson's Floor Covering Inc.   3.5   3   4.5   4.5
135 West 17th Street, New York, NY 10011
(212) 243 - 4993   aronsonsfloors.com

Flooring installation and retail

Who says flooring has to be boring? Though it's one of the oldest flooring companies in New York, Aronson's doesn't think flooring should be stodgy and dull, but fun and cool. A visit to their showroom feels much like a school trip, with the colorful swatches and samples and Aronson's famous "action figures:" Vinyl Vixen, Carpet Cowboy, and Tile Temptress.

This firm has been serving clients in Manhattan, the Hamptons, Westchester, and other areas in the tri-state area since its founding in 1867 by Samuel Aronson. The company is now owned and run by Aronson's great-nieces, Laura and Carol Swedlow. This residential and commercial business sells, installs, and creates custom designs, and does repair work on wood, cork, rubber, linoleum, area rugs, wall-to-wall carpets, and mats. The eighteen-man outfit works with architects, contractors, and designers as well as directly with homeowners.

Clients are delighted with the efficient service and vouch for Aronson's tidy, punctual, and prompt staff. Pricing is per square foot and is said to be fair and competitive.

"It's obvious that customer satisfaction is important to them." "Crews are self-supervising." "Lovely work." "Recommended for mid-market clients." "Fair quality, reasonable prices, and a good attitude." "Wonderful customer service."

Atlantic Hardwood Flooring 3.5 3 4.5 4
276 West 238th Street, Bronx, NY 10463
(718) 601 - 4082 www.atlanticfloorsny.com
Wood and laminated flooring installation and repair

Established in 1984, Atlantic Hardwood Flooring installs, repairs, and refinishes hardwood floors. Helmed by founder Jerry Plunkett, Atlantic serves mostly residential clients on the Upper East Side and in garden districts of the Bronx. The firm's staff of six can work with most any type of wood. Pricing is by the square foot, with minimums falling in the $750 to $2,000 bracket.

Clients appreciate the professional attitude and workmanship Atlantic brings to the job, noting that the reasonable prices are an added perk.

"Extremely well carried out." "Very impressed with workers." "Work executed professionally from beginning to end."

C&C Flooring 3.5 3 4 4.5
4276 Oneida Avenue, Bronx, NY 10470
(718) 994 - 1496
Wood flooring installation and refinishing

We hear that for standard flooring needs at reasonable prices, C&C is a good bet. Founded in 1995 and managed by brothers Bryan and Keith Chapman, the company installs flooring for new construction and existing structures. The firm specializes solely in wood floors and will clean, repair, restore, refinish, create custom designs, and install.

C&C works mainly in Manhattan with some projects in Westchester, serving both residential and commercial clients. The firm's roster includes a number of high-end management companies, decorators, and architects, as well as Columbia University. With a full-time staff of eight skilled workmen, C&C can handle large projects, but is small enough to give personal attention to each client. Insiders say the Chapmans are perfectionists who are on-site at all times to ensure that everything goes smoothly. Clients describe C&C as responsive, prompt, courteous, and well-priced.

"Absolutely superb work—and fast." "Bends over backward." "Extremely reliable."

Capitol Wood Floors LLC 4 4 4 4.5
100 Louis Street, South Hackensack, NJ 10022
(201) 296 - 0123 brian@capitolwoodfloors.com
Wood floor installation, maintenance, custom design, and repair

Formerly the service center of distributor Hoboken Wood Floors, Capitol branched out on its own and established headquarters in New Jersey. Following closely behind were the firm's many devoted fans. Originally founded in 1932 by Joseph Sakosits, Capitol is now run by grandson Brian Sakosits, who carries on the family hardwood business.

The company installs, repairs, restores, sands, finishes, stains, bleaches, and creates custom designs and high-quality borders for wood floors. Capitol works directly with homeowners in addition to designers, architects, and contractors. Pricing is by the job and estimates are free. The firm has done projects for such exacting spaces as the Metropolitan Museum of Art, Carnegie Hall, The Juilliard School, the famed restaurant Nobu, and the Chamber Music Society.

Customers say they appreciate Capitol's efficient service, excellent work ethic, and promptness. Although the work is expensive, clients say it's a good value considering the level of service.

"Never had a problem with them." "My floors are beautiful." "One of the best in the New York area." "Very reliable quality without killing you on price." "They are a professional company, not three guys and a truck."

Country Floors Inc.

15 East 16th Street, New York, NY 10003
(212) 627 - 8300 www.countryfloors.com

Handmade and imported tile sales

See Country Floors Inc.'s full report under the heading Tile, Marble & Stone

Eastside Floor Services   4   3.5   4.5   4.5

129 East 124th Street, New York, NY 10035
(212) 996 - 1800 www.eastsidefloors.com

Wood flooring installation, refinishing, repair, cleaning, custom design, and retail

Established by Gerry Flynn in 1985, Eastside is one of the city's largest distributors and manufacturers of wood flooring. Working with its sister company New York Flooring, Eastside specializes in installing, repairing, refinishing, cleaning, and maintaining wood floors.

The company will do both standard jobs and custom-milled flooring in local and exotic woods. Eastside also deals in unfinished wood such as strip, parquet, and herringbone of all sizes and types. This firm also has the ability to create custom designs and borders in its workshop. In addition, Eastside distributes pre-finished wood flooring from all leading manufacturers. This commercial and residential company serves all five boroughs, the Hamptons, and other parts of the tri-state area. This company boasts such commercial projects as Barney's New York and Macy's. Clients praise the quality of the work and describe Eastside as professional, punctual, and neat. Though scheduling is often difficult due to the firm's busy timetable and sources say it can be tough to get in touch with Gerry, most agree that the "good quality is worth the moderate to ;upper-end prices."

"The only people who touch our floors." "They're very good at what they do." "Gerry is a bit difficult to reach, but someone will always get back to me." "Great refinishers."

H&K Hansen Flooring   4.5   4.5   4   5

580 Old Stage Road, East Brunswick, NJ 08816
(732) 251 - 0989

Wood flooring refinishing and sanding

Established and incorporated in 1990, this family-run business specializes in sanding and finishing wood floors only. Helmed by Kurt Hansen (a third-generation Hansen in the flooring industry) and his uncle, H&K serves only residential clients in Manhattan and parts of the Hamptons, Westchester, and Connecticut. The firm works with decorators, contractors, and directly with homeowners. Pricing is usually per square foot, but for smaller projects H&K will charge by the job.

Sources report that H&K's work is excellent—some say the best in the city—but note that it comes with a certain amount of artistic attitude and prices in the expensive range.

"Best finisher!" "Reliable and pleasant." "Extremely knowledgeable. He gives realistic schedules and the quality of work is superb." "Highest integrity." "Very small company, but good." "Punctual, respectful, knowledgeable, and the quality of work is superb."

I.J. Peiser's Sons Inc.   4.5   4   4.5   4.5

1891 Park Avenue, New York, NY 10035
(212) 348 - 7500   stephen@ijpeiser.com
Wood flooring installation and refinishing

Known for its hand-scraped and hand-finished floors, I.J. Peiser's is one of New York's oldest flooring companies. Owned and managed by Stephen Estrin, the company was established by his great-grandfather in 1909. The company installs, cleans, and repairs all types of wood floors. The firm also takes pride in its custom designs and inlays, which are created in Peiser's own workshop.

This mainly residential company serves most of Manhattan, some areas in the Hamptons, Westchester, Connecticut, and even as far away as Palm Beach and Oklahoma. Estrin also has a strong commercial following, some of which includes prestigious hotels (The Palace and The Carlyle) and some of the top contractor and architectural firms in the city.

Sources describe Estrin as very professional, honest, reliable, easy to work with, and a great craftsman. Delighted customers say the firm meets deadlines, adheres to budgets, and is willing to fix any problem that arises—although some say there's room for improvement in customer service. Happy clients say the quality of the floors and reliable workmanship are well worth the "upper tier" cost.

"Absolutely excellent." "Extremely cooperative." "One of the finest craftsmen around." "Honest." "Been here a long time." "On schedule. Reliable." "Excellent installers."

Lane's Floor Coverings and Interiors Inc.   3   2.5   3.5   4

30 West 26th Street, 6th Floor, New York, NY 10010
(212) 532 - 5200   www.lanes-carpets.com
All types of flooring retail, installation, cleaning, and repair

Sources say Lane's is "excellent to work with" and praise the company's high quality across a variety of materials and tasks. Lane's supplies, installs, cleans, and repairs vinyl, wall-to-wall carpets, wood, linoleum, tile, marble, granite, cork, rubber, and laminates. Established in 1965 by Lane Brettschneider, who comes from a family of experienced flooring folks, this firm does projects around the tri-state area, the Hamptons, Westchester, and along the West Coast.

In business for 40 years, Lane's has built a strong reputation not only among residential clients, but in the trade as well. The company works with designers, general contractors, and noted architects. Some of the company's impressive projects include providing Pope John Paul II's carpet during his visits to New York City in the 1970s and 1995 and doing the floors for the Reuters Building in New York. Lane's has a showroom on Park Avenue, which is open to the public and to the trade. Offering a broad menu of services at reasonable prices, Lane's is a popular choice.

"On time. Responds quickly." "Reliable. Worked out issues well." "Superb service." "Excellent finisher."

Norwegian Wood   3.5   3   4.5   4
942 Grand Street, Brooklyn, NY 11211
(718) 218 - 8880   norwegianwood1@msn.com
Wood flooring installation, refinishing, custom designs, and repair

A specialist in installing, repairing, refinishing, and creating custom inlays, Norwegian Wood has been satisfying customers since its founding in 1989. With fifteen full-time employees, this company handles residential and commercial projects, including new construction and remodeling existing structures around Manhattan and Westchester. Estimates are free and pricing, normally by square foot or by the job, is negotiable. Norwegian Wood is a member of The National Wood Flooring Association.

Many enthusiastic clients praise the company for being easy to work with, pleasant, and dependable. Norwegian's work is described as top quality and lasting. Satisfied customers say they have used the company again and again, and have recommended it to friends. Pricing is by the square foot and costs are described as mid-range.

"My floors look great!" "Good quality and service." "Reliable." "Difficult to reach but will return phone calls." "A solid choice for mid-market projects."

Phoenix Hardwood Flooring   4.5   4   4.5   5
1 Muller Avenue, Norwalk, CT 06815
(203) 845 - 8094   www.phoenixfloors.com
Superb hardwood floor installation, finishing, restoration and repair, custom designs, inlays, and specialty finishes

A well-kept secret among high-end builders and contractors, Phoenix Hardwood Flooring has built a glowing reputation among its clients over the past thirteen years. Established in 1990 by Ed Myers, Ken Myatt, Stan Hill, and Jeff Samoncik, a business that started out with just ten people is now a company with three offices/showrooms (Norwalk, Guilford, and Southbury), two 10,000 square foot warehouses, and 125 employees.

Phoenix installs, repairs, restores, sands, finishes, and creates custom designs, medallions, and inlays for hardwood floors only. The firm does mostly new construction for residential interiors in New York City, Connecticut, Westchester, and beyond. Aside from new installations, Phoenix also boasts museum-quality and historic restoration projects like the Bush-Holley Museum in Greenwich and the Lockwood Mansion in Norwalk.

Sources praise the firm's "excellent customer service" and "creative, problem-solving" workers. The company assigns a project manager for each job, ensuring that the client deals with only one key person from start to finish. There is no set method for pricing, but a flat fee is quoted for each job. Projects can range from a simple $500 refinishing to $350,000 installations.

"Very resourceful. Found us floors in France in order to match what we had." "Can accommodate any design aesthetic." "Easygoing. A pleasure to work with."

	Quality	Cost	Value	Recommend?
	+	$	◆	★

Stanleyco Inc.

| | 3.5 | 3 | 4.5 | 4.5 |

20 Jay Street, Suite 319, Brooklyn, NY 11201
(718) 643 - 3938   stanleycowood@aol.com

Wood floor installation, sanding, finishing, repair, and custom designs

In business for more than thirteen years, Stanleyco Inc. is run by partners Stephen Clementi and Michael Savino. The hardwood specialists at Stanleyco install, sand, finish, and repair floors; they will also create custom designs, borders, and inlays. Stanleyco is known for its expertise in staining.

With ten full-time employees, the firm serves a mostly residential clientele in Manhattan, Long Island, New Jersey, Queens, the Hamptons, and Westchester. References say the firm is professional, knowledgeable about its craft, and reliable. Prices, which are calculated per square foot, are said to be upper-end, but are still considered "a very good deal" by the majority of customers.

"Top of the class!" "Diligent. Excellent at achieving desired color and finish." "They are open to the designer's specifications."

Sutton Carpet Ltd.

417 East 57th Street, 8th Floor, New York, NY 10022
(212) 980 - 5967   www.suttoncarpetltd.com

Rug and upholstery cleaning, repair, and restoration; wood, tile, and carpet flooring retail and installation

See Sutton Carpet Ltd.'s full report under the heading Rugs—Cleaning & Repair

Walsh Flooring

| | 3.5 | 3 | 4.5 | 4 |

1121 Edgewater Avenue, Richfield, NJ 07657
(201) 945 - 9014   info@walshflooring.com

Wood flooring installation, refinishing, and repair

This New Jersey-based firm caters to a high-end residential and commercial clientele throughout the Northeast. Walsh Flooring will supply, install, refinish, sand, and repair floors, and create custom designs. This firm is an upstanding member of the National Wood Flooring Association. Sources say Walsh Flooring takes pride in its excellent client relations and high levels of workmanship—as well as its top-notch materials.

References tell us they love dealing with the craftsmen of this firm, who work with skill, attention to detail, and a sense of humor, and will often put in extra effort to make a job perfect. When one client thought she saw a dull spot, principal Joseph Walsh and his workmen came back and graciously redid the section at no cost. The quality of its work is roundly hailed as some of the best in the area, while prices fall at the middle of the high-end range.

"Really good work—their herringbone design is gorgeous." "May cost a bit more, but gets it done right." "Floors are fabulous!" "My floors still look good after four years."

	Quality	Cost	Value	Recommend?
	+	$	◆	★

William J. Erbe Company Inc.   5   5   4.5   4.5

560 Barry Street, Bronx, NY 10474
(212) 249 - 6400

Museum-quality wood flooring installation, refinishing, sanding, custom designs, restoration, and repair

Flooring as art? At the William J. Erbe Company, it certainly is. Clients, architects, designers—and even other high-end flooring companies—acknowledge Erbe as the best and most expensive producer of handmade and hand-scraped wood floors. The company installs, repairs, refinishes, sands, restores, and maintains wood floors for residential and commercial interiors, and designs some of the most intricate floor patterns. Its workmen are few and in demand, and Erbe himself or one of his sons supervises each project.

Though based in New York, Erbe's projects are mostly out-of-state or outside the country. The firm enjoys an impressive roster of local and international clients such as top designers David Easton and Mark Hampton, the Metropolitan Museum of Art, the White House, and the royal family in Kuwait, to name a few. Known for his custom designs and antique restorations, Erbe scours France looking for chateau owners about to part with their antique parquet floors. He then imports them and meticulously restores the exquisite pieces for clients.

Called "the Rolls-Royce of flooring companies" by *The New York Times*, this family business was founded by Erbe's great-grandfather in 1907 and was incorporated in 1968. Sources say that this firm can reproduce and create any kind of floor, and that they are dedicated, professional, and "the most amazing craftsmen around." Indeed, whether it be Erbe's famous parquet de Versailles, antique or modern finish, with inlays or without, flooring at the William J. Erbe Company has been elevated to an art form. For those for whom money is no object, there's no finer choice.

"As an architect, I would not consider risking a client's floors with anyone other than Erbe; no one can compare." "Seriously the best floor company around." "Exquisite craftsman. Exceeds my expectations." "If there was a New York God for Wood Floors, William Erbe would be it." "They only accept a limited number of projects." "Über flooring."

Hiring a Furniture Repair & Refinishing Service Provider

Does your prized baroque chair need restoration? Do you refuse to get rid of your comfortable thrift store couch, but admit it needs sprucing up? Will your bedroom finally be complete with the addition of a twin reproduction of your favorite antique nightstand? Or perhaps you have a piece that has survived fire or flood damage, a teething puppy, climate changes, or just general wear and tear. Before surrendering your furniture into the hands of a professional, you should know a few things about it and the artisan who will repair, restore, or conserve it.

Where Do I Start?

Before hiring a professional to repair your piece, take the time to verify that your thrift shop bargain isn't a priceless antique in disguise and that your heirloom isn't actually an ordinary reproduction. Inappropriate restoration of an antique can greatly compromise its value. Sometimes a seemingly simple repair can actually cause further, irreparable damage. So be sure to have your piece's history and condition closely examined—preferably by several people—before allowing any work to be done.

Most professionals will visit your home to provide a price estimate and a detailed explanation of how your piece should be treated. Some charge fees for on-site verbal and written estimates, others don't. Estimates should include the cost of labor, materials, and transportation. You should also discuss how your piece will be insured and whether or not a warranty will be provided for the work and under what conditions.

Knowing the value of your piece is important not only in determining the type of work that it needs and how well it should be insured, but also how much to invest in the work. If your thrift store table simply needs its broken leg replaced, you may not want to pay top dollar for labor fees. However, if you're concerned about transporting your original Louis XIV dining room table, you may opt to keep it at home and pay for a specialized restorer to work on site.

On Cost

Many professionals base their fees on an hourly or daily rate that is subject to increase, depending on the condition of your piece, the work it needs, and where the work takes place. As a general guideline, hourly rates can range from $45 to $150. Others restorers, however, charge by the piece. Costs can vary depending on the condition of the piece and how much work needs to be done. In the case of per-piece fees, request an itemized estimate that clearly explains where each charge comes from. Be sure you receive a written contract for the amount of work agreed upon and the cost. If additional work is needed, the professional should notify you before taking action and a new fee should be agreed upon.

Choosing the Right Specialist for You

No licensing bureaus or governing boards regulate furniture restorers, so it is crucial that you take the time to find the right professional for your particular piece. Although furniture restorers tend to be well-versed in all styles and periods, each has a specialty. You wouldn't take a broken toe to an allergist, nor would you want to take your japanned armoire to a caning specialist. Inquire about the professional's area of expertise. For example, if your dining room table needs to be refinished, be wary of a craftsman who wants to use French polish and says you'll be eating from your table within a day or two. French polish is typically saved for show pieces, such as game tables and armoires, and is not used on surfaces that are prone to spills or burns. If you do want French polish, know that applying it is a time-consuming process that requires numerous layers of shellac and alcohol to be applied, dried, and rubbed before being reapplied. Keep in mind that moisture captured between the layers can cloud the surfaces irrevocably, so humid weather will prolong the process. Be patient because a good professional will not want to rush the job.

Also, be wary of someone who is eager to refinish your Federal bureau, or any of your antiques. Much of the value of any antique derives from its rarity, quality, and condition, and an original finish is an important part of this. A real crafts-man knows that a furniture's original patina is what gives an antique much of its character. Be sure to find a professional who is as interested in preserving the unique qualities of your piece as you are.

QUESTIONS TO ASK A FURNITURE PROFESSIONAL

Although your main contact will most likely be the firm's principal, most firms have numerous employees, each with a different area of expertise. Ask who is working on your piece and what that person will be doing. The person who recre-ates the leg of your table may not be the person who finishes it.

Don't be afraid to ask about the firm's expertise, including whether individuals have been trained in a particular style or period. Ask where they've worked and with whom. Also, ask to see their portfolios and to speak with numerous refer-ences. Make a point of speaking with the references. They know the work and will tell you if actual fees exceeded the estimate, if the work took twice as long as expected or—the best scenario—if the work was beautifully done.

FURNITURE CARE TIPS

◇ Protect furniture from direct sunlight, which fades col-ors, bleaches wood, and clouds polished surfaces.

◇ Avoid exposing furniture to excessive heat—do not place it near a radiator or set hot objects upon it, as this damages surface coatings, veneers, and underly-ing adhesives.

◇ Place coasters on surfaces to protect them from liq-uids, which can stain.

◇ Wipe up water-based spills with a towel, but dab alco-hol spills carefully to prevent spreading the spill—alco-hol breaks down finishes.

◇ Invest in a humidifier/dehumidifier to minimize large fluctuations in humidity.

◇ Use a buffer when writing on a table top. Pens and pencils can cause   unsightly indentations.

◇ When moving furniture, lift by the strongest units or rails—never drag!

FURNITURE REPAIR & FINISHING

🛍 FIRMS WITH ONLINE PORTFOLIOS* 🛍

Anglo-Inscape   4.5   4   4.5   5
2472 Broadway, Suite 368, New York, NY 10024
(212) 924 - 2883 www.angloinscape.com

Superior custom furniture with high-end finishes

Clients are so taken with principal Andrew Rouse's good-looking British charm and exquisite work that they invite him to houses all over the country. Rouse studied in the UK and has been in business for fifteen years. In addition to designing a furniture line, he specializes in antique furniture restoration and re-finishing, as well as decorative wall finishes. Rouse's French polish is reportedly magnificent, and we are told he works with impressive facility in oil- and water-based glazes, graining, marbling, and specialty plaster treatments.

We hear Rouse values the integrity of Old World methods and uses only tra-ditional techniques, applying rubs and finishes by hand. Clients praise Rouse's enormous body of knowledge and recommend him for projects that call for pre-serving the character of a valuable piece. Insiders say that in an industry of divas, Rouse stands out for his absence of ego, and his impeccable reliability.

"Work is of the highest quality and is completed within the time specified." "Andrew's work is outstanding and his commitment is unfailing." "Some high-end finishers are difficult to work with—Andrew is not one of these. His pricing is fair, he's there when he says he will be, and he goes the extra mile to make sure the job is done right." "The top, top man." "I needed a marble staircase. We only had a wooden one. Andrew went to work on the staircase. When he was done, the plain wooden staircase was a fabulous marble one." "He's a magician with finishes."

Carlton House Restoration 🛍   4   3.5   4.5   4.5
40-09 21st Street, 4th Floor, Long Island City, NY 11101
(718) 609 - 0762 www.carltonhouse.net

Antique restoration and refinishing, custom furniture design

Principal Kenny Dell is described as an antiques expert who truly loves what he does. Dell specializes in the repair and refinishing of wooden furniture, as well as working with veneers and French polish. Clients laud his abilities with 18th and 19th century fine antiques, particularly English, French, and continental. Since the firm moved to its 13,000 square foot workshop in Long Island City, Carlton House has also been manufacturing custom furniture.

The firm was established in 1995 by Dell, originally a double major in philosphy and music. In 1987, Dell moved to New York and apprenticed with an English restorer, where he learned the ropes. The city's top designers and antiques dealers rave about Carlton House, saying the qualified staff of fifteen can handle bigger projects than most. Insiders particularly praise the staff's fidelity to tradi-tional restoration methods. In addition to working for the best in the interior de-sign trade, the firm also works for private clients. Selected commissions include custom furniture production for The Hudson Hotel and restoration work for Gracie Mansion and The Louis Armstrong Museum. We hear Carlton House is competi-tively priced (usually by the piece) and extremely reliable and organized.

*We invite you to visit www.franklinreport.com to view images of their work.

"They're the best; that's why we've continued to work with them over the years." "We recommend them wholeheartedly." "There aren't many good restorers in New York City, and we recommend Carlton to all our customers, so that tells you something."

ECR Conservation & Restoration Inc. 🛍 4.5 4 4.5 5
515 West 29th Street, 5th Floor, New York, NY 10001
(212) 643 - 0388 www.ecrios.com

Superior reconditioning of existing finishes; repair and reproduction; japanning experts

Principal Eli Rios specializes in the reconditioning of Great American and Regency English furniture, in particular, but also of French and Italian antiques. We hear he shuns the word "refinish," saying antiques are so delicate that to strip them down to refinish would devalue the piece. Instead, Rios relies on his 30 years of experience carving, replacing veneers, reconditioning, and polishing antique furniture. He can also deliver appraisals. Sources say Rios's reproductions are indistinguishable from the originals, particularly his japanning skills, which have been featured by Martha Stewart.

Rios boasts an impressive resume. After training under a German restorer, he was the first employee hired by Sotheby's Restoration, heading that department for six years. He earned a conservator degree from Smithsonian University and continues to teach applied chemistry of historic materials at FIT, NYU, The Cooper-Hewitt Museum and The Harvard Club. He continues his involvement with FIT and NYU by taking on student apprentices.

Rios established the company in 1989 and has seven full-time employees. The firm now has a bigger workshop—10,000 square feet to be exact, which serves as a workshop, storage space, and gallery, where he shows some art. On staff are gilders, French polishers, a japanner and carver with refined chair-making skills, and a metalworker who does extensive boulle work, lock and key repair, and metal inlay. With so much talent around, it's no surprise that quality is near the top of the pyramid.

"Mr. Rios is always very accommodating, professional, and competent. It is a pleasure doing business with him." "Eli Rios has been one of our most informant vendors for the past five years." "An outstanding restorer, Eli also produces the highest quality reproductions."

Elias Conservation & Restoration Inc. 🛍 3.5 3 4.5 4
515 West 29th Street, 2nd Floor, New York, NY 10001
(212) 947 - 4515 www.eliascr.com

Furniture reproduction, polishing, and antiquing

Elias Maldanado may run a small shop, but he has quite a reputation. He has been featured on Martha Stewart's television show and has taught his skills to students from local design schools. We hear that his specialties are French polishing and antiquing.

Maldanado works with members of the trade and private clients, with most work for private clients being done in their homes. Sources tell us that Maldanado does very good work at an extremely reasonable rate, and they appreciate his low-key, gentlemanly attitude.

"He does a faux parchment finish that looks like the real thing." "Sometimes delivery of finished items is longer than quoted." "Very good work at an excellent price." "Very cost effective but hard to get in touch with." "Has done nothing but superb work for my highest-end clients."

Richard Moller Ltd. ▇ 4.5 4 4.5 5
178 Upper Shad Road, Pound Ridge, NY 10576
(914) 764 - 0121 rrmoller@optonline.net
Antique furniture repair and refinishing

Clients call Richard Moller efficient and conscientious. Customers appreciate Moller's ability to work on-site, which protects pieces from travel damage and means clients don't have to go without their furniture.

Moller trained with European craftsmen in New York after which he became head of the cabinet shop at Sotheby's for five years. Moller specializes in 18th and 19th century European pieces. Trade professionals rely on Moller and his staff of two, but we hear he also takes on new private clients. Established in 1977, Moller has a loyal following—sources say many long-term clients' children employ Moller for their collections. Moller was featured in *New York* magazine's Best Of New York 2006.

"He is always available and is completely reliable." "Professionalism and old-school charm."

FIRMS WITHOUT ONLINE PORTFOLIOS

A.R.S. Antiqua Co. LLC 4 4 4 4
118 Eighth Street, Brooklyn, NY 11215
(718) 788 - 3601 www.antiques-repair.com
Antique furniture repair and restoration

Peter Salamonski trained on the job with some of the best craftsmen in his native Poland before coming to America in 1987 and establishing A.R.S. Antiqua in 1989. In fact, some of Salamonski's work can still be seen in prominent museums in Poland and inside Wawel Castle in Warsaw.

Today Salamonski and his team of four specialize in restoring fine antique furniture, including veneer work, inlay, and marquetry repairs. The firm can work with any type of veneer or finish and is well versed with the French polishing technique, as well as with the more contemporary use of shellac and lacquer. At the 5,000 square foot workshop, pricing is by the piece, with typical restoration commissions running from $400 to $3,000 per piece. The firm regularly does conservation and maintenance projects for clients' valuable antiques at $85 an hour.

A.R.S. Antiqua works mostly in Manhattan but also does work in Brooklyn, the Hamptons, and Palm Beach. The solid reputation and excellent results—and Salamonski's laid-back attitude—draw delighted clients back to his shop for repeat business.

"Will use over and over." "Great skill coupled with years of experience—you can't beat that." "Solid prices for excellent work." "Wonderfully efficient." "Sweetest fellow. A pleasure to work with."

	Quality	Cost	Value	Recommend?
	✚	$	◆	★

Anatoli's Restoration

| | 4 | 3.5 | 4 | 4.5 |

344 West 38th Street, 3rd Floor, New York, NY 10018
(212) 629 - 0071
Furniture repair and restoration

Anatoli Lapushner has been in the furniture repair and restoration business for most of his life, studying inlays, carving, and design at art school in his home-land, the former Soviet Union. Insiders say Lapushner has a unique niche restor-ing antique globes and also repairs upholstery, working with all materials other than metal and glass. Established in 1987, his firm has ten full-time employees who were all trained by Lapushner himself. All work is done in his 8,000 square foot workshop.

Many high-end decorators, dealers, and private collectors rely on Lapushner's "incredible skill," but given his impossibly busy schedule, Lapushner is reluctant to take on new clients. The select few he chooses to work with rave about his work and come back year after year. The firm's work has been featured in *The New York Times*, *New York* magazine, and *Elle Decor*.

"I give him carte blanche. I trust him completely." "Anatoli refused to come visit my Park Avenue triplex to see a piece I wanted restored. He said I had to bring it to his workroom—a twelve-foot armoire." "He is a reliable professional. Once he is on your team, you do not need anyone else." "Anatoli has a personality that is not for the faint of heart." "What you see is what you get. His personality is raw and his work is exquisite." "I give him a piece that is a wreck and it comes back to me a work of art again."

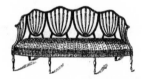

Antiquariato

| | 4 | 3.5 | 4.5 | 4.5 |

150 West 28th Street, Suite 1605, New York, NY 10001
(212) 727 - 0733 antiquariato@aol.com
Gilding and French polish; French-inspired interior design

For more than twelve years, Hicham Ghandour has specialized in restoring gilded furniture, architectural moldings, and ceilings. Trained in Florence and at the Fashion Institute of Technology's Restoration Program, Ghandour has earned a niche in the trade for traditional water gilding, oil gilding, and French polish. His company also does gold and silver leafing to new furniture upon request.

We hear this reliable craftsman is a pleasure to work with and delivers a beau-tiful product. Sources say he works mainly for the trade—including antique deal-ers, major art museums and top designers—but will take on a small number of private clients. Ghandour works both on-site and in his workroom, depending on the piece. Some clients have drawn further on Ghandour's knowledge of French furniture, employing his services as decorator. For his interior design work, he charges a modest design fee and retail on products. Ghandour's work has ap-peared in *Design Times*, *New York* magazine, *House & Garden*, and the French Designer's Showcase.

"He's a real artisan." "All I know is that when we gave him the chair it was a mess. When we got it back, it was beautiful." "High-quality work for a great price." "My frames were flawless when completed."

	Quality	Cost	Value	Recommend?
	+	$	◆	★

Antiquity Preservation LLC

4.5   3.5   4.5   4.5

By appointment only, New Milford, NJ 07646
(201) 261 - 8147 www.antique-repair.com

Museum-quality antique restoration, refinishing, and reproduction

Dennis DeCarlo earns praise from both professionals and private clients for his wealth of knowledge and kind nature. DeCarlo specializes in 18th and 19th century English furniture, but works on continental and Eastern pieces as well. The Merchant House Museum entrusts its collection of American antiques to DeCarlo and even had him teach a seminar on antique restoration.

Sources praise DeCarlo's work in structural repair, marquetry, carving, turning, and French polishing, as well as reproduction and metalwork. Labeled an "expert" with veneers, DeCarlo is said to be completely honest and reliable. Clients appreciate the regular maintenance service the firm offers, which restores and maintains the existing patina of a piece instead of stripping and refinishing it constantly.

Prior to running his company, DeCarlo worked at the Metropolitan Museum of Art, reproducing sculpture that would be sold in the museum's gift shop. He later moved to Sotheby's, where he was senior furniture restorer. In 1992, he established Antiquity Preservation. Pricing for onsite work is $160 per hour for a two-man crew, while in-studio jobs are $80 per hour. With prominent interior designers, architects, museums, galleries, auction houses, and private collectors as clients, this husband-and-wife team has commissions mostly in Manhattan and Brooklyn, with some jobs in the Hamptons, Florida, New Jersey, Greenwich, and Newport.

"As a museum professional, my goal is to preserve the furniture for future generations. I choose Dennis to do that, which should tell you a lot." "He knows his stuff, and his qualifications and credentials are incredible." "Top-notch, no question about it." "I couldn't recommend anybody any better." "One of the best restorers in the field."

Baggott Frank Lockwood LLC

4   3.5   4.5   4.5

1 Celestial Drive, Narragansett, RI 02882
(212) 226 - 6244 twfrank@earthlink.net

Furniture restoration and conservation

Clients praise Baggott Frank Lockwood for achieving top-quality luster and accommodating their restoration needs. Principal Tom Frank established the company in 1981 after a career working for museums, antiques dealers, interior decorators, and private clients. References tell us he's extremely knowledgeable and personable and loves his work. Frank specializes in aesthetic furniture, especially 19th century Rosewood Herte and American furniture. The firm also does minor gilding, replacement of furniture parts, restoration of paint and veneer, and wood turning, and is proficient in the French polishing technique. Everything is done onsite with pricing at $125 per hour. This two-man firm works in Manhattan, California, Detroit, Newport, Boston, and Connecticut, and has been featured in *Architectural Digest*.

"Top, top quality." "I have no hesitations about giving them any work I have." "Gracious and easy to work with."

Budd Woodwork Inc.

54 Franklin Street, Brooklyn, NY 11222
(718) 389 - 1110

Exquisite classical millwork and historic restoration; French specialists

See Budd Woodwork Inc.'s full report under the heading Millwork & Cabinetry

	Quality	Cost	Value	Recommend?

Christophe Pourny Ltd. **5   4.5   4   4.5**

20 Jay Street, Suite 253, Brooklyn, NY 11201
(718) 855 - 8865   pournyc@aol.com

Extraordinary antique furniture repair, refinishing, and custom reproduction

For antique restoration and finishes, custom reproduction of antiques, gilding and French polishing, insiders say Christophe Pourney is among the few best in the business. With a lifetime of experience of restoring furniture and creating antique finishes—as the result of being brought up in a family of antique dealers in France—Pourny started his own firm in 1995. He holds a master's degree from the University of Nice (France) in art history. Pourny is particularly talented with hand finishes on walls and panelings, in addition to the restoration of antique furniture (mainly 18th, 19th, and even early 20th century). He deals with pieces from around the world, including objects from France, Italy, Spain, England, America, and Asia. A large part of the business is French polishing.

For certain pieces that require unique and specialized care, Pourny also has a network of craftsmen around the world at his service. If a job can be done on site, the firm will go into homes for touch up and refinishing. He'll even go into a home while a client is away on vacation and care for an entire collection before the client's return. However, Pourny likes to bring pieces into his 1,500 square foot Brooklyn workshop.

The company has been widely published in magazines such as *Elle Decor*, *The New York Times Magazine*, *House Beautiful*, and *Metropolitan Home*. The majority of the company's work comes through interior designers and high-end contractors, but Pourny also takes on new private clients. However, be prepared for prices to match this firm's high-end reputation.

"Amazing. One of the best in the country." "His finishes are top quality and his mechanical ability (especially working with old locks) cannot be matched." "Handles restoration of pieces owned by kings and presidents with ease." "His work is beautiful and long-lasting."

D. Miller Restorers Inc. **4   3.5   4.5   4.5**

166 East 124th Street, New York, NY 10035
(212) 876 - 1861   www.dmillerrestorers.com

Furniture restoration and sculpture mounting

Loyal clients describe third-generation principal Robin Miller as reliable and attentive, and her work as "brilliant and superb." Established in 1967 by Robin's father, David, a restorer from Brooklyn, this three-person firm restores European antiques and mounts sculpture for private clients, the trade, dealers, and museums. The company's French polish and gilding draw praise, as does its expertise in 18th century European furniture. Clients also love the reasonable prices.

We hear Miller is extremely accommodating and will tailor the restoration job to the quality of the piece, so no job is too small. Over the years, the firm has done work for some of Manhattan's most famous residents. Miller, who received training at Christie's in London, also teaches courses in European furniture construction and connoisseurship of French furniture at NYU. She has also been a guest lecturer at Christie's in New York and Parsons. Miller is a member of The Furniture History Society and The Appraisers Association of America.

"Always on time. Great attention to detail." "Everything they've done for me has been first class. No one else can compare." "I have worked with two generations of Millers and am now on the third. Obviously, I am more than satisfied with their work—in fact, I'm ecstatic!"

Daniel's Custom Upholstery

422 East 75th Street, New York, NY 10021
(212) 249 - 5015

Retail and trade—slipcovers, recaning and antique furniture restoration

See Daniel's Custom Upholstery's full report under the heading Upholstery & Window Treatments

David Linker, Ebeniste   5   4.5   4.5   4.5

300 Observer Highway, 4th Floor, Hoboken, NJ 07030
(201) 653 - 2860 dlinkebn@erols.com

Superb antique restoration and reproduction; ebeniste

David Linker is an ebeniste—one of the few in New York. Taking its name from ebony, an important element in marquetry, the practice of ebenisterie (designing and creating custom furniture for French royalty) arose in the service of French kings in the mid-17th century. Linker's prestigious training and passion for restoration draws awe and affection from his clients, who can hardly articulate their admiration. We hear that Linker dazzles in American, English, and Oriental restorations, and can also build reproductions. Despite his capabilities, we hear Linker isn't at all snobby—he respects each piece and reveres its history, no matter its worth. Insiders describe Linker as committed to preserving the integrity of the materials. He works exclusively in methods true to the period, drawing on his encyclopedic storehouse of oils, woods, and knowledge.

David Linker has appeared twice on Martha Stewart's television show and was profiled in 1999 by *New York* magazine. He has also been featured in *Traditional Home, To the Trade, Time Out New York*, and *The Atlantic Monthly.*

"David's the best I know of in the country, and I know them all." "He is absolutely one of the most reliable people I know." "You can't be an ebeniste without being a five. David is a ten." "David is so charming—my husband and I enjoyed daily breakfasts with him during the months that he assembled French brasserie paneling in our home library."

DF Conservation Inc.   4   3.5   4.5   4

361 Stagg Street, Brooklyn, NY 11206
(718) 381 - 3548 dfuentes98@hotmail.com

Antique restoration and refinishing; Nakashima experts

Decorators and antiques dealers praise principal David Fuentes for his gorgeous finishes and commitment to the project, period, and style for all types of restoration. Fuentes, who started the firm in 1993, is an expert in Nakashima furniture restoration, having reconditioned Columbia University's Nakashima collection. Fuentes also restores museum-quality pieces, especially American and European, and is well-versed in the French polish technique (although he can work with any kind of finish). We hear Fuentes enjoys the challenge of researching and working with rare pieces, but he does not do replications.

Insiders praise his extraordinary French polish and authentic finishes, calling him conscientious, professional, communicative, and timely. Pricing is per hour—$75 per hour for in-house projects, $110 per hour for onsite work. DF Conservation charges a fee for estimates for new clients, but once you are an established customer, the estimates come free.

"David works extremely carefully—not at all mechanically." "He was the only man for the job—he did his research and respected the furniture as much as we do."

	Quality	Cost	Value	Recommend?
	✚	$	◆	★

Fred Agrusa Restoration

3.5 3 4.5 4.5

42-13 162nd Street, Flushing, NY 11358
(718) 961 - 5984
Furniture restoration and refinishing

Fred Agrusa opened his company in 1983 after training with his father, who is still actively involved in the family business. Currently, the Agrusas work with all types of furniture, specializing in antique restoration. We hear this outfit excels in polishing, tightening, refinishing, and veneer, and that in addition to hand caning and inlay, Agrusa will do custom cabinetry on occasion. Antiques dealers say Agrusa responds well to their instruction and accommodates their tastes, while private clients praise him for being very reliable and timely with competitive costs. The firm can do work onsite or in its 3,000 square foot workshop.

Agrusa travels to clients' homes to provide estimates, for which he charges between $50 to $100, a fee that is deducted from the final cost of services. Those in the trade describe his work as very good, a proof of which is the fact that Agrusa has worked with the famed auction house Christie's since 1985.

"They pick up, drop off. It's family owned, they're very reliable, and they're very good." "When Fred does it, it's done right." "Excellent turnaround time and very fair prices."

Joseph Biunno Ltd.

4.5 4.5 4 4.5

129 West 29th Street, New York, NY 10001
(212) 629 - 5630 www.antiquefurnitureusa.com
Artisanal furniture restoration and custom drapery hardware

A third-generation business, Joseph Biunno Ltd. is known for its immaculate reproductions and expert restoration. Additionally, principal Joseph Biunno makes custom furniture, mostly for architects and designers, many of whom call his works masterpieces. In recent years, Biunno has expanded the family business into a diversified workroom, offering custom drapery hardware, custom legs, and antique locks and keys. Sources marvel at his staff of artisans—experts in carving, cabinetmaking, turning, gilding, metalwork, polishing, and painting—and say a visit to the workroom is truly worthwhile.

Clients compliment Biunno's professionalism and reliability, as well as his good-natured personality. He earns respect for his perfectionism and highly analytical mind, which allows him to solve tricky problems. Biunno works extensively with some of the top designers and architects in the city, and also works with some private clients. He was recently featured in *House Beautiful* and *W* magazine's "Black Book" for the "best of the best."

"He can do anything from Art Deco to 17th century Flemish bureaus." "He's enormously creative with special finishes and creates the most marvelous valances and architectural details." "Extremely high quality for an extremely high cost, but worth it." "When I called to inquire about restoring about ten pieces of antiques, he was not very interested." "Good but not fabulous." "Joe restored a 17th century European inlaid cabinet that looked as if it had been in a basement for 300 years, bringing it back to life."

Lore Upholstery Shop

2201 Third Avenue, New York, NY 10035
(212) 534 - 2170 www.lore.qpg.com
Retail and trade—Custom window treatments, upholstery and restoration

See Lore Upholstery Shop's full report under the heading Upholstery & Window Treatments

	Quality	Cost	Value	Recommend?
	✚	$	◆	★

Mary Ann Miles

4.5　3.5　5　5

226 East 70th Street, New York, NY 10021
(212) 988 - 6691

Excellent antique and contemporary furniture restoration and repair

Clients praise Mary Ann Miles as much for her unwavering character and charming personality as for the outstanding quality of her work. Working in the homes of the most pedigreed clientele, Miles has proven herself polite and personable with everyone on the job, right down to the roughest mover. We hear the British government relies on Miles for furniture restoration in its offices and ambassador residences, as do many Park Avenue clients. Clients say Mary Ann Miles is perfectly trustworthy and works independently in the home "without any hand-holding whatsoever." Miles is also said to understand customer service and to go to great lengths to ensure her clients are satisfied.

Insiders say Miles has a genuine interest in history and antiques, but can also repair modern pieces. She will repair anything, whatever its worth, to the full satisfaction of the client. Though she doesn't do gilding, caning, or cast-iron welding, we hear she'll offer references for those jobs. The obvious pleasure she takes in her work strikes a chord with customers, who value her open lines of communication and flexibility. Because Miles' services are in great demand, don't be surprised if there is a waiting list, but clients say "once she does get to you, she knows exactly what to do and does it expediently."

"I was very impressed with the quality of the work—it wasn't overkill." "She's an invaluable resource. She knows who to recommend and where to go to find things, and she'll match a handle or latch because she's just so resourceful." "She fixed a very tricky piece of mine—I don't even know how." "She never fails."

Midtown Antiques Inc.

3　3　4　4.5

310 City Island Avenue, Bronx, NY 10464
(718) 885 - 2820 www.midtownantiquesinc.com

Antique center—dealership, retail, restoration

Mort and Violet Ellis at Midtown Antiques are known to be extremely charming, honest, and kind. The firm was established in 1940 by Mort's father. Besides offering retail antiques with an in-house dealer, we hear Midtown loans antiques to publications and movie studios for creating period looks. Midtown has two restorers on the premises who also make house calls and reportedly does it all—from refinishing and painting restoration to cabinetry repair, japanning, gilding, and gesso. Aside from these services, this husband-and-wife team also gives design consults and sells 17th to early 20th century European furniture and accessories.

The company specializes in libraries, paneling, railings, and doors, and its fine work can be found in several elite locales, including Gracie Mansion, Manhattan's City Hall, and Mayor Bloomberg's residence. Third-generation restorer Mort trained in South America under his father, and sources call his work exquisite.

"A magnificent restoration job." "Such nice people with so much integrity." "They restored our family blackamoor collection that was damaged in an earthquake back to its original state."

Olek Lejbzon & Co.

4　3.5　4.5　4

58 Gould Avenue, Newark, NJ 07107
(212) 243 - 3363 www.oleklejbzon.com

Furniture conservation and historic building preservation and restoration

This group of 30 European master craftsmen has been working in the New York area since its establishment in 1950, servicing a variety of furniture restoration and conservation needs. We hear they offer a full complement of services:

reupholstering, caning, leatherwork, metalwork, marquetry, inlay, water and oil gilding, turning, carving, and pietre dure. They also restore and repair chandeliers and lead canes. Sources say the team at Olek Lejbzon, led by current owner Peter Triestman, can also design custom furniture and build replications, cabinetry, architectural millwork, paneling, and windows and doors in a wide variety of styles, from medieval to rococo to postmodern, and everything in between.

Olek Lejbzon's outstanding quality of work extends to such impressive projects as Grand Central Station, Madison Avenue Presbyterian Church, the Prince George Hotel, Jules Bistro, Queens County Farm Museum, Dyckman House, and the prestigious Cooper Hewitt Museum. Much of the firm's work has been for locations on the National Building Register of Historic Places. The company has been featured in *New York* Magazine and has received The New Jersey Historic Building Preservation Award in 2005 and The McGraw-Hill Project Of The Year Award in 2001.

"I would highly recommend their expertise." "Diligent, meticulous, and artful." "Everyone praises Triestman's down-to-earth and friendly demeanor, though some have had issues with his patience." "Hard to reach, but worth the wait."

Richomme Inc.   4   4   4   4.5
336 West 37th Street, 8th Floor, New York, NY 10018
(212) 226 - 4706
Furniture restoration, reproduction, and refinishing

Clients praise Richomme for its customer service and attention to detail. The company is said to deliver an exquisite French polish and finishes that are authentic to the period. Clients call principal Ian Nicolson extremely reliable and personable, praising his ability to meet deadlines. We hear those in the trade use Richomme to restore paneling and build custom furniture as well as restore antiques. Insiders consider Richomme's prices comparable to other high-end restorers but say the company's customer service goes way beyond the competition. Our sources tell us Ralph Lauren uses Richomme to build custom furniture and refinish antique and new furniture both in his stores and in his private homes.

"Richomme is a small company that is able to fit clients' needs, budget, and timeline." "My business is very deadline-oriented, and they always come through for me."

Robert F. Rohr   4.5   3.5   5   5
310 West 73rd Street, Suite B, New York, NY 10023
(212) 787 - 5420
Meticulous furniture restoration and repair

Robert Rohr earns praise for his skills as both an artist and an expert furniture restorer. He specializes in inlay, French polish, veneering, lacquering, and the restoration of hand paintings. Rohr is respected for being communicative, as well as completely trustworthy.

Customers welcome him warmly into their homes, where he does all of his work in order to eliminate transportation damage and minimize disruption. Clients tell us that Rohr's work never takes more than a few days and is priced very fairly. They describe him as a highly principled and knowledgeable man who will take the time to teach his clients how to care properly for the pieces that he meticulously restores and repairs. Pricing is per piece for Rohr's many private clients, many of whom were referred by Sotheby's. In business since 1985, Rohr's work has been featured in *The New York Times* and *Quest* magazine.

"His workmanship is a joy to behold!" "As usual, he has created perfection." "I'm just thrilled with the way each piece looks!" "It was a pleasure to meet a craftsman in this materialistic world who cares about his work." "He's an antiques doctor—he leaves nothing unattended."

Scottie Donohue

4   3.5   4.5   4.5

PO Box 1368 Cooper Square Station, New York, NY 10276
(212) 477 - 0519

Chinoiserie, lacquer, coromandel screens, and inlay

In business since 1984, Scottie Donohue specializes in restoring 18th and 19th century antiques. Clients praise Donohue's gracious demeanor and accommodating service—she delivers free estimates and works in clients' houses, saving them moving fees and inconveniences. In addition to French polishing, veneering, lacquering, gilding, woodcarving, and structural repairs, Donohue works on chinoiserie, coromandel screens, and inlays in brass, mother of pearl, and ivory. We even heard of a case where she did some decorative painting on a chair, turning an otherwise worthless piece into a show-stopper. Clients repeatedly cite Donohue's perfectionism and meticulous attention to detail.

Private clients and those in the trade value Donohue's versatile skills and extensive knowledge, and she has worked with some of the most noted designers in the city. We heard of several occasions on which Donohue transformed pieces that others had deemed "beyond repair." Sources describe Donohue as communicative, informative, and absolutely trustworthy—and a good value.

"She prices by the hour—an incredibly fair rate—but she's a perfectionist and won't stop short, so some might not want to pay for that." "Anything I have asked her to do she has done to perfection. She gives you first-rate stuff, but she works at her own speed, and you can't rush her." "Her commitment to perfection might be her only flaw, if it can be called that."

Sheelin Wilson Gilding Studio

3.5   3.5   4   4.5

315 East 91st Street, 2nd Floor, New York, NY 10128
(212) 722 - 2089   sheelinw@aol.com

Antique guilding, lacquer, and painted finishes

Trained in London and apprenticed to the Loughcrew Studio in Ireland, Sheelin Wilson now specializes in the restoration and conservation of gilded and painted surfaces, antique furniture, and objets d'art. In business since 1988 in the US, including a term at Sotheby's Restoration, Wilson has built a following among major museums, antiques dealers, designers, and private clients. Sources tell us Wilson loves the challenge of 17th and 18th century Italian restoration jobs, and clients compliment her inlays. We hear Wilson also offers expert lacquering, japanning, traditional and water and oil gilding, exterior and interior architectural gilding, polychrome finishes, and painted finish jobs.

Clients marvel at how Wilson can restore almost anything to its original state. They add that Wilson is easy to work with and has reasonable costs. We hear reports of a wide array of accomplishments, from restoring a Dutch metal piece to creating Art Deco tiles. Insiders tell us Wilson does much of her work for the trade and has taught traditional gilding at FIT. Clients enjoy her witty sense of humor, and find her to be as reliable as she is entertaining.

"No hesitation. I recommend her 100%." "She is very personable, conscientious, and not inexpensive, but she takes care of it and I can count on her." "She finds the original finish and restores it to its original gilding. She's very good, and she knows her stuff."

	Quality	Cost	Value	Recommend?
	+	$	◆	★

Stair Galleries & Restoration Inc.

4.5 4 4.5 4.5

33 Maple Avenue, Claverack, NY 12513
(518) 851 - 2544 www.stairgalleries.com

Exemplary furniture reproductions and restoration; fire and water damage repair

Stair Galleries & Restoration Inc. was created in 2001 as a spin-off from Sotheby's Restoration after the department was closed in a strategic realignment. Colin Stair headed up the internal Sotheby's operation and moved the group to upstate New York. The firm welcomes inquiries from the city which constitutes half the work. Stair Galleries continues to take on numerous project referrals from Sotheby's.

Clients laud Stair for his professional demeanor, friendly disposition, and quality workmanship. His firm handles fire and water damage, repairs and refinishes for all styles and periods of furniture, and also does interior woodwork, paneling, veneering, and polishing. According to references, Stair will also make expert furniture reproductions that clients say can't be distinguished from the originals. One customer told us that when her young daughter's favorite doll's bed broke, a call to Stair was all that was needed. He made a house call, whisked the bed away and within two weeks, the bed was delivered "in perfect condition," for a surprisingly small fee.

Stair spends much of his time traveling all over the country for his clients. He will also assist clients at auctions, providing advice on the worth and restoration potential of pieces. References say Stair performs expert custom work with the highest caliber of integrity and skill—at a price that is considered reasonable.

"When it comes to finishes, he's the best around—and the finish is the most important and difficult task to undertake." "A really nice guy who really is amazing at what he does." "The service is not cheap, but it's not nearly as much as it could be, given the quality."

Thomas Kortus

4.5 3.5 4 5

PO Box 6839 New York, NY 10150
(646) 752 - 0769 www.frenchpolishnyc.com

Antique furniture repair and restoration

Deep in the majestic cathedrals of Prague, the heart of Gothic Europe, Thomas Kortus honed his skills as an atelier. He learned to maintain the intricate woodworking of the medieval masterpieces with skills passed down from generations of artisans in his family. Utilizing the painstaking technique of French polish, developed in the 18th century, Kortus now caters to clients who know the value of their pieces and want them beautiful for life. Reports confirm Kortus is one of the last truly old school artisans still practicing French polish, and the demand for his skills reflects this rarity. We hear Kortus uses shellac, because the finish is cleaner and it is removable. His firm works with all types of wood to re-finish and restore a lasting finish.

After founding the firm in 1990, Kortus took on Manhattan. Servicing a high-end clientele, mostly in the Upper East Side and Brooklyn, this one-man show takes on between two and five clients a month. Kortus provides free estimates and prefers to work on site. Fees are calculated by the job. Clients love doing

	Quality	Cost	Value	Recommend?
	✚	$	◆	★

business with Kortus who claim the firm is "simply lovely" to work with and insist that the upper end prices ($100-$150 per hour) are an excellent value for results that are unquestionably "top of the line."

"Meticulous attention to detail and restoration finesse." "Most cooperative and eager to please." "Insisted on extra application which meant more hours, but later declined an offer of additional charge. Very gracious and professional." "An exceptional craftsman and very reliable." "Diligent, precise, explained all with suggestions of excellent upkeep I could do." "Talented crafstman with personal charm—a winning combo." "They will get my business every time." "Extremely sensitive to the furniture's quality and needs."

Timothy G. Riordan Inc.   4   4   4   4.5

50 Webster Avenue, New Rochelle, NY 10801
(212) 360 - 1246   tgriordan@juno.com
Antique furniture restoration and repair

After working as a furniture restorer on the West Coast and as an antique preservationist in Queens, Timothy Riordan started his highly respected furniture restoration business in 1983. His services include restoring, gilding, gold leafing, repairing, and French polishing of fine antique furniture, mostly from the late 18th and early 19th century.

Riordan will work on-site for minor repair and polishing, and for the work he does in his own workshop, Riordan will come and pick up and deliver your piece at no extra cost, as long as it will fit into his van. For larger pieces, he'll recommend a trucking company—but that will be on your dime.

Riordan works mostly in Manhattan and sometimes in Westchester and Connecticut. He has an enviable background, having worked at Sotheby's during the early years of its restoration program. Over the years, American, French, and English antiques have become his areas of specialty. He works on an hourly basis and does a considerable amount of work on the Upper East Side.

"Knowledgeable and efficient." "Will trust him with my most valuable pieces."

Vitanza Furniture Finishers Corp.   4   3   5   5

728 East 136th Street, New York, NY 10454
(718) 401 - 1022   www.vitanzafurniture.com
Furniture restoration, particularly Art Deco, upholstery

Founded in 1930, Vitanza is known to be dedicated to the restoration of fine wood furniture using handcrafted, traditional methods. Since then, the firm has been involved with some extremely high-profile jobs, including the chair of Pope John Paul and the Sotheby's auction for the estate of Jacqueline Kennedy Onassis. Principal Michael Maytel has gained a reputation for being one of the premier experts in the restoration of 20th century modern design, specializing in Art Deco and 1950s furniture.

We hear the firm's craftsmen excel in both contemporary and antique restorations and are adept with lacquer, polyurethane, antique white, French polish, custom color, and custom finishes. Clients also praise the line of custom-built furniture. Clients say Vitanza uses only the finest materials to reupholster furniture, from fabrics appropriate to the period to horsehair stuffing and coil springs. Sources call Maytel the top in the business and say he works closely with clients, designers, architects, and showrooms on both large and small projects. The firm was incorporated in 1986.

"Michael is simply the man for the job. I've had nothing but good results from him." "Michael is fabulous. The best." "Thorough and has respect for the piece's history." "Satisfies an affluent clientele that expects only the best."

Hiring an Interior Designer or Decorator

The decoration of homes has captivated people throughout recorded history. In 67 BC, Cicero asked, "What is more agreeable than one's home?"—and today, a beautiful home is still among the most treasured of all possessions. Interior designers put their style, creativity, and experience to work to help a home reach its full potential—be it a studio, a loft, or a multi-million-dollar spread.

The Franklin Report has uncovered over 150 design firms that clients consistently praise for their abilities and professionalism. Apart from intangible value (like lifting the entire mood of a room, or creating a pitch-perfect atmosphere throughout a home), clients believe that these firms saved them considerable time and money by finding interesting and unique objects and avoiding costly errors. Each practice has its own style and personality, which we have taken care to describe on the following pages. For our highly competitive New York City edition, we have tended to highlight the most well-regarded, beloved designers—which often translates into higher quality ratings, costs, and minimums. Remember, a "3" rating in quality is still "High-end" and a "4" is "Outstanding" with excellent references and skills. Also, a "5" quality ("Highest Imaginable") often carries with it a "5" cost—over the top and unnecessary for most clients. Additional firms and the most current information may be found on our website (www.franklinreport.com).

Finding a Match

After you fully assess your needs and your budget, we recommend that you gather photographs from magazines and books to share with potential design candidates to communicate your preferences. Through our research, we have found that the best interior decorator-client bonds are founded on common ideas of style and taste. Even the best designers can falter and lose interest in a project if they are not excited by the end goal. So as you gather potential names from The Franklin Report and from friends, focus on the preferred styles of the designers and ask to see their portfolios (or view them on our website)—even if they say they can "do anything."

As you narrow down your list and begin the interview process, think about your working relationship with the interior designer who, for better or for worse, will become a big part of your life. Will you be seeing the principal or the project managers on a regular basis? Are you interested in a collaborative process or are you looking for strong direction? Will you be offered a wide range of budgetary choices? Finally, the prospect of working with this person should feel positive and enjoyable. Given the amount of time and money you are about to spend, it ought to be fun.

On Cost

Only a client can determine the worth of an interior designer's services. The "great masters" of interior design are considered exceptional artists who may charge whatever the market will bear. No one ever valued a Picasso based on a markup over the cost of his materials. That said, the vast majority of designers are not eccentric geniuses, but skilled professionals looking for a reasonable profit.

Interestingly, very few designers earn huge sums, due to the inherent unscalability of the process. Since clients generally want to deal with the Name on the Door and not a senior associate, a design firm can only handle so many projects a year, usually about eight. Therefore, even with an average job size of $300,000 including a markup of 33 percent, annual pretax profits to a designer working with eight clients equal $90,000—a good living but not a fortune (especially compared to their clients).*

Just a handful of designers have the clout to make serious money. This can be done by charging unusually high markups or hourly fees, employing multiple senior project managers, selling custom products (which carry very high, undisclosed markups) and/or accepting only clients with very expensive purchasing habits. While you should know standard industry pricing practices, many clients are more than willing to pay more for additional service or amazing talent (rightfully so). However, if you are paying extra to work with the very best designer in town, make sure you are going to get the maestro's time and views, not the assistant's.

STANDARD INDUSTRY PRICING

There are three fundamental services for which interior designers receive fees: 1) up-front design plans, 2) the purchasing of products (new and antique), and 3) "hourlies" for the oversight of construction and installation. While there is a different formula for each design firm using these basic elements, the total amount you pay should add up to the standards outlined below. The following pricing indications described are what you can expect from a very competent, experienced design professional—neither a part-time designer nor a grand master.

UP-FRONT DESIGN FEES: Many interior designers charge an up-front, non-reimbursable design fee from about $500 (for a cosmetic rehab) up to $1,500 (for an architectural transformation) per major room, or from $5,000 to $15,000 for a whole-home renovation (considered "standard" in *The Franklin Report*). The extent of these plans can range considerably, from loose sketches to extensive architectural drawings with coordinating furniture memos, swatches, and a detailed architectural plan. Qualify these expectations before you sign on.

If calculated on an hourly basis, the cumulative design fee should add up to about the same amounts as described above. Some clients put a cap on the hourly fees, but that can be unfair to the decorator, especially if you have a hard time making up your mind. Alternatively, if you think you have a good plan in mind and are clear about your preferences, you can save money with hourlies by being a quick decision maker. Either way, you should have a clear agreement with the decorator about what the design fee covers. Does it cover all shopping with markups? All the rooms in the house? How many schemes? Are all discussions with the architects and the contractors included? What happens if you add a closet or a wing later? Are drafting fees included? For this payment, you should at least receive a specific furniture layout and the major fabric selections. Certain designers will charge a smaller design fee to repeat customers, and a select few designers have no design fee but larger product markups instead.

*Assumes net/wholesale cost of products before the markup of $225,000 with a designer markup of 33%, totaling $300,000 of retail product cost to the client and $75,000 of markup/gross revenue to the designer. With a 15% profit margin (after all operating costs) net profit to the designer is only $11,250 for a client, or $90,000 for eight clients (before tax).

Some, but not many, will operate on an hourly consultation basis throughout the entire process, with the client doing all the subsequent shopping, purchasing at net and implementation.

NEW PRODUCT FEES BY PERCENTAGE: Designers earn most of their fees by delivering products, such as upholstery, case goods, window treatments, rugs, and accessories. The vast majority of designers charge clients a markup over the net (or wholesale) price. Designers who search high and low for the lowest-cost materials might charge a more substantial markup, but still offer a very good value to clients.

✧ **Product Markup Over Net:** The majority of the designers who work in and around New York charge a 33% to 35% markup over net/whole-sale cost on all new products. This pricing is considered "standard" in *The Franklin Report's* designer reviews. When selling to interior designers, manufacturers usually set the net price at 40% below retail. Therefore, for a fabric with a retail price of $100/yard, the net price is often $60/yard. Thus, when the designer takes a 35% markup, the price to the client is only $81/yard. So even with the decorators' 35% mark-up, customers are still paying well below the suggested retail price—a great deal for everyone. A markup of less than 33% is considered "low" in the book.

✧ **Classic Retail:** Many established designers charge "Classic retail" on products, or close to what the showrooms state as retail. This is generally 50% above net cost on fabrics, 66% on new furniture and 33% on new rugs. For example, if the decorator were charged a net price of $60/yard, the client's retail price would be roughly $90. Workroom costs (at the curtain and upholstery houses) are usually marked up 25% to 50% (this is a very squishy number that should be clarified). This method of pricing is considered "high" in *The Franklin Report's* interior designer reviews.

✧ **Retail Outside New York City:** Fabric and other showrooms ticket the suggested retail price as 100% over the net price 50 miles outside New York City (vs. 50% within the area). So, continuing on with the same example from above, that same $100/yard piece of fabric would still be $60 net, but would run the client $120. This is substantial difference from the standard 35% markup above, or $81/yard.

✧ **Pricing Structure:** Remarkably, virtually no one charges under any other price structure—it is either retail or about one-third up for new products. This is an interesting unifying principle in an industry that contains so many variables.

✧ **Another Consideration:** Clarify whether the designer will charge a markup on the subcontractors. Any artistic endeavor for which the designer plays a role may come with a fee (rightly so). But know what you are getting into. Is there a markup on the decorative painter? The mosaic tile layer? There also may be a product markup or hourlies for overseeing the work of the architect or others (see hourly and oversight fees below).

ANTIQUE PRODUCT FEES: Antiques are tricky. First, the retail price is usually negotiable with the dealer. Once a retail price is established, most dealers offer designers a further discount of ten to twenty percent. This presents a conundrum. For the designers to make their normal thirty to thirty-five percent markup, they may have to charge the client substantially above new retail price (which could be above or below the original retail price). This is further complicated by the fact that most antique dealers are happy to sell directly to the public, and often at wholesale.

The most satisfactory solution used in many successful client-designer relationships seems to be full disclosure with a sliding scale. These designers charge a markup over the new negotiated net price, their usual thirty to thirty-five percent markup for lower-priced items and a smaller markup for larger items (price breaks usually start at $25,000 to $50,000). Many designers further guarantee that clients will never pay over the original or lower negotiated retail price. A few prominent designers appear to be able to hold to a set markup and/or not disclose the net prices. For expensive antiques, an independent appraisal may be warranted (see our listing of Appraisers).

There is an additional point that needs clarification between a client and the designer on antique purchasing. If a client happens to walk into an antique dealer on Madison Avenue or an auction at Sotheby's and finds the perfect sideboard that has been eluding the decorator for months, should the decorator get a fee? Arguments may be made both ways, especially if that piece has been specified in the design plans, the decorator has spent time shopping for it (educating the client along the way) or the client seeks approval from the decorator before making the purchase.

Most decorators have a strong enough client bond to withstand these issues, and the client will not balk if, in fact, the designer deserves the fee. But specific contracts help in these times. An elegant solution put forth by some of the more sophisticated designers is to charge an hourly consultation fee under these circumstances, or to take a much larger up-front design fee to cover all antique and auction purchases.

HOURLY FEES: Many decorators will charge an hourly fee for the time they spend on product procurement for which they are not receiving a product markup. A good example is when the designer picks out the kitchen tile or the marble floors—but the contractor buys them. This is considered "standard pricing" in the interior designer reviews, assuming the amount charged per hour is in line. Also, some designers will charge hourly for every meeting and "look-see" outside of their immediate product areas, and some will not. There should be an understanding of exactly what is covered in the design fee and what is not before you go to contract. In New York (unlike LA), shopping hours are very rarely charged to the client, but are instead covered by the product markups.

A very small but growing number of designers charge clients on an hourly basis for all product procurement, including antiques, and pass the net prices through to the client with no markup. This methodology eliminates confusion and uncertainty on pricing, but introduces debates on how long it can take to order all the trims and fabrics for a sofa (it takes longer than you think). Hourly fees are particularly popular with architecture-trained designers (since that is how architects usually charge). Hourly fees generally range from $75 per hour for a design assistant to $250+ per hour for a grand master, with $150 to $200 as the typical, well-established Name-on-the-Door designer rate.

OVERSIGHT FEES: Rarely, designers will ask for fifteen to twenty percent of the general contractor's net product costs to coordinate the artistic direction of the entire project. While possibly appropriate if the designer has a very large role in the architectural direction or is the project manager, usually these services are covered in the up-front, flat design fee. Anything beyond the agreed-upon design fee scope is usually charged on an hourly basis (see above). Also, it is usually unnecessary to pay this oversight fee if you are using an architect who generally takes on the project manager's role.

FLAT FEES AND OTHER NEGOTIATED TERMS: A limited but increasing number of designers will consider an overall flat fee for all of the services listed above. This fee would remain stable within a specified expenditure and scope, and go up or down if the product costs far exceeded or came in significantly lower than the estimates. But the key lesson here is that most interior designers are fairly negotiable on pricing and other terms, within reason.

CONTRACTUAL AGREEMENTS

Given the wide range of fee structures, it is highly recommended that you and your designer agree upon an explicit price scheme for each type of product and service before embarking upon a project. While not normally necessary, it is not unreasonable to ask to see all bills and receipts. Also, before you sign, it is customary to speak with of one or two past clients (and occasionally, see the projects firsthand). Once the contract is signed, a retainer is often paid to be used against hourly fees or the first payment on the design fee to show good faith in proceeding. Then, design plans are drawn and purchases are made after agreement. Timing expectations should also be addressed in the contract, but in many cases the timing of materials is out of the control of the designer. Therefore, if you have specific deadlines, the designers should be directed to order only in-stock items.

LICENSING OF INTERIOR DESIGNERS

The debate over the potential licensing of interior designers has been spirited. Currently it is not necessary to hold any type of degree or license to legally practice interior design in New York State or Connecticut. However, there are title regulations. In Connecticut, you cannot bill yourself as an "Interior Designer" unless you have seven years of relevant education and experience and pass a test called the NCIDQ. Similar restrictions apply in Florida. In New York State, you must also have seven years experience and pass the NCIDQ to be called a "Certified Interior Designer," but the plain title "Interior Designer" requires no qualifications. Interestingly, only a miniscule percentage of New York's best designers have pursued certification In fact, as of publication, only 214 across the state have gone through the process. Many designers describe these tests as having more to do with health and safety or regulatory issues (such as the height of the kitchen sink necessary to pass handicap standards, a concern generally handled by architects) than with design competency. In fact, the tests do include sections on space planning, historical styles, fabric selection, and all the necessary algebra, but they cannot test creativity or taste.

From a high-end residential consumer standpoint, there seems to be little correlation in our data between the passing of the NCIDQ exam and the satisfaction of the client. Although ASID membership or NCIDQ completion should impress a potential client with the professionalism of the designer, it is incumbent upon the homeowner to do a thorough investigation of the competency of any potential service professional through extensive interviews, referral information, and a competitive analysis. And, as we mentioned above, and must repeat, the best matches between client and designers are ones founded on common ideas of taste—a highly subjective concept. It is incumbent upon the client to figure out what that decorator thinks is beautiful before you take this expensive and time-consuming plunge.

FINAL CONSIDERATIONS

As further described on the following pages, an overwhelming majority of the countless clients we talked with had very positive feelings toward their interior designers. While it may be possible to purchase "trade-only" fabrics in other ways, truly successful decorating is about creating an intangible upgrade in mood and lifestyle that only an expert can accomplish. Professional designers also have the creative energy and resources to manage projects in a cohesive manner from start to finish, realizing clients' dreams more effectively and efficiently.

WHAT YOU SHOULD NOT EXPECT FROM YOUR INTERIOR DESIGNER

❖ That the designer will maintain interest in the project if you cannot make decisions.

❖ That you will attend each shopping trip or will be shown every possible fabric.

❖ That the designer can read your mind.

❖ That there will be no misunderstandings or mistakes along the way.

❖ That the designer will bid out every subcontractor; there's a reason that the designer has been working with the same upholsterer and decorative painter for years. On the other hand, if you have a favorite supplier, the designer should be accommodating.

❖ That the designer will supervise others' work without an hourly fee. (The designer should be there, however, to oversee the installation of his or her products at no additional fee.)

❖ That the designer will become your new best friend.

WHAT YOU SHOULD EXPECT FROM YOUR INTERIOR DESIGNER

❖ That the designer will have a full understanding of your lifestyle and use of your living space.

❖ A full consideration of your interests and opinions

❖ That some of your existing furniture will be integrated into the new design, if you wish.

❖ That you will be shown a full range of options and products—creative ideas well beyond the D&D. However, you should not feel forced to buy whatever they have purchased on their last worldwide jaunt (especially because pricing is particularly fuzzy with those items.)

❖ That a budget will be presented and roughly met (and that you are not tempted with "the best" unless you express interest in it.)

❖ That you will be provided with information about the net cost of every item, if you want it.

❖ That the designer will be accessible and make a proactive effort, taking the initiative to complete the job to your satisfaction.

INTERIOR DESIGNERS & DECORATORS

🛍 FIRMS WITH ONLINE PORTFOLIOS* 🛍

A. Michael Krieger Inc. 🛍

4	3.5	4.5	5

441 Warren Street, Hudson, NY 12534
(718) 706 - 0077 amkriegerinc@aol.com

Updated, eclectic, historically referenced interior design

Almost every designer in America currently describes his or her style as eclectic—but Michael Krieger takes the prize. Creatively charged with a strong desire to please, Krieger converts each project into a diorama of the life of the client. Surprises rule the day, with exotic artifacts and memories of a client's favorite voyage often counterbalancing streamlined, more neutral backgrounds. This is a designer who can do traditional with punch or contemporary with formal antiques. Negotiating this composite can be tricky, but Krieger understands the look and the territory.

With over twenty years' experience in design—including associations with Kevin McNamara, Mark Hampton, Melvin Dwork, and Donghia—Krieger certainly has breadth. He is described as "engaging, smart, and knowledgeable," and supporters remark that his designs do not have the stamp of a decorator. It's no surprise Krieger is noted for his excellent use of antiques—he's the owner of an antiques shop in Hudson, New York.

Krieger charges a flat fee within the standard range, half of which is deductible against future purchases. Classic retail is charged on products. He is happy to start with just a few rooms as long as the budget can support good-quality work. While plans have been known to go over budget, this is compensated for with original, budget-minded ideas for art and accents. Clients are very pleased with Krieger's organized and detailed design plans, contracts, and back office. Furthermore, he seems to have great patience, whether escorting clients to the D&D building or to London. We hear that if the client is not satisfied, he will readily "go back to the drawing board." HB Top Designers, 1999, 2000.

"My husband resisted hiring a decorator but is now begging Michael to review everything, including our landscape plans." "He turned our big vanilla box of a new house into a warm, comfortable home." "I was overwhelmed by our big new house, which had marble everything. He transformed the aesthetic and made it inviting." "He's able to find a beautiful object in what looks like a pile of junk to me." "I purchased some antiques five years ago on Michael's advice. I now realize they were a steal." "Michael can be a little shy." "There's always a slightly rustic edge." "We learned so much in the process." "Michael has a Yankee-cost mentality, which we really appreciated. While he will sometimes use the very best, he will often have an excellent secret source."

Ageloff & Associates 🛍

57 East 11th Street, Suite 8B, New York, NY 10003
(212) 375 - 0678 www.ageloff.com

Warm, engaging, classical residential architecture

See Ageloff & Associates's full report under the heading Architects

*We invite you to visit www.franklinreport.com to view images of their work.

252

	Quality	Cost	Value	Recommend?
	✚	$	◆	★

Alex Papachristidis Interiors    4.5   4.5   4   5
300 East 57th Street, Suite 1C, New York, NY 10022
(212) 588 - 1777   aprpapa@aol.com

Eclectic, luxurious, and traditional interior design

Alex Papachristidis functions as a translator, turning his clients' ideas into completed visions with sophistication and wit. He began at Parsons, after being overwhelmed with commissions, never graduated. Now Papachristidis has an established roster of clients, to which he is "loyal and doting." Recent projects include a contemporary interior for a young businessman; a hip loft for a downtown entrepreneur; and a Park Avenue residence in traditional French for an established older couple. Clients laud Alex Papachristidis Interiors for mixing bargains with rare antiques.

The firm's style is tailored to the individual client's interests and budgets, but most often is classically based with whimsy, and full of rich details. Supporters speak very highly of the designer's focus on service and back-office capabilities. The firm charges a standard design fee (more if it is involved in architectural plans), retail on products, and standard oversight fees. Clients say the firm is as adept with small projects as with larger ones. More recently, the level (read: expenditures) of the firm's clients and the firm's designs have markedly increased. While sensitive to budgets, the firm encourages the use of highest quality products, but can often source them inexpensively. Patrons highly recommend this firm, which works for many families year to year. KB 1997, 2000, 2005.

"Alex always creates something interesting and beautiful." "The first thing he asks about is the budget, then he achieves an extraordinary result within the agreed-upon framework." "Did not spend as much money as he could have." "Alex embraced my concept of Greek antiquity, came up to speed quickly, and together, we found some wonderful examples." "Not only creative, ingenious, and fun, but most of all intelligent." "The firm is honest and sweet but has recently gotten much more expensive." "The process could have been scheduled better, but the end result was terrific." "Incredibly high standards, would rather do a small project perfectly than a large one with concessions." "The Coco Chanel of design. Wonderful dressmaker's details." "Alex absolutely gets the upper, upper look we were after." "After he did my New York apartment, I did not consider anyone else for my Connecticut country home."

Aman & Carson Inc.    4.5   4.5   4   4
19 West 55th Street, New York, NY 10019
(212) 247 - 7577   www.amancarson.com

Updated, classic, American interior design

Championed by devotees, Aman & Carson is considered to be insightful, resourceful, and attuned to their clients' greatest design aspirations. Jim Aman and Anne Carson started their careers in interior design as store designers for Ralph Lauren, and their first clients were friends and employees impressed by the creative pair's polished classic vision. They are known for bringing glamour and elegance to the home without "overdoing it." Clients say that they focus strongly on detail and gracefully incorporate the owner's viewpoint and surroundings.

Established in 1994, the firm's clients now include members of the Upper East Side establishment, Santa Fe ranch owners, Palm Beach traditionalists, and downtown modernists in search of a contemporary interpretation of timeless elegance. References are convinced that this pair is skyrocketing to stardom, and they are trying their best not to let the word out too quickly. The firm is so busy with repeat business (including at least one family with six commissions) that very few new clients are brought into the fold, and current clients have mentioned timing issues.

The team tends to have a classically elegant, more formal design approach, much appreciated by patrons not interested in monochromatic minimalism. The firm charges a standard plus design fee, classic retail on products, and standard oversight fees. Living rooms are generally in the $100,000 to $200,000 range. Supporters commend the firm's resourcefulness in locating high-quality products at good prices. "Expensive but a real value." HB Top Designers, 1999, 2000, 2001, 2003.

"Jim and Anne took a run-of-the-mill condo and turned it into something very, very special." "They are capable of museum-quality work but are willing to stay within a budget." "They are wonderful businesspeople, having succeeded under the demands of commercial pressures." "Jim has amazing vision, a very quick wit, and is such a pleasure. I loved spending time with him." "While offering extraordinary results, they are not really into low-maintenance fabrics or the most functional lamps." "They are good about working things out between the upholsterers and the clients." "The pair did it all while we were away." "They need to slow down and hire more staff." "Jim and Anne offer the preppy look taken to a modern level of refined luxury."

Amanda Nisbet Design Inc. 🏠   4   3.5   4.5   4.5

1326 Madison Avenue, Suite 64, New York, NY 10128
(212) 860 - 9133 www.amandanisbetdesign.com

Lively, elegant, colorful interior design

Guided by an intuitive sense of design, Amanda Nisbet creates interiors that are stylish, upbeat, and graced with a feminine touch. Clients (who usually become friends) admire her ability to create homes that are unique yet livable, even for an active family. Variation is key to Nisbet's method. She prefers not to use the same pattern or fabric twice, and prides herself on delivering something unique to each client. This approach can raise costs, but it yields delightful results, like a plexiglass dining table that doubles up for ping pong on rainy days.

Nisbet has a B.A. in art history from Middlebury College, but, beyond that, interior design is in her genes; her grandmother, mother, and sister have all been in the profession. Spurred on by encouraging offers, she started her firm in 1998, working on large, upscale projects right away. Currently, Nisbet oversees a staff of five, taking on five or six major jobs at a time. Clients are drawn to her charm, easy laughter, and down-to-earth personality. They note that while she "has a sense of humor," she "takes serious pride in a job well done."

Shifting the pricing structure to avoid costly surprises, Nisbet charges a higher upfront design fee (which includes a detailed plan and proposal) and a low markup over wholesale. She prefers to take on complete projects, but Nisbet will design a single room if the space provides a creative challenge. Living rooms are generally in the $100,000 area. Though most of her New York projects have been on the Upper East Side, this uptown girl is also moving into the downtown world, with recent projects in Soho and Chelsea. KB 2004.

"Amanda has a great eye for color, detail, and beauty." "She was able to incorporate much of our existing furnishing that we wanted to keep." "As opposed to many decorators whose work has a distinct 'look,' Amanda has been able to make our apartment

feel like our home...with great style and panache!" *"If you love color, hire her now."* *"She has great taste, which does come at a price."* *"Amanda has fresh, unique ideas and worked well within our budget."* *"She understands the high class look, but there's nothing snobby about her at all."* *"I'll use her for all my future projects."*

Barclay Fryery Ltd. 📷   4.5   4.5   4   4.5
271 Greenwich Avenue, Greenwich, CT 06830
(203) 862 - 9662   www.askbarclay.com
Gutsy, fresh interpretation of classical interior design

Is Barclay Fryery a designer, a one-man media blitz, or a personality? Many argue that this multifaceted whirlwind cannot possibly be all things to all people. But when it comes to decorating, his clients and favorite antiques dealers sing his praises. Taking on just a few large and a few smaller projects a year, Fryery makes a rough sketch of a concept, then turns it into a spectacular reality with his "full heart and soul." Just a few years ago, his designs were described by *House Beautiful* as "updated American Federal." One year later it was "simple, hip and alive." The truth is that Fryery will do whatever pleases the client, as long as it is unabashedly chic with historical references.

Nothing describes Fryery better than his website, which is a multimedia exhibition of the worlds in which he operates: his favorite music, books, art, fashion designers, restaurants, furniture, and events. Fryery is also a frequent contributor to various magazines, radio programs, and TV shows, and the author of *Indulge: 7 Ways To A Fabulous Home.* Despite this hectic schedule, clients say that Fryery will still come when needed "at the drop of a hat" and will graciously deal with all budget levels (not to say that he does not esteem the highest). He is most appreciated for his design creativity, which produces rooms that are "not what the neighbors have." Raised in Mississippi, Fryery's interior design career began in college, where he would decorate his friends' dorm rooms in exchange for cheeseburgers. Fryery moved to Greenwich in 1991 and formally began his design firm in 1995. A minimal flat fee is paid up front, and classic markups are paid on product. HB Top Designers, 2001, 2002, 2003, 2004, 2005.

"He is really a lifestyle guru and proud of it." *"Quite the man on the scene in Greenwich. Not your typical local decorator."* *"The custom upholstery he designed for me was the utmost in quality, including horsehair innards."* *"Barclay was completely on top of our complicated renovation. After a full evaluation he laid out a course of action with a timeline and stuck to it."* *"While he may take four cell calls in the course of one conversation with you, he gets it done."* *"A big personality with a big heart."* *"His creativity is boundless, and he lets it run wild."* *"Prefers to let style dictate the process, not money."* *"Budgets are not a top priority."* *"He is wired in more than one sense—Barclay makes a business of knowing the latest but is not an interior design fashion victim. He develops schemes with beautiful classic lines that will last, then wires the home for the future."*

Benjamin Noriega-Ortiz LLC 📷   4.5   4   4.5   5
75 Spring Street, 6th Floor, New York, NY 10012
(212) 343 - 9709   www.bnodesign.com
Edited, eclectic, elegant interior design

Benjamin Noriega-Ortiz is admired by clients and industry insiders for his charming and outgoing demeanor, modern design outlook, and affinity for rich finishes. With two master's degrees in architecture and six years as head designer for John Saladino, Noriega-Ortiz's distinctive color-saturated forms highlight his work. Clients (a group that includes Lenny Kravitz and Laura Esquivel) describe the spaces he has created as open, clean, serene, and coherent. He is happy to mix Crate & Barrel finds and the client's personal treasures with the finest antiques. While project managers are employed to run day-to-day operations, he is a self-described "control freak" involved with all major decisions.

Noriega-Ortiz works mostly in Manhattan but has a round of other projects throughout the country, especially Palm Beach (he has a house in Florida). He is willing and able to design a bathroom or a 30,000 square foot house from the ground up. Details are warm and thoughtful, including a recent room highlighting silk embroidery on bolt wool, inspired by the Met's Costume Institute. All fees are by the hour, including consultations. Products are purchased at net. HB Top Designers, 1999, 2000, 2001, 2002, 2003, 2004, 2005.

"Benjamin is the perfect example of what professionalism should be." "When the job is over, you're sorry he has to leave." "He has a style, but he's not chained to it." "He is so sensitive to the client's needs and is happy to walk you through the process." "Ben revitalized our apartment with a depth of convivial neutrals that re-energized the space." "He enjoys leaning toward the funky side of modern, but always exquisitely well done." "Benjamin has a complete absence of ego, yet he carries himself with a quiet confidence." "Modern, yes. Prison-like minimalism, no." "We so appreciated his hourly billing system, which gave us complete purchasing freedom." "Uses his architectural training to create really exciting spaces, well beyond the status quo of today's typical interior design."

Birchfield Studio Ltd. 💼   4   4   4.5   4.5
PO Box 1353, Lakeville, CT 06039
(860) 435 - 8016   www.birchfieldltd.com
Streamlined, international-style interior design

Clients report that Birch Coffey collaboratively develops thoughtful designs that often incorporate a restrained, international style and architectural presence. He achieves looks that are refined but relaxed—perfect for dinner parties, but also able to withstand the wear and tear of daily family life. He receives kudos for taking initiative, delivering jobs with fine detail, and building upon clients' visions. Though Coffey has an extensive commercial background in New York, he has recently moved to Connecticut and dedicated his efforts to residential work. Preferring to work individually with clients, he keeps only a minimal staff and makes all decisions himself.

References appreciate Coffey's top-notch organizational skills and professional thoroughness, including strong up-front presentations, excellent documentation, and great follow-up. Clients say it is often unnecessary to hire a separate architect, as Coffey holds both a B.A. and a master's in architecture. The company forgoes product markups and instead works on a straight hourly fee. Clients praise Coffey for offering product alternatives, for staying on schedule, and for respecting budgets. ASID.

"Birch offers the unexpected within a traditional framework—but it is always in good taste." "He orchestrates the entire project—the plans are detailed and they make sure the contractors finish the job." "My husband and I not only like Birch but we also respect his business acumen." "He has an amazing eye. He offers a mix of limited antique and mostly repro to ease the wallet." "When there were issues, he worked them out directly with the contractor, saving me untold headaches." "Never scoffs at the bottom line." "He's given up the hustle and bustle of the commercial work to do what he's always wanted to do: create beautiful homes." "Not as well known, so you get something unique and special." "If he cannot find the perfect piece, he gets it made. I love that can-do attitude." "He makes it happen." "He was so patient, even when I changed my mind a hundred times."

Bonni E. Braverman Interiors LLC 💼   3.5   3   4   4
235 East 73rd Street, New York, NY 10021
(212) 734 - 3032   bonnibrave@rcn.com
Fresh, clean-lined contemporary interior design

After training with Josef Pricci for eight years, Bonni Braverman struck out on her own in 1998 with a clean contemporary mix. Neutral palettes are favored, with judicious accessories adding highlights. Clients with modern art and a fresh view are particularly drawn to this aesthetic, and appreciate Braverman's professional attitude and streamlined looks.

Braverman's clients range from Manhattan bachelors to Westchester families to Midwesterners redoing their NYC pieds-à-terre. Clients report that Braverman will happily do either one room at a time or a complete renovation. Budgets tend to evolve one piece at a time, but generally add up to about $75,000 to $100,000 for a living room. A solo practitioner, Braverman reportedly is very responsive, solution-driven, and client-focused. With an excellent array of sources, she "always finds a way to make it happen."

A standard retainer is taken up-front, and a lower commission on product. If there is no product fee, a standard hourly rate is charged. Clients return for Braverman's practical and helpful approach, and recommend her to friends.

"This was a tough project involving NYC construction and regulations. Bonni did a great job working for me while I was traveling. I didn't worry it wouldn't get done." "Great management skills." "We trusted Bonni to run the entire construction project and will use her again." "Good at creating cozy little spaces out of nothing." "She is so good about following up on the impossibly late fabric manufacturers. She does all the legwork." "Never goes over budget, always preferring the sparse." "Bonni would not show me anything that I could not afford." "My husband is very opinionated and wants to see everything, not just the pictures, before we commit. Bonni worked really hard to make it work."

Bowerbirdhouse Interiors   4   3.5   4.5   4.5

49 East 73rd Street, New York, NY 10021
(212) 988 - 6414 www.bowerbirdhouse.com
Traditional, elegant, comfortable interior design

With an innate sense of style and warmth, Susannah Chapman has developed a cadre of supportive clients. Whether simply renovating a living room or fully redecorating an apartment, Chapman is said to give it her all, finding elegant solutions while keeping an eye on the bottom line. Rooms generally reflect "Old World charm," incorporating chintzes filled with generous down and a clutter of books and mementos that reflect a life well lived. However, Chapman enjoys contemporary projects as well, saying "it's all in the textures, fine art, minimalism, and lighting."

After fifteen years in and out of design in the Boston area, which included training with the venerable Roach & Craven, Chapman moved her business to New York in 1997. A sole practitioner, she is known for doing whatever it takes to make the client happy including freshening flowers, hanging pictures, and general "sprucing up." Many of her current New York clients are busy single parents and professionals who are interested in all the details of comfortable family living, but feel they have too little time to attend to them. Chapman maintains a summer home in Manchester-by-the-Sea, Massachusetts, thus keeping up with her loyal Boston base.

Clients tell us Chapman is pragmatic, using as much of clients' existing furniture as possible. She can work on a reasonable consultation basis or with a retainer and retail on product. Typical living rooms are $60,000+. For those who want to decorate their own homes but appreciate the value of seasoned advice, the firm offers hourly consultations at $150. Chapman's flexibility, focus, and professionalism keep the good buzz swirling.

"Susannah's taste is impeccable, but it is also fun and unexpected at times." "It always looks right for the setting." "She made me comfortable with color, a major step for someone who'd had white walls for over twenty years." "She did it all for us, smoothly and with minimal disruption to our hectic business schedules." "Works well with families. She's not the temperamental artist type." "She consistently over-delivered." "My request seemed almost impossible—to add color and warmth while

maintaining my minimalist preferences. But she did it beautifully." "Susannah has the perfect background, fabulous flair—and she doesn't make heavy weather of it."

Brad Ford ID Inc.

4   4   4   4.5

315 Seventh Avenue, Suite 16B, New York, NY 10001
(212) 352 - 9616 www.bradfordid.com

Intriguing, refined, delightful modern interior design

With a highly edited vision and a strong hand, Brad Ford has developed a spare, modern aesthetic with a warm soul. While the furnishings are few and far between, each is lovingly crafted and wrapped in the most endearing textures. Brushed caramel leather, earthy honed gray marble, vanilla linens, raw iron fixtures, mahogany velvet, and rough-hewn wood exposures charm the otherwise neutral palettes. This clean, fresh approach draws inspiration from the 20th century masters—Jean-Michel Frank, Pierre Chareau, George Nakashima. Ford's desire to please his clients matches his careful and reassuring design sensibility.

Ford grew up in Arkansas, receiving a business and economics degree from Hendrix College. After working in computer programming for a few years, he found his calling in design. Moving to New York, Ford earned a degree in interior design from FIT, working with Jed Johnson for two years, Thad Hayes for three, and starting his own firm in 1998. With a small office and a committed desire to offer personalized attention, Ford takes on about four large and four smaller projects at a time.

Projects can be in the $100,000 range, with many recent clients being avid modern art collectors in the process of establishing a collection. The firm takes a standard design fee and a lower commission (across the board). Hourlies are charged for non-product time.

"Beauty and function come together in Brad's designs." "His keen predilection for clean lines and pure color has transformed our apartment." Brad is one of the few designers that really knows how to make modern livable and responsive." "He can get that mid-century look without looking old-fashioned or backwards." "Brad is a calm and reassuring presence throughout the process, with a terrific sense of humor that also makes it fun." "His knowledge of materials sets him apart from all the cookie cutter modernists." "Have recommended him to family and friends. Everyone was very pleased." "To know Brad Ford is to love him. He is the warmest, nicest person you could ever have the pleasure of working with."

Branca Inc.

4.5   4.5   4   4.5

1325 North State Parkway, Chicago, IL 60610
(312) 787 - 6123 www.branca.com

Luxurious, stylistic, exuberant continental interior design

Peers and clients roundly laud Alessandra Branca for her lavish continental designs, intense creativity, and stylistic flourish. Recognized as among the very best in Chicago, in recent years she has taken on a number of East Coast projects. Credited with extraordinary flair, Branca tends to work best in the classical genre, updated with exhilarating color, a multitude of details—and a wink. Upholstered walls, multiple patterns, rich glazes, and exquisite millwork often factor into the design plans. Italian-born, fine arts-trained, and a mother of three, Branca uses all of her skills and experiences to develop her characteristic design creations.

Branca begins with a physical inventory and plan, and much is retrofitted to the new composition. Clients range from the most established to the young, who may begin with just a few rooms, but all tend to have high quality expectations, classical tastes, and healthy budgets. Very often these clients continue with Branca, finishing the house, expanding to multiple locations, and then moving on to the yacht. European shopping trips often factor into the picture.

Most of the products are custom, with many unusual European sources, creating a relatively expensive but unique setting. There are eleven people at the firm, including three project directors. The firm's hourly rate ranges from low to high, depending on seniority, with a high markup on product (none on millwork). Typical living rooms are in the $25,000 to $125,000 range. Clients tend to be quite loyal, albeit exhausted and clearly enthralled by the end result. HB Top Designers, 2000, 2001, 2002, 2003, 2004, 2005.

"Alessandra has the temperament of an artist, and she produces design masterpieces." "I think that you are born with great style, and Alessandra has more of it than anyone else." "Takes staid, traditional ideas and brings them to life with a shot of unexpected color." "She gives new life and vibrancy to historical spaces, while retaining their original character." "While there were times when I wondered if we would ever make it to the end, I would not consider using anyone else." "She combines the best of Italy with the best of America." "A lovely, outgoing person who speaks her mind but always listens." "She always does it her way, and that's a good thing." "Her star has risen, she's at the top of her game." "As an architect, I applaud her ability to add multidimensional, detailed, layered warmth to the architectural renderings. While it is not always easy, her undeniable talent makes me want to do it again." "I have become a great friend of Alessandra's through this crazy, exciting, and rewarding process."

Brian J. McCarthy Inc. 📇   4.5   4.5   4   4.5
1414 Avenue of the Americas, Suite 404, New York, NY 10019
(212) 308 - 7600 www.bjminc.com

Stylish, strong, articulate, traditional interior design

Whether doing a Park Avenue duplex full of 18th century master paintings or a period-pure 18th century square-cut log cabin, Brian McCarthy does all things to perfection. Admired for his innate desire to create rooms of unique character and grace, McCarthy finds extraordinary pieces that are coherently placed in classic frameworks. Many recent clients are collectors of fine works of art or furniture. The firm has a full-time employee stationed in Paris to assist these clients. Trained by master designer Albert Hadley, McCarthy displays both Hadley's professionalism and his skill in combining the expected and the traditional with elements of more modern or gutsier protocol.

McCarthy's clients are generally very well established, many with substantial apartments or stately homes, and looking to create a personal magnum opus. Most of the work is done in the city, but recent projects also include homes in Pebble Beach, Fresno, D.C., and Conyer's Farm. Supporters say the firm's client service is outstanding—issues disappear and billing is presented clearly. Additionally, McCarthy is hailed for his depth of knowledge and warm personality. About eight active projects are pursued at a time, with nine on staff including three experienced project managers.

References consider McCarthy's work quite expensive, but worth it. Living rooms can be excessively expensive, and that's before the fine antiques. On the other hand, McCarthy recently did a local Arts and Crafts home on a much more reasonable budget, and is said to be quite practical in children's rooms, using washable $15 per yard fabrics. In addition, he is commended for his "amazing sources here and abroad that can duplicate originals for a quarter of the cost." Supporters are protective, considering McCarthy a friend and a fabulous secret source. They cannot wait to embark on another project with this designer.

"Everyone who walks in is blown away by the warmth and details." "Brian is on an intellectual mission to find the beauty in any period." "He strongly encourages you to find your own design viewpoint." "The best part about working with Brian is having a drink with him at the end of a long day. He is such delightful company." "Carries the torch of tradition." "We hired him just to do the public rooms, but fell in love with his work and did the whole house." "The logical descendant of Albert Hadley and Sister Parish." "While you spend more than you care to think about, you are always invest-

ing in pieces of quality." "A quiet, strong personality." "Brian was in the right place at the right time." "Three years later, Brian is more than gracious about finding just one little lamp." "My curtains rival any of Marie Antoinette's dresses." "We couldn't recommend him more highly."

Bruce Bierman Design Inc. 📱

4.5   4.5   4   5

29 West 15th Street, New York, NY 10011
(212) 243 - 1935 www.biermandesign.com

Classical, modern high-end interior design

Bruce Bierman wins accolades for his practical skills, refined aesthetic, and warm personality. Trained in architecture and interiors at RISD, Bierman brings both skills to a project. While he is known as a modernist, clients also appreciate his ability to do traditional work with a lighter touch. Spaces typically feature a few shapely focal points, rather than an overwhelming number of objects. Projects include a large stone house in Greenwich, a penthouse at the Breakers in Palm Beach, a home on Rittenhouse Square in Philadelphia, and a Park Avenue apartment. The work—no matter how large or small the project may be—offers comfort, strong details, and clever storage space, all of which are Bierman's specialties.

Started in 1977, the firm now employs a staff of twenty-five, with five interior designers and eleven architectural designers. Clients happily report the team works well together and makes the process enjoyable. The firm charges a design fee depending upon the scope of the work, a reasonable percentage over net for product, and standard oversight fees. Products are of high quality, but never over the top. Bierman is said to enjoy incorporating interesting electronics and cutting-edge A/V equipment into his work; still, he doesn't shun older objects. Antiques may be purchased on an hourly consultation basis or percentage, depending upon the involvement of the firm. Budgets are meticulously detailed, with living rooms generally in the $75,000 to $200,000 range. Clients strongly recommend Bierman for his sympathetic approach to their lifestyle. HB Top Designers, 2000. ID Hall of Fame.

"I have used many well-known designers over the years, and I felt that Bruce was the only one committed to the project and our family for the long haul." "Bruce is a very special person—mature, calm, and generous. I am happy to say that he is now a friend." "Champions his clients' best interests." "There is a clarity and straightforwardness about what Bruce is trying to accomplish." "We ended up spending more than we wanted to, but it was worth it." "What a professional—he never gets flustered." "Very expensive but very sophisticated designs." "Bruce does things subtly, a touch of Asian influence, a little color there." "Our cookie-cutter apartment now magically looks like a glamorous loft." "I am a very opinionated client. I interviewed 30 people for this job, and I will definitely go back to Bruce for the next one." "So much fun."

Bunny Williams 📱

5   5   4   4.5

306 East 61st Street, Fifth Floor, New York, NY 10021
(212) 207 - 4040 www.bunnywilliams.com

Lovely, exalted, traditional interior design

Awash in charm and elegance, Bunny Williams' rooms enchant clients with a cohesiveness that speaks unpretentiously to a genteel past—and current comfort. Clients report that Williams can expertly execute a range of styles, but that she gravitates toward a refined, welcoming English sensibility, awakened with fresh, modern finishes and unusual pieces of character. An 18th century English chest might be crowned with a 1950s mirror; a French Moderne desk flanked by Regency chairs. Combining this bespoke approach with her extraordinary professionalism, talent, and energy, Williams has attained near-cult status in the decorating community.

Raised in Albemarle County, Virginia (home to Nancy Lancaster), Williams carries on the craft of gracious Southern living. Trained at the venerable Parish-Hadley, she opened her namesake firm in 1988. Her organizational skills and strong back office allow for excellent efficiency and quick project development. The firm has four integrated design teams, each headed by a senior design associate. Williams is said to travel extensively, but she continues to be the design inspiration behind each creation.

Most projects are quite substantial, ranging from a classic Cape Cod-style compound on the Connecticut side of the Sound to Manhattan penthouses to large homes in California, Palm Beach, Atlanta, Maine, Texas, and the south of France. Clients attest to Williams' "ladylike nature" and her ability to "do it all," saying that she is a woman of her word. Prices are reportedly extraordinarily high, but can be brought under control upon request. Williams also has a great passion for gardening. With antiques dealer John Rosselli, she owns Treillage, a garden furniture shop in Manhattan. She is the author of the books *On Garden Style* and *An Affair with a House*, a detailed look at her own Connecticut retreat. HB Top Designers, 1999, 2000, 2001, 2002, 2003, 2004, 2005. ID Hall of Fame. KB 1990, 1998.

"You tell her how much you want to spend, and she develops a design plan very quickly." "We hired Bunny for a relatively modest project and she totally got it." "Much less chintz than you would expect. Bunny is developing a real fondness for simplicity of line." "There is a complete understanding inside and out. She interweaves the mood and the design." "Bunny treats design like a cottage industry—she has an amazing array of specialists at hand that she can dispense at a moment's notice." "Enormous design vocabulary." "The staff is a bit stretched given the substantial client base, but always wonderful." "She also did my friend's apartment, and I was surprised to see some of the same elements as in mine." "Doesn't take anything she doesn't really want to do." "We have meetings every three weeks, and she is always very prepared." "Bunny even showed us how to make the beds in the correct manner." "She is not a prima donna and was very thoughtful in her allocation of our budget." "She is dazzling in a quiet kind of way."

Charlotte Moss Interior Design 🏠   5   4.5   4   5
135 East 65th Street, New York, NY 10021
(212) 288 - 1535   www.charlottemoss.com
Elegant, timeless, English manor house interior design

Charlotte Moss is one of today's great names in interior design. Her success is built upon extraordinary talent, a love of the process, and an indefatigable spirit. This makes the journey with Moss not only rewarding and exciting, but fun, too. She takes pride in getting that luscious, layered, English-with-ease look at a down-to-earth price. Known for mixing exuberant colors, fine antiques, and stylistically engaging pieces of interest, Moss has forged a signature American classic. She is said to listen well and to encourage clients to develop their own distinctive and personal style, using collections or signature colors.

Clients include Wall Street bankers and others who appreciate her professionalism and straightforward approach. Recent projects include New York apartments and large homes in California, Connecticut, Colorado, and the Hamptons.

About half a dozen commissions are ongoing, with a staff of nine. Moss is said to be very warm, quite accessible, and a consummate professional. Previously, Moss spent a decade on Wall Street, which explains her excellent organizational skills and strong back office. She has a large cadre of repeat customers, who appreciate her ability to limit the budget by selecting a few very high quality items, then filling in the rest with flea market or reproductions found worldwide.

In her designing role, Moss advises on garden plans, entertaining needs and the building of book and other collections. She also creates furniture and decorative accessories under license, authors decorating books, lectures widely, and devotes significant time to philanthropic causes. HB Top Designers, 1999, 2000, 2001, 2002, 2003, 2004. KB 1994, 1995, 2006.

"Charlotte allows her clients' visions and taste to shine through, with her inspiration." "She steers you in the right direction with tact and grace." "Charlotte is so real. While now a big time New York success, she is at heart a small-town Southern girl who has been shopping at flea markets since she was a child." "She has embraced e-mail, sending me pictures of potential purchases found during her travels." "A Southern interpretation of the English tradition." "Some people call her the Diva of Design, I call her the Goddess of Design. She's an intuitive thinker with an amazing perspective." "Charlotte did a fabulous job at finding the perfect compromise between my husband and me." "If you listen to her and follow her advice to the letter, you'll end up with a flawless house." "I cannot imagine her working with an indecisive client, it would drive her crazy." "She continues to design because she is passionate about it." "When I came home after a difficult installation, my favorite flowers were planted everywhere." "The day after I finished my house I was offered twice what I put into it."

Christopher Coleman Interior Design ▪   4   3   5   4.5
55 Washington Street, Suite 707, Brooklyn, NY 11201
(718) 222 - 8984 www.ccinteriordesign.com

Colorful, bold, witty, contemporary interior design

Clients appreciate Christopher Coleman's confident mix of geometric shapes, clean lines, exuberant colors, and warm undertones. They also applaud his enthusiasm, charm, and willingness to take design risks. His unique chromatic style and dashing mélange of 20th century items is finding voice on the Upper East Side and in Westchester: an "amazingly practical and uplifting use of each space, so that the family uses it on a daily basis."

After spending five years with Renny Saltzman, Coleman founded his design practice in 1993. Based in Brooklyn, supporters include established professionals and young couples decorating their first homes. Past clients include former *Harper's Bazaar* editor Kate Betts, Helen Henson (Jim's widow), and former Time Inc. chairman Don Logan. Clients credit Coleman for taking time to educate them about the design process—be it on classical historic styles, economic alternatives, or timing. Other strengths include a sensitivity to family living, with notable contemporary art next to the jigsaw puzzle collection. Reportedly Coleman will always create a place for all the children's toys and gadgets, often in stylish Lucite or bleached beech wood. He also enjoys bringing the "inside out and the outside in." References say Coleman is very available, highly attentive, and lots of fun.

Coleman works with a low up-front design fee, a low percentage over net for products, and no hourlies. He is known for his ability to make the most of less with some living rooms in the $40,000 range and a willingness to work in phases. Clients note that Coleman is highly professional and straightforward—all bills and the background paperwork are presented on a regular basis. A new line of Coleman's carpets was recently introduced by Doris Leslie Blau. HB Top Designers, 1999, 2000, 2001, 2002, 2003, 2004, 2005. KB 1997.

"Christopher finds the most unique furnishings. Whatever he cannot find at a reasonable price he has made. His upholstery people can do the highest quality sofas

for half the price of what we expected and deliver in half the time." "He is overtly modern without being rehashed-retro." "Some designers are all about form. Color is Christopher's weapon, and he wields it with panache." "We so enjoy his creativity. Anything can become an interesting design motif to him—country, ethnic, old maps." "Young, hip clientele." "Leading the charge for the younger generation of designers." "My apartment turned out to be spectacular, but it took longer than I would have liked." "He is the only guy in the business who can do red vinyl successfully." "I would even trust him with a spray can of automotive paint in my living room." "When I was after a particular, very expensive Italian look, he found a very good match at Crate & Barrel." "Christopher is a doll." "He has a wicked sense of humor and a hip design sensibility to match."

Christopher Corcoran Incorporated 🛍   3.5   3.5   4   4.5
410 West 24th Street, New York, NY 10011
(212) 741 - 3675 www.christophercorcoran.com
Clean, traditional, balanced interior design

Christopher Corcoran works closely with clients to create tasteful, classic homes that will be as charming ten years from now as they are today. Typically, his projects consist of traditional, classic elements arranged in a logical, uncluttered manner that reads fashionably modern. The look is always collected and mature, with an aura of calm throughout. References praise Corcoran's balance of color and light, saying that he uses them to achieve spaces that are relaxed, yet engaging. Indeed, he originally studied to be a fine artist, and often uses a color scale when envisioning the finished product. Furnishings and antiques will never break the bank, but Corcoran prefers not to dip too heavily into the Crate and Barrel catalog.

After working for Leonard McIntosh and Michael de Santis, Corcoran started his own boutique firm in 1986. With an office of three, he handles eight to ten projects at a time, from full-scale renovations to one room redesigns for existing clients. He charges a reasonable upfront design fee and a standard markup over wholesale. Living rooms are generally in the $75,000 to $100,000 range. Clients, who tend to be in the financial or legal profession, report that he is genteel, polite, straightforward, and eager to please. Corcoran's first clients, now in their 70s, still use him today.

"Chris is both flexible and decisive. Very easy to work with." "There were a few mistakes, but Christopher took complete responsibility and had them fixed." "The first thing people say when they see our house is, 'I can't believe it's new!' It feels like it's been this way forever." "A painter's eye." "From the very beginning, we weren't just on the same page, we were on the same word." "The back office is helpful, always staying on top of things, even if the schedule got thrown off." "Christopher really pushed for a Louis XVI commode in our dining room, but he forfeited his commission on it. He just thought it was the right thing." "He can work with the architect from the very beginning." "A great 'first designer.' Chris can really help you develop your sensibilities." "Christopher handled every aspect of our project, including the structural things like wiring and plumbing. We called him our CEO."

Coffinier Ku Design Ltd. 🛍   4.5   4   4   4
249 East 57th Street, Suite 2R, New York, NY 10022
(212) 715 - 9699 www.coffinierku.com
Grand-to-chic French-inspired design

Known for his distinct Francophile design leanings, exacting details, and imaginative whimsy, Etienne Coffinier has a loyal New York client base. Coffinier practiced architecture and interior design in France for seventeen years before crossing the pond in 1998. With an artistic vision to bring the elegance and skills of continental craft to the United States, Coffinier's designs are based on classical motifs but refined with a modern flourish. Given Coffinier's architectural background and the business skills of his partner, Ed Ku, the firm takes a holistic approach, assuming ownership for all design details, including doors, lighting, room configurations, and the hiring of the contractor. Clients report they are both relieved and impressed.

Coffinier was educated in Rouen and Lille, where he received an M. Arch. In France, he worked for numerous heads of states and many Middle Eastern palaces. Ku, responsible for the day-to-day management of client projects, has an M.B.A. from Columbia and fifteen years of experience in marketing for diverse businesses, from Crest toothpaste to Broadway musicals. Since 1998, the firm has concentrated on residential work, with occasional forays into the high-end restaurant world. Recent projects include the restaurants Piano Due and Frederick's Madison, as well as a 4,500 square foot loft in Soho, which they built from the hardwood up.

New clients range from those refurbishing a bathroom to major home renovations. Clients are billed monthly with hourly rates for all the design and shopping time of Coffinier and low product commissions. Coffinier is said to use a wide range of sources, depending upon the client's interests. As a result, living room costs may vary greatly, from $50,000 to $500,000. ASID. KB 2003.

"Etienne's attention to detail is so impressive. I now have a whole new appreciation of architectural detail." "I'm going to use them for all my future projects." "They have a beautiful aesthetic sense." "They help just as much in space planning as in the decorating." "There's an underlying architectural logic to everything they do." "Both designers really dedicated 100% of their focus on our project." "Their ideas are very chic." "A young, energetic team." "We combined two apartments and they totally guided us." "They are good about keeping the beloved family heirlooms and making them work within the scheme." "Etienne and Ed were able to translate and combine French chic and style with a hip downtown Soho loft." "There were extraordinarily few change orders with Etienne and Ed at the helm." "Just try them and you'll be addicted."

Connie Beale Inc. 🛍️ 3.5 3.5 4 4.5
125 East Putnam Avenue, Greenwich, CT 06830
(203) 661 - 6003 www.conniebeale.com
Dashing, luxurious, updated, classical interior design

Connie Beale is known as an assertive decorator with fine taste who aims for the best in quality materials and products. Beale is described as extremely hands-on, occasionally taking hammer in hand to demonstrate to contractors how something should be done. Beale's design style has been called "casually elegant," featuring modern flourishes and youthful verve. With a fresh, radiant approach, upholstered lines are tailored, layouts are pared down, and a comfortable openness is achieved. References tell us each project is a unique work with Beale being extremely collaborative, yet resolute in her overall vision. Many of Beale's products are of her own design, often forming the dramatic focus point in a room (be it a sculptural iron chandelier or the artistic palm frond finials on a tester bed).

A native of Louisiana, Beale holds a degree from Louisiana Tech and established her practice in 1979. One of a handful of designers in the suburban area that has attracted national attention, she has done substantial residential and commercial work in New York, including the interiors of The Regency Hotel on Park Avenue. There are ten on staff, including three excellent project managers and a draftsman. Beale and senior designer Brian del Toro (who joined Beale after working with New York's prestigious Parish-Hadley and David Kleinberg) oversee all project decisions. References are impressed with the clear paperwork and back office management.

The firm discusses budgets up front in great detail, establishing a standard starting budget that can swell given the client's preferences. Supporters who have used Beale for numerous projects say they completely trust her creative

(and sometimes unorthodox) ideas, and let her work largely unsupervised through much of the project. The firm charges standard hourly rates and classic product markups. Next door to Beale's office in Greenwich there is a hip and evocative 1,000 square foot store, 'Button,' that features vintage and handcrafted goods; Beale makes good use of it. ASID. HB Top Designers, 1999, 2000. KB, 2001.

"She made our house young again." "While I seriously questioned the eggplant walls, she was right and we now love it." "She spoiled us by introducing us to the best. A favorite expression is 'you can do better' and we did." "Not a pushover, but wonderful to work with." "It was virtually decorated overnight. In six months, it looked as if we had lived there five years." "The budget quickly went out the window." "Great integrity." "Not soft, she is no-nonsense and doesn't play games. Says it like it is with no fluff, but she's not a prima donna or a diva." "I am at a point now where I just give her the keys and tell her to do it." "We have nothing but compliments and raves."

Constantin Gorges Ltd. 🏠   4.5   4   4.5   4.5
450 Alton Road, Suite 3210, Miami Beach, FL 33139
(646) 234 - 5686 www.constantingorges.com
Adroit, modern-hued, traditional interior design

Constantin Gorges has impressed clients with interiors that reflect a worldly view, pastiches that are jauntily poised on the leading edge. Designs range from clean 20th century modern to continental traditional luxury, but are typically a mix. This creates an interplay of energy and form that is consistently described as "exquisite." Gorges favors luxurious materials and fine antiques, used with restraint. Architecture usually sets the tone—Neoclassical glam on Fifth, English country in Bedford, funky 1950s on the West Side, hip Deco-Moderne in Florida, New Age on the 77th floor—but all are said to be gracious. Gorges recently moved his operations to Palm Beach, but he keeps one foot in Manhattan, tending to existing clients and taking on new work in both cities.

Gorges is sympathetic to budget constraints, expertly integrating clients' existing furnishings into the design plan. While he knows and offers the best, he always seems to have a well-priced alternative "up his sleeve." Because of his excellent and multifarious training—Parsons, Noel Jeffrey, Peter Marino, and Parish-Hadley's architecture department—Gorges, according to appreciative clients, often becomes the project manager. While he wins accolades for delivering fantastic architectural details (including lighting schematics) and intelligent design elements (Peter Marino at a fraction of the cost), some say he has less interest in selecting the detailed accessories, such as books, picture frames, etc.

Gorges is known to be very fair with his fees, as he is most focused on a perfect end result. He has been known to waive charges for things that are redone even if he originally followed a client decision. He charges a standard design fee and a reasonable percentage over net. Oversight fees may be charged by the hour or on a percentage basis. Clients highly recommend Gorges for his cohesive vision and outstanding project management skills. KB, 2001.

"He has an amazing work ethic—if the client is not happy then Constantin feels he has not done his job properly." "He will find it or create it if you can't afford the real thing." "He is clear on price and there are never any surprises." "Constantin is a trendsetter, not a trend follower." "The living room can be a Bentley and the kids' rooms attractive VW Bugs." "He pre-shops and doesn't waste your time." "He is the kind of decorator that your husband would also like, but he is not going to take the place of your best girlfriend." "There is a tendency for the more formal that you can tone down." "High-minded design that's quite livable." "He's got an eye for detail,

everything is thought through." "Constantin is 100% dependable and particularly effective at getting suppliers to deliver." "He could have prepared us better regarding overall costs." "He will negotiate price very hard on your behalf." "He is always available and has no attitude, and your apartment will have tons of personality.

Craig Nealy Architects

49 West 38th Street, Suite 12A, New York, NY 10018
(917) 342 - 0060 www.craignealy.com

Modern, engaging, innovative architecture and interior design

See Craig Nealy Architects' full report under the heading Architects

Cullman & Kravis Inc.   4.5   5   4   4.5

790 Madison Avenue, 7th Floor, New York, NY 10021
(212) 249 - 3874 www.cullmankravis.com

Exquisite, stately-yet-accessible, traditional interior design

Cullman & Kravis has clearly established itself as a venerable design firm transcending generations. Founded in 1985 by Elissa Cullman and the late Heidi Kravis, the firm is often called upon to design around superb collections of fine art and antiques. Cullman's own Fairfield home is filled with the results of a lifelong devotion to fine Americana, a theme often carried to patrons' country homes. Clients are consistently impressed by the firm's "traditional yet creative" textures, project management acumen, and extreme attention to detail.

Clients have included the CEOs of Philip Morris, Goldman Sachs, Paramount, Solomon Brothers, and Miramax, as well as the estate of John Singer Sargent. While the firm may have as many as 25 projects at any one time (in various stages), a full staff of "super competent" project coordinators helps manage project operations. Cullman's supporters see her as the design inspiration, working from the client's interests. Generally speaking, most clients note that Cullman was fairly available and were pleased with their strong project managers. The firm also wins accolades for its sensitivity to family living.

Customers consider pricing top of the market but worth it. The firm charges a standard design fee, classic retail on product and workroom, standard markup on antiques, and standard hourly fees for oversight. While "no expense is spared," the contract reportedly is followed to the line. The firm's outreach to superior craftsmen is described as "unparalleled." Supporters highly recommended the firm for those who appreciate effective oversight of the highest caliber quality. Many clients have used the firm multiple times—the ultimate compliment. AD 100, 2000, 2002, 2004.

"Very consistent quality." "I really respected Ellie's integrity. With our new home she insisted that we first put the money into the proper architecture, saying that the sofas could be purchased anytime." "The firm's incredible organization skills are very comforting." "Though slipcovers are not Ellie's thing, she did what I asked and made it look great." "Twelve years later, everything still looks fresh." "The only firm to use if you're a serious collector. They understand that mindset." "Many of the same chintzes and tartans are used, even in the same color." "Ellie personally vetted every antique and kept a close eye on the associates assigned to us." "You can end up working with a junior partner a lot, but they're all great." "People have nicknamed the firm 'The Sorority,' with Ellie as the den mother, monitoring the operation carefully." "We lucked out and I loved my young project manager, but things did not work out so well with my friend." "I did not want to be involved on a detailed basis, and I certainly did not need to be—they did it all perfectly." "My husband is crazy about Ellie—and it amazed me that he got involved at all." "They wanted a lot of feedback from us, and they acted on it." "Ellie's knowledge of antiques and rugs is extensive and central to her stately decorating." "Not a bargain but top quality." "She'll throw a curveball from time to time. It helps to avoid a prosaic look." "She delivers an Ameri-

can original—extraordinarily luscious designs that withstand the test of time. Classic opulence meets livable comfort." "A+ service at tip-top prices."

D'Aquino Monaco Inc. 🛍   4   3.5   5   5
214 West 29th Street, Suite 1202, New York, NY 10001
(212) 929 - 9787 www.daquinomonaco.com

Unique, vibrant, warm interior design and architecture

Clients recommend D'Aquino Monaco with warmth and joy. The firm is said to make a personal investment in each project, resulting in vibrant and unique interiors. Carl D'Aquino has been in the profession for over two decades and was joined later in his career by architect Francine Monaco. Clients appreciate the full service capabilities of the partners and also mention their unusually calm and kind nature. The firm is known for its remarkably varied styles, from Italian modernism to resonant color to high Victorian, driven by client preferences.

The firm's recent projects include large houses built from the ground up, chic downtown lofts, Upper East Side apartments, and a penthouse in Knightsbridge. Clients include a wide range of professionals—artists, fashion designers, actors, and Wall Streeters. Bringing charm and character to newly built large-scale homes is a specialty recognized by clients, who benefit from the unusually close ties the firm has established with its supporters. D'Aquino Monaco is also developing a furniture line and recently designed the executive offices for La Prairie, as well as the La Prairie Silver Rain Spa at the new Ritz-Carlton Grand Cayman. It was also recently featured in the *Robb Report's* "Best of the Best" list.

Generally, a standard up-front design fee is charged and products are acquired at a reasonable percentage over net. Oversight fees are in the typical range, and the firm is quite sensitive to budgetary constraints, often shopping outside normally traveled paths and offering creative alternatives. D'Aquino Monaco will also do consultations by the hour. The partners have many repeat customers who think the world of the firm. ASID. HB Top Designers, 2000, 2001.

"Francine and Carl will go the extra mile for their clients—we undertook an exhaustive auction hunt together for the perfect antiques for our house." "They were instrumental in advising me on the purchase of my new apartment." "They are not constricted by the common view of coherency." "Carl and Francine are very cost-conscious, offering several alternatives." "I did not want a traditional, refined apartment, but a fresh breeze. They got it." "Underrated by the industry. All of their work is interesting, and sometimes it's superb." "We were amazed at how they created a room of multiple functions, with folding furniture that looked just fabulous." "Carl's work is lovely, but sometimes he caves in to clients. He should put his foot down and rely on his excellent instincts." "All the firm's interiors make a thematic personal statement, and are tied together with comfortable upholstery." "Heavily conceptual designs that look very natural." "I admit to being a skeptic at first, but they did an incredible job." "Carl and Francine have brought expression and joy to all six of our projects. We are dedicated clients."

Dana Nicholson Studio Inc. 🛍   4   3   5   5
515 Broadway, New York, NY 10012
(212) 941 - 6834 www.dananicholsonstudio.com

Spare, luxurious interior design

A classicist and modernist at once, Dana Nicholson is praised for his cultured, hip, and opulent designs. Frequent references to antiquity and unapologetically decorative furniture often reside in clean and restrained backgrounds. Born on Canada's Prince Edward Island and raised in Germany and rural Maine, Nicholson is able to capture an elegant, yet peaceful harmony of cultures and styles. This aesthetic is said to be beautiful, functional, and comfortable. All customers, especially those unsure of what they are trying to articulate, applaud Nicholson's confident direction.

After graduating from Northeastern University, Nicholson spent five years with Melvin Dwork, mixing interior design with jewelry, photography, and fashion. In 1992, he opened his own studio. Clients include young bohemians and the uptown chic with loft-like aspirations. Some commercial projects have been completed as well, including the Sean clothing store and the advertising offices of Grey Entertainment. Nicholson is said to be very adept at designing complementary lighting fixtures, custom carpets, and intricate hardware. No detail is said to be too small for Nicholson to improve upon its design.

Pricing is said to be quite reasonable, with Nicholson providing a multitude of economic choices. Return clients say they would recommend him to anyone. HB Top Designers, 2000, 2001.

"I can hardly wait for Dana to start my next home." "Dana is so imaginative. He will let you go as far as you want to go." "Fun to work with. No angst." "After he did my loft twice, I recommended him to my mother. She just loved his minimal elegance." "Dana has great vision, but kitchens are not his forte." "I don't know how he does it, but his rooms are both luscious and spare." "Out-of-the-box thinking." "I would not recommend him for traditional spaces, it would be a mismatch." "Dana has strong taste and loves strong colors. You have to be equally strong to change his mind. But the results will always be glorious." "Dana's follow-through is his biggest strength." "Although his personal style is different from my own, it is as though he can read my thoughts and anticipate my needs even before I do."

Darren Henault Interiors Inc.   4   4.5   4   5

180 Varick Street, Suite 424, New York, NY 10014
(212) 677 - 5699 www.darrenhenault.com

Tailored, traditional interior design

"Traditional" is a tricky word, meaning different things to different people. Darren Henault embraces its essence—comfort, familiarity, formality—but forgoes the expected connotation, wall-to-wall chintz and overstuffed pillows. Generally, Henault employs a palette of pale creams, browns, and rich tans for a calm foundation, then livens things up with midcentury furniture, vivid prints, and clever fixtures. The result: upscale yet inviting rooms that convey exquisite detail, whether one is looking at a picture or examining the couch with a magnifying glass. Sources remark that his homes are always comfortable and relaxed for their inhabitants yet always surprising and entertaining for their guests.

On the advice of architect (and family friend) Norman Rosenfeld, Henault left behind a successful advertising career to enter interior design on the ground floor, taking classes at FIT and sewing slipcovers. From there, he graduated to window treatments, upholstery, and eventually his own design firm, which he formed in 1996. Sources say this step-by-step education gives Henault a leg up on the competition: he appreciates the process at all levels.

Henault's firm of five takes on a large number of projects at one time, reflecting its principal's workaholic, Type-A professional style. Clients applaud his breadth of knowledge, his enthusiasm, and his quick wit (Henault on drapes: "A naked window is like a naked 90-year-old man"). Generally, he charges a reasonable upfront design fee and a markup on the higher end of standard. When the project is less involved, Henault will work on an hourly basis. Clients note the expense, then hire Henault anyway, saying "I would work with Darren again and again and again."

"From a contractor's point of view, we have found them very easy to work with, a trait that is not too common among NYC designers." "He is a fun, funny, very easygoing person." "Darren's taste does run toward the expensive and his fees are on the high side of designers we interviewed. However, he did work with us even though we could not afford to do everything at once at the level which he (and soon we) wanted." "In the end a designer's personality may be one of the most important issues to consider when hiring someone. As for Darren, you cannot find a more enjoyable, pleasant,

entertaining and talented individual." "Darren's assistant Michael was a wonderful help." "Occasionally, when he is very busy, it can be difficult to coordinate timing. But in general, he tries to make himself available when it is convenient to you." "Every night I rock our baby to sleep in our beautiful nursery and I thank Darren. It is the most beautiful room in our home."

David Easton Inc.   5   5   4   4.5
72 Spring Street, 7th Floor, New York, NY 10012
(212) 334 - 3820   www.davideastoninc.com

Extraordinary, timeless, elegant interior design

David Easton is universally recognized as one of today's great patriarchs of interior design. His striking ability to instantly visualize the perfect solution, acquire masterful product, and manage (with a large support system) a comprehensive project with the highest standards sets him apart. While best known for interiors that recapture the elegance of the classic English country manor with a modern sweep, he is equally capable of using other styles. Supporters add that Easton is brilliant, funny, and friendly.

Project management is where the firm excels. There are about fifteen to twenty large commissions at a time, and a process for everything—including how to manage the painters. Most of the firm's jobs are exceedingly large and expensive. While Easton is quite involved with the up-front design plans, which are lovingly drawn much by hand (working fifteen hours a day, seven days a week), experienced project managers take over from there. Working within a large library of "Easton-approved" materials, many of them created by exclusive European artisans (with exclusive markups), the managers cannot stray too far from the master.

Most commissions are in the United States, from New York and Connecticut to Aspen, but select projects do reach as far as England, Africa, and Jamaica. Easton has been recognized for his licensed designer collections with Lee Jofa, Cole & Son, Beauvais Carpets, Walter's Wicker, Robert Abbey, and Henredon.

Easton has a devoted following. While his clients generally acknowledge that costs are over the top (reportedly, living rooms of $600,000 to $1.2 million are the norm), most say the firm's extraordinary results and overall client services are worth every penny. AD 100, 1990, 1995, 2000, 2002, 2004. HB Top Designers, 1999, 2000, 2001, 2002, 2003, 2004, 2005. ID Hall of Fame. KB 2000, 2003.

"David instantly connects with people. I learned so much from him." "He has a masterful touch, and his spaces are extraordinary, livable, and timeless." "David understands that things should be built to last." "For Room 101 there is Carpet 101.1, etc. And with their bi-monthly meetings, there are never any surprises." "David looks into the past to predict the future." "While we liked our project manager, I only saw David about once a month, and he was always about to fly somewhere else. While we were very pleased with the end product, we did not enjoy the process." "Flawless design." "His office runs like a well-oiled machine." "The meter is always running." "In Greenwich, there is an easier sensibility that very much relates to the landscape and a calm, genteel living." "They simply get what we want in our home and then make it reality. Is the cost high? The answer is yes, usually!" "His products are all fantastic, and he uses them beautifully in his designs." "All the antiques are vetted and valued, which gives me tremendous confidence." "David's unique products and superior client service are unmatched."

David Howell Design Inc.
200 Park Avenue South, Suite 1518, New York, NY 10003
(212) 477 - 0149   www.davidhowell.net

Creative, contemporary, unique residential architecture

See David Howell Design, Inc.'s full report under the heading Architects

	Quality ✚	Cost $	Value ◆	Recommend? ★

David Kleinberg Design Associates   5   5   4   4.5

330 East 59th Street, New York, NY 10022
(212) 754 - 9500 www.dkda.com

Sophisticated, luxurious, supremely-edited contemporary interior design

Walking into a David Kleinberg home, one is immediately overwhelmed by the plethora of shapely, elegant forms and simultaneously impressed by the understated yet layered grandeur. Everything has a place and a point of view. But first the flow and architecture is reconstituted—moldings, baseboards, mantles, doors are expunged of all extraneous detail and refit as handsome moments of definition. Then comes the ultimate paint job, with at least three shades of crème or gray on the dado paneling to further enhance the dimensionality and add structure to the space. Rugs, furniture, textiles, accessories, and artwork are chosen with extreme care for their sculptural qualities and ability to create harmonious interludes. This often means the real thing—including original, neutral-clad Eugéne Printz, Jacques Adnet, and Clément Rousseaus. And last but certainly not least, the latest amenities are required: motorized window shades, a multitude of kitchen gadgets, and a bathroom wired for stereo in the shower. Clients who make it across the finish line are ecstatic with the outcome.

After sixteen years at Parish Hadley with Albert as his mentor, Kleinberg founded this namesake firm in 1997. In a very short period of time, DKDA became one of the most respected talent bases in the country, with plugged-in New Yorkers clamoring for his time. With a staff of 28, about 10 large commissions are taken on at a time and in-house architectural services are extensive. Recent Manhattan projects include a Park Avenue apartment, an UES townhouse, and a Tribeca loft. Other clients are located in Greenwich, Palm Beach, Little Rock, Maine, Los Angeles, Washington, D.C., Jumby Bay, and London. They include notables Scott Rudin and Jessye Norman. New projects tend to be substantial and elaborate. In addition to designing custom furniture for clients, Kleinberg has recently launched a rug collection with Patterson, Flynn & Martin.

The firm charges a standard design fee, classic retail on product, and standard oversight fees. Kleinberg can find the "most extraordinary antique table base and knows exactly what marble top will highlight it at half the cost of the original." Products tend to be the best available; when needed, the firm has extensive and extraordinary custom builders to fabricate the dream. Clients feel they get a masterpiece at a commensurate price. HB Top Designers, 1999, 2000, 2001, 2002, 2003, 2004, 2005. KB 1998.

"David exudes confidence. And his designs reflect that polish." "We purchased two apartments that David wove together seamlessly." "While clearly aiming to please, he has a particular stylistic point of view that you need to understand before you begin." "Unless you are planning to spend a serious amount, I would not go there." "You buy into the process." "Gorgeous work that both clients and other designers love." "David was great about using our less costly source for the kid's furniture and even did the drawings." "When you are with David, he absolutely gives you his full attention." "We had a team of three on the front lines. This worked very well." "Not the right fit for someone who wants to do part of it themselves." "It always looks right because David visits the upholsterer several times before it is presented to you." "You do not get any bargains anywhere, but it is all perfect."

David McMahon ⬛

155 East 56th Street, New York, NY 10022
(212) 755 - 2551

Pedigreed, transitional residential architecture and interior design

See David McMahon's full report under the heading Architects

	Quality	Cost	Value	Recommend?
	+	$	◆	★

David Scott Interiors Ltd.   4   4   4   4.5

120 East 57th Street, 2nd Floor, New York, NY 10022
(212) 829 - 0703   david@davidscottinteriors.com

Characteristic, joyful, modern-hued interior design

With youthful verve and a dedicated soul, David Scott creates transitional rooms with a view to the future and a nod to the past. Neutral backgrounds often highlight a thoughtful mixture of vintage, antique, and sculptural shapes with rousing accents. Described as "exceptionally knowledgeable, accommodating, and practical," Scott takes great care to understand the client's viewpoint and develop long-term relationships.

Clients tell us Scott is a "design psychologist" who understands their physical and spiritual design thoughts better than they do, and in turn delivers a highly customized product. Scott has been known to wade through clients' closets to better understand their stylistic interests. Scott is on the board of trustees at the New York School of Interior Design and was previously in the hotel and real estate businesses.

The firm charges standard hourly fees for design plans and oversight, and reasonable markups on products with a sliding scale for more expensive antiques. Scott reportedly is flexible about offering a variety of economic alternatives, and is praised for meeting timing deadlines. Most living rooms are in the $100,000+ range. Patrons comment that Scott is very professional, with a laid-back office of four. The vast majority of clients return for additional projects.

"David truly believes the best client is a happy client." "David helped me stay within my budget—something that I am not always good at!" "I enjoy my home as much today as I did three years ago when it was finished." "I never wanted to go into my living room before, and now it is my favorite room." "Not a difficult bone in his body." "David always returns phone calls the same day." "A social and witty person who is passionate about his work." "We reap the benefits of his wonderful relationships with vendors." "Sometimes more expensive than expected, because David is a real perfectionist and only uses the best." "As a businessman, he relies on his contract." "He strives to understand his clients' lifestyles, anticipates practical needs, and executes every project detail with style." "He hooked me up with a fabulous architect and a reliable, honest, professional contractor." "Always listens to the client, no matter what." "He is as nice as he is talented, with real star potential."

Dennis Rolland Inc.   4   4   4   5

405 East 54th Street, New York, NY 10022
(212) 644 - 0537   dennisrolland@verizon.net

Sumptuous, traditional, European and American interior design

Clients continue to champion Dennis Rolland for his cultivated eye, exacting standards, and warm personality. Assembling atmospheres of layered elegance, saturated color, and timelessness, Rolland ably mixes charming objects of lesser value with important antiques. Clients report that they receive a highly personalized design which may embrace "over-the-top" classical grandeur, "perfect suburban," or "funky-exuberant-charming." But what remains consistent is Rolland's commitment to fine quality. Suppliers also respect Rolland, enabling him to deliver the highest quality to clients.

Rolland started his own business in 1987 after six years with mentor Mark Hampton. Clients currently include world-renowned businessmen, European dowagers, the Greenwich establishment, and some second-generation young couples with high standards and healthy budgets. He is willing to do a few rooms at a time, knowing that the initiated will come back for more.

Most clients do not have a set budget, with many living rooms in the $250,000+ range before antiques. The firm has an excellent business reputation. There is no design fee and products are purchased at retail. KB 1990, 1994.

"Dennis is such a gentleman. I call him my personal Fred Astaire." "I can't say enough about Dennis. He will come to your house to hang the pictures himself and fluff the pillows before a big party." "Dennis updated my entire house, simultaneously making it fresher and more traditional." "Dennis coaxed out aspects of my style that I didn't know I had." "He arrives at my house with five or six shopping bags to see how I will react. If I don't like them, he goes back and does it again." "Dennis is extremely patient." "There are some things he absolutely insisted on, which was initially a source of tension. Dennis turned out to be absolutely right." "My husband is an antique furniture collector and very much respects Dennis's knowledge and sophisticated eye." "He certainly showed us expensive things, but was never pushy when it came to the budget." "He is perpetually hired in our house and has become a real friend."

Dessins LLC/Penny Drue Baird 🏠   4.5   4.5   4   5

787 Madison Avenue, Third Floor, New York, NY 10021
(212) 288 - 3600   pbaird@attglobal.net

Detailed, thoughtful traditional and modern interior design

Known for her traditional yet extraordinary European style, clients applaud Penny Drue Baird's insight, taste, and talents. Her attention to detail, unique perspective, and exacting standards of quality also set her apart. Baird is said to take great pains to match the interiors to the architecture of the house and the personality of the client; attempting "to fulfill each client's fantasy." Baird has a second residence in France, and her work often takes on a Gallic hue, including many an object found at the French flea markets (reclaimed antique ceiling beams, a full-wall 19th-century walnut boiserie, antique carpet runners) and French-inspired craftmanship (fabric upholstered walls, unique lozenge-shaped door handles). Though her designs have ranged from timeless Givenchy classic to Calvin Klein sleek, each is consistent in theme throughout.

A former psychologist, Baird received her doctorate in child psychology from the Albert Einstein Medical School. After receiving a degree from NYSID, she adeptly used her psychological training to understand the client's lifestyle and what works best over the long term. With her easy and gracious manner, Baird develops excellent relationships with her clients, who often become friends. There are four assistants to help coordinate about ten medium to huge projects at a time, but Baird does all the shopping herself.

Multiple layers of intricacy play their roles, subtly adding to the effect and to the cost. Most everything is custom and top of the line. Living rooms tend to be in the $175,000+ range. The firm charges higher design fees (for a very complete package) and standard product markups. While thought to be outside of many budgets, those who can secure her services consider her worth every penny, often returning for later projects. AD 100, 2004. KB 2000, 2005.

"Impeccable taste." "Penny has unbelievable vision and creativity." "Unending resources, efficiency, speed, and imagination." "She came into my living room and did five things, transforming it from a frumpy, grandmotherly look to the hip and now. My friends and I were amazed." "She is so busy. It would help if she hired a few more office people to leverage her time and answer the phone." "She does not clamor to work on a budget." "Penny and her staff make every project a pleasure." "Penny is incredibly creative and has a great sense of proportion and color." "Amazing work,

but she needs space and scope—not a 'one room' decorator." "My house is filled with beautiful objects from Paris and London." "We couldn't imagine our surroundings without her." "It was a huge pleasure to watch Penny transform our house." "If I won the lottery, the first thing I would do is hire her again."

Dineen Architecture & Design PC
56 East 81st Street, New York, NY 10028
(212) 249 - 2575 www.dineenarchitecture.com
Modern, romantic, comfortable residential architecture

See Dineen Architecture & Design PC's full report under the heading Architects

Drake Design Associates Inc.   4.5   4.5   4   5
315 East 62nd Street, 5th Floor, New York, NY 10021
(212) 754 - 3099 www.drakedesignassociates.com
Bold, stylistic, colorful interior design

Jamie Drake is heartily endorsed by clients for his inventive refreshing style, attention to detail, and warm personality. Well known for his invigorating palette of vibrant color, fashion infusions, and over-the-top embellishments, Drake also works well with more moderate customers. Clients report that he is happy to take their lead, while gently nudging them in a coherent direction.

Drake established his firm upon his graduation from Parsons in 1978. There are two senior designers and a registered architect on staff. While there is a (not surprising) substantial minimum for new clients, Drake will work with a client in phases, and can be very budget-minded. Clients span a wide range of ages and design interests, but all speak warmly of Drake and his work. Commissions include Gracie Mansion, Mayor Michael Bloomberg's Manhattan townhouse (a client for seventeen years), Madonna's lush, dramatic LA residence, and Victor Gramm's retreat on Martha's Vineyard. References all conclude that Drake offers wonderful customer service.

A standard design fee is charged, with all products at a reasonable markup. Oversight usually falls under Drake's purview—at higher rates. Younger clients often do living rooms in the $100,000 range, with more established clientele in the $500,000 range. A number of clients are repeat customers: one devotee has done nine projects with Drake, including two planes, a helicopter, and a boat. ASID. HB Top Designers, 2000, 2001, 2002, 2003, 2004, 2005. ID Hall of Fame. KB 2002, 2004.

"His designs tell creative, fashion-based stories." "Jamie has an infallible eye and a great sense of humor." "They have given me the best service imaginable." "He is an original with very high-quality standards." "Jamie transposed my estate-sale apartment into something absolutely fantastic with creativity and color." "I follow his lead without question." "He works best when he's allowed to make his own decisions." "His sense of color is unmatched." "Luxury, glamour, and sensuality." "Jamie holds the line between inventive forward thinking and being out of control." "In all the years I have dealt with Jamie, I cannot remember a single lapse." "A perfect match of wondrous creativity and a well-run business." "Decorating with Jamie is like FAO Schwarz for big kids."

Dujardin Design Associates   4.5   5   4   4
PO Box 5202, Westport, CT 06881
(203) 838 - 8100 www.dujardindesign.com
Elegant, comfortable, environmentally conscious interior design

While most clients hire Dujardin Design Associates for its evocative, high-quality, classic lines of yesteryear, many are also attracted to the firm's philosophic predilection for green, allergy-sensitive materials. Supporters say princi-

pal Trudy Dujardin is like a scientist, with an amazing knowledge of materials. Designs often feature strong, traditional, handsome millwork that juxtaposes comfortable, clean, neutral settings with a touch of country chic.

Dujardin began her firm in 1982, determined to meld tasteful design with environmentally-smart decision making. Most of her work is in Connecticut, Manhattan and Nantucket, where Dujardin has a home. Responsive to the client's interests, Dujardin leads the design decisions and the project managers implement. The firm also provides a turnkey service including linens, cookware, and houseplants.

Clients say that Dujardin is quite expensive, but well worth it if you are particular. The firm charges a flat design fee and standard retail, and also offers hourly environmental consulting. Dujardin is generally regarded by industry leaders as an expert in the world of green design; she is a board member of the Joslyn Castle Institute for Sustainable Communities and the Design Futures Council. Clients reap the benefits of Dujardin's green efforts, but note that she can work in other colors as well. ASID.

"Everyone in the office is very nice and helpful." "Green design doesn't just mean environmentally conscious materials. Trudy really thinks about how people live, not just what looks good." "Every piece of hardware and plumbing is an exact reproduction—no detail is too small for Trudy to have custom made." "We did not do the environmental thing with her and found her attention to detail to be excellent." "Trudy and Price Connors were very helpful from the beginning—they worked with our architects and provided helpful guidance on every decision." "Having Dujardin Design Associates on board before we started building was a godsend." "They are most aware of the environment and the importance of designing in harmony with it." "Not cheap, but no more expensive than anyone on her level." "Really really smart design." "Trudy can be hard to reach given her multiple locations and multiple commitments." "Although almost everything was new, I immediately felt completely at home." "She is the first decorator that we will use again."

Elaine Griffin 🛍   4   3.5   4.5   4
315 West 39th Street, Suite 1203, New York, NY 10018
(212) 239 - 3090 www.elainegriffin.com
High-end residential interior design

Elaine Griffin builds interiors of comfort, starting with the client's personal treasures and memorabilia. Known for her sensitivity to lifestyle and her practicality with a budget, Griffin strives to create effortless, elegant spaces that look as if they evolved over time. Rooms are calm and inviting, enticing the inhabitants to linger.

Raised in Georgia, Griffin majored in art history at Yale and interior design at NYSID. She worked as a publicist in New York and Paris for nine years, and then joined Peter Marino. Clients say her "colorful and spunky, but not over the top," personality matches her designs perfectly. Griffin opened her own firm in 1997 and has been earning good press and solid client recommendations ever since. HB Top Designers, 2000, 2001, 2002, 2003, 2004, 2005. KB 2003.

"Elaine's peppy personality adds to the charm of working with her." "The first thing that struck me about her was she is clearly an expert, but respects and appreciates that the home is mine—a place where I am going to live, not just a showpiece for her book." "A ton of fun to work with." "She's always laughing and having a blast—nothing seems to get her down." "The outcome was great but the process was slow going." "We love working with her, and would do so again in a heartbeat." "Smart, witty, and on the ball."

Eric Cohler Incorporated 🛍️   4   3.5   4.5   5

872 Madison Avenue, Suite 2B, New York, NY 10021
(212) 737 - 8600   www.ericcohler.com

Updated, traditional, ingenious interior design

Mixing the classically enduring and beautifully erudite with excessive fun is Eric Cohler's modus operandi. Known for realizing his client's visions with a dedicated interest and an edge toward the future, Cohler is said to have his client's view at heart. With a confident countenance, this designer deftly composes the fine and the found, the traditional and the postmodern. Appreciated for his architectural inventiveness as well as his design skills, Cohler effectively works with the client's architect from a project's inception, adding significant architectural enhancements.

Clients laud Cohler for his helpful, reliable, and diplomatic nature, saying he quickly understands their intentions. Cohler's training includes a B.A. in art history and an M.S. in historic preservation and design from Columbia University. On his own since 1990, he comes recommended by more established designers and the trade as a rising star in the industry. He currently has a staff of six, including two senior designers, but clients note that Cohler remains very accessible.

The firm works with a low up-front design fee and a reasonable markup over net for products. Alternatively, it can work on an hourly fee basis when shopping for products. Standard oversight fees are charged on a percentage basis. Cohler gravitates to the best quality the budget will allow, but he is perfectly willing to mix his aesthetic with the client's existing furniture and new Crate & Barrel items. Known as Mr. Answerman, Cohler has wide-ranging resources and can accommodate many budget levels, remaining value-conscious whatever the price. He recently debuted a substantial couture-inspired line of fabrics at Lee Jofa with a wide range of price points. Professional, businesslike, and generous, Cohler has an excellent reputation with past clients, who frequently ask him back. HB Top Designers, 1999, 2000, 2001, 2002, 2003, 2004, 2005. KB 1994, 1999, 2001, 2004, 2006.

"Eric is so easy, quick and has so much range. He is as good with his left brain as his right—creative and yet so practical." "When my architect and I were perplexed as to how to treat the walls adjoining the three floors in our apartment, Eric envisioned the solution with just one look." "Eric willingly and lovingly helped design our Christmas decorations last year and never asked for a fee. He did the same for my friend's Rosh Hashanah dinner." "Refined, immaculate, and sincere." "He could even make items purchased at Ethan Allen sing on Park Avenue." "Eric has an encyclopedic knowledge of furniture, antiques, fine art, and what's happening on the Upper East Side. He's a fantastic designer and a great conversationalist." "A master of design, but blueprints are not his forte." "Eric is my insurance policy because I know everything he suggests will be correct." "There is no question that Eric's decoration was the reason I was able to sell my house so quickly and profitably."

Eric Lysdahl Inc. 🛍️   4   3.5   4.5   4.5

960 Madison Avenue, New York, NY 10021
(212) 717 - 5121 www.ericlysdahl.com

Enchanting, composite, fluid interior design

Eric Lysdahl receives accolades for his resourcefulness, patience, and designs of familiar warmth. Whether it be a six-story townhouse, a new house in the Hamptons, or a set of curtains, he is known to give his all in developing unique and personalized designs. With a view grounded in tailored neoclassical reference, his compositions show knowledge of the greats but also evoke a strong,

metropolitan modernity. Bringing elegant lines to Fifth Avenue and stylish, comfortable chic to the Hamptons, Lysdahl successfully wraps his creations around his clients to fit their lifestyle.

Lysdahl is said to have the winsome personality of a small-town Midwesterner (where he was raised) and the expertise of a designer with degrees from both FIT (in fashion) and The New York School of Interior Design. A recent *New York Times* article described him as "outwardly mild-mannered...but with a maverick attitude and a sure-footed sense of drama." After training with Bunny Williams, Lysdahl started his own firm in 1998. Aided by a single assistant, he takes on about three larger jobs and a handful of smaller jobs at a time. Current projects include the renovation and decoration of a manor house in Connecticut, an historic Palladian-style mansion in Wetschester County, a Japanese-inspired Arts and Crafts home in Bridgehampton, and a grand apartment in The Riverhouse.

Clients say Lysdahl produces a luxury look at a realistic price. He is known to shop everywhere, seeking "that special find." Shopping with clients is the norm, with all pricing discussed up front. The firm charges a modest design fee and reasonable markups. Vendors are off the beaten path, with Lysdahl "staying on top of every detail." ASID.

"In his very clever American way, he was able to combine some inherited antiques with contemporary furnishings to create a scheme which is both chic and timeless." "Posh without pretense." "Eric rescued my apartment and me from a horrible start with someone else." "With friendly colors, textures, and lots of quirky antiques, he created warmth and a home with heart." "I would never even buy a napkin ring without his approval." "Before Eric, my collection of English and continental antiques looked like a jumble. He created a unified look that sings." "While it cost a bit more than I'd imagined, the end result was worth it." "His professionalism, pleasantness, and personal eloquence are evident the second he walks through the door."

Erica Millar Design Inc.   4   3.5   4.5   4.5

16 East 65th Street, 5th Floor, New York, NY 10021
(212) 439 - 1521   emillar@emd-rra.com

Upscale, understated, serene interior design

Dealers and clients alike applaud Erica Millar for her deft designs and rooms of unassuming beauty and refined elegance. Clients appreciate these rooms for their comfortable, welcoming air and appropriateness to their lifestyles. We hear Millar often teams up with her architect husband, Russell Riccardi, resulting in very streamlined, successful collaborations.

After earning a degree in painting, Millar worked for Frank Gehry, Robert Stern, and Ward Bennett before striking out on her own in 1988. The firm does mostly substantial Manhattan residential renovations. While there is a good amount of staff support, Millar is the primary client interface and does most of the shopping herself. References say she is quite demanding of the dealers, having them restore every little scratch before delivery. If the perfect piece is not readily available, Millar has the resources to create it through her furniture partnership with the manufacturer Walter P. Sauer.

Millar charges a low design fee, a reasonable markup over net on product and an hourly consultation fee for oversight. Living rooms are generally in the $150,000 range, before major antiques and carpets. Many customers have done several projects with Millar, and recommend her "whenever they can."

"Erica's designs work perfectly for both toddler play dates and highbrow cocktail parties." "Her sense of style, color, detail, and scale is impeccable." "You feel as if Erica cares as much about the outcome as you do." "She has done three large residences for us as well as offices. What more can we say?" "My friends are always struck by the calm simplicity of the apartment." "She is not afraid to put Crate & Barrel alongside the finest antiques—and it works." "She feels that her job is not done unless the client is totally satisfied." "Our homes are a source of great comfort and pride."

	Quality	Cost	Value	Recommend?
	➕	$	◆	★

Eve Robinson Associates Inc.

4   4.5   4   4.5

2091 Broadway, Third Floor, New York, NY 10023
(212) 595 - 0661 www.everobinson.net

Clean, comfortable, modern interior design

Eve Robinson is appreciated for her creative use of natural materials, and cohesive compositions of forward-thinking interior elements. Client collaboration is a strength, with Robinson being described as "accessible" and "thoughtful." Clients say Robinson makes her modern aesthetic warm and comfortable by adding traditional elements and accent colors. She is known for her use of high-quality fabrics and fine workmanship.

Robinson studied art history at Vassar, worked in fashion for Polo/Ralph Lauren, and then studied interior design at Parsons. After a year with Victoria Hagan, Robinson founded her firm in 1990. Recent projects include a Manhattan townhouse, a classic Park Avenue apartment, and a house in Westchester. Robinson presents lots of options to clients, often accompanying them on shopping trips. Robinson often works with her husband, the owner of the contracting firm SilverLining, a teaming that reflects her collaborative approach and reportedly elevates the experience.

To start a project, Robinson's firm charges an hourly rate for design concept and shopping, with a commission for product. Oversight fees are in the standard range. Robinson stays to the reasonable side in her product selections and no hourly product fee is charged if a client is paying for oversight services. Living rooms are generally in the $130,000 realm. Clients say they continue to come back to Robinson for livable interiors that are simple yet elegant, on time, and without any surprises. HB Top Designers, 1999, 2000, 2001, 2002, 2003, 2004, 2005. KB 1998, 2001, 2004.

"Eve pushes me to consider items I would not have looked at otherwise." "She saved me from being boring." "When the tile layer had a problem matching a pattern Eve came right up and straightened it out." "She finds furnishings that tread that fine line between unusual and livable." "Elegant, witty, and slightly edgy." "Intellectual bohemian work. Exciting but sophisticated." "Everything she did for us we think we will keep our entire lives." "Her designs are well-received by the younger crowd." "She was very patient about working with us in multiple phases, one project at a time over four years, and we are still going." "Eve has great vendor relationships and sources that I would never dream of." "I've never made a mistake when I have used Eve. I have worked with other decorators to save money, but will not do so again." "For people who want the best and are not particularly price sensitive, Eve comes highly recommended."

FDS Inc.

3.5   3.5   4   4.5

200 Byram Shore Road, Greenwich, CT 06830
(203) 532 - 2944 www.fdsdesign.com

Integrated, full-service, modern-hued interior design

Lori Feldman wins kudos from clients for her excellent organizational skills, extreme attention to detail, and consistent, modernistic design layouts. Clients note that she takes great care to incorporate the lifestyle of the client into the character of the site. Feldman's practice distinguishes itself by focusing solely on complete turnkey designs, with the firm becoming the client's designated representative, managing the architect, contractor, subs, suppliers, and the design and interior decoration. This often includes the wiring scheme and tile placement, and even the fish tanks, sheets, and dishes. Sometimes, Feldman will even go to the level of the flowers, the cutlery, and the music.

Feldman received degrees in interior design and textile design from Syracuse University. Prior to starting her own design firm in 1998, she worked in the fashion trade with Nine West and Liz Claiborne, and in interiors with A Touch of Ivy. Located in Soho, the practice has completed projects throughout Manhattan including the Upper East Side and downtown Tribeca lofts, and as far afield as the Hamptons and Boston. Clients remark on Feldman's "concentrated effort to make it as painless as possible for the client" and her yeoman efforts to deliver a beautiful and appropriately priced product.

"Lori was instrumental in every aspect of the project." "Her drawings and renderings are planned to the smallest detail." "Unlike previous designers, she listened to our request and created the perfect retreat." "Our bedroom is both restful and exciting." "She gets along with everyone from the architect to the electrician and the suppliers." "Lori is so resourceful. Terrific ability with quality furnishings." "She was always there when we needed her, and our place was completed in less than six months." "Amazing communication skills and professionalism." "Her keen eye for space planning turned a so-so loft into a spectacular home."

Fox-Nahem Design   4.5   4.5   4   4.5
82 East 10th Street, New York, NY 10003
(212) 358 - 1411 www.foxnahemdesign.com
Modern, sumptuous, high-end interior design

As the creative force behind Fox-Nahem, Joe Nahem oversees the firm's striking and elegant interior compositions with a confident hand. Fox-Nahem is acclaimed for a wide range of looks, from traditionally based townhouses to Americana farmhouses to more tailored, even minimalist beach houses, all with a dash of sparkling wit. Fox-Nahem's designers are regarded as first-class professionals who work collaboratively with clients as well as architects and painters. With an architect on staff, the firm is also adept at creating spaces that are in balance with—and sensitive to—the architectural perspective.

This firm of five, founded in 1980 by Nahem and the late Tom Fox, takes on eight to fifteen projects annually. Nahem, who graduated from Parsons New York and Paris, is said to have substantial involvement in each project, down to the selection of the linen and china. For a number of clients the firm even interviewed and hired housekeepers. Clients tend to come with an open outlook and a healthy budget. Most of the work is high-end residential, with a booming business in the Hamptons, where Nahem keeps a second home and satellite office.

A typical living room is in the $250,000+ realm. Standard design fees are taken up-front, with reasonable product markups. Clients say the firm is wonderful about switching out any furnishing that doesn't strike a chord, and highly recommend it to friends. HB Top Designers, 1999, 2000, 2001, 2003, 2004, 2005.

"Joe strikes that perfect balance between the sumptuous and the seriously hip." "Joe gives his project life, sophistication, and sensibility all at the same time." "They created some really bomb-proof designs with my kids in mind, but it's still fun and incredibly attractive." "Cool and down to earth." "Joe is not a prima donna, but honest and easy to work with." "Stunning, very dramatic work." "They are little pit bulls with suppliers. If anything is late they will make it happen." "We did not have one disagreement throughout the whole process. Very much a joint effort." "Certainly not cheap, but so beautiful." "I asked for Chanel with combat boots and they more than delivered." "I only wish I had taken every suggestion they offered."

Fraser Associates   4.5   4.5   4   4
133 East 64th Street, New York, NY 10021
(212) 737 - 3479 clarefraser@nyc.rr.com
Luxurious, elegant, updated, classical interior design

Generations have depended upon Clare Fraser for her ability to create traditional spaces laced with glamour, well before it became the style du jour. Patrons say that her taste is absolutely faultless, her creativity unique, and her execution impeccable. Every project is uniquely dramatic, employing rich color, exquisite details, and many custom elements. Fraser is very involved with each project. She is good at listening and involving the client, but is said to show firm resolve when necessary to keep the project on track. Clients implicitly trust her design judgment and defer to her good taste.

According to clients, Fraser and her assistants handle every last detail. About ten assignments are taken on at any one time. Residential commissions are generally concentrated in Manhattan's Upper East Side and Greenwich, Connecticut. Hobe Sound/Palm Beach is another oft-visited region. Commercial projects include suites at the Waldorf Towers and the Plaza, the Lyford Cay Club, and the Hudson National Golf Club.

The firm operates with no up-front fees for current clients and charges retail on products, a reasonable markup on labor, and a negotiated oversight fee. Fraser reportedly prefers jobs with budgets that can support the highest quality fabrics and furnishings. Living rooms are often in the $150,000+ range. While clients clearly appreciate her high standards, some felt that Fraser went "a bit too far," urging them to replace moldings and doors that looked just fine. Clients highly recommend Fraser for a timeless, yet remarkable statement of personal style. KB 1993.

"She metaphysically puts your signature in the room. It looks just like you." "I never feel as though she is giving me the cookie-cutter approach." "With Clare, you die when you get the estimate. But when the furnishings arrive, you are always floored by the look and happy with the investment." "She can do the ultimate Waspy-calm for the country and super-chic for the city." "She can do a guy's apartment with perfect taste, and without it looking too fussy." "I know that Clare Fraser's clients are mostly wealthy or well known. I am neither, but my home looks like it now." "If she doesn't agree with you, she'll say so, and you'll usually end up on her side." "Simultaneously functional and drop-dead gorgeous." "There's definitely a 'look.'" "I frequently see the retail prices as we have shopped for years, and that is what I am billed." "She inherently knows how to create that 'je ne sais quoi' that is stunning, but always in good taste."

Frederic Jochem Inc.   3.5   3.5   4   5

135 Fifth Avenue, New York, NY 10010
(212) 956 - 1840   www.fredericjochem.com

Updated, refined, continental interior design

Frederic Jochem is acclaimed for his calm continental style, excellent oversight capabilities, and focus on the client. Described as traditional with a twist, Jochem's decorating incorporates his client's tastes and personality with his own confident and open-minded style. Jochem is said to have a particularly good sensitivity for and relationships with patrons hailing from his native France.

With extensive experience in planning, architecture, landscape, and interior design, Jochem has worked for a range of well-known families, from the Rockefellers to the Cartiers to the Hermes. Commissions range from Beekman Place to Casa del Campo to Bermuda and the Left Bank. Commercially, his work can be found in Fifth Avenue lobbies, showrooms, and high-end office spaces. Jochem holds a B.A. from the Paris Law University, Rue d'Assas, and from the École d'Architecture de Paris, as well as an M.B.A. from the Paris Business School, École des Cadres. He also attended the New York School of Interior Design.

The firm charges a standard product fee and a standard oversight fee. Jochem's clients report that he is specific and precise with his contractual agreements. His back office is said to be highly professional. Jochem is consistently noted for his troubleshooting capabilities, his managerial abilities, and his ability to meet budget. Many supporters have returned for a second phase or a second project over the last year. ASID.

"He made my home express my personality and reflect my multinational interests and background. He makes sure the client is totally satisfied." "As newlyweds, we each had our own things as well as our joint possessions, and Mr. Jochem found ways to in-

tegrate all of this with a very fine sense of our tastes." "On the human level, he proves his honesty, loyalty, patience, tenacity, and flexibility of mind. On a professional level, Frederic brings a wealth of experience and talent to any job." "His subcontractors weren't as good as he was." "Our requirements were exacting, if not strenuous, but Mr. Jochem totally stayed on the program." "We appreciated his respect for our requirements and our budget." "His assistants dealt with our difficult building, Frederic dealt with the aesthetics." "Every phase of the project was completed in advance of the original schedule." "The results were gorgeous, comfortable—and totally us."

Geoffrey Bradfield ▉   4   4.5   4   4.5

116 East 61st Street, New York, NY 10021
(212) 758 - 1773 gnbradfield@aol.com

Opulent, modern interior design

Known for his unique perspective, Geoffrey Bradfield brings opulence, quality, and verve to his projects. He often bases his designs on 1930s glamour with a contemporary lilt, highlighted with antiques and objects from different centuries and continents. Art Deco often factors into the picture. Art collectors often become clients and clients often become art collectors, owing to Bradfield's passion and knowledge of contemporary art. Clients say he is particularly adept at designing a room around a single masterpiece.

After working with McMillen for a brief period, Bradfield joined the late Jay Spectre in 1978 to pursue his more contemporary style. Recent projects include spacious Central Park West and Park Avenue apartments, substantial apartments in Chicago, grand private homes in Palm Beach, private jets, yachts, and offices with character. Clients appreciate his responsiveness, and say Bradfield makes it very easy to have a long-distance relationship.

The firm charges a standard+ up-front design fee, standard product markups, and hourly rates only for hours where no commission is otherwise received. Bradfield tends to work with only the highest-quality materials, including elegant silks and sateens. Living rooms tend to be quite well over $100,000, although sisal can also be used with style. While many enjoy Bradfield's fulsome personality, others say he can be a bit overwhelming. Overall, clients roundly praise Bradfield for his attention to detail, resourcefulness, accessibility, and style. ASID. AD 100, 2000, 2002, 2004. KB 1993.

"Geoffrey has endless imagination and a riotous sense of humor. This makes for wildly amusing interiors." "He took a shell of a house, my dream concept and my color scheme, and transposed the property into something magical." "Very talented and very expensive." "While always respectful and professional, he was not thrilled when I pushed the aesthetic line toward practicality." "I feel as if I am happily floating on a cloud in my high-rise living room." "There is no challenge he won't attempt. He doesn't cower in the face of convention." "Jean Harlow would be at home in one of his interiors." "He spares no expense, even flying out his favorite upholsterers to Japan to work on details." "More than elegant and a step past grand." "Their work is flawless." "As a fine furniture dealer, I can say that he has an excellent eye." "A joy to work with and he never makes a mistake. Good thing, because compromise is not favored." "We were a team and I loved the experience." "I cannot tell you how many people are dying for a dinner invitation just to see the house." "We trust him 20,000 percent."

Gleicher Design Group ▉

135 Fifth Avenue, 2nd Floor, New York, NY 10010
(212) 462 - 2789 www.gleicherdesign.com

Handsome modern residential architecture

See Gleicher Design Group's full report under the heading Architects

	Quality	Cost	Value	Recommend?
	✚	$	◆	★

Glenn Gissler Design 🛍

4 3.5 4.5 5

36 East 22nd Street, New York, NY 10010
(212) 228 - 9880 www.glenngisslerdesign.com

Calm, considered, edited interior design

Hailed for his cool, clean, sophisticated rooms in cohesive colors, Glenn Gissler is equally noted for being hot on design details. It is said that nothing escapes the notice of this consummate "finisher." Sources report that Gissler goes out of his way to understand clients' needs, examining their lifestyles and interests and educating them throughout the process. Knowledgeable about antiques and passionate about design history, Gissler places objects with historical significance in new contexts. Clients feel privileged to work with Gissler, whose Midwestern roots make him "appealing" and "approachable."

Before striking out on his own, Gissler worked with Rafael Vinoly and Juan Montoya. Gissler is known to start as the designer on a job and evolve into the project manager. While primarily an interior designer, Gissler has a degree in architecture from RISD and often designs and supervises complete renovations. Projects range from small to large apartments in the city to houses in the Hamptons, Martha's Vineyard, and Naples. Clients range from first-time homeowners to curators with apartments full of fine art. Most clients continue to seek this designer's advice well after the project is formally completed, and very often hire him again.

A standard design fee is charged and the firm then works at a reasonable percentage over net. Oversight fees run in the standard range. Any issues (all small) are reportedly handled very professionally and with Gissler taking full financial responsibility. Living rooms generally are in the $100,000+ range, and Gissler sometimes works on a consulting basis. ASID. HB Top Designers, 1999, 2000, 2001.

"While my architect was only so-so, and my contractor left me high and dry, Glenn was a dream." "Glenn's designs and his ways of thinking are good for a lifetime." "Glenn distinguished himself by asking really good questions about how we lived and worked, not about which Louis we preferred." "He can make objects with great historical significance dance with purchases from Pottery Barn." "He's incredibly talented, but I found him somewhat unavailable." "His subs are of the very best quality." "Good work, but it took longer in the design phase than I would have liked." "I have taken Glenn's furniture and designs to four larger apartments and a house (which I renovated around his designs, and which sold over the asking price when I needed to move)." "Good, solid work. Clean lines, and thoughtful modern style." "He kept the rooms open enough for us to enjoy the luxury of space." "I don't know how he did it, but he took my sketchy concept and translated it into an apartment of clarity and beauty."

Gomez Assoc./Mariette Himes Gomez 🛍

5 5 4 4.5

504-506 East 74th Street, 3rd Floor, New York, NY 10021
(212) 288 - 6856 www.gomezassociates.com

Modern, elegant interior design

Mariette Himes Gomez is considered a master by peers and one of the prime innovators of Warm Modernism, the gold standard sweeping the design world today—fulsome upholstery covered in beige linen or oatmeal raw silk piqued with exquisite dressmaker details. While she has a healthy respect for tradition, Gomez is better known as a master editor who refines spaces with clean yet curvaceous lines, solid textiles and jaunty 1930s French or English showpieces. Best known for her trademark neutral colors, she will incorporate soft hues at the client's request. References say that Gomez is not, however, the person to hire for flounces or frills, and that she has a very specific view of what she believes will work.

Gomez graduated from RISD and NYSID, and began her design career with Parish-Hadley, and then architect Edward Durrel Stone. The firm is quite large by industry standards. Recently Gomez's daughter Brooke has been spearheading projects, while senior manager Dominick Rotondi is noted as gracious and extremely accommodating, running a tight organizational ship with excellent follow-through. Historically, demand has far exceeded Gomez's available time, especially since about a third of her time is spent in London. More recently, the firm is only taking on a handful of large, new projects each year to meet client service expectations. High-profile bankers and a large number of entertainment moguls count among her clients, including Harrison Ford and director Ivan Reitman. In 2001, Gomez opened a 2,000 square foot showroom, The Shop, at the above address, highlighting hand-picked antiques, a custom furniture line, and intriguing accessories.

Clients seem to be very pleased with Gomez's fee structure, which is somewhat unique in the industry. A substantial design fee is charged, based upon anticipated hourly reviews and a standard design fee is taken for the product purchases, based on the estimated budget. Clients speak lovingly of her designs, and if imitation is the sincerest form of flattery, she wins the prize. ASID. AD 100, 2000, 2002, 2004. HB Top Designers, 1999, 2000, 2001, 2002, 2003, 2004, 2005. ID Hall of Fame. KB 1991, 1994, 1996, 1999, 2001, 2003.

"She is the champion of minimalism, yet hearteningly eloquent." "Mariette is particularly good at solving functionality challenges—every room is used to the maximum potential." "Modern design approached from a warm, traditional perspective. It's the best of both worlds." "It is not easy to get Mariette on the phone." "Luxurious living spaces, less focus on the kitchen and bath." "She was amazing with my major new house, collaborating with me and our serious architect. But when it came to renovating my Manhattan apartment, she was less interested." "You can't always get her directly involved with your project, but if you can, you've got the best." "Her spaces reflect her personality—warm, comforting, and professional." "A brilliant editor and a consummate professional." "Our house is a youthful vision of traditional." "She finds the most sublime furniture in England that is grand without being presumptuous." "Brooke Gomez's interiors get better every year." "Dominick is the backbone of the office, always helpful and always straightforward." "Her rooms delight the senses and warm the soul."

H. Parkin Saunders Inc. 💼   4   4   4   4.5

38 East 57th Street, 5th Floor, New York, NY 10022
(212) 421 - 5000 www.hparkinsaunders.com
Gracious, edited, luxurious traditional interior design

With a Southern touch that harkens back to his Little Rock, Arkansas roots, Parkin Saunders has built his business on relaxed, well-chosen, sophisticated designs, and discretion. Beginning with the background, including stately architecture, Saunders works in detailed layers to create designs uniquely suited to a client's lifestyle. Concept discussions include a talk with the housekeeper to properly understand what kind of soap will be placed in the soap trays and the client's favorite food for presentation on the night they move in. Generally following a solidly traditional framework, as preferred by his clientele, Saunders enjoys leading his patrons to an edited and luxurious version of traditional. Outstanding English and French antiques are sparingly placed and often clothed in neutral tones, creating a more dramatic and peaceful venue than one may have anticipated.

After attending the University of Arkansas and NYSID, Saunders apprenticed with a prominent New York designer before establishing Saunders and Walsh with the late Christopher Walsh in 1984. One of the firm's most notable projects was the decoration of David Koch's oceanfront Hamptons estate, "Aspen East," in less than six months, including monogrammed note pads and monogrammed hangers in each room. Other highlights include the Southampton homes of Anne Ford and Teddy Forstmann and the Grosse Pointe Farms lakeside compound of Edsel Ford, II and Nelson Doubleday.

Currently, there are three on staff including an interior architect. Three to four major projects are undertaken at a time. The practice will take on a few rooms, if the budget is "realistic." Generally living rooms are well over $100,000 with one topping out at over $4,000,000, including fine art and the best Georgian furniture. There is no up-front fee, but an hourly design retainer, and classic retail on products.

"Parkin was wonderful about opening my eyes to a more refined, less cluttered approach." "We really had fun all the way through the project." "Parkin cares very much about the client's viewpoint and preferences." "He takes the time to also make sure you have great sheets, beautiful flatware, and all the other comforts of gracious living." "Parkin shops nationally and internationally for the most unique items." "I have done two homes with Parkin: one traditional and one contemporary. Both are extremely livable and stylish." "Mr. Saunders and his staff are thoughtful, talented, and unfailingly courteous." "While it may take longer than you like and be quite expensive, every detail is perfect and never has to be changed."

Harry Schnaper Inc. 📱   4   3.5   4.5   5

692 Madison Avenue, New York, NY 10021
(212) 980 - 9898 harry@harryschnaper.com

Streamlined, traditional interior design

Upholding very high design standards while maintaining a practical sensibility, Harry Schnaper continues to impress clients and peers. He ably incorporates French, Regency, or Deco furnishings with clean lines into classic spaces, creating interiors that are "breathtakingly appealing," livable, and timeless. Schnaper is said to favor schematic design themes, a tact that translates into artful consistency. Clients also praise Schnaper's intent client focus, expedient intelligence, effervescent optimism, and sense of humor. He is said to be particularly adept at maximizing the living space in New York apartments.

Equipped with a degree in clinical psychology and schooled at the Chelsea School of Art, Schnaper worked with Gay Matthaei and Robert Metzger prior to opening his eponymous firm in 1989. While most of Schnaper's work is in Manhattan (including a project for RCA Music Group Chairman, Clive Davis), other projects have taken him to Southampton, Philadelphia, Washington, DC, and New Jersey. A small boutique, Schnaper's outfit generally only undertakes three to four major projects at a time. The firm's fees are considered to be very fair. Some say that Schnaper can be very economical, while others indicate that budgets are not a strength of the firm. Project costs have varied, from $40,000 to well over a million.

Many clients are repeat customers, crediting Schnaper's handsome designs, solid implementation skills and charm. AD 100, 2000, 2002, 2004. HB Top Designers, 1999, 2000. KB 1996.

"Everyone's just wild about Harry and his designs. I keep expecting him to become huge, but he is not a self-promoter." "He successfully worked with John McEnroe, so I knew that he could handle my husband. He is delightful and charming." "While his love is the more modern, he has a great range of styles that he does so well." "Harry understood the requirements of being newly divorced—how to make the apartment kid friendly but also sophisticated for my new life." "He works really well with architects, but should not be allowed outside without one." "He looks forward rather than backward. A true 21st century designer." "He's worked in New York long enough to know that sometimes you have to be gentle, and sometimes you have to put your foot down." "My husband and I are fanatics and this team respects that." "Harry was always there to supervise." "While I know he has a reputation for being expensive, he worked around my meager budget wonderfully."

	Quality	Cost	Value	Recommend?
	✚	$	◆	★

Haynes-Roberts Inc.

	4	4	4	4.5

601 West 26th Street, Suite 1655, New York, NY 10013
(212) 989 - 1901 www.haynesroberts.com

High-end residential interior design

Timothy Haynes and Kevin Roberts create modern distillations of classic design that are spare, elegant, and inviting. After defining handsome architectural backgrounds, comfortable upholstered furniture is selected, ranging from 18th century to mid-century modern, suiting the interests of the client and the setting. Much attention is paid to the objects' sculptural interest and character. Finally, well-edited accents and artistic expressions are added to the composition. Clients speak glowingly about the partners' careful planning and their considerate, delightful natures.

Haynes and Roberts founded the firm in 1991. Haynes, a registered architect, obtained his master of architecture degree from Harvard and worked for Robert Stern. Roberts holds advanced degrees in cultural anthropology and previously worked for the Aga Khan Award for Architecture in Geneva, Switzerland. Since their very first project was published on the cover of *Metropolitan Home* in 1992, they've never looked back. Recent projects have included large gut renovations on Park Avenue and Cape Cod, Sagaponack, Boston, Palm Beach—not to mention the interior architecture and decoration of a 24,000 square foot chateau in the Loire Valley.

Typical projects start around $500,000 and go up from there. The firm is willing to work on a standard design fee plus product commission, but most clients prefer a flat fee based on estimated overall cost. This allows the team to deliver the product at net and "go to bat for the client," negotiating on the high end and interspersing Crate & Barrel when appropriate. Patrons also report that they develop wonderful, personal relationships with the principals, who are highly accessible. HB Top Designers, 1999, 2000.

"Excellent taste with an intelligent analytical approach." "Always pleasant—indeed, charming and warm." "Great people, honest and fun to work with." "Organized, budget conscious, and very, very chic." "Witty gentlemen. Serious design." "No complaints other than the timing, which always takes longer than you hope." "Superb taste and extremely knowledgeable in the fields of both architecture and interior design." "They love basing their designs on collections of art and antiques." "They see the project through to the sheets, towels, and dishes." "They never lose patience or enthusiasm, even if the client balks and they have to rethink an aspect of the scheme." "Great sensitivity to the character of each location and our lifestyle." "Very reliable—would work with them again in a heartbeat."

Housefitters Inc.

	3.5	3	4.5	4.5

57 East 93rd Street, New York, NY 10128
(212) 348 - 2417 www.housefittersinc.com

Classical, warm interior design

Ruth Ann McSpadden is lauded by clients for designs with Old World comfort that incorporate strong classic architectural details and warm palettes. Mixing excellent antiques with reproductions, she creates environments that appear to have evolved over generations. Mindful of the budget, McSpadden offers a range of fabrics and furnishings, but always creates a high-quality ambience. While she personally prefers lively colors and a mix of patterns, we're told that

McSpadden is very accommodating. She has completed at least one highly successful monochromatic apartment that sold weeks after redecoration at 20% over the asking price. Clients say that McSpadden is especially good with family environments, choosing practical and inviting fabrics.

McSpadden officially opened Housefitters for business in early 1999, after undertaking numerous personal projects for herself and her friends. Recent jobs include an Upper East Side townhouse, an East End apartment, and houses in Quogue, Newport, and Sun Valley. Extremely reasonable in her pricing, she will do just one room or a whole townhouse. A one-woman-band, McSpadden limits the number of jobs taken during any particular period of time. Recommended from friend-to-friend for enhancements or for a complete renovation, Housefitters "fits the bill."

"Ruth Ann is a delight to work with. It was as if I was redecorating with my best friend." "She was incredibly helpful mediating style issues between myself and my husband." "She has an uncanny sense of color, distinguishing shades that elude me to this day." "Ruth Ann's strength is in her friendly approach, not her business side." "She has a clear view that she will tailor to your needs." "Time is an issue; she really needs an assistant." "Lots of repeat customers, which is the best recommendation." "Ruth Ann has to be the most honest decorator in New York—she spent an inordinate amount of time talking me out of unnecessary purchases." "A generous and kind person with a classically refreshing sense of design."

Ingrao Inc.   5   5   4   4.5
17 East 64th Street, New York, NY 10021
(212) 472 - 5400   ingrao@ingrao.com
Luminous, extraordinary, near-epic interior design

Tony Ingrao's projects range from baronial splendor to contemporary grandeur. Considered among the most indefatigable of designers, Ingrao's first project over twenty years ago was a spectacular seven-year transformation of a 1920s Norman chateau in Greenwich into an extravagant Louis XIV fantasia with a level of detail that rivals the great European houses. Even Ingrao's more modest projects are filled with important 16th century consoles, paired George II mahogany chairs, and floors refinished by experts flown in from France for the ultimate layered glow. Clients are undeniably drawn to the firm for its vast knowledge of architecture and furniture, and for an innate sense of elegance and luxury.

After attending RISD, Ingrao opened his firm which now includes seven designers, five architectural specialists (non-licensed), and several in administration. In October 2002, Ingrao and partner Randy Kemper opened a dramatic three-story antiques gallery at 17 East 64th Street in Manhattan with gleaming white marble floors and sinuous walls, primarily showcasing extraordinary 18th to 20th century continental furniture and cutting-edge contemporary art.

Interior design projects vary in size and shape, with some going into multiple millions. Clients include GE legend Jack Welch, Kim Cattrall, Goldie Hawn, The Related Companies Chairman and CEO Stephen Ross, and financial managers Steve Cohen (SAC Capital), Marc Rowan (Apollo Management), and Dan Och (Och-Ziff Capital Management). The firm charges standard architecture fees, project management fees, millwork and painting fees, and classic retail on product (except antiques, which are purchased on a scaled fee schedule). Clients looking to experience the design dream of a lifetime are drawn to Ingrao.

"Tony delivers flawless, singular creations that are clearly over the top, but never gauche." "Only for families that live comfortably with museum quality art and antiques." "Tony makes your design fantasies into a reality—it may take a while, but it will be amazing." "The journey is just as much fun as the end result."

	Quality	Cost	Value	Recommend?
	✚	$	◆	★

Jackson Siegel Aaron Ltd.

4   4   4   4.5

306 East 61st Street, 2nd Floor, New York, NY 10021
(212) 593 - 0117 www.jacksonsiegelaaron.com

Coherent, polished interior design

Joining forces and design visions, Lisa Jackson and Catherine Aaron have recently partnered with architect and designer Stephen Miller Siegel. Cohesively melding their abilities, the team members are known for their skill in blending the patina of traditional with the delights of the modern. Architectural detail and calming color tones are also said to be a strength, forming the underpinnings of a coherent and sophisticated result. With a proclivity for handsome and daring furniture, rooms are admired for their understated, yet distinct personalities. Supporters say that they listen well and always make the most of their clients' spaces—all with measured professionalism.

The firm's retail shop has also been renamed Jackson Siegel Aaron, and now features a new line of furniture designed and produced by the threesome (306 East 61st Street). Many high profile designers frequent the store, allowing an easy exchange of design concepts that often surface in their private client work. Siegel also maintains his independent architectural firm, Stephen Miller Siegel (SMSA). Siegel worked with Peter Marino for eleven years and is a licensed New York architect. Notable projects have included the Wathne stores, Bergdorf Goodman Men's Store, and the Escada flagship on 5th. Not surprisingly, Jackson Siegel Aaron often brings in SMSA on their projects and vice-versa.

The firm takes on about six major projects at a time, mostly in Manhattan, the Hamptons, and Connecticut. A standard design fee and reasonable product markups are charged for services, and retail on antiques. The bills include vendor paperwork. The firm is said to be good about working with the client's existing furnishings, finding alternatives, and staying on budget. Supporters highly recommend this trio for its creativity, grace, and commitment to quality. HB Top Designers, 1999, 2000.

"They completely understand the look and world in which we live, and what we are trying to accomplish." "Classic American taste with a touch of genius." "Beautiful sophisticated work that never feels too decorated." "They keep the strategic design on target, while being practical about the costs and the children's rooms." "Over the summer, there can be timing lags, but nothing major." "Even though I hate the process of decorating, they made it fun." "They endeavor to provide interesting, modern solutions that you can also entertain your Club friends in." "There is a spirituality about the work."

James Rixner Inc. ◼

4   4   4   4.5

121 Morton Street, New York, NY 10014
(212) 206 - 7439 www.jamesrixner.com

Dramatic, engaging, individualist interior design

Whether he's doing high-voltage Art Deco glamour or Neoclassical with panache, James Rixner's interiors radiate warmth and charmed elegance. Known for details rather than a rubber-stamp look, Rixner listens carefully to the client and often takes a project management role. Given his background in architectural planning, clients are comfortable when Rixner takes the works back to the skeletal bones and reconstitutes the space with architectural flair. Lighting is also a strength. Custom cabinetry, kitchens, and baths are often part of the remix, with clients very pleased with the results.

Rixner received a master's in urban planning from the University of Pittsburgh before coming to New York and working for Harry Hinson in his interiors group. After working at Bloomingdale's and for the architectural firm HLW, Rixner went out on his own in 1983. Currently there is a staff of four, with about eight projects ongoing. Known for his work in high-end lofts (Rixner lives in one), recent projects include a floor-through Tribeca loft done in a Tuscan motif and an estate in Alpine, New Jersey in the Hollywood Regency style. He is also overseeing the restoration and decoration of a historically significant estate on Long Island.

The firm will take on a few rooms for new clients and is known for its excellent up-front presentations, including floor plans, elevations, and lighting schemes. There is a standard flat design fee, lower product markups, but also standard architectural commissions on millwork and painting. Most living rooms fall in the $100,000 range. ASID. KB 1997, 2003.

"What used to be a plain white wall now has the most amazing glow—the painters took six months but it was clearly worth it." "James was great about following my lead if I pointed him in a direction—no ego issues." "Clearly a preference for high-end materials." "James doesn't just think about color and fabric, he really rethinks the space." "My bedroom is truly amazing, shades of gold, silver, and black. I never could have pulled that off alone." "Can get unique materials and results that no one else can." "Wildly different looks from one house to the next. His ability to do different styles is admirable." "A little below the radar, he doesn't have an attitude and always does a nice job." "Jim is great about trying to steer us in the direction of reasonably priced antiques. We did not listen, but that was not his doing." "When the electricians tore up my brand new mahogany library, Jim had it all restored at no cost to me." "You pay for the best and get it with Jim."

Jane Hottensen Interiors 👜   3.5   3.5   4   4.5
863 Park Avenue, New York, NY 10021
(212) 831 - 5764   hotter3@aol.com
Comfortable, traditional, generational interior design

Appealing to those seeking timeless rooms that looked as if they evolved over generations, Jane Hottensen takes on a few jobs at a time and develops excellent relationships with her clients. The spaces are understated and undeniably traditional, successfully achieving that "not decorated look." Said to be Southern in tone, toiles, checks, and chintzes predominate her work outside the city, with the Manhattan designs receiving a somewhat more tonal treatment. A mother of three, Hottensen is appreciated for her sensitivity to "lifestyles built around the kids and dogs."

Hottensen grew up in Wisconsin, graduated from Skidmore with a degree in marketing, and received her M.B.A. from Boston University. Ten years later, she earned a two-year certificate at NYSID and jumped right into the business. A sole practitioner, Hottensen takes on a manageable number of projects: four at a time, split evenly between large and small jobs. The vast majority of her work to date has been for friends or friends of friends. About half of her jobs are in the city (usually Fifth or Park) and the other half are in the Millbrook area, where Hottensen rides with the hunt and has an 1835 Greek Revival home. Other homes have been completed in New Canaan and Darien.

Said to be practical and reasonable, Hottensen will start with projects as small as a master bedroom. Also, the cost of product may range considerably with an understanding that not everything must be of the finest provenance. "Robbing Peter to pay Paul" is often the case; for example, Hottensen will take an existing dining room rug and redeploy it to greater effect in the bedroom. Oriental rugs are often used, but there may be sisal in the next room. Fees are lower than standard, but due to the small size of the firm, timing can be less predictable. Clients "in the know" highly recommend Hottensen to their friends and family.

"We first did our city apartment with Jane, and then she helped us in New Canaan." "I started the project but just ran out of steam for the main rooms. Jane was wonderful about pulling it all together." "She mixed patterns and colors in ways that I would not have thought about." "Jane would suggest a fabric and I would not care for it at all. Then, days later, it would dawn on me that she was right all along." "There was no particular budget, it all evolved." "Jane made everything fun and easy." "I met Jane through the project and now consider her a good friend."

JD Bell Inc. 💼   4.5   5   4   4
155 Sixth Avenue, 15th Floor, New York, NY 10013
(212) 339 - 0006 www.jdbellinc.com
Classic, versatile, high-end interior design

Raised in the South and trained at the old-line powerhouse firm of Irvine and Fleming, Jason Bell executes traditional work with panache, be it English country or stately Georgian. He is also frequently called on by young couples to combine two distinct sensibilities into one home. This calls for tricky footwork—how to make his Bauhaus desk fit in with her Victorian four-poster, without compromising the overall design. Though the materials can be a hodgepodge, references say the results are anything but. Specifically, clients praise Bell's ability to achieve a harmonious, unified look that is artful but not over-designed. They also single out his exemplary project management skills, saying, "Jason knows how to make things happen."

Bell studied interior design at the University of Alabama before moving to New York and working for Irvine and Fleming. He stayed there for seven years, was named partner, and continued on for three more before striking out on his own. Currently he fields a staff of six, working on projects throughout Manhattan and Connecticut. The firm has also shipped its design work overseas, to relocated clients as far afield as London and Geneva. Generally, Bell charges an upfront design fee and retail on product. Clients report that while his prices are high, the final product is always gorgeous, comfortable, and distinct.

"Traditional with a modern edge." "I gave Jason a warehouse with furniture stacked twenty feet high, and he sorted out what to use beautifully." "Jason is an absolute professional, but he still manages to have a lot of fun." "Jason was great at handling 'curveballs.' A real problem solver." "He's relatively new to the game, but he's got a lot of tricks up his sleeve already." "The billing process went exactly as we expected." "He turned a Park Avenue wreck into a little jewel." "Jason took the furnishings from two different homes and the work of another designer and managed to combine them seamlessly." "He didn't show us fabrics that were out of our price range." "He doesn't have an 'in-your-face' New York attitude."

Jed Johnson Associates 💼   4.5   5   4   4
32 Sixth Avenue, 20th Floor, New York, NY 10013
(212) 707 - 8989 www.jedjohnson.com
Thoughtful, edited, exceptional interior design

Design director Arthur Dunnam continues to set standards in the industry. Clients, peers, and vendors consistently and wistfully speak of the firm's impeccable taste, inspired style, and remarkable quality. Dunnam worked closely with the late Jed Johnson for ten years, and reportedly has maintained the ideals and forward-thinking design momentum of the firm. Known truly as a full-service operation, Jed Johnson Associates will provide architectural as well as design services. Patrons praise the firm's ability to shop and install its product to the very last detail.

References compliment the team's color sensibility and knowledge of all sources, especially antiques and lighting. Twenty members strong, the firm is said to diligently deliver a finished product. Buzz Kelly, Christine Cain, and Andy Clark, each with extensive experience at the firm, are noted as exceptional designers in their own right. Jed Johnson Associates takes on roughly fifteen projects at a time. While some would like to have been more involved in the design process, all applaud the firm's efficiency.

The firm asks for an up-front retainer and charges retail for new products and net plus a percentage for antiques. Cost-conscious clients caution that the firm much prefers couture products, which are very difficult to return, but will present less costly alternatives if urged. Living rooms may start at $150,000, but can run as high as the imagination can run wild. Recently, the company launched a line of Jed Johnson fabrics and home furniture, both sold at John Rosselli in New York. This design team is highly recommended for thoughtful, modern-edged, classic design. HB Top Designers, 1999, 2000, 2001, 2002, 2003, 2004, 2005. ID Hall of Fame.

"They made it incredibly easy. Poof and it was done—I did not have to do a thing." "They do everything to the point of perfection. Mundane drawer handles become an opportunity to create artistic, interior jewelry." "Their first instinct is to create custom product. However, if I insist on pret-a-porter, they usually can find an excellent alternative." "The paragon of good taste." "Even their design peers are inspired by their creativity." "Christine Cain is a consummate professional." "They made the maddening process of interior design seem easy and almost fun...I only wish figuring out their invoicing system was as fun." "They are very focused on the bottom line, which can be tricky if you do not like a delivered item." "They found some upholstery silks that are so gorgeous and unusual—I'm still astounded three years later." "Everything they do is beautiful, custom, expensive, and worth it." "They deserve all the praise they get." "We travelled together for nine days in Europe. Then Arthur created my dream."

Jeff Lincoln Interiors Inc.   4.5 4 5 4.5

315 East 62nd Street, New York, NY 10021
(212) 588 - 9500   jtlincoln@verizon.net

Classical, comfortable interior design

Recently developing a more edited version of classically chic, Jeff Lincoln continues to balance the correct with the au courant, keeping the fashionable of Park Avenue and Darien up-to-date. Warm and resonant colors, refined fringes, Old World craftsmanship and creative details are revisited with a modern eye, creating a sophisticated presence. References also praise Lincoln for his knowledge of fine antiques, European and Scandinavian historical details, and unusual custom sources. With restraint and practicality, the serious is set against the comfortable, the economic against the outstanding.

Clients include many young sophisticates, who relate to Lincoln's easy manner, genteel sensibility, and businesslike approach. Supporters also appreciate his artistic vision, saying that each project is unique to the setting and taste of the homeowner. While some express concern that he starts slowly, he always wins the clients' hearts with an outstanding end result.

The firm charges a standard up-front design fee and classic retail on product. Lincoln is capable of going as high as a client would like in the quality spectrum, but is equally open to less costly alternatives. Living rooms are generally in the $200,000 realm. He is highly recommended by many of the most discerning shoppers in New York for timeless comfort. HB Top Designers, 1999, 2000, 2001. KB 1995, 1998, 2001, 2004.

"More recently, there is this cleaner, more contemporary thread that is weaving its way through Jeff's work. Holly Hunt visits Darien but is sidetracked by silk taffeta." "His rooms are full of happy luxury without being over the top. And he can add a bit of whimsy, which we really appreciate." "The rooms are never pretentious and are always beautiful." "An emerging talent who is just coming of age. While prone to a few bumps, the outcome was fabulous." "Five of my friends in town have used Jeff. All the homes look different and all are fabulous." "Its all about lighting and patina." "If you do not like it, he will take it right back in his truck." "Always has a good time and makes sure the client does too." "I have only positive things to say about Jeff. He has great taste and is a great guy." "His balance of the comfortable and the formal exactly matches our lifestyle." "He really listens and responds appropriately."

Jennifer Post Design 🛍   4   4   4   4.5

25 East 67th Street, Suite 10E, New York, NY 10021
(212) 734 - 7994 www.jenniferpostdesign.com
Polished, classical, progressive interior design

Tearing into a project, both literally and figuratively, Jennifer Post and her clients have concurrent epiphanies. Post knows her style and her clients applaud her ambitious transformations of boring or staid apartments into streamlined visions of classical contemporary. Her spatial insights and ingenuity usually translate into the raising of doorways, lowering of floors, and elimination of superfluous details. These new spaces are also commended for their strong bias toward comfort and livability, often with monochromatic built-ins. Historically, Post favored a white palette juxtaposed with dark floors and accents. Lately, she has favored more homogeneous tones, judiciously adding vibrant color to the mix. Supporters admire Post's can-do attitude and tenacity with contractors and suppliers, which enables her to wrap up projects in "record time." Post can also be adamant regarding the cohesive nature of a design.

Post's clients include a number of celebrities (Jennifer Lopez, Matt Lauer), high-profile executives, and other progressive, high-end homeowners. While most clients applaud her ability to give you a great look at a "decent price" and within budget, others say the price can be high. Living rooms generally range from $60,000 to $150,000+. Post holds a graduate degree in fine arts and design, with a minor in architecture. Supporters recommend her for a specific, sleek, and polished contemporary look. AD 100, 2004. HB Top Designers, 1999, 2000, 2001. KB 1999.

"An easy-to-work-with perfectionist who is worth every penny." "Jennifer represents the beginning of the next generational wave in interior design." "I fell in love with her upon our first meeting. She is committed and is a ball of fire." "She is very dedicated and energetic—she would call me back immediately whether she was in Italy or Paris." "Not afraid of serious architectural alterations." "Her office staff can be a bit brusque." "Her sense of space and color is excellent, and she takes her work completely seriously. She doesn't let the details go." "Jennifer tends to keep the design details in her head instead of on blueprints. But everything worked out beautifully." "Won't give up on her ideas easily, but everything is always extremely well thought out." "She did my entire apartment in two months." "Really takes the time to figure out how you live and designs accordingly." "She took my staid, box of an apartment and created an environment of excitement, polish, refinement, and warmth." "Her designs elevate the spirit." "She is a force."

John Barman Inc. 🛍   4.5   4.5   4   4

500 Park Avenue, New York, NY 10022
(212) 838 - 9443 www.johnbarman.com
Distinctive, stylistic, mid-century modern interior design

John Barman has staked out an iconoclastic design niche with resonant colors, lush fabrics, and courageous appointments. Vibrant arabesque taffetas meet hot pink custom carpets, vivid red walls exaggerate linear space, and French modern furniture converses with acrylic. Drawing from mid-century design emblems or the historically referential, Barman intensifies and enlivens. Or Barman can do a modified, more discreet version by using distinct colors to freshen a more traditional construct. To his clients' delight, Barman builds such themes upon their interests and then retrofits to their lifestyles.

This firm of seven was established by Barman more than fifteen years ago. It assumes about thirty assignments annually, six or eight of which are major. Clients say Barman is backed by a "first-class" support staff that keeps meticulously detailed budgets and status reports. Additionally, Barman is said to work extremely well in collaboration with architects and contractors to ensure that the final product is the client's true vision.

Barman conducts the majority of his business in Manhattan, including a recent two-apartment renovation for Wynton Marsalis, but also works in the Hamptons including some unusual decorating assignments, such as yachts. A satellite LA office opened in the summer of 2003. Typical living rooms run about $100,000 to $150,000, with the firm charging standard design fees and standard markups on product. Budgets can be set or evolve, but Barman is trusted by clients to stay sensible. ASID. AD 100, 2004. HB Top Designers, 2000, 2001. KB 2000, 2001, 2003.

"His rooms are always dazzling compared to other designers." "Snappy, with vision." "You have to see his portfolio to believe it. We love him, but he would not be for everybody." "His style is so varied—he's able to do whatever the project calls for, but he works really well with themes." "He rescued the architect and the contractor from what could have been a disaster on the house we built in the country." "Timing can be an issue, especially if the project is not focused." "Not inexpensive, but for a certain look, he's essential." "Crisp modern work with expressive lines." "John is an earnest and straightforward character with a bottomless pit of untapped creativity." "After wandering in the design forest, John has really found his groove." "He respected issues of economics and authenticity, and was very understanding about my choices." "As long as it looks good, he will go to Crate & Barrel." "He selects fabrics and furniture with such character. He would not settle for anything less."

Juan Montoya Design Corporation ▮   4.5   5   4   5

330 East 59th Street, 2nd Floor, New York, NY 10022
(212) 421 - 2400 www.juanmontoyadesign.com
Neoclassical and contemporary interior design

Juan Montoya is highly respected by clients and peers for his exquisite juxtaposition of cultures and periods, dramatic yet restrained taste, and exceptional good manners. His contemporary design work is seen by past clients as sleek and eclectic, often merging bold South American and Asian elements into a neutral palette. More recently he has developed a neoclassical design sensibility that integrates exquisite fabrics, fine antiques, and rich colors. Clients applaud his ability to offer sophistication to any design construct, be it idealized cowboy or an Arts and Crafts yacht.

The son of a Colombian diplomat who worked in Paris and Milan before settling in New York, Montoya tends to have an international following. Many clients are very well-established New Yorkers or South Americans with impressive collections. Many are loyalists—at least one client has completed fourteen projects with Montoya over two decades. Montoya and his office are commended for being highly professional. Experienced project directors are assigned to each commission, yet Montoya makes all design decisions down to the buttons on every cushion. A detailed 380-page monograph of his work was published in 1998 by Villegas Editores.

The firm will work on a percentage basis or for a flat fee. Costs are said to fall at the very high end of the range, with most living rooms well above $100,000.

Patrons report that there is a healthy respect for schedule and budgets, and that Montoya is always happy to discuss alternatives. Most clients consider Montoya to be a master and continue to use him whenever possible. ASID. AD 100, 2000, 2002, 2004. HB Top Designers, 1999, 2000. ID Hall of Fame. KB 1992.

"Juan is a total gentleman with a joyful outlook." "I was amazed how he integrated Aztec, Art Deco, and Egyptian in an artfully masculine way." "I wish that I was still a priority client for him. When he is focused on your project, no one can match that richness and complexity." "He works like he's solving a Rubik's Cube, carefully lining everything up until it all matches perfectly." "I feel as if he would spend all the time in the world with me walking up and down Madison Avenue, until we find the perfect solution." "He has done an excellent job, evolving over the years with my changing lifestyle and design interests." "He's expensive, but he gets it." "Likes to show you high end furnishings, but will go a level down if you faint at the price tag." "Definitely not a prima donna, he's happy to discuss every detail with you." "Not speedy, he takes the time to find things that you'll like ten years from now." "I gave him my mish-mash of a priority list and he delivered a gorgeous, coherent product."

KA Design Group

4   4   4   4.5

595 Madison Avenue, 16th Floor, New York, NY 10022
(212) 223 - 0314   www.kadesigngroup.com
Abundant, detailed, traditional interior design

With outstanding client service as their fundamental axiom, principals Kenneth Alpert and Andrew Petronio take a sincere, focused, and personalized approach to each project. While best known for a traditional-to-the-max style, bedecked with chintzes, toile, and elegant trims, founder Alpert is also fluent in Art Deco, minimalist, and formal French. Regardless of the style, the firm delivers comfortable, full-sized, family-oriented designs and brings attention to detail to an unfathomable level.

Alpert holds a B.S. from Wharton and an M.B.A. from NYU. While attending classes at the NYSID, he founded the firm almost 30 years ago. Petronio, who holds degrees from Fordham and FIT, joined in 2000. With fourteen on staff, about forty projects are undertaken annually, ten of which are of substantial size and scope. While there are four senior designers, all significant design decisions are made with Alpert or Petronio. Clients say they do not doubt Alpert more than once "because his ideas are always better." Most of the firm's work takes place in Manhattan and Long Island, with additional client bases in New Jersey, Westchester, Fairfield, and Florida.

References appreciate KA's formal presentations, and also comment on his excellent budget layouts and refined professionalism. Clients express equal confidence in the back office. The firm charges a standard design fee and classic retail on product, with a typical living room baselining at about $150,000. Clients say Alpert and Petronio "are not budget designers," but they are practical. Also if there is ever an issue, the team is known to fix it "faster than you can blink." KB 2003.

"Ken is the most organized person I have ever met." "They interpret what I like and make sure it is in good taste." "Ken and Andrew get the job done: bing, bang, boom." "A real straight shooter." "They were very receptive to using the furniture that I already owned." "Ken is in his office from 7 AM to 7 PM every day." "The project managers did a really efficient job day to day." "If we did not get it the first time, they were really patient, going at it until we find something we both like." "They understand family living, making sure that the floors in the rec room near the pool were not slippery." "A busy team that is available 24 hours a day." "I know we were not a huge client for Ken and Andrew, but they always treated us as if we had 22 rooms." "The hardest working men in decoration." "Keeps to a certain look and does it well." "Ken aggressively pursues what's right for his clients." "I turn to them for so many design

situations well beyond the decoration of my home—from what to wear to vacation choices to dinner party options."

Kathy Abbott Interiors 🛍   4.5   4   4   5

398 Cross River Road, Katonah, NY 10536
(914) 232 - 1934   www.kathyabbottinteriors.com

Fresh, elegant, livable, traditional-based interior design

Dexterously blending inherited and found antiques, fine streamlined forms, and handsome counterpoints of provenance, Kathy Abbott impresses clients with her creative thinking and professionalism. Juxtapositions are a trademark, adding flair, freshness, and interest to the predictable. Fortuny in sherbet hues can cover traditional profiles, and contemporary art renderings may be placed in an otherwise traditional setting. All is done with a light hand and from a livable point of view.

With a B.A. in studio art and art history from Claremont College in California, Abbott has always focused on the aesthetic. In 1987, friends began asking for advice on interiors, and soon afterwards, a business was formed. Pursuing the trade with a clear focus, Abbott is a sole proprietor appreciated for her client attention and ability to "speak the language of the painters." References also credit Abbott for guiding a unique group of "incredible sources, especially craftsmen." Abbott does about five or six good-sized projects at a time. The bulk of her work is done in Manhattan, Connecticut, and Westchester, but Abbott has gone as far afield as Rhode Island, Florida, and Colorado.

While many of her clients do not have a specific budget and Abbott is known to prefer excellent quality, she is said to mix it up—allocating enough for a fabulous sofa frame and saving somewhere else. A minimal contract fee is charged with classic retail on product.

"It was amazing. Kathy got much of the house done while I was in Japan for a few years. She is so organized and would send me packages of samples." "Kathy is an absolute perfectionist. She sent the sofa pillows back three times to the workroom." "My husband and I were overseas and we picked up a fair amount of stuff. Kathy was wonderful about using what we had and gently telling me if something needed to be replaced." "It was a collaborative process, but Kathy would bring me a variety of options and I would choose. Not like looking for a needle in a haystack." "Wonderful with color and texture. Everyone comments on how warm and inviting our home is." "Though Kathy steered us towards more expensive materials, there's not a single purchase we regret." "Kathy knows how to treat craftspeople, and so you always end up getting their best work." "If a lampshade is not quite correct, it will really bother her until it is replaced." "She is available seven days a week, always gets right back to you."

Katie Ridder Design & Decoration 🛍   4   4   4   4.5

432 Park Avenue South, 11th Floor, New York, NY 10016
(212) 779 - 9080   www.katieridder.com

English meets eclectic interior design

Katie Ridder is acclaimed for her ability to strike a design balance between style and discretion. Clients say that she takes care to preserve the integrity of classic elements while incorporating the unexpected. Innovative hues, whimsical accents, and eclectic objects are often layered on to more traditional backgrounds, making spaces more comfortable and friendly. References say she is very conscience of their lifestyles, and is interested in making the most of each room.

After working as a decorating editor at *House & Garden* and *House Beautiful* and establishing a retail home furnishings store on the Upper East Side, Ridder founded the firm in 1995. About ten projects are undertaken each year. The majority of commissions are in Manhattan and the surrounding areas, but Ridder has taken on projects as far afield as New Zealand. Clients say Ridder's affable, organized, helpful manner really puts them at ease, and that she is always the primary client contact.

The design firm has an unusually strong computer capability, using CAD to map out every project to a budget beforehand. Charging a standard design fee and retail on product, a typical living room costs around $125,000, starting from scratch. Ridder is highly recommended for her updated classical style and intelligent view. HB Top Designers, 2000, 2001, 2002, 2003, 2004, 2005. KB 2002.

"The most tasteful and creative person I have ever worked with." "Not at all cookie cutter." "She worked very well under tight deadlines and she did it with a smile." "She's so friendly that I look forward to her phone calls and meetings." "Katie is very innovative, but she always makes you feel like you came up with the idea. She's gracious and ego-free." "She breathed new life into our traditional Tudor home." "Her colors were so unusual and so perfect." "Left of center enough to grab your eye, but not too far left." "Bohemian elegance." "Katie's organizational skills are phenomenal." "We were so impressed with her efficiency. On the other hand, the upholstery choices went a little too fast for us." "Furniture placement is definitely a strength." "She and her colleagues are extremely attentive and prompt with follow up." "Her ideas come from the heart, not the wallet." "We immediately connected. She's so intelligent, compassionate, and talented. What more can you ask?"

Lafia/Arvin 📖

4.5   4.5   4   5

741A 10th Street, Santa Monica, CA 90402
(310) 587 - 1141 www.lafiaarvin.com

Articulate, luxurious, classic interior design

Discreet and calm, Lafia/Arvin has raised the concept of client service to an art form. Their goal is to make decorating easy and fun for the customer, while creating unassuming, classically beautiful homes. Interiors are graciously appointed in the finest antiques and some repro, with every possible comfortable detail considered. Designs range from formal traditional with sparks of leather to comfortable relaxed clubby looks using dark woods, light fabrics, and eloquent antiques. Monique Lafia takes the lead on design while associate Chris Arvin, heads up the business end.

Lafia graduated from UCLA's design program, worked in commercial interiors and designed with legendaries Waldo Fernandez and Hendrix/Allardyce. Arvin is an attorney with a passion for design. Established in 1997, the business is rounded out by six others who supporters say are on top of every detail. Clients seem to truly be "in love" with Lafia's design sensibility and her kind manner. Many have signed on for multiple projects, including four for Victoria Jackson (including, currently, the Buster Keaton estate), three for Courtney Thorne-Smith, two for Josie Bisset, and several for Andy Conrad. Other clients include Wayne Gretzky, Rob and Sheryl Lowe, Lyndie and Kenny G, Bernadette and Sugar Ray Leonard, and Lilly Tartikoff. In New York, the firm's work combines the best of their Californian penchant for light and space with cultivated local sources.

Perfection comes at a cost when the best products are used. Fees are standard (but the cost and quality of materials is high to meet client expectations), including up-front design fees and product markups, with no hourlies. The pair is said to be good about recovering the old and finding a home for many of the client's current possessions. NCIDQ, CCIDC.

"Monique learned from the masters and applied her own understated elegance." "There is a controlled calm to their style that works with Gap and also with Prada." "Lots of accessories, lots of work." "Millions of questions are asked of everyone, including the kids and the housekeepers." "They bend over backwards to make sure that everything is perfect." "I just hope they do not get too big, as their charm is in their individualized attention." "They do expect a certain high level of quality, but can

work with you if you set limits." "I totally trust Monique. She saved my life on our last project, taking it from humdrum to amazing, yet it was still comfortable." "Right after I had my baby she was there, making everything easy." "They have become indispensable and also friends." "They came highly recommended and fulfilled our expectations."

Larry Laslo Designs 🛍   4   3.5   4.5   4
240 East 67th Street, New York, NY 10021
(212) 734 - 3824 llaslo@aol.com
Contemporary, lively residential interior design

Loyal clients return to Larry Laslo for his clean lines, vibrant colors, and dedicated nature. He is said to be excellent at restraining clients when "necessary" and also encouraging them to stretch beyond their general inclinations. Even plain white is developed into more painted shades than the imagination can contemplate. Clients find Laslo to be a wealth of historical information and enjoy his incorporation of varied periods and styles, from ancient classical Egyptian to Italian 1940s. It is said that nothing is off-limits to this intrepid designer, who can meld various periods with élan. A man ahead of his time, Laslo was doing "mid-century modern" before the term was coined. But all is done with a nod to glamorous irreverence.

Laslo began his design journey as an oil painter and fashion illustrator. After working with Bergdorf Goodman for several years in store design, he worked with Mikasa and Takashimaya, developing their United States look. His interior design firm was founded in 1985 and remains small, with Laslo doing all the shopping. Clients tend to be the young and less conservative in Manhattan and the metro area. Laslo also likes to be involved with the architectural details and spends a good deal of time with clients understanding their lifestyle before anything is purchased.

The firm charges a typical design fee and reasonable product fees. Depending upon the clients' interests, living rooms can range from $50,000 to $300,000+. He is said to much prefer just a few pieces of higher quality than a full room. Clients are shown all invoices and often pay directly. His own furniture products may be purchased through John Whitticomb, Directional, and Interior Craft, with a new pottery line via Haeger. HB Top Designers, 1999, 2000, 2001. KB 2001, 2003, 2006.

"While gold was not something I would have thought of, Larry advised me to go for the ultimate gold dining room—walls, chairs, and skirted table all in gold. We absolutely adore it." "He places furniture in a room like jewels in a necklace." "He is a visionary. He found treasures in dusty antiques shops in London that looked like nothing to me." "Inventive, colorful, and an actual bargain." "Really pushed us to think outside of the box." "Always does a spot check to make sure the project comes out perfectly." "He took our historic mansion and added modern life and great cheer." "He offers a broad range of economic alternatives, pointing you to Bloomingdale's if that makes sense." "Injects a sense of fun into everything he does." "You don't have to worry about the architect, because Larry will provide all the inspiration."

	Quality	Cost	Value	Recommend?

LBDA/Laura Bohn Design Associates   4 4 4 4

30 West 26th Street, 11th Floor, New York, NY 10010
(212) 645 - 3636 www.lbda.com

High-end, contemporary, harmonious interior design

Calmness and character abundantly and integrally offer a counterpoint in thought and form in the spaces designed by Laura Bohn. Clients applaud Bohn's unpretentious, intriguing style and helpful attitude. They also appreciate her extensive design background, which includes a degree from Pratt, training with John Saladino (leading to the senior designer position), and over twenty years of practice in her own firm. Bohn's taste tends toward clean contemporary lines mixed with unusual antiques, quirky highlights and brushed in layered, muted neutral hues. There are often more than eight different fabrics in a room—usually in the same hushed tones, yet in different textures.

References report that Bohn is most comfortable doing a few complete renovations of substantial size per year, working with a full budget. Known to be flexible and practical, with "form following function" and comfort ruling all, furnishings are full-sized and welcoming. Bohn is reportedly very organized and available, with a strong back office that can answer most any day-to-day questions. Recently, she is said to be lightening the workload, taking on fewer clients (generally only those with bigger budgets) as her status in the industry allows. When she does take on work, Bohn often teams with the contracting firm of Bohn-Fiore, owned by her husband.

Bohn charges a design fee of approximately 10% of the budget and then charges a reasonable markup over net on products. Mindful of the customer's expenses, Bohn is willing to combine expensive antiques and exquisite Italian lighting with the latest from IKEA or Conran's. HB Top Designers, 1999, 2000, 2001. ID Hall of Fame. KB 1992.

"The queen of soft modern." "She is a seasoned professional. What she sketched is exactly what you get, and it is always perfect." "Laura has a very defined portfolio. If you share her perspective, then you will love what she does to your house." "Functional for family use." "The firm has an extensive library of resources at the office that makes most decision making a breeze." "She uses the unexpected, but in a relaxed way." "I paid most vendors directly, so I knew exactly where we stood financially." "She doesn't back down from her decisions." "She is strong enough to voice her opinion but good about listening to the client." "You're dealing with a true artist, which means the results are great, but sometimes the process is vague." "I was hysterical when she used six different shades of green in a single space, but she was absolutely right—it looks rich, yet homogeneous and peaceful." "Bohemian, urban, chic." "Unbelievable sense of color, every room is gorgeous and exciting. She delivers the highest quality."

Leta Austin Foster   3.5 3.5 4 4.5

424 East 52nd Street, New York, NY 10022
(212) 421 - 5918

Historically minded, traditional interior design with panache

Sallie Giordano heads up the New York office of this renowned Palm Beach firm, begun by her mother more than a quarter of a century ago. Guided by their young soirée-set client base, 90% of the work is traditional with a kick—Greenwich meets Lilly Pulitzer by way of Ray and Charles Eames. Supporters often mention Giordano's creativity, citing a range of styles that can be competently executed, including 1930s Art Deco and more contemporary. Still, most rooms are anchored by traditional American casegoods and custom linen textiles. It is also mentioned that the firm is very well organized, fun to work with, and committed to building on the client's thematic cues.

Giordano graduated from Georgetown and was a journalist for several years before joining the family practice about fourteen years ago. The practice has recently completed several first apartments for young New Yorkers, a range of Greenwich and Long Island homes, and several vacation homes across the country. A few rooms are often the starting point.

Working with no design fee, a classic retail is charged on products, with standard oversight fees. Clients mention that Giordano will offer a variety of quality product choices, allowing the client broad economic and stylistic latitude. It has been mentioned, however, that she can be quite adamant that her clients make sound design choices, and that she would rather go back to the proverbial drawing board than settle for anything less.

"They are practical, helpful decorators who just get it." "Sallie will bring 20 to 30 fabric samples and will have an elaborate discussion about them. But if we do not agree, 30 more will be here the following week." "You don't feel like you're living in your grandmother's house, but that you've inherited some of her better pieces." "Though she has a full life outside decoration, she makes up for it with incredible energy and dedication." "Helped to guide me in the right direction despite my initial reluctance. Now, I'm so glad she was persistent." "Not a superstar, but a real pro." "Sallie is perfect for the client with strong ideas and wants a very active relationship with their designer." "When we first saw the space, we wondered where the money had gone. But after living in it for a while, we realized it had been worth it. With Sallie, you don't see the quality, you feel it." "Sallie will custom color the Bennison in a imperceptibly different shade, which makes all the difference." "She never runs out of steam, just keeps going until the last lampshade is completed."

Lichten Craig Architects LLP ▣
6 West 18th Street, 9th Floor, New York, NY 10011
(212) 229 - 0200   www.lichtencraig.com

Distinguished, classical residential architecture and interior design

See Lichten Craig Architects LLP's full report under the heading Architects

London Bridges Interiors ▣   3.5   2.5   5   4.5
1111 Park Avenue, Suite 2A, New York, NY 10128
(917) 592 - 2611   jennyelmlinger@aol.com

Timeless, English, traditional interior design

Clients appreciate London Bridges' understanding of the Manhattan family lifestyle and their realistic views on budget. Heather Harper and Jenny Elmlinger, sisters with an eye for timeless designs and excellent details, run the firm. Supporters tell us they work effectively and efficiently to achieve the client's vision, be it traditional English with a twist or stark white modern, all in appropriate good taste.

Many clients are Park Avenue families signing up their first "real" decorator. Clients report that one of the firm's great strengths is an understanding of family traffic patterns and interests. The team will undertake a wide variety of projects, from home "facelifts" to gut renovations. While scheduling is usually not an issue, these partners are moms whose first priority is to their kids, according to clients.

London Bridges charges a low design fee and a very reasonable markup on product. Oversight fees or consultations are billed at reasonable rates. Living rooms fall in the $75,000+ range. The firm taps only the best suppliers and has great industry relationships. This team can also work on a phased approach or a consulting basis. Clients say they feel no pressure to purchase items they do not love. Harper and Elmlinger are reportedly very professional, and many repeat customers highly recommend them.

"You want to sit down and have tea with Heather and Jenny." "I was a little worried that their family obligations might hinder the progress of my renovation, but their efficiency compensated for any scheduling conflicts." "I was so grateful that they

found an excellent contractor for us, and stayed on top of him." "Wonderful, warm, down-to-earth people." "They solved any misunderstandings, and absorbed the cost." "Great to work with. The only downside, if you can call it that, is that they have a life outside their business." "They work together as a team, so that one of them is always accessible." "A great strength is that they have great empathy for my life with kids." "They are very practical, suggesting the highest quality for certain pieces and keeping the rest of it under control."

M (Group) LLC   4.5   4.5   4   5

152 West 88th Street, New York, NY 10024
(212) 874 - 0773 www.mgrouponline.com

Chic, urban, classic interior design and architecture

Gracious and grateful clients "thank their lucky stars" that destiny has led them to Carey Maloney and Hermes Mallea, partners of the M (Group). This collaborative team is well-known for strong architectural details, complex layering of classical effects, good manners, and wit. Experience and success have allowed the pair to cultivate an original style based on classic forms but more confident in its bolder, handsome lines. With Maloney (an M.B.A.) focusing on design and business and Mallea (AIA) focusing on architecture, clients report a seamless exchange of ideas and no production hassles.

Mallea was raised in Miami and Maloney in Beaumont, Texas. The subtleties of their classic Southern taste and charm are evident in both their work and their relationships with clients. They win accolades for interpreting patrons' visions into beautiful, tangible products, be it bohemian or high neoclassical. Clients report that the team uses their strong regional connections to find great furniture buys well outside the normal paths. Going beyond the call of duty, references report that the pair makes sure clients "never commit any social or design faux pas."

The firm is in high demand and only works on a few projects each year. Clients include Barbara Warner (of Warner Bros.), illustrious entertainment players, and notable businessmen. About two-thirds of the projects are in Manhattan and the rest worldwide. Supporters say that the partners spend quite a lot of time up-front on design plans, and that there are no surprises concerning budgets or timing. While noted as extremely expensive, clients believe the result to be well worth the cost. AD 100, 2000, 2002. HB Top Designers, 1999, 2000, 2001, 2002. KB 1993.

"Carey and Hermes can redefine spaces. I bought an ugly new house in the suburbs with absolutely no character. They made it look wonderful with gorgeous colors and subtle detailing." "Their style has evolved over the fifteen years I have worked with Carey and Hermes, more than ever incorporating an international patina." "While they might use eight coats of paint for an effect on my living room wall, it does not look ostentatious. You can feel the quality, but you cannot identify it." "If I had the money, I would hire them without question." "When I asked them to slow down due to the uncertain economic environment, they could not have been more gracious." "They know when to push and when not to, in their quest for serious excellence." "Not a cheap date." "Southern gentleman with immaculate taste." "There is no attitude. They even included my Goodwill Bombay side table in the design." "The end result is also always beautiful and warm without being overdecorated."

M. Jane Gaillard Inc.   3.5   3   4.5   4.5

167 East 74th Street, New York, NY 10021
(212) 988 - 3356 mjgnyc1@aol.com

Classic-to-updated Old School interior design

"Consummate professional" Jane Gaillard is seen as a calming, clear influence in a world of possibilities. Gaillard counts many a Park Avenue resident among the admirers of her "tony" and "appropriate" designs, with the English and French 18th century as major influences. Lately, some clients have been asking for a more tailored, structured look, and Gaillard is happily taking their lead. While she is noted to be a helpful, confident, and excellent second opinion for customers who are actively engaged in the design process themselves, she also offers complete solutions for others who don't know where to begin.

References say this is a small operation, with Gaillard the clear client contact and very accessible. Only a few major projects are on the roster at any one time, keeping schedules in line. Recent undertakings include a traditional country house in Connecticut and a French Art Deco pied-a-terre on the Upper East Side. Gaillard often starts with the public rooms, moving to other quarters at the request of the satisfied client. The designer can work on a consulting or a project basis. For defined projects, a minimal design fee is charged with reasonable product markups. Living rooms tend to be in the neighborhood of $100,000. Ethan Allen is considered for the children's rooms.

"If you are not sure what you want, Jane will ably guide you." "We started with just the living room, and ended up doing two apartments and the country house." "Traditional, but Jane has a good range within that style." "Jane was amazing at breaking the deadlock my husband and I had over the last two years." "She never assumes that the sky is the limit—she is reasonable and practical." "Never any surprises, just solid, charming work." "We attended her twenty-year anniversary party at the Colony five years ago, and met the loveliest group of past clients." "Not the decorator to use if you are trying to make a statement. Perfect for the low-key, just-so couple." "Great kitchen redesign." "She never nickel-and-dimes you." "I thought that I knew a lot, but Jane brought the apartment to a new level." "There is a tremendous comfort level in using Jane."

Marc Charbonnet Associates   4   3.5   4.5   4

222 East 46th Street, New York, NY 10017
(212) 687 - 1333 www.mecaproductions.com
Updated, classical comfortable interior design

Marc Charbonnet has cultivated a group of dedicated clients by offering a highly individualized look. Supporters consider him to be a very knowledgeable social and design historian, and they enjoy the education he provides along the way. Charbonnet often recommends the commission of high-quality custom furniture and rugs, as well as imaginative decorative paintings integral to the design. We hear the very attentive Charbonnet allows clients to be as active as they wish in the design process.

Raised in New Orleans, Charbonnet worked for Peter Marino before starting his own firm in 1991. Current clients include Michael J. Fox and other prominent New Yorkers. Many former city dwellers have subsequently brought Charbonnet with them to other parts of the United States. Charbonnet leads all design decisions and is bolstered by a solid back office.

The firm charges reasonable up-front and product fees, with additional hourlies for the design of newly created product. It is said the firm will work endlessly to find a client well-priced alternatives. Non-structural architectural design details are also well incorporated, with clients noting that Charbonnet works quite well with architects. References applaud Charbonnet for his incorporation of their existing furnishings, and for the seamless use of Crate & Barrel when appropriate, balanced by substantial custom pieces. Fees can range considerably, with living rooms from $30,000 to $300,000. Though Charbonnet notes he has "clients with lovely Louis XVI reproduction furniture, clients with period Louis XVI furniture, and one client with Louis XVI's actual furniture, all find him to be funny, fair, and honest, delivering a very high-quality product at a strong value. AD 100, 2000, 2002, 2004.

"While he is extremely knowledgeable about antiques, he is not a snob. He will scour all parts of town to find the most cost-effective solution." "He even identified an

estate sale the week before it went to Sotheby's. We had a field day." "Working in a creative field myself, I was overwhelmed by Marc's attention to detail." "He offers comfort that can be enjoyed in diamonds and high heels, or bare feet." "No one can beat Marc on value—he has incredible resources." "Impeccable design work, the billing process could have gone more smoothly." "Great to work with." "Beautiful beautiful work, and Marc is insistent on every detail." "He considered my lifestyle in designing each aspect of the project. While being very stylish, he did not sacrifice comfort or functionality." "Our experience with Marc on our New Jersey home ten years ago was so successful that we have been working together on a new construction project in Florida."

Mario Buatta Inc.   5   5   4   4.5

120 East 80th Street, New York, NY 10021
(212) 988 - 6811

Elegant, classical residential interior design

Mario Buatta continues to be in a class of his own. Of course, if you have met Buatta, even briefly, this distinction initially applies to his irreverent sense of humor. But then, as a client, a potential client, or an industry peer, one is immediately swept away by the breathtaking balance, supreme subtlety, and integrated flow of Buatta's rooms which are "nothing short of masterful." Known as a consummate colorist, Buatta is said to create looks that "last a lifetime" by combining shades of color and textures unimaginable to others. Buatta can also make a fabulous room from pieces clients would have otherwise discarded, adding a small accessory or trim to tie it all together. Clients further report that Buatta can regularly solve the issues that confound architects and contractors, often "with just one look."

While Buatta does not have a consistent office staff or any design associates, clients appreciate the fact that this "one-man maelstrom" is involved in all the design decisions himself. Patrons note, however, that getting Buatta to focus can sometimes be an issue. Accordingly, he generally limits the number of his new clients, taking on just a few of very substantial means. In addition to the White House guest quarters, Buatta has done projects for Barbara Walters, Billy Joel, Malcolm Forbes, Nelson Doubleday, and Mariah Carey. Interestingly, Buatta will sometimes play a much more limited role, especially for family members of past clients, acting as a consultant without sourcing the main fabrics or furnishings.

Buatta works on a significant retainer that is fully reimbursable against product purchases. Products are acquired at retail and there is a 25% oversight fee. His out-of-town daily rate is $3,500. Bills are reportedly always late and typically extreme, but quite clear. Clients recommend Buatta for those who want the ultimate look "at whatever cost." AD 100, 2000, 2002, 2004. HB Top Designers, 1999, 2000, 2001, 2002, 2003, 2004, 2005. ID Hall of Fame. KB 1990, 1997, 2000, 2006.

"Mario is the most gifted decorator of our generation." "He has such a beguiling personality that it becomes a great, amusing adventure." "Once you get him going, there's no one better. He was molded from the great masters." "For a person of such stature, Mario is not a snob, remarkably down-to-earth, and proud of his local roots." "While Mario's fees are relatively reasonable, project costs can get out of control." "Mario is used to dealing only with the ultimate—read: exorbitant—craftsmen." "While the project took much longer than expected, Mario is incredible under deadlines. Once I sent out invitations for a large party, he magically finished." "He is clearly a genius, but will drive you to drink." "He hangs Peale portraits and field hockey sticks with equal skill and enthusiasm." "Mario believes that a house grows like a garden, and is never completely finished." "Mario is a true friend, taking client relationships well beyond the business level." "He is not for the faint of heart, but well worth it."

	Quality	Cost	Value	Recommend?
	✚	$	◆	★

Mark Cutler Design Inc. 📷   4   3.5   4.5   4.5

8656 Holloway Plaza Drive, West Hollywood, CA 90069
(310) 360 - 6212 www.markcutlerdesign.com

Streamlined, stylish, tradition-based interior design

Maintaining a classical European-American tradition while welcoming the charm of modernity, Mark Cutler offers an updated take on the expected. With the greatest respect for historical lines, Cutler takes a space and creates a personalized portrait of the client. This may translate into a modern take on traditional or a "soft and warm" take on modern, depending on the client's preferences. Distressed woods may be used to create a more formal cadence, or modern fittings may be used in a farmhouse to create balance. In all cases, Cutler has won the confidence of his clients, who consistently compliment his professional and personal skills.

Raised in Australia, Cutler received a degree in architecture at the University of Queensland. Starting his career in New York, he was soon lured to LA. Working under the tutelage of Bill Hablinski in the interiors department for nine years, Cutler struck out on his own in 2000. Now with his own very competent team of six, Cutler takes on about six major commissions a year, devoting serious time to each. When working in New York, he sets up camp on this coast, shipping in certain LA resources but using local craftsmen for finishing to maintain a sense of context. References say Cutler brings a refreshing perspective to the City, designing elegant, intelligent homes and creating a sense of "California spaciousness" in even the most cramped apartment.

Clients and contractors credit Cutler for his comprehensive CAD floor plans, which detail every item. The company is also commended for "value engineering" budgets and its reasonable, businesslike approach. Standard design fees are taken up front with standard product fees taken on purchases. Clients in New York are typically young or middle-aged professionals with a unique, creative perspective on their homes.

"Mark really has a special ability to get inside a client's head and understand their vision." "All my rooms are my favorite." "The nicest guy in the world to work with. And humorous to boot." "Extremely hands-on." "A genuine team player with the remodeling staff." "My husband is a builder with exacting standards. He is very pleased with Mark's professional, knowledgeable, creative skills. I never thought it would be this easy." "If we said 'go for it' the costs would be too much, but he is excellent about meeting a specified budget." "He saved us tons of money in potential plumbing mistakes." "I never felt pressured in any way." "He would always come back with alternatives if we asked, which was the case with the practicality of the children's fabrics." "We are really opinionated and Mark always respected our viewpoint." "While Mark is a busy guy with lots of clients, he was always accessible." "He made it so easy."

Mark Hampton Inc. 📷   4.5   5   4   4.5

654 Madison Avenue, 21st Floor, New York, NY 10021
(212) 753 - 4110 www.markhamptoninc.com

Sumptuous, classically inspired, detailed interior design

Not resting on her family laurels, Alexa Hampton is continuing to evolve as a gifted designer and a manager. Building upon her innate design sensitivity, commitment to quality, and range of scope, there is a freshness of line with a wealth of historical reference. Hampton is also credited for her attention to detail, professional demeanor, and charming personality. Hampton assumed the reins of Mark Hampton Inc. after the death of her father in 1998. Hampton has ably gained the confidence of past clients and has built a base of her own, reflecting her spirited approach with a pastiche of the finest Chippendale antiques intermingled with the likes of Jean-Michel Frank. In the country, there is a nod to contextual suitability, but "it is very much a catered affair" with the same ultimate resources being trucked in.

Hampton graduated from Brown and studied at the Institute of Fine Arts at NYU. At age thirteen, she began working in her father's office, developing what clients say are her well-honed design instincts. Hampton's versatile capabilities are reflected in her recent projects. These include a new Louis XIV-style home in Atlanta, a Balinese-style Florida retreat, a formal Anglo-French home, a traditional boat with modern backgrounds, and several New York apartments, ranging from modern eclectic to streamlined traditional. Clients (a group that includes Susan Burden and Teresa Heinz) say that the common thread is a desire to steer the project to the absolute highest standards, and a substantial budget. To the delight of clients and the detriment of the schedule, design delegation is not Hampton's forte, and there are usually about five large and twenty smaller ongoing projects.

The firm works with a fairly high design fee (but this includes oversight services and auction consultations) and classic retail on products. Hampton is known to mix it up to meet budgets—De Angelis for the living room and Classic Sofa for the playroom (with some unique tweaks). While most projects are large, the firm is happy to work on smaller assignments. AD 100, 2002, 2004. HB Top Designers, 1999, 2000, 2001, 2002, 2003, 2004, 2005. ID Hall of Fame. KB 1997, 1999.

"Once you have seen the exemplary quality 'Down the Rabbit-Hole' and experienced the joy of Alexa's dry wit, it is hard to turn back." "While not cheap, Alexa is quite fair. Getting it right is a matter of pride and family tradition." "I am pleased to report that Alexa is quite busy. But this can mean less of her time for the smaller clients." "The ballast is firmly in the keel, the sails are on course." "There is a new focus." "She's got a lot on her shoulders, but she shoulders it well." "A lot of fun, and each interior is better than the last." "I have been in the real estate development business for over 30 years, and I have not seen anyone with the project management skills Alexa has brought to the table." "Walking through the D&D with Alexa is like being with royalty, everyone rushes to her side." "Architectural details have fallen between the cracks, but the interior design is fabulous." "Alexa has a unique eye. We will go through 200 samples at the D&D and she will know exactly which blue will work. It is amazing."

Mark Weaver & Associates Inc.   💼   4   4   4   4
519 North La Cienega Boulevard, Suite 12, West Hollywood, CA 90048
(310) 855 - 0400 www.markweaver.com

Calm, content, traditional interior design

A gentle warmth is reflected in Mark Weaver's work, a glow that invites the onlooker to come and take a seat. The firm prides itself on active collaboration with the client, finding a seamless balance between the traditional and the more contemporary, with comfort as a primary goal. With headquarters on the West Coast, Weaver favors California forms in soothing neutrals, with punches of graphic art throughout. Italian influences also may be seen, with frequent trips abroad. References report that not only are the rooms calm, but so is the process.

Raised in Southern California, Weaver moved to LA to attend Woodbury College, and soon thereafter worked with respected old-line designer Frank Austin. In 1969, he set up on his own and soon had a society editor client. There are five members of the team, including Darrell Wilson, who received a master's of architecture at Princeton and a master's of fine arts at the Otis School. The firm can do the most complete jobs, down to placing the clothes in the closet and lighting the fireplace, but it is also open to refurbishing a few rooms. Though Weaver has connections in New York, his unique California sources can help break the mold, and usually at a lower cost.

Clients report that the process is quite clear, with a specific letter of agreement. The firm charges a standard up-front design fee and standard markups on product. Weaver has maintained the loyalty of clients over his 35-year career, now doing several children's and grandchildren's homes.

"As a dealer, I see them all. Mark is really a terrific person." "He gave us the confidence to take on a new look, but never pushed us beyond our comfort zone." "Mark has a very clear-cut approach. There is continuity in his work." "He absolutely helped us avoid trendiness and errors in judgment." "Mark can do everything in Crate & Barrel, bring in the finest Pompeiian artifacts, or get an antique Grecian bed reproduced." "Everything is so well defined with an excellent road map."

Markham Roberts Inc.   4.5   4.5   4   4.5

1020 Lexington Avenue, 2nd Floor, New York, NY 10021
(212) 288 - 6090   www.markhamroberts.com

Eloquent, alluring, classic interior design

With a strong knowledge of the most sublime traditions, Markham Roberts creates designs of timeless and gracious appeal with a modicum of radiant wit. A sumptuous neutral background may be a foil for a blood-red felt table edged in parchment white, brandishing delicate ostrich eggs. Clients may come to the party with family heirlooms, or seeking a fresh start. Roberts will insist upon classical architectural bones, an exquisite paint finish, and a minimum of one or two fine antiques, with the rest dictated by budget. Supporters consistently say the result is the very definition of chic.

An art history and architecture major at Brown, Roberts embarked upon his design career after working for Mark Hampton for five years. In 1997, Roberts began an independent firm which now has six others in staff, including two project managers and a licensed architect. Two or three major projects are taken on at a time, with many smaller undertakings accepted for past clients. About half the work is on the Upper East Side and in the suburbs (Greenwich, Rye, Katonah), with the rest spread across the United States. The entire team is consistently complimented for its well-honed organizational skills, with Roberts serving as the primary client contact.

The firm takes a good-sized design fee to start and bills classic retail on product, but charges no hourlies and low workroom markups. An array of amazing-to-outstanding sources is used depending on budgets, with Roberts coaching the lesser vendors to deliver fine goods. He is particularly applauded for his creative abilities with younger family clients, designing pieces which are simultaneously functional, fanciful, and rugged enough to withstand the PB&J set. Original pieces of his furniture may be purchased at the office/showroom Roberts shares with James Sansum at the address above. Budgets tend to be incremental, with the sky as the limit. Clients believe they are getting excellent value for the money, and have fun in the process. HB Top Designers, 2002, 2003, 2004, 2005.

"Markham is fastidious. My husband is an organization fanatic, and even he was impressed." "Mark was there for us on Saturday mornings when that was best for us." "Sensitive to our family needs, Markham put a indestructible paisley covered table in the foyer to hide the stroller." "Takes his designs seriously, and it shows." "My son's Louis XVI daybed is truly unique, but is functional and does not look overdone." "James Sansum's shop is wonderful—a treasure trove hidden away on the second floor." "He trained with a master and has gone on to make his own mark." "Sets up a traditional room, then adds one quirky piece and the whole thing comes alive." "Understands when patterns are appropriate and when they are not." "Picture-perfect designs that don't read like showpieces." "You get him, not an assistant." "There was give and take in the budget—when we got sticker shock, he would find another. But

when he said it was important, we would bend." "There is huge respect for Markham when he walks into a store. He can get it done." "I have redecorated my apartment three times before, but this is the first time I was completely happy."

Martin Raffone Interior Design  4 3.5 4.5 4.5
247 Centre Street, 7th Floor, New York, NY 10013
(212) 243 - 2027 www.martinraffone.com
Luxurious modern interiors inspired by natural materials

Commended for his enthusiasm, dedication, and his unique take on modernity, Martin Raffone creates consistently handsome, elegant, and chic interiors inspired by his love of natural, authentic materials. Harmonious juxtapositions of color and texture are a trademark. Furnishings are generally kept to elemental modern forms but mixed with an unexpected twist of the antique and exotic. Despite the textural diversity, an underlying sense of calm is felt by clients, who are avid supporters of Raffone. The designer is applauded for being "super-organized" and for an excellent understanding of the practical: storage, lighting, and architectural detailing. Clients also report that Raffone is open to a wide range of sources in the belief that "each has its moment."

In practice since 1997 and bringing 10 years' experience at top-name firms to the job, Raffone has attracted a following of sophisticated clients, creating modern homes both downtown and up. Current projects include several loft renovations in Chelsea and Soho—and projects as far afield as St. Barts and Morocco. Raffone's projects consist of a mix of entire renovations, fully detailed decoration, and at times, just a few good rooms for a sympathetic client.

Budgets start at $200,000, with living rooms running from $75,000 on up. Budgets are professionally detailed and discussed upfront, and a standard design fee and commission are charged. Hourly consultations are available with a minimum. Architecture percentages are taken for structural oversight. HB Top Designers, 2000, 2001.

"Martin defines a look that is an unusual twist on the mundane, but always classy." "Conceptually brilliant, and thoroughly and practically executed." "No one else would think to have a modern steel table with historic Chippendale chairs and a plastic laminate sideboard. We so appreciate the creativity." "Martin is not a snob, but really appreciates and can deliver top quality." "Approaches each project with unique vision." "He understood the perhaps eccentric nature of my needs." "I am not an easy client, but Martin dealt with me so well. I really trusted him." "He has a distinct look, and makes it work for the client's particular work and family requirements." "It is not only unique, but so well executed in the time frame allotted." "Martin is an absolute pleasure."

Matthew Patrick Smyth Inc. ▮ 4.5 3.5 5 5
136 East 57th Street, Suite 1700, New York, NY 10022
(212) 333 - 5353 www.matthewsmyth.com
Uplifting, refined, tranquil interior design

Appropriate scale, harmony of light, and crystalline placement are the trademarks of Matthew Smyth. Mixing the historically relevant with modern élan, rooms are streamlined with fine antiques and original thought. Clients, peers, and the trade speak with great affection for the designer, noting his general good judgment and accommodating nature. Architecturally, his design plans are said to be very clear and helpful, giving the client a visual basis for informed decision making. The firm is small, and clients note that they receive Smyth's full attention.

After studying at FIT and spending five years with David Easton, Smyth started his own firm in 1987. Most of his work is in Manhattan and the regional area, although clients are found worldwide. He often decorates second or third residences, and many of his new customers are family referrals. He is willing to do small projects for interesting new clients but usually undertakes complete renovations. Smyth spends time regularly in Paris (he has an apartment there), adding a continental inspiration to his lines.

Smyth charges a standard design fee and a reasonable markup on product. Living rooms are in the $75,000+ range. All bills include the net costs. While he personally tends toward the modern, clients report that he is successful with any style—including highly traditional—or with a dexterous blend. HB Top Designers, 2000, 2001, 2002, 2003, 2004, 2005. KB 1995, 1998, 2001.

"I cannot fully describe his respect and concern for his clients." "He is involved in everything right down to the last trim selection." "Matthew understood the house much better than I did and would come out to visit whenever necessary." "His demeanor and his billing are so straightforward." "Sometimes he pushes too hard on certain touches." "A Francophile, but he loves to mix it up with items for the American Federal period." "He has multiple homes, but he stayed on top of everything." "Dealers are always surprised that he speaks of the net price in front of the client." "His architectural talents are better than any architect I have ever known." "Refined, not snobbish." "Likes to work with a certain group of subcontractors." "He is unique within the industry. He always makes it right." "I just love being with Matthew. He is tons of fun and has a wide range of interests." "He not only understands peoples' design interests but also their values." "He can deal with any circumstance. I had to move in a week, and Matthew made it happen." "Matthew kept us so calm. I would recommend him to anyone."

Maureen Footer and Associates 💼   4   4   4   4.5

136 East 57th Street, Suite 503, New York, NY 10022
(212) 207 - 3400   info@mwfooterdesign.com

Classic, clever, French-accented interior design

Maureen Wilson Footer's work is guided by warmth, color, and a playful intellect. She is equally comfortable executing witty historical references (one showhouse bedroom featured Proust's legendary cork-lined walls) and touching details, such as Robert McCloskey prints in the children's rooms of a literary family's Manhattan apartment. Footer's love of antique furniture means that many of her interiors end up with a historical flavor, though the effect is never overwhelming. Indeed, when these items are paired with contemporary fabrics and cheery color schemes, she unquestionably earns the title "modern classicist."

Footer has a multifaceted educational background, with an M.B.A. from Columbia, time spent in the interior design program at FIT, and graduate studies in 18th century French interiors at the École du Louvre. Her experiences in Paris continue to inform her work today, which is often complemented by French accents. After working as a senior designer for J.P. Molyneux and founding the interior design department at Jones, Footer, Margeotes & Partners, she started her own firm in 1998.

A recent project found Footer working in an original Trumbauer mansion, transforming a "dreary 20th century developer's hell" into a French Neoclassical flat. She has also recently completed a maisonette for two modern art collectors in Manhattan, a country house on Long Island Sound, and a Fifth Avenue co-op. Prices tend to be on the higher end of the scale, reflecting Footer's appreciation for fine antiques and quality materials. Clients report that she is warm, enthusiastic, intelligent, and that though she can get "carried away with the details," her work is "impeccable." KB 2005.

"I would not go to anyone else for my next projects. Maureen Footer over-delivers on style and quality; is always on time and on budget; and is a pleasure to work with." "We bought a pre-war co-op that hadn't been touched in 25 years. Maureen made it elegant in a period-sensitive but fresh way." "She has a very good sense of taste and imagination, and a network of outstanding subcontractors who are very high caliber." "There were no monetary/contract issues. Maureen Footer abides by the contract."

"She did an excellent job in designing our New York apartment in the spirit of France." "Fun, feminine, and French." "She sweats the details. Sometimes it can make things more expensive, but the result is great." "Our building has very strict renovation rules, and she worked through them masterfully." "Our project involved everything—furniture layout, kitchen cabinetry, bathrooms, room flow, lighting, and finishes. The quality of her work is outstanding, and I would highly recommend working with Ms. Footer to others."

McMillen Inc.

4.5   4.5   4   4.5

155 East 56th Street, 5th Floor, New York, NY 10022
(212) 753 - 5600   designdept@mcmilleninc.com

Classical, staid, proper interior design

McMillen is known as one of the tried-and-true in the business, as generation after generation of discreet old-money clients continue to favor the firm's timeless designs. Founded in 1923 by Eleanor McMillen Brown, the firm's guiding lights are now Betty Sherrill (who joined in 1951), Luis Rey (1972), Mary Louise Guertler (1965), and Katherine McCallum (1982), who lead a strong team of experienced senior designers. Ann Pyne, Sherrill's daughter, is also a designer with the firm. McMillen can deliver a surprising range of styles (way beyond just chintz) and undertakes most of the related architectural work. It focuses on the highest quality product available, avoids any and all trendiness, and often cultivates unique sources. At a client's request, the staff will even provide the books on your shelves.

McMillen's list of highly satisfied customers is extensive. Many have a habit of owning several homes over time, all decorated by McMillen. The firm takes great pride in retrofitting clients' old curtains and upholstery to new venues. The company is open to new clients, especially ones that will grow with the firm. The very professional office of 22 is said to deliver the ultimate in customer service, exchanging items until the client is satisfied. Dozens of projects are taken on annually, each headed by a senior designer.

The firm charges a standard design fee (for an average-sized project), standard oversight fees, and classic retail on products. Most projects are full-scale renovations. Patrons say that the net product pricing is unknown to them, but that McMillen perfection is worth any price. AD 100, 2000. HB Top Designers, 1999, 2000, 2003, 2004. KB 1993, 1997, 2005.

"It would never occur to me or my family to think of using anyone else." "McMillen functions seamlessly. A senior designer was always on-site, and they faxed my office with any decisions I had to make." "Luis made me stick to my budget, even stopping me from buying certain antiques." "Managing to a budget is not really their thing past the major pieces." "We had to choose between a new car and the McMillen curtains. Thirteen years later, the curtains still look fresh, and the car would have been long gone." "My apartment is contemporary, and it will still be fresh in 25 years." "McMillen represents a system which works, but they are not the most innovative designers." "These are schooled professionals that are not worried about invitations to the south of France." "They are never condescending or haughty. These are practical people who get the job done without an attitude." "Betty, quite frankly, just likes things that are 'pretty.' It's a simple, commendable approach, and thankfully it has filtered down to the associates." "Their large size gives them a lot of clout, and my project was done completely on time and on budget." "It is a well-oiled machine." "I wish I had another home to do with them." "They are embarking on a new phase of the McMillen story."

Meg Braff Interiors Inc.   3.5 3.5 4 4.5

107 East 63rd Street, New York, NY 10021
(212) 355 - 2482   mwbraff@aol.com

Warm, tailored, traditional interior design

Clients gratefully turn to Meg Braff for her engaging and "uplifting" design style and friendly, yet professional demeanor. While she takes her cue from the client, Braff usually favors an updated traditional style with "happy yet sophisticated colors" and creative details. She will do as little as two rooms up to a complete redesign. References appreciate the firm's unusual secret sources, many from the South where Braff was raised. She is a favorite of many young uptown New Yorkers, more established suburban clients (Locust Valley, Greenwich, Bronxville) and families in Newport and Palm Beach.

Braff earned a B.S. in developmental psychology from Vanderbilt University and an A.A.S. from Parsons. She opened her own shop in 1992, applying her background in psychology to create beautiful spaces that conform to the personalities of their inhabitants. Recent projects include a twelve-room apartment on Fifth Avenue decorated in finely modulated color harmonies, and a furniture showroom in High Point, North Carolina done in conjunction with Scalamandre.

Sensitive to cost constraints and able to work with a budget, Braff often incorporates moderately priced pieces from a large resource library. She is further commended for her "quick and appropriate action" if any issues arise, despite a relatively small office. While Braff is sometimes over-committed, her clients say that she always comes through. Fees are based on a standard design charge and the retail cost of products the company sources. Living rooms often are in the $75,000+ range. The firm is referred from friend-to-friend with the strongest commendations.

"I can always count on Meg, especially for that just-so Town & Country look." "We were so impressed that she took our very fine Oriental rug (to which we were attached), and had it magically transformed to fit our new apartment." "We are so appreciative of their resourcefulness, willingness, and the quality of the work." "Very flexible with billing." "I actually think she's too cost conscious. Sometimes you just have to go for it." "She has a life outside decorating, but she won't take on any more projects than she can do a perfect job on." "Meg is so professional and gracious, she can even work with friends." "Meg is amazing with fabrics." "The rooms turned out exactly like the pictures they drew."

Michael Formica Inc.   3.5 3 4.5 4

95 Christopher Street, New York, NY 10014
(646) 510 - 4848   www.michaelformica.com

Contemporary, mid-century, modern interior design

Michael Formica is known for an edited, "cool and hip" look that incorporates quality furnishings and neutral backgrounds. Formica works in restrained colors, clean surfaces, serious mid-century furnishings, and "moments of folly," creating from a thoroughly modern point of view. Formica is also skilled at drawing inspiration from the 1940s and 1950s to create a happy marriage between contemporary living and the simplistic functionality of yesteryear. Sources applaud Formica's intelligent juxtaposition of furnishings and colors to maximize ambient light reflecting the open spaces. He is also reportedly adept at installing clients' existing possessions—particularly artwork—into refreshing and inspiring interiors.

Formica was trained at RISD but now lives downtown, and his clients tend to reside in the New York metropolitan area. Recent projects include a Park Avenue penthouse, a Tribeca loft, a Cobble Hill townhouse, a North Shore residence, and a Sands Point shingle cottage. His enthusiasm for his work is said to be heartily appreciated by clients, dealers, and vendors. HB Top Designers, 1999, 2000.

"He is not a slave of period architecture. Regardless of the exterior, the interiors are edited and light as if filled by a breeze." "He really came up with an effective use of lesser, yet larger pieces of furniture to dramatize the space." "I never thought 'groovy' could be of such quality." "Some people try to get that sort of retro modernist look. Michael doesn't have to try, it isn't a conceit for him, he just does it." "Friendly, funny, and eccentric."

Michael Simon Interiors Inc.   5 4.5 4.5 5
3 East 54th Street, 9th Floor, New York, NY 10022
(212) 307 - 7670 www.michaelsimoninc.com

Historically derived 18th century French interior design

Michael Simon's passion for quality French design is apparent to all who view his work. Clients are convinced that he lived a past life in 18th century France, furnishing the finest chateaus. Many extol Simon's encyclopedic knowledge of Louis XIV to XVI design, unique resources, and "ideas beyond anyone else's imagination." He is also noted for intricate planning, highly developed backgrounds (wall paneling/floors/ceilings), and comprehensive project management skills. While his interiors certainly have a historical point of view, clients mention that they do not appear stuffy, due to cleverly reformulated motifs. They also report that Simon can also do English country extremely well.

Trained as a musical composer, Simon went on to work in the design group at Citibank for eleven years before starting his boutique firm. Most of his clients are well established, have traveled widely, and have been exposed to important homes and museums. While Simon is accommodating and realistic about his clients' interests, he has been known to be adamant about certain design decisions. There is a small back office, with Simon on the front line meticulously executing his detailed designs.

The firm charges a substantial percentage-based, reimbursable design fee, reasonable percentages over net, and standard oversight fees. City living rooms generally run in the $150,000 to $300,000 range (before serious antiques). Country home living rooms can be developed for far less. Clients say that Simon offers many alternatives, and that his years in commercial design enable him to meet schedule and budget. However, the nature of these undertakings, most of which incorporate elaborate custom fabrics and architectural detailing, can result in very expensive projects that take up to two years to complete. KB 1998, 2000, 2003.

"Michael is nothing short of a genius." "While his specialty is clearly 18th century French, I would use him for any challenge." "Michael's detailed craftsmanship and quality is as good as David Easton's at half the price." "He was very understanding about the fact that we are at the mercy of our children and dogs and designed with them in mind." "Supportive and pleasant, but could use more support staff." "Michael looks at a room at different times of day and in different lights before starting on it. He is a completionist." "Speeds rapidly towards being too French and then stops just short. He knows where the boundaries are." "He brought fabrics in all price ranges from $49 to $300, all of which were great choices." "Not the fastest project I've ever seen, but he was upfront about it, and met all the deadlines." "His design plans are amazing—each page, room, object, and light socket is key-coded to each other and to a price schedule." "He lives the 18th century today." "After working with him, clients feel like they've taken a college course, he's that knowledgeable." "There are no surprises and I did not need an architect." "Vendors in the D&D will pull you aside to exclaim how much they admire Michael."

Miles Redd LLC 🛍️   4   4   4   5

77 Bleecker Street, Suite 77, New York, NY 10012
(212) 674 - 0902   miles@milesredd.com

Dashing, elegant, traditional interior design with sparkle

Miles Redd is hailed for developing glamorous rooms full of bountiful color and alluring forms while still maintaining a decorous balance. With an original sense of design wit and flair applied to things once traditional, Redd has reconfigured the concept of updated neoclassical. Monogrammed pillows lay atop a rock star's festooned bed, sequins edge Brunschwig chintz swags, and Kentshire antiques banter with burlap walls. Clients say Redd's signature style is layered and full, with intricate detail and perfect placement, resulting in a balanced and open feel. In the country, it reflects a dialogue of the ages, resulting in a playful yet quiet sophistication.

Redd started the firm in 1999 after spending five years with Bunny Williams. He takes on a wide scope of projects, from small downtown apartments to uptown remakes to large homes in Millbrook. With his flexibility and excellent collaborative abilities, Redd has pleased a diverse clientele that includes empty nesters, young professionals, and families. Running a very small office, Redd is highly accessible.

The firm charges a flat design fee and low markup on product. There is as much appreciation for flea market finds and forgotten closet items as for exquisite Louis XV antiques. While more modest projects are artfully arranged thrift-store stunners, others are more Fendi meets F. Scott Fitzgerald. HB Top Designers, 2000, 2001, 2002, 2003, 2004, 2005.

"The designs are spunky but are also completely genteel." "It is the very definition of a collaborative effort. Miles is so enthusiastic about all of your ideas, but at the same time he reins you in to make sure that you have a polished result." "In the right setting, with the right fabric, he can take others' throwaways and make them grand." "Miles has a wonderful foundation of knowledge that he builds upon and runs with." "Preppy version of new millennium glamour." "He took the 18th century style curtains that I refused to get rid of and bordered them with Indian gossamer fabric, adding spice to a tired concept." "Very talented and very good at capturing the moment." "He is such a gentleman—suave and sweet." "Projects have gotten bigger and more extravagant." "Miles is 100% responsible, great at returning phone calls, and would always keep us in the loop." "Not only a great designer, but Miles is also so practical." "He has exquisite taste, imagination, and wit, as well as a beautiful sense of color."

Milly de Cabrol Ltd 🛍️   4   3.5   4.5   4

150 East 72nd Street, Suite 2C, New York, NY 10021
(212) 717 - 9317   millyltd@yahoo.com

Unabashed, continental, bohemian interior design

Highly regarded for her fanciful flair and almost-over-the-edge creativity, Milly de Cabrol is said to "transport" clients with her designs. Recently, de Cabrol has developed a Provence-meets-Tuscany genre which is like "taking a vacation and checking into a five-star hotel," grateful clients report. While ably using a diverse palette of textiles and colors and strong pieces of character, the designer's editing skills are said to be as remarkable as her versatility. Clients appreciate the fact that de Cabrol is the sole contact and inspiration for projects, and that she works highly collaboratively with the client.

Born into an aristocratic and artistic Italian family, de Cabrol lived in London for ten years and traveled extensively in the Far East. In 1984 the designer moved to the States and started her career in interior design. We're told she most enjoys unusual design projects, which she "pours her heart and soul into." Recent projects have included a French chateau-like house in Westport, an Indian-Swedish apartment on Fifth Avenue, a grand English duplex on the West Side of Manhattan, and a New York pied-à-terre filled with modern art. She is said to have a particularly good touch with collections.

The firm charges a standard design fee and low product markups. De Cabrol is lauded by supporters for her hardworking attitude and helpful nature. HB Top Designers, 2000, 2001, 2002, 2003.

"Milly is the perfect designer for an interesting, sophisticated couple or a tycoon who wants to stand out from the pack." "She does formal that is also so comfortable with extreme panache." "Milly is talented, chic, and charming with a wonderful eye for color, composition, and placement." "She is the complete opposite of stuffy, but at the same time classy—just what we were looking for." "I am so impressed by Milly's skill at combining so many styles into the livable, tasteful composite I call my home." "Milly is a hardworking artist type, not a corporate-type organizational commando." "Milly found these amazing crystal chandeliers from a private collection that were not even available to the public." "She has a very strong ability to choose just the right amount of 'ethnic style' to give a room verve without it looking overdone." "I love Milly and would absolutely use her again, but she really could use a bit more support." "She decorated my apartment as if it were her own."

Muriel Brandolini Inc. 🛍️   4   3.5   4.5   4

525 East 72nd Street, New York, NY 10021
(212) 249 - 4920 www.murielbrandolini.com

Idiosyncratic, exuberant interior design

Muriel Brandolini is commended for an abundance of creative exuberance, featuring colorful sweeps of fabric and dramatic details. She is well-known for her bold new ideas, unusual combinations, and strong point of view. Her high-energy interiors are inspired by her intriguing heritage. Born in Saigon, raised in the Caribbean, educated in Paris, and married to an Italian aristocrat, Brandolini brings a unique scope to her work. Clients' interiors reflect their families' needs, and become warm cocoons of joyful, comfortable elegance.

While Brandolini's business is small, her clients are big names, including the Crown Prince and Princess Pavlos of Greece, Christopher and Pia Getty, and several media moguls. She is known to show clients a plethora of opulent fabrics, much to their amazement and delight. While most happily remark that she often beats their deadlines, some suggest that Brandolini is more about the overall look than the details.

Often her clients are the young and very chic, who appreciate Brandolini's design talent and ardent love of color. They say she can bring fantasy and fun to an otherwise boring Upper East Side apartment. Though some find her style a bit overwhelming, supporters recommend her for exhilarating projects incorporating the Brandolini style. HB Top Designers, 1999, 2000, 2001.

"Muriel's range is mind-boggling—she can go from the smallest loft to the grandest Park Avenue apartment, and have great fun with both." "Nothing intimidates Muriel, either stylistically or process-wise." "Muriel thinks decorating should be fun and does not take herself too seriously." "She can visualize many different uses for a room which is amazingly helpful for New Yorkers living with kids." "Nothing Muriel does can be described as quiet or small." "Did an exciting, colorful, regal design, like the apartment of a well-traveled princess." "Her antique sources in Paris are unbeatable." "She is a whirlwind of style, opulence, and the unexpected."

Orsini Design Associates Inc. 🛍️   4.5   4.5   4   5

330 East 59th Street, 3rd Floor, New York, NY 10022
(212) 371 - 8400 www.orsinidesignassociates.com

Updated traditional, high-end interior design

Assured, clear, and immensely capable, Susan Orsini quickly assesses each client situation and delivers the appropriate product. Leaning toward updated traditional designs reflecting the interests of her client base, she also has successfully completed Art Deco and more contemporary works. All designs are appreciated for their bold, tailored lines and their livability.

The majority of the firm's work is residential, mostly for prominent business executives (including their boats and planes), though Orsini is open to smaller projects with new clients. The firm also delves into office, commercial, and hospitality work, including projects for Chanel, Goldman Sachs, Disney's first two cruise ships, and notable US embassy residences. In all cases, Orsini is commended for her acute attention to detail, professional manner, and excellent client service.

Orsini is reputed to deliver exactly on budget and on schedule. New clients are charged a design fee and products are purchased for a reasonable percentage over net. The firm spends a great deal of time with clients doing research and planning, and often recommends complete reconfiguration. All types of products are considered, from the finest French silks to Crate & Barrel. The firm often implements winter and summer maintenance programs for its customers and has embraced new home technologies such as state-of-the-art home theaters.

While there is a "very capable" staff of 16, Orsini oversees all client relationships. She has been on *Interior Design* magazine's list of the top 200 decorators every year since 1985. Many of her first clients of 25 years ago are still with her today. HB Top Designers, 1999, 2000. KB 1996.

"Susan's style reflects the ease and comfort necessary for very busy people, who often have several houses to keep up." "She has a strategic plan for everything, which was very appealing to my husband who is used to that sort of thing." "She was the first designer in New York to understand our interest in a California modern comfort." "Can bring grandeur to even the smallest Manhattan apartment." "They are open 24/7 and can make things happen faster than a speeding bullet, even if Susan is out of town." "Her designs work. There is always an electrical outlet where you need one." "She has gotten to know my design preferences so well that she will send me the same photo in this month's AD that I planned to send her, before I get to it." "A real businesswoman—professional, through and through." "She has no patience for slackers." "Susan checks every penny the contractors spend and will always win any disputes with them."

Paula Perlini Inc. ▇   4   4   4   4

165 East 35th Street, New York, NY 10016
(212) 889 - 6551

Warm, richly-toned, traditional interior design

Paula Perlini wins the respect and loyalty of clients with excellent resources and strong creativity. When one client wanted to wait to find the ultimate Oriental rug, Perlini had a facsimile of a Sultanbad Persian painted on sisal. Now the client considers the sisal rug one of her favorite possessions. Perlini is known for her intermingling of the fine and the found, creating friendly environments comfortable for adults, children, and pets alike. Rooms tend to be quite traditional, with distinct colors offering depth and character.

Perlini spent her student years in Italy and Switzerland, studying at the Accademia di Belle Arti in Rome and absorbing the artistic wonders at hand. Returning home to Cincinnati, Perlini worked in interior design locally, then headed to New York to work for brother-in-law Mark Hampton for almost a decade, eventually becoming the head of design. Perlini then formed a design partnership with Alan Tanksley for six years, and ultimately went out on her own in 1993. Currently, there are about five large projects going on at any one time, generally in Manhattan and the surrounding areas.

While Perlini usually encourages the client to invest in some excellent upholstery and some interesting antique accents, she is good about designing custom

casegoods to help meet the budget. On top of the process and the economics, Perlini has a New York-type design fee and charges classic retail on product. Contented clients say they would not hesitate to recommend Perlini to a friend.

"I would define her style as classic, but with an eye for practicality and freshness." "We have learned to totally trust her judgment." "Paula is way beyond just color and proportion. She always gets it right. My husband used to think he had perfect design sensibilities. But now he fully admits that Paula is way better." "The workmen she brings to the job are of the highest quality—both as artisans and responsible businesses." "While Paula has her own definitive taste, she was open to my definitive style as well." "Paula can find a treasure among random things in the garage. She has such an eye." "We always have either a small project or a large project going on with Paula." "We have never had to ask her to take back a thing." "Paula is so much fun. It is a gift to be around her."

Philip Gorrivan Design 🛍

3.5   3.5   4   4

155A East 71st Street, New York, NY 10021
(212) 452 - 1717 www.philipgorrivan.com

Tailored, traditional-to-hip interior design

Philip Gorrivan designs with an eye towards the future and a foot in the past. While the components may sometimes include antiques, the result is always modern: symmetrical arrangements, open space, and the careful balance of muted and bright colors. Clients praise Gorrivan's ability to liven up a room inexpensively, saying he adds glamour with just a coat of gloss, or class with one well-chosen piece. Indeed, many recent projects have seen this young firm finishing incomplete designs and touching up lackluster rooms. When the project is more extensive, Gorrivan works with clients to create spaces that are "tailored and comfortable" but "full of the unexpected." The outcome is Park Avenue panache for the younger, more eclectic crowd.

Before opening this boutique firm in 2001, Gorrivan spent time as both a private dealer in Old Master paintings and as a venture capitalist for JP Morgan Chase. Associate Robert Lindgren has a background in the art world, working for Sotheby's and Christie's as a specialist in Impressionist paintings and French furniture, respectively. He also spent nine years as a design associate for Meg Braff. References say Gorrivan is the starter—he generates the creative ideas that guide the project—and Lindgren is the relief pitcher—attending to the details and making sure the process is buttoned up properly. Together they take on a small number of projects each year, primarily on the Upper East and Upper West Sides. Clients, who tend to be young families, say that Gorrivan is "lovely" and "easy to work with," and that calls were returned quickly. The firm charges a reasonable upfront design fee and a standard markup over wholesale. Living rooms are generally in the $75,000+ range.

"Philip took some of my mother's midcentury chairs and painted them black to update them. It was the perfect mix of something old and something new." "More inclined towards interesting mixtures than straight traditional or straight modern." "They're definitely there for me. I say it once and it's done." "Philip gets the ball rolling. Robert figures out a way to do it practically, and makes sure all the details are taken care of. They're a great team." "Robert would sometimes return my e-mails in a space of a minute." "A young firm to grow with, not an established master who won't give you the time of day." "They introduced me to a contractor I just loved." "I wouldn't hesitate to use Philip again." "Robert knows so much about art. It was so much fun going to galleries and auctions with him." "I wanted an up-and-coming firm that would take my phone calls and work hard for my business. That's exactly what I got." "I've had bad. They're really good."

Randall A. Ridless 🛍   4.5   4.5   4   4.5

315 West 39th Street, Suite 1101, New York, NY 10018
(212) 643 - 8140   randallridless@msn.com

Exquisite, chic, high-end interior design

With an endearing appreciation of the great moments in design, Randy Ridless has the unique ability to select among the finest examples, creating rooms of dynamic substance and undeniable allure. His stylistic interests range from Federal to Swedish, African to country folk, all reflecting Ridless' knowledge of (and passion for) defined historic periods. Conventions honoring the hallowed past are twisted, with a heartened sense of the new. Clients continue to be agog, speaking glowingly of his design élan and businesslike manner.

Ridless draws upon his extensive training: first at RISD, then in the corporate world at I. Magnin (prototype stores) and Macy's (antiques buying), plus two years with David Easton and a recent post at Saks (store design). His residential design firm was founded relatively recently with VP Elizabeth Martell, but his clients are numerous, many dating back to his days with Easton. While Ridless devotes about half his time to corporate endeavors (Burberry's acclaimed makeover and Bergdorf's shoe salon), patrons find his residential design skills extraordinary, citing his chic, comfortable detailing. The practice selectively takes on about five residential projects at a time, with minimum fees at $100,000. References tell us they feel as if theirs is his only project.

Ridless reportedly understands clients' desires very quickly and works hard to fulfill their vision. He can collaborate with clients or assume all angles, which he often does for vacation homes. The firm works with clients to determine a fee construct that works for both parties. This could include a percentage over net or a flat fee. Customers remark upon Ridless' willingness to always offer "another option" to satisfy expense or style inclinations, and highly recommend the firm. HB Top Designers, 2000, 2001, 2002, 2003, 2004, 2005. KB 2000, 2004.

"I know that he is busy, but he made us feel so special." "I interviewed six potential decorators, but Randy was the obvious choice." "We gave Randy some clippings and some ideas and two weeks later he had the whole thing planned out. We were amazed." "He has an incredible touch: perfect, but not over-decorated. And not insanely expensive to boot." "He picks his clients carefully. Chemistry is very important to him." "He encourages us to have a fabulous living room but use Pottery Barn in the kids' rooms." "Randy goes back and forth between commercial and residential work, so make sure his schedule is free. He's worth waiting for." "He will make your old ABC chair look as if it came from Kentshire." "Randy sets the stage and picks the important pieces, and Beth is equally wonderful at finishing up." "Always has a smile on his face." "When the antique pillows fell apart a few months later, they had twenty alternative choices for us the week after we called." "Even when he offers me choices, he always knows which one I am going to pick." "He is the only one I would trust to go Italian neo-baroque. He is so open and enthusiastic, yet executes with confidence and class."

Robert Couturier Inc. 🛍   5   5   4   4.5

69 Mercer Street, 3rd Floor, New York, NY 10012
(212) 463 - 7177   www.robertcouturier.com

Dramatic, stylish, lush interior design

Robert Couturier takes the art of interior design to an ethereally remarkable level, but neither Couturier nor his work loses its sense of levity in the process. He is renowned for creating visions that relate to historical moments, yet are infused with the presence of today. Couturier's French influence (he spent years studying in Paris) often finds its way into his work, usually in the form of unbridled surrealist-minded folly. Clients stand back and watch in "serious amusement," remarking that Couturier takes them on a personal journey and delivers spectacular and original thought.

While many projects are undertaken for a variety of English, French, and American tycoons (Jimmy Goldsmith's 60,000 square foot Mexican castle, Princess Wolkonsky, Anne Hearst), younger clients also enjoy working with Couturier. There is a sophisticated team of 17 supporting Couturier, detailing each step along the way. He is willing to begin just one room at a time, knowing that the budget-constrained will return when they are able. Alternatively, he is capable of mobilizing an entire village of 2,000 workers in a remote location to get the job done correctly.

While some balk at his prices and uncompromising taste in expensive fabrics, all find him honest, and his staff helpful and responsive. Living rooms are typically in the $100,000 to $300,000+ realm. Well-heeled references commend Couturier for helping them to make wise design investment decisions. He readily admits and absorbs mistakes, and most feel the high costs are justified for the ultimate in upscale chic. AD 100, 2000, 2002. HB Top Designers, 1999, 2000, 2001, 2004. KB, 2004.

"He can see a room and instantly know how to make it fabulous." "Brilliantly creative, yet he always listens to the client." "We hired him after not being pleased with our former decorator—what a difference." "Works with the most influential people in the world—and with my friends, who own rather small apartments." "He brought cheer and wit into our dreadfully boring Park Avenue digs." "He is an ingenious master who knows every historical reference, but he does not take himself too seriously." "Patient yet timely, opinionated yet accommodating." "His sense of proportion knows no equal, his designs span the centuries." "If ever there is an issue, he says, 'Don't worry about it' and magically finds a solution." "The harmony and tranquility one feels when one enters my apartment belies the fact that we are in NYC." "Robert provided a heart for my home." "He has become a significant presence in my life and a friend."

Ronald Bricke & Associates Inc. 🛍   3.5   3.5   4   4.5
333 East 69th Street, New York, NY 10021
(212) 472 - 9006   mail@ronaldbricke.com
Innovative, chic, refined interior design

Ronald Bricke is best known for a "fabulous unfused modernism" that borders on funky. He is also said to be quite facile with 18th century period spaces with an affinity for French and English pieces. The common thread, reportedly, is Bricke's painstaking attention to detail and his strong desire to please the client. Clients say that Bricke is simultaneously adept at creating luxurious, eye-pleasing interiors and taking into account the overall comfort of the space.

Bricke, the sole principal of this three-person firm, is a graduate of Parsons and started his practice in 1972. We are told he is extremely hands-on and has excellent follow-up practices—always returning phone calls and making himself available to his clients. Bricke is said to quickly come up with drawings and usually formulates five plans for the client to choose from. The firm generally takes on about five major projects each year (about twenty overall).

Projects start around $75,000 and clients say Bricke is excellent at working within strict budgets. In addition to his many New York City clients, Bricke has taken on work in London, Florida, Texas, California, and Maine. Brick charges a standard retainer applicable to the last bill and retail on products. Clients trust Bricke to creatively incorporate clients' existing furniture and save money in the process. HB Top Designers, 1999, 2000. KB 1994.

"He is just so creative and knows how to get things done on budget." "He has the patience of a saint. Never talks down to you or scoffs at ideas or questions." "Can make even the dustiest antique seem modern and fresh." "Great quality for a price that was

less than it could have been." "Absolutely delightful in personality and design." "Creates the most whimsical updated French that knocks your socks off." "He is a big fox terrier in personality. He wants to do a good job and will bring you the bone."

Russell Bush 📷   4   3.5   4   4.5

4 Park Avenue, New York, NY 10016
(212) 686 - 9152

Refined, transformational, singular residential interior design

Extolled for his personal style and stylish interiors, Russell Bush can completely transform a space or "magically weave a new facade" into an existing framework. While known for his refined, essential layouts featuring spare, astute antiques, and tailored, detailed upholstery, Bush works really hard to reflect the personality and taste of the owner—so much so that clients hand over the keys to Bush and walk away, knowing that they will love the results. A self described "camouflage decorator," Bush can do a Zen makeover or a Bijou alteration with both parties claiming him to be an interior artist. Bush reportedly thinks of the process as a spiritual exercise with the epiphanic goal being client satisfaction.

Bush entered the design world via fashion, working at the Costume Institute at the Met under Diana Vreeland for seven shows. After taking classes at the New School and Parsons, Bush did interiors for Peter Marino for ten years, becoming the head of the interiors department. In 1997, Bush started his own boutique firm, now with four on staff.

Whether it's providing museum-quality decor or quickly assembling a becoming guest room from Crate & Barrel, clients say Bush is equally talented and handles himself in a most professional manner. Budgets usually evolve throughout the course of the project and are always dictated by the client. The firm takes on about three projects at a time (with small touchups ongoing) and charges standard hourly fees and lower product markups. ASID. HB Top Designers, 2000, 2001, 2002, 2003, 2004.

"So organized, professional, and gentlemanly." "He respects any budget and always remains calm—both such rarities in this business." "He did a five-story townhouse renovation for me and extensive work for a friend of mine with very different taste, and both are entirely true to the spirit and style of each of us." "It's a stretch for him to juggle all his projects at once, but he manages it." "Will never foist you off on an assistant, very hands-on." "He never imposes his taste, but gently guides you to the perfect solution." "He's not too precious to use 'low' when it works and will add some interest to a room." "I appreciate his extraordinary talent and his intellectual mind. We discuss the historic perspective of it all: furniture, fashion, people."

S. Russell Groves 📷

210 11th Avenue, Suite 502, New York, NY 10001
(212) 929 - 5221   www.srussellgroves.com

Restrained, elegant modern residential and retail architecture and interior design

See S. Russell Groves's full report under the heading Architects

Sandra Nunnerley Inc. 📷   4   4.5   4   4

41 East 57th Street, New York, NY 10022
(212) 826 - 0539   www.sandranunnerley.com

Tailored, organized, consistent interior design

Sandra Nunnerley is known for blending periods and styles into functional and fashionable interiors, as well as her ability to solve quirky architectural challenges. Clients say Nunnerley's style is specifically tailored and eclectic, filtering in the client's lifestyle, attitude, and needs. A trained architect, Nunnerley is said to take control of projects from the start, having a hand in most details from the architecture to the moldings and furnishings. We're told her approach to design can be rigid—she does not shop with clients, and she can be quite demanding of other service providers working alongside her. However, sources praise Nunnerley for being a great buffer between the client and subcontractors, and say she collaborates well with clients.

Nunnerley is said to have a professional and efficient back office, with assistants who are very knowledgeable about most projects. We are told her staff handles many clients' inquiries in between Nunnerley's brief site visits. Sources say Nunnerley is intense, organized, intelligent, and completes projects swiftly and accurately. In addition to her Manhattan clientele, Nunnerley also works in the Los Angeles area. Project costs tend to be standard and start around $400,000. AD 100, 2002, 2004. ASID. HB Top Designers, 1999, 2000. KB 1992.

"Sandra can really get it done, but she is best with a full-fledged project." "She's so professional, talented, and creative." "Can combine styles and periods, and make it work." "She did everything from the ground up—the lighting, moldings, and the paint." "Sandra has a singular vision and pursues it." "Has expensive taste, but her rates are fair." "Her supreme self confidence allows her to take the client's view into consideration." "A good businesswoman." "As the architect, I appreciated that she was respectful of the backgrounds." "While she can be tough on the employees, she gets it done." "She did encourage us to spend more than we planned, but it was our choice." "Not all things to all people." "You buy into a specific, refined look when you hire Sandra and she delivers it."

Sara Bengur Interiors 🛍

4	3	5	5

601 West 26th Street, Suite 1509, New York, NY 10001
(212) 226 - 8796 www.sarabengur.com

Exotic, cohesive, classical interior design

Dexterously blending enticing Old World objects and chic cosmopolitan furniture, Sara Bengur and her clients are shaking up the Upper East Side and the suburbs. Drawing upon her Turkish heritage, Bengur creates a highly customized look that is fresh and original, yet comfortably appropriate for family living. Instead of the expected Roman shades, there are goblet pleats in ocher linen. Continental antiques live beside a Jean-Michel Frank in natural duck with antique textile pillows. Sources report that Bengur initially invests a great deal of time to understand clients' interests and takes deep pride in creating something special and unique.

After working on Wall Street for a few years, Bengur studied at Parsons, then managed large projects for Stephen Sills. She went off on her own in 1992. Recent projects include homes in Manhattan, Connecticut, Maine, and the French West Indies. The firm has a "highly collaborative and fun attitude."

Clients praise Bengur's close attention to "every little detail" and her strong sensitivity to family traffic. Entire homes are usually undertaken, sometimes in stages. The firm generally charges a standard design fee, a standard percentage over net on products (same on antiques), and hourly fees for oversight. HB Top Designers 2000, 2001, 2002, 2003, 2004, 2005.

"You get to the point where you just trust her reflective designs. I never would have picked these colors, but I love them more each day." "Sara will never do the same thing for any two clients, right down to the last lampshade." "She tirelessly searches up and down the eastern seaboard to find unique antiques and objects." "She organized a big group of subcontractors, all of whom turned out to be great." "While she does not push, she will encourage us to go for the highest quality we can afford without spending a fortune." "She's not fussy, silly, or puffed-up. She's a very sincere, intelligent person." "An amazing colorist." "Sara would never purchase mass market, preferring small shop treasures at the same cost." "She has a wonderful sense of human scale and a delicate understanding of propriety, especially for someone so young." "Sara insisted on going to my attic to see if we could reuse any of my family pieces. That meant so much to me." "I have worked with her on four homes over the past three and a half years, and I'll continue to work with her in the future."

	Quality	Cost	Value	Recommend?
	+	$	◆	★

Scott Salvator 🛍

4   4.5   4   4.5

308 East 79th Street, New York, NY 10021
(212) 861 - 5355 www.scottsalvator.com

Becoming, fastidious, traditional interior design

Scott Salvator and Michael Zabriskie win accolades with their businesslike manner, personable natures, and elegant, updated formal style. Clients also praise the firm for its strong use of color and intricate layering of fabrics and coordinated trims, saying that it constructs the ultimate "traditional, but not stuffy" home. Modern art and glass mosaics sometimes infiltrate the look, as does the occasional flat-screen TV, but the result is consistently one of serious design intent. Salvator is considered to be accommodating, detail-oriented, deeply tied to his work, intense, smart, practical, and fun. Though some say his "micro-management" and legal background can, at times, slow progress, all are effusive about the end results.

Salvator received a B.S. in accounting and a J.D. in law, then studied interior design at FIT and Parsons. Before starting his firm in 1992, he worked for Mario Buatta, Gary Crain, and Robert Metzger. Zabriskie, an associate at the firm, graduated from Parsons and worked with Mario Buatta, McMillen, and Parish-Hadley. The duo's technical competence is often mentioned as a key differentiating strength. After the apartment on Park or Fifth is done, clients often hire the firm for a second home, done with printed linens, hooked rugs, and fewer tassels and trims. Homeowners interface directly with Salvator or Zabriskie, who do all the shopping themselves and "work eighteen hour days." The back office of four is known for its strong follow-up.

The firm asks for a standard design fee that is deductible against future purchases. Products are marked up at classic retail. Though the firm enjoys high-end product, references say "they were not snobs about it when we purchased some items at Home Expo." Said to offer a highly personalized result that is "clearly not off the rack," Salvator's firm evokes a strong reaction from clients, with most becoming lifelong devotees and a few that just don't click. HB Top Designers, 1999, 2000, 2001, 2002, 2003, 2004, 2005. KB 1994, 1999, 2002.

"From city house to country house and back again. All were lovely and appropriate." "Everything is analyzed to perfection—they spent more time on the sofa's seat depth and pitch than I did discussing my wedding vows with my husband." "For that kind of money I did not want to talk to an assistant, and I never had to." "I know they are busy, but Scott spent three hours with me at E. Braun picking out linens." "A bit American, a bit French, a liberal sprinkling of chintz." "While Scott can talk up a storm, the end product is just right." "I would not use him for my country house, but love his urban vision." "They are traditional without being frumpy." "Deliberate design—some would say heavy, others would say opulent." "He can lose interest in a project, but if he's into it, nothing can stop him." "Everyone is so attracted to the rosy colors and the oversized pieces that are even comfortable for large men." "Scott's glamorous couture product stands out in a sea of neutral sameness." "It was rare when I said no, but if I did, he was good about finding an alternative." "We went through several possible schemes with Scott, but we never really connected." "I did not have to interfere because he totally understood. He is great for people with limited time." "Scott has a great, very dry sense of humor." "I recommended him to a friend but they just couldn't participate in this price range." "Scott has a real flair for living and livability. We continue to go to the movies together."

Scott Sanders LLC

4.5   3.5   4.5   4.5

27 West 24th Street, Suite 802, New York, NY 10010
(212) 343 - 8298   www.scottsandersllc.com

Jaunty, engaging, classic American interior design

With sparkle, wit, and focus, Scott Sanders gives traditional forms a new meaning. Master portraits are juxtaposed with crème lacquer walls, bedboards are painted fire engine red, and navy ticking stripes cover nail-headed antiques. Sanders brings a classically based, comfortably nostalgic, yet fresh sensibility to his interiors. Clients turn to him for an original vision and highly personalized interiors, from the metamorphosis of an elegant Fifth Avenue apartment with limestone, camel hair, and tattersall to a 12,000 square foot new home in Bridgehampton, decorated to look as if it had been there for generations.

After graduating from Parsons and spending ten years at Polo Ralph Lauren (where he established the company's interior design department) Sanders opened his eponymous firm in 2000. It is a small operation, so clients get Sanders' full attention. They tell us he is amazing at follow-up, both during and after the project. Projects have included residences in Manhattan, the Hamptons, Palm Beach, Greenwich, Bedford, Palm Springs, Paris, and London, and have ranged from understated New England gentility to beachside Art Deco. Sanders' redesign of The Beach House Bal Harbour in Miami created a media stir when he transformed it from run-down to desirable with Nantucket-style wainscoting, baskets full of starfish, and Nintendo consoles in every room. Sanders is comfortable working on large or small projects, and is often asked to do the client's vacation home.

Clients welcome the firm's unusual methodology of pricing: Sanders charges a flat fee, based on a reasonable mark-up of estimated project costs. Completed projects start at $100,000. Sanders is said to be equally adept at redecorating a few rooms as working with architects on new construction. Clients highly recommend Sanders for addressing their practical needs while simultaneously creating inspired designs.

"I really am grateful for Scott's inherent understanding of my traditional view." "It is like living in a Polo fantasy, with patina." "I use Scott as an example to my staff as to what good customer service means." "Guided by color, Scott's designs are both classic and clever." "He finds a solution even under tight budget situations." "Scott takes flea market finds to an automotive spray shop, and voilà, they are amazing." "A wonderful sense of humor that's key for when the going gets rough." "Scott has a distinct 'well-groomed' style that is organized, but unpretentious." "He cares about each job and is careful to only take as many as he can handle." "Scott first develops the overriding concept with the client and the rest flows naturally. It is like going to a world-class theme party strategy session." "Scott really loves what he does and is an absolute pleasure to work with."

Scott-Ulmann Inc.

4   4   4   4.5

71 Hill Street, Southampton, NY 11968
(212) 755 - 4306   su575@aol.com

Robust, classical, English-hued interior design

Known for her thoughtful designs reflecting a classic English sensibility with all-American comfort and zest, Priscilla Ulmann has built a steadfast clientele. Strong, warm hues of red, green, and yellow are often featured on traditional silhouettes with continental flair. Quirky pieces with personality may also be seen, with few perfectly matched pairs. Ulmann is said to work with the customer to realize their design goals, within the framework of "classical with patina."

After graduating from the New York School of Interior Design and working as a fashion editor for *Town & Country*, Ulmann ran her own design firm for over twenty years before joining McMillen in 1995 and Parish-Hadley in 1997. In 1998, she revived her firm with a team of three. About twenty projects are underway at one time, ranging from the recovering of a few chairs to substantial new construction. Most of all projects are in the New York area, with much in the Hamptons, where her new office is located. Celebrity names seek her designs as well as the most socially prominent. Clients are delighted to receive excellent attention from Ulmann, whom they describe as "very buttoned-up" and smooth.

The firm charges a standard retainer and retail on product. Products are said to range appropriately in price, depending upon the setting. Ulmann is highly recommended for an updated traditional look that is always "in good taste." HB Top Designers, 2001. Kips Bay 1997.

"She absolutely opens your thinking and vision but is very sensible on budgets and timetables." "She would not consider showing you a piece unless she likes it enough to use it herself." "I would highly recommend her for all classical motifs, but she does not like modern design." "Priscilla will look forever for you in the antiques shows to build up a collection of accessories that look as if they were created by you over time." "Priscilla likes things in order but recognizes the reality of everyday living." "She can decorate as well for men as for women." "She will creatively work with you to make a great effect with less money." "Priscilla took the time to really learn how we used the space. She earned our trust and confidence."

Seborn Ragsdale Interiors 📷 3.5 3.5 4 4.5

1133 Broadway, Suite 702, New York, NY 10010
(212) 741 - 1435 www.sebornragsdale.com

Enlightened, overscaled, colorful traditional design

With a love of color, an energetic scale, and classically traditional lines, Seborn Ragsdale is adding verve and polish to the Upper East Side. Ragsdale's North Carolina roots influence a predilection toward traditional lines and layouts, but there is a modern energy that is transmitted through the work. Hot pinks warm the classic striated walls, bold greens highlight the libraries, and shades of Tiffany blue edge the bedrooms. Full-scaled pieces and modern accessories bedeck the hues, increasing the impact. Clients enjoy the process and the result.

After receiving a B.S. from UNC-Greensboro in interior architecture, Ragsdale did photography sets for fabric and wallpaper manufacturers, then worked for numerous companies in the D&D building and elsewhere in styling and showroom layout (Jim Thompson, Lee Jofa, Holly Hunt, Calvin Klein). After working with Thomas Jayne briefly, Ragsdale then did interiors with Lichen Craig for three years, and went out on his own in 2002. Maintaining a boutique feel and a hands-on approach, there are two in staff and about seven jobs are ongoing at a time. Most of the work is in Manhattan and Vermont.

Smaller jobs are taken on with reasonable budgets—living rooms of $50,000 are not uncommon. A standard flat fee is taken upfront with lower product markups. Ragsdale is said to work diligently for clients providing detailed floor plans and architectural direction. We hear he is building his client base with charm and delight.

"Seborn's enthusiasm about design is infectious. It is so much fun to work with him." "He takes his work seriously but adds levity to the process." "When people get sick of dealing with a large, impersonal design company, they call Seborn." "Seborn is not afraid to make bold color statements, brightening up the usual staid view." "He inherently understands youthful vision with a sense of propriety." "Seborn is developing his own genre of fanciful classicism." "Seborn, Sarah, and their team are organized, thorough, and thoughtful. We appreciate all they do for us."

Sherrill Canet Interiors 🏠   4   3.5   4.5   4.5

3 East 66th Street, Suite 4B, New York, NY 10021
(212) 396 - 1194 www.sherrillcanet.com

Updated, traditional interior design

With polish and stylistic ease, Sherrill Canet sets the stage for gracious Long Island Gold Coast and city living. Clients praise Canet for her personalized designs, knowledge of fine English and French antiques, and accommodating nature. Designs are said to start with the architecture and to develop based on the clients' interests and lifestyle. While offering a range of choices, the interiors are generally based on a clean, traditional style with unique objects and details. Discreet clients commend Canet for her designs of understated elegance, and for her ability to find unique harmonies between the old and the new.

Canet, a veteran of the London antiques scene, first studied economics at Fordham and then design at the Inchbald School of Design. Beginning her business on the retail side with Bellwether Antiques in Locust Valley, interior design was a natural evolution. With a staff of eight design and project management professionals, the firm accepts approximately a dozen projects annually, many of which are substantial in scope and budget. While the bulk of its work takes place in Long Island (where it has a satellite office), Manhattan, and Fairfield County, the firm has also completed commissions in Palm Beach, San Francisco, and London. Clients are charged standard design fees and reasonable product markups, with lower hourly rates for drawing and drafting. Living rooms are typically in the $75,000 to $100,000 neighborhood. KB 2003, 2006.

"A total professional with a unique view on traditional design." "She was amazing at finding a compromise between my husband's taste and mine." "She kept us on the straight and narrow, focusing on classic, workable designs that made sense for our family." "Very chic—she shook up the classics and got something unexpected but still elegant." "Sherrill found some really interesting pieces that distinguished our apartment but were in good context with the rest of the plan." "Sherrill is the best. Make sure you work with her directly." "She is a real professional, executing the job with a good eye." "She understood that we did not have an unlimited budget." "My husband likes to get involved with every single design decision, but after a while he had such confidence in Sherrill that he let her run with the project. That says a lot!"

Shields and Company Interiors 🏠   3.5   4   4   4.5

149 Madison Avenue, Suite 201, New York, NY 10016
(212) 679 - 9130 shieldsint@aol.com

Eclectic traditionally inspired interior design with rich color tones

Insiders say Gail Shields-Miller's deft use of vibrant color tones works in perfect harmony with her more muted earth tones and rich materials. Comfortable in settings ranging from ornamental period interiors to clean and contemporary homes, Shields-Miller is well known for being versatile without being watered down. We are told the firm excels in traditional detailing to create refined spaces without coming across as precious. Shields-Miller is known to incorporate colorful and exotic rugs to pick up on subtle hues throughout the spaces she creates, resulting in an understated continuity from room to room.

In addition to bringing together antiques, pottery, and sculptures from around the world, the firm will also use refurbished materials from the existing space such as fixtures and hardware to add character, patina, and a sense of history to renovations. Clients praise Shields-Miller and her staff for being "true collaborators" and encouraging active involvement from her customers from day one. Moreover, we're told her support staff is friendly, courteous, and outright knowledgeable.

Shields-Miller assumed ownership of the firm in 1988, which was established by her mother in 1961 in Great Neck. Now on Madison Avenue, the office serves mostly a Manhattan clientele—and their second homes in Long Island and Fire Island. Shields-Miller, who holds degrees from Adelphi and Parsons, currently has a staff of five, which handles about ten new projects each year. A typical living room will generally carry a budget of $50,000 to $75,000. The firm charges standard design fees and classic retail.

"There is no period she can't work in." "She uses eclectic objects but ends up with surprisingly unified looks." "Livable and lovable interiors." "Her use of greens and burgundies to complement the beiges and camel colors was superb." "She was able to find wonderful and unique fabrics." "Folk art can often play a key role." "You won't see her try anything revolutionary, but her designs are cozy, lovely, and often quite clever." "Everyone at the organization is fantastic, I never had to worry about checking up on anyone." "I had a problem with the dining room table and she sent it back to be redone without hesitation."

Siskin Valls 💼   4   3.5   4.5   5

21 West 58th Street, Suite 2B, New York, NY 10019
(212) 752 - 3790 siskinvalls@hotmail.com

Stylish, practical, modulated interior design

Interweaving unique objects of wide provenance that share common threads of calm simplicity and careful thought is the trademark of Paul Siskin. A balance of the expected and the unexpected, the traditional and the modern also add to the flow. But most important to Siskin is the livability of the space, reflecting the personality and the needs of its inhabitants. This flexibility and reality allows Siskin to work collaboratively with a variety of clients over the long haul, instinctively reformulating as appropriate.

Siskin was born and raised in Beverly Hills, receiving antiques training in the family's furniture business early on. After earning a B.F.A. from Parsons at the crest of the contemporary modernist cycle, Siskin worked for John Saladino for several years. Opening his own firm in 1984, he offered a window to the past countered by the intrigue of the future. His current staff of four is said by clients to be highly effective and helpful.

The practice is noted to be "more than fair on pricing, going for the look, not the history." Living rooms tend to run about $75,000+ with a standard design fee, lower product commissions, and no hourlies. Clients comment that Siskin is very responsive and easy, making the process a pleasure. HB Top Designers, 1999, 2000, 2001. KB 1994.

"Paul favors downtown resources and a downtown timbre that translates beautifully uptown." "Deep brown is a favorite, which is very comfortable and practical." "He understands. Our apartment looks like an adult space but is also kid-friendly." "There are absolutely no ego issues with Paul." "We are always doing something with him. Paul knows what we like and takes the initiative." "He thinks everything through, considering your lifestyle, the surrounding environment, and the budget." "Knows when to go neutral and when to splash on the color. He doesn't do the same thing for every interior." "Seven years later one of our pillow seams ripped in the study, and he took care of it at no cost." "While he can certainly identify the best, Paul is excellent about finding pieces that just look nice and are not expensive." "The designs are neither trendy nor boring." "He is a keeper."

Stedila Design 💼   4   4   4   4

135 East 55th Street, 5th Floor, New York, NY 10022
(212) 751 - 4281 www.stediladesign.com

Classical, creative, fanciful high-end interior design

Stedila Design, led by John Stedila and Tim Button, is applauded for thematic classical elegance infused with spirit and whimsy. Supporters say that they are incredible with creative clients who are interested in design adventures. The two principals have different ways of working: Stedila is known to be more engaged in extraordinary decorating projects, while Button takes on a wide range.

Recent projects include a mansion on the northern shore of Long Island, a 16th century château, a Southampton Tudor oceanfront, a Palm Beach Venetian palazzo, and a contemporary Victorian house in New Jersey, with commercial clients like Perry Ellis and Calvin Klein. Stedila has done seven different houses for at least one client. Button's stamp can be found on the Clintons' home in Chappaqua, finishing less than a year before it was sold to the former president and the New York senator. The firm is also branching out to working with sustainable materials; Button has done three "green" high-rise projects for Albanese Development. We are told both principals are adept at building extensive and valuable collections for clients and at mixing reproductions with antiques. Supporters claim each is very accessible and freely admits and corrects any concerns.

The firm charges a standard up-front design fee, reasonable percentages over net for products, and a significant oversight fee. Hourly fee arrangements can also be made (though are not preferred). Stedila clearly gravitates toward more expensive fabrics and furniture, but can offer a range of options. Button is more flexible, but also favors excellent quality. Supporters highly recommend them for unique, exciting projects. HB Top Designers, 1999, 2000. KB 1993.

"Tim and John offer all the best in interior design." "John is a passionate decorator. Not the guy to use if you want a neutral palette." "John is best with clients who have a specific point of view. If you are wishy-washy or uninspired, he loses interest." "If you click with John and capture his imagination, together you can create something truly incredible. I would never consider using anyone else." "Tim went along with our program, with the greatest integrity and quality. We enjoy mixing unusual and quirky objects and he did it with grace." "Tim orchestrated our project like a symphony!" "Tim's sketches are so good they are a virtual reality." "Tim has many celebrities and dignitaries as clients but gives you the same level of service." "Tim was great about coordinating all the construction details." "They are world-class, but have real personalities."

Stephanie Stokes Inc.   4   4   4   4

139 East 57th Street, 4th Floor, New York, NY 10022
(212) 756 - 9922   www.stephaniestokesinc.com

Understated, elegant, traditional interior design

Stephanie Stokes continues to uphold the classically traditional with strong lines, detailed millwork, and unfettered tones. Clients say that she quickly develops a design vision that is pursued with focus and energy. Designs often have an English heritage but are said to be brought to life with unexpected intricate patterns, thoughtful accents, and rich complementary colors, based upon customer preferences. Patrons include those from the more prominent neighborhoods of Manhattan, as well as Long Island, Westchester, Colorado, Florida, and Washington, DC. For younger clients, a classic contemporary is approached with solid fabrics, warm backgrounds, and a calm serenity.

Stokes started her design company in 1982, after working as a securities analyst for White Weld, a photojournalist for *Gourmet* magazine, and learning the trade with Mark Hampton and Harrison Cultra. Her varied background has produced a variety of strengths. Clients appreciate the way she embraces their style interests and comment on her energy, efficient professionalism, strong ownership—and her sensible, clever choices. The majority of clients enjoyed the design process and are very happy with the result. We're told Stokes can take complete leadership, bringing the project to final move-in condition for out-of-town clients. However, clients with less design experience or less-formulated views can occasionally feel overwhelmed by the process.

Stokes charges a standard up-front design fee and retail on product. Oversight charges are in the standard range. However clients note that her experience, knowledge, and organizational skills often allow for expedited design decisions, and since Stokes is personally involved with every client, the fees seem more than reasonable. Many clients use the firm repeatedly and recommend it liberally. HB Top Designers, 2002, 2003, 2004, 2005.

"Seeing Stephanie's work is what made me hire her." "Brought me so many choices to review. We even shopped in the D&D together." "She has extraordinary vision." "While I may have been ambiguous at times, we did not get to the result I had hoped for." "The staff always seems to be changing." "When the chair in the bedroom was too large, she worked with the upholsterer to find an excellent solution." "She took care of every detail for me." "I have known Stephanie since I was fifteen and would never consider anyone else in New York."

Studio Sofield 🔖   4.5   4.5   4   4.5

380 Lafayette Street, 4th Floor, New York, NY 10003
(212) 473 - 1300 design@studiosofield.com

Stylish, modern, gritty design and architecture

William Sofield confidently and uniquely stimulates the senses with interiors that look hip, glamorous, and slightly decadent all at once. Columns with gilded fluting, floating ceilings, polished concrete floors, and a maximization of the natural lighting are signature elements. Sofield is best known for his interior design of the Soho Grand Hotel and many other boutique hotels, the worldwide redesign of the Gucci, Boucheron, and Yves Saint Laurent stores, and the executive offices for Disney. Equally comfortable with young and old, he reportedly is just as happy working on the first apartment of young newlyweds as for the most esteemed. But for all, it is understood that every detail must be precisely designed and executed.

Sofield graduated from Princeton with a degree in architecture, urban planning, and European cultural studies. After receiving a Whitney Museum fellowship, he apprenticed with a variety of architectural firms and craftsmen, forming his own practice in 1989. In 1992, he co-founded Aero Studios, and in 1996 launched Sofield Studios with a strong interdisciplinary approach. Known for its original looks that redefine the structural underpinnings and combine historical and modern materials, the studio's work is defined by some as "bohemian meets grungy chic." About thirty people strong, the firm takes on a wide variety of residential projects, ranging from metropolitan apartments to expansive estates with extensive landscaping, including Ralph Lauren's personal residences. Project costs can range greatly as the firm often mixes pricey artifacts with a client's existing collections. Clients find the resulting decors have personal importance as well as substantial monetary worth. HB Top Designers, 1999, 2000, 2001, 2002, 2003, 2004.

"He rises to all challenges with commitment and the ultimate execution." "He is dedicated to bringing the finest craftsmanship to interior design—inlaid leather, Italian carvings—nothing is too much to pursue." "Sofield's main interest is the successful marriage of functionality and fine detailing." "Bill is the only one who can make loft sweeps look grand."

T. Keller Donovan Inc. 🔖   4   3.5   4.5   5

325 West 38th Street, Suite 1101, New York, NY 10018
(212) 760 - 0537 tkellerd@aol.com

Fresh, colorful, traditional interior design

With joie de vivre balancing focus and professionalism, Keller Donovan knows how to keep the process moving and fun for the client. With an appreciation of the historic and a love of contemporary flourish, Donovan is noted for a sophisticated approach that "does not look decorated." He favors tailored lines, comfortable furniture and colorful geometric shapes that either coordinate or juxtapose. Donovan studied at Parsons and then held apprenticeships with Barbara Darcy, Tom O'Toole, and David Easton. His client base is centered in New York and the southeast (his second residence is in Miami).

Donovan is known to be resourceful, with an eye toward economical solutions, successfully mixing Hyde Park or Pottery Barn with clients' existing furnishings. He also enjoys finding wonderful objects in Europe. Donovan does everything himself and wouldn't have it any other way, focusing intensely on client service, according to his many supporters. He can start with just a few rooms or coordinate an extensive renovation.

The firm works with a design fee and a reasonable markup over net on products. Living rooms are often in the $70,000 arena. References say Donovan knows exactly what is appropriate for their budget so there are never any uncomfortable conversations about economics. Even other decorators say they would happily hire him. HB Top Designers, 1999, 2000, 2001, 2002, 2003, 2004, 2005. KB 1993, 1998, 2002.

"Keller is such a sweetheart. I love his use of color and bold patterns." "I appreciate the way he mixes high style with comfortable living. He had very appropriate ideas, given the way we live." "He never gilds the lily." "An incredible colorist that other decorators really admire." "Knows when to pull the punches and when not to." "The key to his decorating success is that our house does not look decorated." "Keller's rich colors are so simple, yet so compelling." "He and his staff make a great team—they've got an excellent relationship." "Your house doesn't have to be an architectural masterpiece. He is comfortable doing something on a more modest scale." "He taught us everything, including how to arrange the books on the shelves." "He works 24/7. When he is not working, he is dreaming about improvements." "Any questions would be answered or fixed immediately." "He honored our economic priorities." "From the storyboards on, he knew exactly where we were headed." "We call him our Keller, taking great pride in his success."

Thad Hayes Design 📷   5   4.5   4.5   5

80 West 40th Street, New York, NY 10018
(212) 571 - 1234 www.thadhayes.com

Classic, modern interior design

Known to some as an intellectual purist and others as master of the ultimate integrated modernist experience (and both to many), Thad Hayes continues to hone his unique approach. Using discrete elements of classic mid-twentieth century furniture, fine art, and sculptural compositions, there is a softened edge that seamlessly flows from room to room. Calm backgrounds, spare and serene furnishings, intimate settings and warm neutral colors maintain the restraint and create elegance. Often he will maximize the space in New York apartments with a good deal of high-caliber, built-in furniture embellished with clean, wood-toned trims.

Clients are often art collectors, the young establishment seeking the new classic style, or modernists in search of the very best quality. Though Hayes is in high demand, he aims to please every client. He is described by customers as a warm and engaging man who is helpful until the end. Many applaud his drawings, including several architects of great note. Clients say he often will completely transform the character of their living space, including the artwork. Born in Louisiana with a modernist heart, he began his career with Robert Bray and Mike Schaible, and then started his own firm in 1985. The office includes eight and is said to be highly efficient.

Considered expensive but very fair, the lowest project cost is around $750,000 and can easily go into the millions. He is highly recommended for clients that share his essentialist, modernistic vision. AD 100, 2000, 2002, 2004. HB Top Designers, 1999, 2000, 2001.

"Historic provenance meets the machine age." "The minute that I saw his work I knew that I wanted to live in it, and I was right." "He completely revitalized the utility and atmosphere of our apartment." "A forward-looking modernist with warmth." "Thad is very concerned that every welt and every hem are exactly correct." "Thad is philosophically devoted to the aesthetic melding of disparate notions that meld exquisitely in his hands. But you have to be on that program." "The amount of thinking that goes into each design is staggering, especially given the minimalist outcome." "He is perfectly suited to his line of work—very disciplined yet a delight to be with."

Thomas Hays Interiors   3.5   3.5   4   4.5
248 West 23rd Street, New York, NY 10011
(212) 741 - 8548   www.thomashaysinteriors.com
Eclectic-to-modern interior design

Clients praise Thomas Hays for his clever transformations and his "out-of-the-box" creative thought. Turkish carpets and Indian camel carts may make appearances in his work. Other projects incorporate a cleaner palette, evocative of a more natural setting. Hays uses line and form to distinguish his work, usually incorporating a range of eclectic elements and a splash of color. Clients note that there is often a focus in each room, highlighting a unique and creative object. Hays is appreciated for his talent for blending clients' interests and existing furnishings with his own design sensibilities to conjure a balanced whole.

Hays received an M.B.A. at Northwestern and worked as a banker in New York and London before studying at numerous design institutions, including London's Chelsea School of Design and the National Academy of Art in New York. Founded in 1996, Hays's firm is lauded for its unusual resources, both local and international. Moreover Hays is said to be just as skilled at doing a few rooms as an entire renovation.

Design fees are based on a reasonable hourly rate and products are purchased at a very reasonable markup over net. While Hays encourages clients to purchase high-quality products, they note that he is sympathetic to economic constraints. Living rooms are generally in the $75,000 to $150,000 realm. Clients believe that hiring Hays saves time and money with his "extraordinary" coordination skills.

"I have used Thomas for three projects in three years. He has that rare blend of a clear passion for design and financial savvy." "Every room has a different mood, but there's nothing jarring." "He's fantastic with colors and found truly unusual pieces for my kitchen and bathroom." "He was great at working with us as a couple. We had our own disagreements, but both my husband and I deferred to Thomas." "Thomas' designs let me escape New York City while I'm home." "He remains calm and professional at all times, and keeps the project running without any hoopla." "He's a very hip designer, but not trendy." "My roots are in Italy, and Thomas helped me bring that look to the Upper East Side." "When people come to dinner, they fall in love with the house." "Thomas went out of his way to find some really stunning pieces." "Don't use him if you want to mix with Ikea. He insists on the highest quality." "One area floats into the next—people are amazed." "He stuck to the budget and the timeline." "He was on call like a doctor." "A perfectionist who will never rest until the job is done right."

Thomas Jayne Studio Inc.    4.5   4.5   4   4.5
136 East 57th Street, Suite 1704, New York, NY 10022
(212) 838 - 9080   www.thomasjaynestudio.com
Historically-based, individual, spirited interior design

Consistently described by clients and peers as a scholarly genius with a passion for historic design, Thomas Jayne effortlessly builds character, dignity, and humor into his compositions. He can do either a preservationist's perspective or a more lighthearted tilt with high-spirited colors and modern accents, but all offer a heightened reality. Best known for his designs showcasing fine American heritage, his work broadly runs from Colonial Revival to Continental, but references say it is always gorgeous. Most clients note that Jayne is also captivating company, highly focused, and charmingly intent.

Jayne received a master's degree in American architecture and decorative arts from the Winterthur Museum. He then trained at Cooper Hewitt, Christie's, and Parish-Hadley. Clients say he takes his training seriously and believes in "period-pure" rooms without "gimmicks" or reproductions, though he will mix styles to give these rooms a comfortable, sophisticated touch. Jayne also has creative takes on classic favorites: stenciled floor cloths in unexpected tones, hand-painted Greek key shades, framed antique scarves for color. But "the architecture must be correct before the fun can begin."

Jayne's clients tend to be well-funded art and antique collectors, many of whom hail from the South. Projects have included many an uptown Manhattan townhouse and apartment, as well as a variety of homes in Connecticut and Westchester, ranging from a small saltbox to a 30,000 square foot Greenwich estate. The smaller commissions are often less saturated with antiques and more filled with color. Many clients are repeat customers, with one or two loyalists owning five residences, all decorated by Jayne. They tell us with delight that by the time the fifth house is completed, it's time to do the first over again. Jayne reportedly has a hard time saying "no" to a client, sometimes accepting more jobs than he can handle. All, however, remark that he meets the important deadlines and is "very conscientious."

The firm charges classic retail on products and a standard markup on antiques. Customers say Jayne has a strong preference for high-end fabrics (some quite over the top) and serious rugs. Living rooms can start low for "guerrilla decorating," and can go as high as the imagination with fine antiques. All believe that Jayne is quite earnest and honest. He is highly recommended by major collectors of American antiques and others who are looking for intelligent quality with a modern twist. HB Top Designers, 1999, 2000, 2001, 2002, 2003, 2004, 2005. KB 1996.

"No one knows how to make formal Americana sing more joyfully than Thomas." "If you give him free rein, you will get full attention." "Working with Thomas is like a really good addiction, it is hard to stop once you get going." "He knows when he is right, but patiently waits for you to come around." "Timing used to be an issue, but now he has a hyper-efficient back office." "Tom is a one-of-a-kind gem. He has done eight projects for us, designing close to 100,000 square feet in total, including the family mausoleum." "He lets it slide for the kids' rooms, but otherwise all the period antiques were upholstered in period-appropriate fabrics." "Formal and refined, there's not a gaudy bone in his body." "He prefers to work within a certain vernacular." "As one of Thomas' more modest clients, I appreciated his directed priorities and his ability to edit, edit, edit." "He inspired my husband to Think Pink." "He has a passion for doing things the right way, starting with the architectural bones." "When the rectory of his church was in disrepair, he took it upon himself to refurbish." "He has amazing common sense, great judgment, and an original dry wit." "He is so calm, yet so specific—and clearly a genius." "I would recommend him to anyone with good taste."

Timothy Whealon Inc. 🛍   4   4   4   4.5
23 East 69th Street, Suite 2, New York, NY 10021
(212) 249 - 2153 www.timothywhealon.com

Classic, simple, elegant interior design

Timothy Whealon is a young designer with mature taste. His projects display a sense of decorum and a respect for the classic themes of design. Though, like many of his peers, he's not afraid to mix a mid-century dining table with an antique chandelier—just as long as both posess a quality of simple elegance. More recent projects have found Whealon editing the look down for younger couples: fewer flourishes but still the same "beautiful proportions" and "well-earned patina" that comes from an abundance of custom pieces. Whealon can also pare down the number of provenanced items, though clients caution that it would be a waste not to take advantage of his fine arts background. A former Sotheby's employee, Whealon will often base an entire room around a client's favorite work of art.

Whealon holds a degree from Kenyon College and studied art history at the University of Edinburgh. He founded this eponymous firm in 1994, immediately taking on large-scale projects. Currently, Whealon fields a staff of five. He is responsible for all the design decisions, while associates handle follow-up and purchasing. Clients describe the team as helpful and honest; Whealon himself as "charming" and "modest," though some stress that "it doesn't hurt to pat Tim on the back from time to time." Not one for small projects, Whealon doesn't usually take jobs with a total budget of less than $400,000, though exceptions are made. He charges an upfront design fee and a standard markup on product. Clients note that Whealon doesn't skimp on custom items, but that he can figure out ways to stick to the budget. Above all, they commend his affable manner, deep pool of knowledge, and impeccable taste. KB, 2004.

"His taste is classic with a modernist touch." "No real overwhelming sense of a particular style." "I didn't like any of the bathtubs that he showed me, so he managed to get something from Italy that had never been imported to the US before." "Sotheby's trained, he has a great eye for works of art across the spectrum." "Everything was original, everything was custom." "His style is sophisticated while his execution is reliable and timely." "Very simple, luxurious materials." "Likes working with young couples." "Couldn't have been sweeter with my children." "He is a true artist in his field and as such, bears many traits of an artist's temperament." "Can work within a budget, but doesn't love talking money." "He's never insulted if you want to go with something different than what he chose." "I trust him for everything nonstructural." "Really went out of his way for us." "Tim deeply cares about giving you something that's perfect for you."

Todd Klein Inc. 🏠   4.5   4.5   4   4.5
27 West 24th Street, Suite 802, New York, NY 10010
(212) 414 - 0001   www.toddklein.com
Modern interior design with traditional grounding

Color, candor, and confidence draw clients time and time again to Todd Klein. Known to the upper echelons of New York society as well as appreciative newlyweds, Klein focuses on comfortable, classic designs highlighted with modern accents and punches of color. Spectacular window treatments are a signature, often featuring fashion couture lines and contrast trims. This spirited give and take between the modern and the historic is what makes his designs come alive, according to loyal clients.

Klein developed his soft spot for the traditional growing up in Louisville, Kentucky. After majoring in art history at Denison, Klein returned to his hometown, first working as a retail banker, then embarking into interior design, where he received a historic preservation award for his work. On moving to New York, he trained with master Albert Hadley for several years. In 1999, he formed his own firm and has been jetting around the country every since. A staff of four assists Klein, always the primary client contact, with three major projects a year. Clients include Caroline Kennedy and Ed Schlossberg. Budgets start at about $100,000 and easily fall into the million-dollar range, evolving with the process. The firm will work with new clients on just one room if the chemistry is right.

Taking its cue from architects, the practice will work on an hourly consultation basis at standard levels (especially for clients with lots of existing antiques) or on a standard up-front design fee, a commission on product, and hourlies for non-product consultations. Clients enjoy Klein's intelligent choices and his practical, long-term approach. HB Top Designers, 2000, 2001, 2002, 2003.

"Todd introduced me to colors I never even knew existed. Now I love them." "While ABC remnants are not his normal stomping ground, he was very amenable for the kids' rooms." "Todd has the most amazing ability to see how things will come together. I could never have imagined it would have been so great from the swatches." "Learned a lot from Albert Hadley but completely has his own style." "He really knows his antiques, incorporated mine, and has unique economically viable Southern sources." "Todd stuck to the budget and encouraged us to finish over time." "Todd just gets it, which really takes the pressure off." "He has Southern charm and New York edge."

Tori Golub Interior Design 🖼   3.5   3.5   4   4
162 East 80th Street, Suite 8A, New York, NY 10021
(212) 879 - 0680   www.torigolubinteriors.com

Modern, classic interior design

Drawn to her clean, modern aesthetic, clients are gravitating to Tori Golub for "great design" that is also comfortable, reasonably priced, and functional. Supporters say Golub leans toward an edited style with a felicitous juxtaposition of period decor alongside more modern furnishings and unique character finds to give the look an edge. Sources tell us Golub generally favors muted hues, with shots of color. Although her designs are simple and clean, they are not cold, and they very much speak to the wishes of the client. Golub understands all phases of architectural design and construction and "stands by her work, never leaving anything undone."

Golub has been on the forefront of style for many years, first in the fashion business, then as a freelance stylist, and then with Andrew Frank in interior design. She struck out on her own in 1996, and takes on about seven major projects each year. Most current projects involve interior architectural reconfigurations, including kitchen and bath re-dos and custom cabinetry enhancements. Many clients are young singles or young couples with families, who appreciate her sensible budgets and chic refinements.

Golub is said to have an open view on the clients' existing furnishings and to exhibit an excellent touch with thoughtful layouts, "creating the best possible result for a reasonable price." Clients remark that she is as equally talented in designing the "smallest detail as she is a large room divider." The firm charges standard design fees and reasonable product markups. A typical living room starts at $60,000 and is based on a detailed budget, after presenting several design alternatives. Clients highly recommend Golub for understanding their design needs better than they do. HB Top Designers, 2000, 2001.

"Tori grabbed the essence of what I was trying to accomplish very quickly and worked with me hand-in-hand to get it done." "Tori is a delight to work with—she has a clear vision but is not egotistical." ""She was really sensitive to the fact that it had to be safe and functional for the kids, but still stylish for us." "A very comfortable, homey version of modern." "Not at all snobby, with a gorgeous touch." "Tori was great with some architectural details, designing millwork that worked as a bar, bookshelf, and entertainment center." "Tori has an excellent understanding of unusual finishes and natural materials, which makes for a very special result." "She adds a bit of glamour to all her work." "She is so hip and now—she totally transformed my space into a joyful refuge."

	Quality	Cost	Value	Recommend?
	+	$	◆	★

Victoria Hagan Interiors 💼   5   5   4   4.5

654 Madison Avenue, Suite 2201, New York, NY 10021
(212) 888 - 1178 www.victoriahagan.com

Elegant, eclectic, edited interior design

Noted for her sculptural, harmonious, monochromatic designs and her professionalism, Victoria Hagan stands out from the new crowd of contemporary designers. Clients praise the quality of her workmanship, her handsome and spare forms, and her incorporation of every modern comfort. Warm velvets and cashmeres enhance clean, cerebral lines. Hagan's work is further distinguished by a generous use of fine antiques, strong architectural details, natural materials, and eclectic embellishments. Designs are thoughtfully integrated into the settings. While references say that she is firm in her design opinions, they also acknowledge that she is determined to make clients happy. Hagan reportedly presents several options and works with the clients to lead them through the process.

A graduate and board member of Parsons, Hagan founded her firm in 1991. She accepts only a few projects per year and devotes significant attention to each one. Clients include Jack Welsh in Fairfield, Revlon head Ronald Perelman, movie director Barry Sonnenfeld, and the Bronfmans. While lesser-knowns are taken on, project scopes remain large and serious, and none are undertaken without a specific commitment. Recent projects include several Manhattan apartments, a Greenwich manor house, a Westchester country home, and a bucolic South Carolina retreat. An exclusive architectural consultant often works on projects with Hagan.

Clients are frequently repeat customers. It is said that the cost of Hagan's work is quite high (with budgets usually in the generous six figures), but true to budget and well worth the expense. AD 100, 2000, 2002, 2004. HB Top Designers, 1999, 2000, 2001, 2002, 2003, 2004, 2005. KB 1990.

"Victoria is thoughtful, smart and interesting to work with, but she is no pussycat. She gets it done." "Her ego does not get in the way. She does what is best for the client." "There is a peacefulness to the finished product." "While a model of restraint, her designs have energy, with the unexpected in scale or form." "Her office does all the shopping for you. She presents three choices and does not overload you." "We asked Victoria to come look at the historic restoration of an important building, but she would not even talk to us without a consulting contract." "She makes a conscious effort to have a small, select clientele so as to not spread herself too thin." "To her credit she is at my girlfriend's house almost every day. But it is a 30,000 square foot house—there is a lot to do." "Her designs are so livable—full of sunshine and with room to breathe."

White Webb LLC 💼   4.5   4.5   4   4

167 Madison Avenue, Suite 603, New York, NY 10016
(212) 889 - 2900 www.whitewebb.com

Inventive, eclectic, elegant interior design

Blessed with "incredible skill" and boundless enthusiasm for the craft, Matthew White and Frank Webb create interiors that radiate energy and wit. Not a firm for genre pieces or cookie-cutter looks, White and Webb work with a client to find a central theme—then find inventive ways to carry it out. In different contexts, a pair of Parthenon-shaped end tables might be a nod to Greek antiquity or a cheeky Pop Art moment. Whatever the project, the firm is known for bringing together bold colors, quality antiques, and up-to-the-minute technology. When carefully edited, the result is classic, tailored, and charged with the power of ideas.

White has an atypical résumé: He was a dancer for the Los Angeles Ballet before executing a neat jeté into graphic design, then antiques, then interiors. Webb, who oversees project management and collaborates with White on design, spent seventeen years in finance before giving in to the artistic impulse. The two joined forces in 2004. Clients praise the excellent teamwork, noting that Webb's pragmatism and White's delight in the design process fit together well.

The firm charges an upfront design fee, an hourly design fee, and a markup only on furnishings and labor. Prices reflect the high level of innovation and the quality of materials. Sources agree that White and Webb are "in it for the right reasons" and that "the only danger is that you'll have too much fun." AD 100, 2004. KB 2005

"Matthew White is a charming man, a talented and inspired designer of impeccable taste who seemed to know exactly what my desires were." "Matthew does not shy away from bold ideas." "They're not a traditional firm, and they're not a super-modern, minimal firm. They're just great designers." "They really love their work. It makes the process fun." "They design with ideas." "Mr. White researched and chose specific antiques, selected beautiful fabrics, and developed decorating ideas that included my particular interests in music and classical art." "They enjoy getting carried away with concepts and themes." "What a wonderful team! Together, they don't let anything through the cracks." "For several years now, I've been enjoying my well-designed— yet homey—space."

William Green & Associates 🛍
6 West 18th Street, 7th Floor, New York, NY 10011
(212) 924 - 2828   www.wgaarchitects.net
Classical, detailed, residential architecture and interiors

See William Green & Associates' full report under the heading Architects

William Hellow Studio Inc. 🛍   3.5   3   4   5
231 West 29 Street, Suite 1407, New York, NY 10001
(212) 868 - 1262   www.hellowstudio.com
Funky colorful meets classic modern design

William Hellow Studio is the next generation of the American Design Company (Hellow renamed the firm after a longtime partner left to pursue other interests), and it carries on that firm's reputation as a beacon of lively modernism. Clients praise Hellow and his team for their innovative finish materials as well as their attention to practical detail. The company's interior design work often mixes mid-century furniture with classic pieces to create a fun and dynamic atmosphere. Clients laud this innovative use of space and the company's ability to adjust the style to suit customers' individual tastes, resulting in "spicy sophistication."

William Hellow has a wide range of experience in both commercial and residential interior design. In fact, he often ends up designing the homes of his commercial clients. His back office is said to be excellent and professional, enhancing the firm's client service strengths. The team is also applauded for its ability to respond well to any client requests, including major design changes.

Residential projects range from lofts to townhouses, with budgets supporting products from industrial catalogs to luxurious high-end showrooms. Clients say the firm sticks to budget and is financially accommodating. The company is also reputed to be extremely flexible and caring, taking full responsibility in solving any mishaps.

"Starting with industrial building products not usually associated with indoor construction, they add pinches of vintage and interesting, yet subtle color. The result is a delicious combination of the practical and the unpredictable." "Although modern decor is often considered somewhat cold, they have the ability to make it warm with natural woods and polished glass." "Down-to-earth people who don't think everything has to be expensive antiques." "The work is exciting without being theatrical." "They are professional, have excellent taste, and are easy to work with." "While there were no issues, I would not say budgets are a strength." "Very creative and impressively

knowledgeable in all areas of design and construction." "Every detail is extensively discussed." "When guests admire my apartment, I am reminded of just how much I love it."

Zeff Design 🏠   4   3.5   4.5   4.5

515 West 20th Street, Suite 4W, New York, NY 10011
(212) 580 - 7090 www.zeffdesign.com

Eclectic, hip-to-traditional interior design

Mark Zeff believes that design is natural fusion of aesthetic sensibilities, knowledge, and technology—which, when brought together, create potent synergistic energy. This cohesive philosophy has intrigued and attracted New York clients since 1984, when Zeff made his first foray into interior design. A native of South Africa, Zeff is known for his "uncanny" ability to blend airy colors with exotic textures, producing an eclectic amalgamation of periods and styles witnessed during his extensive travels. Handsome woods, custom ironwork, English antiques, and 1930s French Moderne may co-exist. With his pared-down, worldly style, Zeff tends to work with a younger clientele looking for a unique and romantic construct.

Zeff studied furniture and industrial design and received his masters in architecture from the Royal College of Art in London. Residential projects are of all sizes, with about 30 completed per year. Currently Zeff Design has fifteen interior and architecture projects underway, including five large townhouses in Manhattan, three modern barns in the Hamptons, and an oceanfront estate in Palm Beach. Clients include Anne Leibovitz and Hilary Swank. More than just an interior designer, Zeff runs a full-service design agency with services that include brand identity, packaging, and multimedia graphics. Some of his commissions have included branding assignments for Moulton Brown (the bath and body retailer), Just for Feet retail stores, and The Red Cat restaurant. Other commercial ventures include the restaurant Social for Jeffrey Chodrow, and a collaboration with Vikram Chatwal on Night, an 80-room boutique hotel in the theater district.

Clients say the firm is quite professional with a deep, talented staff, and that one design venture stimulates highly imaginative thinking for the next. Prices are standard given the comprehensive nature of Zeff's services. HB Top Designers, 1999, 2000.

"Mark can do anything—and he's been successful at every endeavor he's taken on." "While Mark is a bit stretched between the commercial ventures and the interior design, the project was very professionally managed." "Creative, but realistic. He doesn't do these flimsy fantasy designs." "There are often interesting historical references in his work. He researches the history of the space." "Very busy, but never leaves you hanging." "He takes a holistic view of design, thinking about the mind and the spirit as well as the look." "Very talented and uncompromising in his vision." "Mark is very full-service, conscientious, and diligent, even post-project." "A point person was available at all times, and there was personal attention from Mark Zeff, himself, who was always on call."

FIRMS WITHOUT ONLINE PORTFOLIOS

Aero Studios/Thomas O'Brien   5   4.5   4.5   4.5

419 Broome Street, New York, NY 10013
(212) 966 - 4700 www.aerostudios.com

Contemporary, comfortable, refined interior design

Praised for spotting the trends before they become trends, Thomas O'Brien creates distinctive, refined environments based upon a Moderne aesthetic and saturated with neoclassical warmth. A master creator of mood, O'Brien studied

architecture at the Cooper Union and then worked as the director of the Ralph Lauren Home Collection. At Aero, he has created his own comfortable modernism that fuses bold architectural furniture with serene backgrounds, shots of color and bargain finds. This look, which is the envy of his peers, is available at Aero's Soho retail store or through a variety of showrooms (Hickory Chair for furniture, Lee Jofa for fabric, etc.). O'Brien also has a line of products at Target.

O'Brien wins accolades from supporters for being extremely loyal—he reportedly went to the "ends of the earth" to finish a project before a big wedding. His projects range from an apartment for Giorgio Armani to large-scale houses in Greenwich to major commercial undertakings (Donna Karan showrooms, David Barton gym, Soho Grand Hotel). Satisfied clients (a group that includes Giorgio Armani and Ralph Lauren) testify that he is very involved in the initial design concept and then hands the projects over to strong project managers. Smaller clients can get less attention.

The firm's fees reflect its stature in the marketplace. Up-front charges are substantial, and products are generally offered at retail or above. Hourly fees are charged for oversight, varying considerably based on the seniority of the designer. Despite the chic, relaxed result, patrons say that well over half of the contents are custom made, from furniture and fittings to fabrics and carpets. HB Top Designers, 1999, 2000, 2001, 2002, 2003, 2004, 2005. KB 1999.

"Everyone looks to him for the next step." "He was very good about integrating a modern design sensibility into my more traditional home. He would use chintz, but in a fresh way." "He is extremely expensive, but you get the best." "With new lines coming out all the time, he's got a lot on his plate, but still puts a lot of care into the exciting projects." "His rooms are modern, yet brushed with a nostalgic, silver-hued patina." "Incredibly innovative work that's not in the least bit trendy." "He's got a lot of products to worry about, but he doesn't take jobs he can't handle." "Thomas's designs are both beautiful and functional." "He often does an exaggerated Jean-Michel Frank in neutral shades, but can also do a more traditional look with unexpected pizzazz." "I cannot decide which room I love the most." "He can make a suburban Georgian manor house look hip and now." "Aesthetic restraint with a passion."

Albert Hadley Inc.   5   4.5   5   5
24 East 64th Street, New York, NY 10021
(212) 888 - 7979 ahi@alberthadley.com
Masterful, high-end interior design

Surprising even himself with his ability to top his past work, Albert Hadley is doing a brisk business, once again (with the help of a few younger associates) on the leading curve between urban chic and the perfectly appropriate. An icon of 20th century American design, his signature rooms offer a knowing sophistication based on classic furnishings with a kick, complementing the architecture and the setting. Hadley's compositions include everything, from his signature zebra-pattern hooked rugs to historical, tufted chaises to French mid-century faux tortoiseshell. His edited looks herald luxury, quality, and comfort, with a nod to innovation.

Originally from Nashville, Tennessee, Hadley studied (and later taught) at the Parsons School of Design. He worked at McMillen for many years before starting the famous design firm Parish-Hadley with the late Sister Parish, where young designers like Mark Hampton, Bunny Williams, and David Kleinberg got their start. Hadley's masterly designs are not all that is praised. He is extremely conscientious with his clients, involving them in the process and always taking their personalities into account. Past clients have included Brooke Astor, Happy Rockefeller, Al and Tipper Gore, and Oscar de la Renta. While he closed the eighteen-person office of Parish-Hadley several years ago, stating his intention to retire, Hadley is still going strong at age eighty-five, currently with three associates. He is reported to be having more fun than ever.

Not content to rest on his well-earned laurels, Hadley remains very involved in the design industry, giving generously of his time to inspire new designers and contemporaries alike. All agree that Hadley has permanently shaped interior design. He recently debuted a new collection of fabrics at Hinson & Company, and a career retrospective was recently published by Rizzoli. ASID. HB Top Designers, 1999, 2000, 2001, 2002, 2003, 2004, 2005. ID Hall of Fame. KB 1992, 1997, 2002.

"Without the weight of Parish-Hadley he is free to pursue his design passions." "It is simultaneously WASPy-correct and urban chic, without being forced." "His designs have never aged, and are particularly current today. Everything he has designed for me is still fresh." "He'll fill a room with antique furnishings, then cover the ceiling with modern, abalone-colored tiles. Brilliant little twists." "He has relaxed his schedule a bit, but is still going strong." "If you can get him, go for it." "Albert guides the first phase, then hands it down to one of his extremely competent disciples." "Everyone in the business loves him. A designer's designer." "A true gentleman who always knows just how to treat his clients and how to treat a room." "A living legend." "He's saved many an old-line family from looking like white-shoed snobs." "He abides by his mantra—never more, never less."

B Five Studio LLP   4   4   4   5

160 Fifth Avenue, Suite 702, New York, NY 10010
(212) 255 - 7827   www.bfivestudio.com

Classic, progressive high-end interior design

With a heightened sensitivity to the relationship between interiors and architectural design, B Five Studio offers a unique and integrated approach that clients applaud. This large firm is made up of five principal architects and decorators well versed in a panoply of styles and techniques. Consequently, references report that they are able to "handle anything," from confident traditional with a splash to wildly modern. All the work is said to be of the highest standards, "great fun," and "exclusive and rarified." Clients describe the firm's signature style as "classic progressive," with a fusion of strong modern gestures and classic, historically referenced furnishings. The firm is also known for its effective use of strong sweeps of color and luxurious fabrics, and its skillful incorporation of modern art.

The vast majority of B Five's work is residential, and more than half of all its projects take place in Manhattan. The firm was established in 1981 and currently employs 24. The five partners of the practice are Ronald Bentley, Victoria Boris, Charles Capaldi, Salvatore La Rosa, and Franklin Salasky. The firm accepts approximately 40 projects each year, most of which are done on substantial budgets. B Five is said to quickly provide detailed sketches that truly reflect the client's input. Clients praise the designers for creating many original pieces by hand using imported materials, an effort that typifies the firm's highly customized approach.

Reaching well beyond Manhattan, B Five also does work around the country, especially in Philadelphia, where there is a second office. Most clients tend to have discriminating taste and large budgets and to share the practice's methodical, patient approach to interior design. We are told the firm provides high-end services for a high-end fee. HB Top Designers, 1999, 2000.

"They did everything from top to bottom. One-stop shopping." "Their resources are amazing, particularly their relationships with unusual and fine craftsmen." "The work they did is elegant, approachable, and bathed in beautiful pale golds, olives, and lovely shades of contrasting greens." "No fussiness, but beautiful, luxurious fabrics that speak for themselves—mohairs, damasks, silks." "They certainly don't rush the job and I appreciate the time and care that went into my home." "A bit too architectural to be brilliant." "Not only are the doorknobs custom but so are the screws." "Their subcontractors are great and easy to work with." "B Five brought fun and life to my

boring Park Avenue apartment." "It is a substantial commitment to hire B Five—so extravagant, but so worth it."

Bilhuber Inc.　　　　　　　　5　　5　　4　　5

330 East 59th Street, 6th Floor, New York, NY 10022
(212) 308 - 4888　bilhuber@aol.com

Gutsy, handsome, modernly classical interior design

One of the primary architects of the New American classicism, Jeffrey Bilhuber has clearly influenced the design world. His compositions—featuring streamlined neutrals highlighted by touches of eminence simultaneously—speak to modern comfort and mid-century elegance. Clients and peers alike regard him as one of the great talents of his generation. Bilhuber has an established look which is elegant and chic, yet simultaneously welcoming. For families, he brings a fresh, modern, yet appropriate spirit, recently incorporating light chintzes upholstered inside-out near antique benches bleached white by years in the sun. While some may say he is a marketing machine with a very distinctive point of view, his work remains respected by all.

The design firm, established fifteen years ago, takes on about ten projects at a time. Clients have included Randolph Duke, Anna Wintour, Elsa Peretti, Peter Jennings, Iman and David Bowie, and the new NYC City Club Hotel—but Bilhuber is also open to doing less prominent projects. He will do a few rooms, if there is a connection with the client. His office is said to be very professional and responsive, even six months after the project's completion. Bilhuber wins accolades for being "completely dedicated to getting things done on time and on budget."

Pre-shopping effectively, Bilhuber is not the kind of guy to spend the day at the D&D with clients on a daily basis. Living rooms can run in the $250,000 neighborhood, but Bilhuber has also won the hearts of those clients with much lower budgets with a mix of "the humble and the high." He is also known to make great architectural suggestions and will ship back anything the client does not like "in the blink of an eye." AD 100, 2002. HB Top Designers, 1999, 2000, 2001, 2002, 2003, 2004, 2005. KB 1991.

"He has a very large personality but is always very professional." "The most chic person in Greenwich was amazed at what Jeffrey did. She dragged me away from my guests to see every room." "Gives many newly wealthy clients a distinct design voice making sure they take the edge off." "Very intelligent and very hands-on—and he's always been that way. The name hasn't gotten to his head." "While our budget was minuscule compared to others, he made us feel like his only client." "He started out as a concierge, and he still has all the answers." "He takes your personality and turns it into a design vision. But you have to appreciate his perspective to start." "He listens and then pushes the envelope." "We have done sixteen houses with Jeffrey and would not consider doing it any other way." "His spirit is contagious."

Christopher Maya Assoc. Inc.　　4.5　　4.5　　4　　4.5

60 East 66th Street, Suite 3B, New York, NY 10021
(212) 772 - 2480　www.christophermayainc.com

Integrated, polished, tailored interior design

Clients and peers are consistently impressed with Christopher Maya's dedication, his skillful and comprehensive approach, and his designs of timeless appeal. Noted for their finesse, Maya's well-integrated designs are a blend of tailored, historically referenced, understated elegance—classically based, with a touch of Jean-Michel Frank. There is a certain easy rhythm to the work, with loose weave cottons and aged leather resting against calming, handsome frameworks. It is often mentioned that Maya listens well to his clients, then designs with their individual concerns in mind. References remark that he never "violated the realities of our family circumstances (children) or our strict financial parameters." Maya also can ably take on the project management role, "implicitly challenging all involved to raise their standards of performance."

Maya began his design career as a set designer for print, television, and film. From there he segued into interior design, working for Jed Johnson for several years while attending the Parsons School of Interior Design. In 1998 Maya established his firm, which is small by industry standards, but said to be extremely efficient and accommodating, "making the process actually enjoyable." He manages projects both large and small, from Manhattan apartments and townhouses to estates in Connecticut, Westchester, Long Island, and New Jersey. The firm will take on a few rooms for a new client, but usually handles commissions in the $200,000 to $1 million range. Clients say Maya is highly skilled at architectural detailing, which he will take on for an additional hourly rate. Product markups are standard, as are antique fees. Maya is highly regarded by clients and often recommended. KB 2006.

"Christopher spent a lot of time getting to know our family and our needs." "His selections were on target on the very first try an overwhelming percentage of the time." "A master of texture, warmth, and subtlety." "Christopher delivers on the details." "His business skills match his design skills, even earning the awe of the general contractor." "Christopher is well educated, well trained, and has the experience to start and complete a large project under less than optimal circumstances." "Very businesslike." "Tasteful, charming, easy to work with." "Pays homage to the past but doesn't skimp on the niceties." "Great for clients that do not want to live in a date-stamped interior." "We can not recommend Christopher strongly enough for those committed to achieving the best possible results." "I'm excited to have my friends use Christopher."

Clodagh Design International

	Quality	Cost	Value	Recommend?
	4	4	4	4.5

670 Broadway, 4th Floor, New York, NY 10012
(212) 780 - 5300   www.clodagh.com

New age high-end interior design

Clodagh is known for her innovative use of form, lighting, and harmonizing materials to create life-enriching environments. To this designer, a job is complete only if it involves all of the senses and the elements. This often translates into the use of natural, low-maintenance, and environmentally friendly materials. Her young and spirited team takes great care to understand clients' interests, a process that can include lively discussions of energy fields or astrological signs. Clients also appreciate Clodagh's strong ties to many local artisans worldwide.

Clodagh began her career as a highly successful fashion designer in her native Ireland. Moving to Spain and finally New York City, she shifted her focus to architectural and interior design, opening a New York City firm in 1983. Residential projects include smaller Chelsea lofts and larger uptown penthouses. Recently she has expanded into landscape architecture, commercial projects, lighting design, furniture, and textiles. Past clients include Robert Redford and Mo Vaughn.

The firm charges by the hour for consultations (design, feng shui, environmental) or can work on a retainer. Clodagh is recommended by clients and peers alike for her creative, sensitive design approach. HB Top Designers, 1999, 2000, 2001. ID Hall of Fame. KB 1992, 1995, 1998.

"We respect and adore Clodagh." "She has a magical touch. The cement floors glow a rich taupey gold, but it is still very subtle." "She completely upgraded our life by adding a sink area in the bedroom, so my husband and I can get dressed in the morning at the same time." "She's got a lot on her plate at the moment, but manages to keep her clients ecstatic." "Clodagh fixed all the idiotic things the contractor did, and was extremely fair about the costs." "She asks you to close your eyes when choosing a fabric, to experience the texture." "I am very fussy, and she captured exactly what I

wanted by asking careful questions." "If you're doing a large, intricate project and you want it environmentally conscious, she's the only person to call." "She's not for everybody, but people who are right for her absolutely adore her." "While she is clearly expensive, there were never any issues." "My home is now a work of art."

Courtney Sloane/Alternative Design   4   4   4   4
21 West 16th Street, Garden Level, New York, NY 10011
(646) 230 - 7222   www.alternativedesign.com
Holistic, progressive modern interior design

From record moguls to professional athletes, interior designer Courtney Sloane has built a loyal clientele who admire her cross-cultural, multidimensional style with a modern twist. Sloane undertakes projects with younger, hip downtown clients and also with large commercial entertainment and marketing companies (Sony Recording Studios, Fila showrooms), all of whom share her global and progressive perspective. This firm of five was established in 1993, and takes on three to five projects of substantial size and budget each year. We are told the entire firm collaborates on each project, dividing responsibilities into phases, with Sloane directly involved in each endeavor.

Approximately 75% of the firm's work takes place in Manhattan, with the cost of a typical living room ranging from $70,000 on up. Budgets tend to evolve with the design process. Insiders tell us the firm employs high-tech design software and creates 3-D animated walk-throughs for clients. Clients include Sean "P. Diddy" Combs and Queen Latifah. The firm charges standard design and retail on product. Clients say Sloane inherently understands their design objectives and delivers a comfortable and unique product. HB Top Designers, 1999.

"Really unique spaces with some imaginative elements—it can be over-the-top funky or twisted traditional." "Courtney melds numerous cultures and styles into her design. It really is a reflection of how modern, edgy American design is evolving." "You have to see her work. Words do no justice to this kind of imagination." "Does retail work, but you'd never guess it if you saw her living rooms." "She forced me to focus on the important elements of the structure up front, so there were no surprises." "Courtney breaks out of the box, offering not just design, but a new identity."

Diamond Baratta Design   4.5   5   4   4.5
270 Lafayette Street, Suite 1501, New York, NY 10012
(212) 966 - 8892   wdiamond@diamondbarattadesign.com
Exuberant, colorful, American interior design

Principals William Diamond and Anthony Baratta have conceived a distinct, energetic, fantastic take on the Americana aesthetic, employing oversized patterns, vibrant colors, and an unconventional twist on the expected. The firm's indelible signature is this new-wave American vernacular—bright, larger-than-life houndstooth, bold stripes, classic-shaped furniture updated with exuberant color, contrasting millwork, and plaid rugs. They have also designed refined Upper East Side townhouses and stately Westchester homes with dignity and flair. Clients praise the principals' "extraordinarily innate sense of the appropriate" and their leanings toward the highest quality materials and outstanding attention to fine details.

Diamond Baratta Design was established 30 years ago. References praise the firm's sources for collectable furnishings (ranging from 18th century English to 1930s vintage) and its "unbelievable craftsmen," who can reputedly match any historic sample to create the perfect pair. New York City and Westchester projects account for most of their work. Though the firm charges high fees, clients report they are very satisfied with the results. After receiving great acclaim for its successful and original Lee Jofa fabric line, the firm's projects now range from $1 million to $10 million. Even with the sky-high pricing, Diamond Barratta is beloved for its significant architectural contributions and remarkable breadth of scope—just don't ask for beige. HB Top Designers, 1999, 2000, 2001, 2002, 2003, 2004, 2005.

"They restored and dignified our house with fine interior architectural details. Then they added charm with fresh colors and bold chintzes." "They do traditional with merriment, really adding joy to our lives." "They transformed my brainstorm—it has more classic, essential character than I could have thought possible." "The pair was very willing and very able to adapt to my desire for a classic house with understated decoration. They are first-rate designers." "They have an extraordinary eye for architectural concepts, but let someone else draw the blueprints." "It was amazing how they could come up with a solution right then and there. Then they would draw it freehand on the wall for the contractor to implement." "They are not great about babysitting the subs." "They pretty much lost interest at the end of the job." "We could not be happier with the result."

Irvine & Fleming Inc.   4.5   5   3.5   4.5
327 East 58th Street, New York, NY 10022
(212) 888 - 6000 www.irvinefleming.com
Traditional English interior design

For over 45 years, Keith Irvine and Tom Fleming have maintained the standards of traditional English style with rich fabrics, warm colors, and 18th century formal-to-bohemian classicism. The firm has maintained the highest standards of quality, and the designers are regularly praised for their knowledge and effective management process. Clients will often give them carte blanche to design, implement, and detail a new home, though the practice can also take cues from clients' preferences. Judiciously mixing exquisite antiques with vernacular straw rugs and paint-chipped furniture, homes take on a look of well-heeled living for generations.

During its tenure, the firm has decorated historic homes, ranches, airplanes, and railroad cars in the New York area and throughout the world. While the partners are known to be fond of the highest-priced fabrics and furnishings (with living rooms generally well above the $150,000 level), they encourage clients to re-use existing furniture in new settings or with updated coverings. Their efficiency pleases most customers, but some find the process overwhelming and too hurried. The firm is among the standard bearers of the industry and has a reputation for avoiding the flavor of the month. Among the very few design houses to successfully pass on the mantle, many second-generation clients are now signing on. AD 100, 2000, 2002, 2004. HB Top Designers, 1999, 2000, 2001, 2002, 2003, 2004, 2005. KB 2002, 2005.

"Sumptuous is an adjective that immediately comes to mind." "Their effective process and the gorgeous results earn them superstar status in our minds." "I really wanted to choose the rugs first, but they were focused on the fabrics and on getting the project done quickly." "I'm on my second 'Keith Home.'" "Keith's choices of colors, textures, and patterns are always unexpected but well bred." "While upholding the traditional standards of the '70s and '80s, we were ready to move into the 21st century." "Can rush through the smaller projects." "They are the only choice for the English Belle Epoque look, and can do so much more." "Old-World charm at its finest with clients that are in the very upper echelons of old, quiet New York society."

J.P. Molyneux Studio Ltd.   4.5   5   3.5   4
29 East 69th Street, New York, NY 10021
(212) 628 - 0097
Lavish residential interior design

With artistic flourish, architectural support, and stylistic detail, J.P. Molyneux is known for his insistence on the very best quality. Clients say he has brilliant vision and can shape a room with just one look. Molyneux's many enthusiastic clients extol his "stunning" taste and exquisite design skills. Many creations are an ingenious amalgam of fantasy and opulence, combined with the comfort and richness of neoclassical traditions. Grand entryways are said to be important to Molyneux's strategic thinking, and often reach a level of splendor "beyond the imagination." A good example of the designer's palatial creativity is his glorious commission of the Palace of Treaties outside St. Petersburg for the Russian government.

Born in Chile, educated in modernist architecture in Santiago and in classical design at the École des Beaux-Arts in Paris, Molyneux is a man of many continents and influences. After working in Santiago and Buenos Aires, he settled in New York in 1987, with satellite offices in Paris and St. Petersburg. Commissions include many impressive Park and Fifth Avenue apartments and sumptuous homes in Hobe Sound, Lyford Cay, Palm Beach, and other major vacation spots. Most of his satisfied clients do not need to think about budget and do not become overly involved in the design process. The results, they say, are spectacular, and can be seen in the Rizzoli monograph of his work published in 1997. Clients also remark that he is most accommodating, offering helpful advice years after project completion.

His strong vision can overwhelm, as when he chooses and delivers furniture or a rug to a client without much discussion. While this is a blessing to some, others find it difficult to say no to Molyneux, and find it hard to resolve any design issues. All clients lavishly praise Molyneux's talent, charming personality, and the quality of the end results, but some characterize the design process as exhausting. AD 100, 2000, 2002, 2004. KB 1992, 1995.

"J.P. is worth every penny if you can control him or completely buy into his vision." "I never worried, as he has the most refined eye of anyone I have ever met." "Guests remark that our house is among the most beautifully decorated jobs they have ever seen." "He created the most lavish and spectacular rooms—better than I ever imagined." "Everything is done correctly, nothing is ever makeshift." "I thought he could have made my house just as beautiful without redecorating quite as much as he did." "He is the type to say, 'Take the roof off and move it up three feet,' without much regard for cost." "The project's price-quality ratio was very high." "His design choices can be audacious or more subtle, but are never boring." "If ever I disagreed with his vision fully, I became distressed because I did not want to upset him." "Years later we still count on his advice." "We would absolutely hire him again."

Julia Durney Interiors Ltd.   3.5   3   4.5   4.5
79 Putnam Park Road, Bethel, CT 06801
(203) 798 - 7110   juliadurney@snet.net

Engaging, timeless, traditional interior design

Hailed for her generosity of spirit and a breezy elegance, Julia Durney has delighted a cadre of loyal clients. Many applaud her easygoing manner, great listening skills, and attention to detail. All say that Durney takes pleasure in developing their design visions into refined outcomes. They also applaud Durney's understanding and willingness to accommodate the needs of family living and realistic budgets. While most of her rooms are filled with warm colors, classic lines, and multigenerational ingredients, they are also said to be "bomb-proof," impervious to damage by children.

Durney began her career as a bond trader, attended Parsons, and then started her design business in 1990. About two-thirds of her time is spent in Connecticut, and the balance on New York City's Upper East Side (her primary residence for many years). The Nightingale-Bamford School recently commissioned Durney to redesign its boardroom. While Durney is essentially a one-woman shop, clients note that she is very accessible and "conducts herself like a real professional, due to that banker training."

The firm charges no design fee and low markups on product. Hourly consultations are also reasonably priced and fully reimbursable against product fees if Durney is subsequently hired on retainer. Many of her clients are repeat customers, including one family who has completed six projects with Durney, each in a different genre.

"Julia's ideas are well-formed, bright, and imaginative." "She was so good about doing our apartment on a project-by-project basis, over time, as the budget allowed." "Julia's patience was a godsend. She dealt with everything from the countertops to the lighting to the bedding. And not one item was wrong." "She will work around your grandmother's sofa and make it work beautifully." "Her ideas are unique and gorgeous, and she also minds the budget through creative thinking." "A true pleasure, she makes it easy."

MAC II LLC   4.5   5   4   4.5

125 East 81st Street, New York, NY 10028
(212) 249 - 4466 macII@mac2design.com
Memorable, comfortable, high-styled interior design

Mica Ertegun has won recognition over the last several decades for her panache and spare design sensibility. With the late Chessy Rayner, Ertegun founded MAC II on a whim in 1967. The firm's design approach has always combined simple fabrics with sparse yet substantially sized furniture, all carefully edited and with a flash of glamour—in short, showing a remarkable intuition for the design preferences of the 21st century. MAC II insists on several high-quality antiques for each room, though not everything has to be of the utmost provenance. This translates to serene, uncluttered, yet opulent environments. In keeping with her philosophy of mixing the fashionable with the finest, Ertegun won't shy away from using a brushed steel table alongside FFF.

Clients are predominantly the very well established, including many top-echelon businesspeople. Many of the firm's clients have multiple homes, all decorated by MAC II. Commercial clients include the late Bill Blass, Warner Communications, Kenneth Jay Lane, and the Carlyle Hotel. About fifteen projects are ongoing at a time. More recently, certain clients have mentioned less personal attention to detail and follow-up. The large staff is reportedly quite professional, with strong project managers. Pricing levels are said to match the firm's commitment to the highest quality products. AD 100, 2000, 2002, 2004. HB Top Designers, 1999, 2000, 2001, 2002, 2003, 2004. ID Hall of Fame.

"As an architect, I have admired the structural beauty of her work for years." "Clients tend to be the well-heeled and well-traveled." "She delights in finding the most unusual furniture specimens, from unexpected sales markets in Europe to the world's finest antiques dealers." "So expensive, but it is the real deal. Worth it." "She will say: look at this beautiful rug. I know it is ridiculously priced. We will find something like it at a better price point." "Mica doesn't have to stretch to recapture that aura of midcentury glamour, she lived it and does it effortlessly." "Less follow-up than we expected. Then again, it is hard to maintain a villa in Bodrum, Turkey and worry about every last client interest." "Often in a hurry, but she gets to the bottom line effectively and then an excellent staffer will follow." "Not someone who will stay for lunch." "They're more selective with their clients now." "It is not about the money for her, but in creating something beautiful." "So honest, huge integrity." "I have been through five contractors, yet am so loyal to Mica. She keeps me calm and delivers incredible elegance." "Consistent in her reserved demeanor, Mica's designs are also reserved, yet so comfortable and opulent at the same time."

	Quality	Cost	Value	Recommend?
	✚	$	◆	★

Marcy V. Masterson Inc.

| | 4.5 | 4.5 | 4 | 4.5 |

140 West 57th Street, Suite 12D, New York, NY 10019
(212) 541 - 6076   mastersonnyc@aol.com

Tailored, considered interior design

Hailed as a perfectionist and a connoisseur of fine furnishings, Marcy Masterson is held in great regard by clients. Though interiors may be Russian Neoclassical, slick Moderne, or Nantucket American, all are carefully researched and intellectually focused—yet user-friendly. As an expert on 18th and 19th century English and continental furniture, Masterson is said to passionately research and pursue the ultimate pieces. Clients report they have a great deal of confidence in Masterson, usually taking her design lead.

After a year with McMillen and ten years with Jed Johnson, Masterson established an independent firm in 1995. This full-service organization of six includes several project managers, but Masterson is reputedly very much on top of every shopping trip, installation, and architectural detail. About seven very large renovations are taken on at a time, with most in the New York area. Many clients have very large collections of antique furniture or important art, but not all clients are collectors. Masterson is said to listen very carefully to requests, but sources note she can be persistent in her quest for design integrity.

A reimbursable standard+ design fee is charged up-front with retail on product. Living rooms are typically well over $100,000. Careful consideration is given on all fronts, and while there are no surprises, projects tend to evolve as new possibilities are recognized. Patrons appreciate the masterful framework and the great effort to purchase components of value.

"Dealers are her biggest fans as she expertly appreciates every piece." "Marcy will work herself into the ground to get it just right." "After dinner, she insisted upon seeing my apartment one more time, rearranging everything in her high heels." "A fondness for muted colors and continental antiques." "Marcy will hold out for what she believes is right." "Beautiful harmonies of color, light, and form." "She has antiques down." "Only Marcy could find a 1580s Milanese table and an 1820s Russian Tula piece that worked together in perfect sympathy." "I would never second guess Marcy, she will get frustrated and you will be wrong." "If anything, I think she underbills given the vast amount of time she dedicates to each project." "My interiors positively glow with quality and warmth."

Marshall Watson Interiors

| | 4 | 4 | 4 | 5 |

105 West 72nd Street, New York, NY 10023
(212) 595 - 5995   marshall@mwinyc.com

Classical interior design with a twist

Marshall Watson has a strong group of clients who are consistently pleased with his classically elegant interiors, which often find inspiration in historical sources. He employs soft flowing fabrics, stately yet comfortable seating areas, and a welcoming palette of warm colors. Customers say Watson is a very engaging man who tries to please by matching his designs to their lifestyles and interests. Younger clients on a budget—as well as more established patrons with very substantial projects—give the firm high marks.

Watson originally studied set design at Stanford University and currently has his own line of furniture produced by Lewis Mittman. There are seven in staff at the firm, including four senior designers. Resources applaud him for his dedicated philanthropic work, particularly in the area of the design arts.

The New York-based Watson's clients reside mainly in Manhattan and the Midwest, with others in the Hamptons, Nantucket, London, and Spain. Recent projects include a large Adirondacks-style vacation retreat in Missouri and a substantial Italianate home in Medham, New Jersey. While some sources feel Watson's follow-up could be a bit better, most find him to be highly effective— fair, honorable, and helpful to the end. Watson's up-front design fee and product and oversight fees are very reasonable, and he will find unusual and interesting pieces to fit a budget. Project costs vary greatly, from $100,000 to $2 million. The firm is highly recommended for the beauty and comfort of each design.

"He has the warmth of a Midwesterner and the sophisticated design sensibility of a New Yorker." "He quickly understood what we wanted and became part of our family." "He designs for the real world, not for Architectural Digest photo shoots. There is a good reading light near every sofa." "Quality designs for real people." "Many a Goldman partner has commented that we have the most stunning dining room he has ever seen." "He speaks with authority. The real deal." "He'll take pains to make sure it's right the first time, but it's difficult to get in touch with him directly after the job is done." "He does it all—designing, teaching, philanthropy. He's very plugged in, very busy, and very knowledgeable." "He has excellent ideas but does not take himself too seriously." "As we gutted our big, old house, he carefully instructed the contractors to place every AC duct and every light switch correctly." "He delivers great quality without killing you on the budget." "I am very fussy and we take great pride in his work." "He listened well and delivered. A+."

Michael Christiano   4   4.5   4   4.5
215 East 58th Street, New York, NY 10022
(212) 371 - 9800
Luxurious, imaginative interior design

Michael Christiano is well regarded for his sumptuous Baroque, Georgian, Neoclassical and Deco designs. Well-heeled clients adore Christiano for his attention to detail and his inability to accept anything less than the best quality. He is known for his penchant for large-scale design statements, which are based upon toned, thoughtful, contemporary backgrounds. Luscious satins, saturated colors, and handsome lines often play a role.

Christiano majored in architecture at Berkeley, worked in the interiors department at Skidmore, Owings & Merrill, and then partnered with the late Robert Metzger. While about twenty projects are ongoing with a third in major stages, clients say Christiano is very accessible and reliable. The firm produces computer-aided drawings architects and contractors applaud.

The firm requires a design advance, charges retail on product (including antiques) and a standard hourly fee. Living rooms are often in the $250,000 to $300,000 arena, with lots of clients interested in fine antique rugs. Christiano is highly recommended by references for potential clients seeking an exquisite interior with no budget constraints. AD 100, 2000.

"Michael can fulfill your individual design fantasies." "He has a kind heart and a wicked sense of humor." "He can do drop-dead Deco and over-the-top 'Ocean Mediterranean' with equal ease." "While known for color, our home was exquisitely done with a neutral palette, and touches of color." "We adore him as a friend and think he deserves more press." "As a contractor, I was impressed with his detailed drawings and the client's respect for Michael." "When we said that the console was just too costly, he found an alternative we liked a thousand times more." "He is an architectural thinker, with a great understanding for form and shape." "Prefers to work custom over catalog any day." "We nervously bought several pieces based solely on photographs sent by Michael from Paris. Each piece was sheer perfection." "He is a one-armed paperhanger, working so hard for his clients." "He is so gracious, and really there for you."

Nancy Mullan/NDM Kitchens Inc ASID, CKD
By appointment only, New York, NY 10021
(212) 628 - 4629 www.nancymullan.com

Gourmet kitchen design, interior design, and space planning

See Nancy Mullan / NDM Kitchens Inc ASID, CKD's full report under the heading Kitchen & Bath Design

Noel Jeffrey Inc.   4.5   4.5   4   4
215 East 58th Sreet, New York, NY 10022
(212) 935 - 7775 www.noeljeffrey.com

Substantial, comfortable, traditional interior design

Clients consistently describe Noel Jeffrey as a gentleman and as an expert creator of upscale luxe. He began his design career 30 years ago, studying design at Pratt and architecture at Columbia. While he is now known for a strong classical-to-eclectic look, his early preference was for Bauhaus. This broad range lends Jeffrey a fluency of stylistic interests, enabling him to meet clients' various whims, all with punch. Even his traditional has intrepid colors and modern juxtapositions to surprise the eye.

The firm usually undertakes complete renovations of substantial size, with budgets large enough to maintain the highest quality. Given his large staff of resident designers and architects, Jeffrey and Company have the capability to manage every aspect of a project and to keep it synchronized. Jeffrey offers customers economic choices in the up-front design stages (e.g. reproductions vs. antiques) and quickly assesses the budget. Clients compliment him for taking complete control of their projects and for staying within budget. Supporters agree that Jeffrey's is as accessible as his staff is excellent.

The firm charges a standard design fee and standard markup over net, with product costs on the higher end. Clients feel that Jeffrey is very expensive, but quite worth the cost. He has published a book entitled *Design Diary: Innovative Interiors* through Rizzoli. ASID. HB Top Designers, 1999, 2000, 2001, 2002, 2003, 2004, 2005. KB 1991, 1994, 1998, 2001.

"Noel is the consummate professional." "Knows high class but doesn't feel stuck in that mold." "He is always staying current, never stagnating." "He offers a guiding hand, to shape our style with his strong vision." "Not a Crate & Barrel type of guy." "He would always be there for you, constantly in touch." "He even faxed things to me from Paris for approval." "I felt that he took a strong personal interest in our project." "Quite a varied clientele." "No one can do curtains like Jeffrey—full, rich, and dramatic." "Noel offers a historic dialogue without seriousness." "I was impressed by the entire office's desire to please the client." "We so appreciated the generous proportions of the design." "Very exciting process. We had a ball."

Pamela Banker   4.5   4   4.5   4.5
136 East 57th Street, New York, NY 10022
(212) 308 - 5030 www.pamelabanker.com

Classic, traditional, and elegant modern interior design

Pamela Banker is well respected by clients and the trade for her efficient, capable professionalism and her strong, clean designs in the Parish-Hadley tradition. With a calm hand, Banker will remix classic traditional concepts, yielding comfortable, crisp, handsome results. Clients say that she makes a particular effort to save and restore the architectural bones—then trims away any unnecessary embellishments. Room identities are then created through a structured process based upon color preferences, design themes, and functionality.

Banker wins accolades from clients for her clear approach, although some say she could be a bit less focused. Patrons remark favorably upon her excellent commitment to budgets and schedule, which has led to a number of recent high-profile country club commissions including the distinguished makeovers of the Cosmopolitan Club in New York and the Round Hill Club in Greenwich.

In the late 1960s Banker started her own firm. After twenty years in the business, she joined McMillen at a senior level, and then went with Parish-Hadley after Sister Parish retired. With the quasi-retirement of Albert Hadley, Banker reestablished her namesake firm. Currently, there are six on staff including two strong senior associates. Customers are appreciative that they get Banker as the design leader, with a good amount of delegation. Many clients and families have followed Banker wherever she goes. Now younger generations have followed suit.

Classic retail is charged on all products, with a standard design fee covering hourly costs. While her many clients appreciate her gracious, timeless approach, others say that it can be impeccably predictable. But the work is said to always be completed accurately, professionally, and meticulously, and many devoted clients would not consider using anyone else.

"After 30+ years, she has seen it all. She is the consummate professional." "Sister Parish without the ruffles." "Bold, contemporary jungle prints at the beach and more rarified, traditional silks on Park Avenue. She has a very broad range and really meets the client's objectives." "Pam is an excellent listener up front, but once you are in the implementation phase—watch out! She gets on a roll." "There is no nonsense with Pam." "She's one of the most efficient decorators in the city." "She will inspect the upholsterer's work on her hands and knees to make sure he has it right." "She was only doing a kitchen for me, but she took the whole apartment into consideration when she made choices. As a result, the whole space makes more sense." "Trendy is not in her vocabulary." "I wouldn't recommend her to the younger crowd, but she's fluent in any design language." "There were some scheduling setbacks, but they weren't Pamela's fault, and she got the kitchen done in time for a great Thanksgiving." "She would come out to the country for all the meetings in the beginning and was personally there for installations." "She was on budget to the dime." "Our family has depended on her for years."

Patricia Hill Designs   4   4   4   5

13 Meadow Wood Drive, Greenwich, CT 06830
(203) 869 - 1719   phill97236@aol.com

Classical, inviting, comely interior design

Creating rooms that look as if they had evolved over generations, Patricia Hill guides clients with focus, thoughtful reflection, and a soft hand. Offering a richness of form, designs are broad in scope and provenance, commingling the fine and the personally meaningful. Whether starting with a new construction or an historic home, detailed painted millwork, unusual fabrics and textiles, and Sheraton mahogany often make a statement. Contributing to both the architectural construction and the building implementation, Hill is appreciated for her skill and practical nature all the way.

Hill learned both the design and the business aspects of the field from the best. She began her career on a trading floor at DLJ, went on to work with Ron Perelman at Revlon, and then delved into the design trade with a master, Thomas Jayne. On her own since 1992, there are now four people in the firm, with Hill as the designer, doing all the shopping and client meetings. She also has a varied and professional group of specialty painters and craftsmen. Many of Hill's clients are using a designer for the first time and say they "could not imagine ever doing it without her."

Using everything from Fortuny to Pottery Barn, Hill is excellent about starting with just a few rooms and going in phases. The firm charges a standard design fee and reasonable markups. While most of the work is done in the Connecticut region, Hill has done numerous projects over the years in New York City, including Jack Welch's office.

"She professes to love 'ugly' colors, but they look wonderful to me." "Patricia took our 1916 house back to the way it was supposed to be." "Classic top-notch Greenwich with family comfort." "Not a formal person, but completely on the ball." "She kept the builder on track and got a huge construction project done. We started with a pile of rocks and ended up with a townhouse, and it's all because of her." "My husband was highly predisposed to not get along with any decorator, but Patty completely wowed him." "Classic good taste." "While she is busy, you never felt rushed." "She will always make time for us, even if it has to be late at night." "Patricia understood what we wanted from the moment she walked in."

Patrick Gallagher Decoratives & Design Inc.

4   4   4   4.5

65 Water Street, Stonington, CT 06378
(860) 535 - 1330 www.patrickgallagherdesign.com
Crisp, timeless, balanced traditional interior design

With clarity of purpose, honesty of design intent, and refined simplicity, Patrick Gallagher has been impressing clients in the Stonington area and beyond since 1992. While usually bent toward a classic English Regency that reflects his established clientele, Gallagher pares it down, highlighting sleek lines, symmetrical proportion, and a modern palette. Noted as highly responsive, the firm develops plans within context and budget, be it a sleek New York City pied-à-terre, a rambling Pound Ridge estate, a Watch Hill mansion, or the traditional Inn at Stonington.

With Midwest roots and FIT training, Gallagher has ventured into many design endeavors, including retail merchandising and buying, showroom design, and photographic styling. After several years as the director of Visual Merchandising at F. Schumacher, Gallagher started his own interior design firm. With three on staff, the firm is said to be highly professional and proficient, employing the latest CAD techniques. For new clients, the group will take on a few rooms, which usually evolves into many more.

Budgets range considerably, based on the specific situation. The firm works with standard hourly fees on the up-front design, and takes classic retail on product with oversight fees. There is much repeat business, with at least one client working on a fourth project with the firm.

"Patrick is thinking 24/7 about his clients." "Balance is his watch word, which applies to both the designs, the comfort factor, and the economics." "Patrick just gets it. He is as professional as he is nice." "I've known him for a long time, and he's always upheld a high standard." "Perfect for people who want design with a slightly rustic edge." "He can take the quality to the highest level but is sensitive to the client." "He makes himself happy by making the client happy."

Peter F. Carlson & Associates LLC

4.5   4.5   4   4.5

162 Joshuatown Road, Lyme, CT 06371
(860) 434 - 3744 pcarlsonassoc@aol.com
Progressive, structured, sophisticated interior design

A master of the sleek yet soothing, Peter Carlson is a creative force pushing toward the future of interior design. With a love of furniture design, Carlson's forms are elegant and streamlined, sinuous and sensual. Proportion and line take a leading role over the palette, which is often monochromatically interwoven into the architecture. Functionality and quality are always major considerations, and curved wall units full of custom storage may stand near Fortuny-covered chairs and an 18th century Italian reeded settee. For his Connecticut clients, Carlson can do a toned-down version of chic.

After studying theatre in college and briefly working as an actor, Carlson established his design firm in Stonington in 1980. With four assistants, about four major and several smaller projects evolve at a time. Generally, a quarter of the work is done in the local area. Client service is a high priority, with Carlson reportedly being very hands-on, even buying the linens and stocking the fridge upon request. It is not unusual for Carlson to complete three or four projects with a longstanding client.

A standard hourly fee for all hours and reasonable product markups are taken. Carlson is also well known for his lighting products company CL Sterling & Son, launched in 1991. HB Top Designers, 1999, 2000, 2001. KB 1985, 1990.

"It is very hard to make the design look this elegantly simple." "Peter can do understated glamour, which makes sense even in this motherland of center hall Colonials." "I can only say nice things about Peter. He will get on a plane and come visit me whenever necessary." "Peter is a total diplomat." "His rooms are a breath of fresh air." "A decorator from the old school with a pleasantly old-fashioned attitude towards taking care of clients: he does whatever it takes." "He always wins any discussions, and that is because he is always right." "He did traditional for me and only beige and gray for my friend. Both were beautiful." "Twenty years later the design held, he just had to reupholster a few pieces." "His designs work well in both the city and the country."

Pierce Allen   4   4   4   4.5
80 Eighth Avenue, Suite 1602, New York, NY 10011
(212) 627 - 5440 www.pierceallen.com
Eclectic, fun, colorful interior design

With Michael Pierce on architecture and DD Allen on interior design, many clients feel that they have found the "dynamic duo" of leading-edge style, radiant with character and warmth. The pair is said to be particularly creative with color (eggplant, lime ice walls) and original materials (leather floors, pony-skin chairs, stainless steel tables), and known to take the edge off with antiques. They take pleasure in incorporating the clients' view and are said to be easy to work with and "not stuffy."

While the firm can claim a roster of high profile clients, including many Hollywood superstars (Matt Damon, Tommy Tune, Ellen Barkin, Tracey Ullman, Ben Affleck), "regular" clients also sing their praises. Pierce holds a master's in architecture from Harvard and Allen the same from Columbia. The firm was founded in 1986 and about half its clients call on Pierce Allen for both disciplines. The back office is said to be very professional and committed.

The firm works with a standard design fee, a reasonable markup on products, a lower markup on antiques and a standard architectural fee (which eliminates the need for an oversight fee). References report that they are "not exactly budget conscience" but not outrageous either. City living rooms run in the $250,000 to $350,000 range with beach houses at less than $100,000. Bills are sent periodically with no surprises. Patrons say that the partners have the pulse of every secret source in New York and recommend them highly. HB Top Designers, 2000, 2001, 2002, 2003, 2004.

"A New York treasure—they have superb taste and follow through flawlessly." "Fabrics in the $400-per-yard area do not faze them. They are committed to the highest possible quality and do it up." "They are real people who will artfully handle normal jobs." "While I first engaged them before they were known, they happily updated just one room for me." "DD is a true artist." "Ordinary apartments become dashingly dapper." "Since their star has risen, they haven't been as available for smaller projects, unless it's something interesting." "They should be on the American Team (of architects and designers) at the 2008 Olympics." "Thoughtful, relaxed and very, very smart." "Discreet and protective of their clients." "I recommend them to everyone." "They find fresh ways to incorporate the city into their designs. True New Yorkers." "Fun with a capital 'F.'" "I have used them on six projects over six years and have always been thrilled with the results."

Richard Keith Langham Inc.

153 East 60th Street, New York, NY 10021
(212) 759 - 1212

Quality	Cost	Value	Recommend?
5	5	4	4.5

Lavish, colorful, inventive interior design

Keith Langham's motivating factor is fun. And the way Langham has fun is to make the world stop and gasp (ever so politely) at his interiors. While this form of entertainment can take many different forms: from outrageously oversized bucolic interiors to excessively embroidered hallways to tie-dye curtains floating in the wind, Langham is dedicated to creating masterpieces. The Alabama-raised Langham began favoring a stylistic English-toned sensibility twenty years ago—first at Parsons and FIT, and then with Mark Hampton and Irvine & Fleming. After he started his own firm in 1990, the creative energy grew exponentially. While he can be humble with clients, he has worked with some of the most fabled, including Jacqueline Kennedy Onassis, who said to him, "You have a sorcerer's eye. How lucky I am to be a beneficiary." While Langham is open to new clients and can keep to a budget, the budgets tend to be capacious.

The back office is quite large and reportedly strong, with most clients who demand Langham's personal eye generally satisfied with his accessibility. Supporters say that he is very demanding of himself and of the quality of his work. While he may willingly use less expensive fabrics, they are always cut and sewn to exacting specifications. Strong primary colors, saturated cashmeres, and exquisite trims are usually part of the program.

The firm charges a standard design fee, a percentage over retail for products, and hourly oversight fees. The public can get a taste of Langham's timeless designs by visiting his upholstery and antiques showroom (at the above address). Patrons strongly recommend Langham for potential clients with significant and once-in-a-lifetime projects. HB Top Designers, 1999, 2000, 2001, 2002, 2003, 2004, 2005. KB 1998.

"I feel privileged to work with Keith. In time, I feel that he will be recognized as one of the world's legendary designers." "He is a control freak and can be very adamant about certain choices. But I trust his taste." "If you draw a line in the sand, he will flex and do it your way." "Even when it's stressful, he makes the process fun for his clients." "He can do less expensive country houses, but the detail work is still remarkable. Anything less kills him, and he loses interest in the project." "His dedication to the projects he loves is unbelievable. My builder vanished from the job site a week before a big party. Keith took paintbrush in hand for six straight days." "He is the definition of fun. I am sad it is over." "He doesn't even know how much anything costs—he goes by aesthetics alone." "He is not a small potatoes kind of guy. Big projects, big clients are his forte." "My curtains are nicer than any of my couture clothing." "He does not like to talk about money, but all the proposals and bills are clear." "I absolutely trust and adore him beyond measure."

	Quality	Cost	Value	Recommend?
	✚	$	◆	★

Roger de Cabrol Interior Design Inc.   3.5   3   4.5   4
135 West 29th Street, Suite 1103, New York, NY 10001
(212) 213 - 4419 www.rogerdecabrol.com

Modern-edged, European-influenced interior design

Conversant in both continental elegance and modern chic, Roger de Cabrol mixes it up to suit the interests and lifestyle of the client. Many projects begin with a traditional European background, which de Cabrol accents with playful and elegant mid-century inspirations, yielding a result that is contemporary and livable. His clients report that he can either take the lead or work closely with them, keeping priorities such as budgetary constraints and children in the front of his mind.

Educated in France at L'École des Roches and L'École des Beaux-Arts in Paris, de Cabrol has worked with such names as Baron Fred de Cabrol (his uncle), Valerian Rybar, and Jacques Grange. He started his own firm in 1987 and works with a mostly Manhattanite clientele. Clients very much enjoy the design process with de Cabrol and note that he strives to produce a comfortable, gorgeous living environment. We're told de Cabrol keeps his practice small to focus on client relations, and to have an active role in every project. He has been known to call repeatedly while on vacation to check up on items as small as a doorknob.

The firm charges a standard design fee with a lower markup on product—or de Cabrol can work on a consultation basis at reasonable hourly rates. A typical living room starts at $75,000. The designer will take on a few rooms for new clients and is known to offer a wide range of product selection and price ranges. Clients say that he is patient, honest, never pushy—and offers a stylish look that is practical and affordable. AD 100, 2002.

"Roger's scope is really remarkable. We did three projects with him: one French traditional, one contemporary, and one modern. My friend did ultra-traditional with him." "Roger was great about including our existing furnishings and artwork." "His European background is evidenced in his biases regarding furnishings and fabric—not a lot of chintz here." "Fantastic and very quick realization. Expensive but worth it." "He is reachable all hours of the night and day." "He's not one of those hotshot decorators out to set the world on fire, but that's not necessarily a bad thing. He's reliable and gets the job done." "Great flexibility and always extremely courteous." "Roger is totally willing and able to deal with the contractor and architect." "He is an ideal decorator for people who are time-deprived." "In an amazingly short three months and just three shopping trips with Roger, my apartment was on the cover of Architectural Digest." "Roger came highly recommended to us, and now I see why."

Russell Piccione   4   4.5   4   5
131 East 71st Street, New York, NY 10021
(212) 288 - 3033 russellpicione@msn.com

High-end residential interior design

Russell Piccione has developed a discreet group of loyal patrons who tell us they benefit from his expansive knowledge and attentive nature. Piccione signs on only a few clients a year and takes an extremely hands-on approach to the client, the details, and the overall quality. He is known to advise on every kind of design-related family decision, including helping the husbands choose jewelry for their wives. Most of his clients are on Manhattan's Upper East Side, with a few downtown and across the region. Piccione's set are generally quality-biased and tradition-minded, and often appreciate fine art and antiques. This works well for Piccione, who is known for his encyclopedic understanding of continental furniture and art.

The firm asks for a small design fee, but requires a substantial retainer. Products are purchased at standard markups with a sliding scale for higher-priced antiques. Piccione reportedly favors higher-quality/cost fabrics and furnishings. The dedicated designer has developed an equally dedicated fan base.

"Client relationships are so important to him that he interviews you, not the other way around." "His patience is limitless, he will take me to the D&D all day just to find the right trim." "He has a very small group of clients that he takes care of very well." "He doesn't fool around with lower quality fabrics and is not one to focus on price tags, but he does not spend money stupidly either." "He takes great care to understand and appreciate his client's particular interests and needs." "Grander than grand." "He is a maniac for quality, but will use Crate & Barrel for the beach house." "Anyone who uses him loves him."

Scott Snyder Inc.   4.5   4.5   4   4
150 East 58th Street, Suite 2460, New York, NY 10155
(212) 230 - 1811   ny@scottsnyderinc.com, pb@scottsnyderinc.com
Luxurious, continental interior design

Building upon a loyal Palm Beach following, Scott Snyder is winning advocates in New York with his easy manner and design dependability. Best known for his classical and neoclassical decor in sprawling Florida estates, Snyder is adapting to his metropolitan clientele by incorporating a more contemporary feel to the neoclassical backdrops. An avowed traditionalist, Snyder favors interiors with an acute sense of symmetry, scale, and perfect proportion. Sources tell us Scott Snyder has such an instinctual eye for design that he can decide the layout and general direction after just a few minutes of observation.

Snyder is noted by insiders as "making the most" out of New York's tight living spaces by utilizing grand mirrors and crafty color schemes to greatly enhance the perception of open space. We are told Snyder is amazing at melding the interior of any given home—be it in the subtropics of Southern Florida or the concrete jungle of Manhattan—into the existing landscape to create a harmonious balance. He is also noted for a highly efficient and organized office.

Clients are grateful for the firm's customer service and say that while the prices are high, they are not outrageous. Snyder is known to highlight one or two major pieces in a room and keep the rest in line. References say Snyder is a "wonderful, yet dependable extravagance" who will do all he can to make the client happy. AD 100, 2002, 2004. KB 2001, 2004.

"He does it all right down to the flowers, candles, and music." "It's amazing—the rooms appear to have a grandeur and symmetry, even though they began as fairly odd shapes." "The place looks so much bigger than it did when it was completely empty. We were impressed." "His work is always large in scale." "An architect at heart." "He knows where to draw the line. I had wanted a more updated look, but Scott made sure we stayed true to the architecture of the house." "Scott very much gets involved with the architecture as well as the design to make sure it all flows." "Turned a cheesy eighties decor to something classic." "Takes pleasure in complete overhauls. Scott likes to throw everything out and start fresh." "He is excellent at understanding the just-so Palm Beach look and will take care of you." "While the furnishings are indeed traditional, he encouraged us to break it up with some amusing contrasts." "Even after several years, I am so comfortable in his beautiful classical work." "I would use him 100 times over."

Sharon Simonaire Design   4   4   4   4.5
216 West 18th Street, Suite 1102, New York, NY 10011
(212) 242 - 1824   ssimonaire@aol.com
Alluring, reflective, elegant modern interior design

With a worldwide jetsetter clientele and a love of the bucolic Hudson, Sharon Simonaire has brought a tactile warmth to the mid-century mindset. Taking the oft-presented modern mold to an unpretentious, almost camp level, Simonaire installs Tibetan yak wool around the McMakin daybed and a Chinese altar table under the geometric artwork. Instead of botanical prints, there are pressed botanical specimens found in Paris. Wood paneling, flooring, and furnishings are also a favorite, polished in the "most extraordinary matte finish available." Each room is a disciplined presentation of the life and times of its inhabitants, who exclaim that each piece she finds is like a "long, lost friend."

Simonaire's joy in the evocative is well founded in her varied training in the arts. Beginning as an accessories designer, she soon gravitated to photo styling and then cinema costume and set design. A dedicated traveler, Simonaire would discover the exotic before its time; from this habit began an eclectic retail operation in LA. After moving back to New York with her husband (Saturday Night Live producer Jim Signorelli), Simonaire's interior design interest took a serious turn when clients such as Meg Ryan and Dennis Quaid, Robert De Niro and daughter Drena, and Richard Gere and Carey Lowell (who Simonaire introduced) prevailed. About three large and another seven smaller projects are pursued at a time, mostly in Manhattan and Westchester.

Simonaire will start with a few rooms and a practical budget, aiming for a characteristic look that evolves, not a showpiece. A substantial design fee is taken up front and reasonable markup is taken on product. While many clients report that they "fell in love with many pieces that were way over budget," Simonaire is able to balance budgets by locating great flea market items with finesse.

"Sharon creates a better version of what you thought you wanted." "She not only found the perfect mid-century pieces but she also located the historical references in books for us, educating us along the way." "Sharon absorbs what she sees in Paris and with appropriate grace. She applies incredible chic to Westchester." "We did go way over budget as we started a serious furniture collection along the way." "Sharon will override the architect to get a better look and save you money in the process." "Despite her own full family life, Sharon always gets back to you right away." "There was no angst whatsoever solely due to Sharon's professionalism and inherent understanding of a reasonability factor." "She is so dedicated to the final product."

Sheila Bridges Design   4   3.5   4.5   4.5
1065 Madison Avenue, 4th Floor, New York, NY 10028
(212) 535 - 4390 www.sheilabridges.com
Luxurious, contemporary interior design

Sheila Bridges is lauded by clients and peers for her deft use of eclectic vintage furnishings, artfully placed in minimalist settings. While focusing on the comfortable, she fuses bold, richly colored upholstery, weathered sideboards, and soothing backgrounds of cream, taupe, and white. Bridges reports that she designs "low-maintenance homes for high-maintenance people." Clientele include former President Clinton (for his Harlem office space), software designer Peter Norton, and novelist Tom Clancy. Other clients include bankers, artists, and entrepreneurs. Bridges is recognized for being flexible and open, while introducing clients to interesting new options.

Educated at Brown and the Parsons School of Design, Bridges worked with Shelton Mindel and then with Renny Saltzman, each for two years. Bridges formed her own firm in 1994 and it remains small, with Bridges handling all issues personally. While most of her work is in New York, other projects have taken her to Boston, New Orleans, LA, and London. Bridges' first book, *Furnishing Forward*, was published in 2002.

The firm charges a standard design fee, reasonable product fees and high oversight fees. A wide variety of sources are cultivated from the Upper East Side to upstate New York to Paris. Patrons recommend Bridges for her functional, beautiful designs that accommodate busy lifestyles. HB Top Designers, 1999, 2000, 2001, 2002, 2003, 2004, 2005.

"Your learn so much from Sheila. She always has a new thought and a new historical reference." "Design is not a mystery with Sheila, but an evolving practical process." "She offers comfortable, livable spaces that are lovely but not pretentious." "Sheila is clear, reasonable, professional, and smart." "She knows how to persuade you without

being overbearing." "A uniquely strong personality in a sea of individuals." "While at first I thought the budget was outrageous, I now think every penny was worth it. I would have made costly mistakes and she did it just right." "Extremely talented and outspoken on design ideas." "I am always able to reach her and the two projects came in right on budget." "Sheila took us from a college black leather sofa look to an eclectic, sophisticated style that looks better every year."

Sills Huniford Associates   4.5   5   3.5   4
30 East 67th Street, 4th Floor, New York, NY 10021
(212) 988 - 1636 www.sillshuniford.com

Luxurious, neoclassical, mood-bending interior design

On the forefront of the harmonic integration of classical antiquity into early 20th century modern, Stephen Sills and James Huniford operate at the highest levels of quality. Known as grand yet restrained, their interiors join ages past with the comforts and flourish of today. Architectural backgrounds are said to exceed any seen before, with intricate painting, strong moldings, and elaborate floors. Contractors and architects remark that the firm maintains extraordinary control over jobs, making sure that every subcontractor knows just what to do and exactly how to do it. Patrons say the firm always develops highly customized design plans that incorporate customers' particular interests.

The firm's long and exceptional list of clients includes Tina Turner, Vera Wang, and Nan Swid. The partners are known to make frequent worldwide shopping trips in search of unique furniture, storing the items in their large warehouse for current and future clients. Given the firm's large volume of clients with vast residences to fill, they also are well known among New York antiques dealers. According to clients, Sills and Huniford stress the importance of strong client relationships based on "understanding and trust." Apparently, if client and firm are not on "the same wavelength," Sills and Huniford turn down a potential assignment. About ten substantial projects are ongoing, most recently in Manhattan, Long Island, London, and France.

The partners are loved by many of their clients for delivering the very best product available, usually in a very timely manner. For years, however, peers, dealers and the media have asked about the famed firm's ambiguous fee structure in which certain products are purchased at an "agreed upon price" instead of a set markup. Clients say they are comfortable with this structure and can always say no. The duo have launched a book, *Dwelling: Living with Great Style*, and a showroom called Dwellings Home, including new and vintage pieces. Supporters recommend the pair for the ultimate, innovative design journey. AD 100, 2000, 2002, 2004. HB Top Designers, 1999, 2000, 2001, 2002, 2003, 2004, 2005.

"Head and shoulders above anyone else, if you can afford them." "Sometimes the craftsmen's work is so painstaking, I wonder if it is worth it. But it looks great." "Editing is their credo." "Not the right temperament for everyone." "They are uniquely able to construct magnificent settings, combining various objects from different periods in a cohesive and beautiful manner. When others do this, it just looks like a mishmash." "Understated and subtle. Words like 'edgy' and 'trendy' make them cringe." "They have a look, but they don't go overboard with it." "Even their cottons are custom dyed." "Couture design for those with an open checkbook." "While they do love objects of serious provenance, they are good about mixing it up." "I am so grateful I found these guys—they have completely upgraded our lifestyle." "I am spoiled by working with these two, but they are beyond expensive."

	Quality ✚	Cost $	Value ◆	Recommend? ★

Susan Zises Green Inc.   3.5 3.5 4 4
475 Fifth Avenue, Suite 1200, New York, NY 10017
(212) 824 - 1170
Warm, layered, traditional interior design

Clients turn to Susan Zises Green for her consistently tasteful design, her three decades of experience, and her knowledgeable, professional staff. Many of Green's clients repeatedly seek her services—some have had a working relationship with Green for a decade or more. We are told Green is exceptional at generating refreshing combinations of strong painted hues, clear patterns, and rich chintzes reminiscent of the English cottage or manor house. Clients also applaud Green's warm and cheerful updated takes on traditional design.

Green fields a variety of projects, from those with modest budgets of $50,000 to larger full-scale design endeavors in large single-family homes. The firm is reputedly "very organized" and handles seven or eight projects each year. Many of Green's staff members have been with the firm for more than fifteen years. Most work takes place in Manhattan, but Green has also designed for clients in Palm Beach and elsewhere. The firm generally charges standard design fees and markup on products, but will also work on a consulting basis. Clients say Green truly loves her work and is continually looking to connect both stylistically and practically with her clients. ASID. HB Top Designers, 1999, 2000, 2001, 2002, 2003, 2004, 2005. KB 1990, 1993, 2003.

"Such a refined and elegant look, but amazingly comfortable and inviting." "I can always look to her for solid, tasteful design." "Everything was organized—from the initial design consultation right down to the itemized invoices." "Not going to change the design world, but she knows what her audience wants and she delivers it." "She brings all the comforts of home." "Susan is impervious to fashion, much to our delight." "Susan's designs make you think of a more relaxed era."

Thierry W. Despont Ltd.   5 5 4 4.5
10 Harrison Street, New York, NY 10013
(212) 334 - 9444   www.despont.com
Extraordinary, opulent interior design and architecture

Thierry Despont's name is only spoken with awe. As the interior designer of Xanadu, Bill Gates' $50 million house, and The Getty Center, the world's richest museum, he is in a class by himself. Other recent projects include the homes of Calvin Klein, John Gutfreund, Leslie Wexler, Oscar de la Renta, the Frick mansion, and Ralph Lauren's flagship store in London—appropriate assignments for a man who is said to receive the greatest pleasure from fulfilling his clients' dreams.

Lauded for his interior design, Despont often takes on the architect's role as well. He is recognized as one of the few architects or designers who can orchestrate the building of a gargantuan new home and make it look as if it had existed for generations. Classically inspired and stylishly forward-thinking, Despont is said to worship the work of Palladio. Rotundas are Despont's favorite design element, which to him are "spaces with magic poetry." Despont's genius lies in his ability to make use of the most current technology to produce timeless masterpieces. Despont's attention to detail is legendary, while his presentation skills are the stuff of lore. For Wexler's review of the plans for his 64,000 square foot Columbus, Ohio, home, Despont placed the large-scale model in a blackened room. Upon Wexler's arrival, a simulated sun rose over the house, complete with mist and George Gershwin music.

While he maintains a residence in Paris, most of Despont's time is spent in New York, where his firm was established eighteen years ago. He studied design at L'Ecole des Beaux-Arts in Paris, urban design and city planning at Harvard—then worked on the redesign of Tehran for the Shah of Iran. Refer-

ences call him extremely charming—dressing, speaking, and decorating with the grandeur that only the French can summon with grace. We are told that he can decorate equally well in the English tradition and in contemporary styles. Patrons say that the net cost of the products and the corresponding fees of the firm are "inordinately" high, but for the most part, they continue to pay the bills happily. ID Hall of Fame.

"An extremely organized, professional outfit." "It is not unusual for projects to take three to four years." "Excellent architecture, but the designs can be over the top." "Thierry brings taste, class, and prestige to whatever he does." "Several times, daggers have been drawn at the end of an extended project." "He's in another world, only taking on projects at the top of the top." "Clients believe that they are buying the best for the most and I agree." "Thierry draws and paints continually, honing his stunning artistic abilities." "He will do nothing but the best—pursuing authenticity both in the methods and materials." "Not for the light-hearted. It is a serious endeavor to bring Thierry on board."

Thomas Britt Inc.   4   5   3.5   4.5
136 East 57th Street, Suite 701, New York, NY 10022
(212) 752 - 9870

Imaginative, colorful interior design

Like any master designer, Thomas Britt works with form, shape, and color, but his central preoccupation is scale. As a result, his designs often take on a tone of grandeur; Britt works in assertive statements, not understated gestures. Bold patterned floors, deep silk upholstery, pairs of tall classical mirrors, and limited use of objects are a few of the designer's trademarks. Not one to back down from a challenge, Britt will achieve a significant sense of scale "in stone or in cotton—whatever's available to him." He particularly enjoys transforming ordinary spaces into spectacular showplaces through the use of unexpected colors and eclectic groupings of artwork and furnishings. More recently there has been a restrained calm along with his trademark symmetry and oversized furnishings—Britt still makes broad gestures, but to more refined effect. Though Britt registers as "a distinctive personality who hardly thinks twice before suggesting the removal of walls or the raising of ceilings," all describe the finished rooms with wonder, delight, and a sense of wit.

Britt freely mixes reproductions with fine antiques, and will combine pieces from different geographic styles and various historical periods. Jansen side tables can appear next to Georgian side chairs, with ethnic antiques rounding out the picture. Many of the larger pieces Britt incorporates into his designs are purchased during his extensive worldwide travels. His knowledge of historical design borders on encyclopedic, but he does not feel bound to a particular period or style. Rather, he strives to achieve appropriate looks for each of his clients' homes (and they often have many)—vibrant colors in the California desert, cool blues in Carmel, and muted beige on Park Avenue.

A native of Kansas City, Missouri, Britt studied at Parsons in New York and in Europe, and established his namesake firm in 1964. Britt has a loyal base in New York and in Kansas City, and has completed interiors worldwide. Clients say his prices are quite high, but highly recommended for those without budget constraints. ASID. AD 100, 2000, 2002, 2004. HB Top Designers, 1999, 2000, 2001, 2003. ID Hall of Fame. KB 1995, 1997, 1999, 2001.

"He marches to his own drummer. His work is interesting and spectacular." "He drives the bus." "If I won the lottery I would definitely use him." "He is neither short on imagination nor gusto." "One of the giants of interior design. His work is generally quite large-scale as well." "He developed our unique, personal statement." "He operates on another level." "Doesn't back down from big structural changes if they're key to the design." "He's still working on a big scale, but has been more restrained."

	Quality	Cost	Value	Recommend?
	✚	$	◆	★

"As a contractor, I must say that he is not easy to work with. But the results were dramatically impressive."

Todd Alexander Romano Interior Design   4   3.5   4   4.5
1015 Lexington Avenue, New York, NY 10021
(212) 879 - 7722   toddaromano@earthlink.net

Classical, high-end, residential interior design

A darling of the uptown club set, Todd Romano calmly offers an easy propriety with just enough verve. Many of Romano's settings are founded on classical American motifs, highlighted with unexpected colors, inherited furnishings, and rich details. He is known to interweave fine antiques with quality reproductions, creating a finished product at a reasonable price. Romano often works with architect Patrick Carmody, and clients say the two make a terrific team.

The firm works with standard design fees, standard percentages over net, and reasonable hourly oversight fees. Romano is also available for hourly consultations. Most clients are the young families of Park Avenue or those in the suburbs referred by friends to their first real decorator. Other clients include more established homeowners who appreciate Romano's breadth of product choices. References report that Romano is willing and able to take the quality to the highest level, but that he never pushes and has many interesting sources. Project costs average in the $250,000 to $500,000 neighborhood.

Romano recently opened a shop at the above address with furniture ranging from 18th century English to 1970s Lucite. He is highly recommended by clients for the "right look" created with good humor, thoughtfulness, and high-quality workmanship. HB Top Designers, 2002, 2003, 2004.

"He took my inherited English and funky Victorian and created something beautiful." "He has great Texas warmth." "He was able to do a great job with our first apartment, and then he created a whole new, more sophisticated and polished look for our Park Avenue apartment. I can't wait to see what he will do with the country house." "The cost of the children's beds was more that I expected, but they looked great." "He is a real gentleman. While my project was not very large, I got lots of attention." "Todd even considered what colors I look best in, and flooded the house with those tones." "If I didn't like it, he would take it back." "Todd oversaw the entire operation really well." "Very couture. He doesn't like to do the catalog thing." "He has a great group of custom vendors. The light fixtures were particularly fabulous and changed the whole construct of the apartment." "Timely, likable, straight down the fairway."

Tom Scheerer   4   3.5   4   4.5
215 Park Avenue, Suite 1701, New York, NY 10003
(212) 529 - 0744   info@tomscheerer.com

Spare, comfortable, articulate interior design

Though he is self-described as a relaxed modernist, clients claim Tom Scheerer is neither. While the designs clearly have a tailored crispness, the enticing textures, sumptuous tones, and moments of joyful flourish speak to a deeper substance. Diligent and clear in purpose, Tom Scheerer is as particular about his clients as he is about his designs. This obviously works to the advantage of both, as his supporters claim he can "read their minds"—inherently understanding their lifestyles and design interests. Mixing the seriously chic with closet-finds and crafted custom, Scheerer creates design amalgams with ease and panache. Practical with the budget and clever with resources, restrained visual flows are punctuated by distinct pieces of personality that function beautifully. This may include the juxtaposition of a white laminate Saarinen tulip table with a Victorian étagère and wicker attic chairs.

After graduating from the Cooper Union with a degree in architecture, Scheerer formed a partnership with Jeffrey Bilhuber. In 1995 he established his boutique decorating firm, which has recently completed projects in Manhattan, the

Hamptons, Nantucket, Aspen, and Harbour Island (where he also owns a home). Of particular note was the extremely well-conceived and well-received renovation of the Little Club at Lyford Cay with an incredible tented ceiling and sophisticated bamboo details. Clients have included the stylish Gucci CEO, but are mostly hip, young professionals referred by friends.

Scheerer is comfortable starting with just a few rooms as long as the budget allows for excellent potential. Living rooms can start at $75,000 but are usually $100,000 to $150,000. The firm works with a design fee and retail on products. Approaching each project with design insight and acumen, the respected Scheerer finds that his clients often become friends. HB Top Designers, 2000, 2001, 2002, 2003, 2004.

"Tom had no pretensions, but is focused and executes with grace." "A genius at adding modern sensibilities to a background of Old World charm." "The designs are both inventive and playful—adding joie de vivre to the atmosphere." "He comes to the party with no preconceived notions, but gets the picture immediately." "His designs completely uplift your lifestyle. It is no longer a struggle to stack the glassware or find a coaster." "Tom remembers every little detail and puts it to good use." "He is not a snob. Crate & Barrel and Ikea are realistic options for the right space." "The only guy who can make wall-mounted storage grids look glamorous." "I foolishly second-guessed him a few times and was always wrong."

Tonin MacCallum Inc.　　　　　3.5　　3.5　　4　　4.5
21 East 90th Street, New York, NY 10128
(212) 831 - 8909

Fresh, color-saturated, traditional interior design

With professional verve, a classic sensibility, and strong integration skills, Tonin MacCallum has been working with high-end interior design clients for over 40 years. Designs are often traditionally based with a dynamic twist, but sources say the designer is very flexible in delivering a wide range of styles. Reportedly, contemporary is executed with the same excellent flair as traditional. Clients say MacCallum spends a great deal of time up front, learning about their lifestyles and interests.

Clients range widely in age and in the scope of their projects. There is no minimum and MacCallum is acknowledged for her willingness to take a project in stages. While most of the work is in the New York area, past clients have enticed her to journey to Florida, California, New Orleans, London, and Venezuela for second homes. Clients report that MacCallum is very much in control of the tradespeople, who know to remove their shoes before entering a client's home.

Budgets have been known to be specific or to evolve. Pottery Barn is used as well as finest custom upholstery, and the client's own furnishings are often incorporated into the plans. MacCallum's frequent travels often lead to unique resources and the discovery of "little jewels." A design fee is charged at higher hourly rates, with retail on products. An individualized letter of agreement, detailing the job and its costs, is signed at the start of all projects. ASID. KB 1991, 2000, 2006.

"She really gets the laid-back Old World look that does not have that decorator feel." "While the preppy look has just come back in style, it is something that never went out of style in Tonin's designs." "My tired, old apartment has become something remarkable under her guidance." "She is on the case daily." "Tonin's style expands to meet the clients' desires." "While her focus can be a bit overwhelming to others, I love that can-do attitude." "I think I have the most extraordinary apartment in New York, thanks to Tonin."

Vicente Wolf Associates Inc.   4.5   4.5   3.5   4

333 West 39th Street, 10th Floor, New York, NY 10018
(212) 465 - 0590   www.vicentewolfassociates.com

Dramatic, contemporary interior design

Vicente Wolf is known for his distinctive design style, which includes handsome, strong lines and a noticeably lean palette. Clients appreciate the drama in his work that is created with sophisticated monochromatic fabrics, compelling background textures, sculptural furnishings and careful editing. Supporters note that he is a passionate designer with a true love of the creative process. The firm usually adds its architectural prowess to projects as well, recently amazing a client with a fireplace built into an exterior wall of glass.

Wolf was raised in Cuba and moved to Miami during the revolution. Persistence has paid off for Wolf, who started out folding samples in the D&D showroom, eventually worked with Bob Patino, and established his own business in 1988. While Wolf is clearly the guiding light on each account, there are eight capable members of the firm who serve as project coordinators on each job. Customers include major entertainment executives, investment bankers, and appreciative suburban homeowners. While many clients relate to and praise Wolf's signature style, others wish he would incorporate more "family character."

A well-known traveler and insatiable collector of eclectic furnishings, Wolf has a 3,000 square foot retail space near Hell's Kitchen that showcases these purchases and his line of custom furniture. Many of these products are incorporated into his clients' designs at prices set by the firm. A number of commercial undertakings have also been completed, including L'Impero restaurant in NYC, the restaurant and retail store of Steve Wynn's new Las Vegas hotel, and the executive offices of J Records for Clive Davis. The firm charges a standard design fee, standard markups on products, and higher oversight fees. Sisal rugs and over-the-top originals are used with equal aplomb. AD 100, 2000. HB Top Designers, 1999, 2000, 2001, 2002, 2003, 2004, 2005. ID Hall of Fame. KB 1990.

"Vicente is the Richard Gere of interior design. He has the charm and spirit of an artist." "He is passionate about the creative choices. When I was not sold on a brick floor for my kitchen, he came down to my office on Wall Street to convince me with the samples in hand. He was right." "He has a photographer's eye and a clear vision, which he sticks to." "There is often one dark room, which he thinks is mysterious and sexy." "He will clearly state that he is the professional and should hold the painter's brush." "While some of the fabrics are impractical and way expensive, they look amazing." "You basically know the look he will deliver, only it was 100 times better that I expected." "Vicente clearly makes all the firm's creative decisions and is quite available." "It was way easier than I imagined. Expensive, but easy." "He orchestrated a metamorphosis of my home from a jumble of small rooms to something magnificent." "If you don't use Vicente and his team, you can only hope for second best."

Hiring a Kitchen & Bath Designer

The perfect kitchen won't make you a great cook, and a decadent bathroom will still need cleaning, but the fact remains that a kitchen or bath remodel can make your life at home much more pleasurable on a daily basis. They are often the two rooms that see the most use, so their planning and construction deserve careful thought. A good kitchen and bath designer will listen attentively to a client's desires and incorporate them into rooms that are as functional as they are beautiful.

Finding a Designer

Some architects, interior designers, space planners, and certified remodelers dabble in kitchen and bath design. There are even "designers" who work for manufacturers and home improvement stores. But if your sights are set on a specialist, you'll want to look for a Certified Kitchen Designer/Certified Bath Designer (CKD/CBD). To get certified, the designer needs at least seven years of hands-on experience in addition to coursework, and must pass a series of tests administered by the National Kitchen and Bath Association (NKBA), the field's main professional organization. Even after certification, continuing education will enable a designer to stay abreast of current styles and the latest advances in equipment.

Most designers have either a showroom or portfolio to give you a sense of their particular style. You may think you are on the same page when you talk on the phone, but when you see the ideas embodied in a room you may find that you have very different takes on what a word like "contemporary" or "traditional" means. You'll be a giant step closer to getting what you want if you can find a designer whose style is similar to your own. Take a look at your prospective designer's recent work history while you're at it. At the very least, a designer should be able to produce three current references, and a history of two or more projects per month shows a healthy demand for the professional's work. Another good idea is to ask if you can go see a project that is in progress (which lets you see if the workmen are neat and clean in the house).

Finding someone with whom you feel compatible will make the whole process more pleasant and productive—especially if you see eye to eye on budgetary considerations. It will also help to alleviate some of the inevitable stress. With the right designer, you'll be able to openly discuss such issues as project cost, time frame for completion, product information, and warranty issues. You should feel comfortable asking for advice on the logical and functional placement of appliances, how to make cabinets child-proof, lighting alternatives, your storage needs, personal preference for gas or electric stoves, the upkeep involved in tile kitchens vs. stainless steel, and other design considerations. Also, do you want to work with the appliances you have or completely replace them? If you want new appliances, the designer may or may not coordinate their purchase. Don't assume that a designer can read your mind and know that you will not, under any circumstances, part with your matching canary-yellow refrigerator and stove.

On Cost

There are generally two ways in which designers can charge for their services. The first type of pricing structure is a percentage—generally about 10%—of the project's total cost. This type of fee schedule is common when the designer both coordinates the entire project and supplies the artistic template.

Coordinating the project includes ordering all materials and finding and managing the workers. This approach is often a good value. It also relieves you of having to find someone else to carry ou t the project or immerse yourself in the hassles of ordering and overseeing.

The second method of pricing is an hourly fee called a pure design fee. Your money buys only the designer's ideas and plans for creating the kitchen or bath of your dreams. The price will depend upon the designer's experience, education, and general reputation. Hourly charges range from $75 to $200 or more per hour.

It is imperative to discuss total cost prior to starting the job, of course, so you know what to expect. If you have your heart set on a new kitchen layout that requires new plumbing and electrical work, for example, know that this will be a more expensive renovation than one that involves existing systems. If the cost of such a renovation is more than you'd like to spend, work with the designer to match your dreams with your budget.

Once you've chosen a designer, you'll need a contract to protect both parties. No professional will be offended if you request one. The contract should spell out the services you're expecting and include a timetable for payment. Expect to part with a down payment of 40% to 50% to secure a good designer.

Many designers are sole proprietors, which means that the designer may be the only employee of the company. Others are part of a large firm with designers representing a range of specialty areas. Deciding whether or not to use an individual or a firm is a choice that depends upon your own style and the scope of your project: a firm's diverse collection of talent may come in handy if your project is especially complex. Some clients prefer dealing with one person, while others may feel more confident having a number of designers available. If, after speaking to a few of the vendors in this book, designers from both large and small firms interest you, make some comparisons, such as their availability to begin work and how long they anticipate it will take to complete it. Their answers may help you narrow your search.

As with any major home project, you'll go through a period of upheaval when everything—including the kitchen sink—gets overhauled. But the result will be worth the trouble, whether your fantasy is to cook dinner for twenty with ease or to sink into a tiled Roman bath.

OPEN YOUR MIND: TREND IDEAS

- ✧ **Pay Close Attention to Lighting:** Talk to your designer about the latest lighting trends (use glass tiles as a backsplash to reflect the light).

- ✧ **In the Bathroom:** California living often means bringing the outdoors inside. Many designers are adding large windows and doors and opening this space up to a sanctuary garden or small terrace.

- ✧ **In the Kitchen:** Use an open cabinet for storing your everyday dishes and glassware. This will break up the monotony of all-doored cabinets and come in handy when washing dishes—you'll duck beneath open doors less frequently. Placing your everyday dishes in open cabinets may also motivate you tto clear out any mismatched pieces and to better organize your frequently used tableware.

Kitchen & Bath Designers

📷 FIRMS WITH ONLINE PORTFOLIOS* 📷

American Classic Kitchen Inc. 📷   3.5   3   4.5   4
150 East 58th Street, 9th Floor, New York, NY 10155
(212) 838 - 9308   design@americanclassickitchens.com
Kitchen design and installation; appliance sales

American Classic Kitchen is praised for offering clients personal attention from the earliest stages of a project. A knowledgeable design staff works diligently to complete each job according to client requests and in compliance with the firm's high-quality standards. Customers describe this firm as thorough, noting that it not only oversees the cabinetry design and installation, but also ensures accuracy from its flooring and countertop contractors. We're told that should anything go awry during the process, the "great problem solvers" on staff will get involved.

American Classic Kitchen has a showroom, open to the public, which features seven full-kitchen displays at any given time. The firm is a certified dealer of Wood-Mode and Brookhaven cabinetry, and we hear American Classic retails all appliances at just 10% above wholesale price.

"They taught us how to make the correct decisions along the way instead of dictating what we 'need' in our home."

Cabinet Fair Inc. 📷   4.5   3.5   5   4.5
241 37th Street, Brooklyn, NY 11232
(718) 369 - 1402   www.cabinetfair.com
High-end custom kitchen cabinetry, bathroom vanities, and wall units

This "can-do" company keeps up with market trends and can offer clients the best in almost any style of kitchen cabinet design. With manufacturing honcho AJV Prime Source acting as the powerhouse behind Cabinet Fair, the firm boasts a turnaround time of six to eight weeks—one of the quickest in the city. Established in 1993 by Jake Blekhtser, the company is now helmed by his wife Marina, his daughter Donna, and one of firm's long-time partners, Avi Shoshan.

Cabinet Fair works with homeowners and some of the most prominent designers, architects, and contractors in the industry. This 50-man company has a 30,000 square foot factory and works with all species of wood as well as laminates and Thermofoil. From classical architecture's ornate arches and cathedral lifts to the smooth, clean lines of modern design, Cabinet Fair can create them—and create them fast. This full-service company designs, cuts, manufactures and installs custom kitchen cabinetry and moldings, bathroom vanities and wall units. Armed with CNC Routers and a new gigantic Schelling saw, the company keeps pace with the latest technology in millworking but never sacrifices craftsmanship—and with four finishers on staff, discerning clients can be sure that "any stain, color, and finish on the planet" can be achieved.

A member of the National Kitchen & Bath Association, its work has been featured in *New York* magazine (2005 and 2006), This Old House, and the coffee table book *The Perfect Home*. Typical projects run from $20,000 to $70,000, but

We invite you to visit www.franklinreport.com to view images of their work.

the firm will not scoff at smaller-scale (read: $12,000) installations. Individual vanities and units are in the $1,000 to $5,000 realm. Cabinet Fair's work can be seen in interiors in New York, Connecticut, New Jersey, Westchester, and Florida.

"Will hire again for my next house!" "Superb customer service." "Our kitchen was a challenge and not a thing went wrong." "Craftsmanship is impressive." "We did not have to keep calling to get a response." "Unquestionably top-notch."

Chelsea Fine Custom Kitchens Inc.   4   3.5   4.5   4
325 West 16th Street, New York, NY 10011
(212) 243 - 5020   www.chelseakitchens.com

Kitchen and bathroom renovations; custom cabinetry and decks

Clients have been known to hug Arthur Tanturri after a project's completion. Tanturri, whose former company was the venerable Clean Cut Construction, has turned Chelsea Fine Custom Kitchens into a one-stop shop for all types of renovations, additions, cabinets, kitchens, and bathrooms. Known as a contractor to the stars, Tanturri's dedicated staff handcrafted a 23,000 square foot solid mahogany outdoor deck for one discerning client.

We're told that the "friendly" and "easy to work with" employees take a hands-on approach to every job, and that Tanturri personally ensures that his company can handle it all—from interior design, to custom woodwork and general contracting. (They never hire subcontractors.) All this praise, plus a new line of German cabinetry, has satisfied customers itching to hire the firm for another project.

"Project was on-time and on budget." "Professional, and most importantly, reliable." "Arthur personally addresses all of the client's concerns." "Dedicated and inspired." "In the heat of the summer they hand-built a three-level mahogany structure with three pergolas, all done with Arts and Crafts-style detailing. Our gardener said it was the most beautiful outdoor space in the city."

Culin & Colella Inc.
632 Center Avenue, Mamaroneck, NY 10543
(914) 698 - 7727   rculin@hotmail.com

Custom millwork and furniture

See Culin & Colella Inc.'s full report under the heading Millwork & Cabinetry

Designers Home Improvement Inc
160 East 84th Street, Suite 3E, New York, NY 10028
(212) 249 - 5696   cjg160@aol.com

Well-managed renovations and kitchen and bath design

See Designers Home Improvement Inc.'s full report under the heading Contractors & Builders

	Quality	Cost	Value	Recommend?

Kitchen Solutions Inc.

4   4   4   5

1086 East Gun Hill Road, Bronx, NY 10469
(718) 547 - 6100   www.kitchensolutionsinc.com

Custom kitchen and bath design; countertop and cabinet sales

In its 46 years, Kitchen Solutions has done multimillion-dollar jobs in some of the toniest neighborhoods in New York City. Even more impressive than the firm's high-end work is its extraordinary ability to customize and "make any project work." Specializing in high-end cabinetry such as Rutt and SieMatic, the firm constantly adds to its showroom, which now features Pyrolave, an illustrious form of French lava stone. Satisfied customers tell us how much they enjoy working with a staff that can "anticipate a client's needs." Although the company does not install, we hear its staff has a knack for recommending the right person for the job.

"They act as liaison between architect and client, so all facets of design are accounted for." "The Rutt looks beautiful—I never thought the design would work as well as it does." "I return again and again because they really bend over backwards to customize for my clients." "Kitchen Solutions renovated my Park Avenue kitchen and they were helpful throughout the entire process."

Knockout Renovation Services Inc.

300 East 95th Street, New York, NY 10128
(212) 599 - 5060   www.knockoutrenovation.com

Complete residential interior remodeling; kitchen and bath specialists

See Knockout Renovation Services Inc.'s full report under the heading Contractors & Builders

MyHome

353 West 48th Street, New York, NY 10036
(212) 666 - 2888   www.myhomeus.com

Comprehensive design/build services

See MyHome's full report under the heading Contractors & Builders

One to One Studio

4   2.5   5   5

209 Westminster Road, Brooklyn, NY 11218
(347) 452 - 9594   www.121studio.com

Kitchen and bath design; color consultations

Formerly a project editor of a do-it-yourself magazine, Clare Donohue brings a wealth of ideas to projects and takes "one to one" to heart when it comes to working with her clients. Founded in 1996, the small firm offers personalized design services for kitchen, bath, and home office as well as color styling and decorative painting. Specializing in creative solutions for space-constrained New York City apartments, Donohue is said to translate a customer's self-proclaimed "vague ideas" into beautiful results.

One to One does not have a showroom. Rather, Donohue prefers to allow clients to choose products without pressure or bias towards a particular brand. They appreciate her expertise in "narrowing down" selections and note that whether she's using high-end custom built or IKEA, Donohue knows how to get the perfect end result. With a personal style that is described as sophisticated and elegant and a keen eye for color selection, Donohue is known to suggest wonderful extras that the client would never have thought of. Fans say they come back project after project for her practical, down-to-earth approach.

In addition to her creative talent, sources tell us Donohue's "business side" is professional and organized. Fee structures are said to be fair and bills are accurately estimated from the outset, which many feel makes using One to One Studio an utterly pleasurable experience.

"She turned my tiny kitchen into a very workable space." "She deeply cares about getting great results." "Responsive, energetic, and neat as the proverbial pin." "Clare Donohue is an intelligent, charming, well-mannered artist with warmth and wit." "She immediately tuned into where we were headed and then made it much more." "Clare is unsurpassed at choosing colors." "Her attention to detail made all the difference." "A real find."

The Renovated Home

1477 3rd Avenue, Suite 2, New York, NY 10028
(212) 517 - 7020   www.therenovatedhome.com

Entire apartment renovation; kitchen and bath design and installation

See The Renovated Home's full report under the heading Contractors & Builders

Rusk Renovations Inc.

583 West 215th Street, Suite A5, New York, NY 10034
(212) 544 - 0986   www.ruskrenovations.com

General contracting and kitchen and bathroom remodels

See Rusk Renovations Inc.'s full report under the heading Contractors & Builders

Smith River Kitchens   4   3.5   4.5   4.5

25 Cedar Street, East Hampton, NY 11937
(631) 329 - 7122   www.ericabrobergarchitect.com

Kitchen design and installation, color consultations and cabinet fabrication

With a strong architectural background as the backbone of this young company, Smith River Kitchens is a name to watch out for. Helmed by the firm's founders, architect Erica Broberg and project manager Scott Smith, Smith River Kitchens was established in 2000, due to Broberg's frustrations with kitchens that "don't flow with the house's architectural structure."

With a staff of three architects and one kitchen designer, the company serves mostly residential clients in Manhattan, the Hamptons, and Long Island. From designing the actual kitchens to choosing the color palette to fabricating the cabinetry and millwork to picking appliances and finally orchestrating the installation process—Smith River can do everything themselves or work with the client's architect or designer. Pricing is usually a flat rate per project. The firm doesn't scoff at mid-range projects and will happily tackle an $18,000 kitchen with the same fervor as a $200,000 one. Although installation is subcontracted, everything is heavily supervised by Smith himself. Priding itself on its rigorous design process and architectural background, the firm has a steadily growing list of satisfied, high-end clients, who claim that the prices are a "great value" for services that are unquestionably "top-of-the-line."

"Erica is a joy to work with. She really knows her stuff." "Helped me get over my fear of color." "A huge, chiffon-yellow kitchen would have been an eyesore, but Smith

River Kitchens pulled it off effortlessly." "Beautiful, functional kitchens that won't break the bank." "Took the time to go over details. Love their work."

Tom Law and Associates   4   3   4.5   4.5

202 West 78th Street, Suite B, New York, NY 10024
(212) 362 - 5227   tlaltd@nyc.rr.com

Complete apartment renovations, kitchen plus bathroom renovations

After having a terrific experience with Tom Law and Associates, many clients exclaim they "are no longer afraid of doing renovations." The firm offers a diverse blend of professional services including design and planning, general contracting, and project management for kitchen, bath, and full apartment renovations.

Clients say husband-and-wife team Tom and Caroline Law plan each project to perfection. They tell us Tom "quickly understands the client's taste and selects appropriate fixtures and details" while Caroline's "excellent time management" leads to the pleasurable execution of projects on or before scheduled completion.

"I have had the delight of working with Tom Law on several high-end residential projects, where demanding clients appreciate their many years of experience and professionalism." "I have worked with Tom and Caroline Law for the past two decades and I have found their work to be outstanding. I cannot recommend them highly enough." "My granite countertop is still too beautiful for words and the spacious kitchen will make life much easier." "The bathrooms are absolutely smashing." "They were diligent, professional, and trustworthy. The design for the kitchen made smart use of the space we had and the result looked great." "Caroline handles the packages for co-op board approval. In my case, her package was so complete that it was approved within days, without the need for any outside review."

Whitney Interiors Ltd.   4   3   5   4

537 Broadway, 5th Floor, New York, NY 10012
(212) 219 - 9654   www.whitneyinteriors.com

Kitchen and bath design, expert color work, space planning, and total project management

Whitney Interiors has a lot to offer NYC homeowners seeking complete designs for kitchens, baths, and other rooms. References report that owner Colette Whitney excels in anticipating client needs and crafting good-looking designs to accommodate them. We hear the firm's home design review is helpful to those clients who are in the primary stages of project development and are in need of educational and creative guidance.

Working with homeowners, and in concert with architects and designers, the company is flexible in its style and is reputedly able to satisfy most tastes—on a moderate budget. Customers report that Whitney herself is easy to work with and that her friendly, professional staff strives to understand and deliver on client preferences. Whitney was the founding president of the Manhattan Chapter of the National Kitchen and Bath Association.

"Colette is a consummate professional, and a delight to work with. She provided creative, original, and affordable solutions for our kitchen." "I couldn't be more satisfied." "When Plan A didn't work, she had appropriate alternatives ready." "Colette Whitney has an excellent eye." "Listens to your requests and understands." "Colette put us in touch with the city's most professional product suppliers and retailers— great contacts!"

	Quality	Cost	Value	Recommend?
	✚	$	◆	★

Al & Dave Reglazing   3.5   3   4.5   4.5
16 Shenandoah Avenue, Staten Island, NY 10314
(718) 761 - 5800
Bathroom tub and tile refinishing and reglazing

Clients adore the staff at Al & Dave Reglazing, calling Dave a "real teddy bear." Fans report that the firm offers an affordable alternative to renovating an entire kitchen or bath and provides great service. The firm specializes in spraying and refinishing tubs, tiles, appliances, and wood panels with both synthetic and enamel finishes.

This family business has spent over 37 years servicing clients in Manhattan, the outer boroughs, and lower Westchester County. We hear the work crew is not only neat and tidy, but also offers friendly and competent service throughout the duration of the project. Clients appreciate the company's free consultation service, and attest to the accuracy of Al & Dave's own motto: "What Al & Dave sprays on, stays on!"

"Realistic and honest about the product." "Would recommend to friends."

Ann Morris Interiors Ltd.   4.5   3.5   4.5   5
515 Madison Avenue, New York, NY 10022
(212) 688 - 7564   annmorrisints@bellsouth.net
Complete kitchen and bath design and consultation

Insiders say that Ann Morris designs for every room of the home, but specializes in beautifying kitchens and bathrooms. She has a reputation among clients for working within a range of styles—from ultra-contemporary to the more traditional, and her designs have appeared in a number of national publications like *House Beautiful* and *Kitchen & Bath Designer*. Her work was also shown on HGTV. Morris is praised for her ability to incorporate a homeowner's wishes into her work.

We hear Morris excels at communication and trust-building, especially when working with other members of the industry. Many former clients, now friends, return to her repeatedly for design consultation on outside projects. Morris has also been awarded the CMKBD (Certified Master Kitchen & Bath Designer), which is the highest level of certification given by the NKBA. In addition to her main office in New York, she also has an office in Florida.

"Ann's work on my apartment is a testimony to her qualifications. My family and friends as well as neighbors are highly impressed by the functionality and the beauty of my kitchens and bathrooms." "Ann was responsible and always available during the project. We named her this year's 'greatest find.'" "Her designs have such personality."

Beverly Ellsley Design Inc.   4   4   4   4
179 Post Road West, Westport, CT 06880
(203) 454 - 0503   www.beverlyellsley.com
Kitchen and interior design, custom handmade cabinetry

References laud this mother-daughter interior design team for their expertise in high-end kitchen design and construction. Best known for her exquisite

custom cabinetry, Beverly Ellsley—along with daughter Rebecca and their 37-year-old firm—will design, build, and decorate kitchens for clients in Manhattan, Westchester/Fairfield counties and abroad. All cabinets are handmade, with Ellsley's firm "building what they design." We're told that "rustic elegance" is often the hallmark of a Beverly Ellsley kitchen.

The design staff is praised for interacting heavily with clients from the beginning stages of wish lists and floor plans all the way through project completion. The staff "leaves little room for mistakes," and furthermore, the firm offers a lifetime guarantee on all its work. The company's workmanship has been featured in publications like *House Beautiful.* KB 1992, 1996, 1998, 2000, 2004.

"Beverly is so knowledgeable, not only about kitchen cabinets, but about the way her clients will use the space." "She takes the homeowner's lifestyle into account and designs a functional kitchen to match."

Bilotta Kitchens of New York   4   3   5   5
150 East 58th Street, 9th Floor, New York, NY 10155
(212) 486 - 6338   www.bilotta.com
Kitchen and bath design and installation

Responsive customer service and high-end product at a reasonable cost have boosted this firm's popularity. Known to have some of the city's best designers and a favorite among architects, designers, and retail clients, Bilotta takes kitchen and bath renovations from initial designs through installation. Showrooms carry product lines like Rutt, SieMatic, Wood-Mode, and Clive Christians cabinetry, along with a wide selection of natural stone and ceramic tile for countertops.

Jim Bilotta Sr. established the family business now run by his three children in 1985. Regina, Maria, and Jim Jr. oversee the company's main center in Mamaroneck, New York, and its showrooms in midtown New York City, Greenwich, Connecticut, and Westchester. KB 2004.

"The Bilottas have been such wonderful people to work with. They always returned my phone calls." "An honest company that offers quality service."

Bloom & Krup   3   3   4   4
504 East 14th Street, New York, NY 10009
(212) 673 - 2760
Appliance sales and installation, kitchen and bath products

Since 1928, this well-established, high-end dealer of kitchen and bath appliances, hardware, fixtures, and cabinetry has served clients in all five boroughs, often working in concert with architects and interior designers. The firm's newly renovated showroom is now the largest of its kind in Manhattan, and insiders say the company delivers to virtually anywhere in the country.

The impressive showroom is equipped with everything from Sub-Zero refrigerators to kitchen and bath hardware. Bloom & Krup also features an extensive Viking display and the latest in Miele convenience technology, including the steam oven and the complete coffee system. While the installation work Bloom & Krup does is limited to appliances, the firm will recommend contractors for other projects. Clients say a knowledgeable staff is always on hand to help. However, we hear the Manhattan showroom is often busy, so be sure to make an appointment.

"I have been using them for fifteen years. It's a great operation."

	Quality	Cost	Value	Recommend?
	✚	$	◆	★

Boffi Soho
4.5 4 4.5 4.5

31 1/2 Greene Street, New York, NY 10013
(212) 431 - 8282 www.boffisoho.com

Sleek Italian kitchen and bath design

This Soho outpost of an Italian firm dates back to 1934, and is well known for its striking cabinetry work, top-quality designs, and sleek yet adaptable component systems. Exhibits at the Museum of Modern Art in New York and at the Triennale in Milan have only increased Boffi's recognition, and we are told its kitchens have been chosen by such noted architects and designers as Robert Stern and Jeffrey Bilhuber. The different kitchen and bath systems integrate clean, well-defined lines with the functionality and ergonomics that modern living demands. Boffi emphasizes the use of environmentally friendly materials.

Broadway Kitchens and Baths Inc.
3 2.5 4.5 4.5

819 Broadway, New York, NY 10003
(212) 260 - 7768 www.broadwaykitchens.com

Kitchen and bath design, installation, and appliance sales

No, the UKW is not an industry association. Rather, it stands for the "Ultimate Kitchen Warrior"—a nickname given to manager Jeff Chinman for his quality kitchen creations. Since 1995, Chinman and his staff at Broadway Kitchens have been servicing the New York City area in everything from custom kitchen design to supplying faucets and plumbing fixtures. We hear Broadway's 2,000 square foot showroom is a manageable resource for clients—equipped with a knowledgeable staff, computer aided design technology, and a unique selection of "New York City-friendly" appliances. Cabinetry lines stock includes Canac by Kohler and Plain & Fancy. Bargain prices increase this solid firm's appeal.

"Once everyone moved into their condos, we gave Jeff a punch list of minor repairs or adjustments. The residents were so impressed with the quality of the kitchens and service that they began ordering additional cabinetry." "Aces across the board." "I was so pleased with their work for my construction firm, I'm hiring them to do my kitchen at home."

Bulthaup
4.5 5 3.5 4

578 Broadway, Suite 306, New York, NY 10012
(212) 966 - 7183 www.bulthaup.com

Sleek, minimalist, contemporary German cabinetry

Bulthaup's superbly crafted contemporary cabinetry has earned it the nickname "the Mercedes of kitchens." Founded in 1949 in Bavaria by Martin Bulthaup, the company has long been a household name in Germany. Since its recent arrival in New York, it has been winning over architects and designers who often turn to the firm for sleek, minimalist designs.

But according to clients, there's a lot more to Bulthaup than its trademark minimalism. The firm offers a broad array of styles, from ultra-contemporary industrial looks to muted kitchens with more traditional appeal. Most of the company's business comes from the trade, but its much-praised staff members are more than happy to work with retail customers.

"Totally apart from other kitchen companies—they have much more in furnishings and free-standing units." "They really have captured that sharp European look I wanted for my client's new kitchen, and the space remains warm and inviting."

	Quality	Cost	Value	Recommend?
	+	$	◆	★

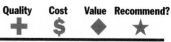

Cardinal Sales Inc.—Kitchens & Baths

| | 4 | 3.5 | 4.5 | 4.5 |

301 East 58th Street, New York, NY 10022
(212) 888 - 8400

Kitchen and bath design, installation, flooring, lighting, and electrical work

At Cardinal, quality kitchen design and installation is a third-generation family affair. For more than 50 years, the staff at Cardinal Kitchens has been serving residential and commercial clients in Manhattan and the surrounding area. The firm's craftsmen perform a wide range of services, from design to gut renovation. Working as contractors for larger projects, the staff does flooring, countertops, lighting, and electrical work in addition to its standard services. At the Cardinal showroom, there are four full kitchens on display and several smaller setups. The firm also has its own manufacturing facility.

Cardinal is a certified dealer of CE cabinetry. Clients remark on the company's friendly showroom staff and compliment the "good quality" workmanship at a reasonable cost. While many references praise the firm for big-ticket projects, others say smaller projects tend to get lost in the shuffle and could be better supervised.

"This group knows kitchens and they do them well." "The day after the 2003 black-out, the plasterer came to the apartment ready to work. What more can I say?" "The workers were efficient, polite, and helpful—just a wonderful crew of people." "They were the best part of my renovation job." "They promised completion of the project within 60 days and finished in 52." "Throughout the entire job, they always kept me updated." "The most innovative staff."

Christopher Peacock Cabinetry

| | 4.5 | 4 | 4.5 | 4.5 |

34 East Putnam Avenue, Greenwich, CT 06830
(203) 862 - 9333 www.peacockcabinetry.com

Highly detailed custom cabinetry

Happy clients can't wait to show off their cabinets from Peacock. Christopher Peacock Cabinetry opened over twenty years ago and has established a reputation for some of the finest cabinetry manufactured in the United States. We're told each piece is carefully constructed with strict attention to the smallest detail. Cabinets are primarily patterned on fine traditional English style and craftsmanship.

Once a customer's cabinets have been commissioned and completed, the company's professional installers make sure that each piece fits perfectly and that moldings and cornices are scribed on-site. Peacock offers a wide selection of stains and finishes, and its artists work to achieve the exact shade, including various painterly effects, that each client wants. KB 2002.

"Extraordinary." "Quality work." "I am so happy with my beautiful kitchen cabinets." "I don't believe people can be perfect all the time, but always accountable. That is Christopher Peacock." "You get a creative, custom look for considerably less than custom prices."

Custom Spraying and Reglazing

| | 3.5 | 3 | 4.5 | 4.5 |

15 Watson Avenue, Staten Island, NY 10314
(718) 556 - 5996 www.customspraying.com

Porcelain and kitchen appliance reglazing, wet electrostatic refinishing

After more than thirteen years of service to both residential and commercial clients in all five boroughs, James (Jimmy) White and his staff can claim the expertise that only comes with experience. Insiders say this small operation handles a very large list of prestigious clients, including Lincoln Center and the Waldorf Astoria.

Custom Spraying and Reglazing offers a strictly cosmetic service, refinishing both porcelain and metallic surfaces for tub, tile, and major appliances. This

Quality	Cost	Value	Recommend?
✚	$	◆	★

firm specializes in wet electrostatic refinishing, which is said to be safer and more efficient than traditional methods and is often requested by clients. Fees are based on labor and cost, with a two-year conditional warranty, and over-the-phone quotes are available.

"I had both my bathtubs and sinks reglazed by Jimmy. They were a disaster and he made them look brand new. I didn't even have to be home to supervise the work."
"Jimmy and his staff are experienced and reliable. I've been using them for years."
"For a guy with a small operation, he does a very good job."

Dura Maid Industries   3   3   4   4

130 Madison Avenue, 6th Floor, New York, NY 10016
(212) 686 - 0246   www.dura-maid.com

Kitchen and bath design and installation and complete renovation

Flexibility is what clients say draws them to Dura Maid Industries for their renovation projects. We hear this firm works with every type of style—and designs everything from kitchens and bathrooms to entire apartment renovations. Dura Maid can accommodate budgets ranging from middle-market to high-end. This clean, efficient operation makes a good impression on clients.

Dura Maid carries Wood-Mode, Brookhaven, Christiana, Merit, and Jay Rambo cabinets and several top lines of appliances, including Viking, Sub-Zero, and KitchenAid. The firm works primarily in Manhattan, but will accept jobs in the Hamptons, plus Westchester and Fairfield counties. Dura Maid's clients often pass on business by way of personal recommendations.

"I was very pleasantly surprised at Dura Maid's cleanliness both during and after the renovation, it was one less thing for us to worry about." "Really on top of her projects. She took me shopping around town for the products I had in mind and made great suggestions, especially for my flooring."

Euro Concepts Ltd.   4   4   4   4

1100 Second Avenue, New York, NY 10022
(212) 688 - 9300   www.euroconceptsltd.com

High-end kitchen cabinetry design and installation

Insiders say that this top-tier firm creates kitchens for the "decorator's decorator." The professionals at Euro Concepts offer design and installation services, in addition to carrying a variety of high-end appliances. After more than 30 years in business, this firm has gained quite a following among clients, who are quick to praise its innovative kitchen designs. Now with two showrooms (one in Manhattan and another in Huntington), the company carries Downsview cabinetry and offers every imaginable style, from country to modern to classical.

"Their design team is ingenious. They were actually able to harmonize my husband's and my wacky tastes with something simpler." "They were able to create a classic yet modern space that is timeless and elegant." "It turned out better than our highest hopes, and was done in the time frame and price promised."

Gracious Home   4   4   4   4.5

1220 Third Avenue, New York, NY 10021
(212) 517 - 6300   www.gracioushome.com

High-end kitchen and bath fixture retail and service

Fans recommend Gracious Home as a terrific place to shop for kitchen and bath appliances. With a "no hassle" return policy, Gracious Home enables you to bring home different bathroom fixtures and accessories so you can really see what looks best in your own home. However, the store does not offer any design or installation services.

Gracious Home's service department provides repair services for all small household appliances, such as vacuum cleaners, toaster ovens, irons, blenders, etc. They are factory-certified to perform repairs on Hoover and Miele products and offer a three-month parts and labor warranty on all their repairs. While they don't respond to round-the-clock service calls, Gracious Home is open seven days a week and has surprisingly quick turnarounds.

"As soon as I walked through the door, a salesperson assisted me. However, there was none of that high-pressure salesmanship." "An amazing selection of appliances." "They totally get the upscale marketing and are so service oriented." "Reliability exemplified." "We practically live at Gracious Home."

Homeworks   3   3   4   3.5

132 West 17th Street, New York, NY 10011
(212) 620 - 7070 homeworks1@nyc.rr.com

Contemporary and traditional kitchen and bath design and installations

Homeworks has garnered a multitude of clients, including homeowners and trade professionals alike, since opening its doors in 1990. The firm offers full design and installation services and has both custom and semi-custom cabinetry such as Brookhaven and Paris. Homeworks' 3,500 square foot showroom has ten kitchen and five full bath displays, with something for everyone. Although Homeworks does not sell tiles, the firm does install all kinds of flooring and tile, including marble, granite, limestone, and ceramic.

"I had a little ugly New York City apartment kitchen. I now have a kitchen that opens to my dining room, four times the counter space, all new appliances, and rave reviews from friends." "They handle the design through the installation of full kitchens and floors at a good price."

Kitchen & Bath Creations Inc.   4   3   4.5   4

1908 Coney Island Avenue, Brooklyn, NY 11230
(718) 375 - 7535 www.kitchen-bath-creations.com

Kitchen and bath design and installation

Kitchen & Bath Creations claims to ease the process of renovation by handling every stage of the project from beginning to end. Sources confirm that the staff has a unique approach to the entire process that eliminates subcontractors: offering free consultations, having an architect on staff, and ensuring that all services are provided in-house. Clients say they enjoy working with this family-run firm, commenting specifically on its insightful staff and its facility in handling the overall project.

With two showrooms in Brooklyn, Kitchen & Bath Creations is the exclusive New York City dealer for Quality Custom Cabinets, and also carries lines such as Medallion and European. All products are covered by the manufacturer's warranty, and, in addition, Sam Zangi and staff attach a lifetime guarantee to their work, improving what was already a terrific value.

"One of the best and most responsible vendors I've worked with so far—and I've worked with many, since I'm renovating my entire house." "The kitchen is now the highlight of our 100-year-old home." "Experts on both technical and creative issues."

Kitchens Etc.   3   3   4   4

149-42 Cross Island Parkway, Whitestone, NY 11375
(718) 352 - 8818 joel@culbertsonbc.com

Kitchen remodeling, architectural detailing

In business since 1959, Kitchens Etc. designs and installs kitchens and baths for clients in Manhattan, the outer boroughs, and Nassau and Westchester counties. The firm also does custom architectural work. We hear these professionals can accommodate all styles of cabinetry at reasonable prices.

For most projects, the shop designs and does some of the installation work in-house, with the remainder of the job assigned to a team of outside subcon-

tractors. The staff at Kitchens Etc. encourages clients to visit the company's showroom in Whitestone which features cabinet lines such as Wood-Mode and Brookhaven, as well as a selection of kitchen appliances.

Krup's Kitchen and Bath   3   3   4   3.5
11 West 18th Street, New York, NY 10011
(212) 243 - 5787
Exclusive kitchen appliances and bathroom fixtures

The staff at Krup's deals in high-end appliances sold to the trade and the public, and has been doing so since 1988. Although some clients report delays, others say the company takes the necessary steps to prevent or correct any issues. Many award the company a high-quality rating, citing its reasonable pricing to boot.

Krup's showroom is open to the public and features both European and domestic lines. The firm carries a wide selection of appliances, domestic and international, including AGA (England) and La Cornue (France). This downtown company has a reputation for staying on top of current trends by constantly attending trade shows and keeping the latest product lines in stock.

"Anything and everything they carry is state-of-the-art." "When our stove delivery was held up, they promptly tracked it down for us and had it brought to our home." "They're on time and on price—I use them for all my kitchen jobs." "Best prices in NYC."

Leesam Kitchen and Bath   3.5   3   4.5   4
124 Seventh Avenue, New York, NY 10011
(212) 243 - 6482 www.leesamkitchens.com
Kitchen and bath design and installation

Family owned and operated, Leesam has been designing kitchens and baths in the New York metro area since 1932. Insiders say this firm uses computer-generated designs at its showroom to work up stock, semi-custom, and custom plans for its clients, who are mostly residents of the Upper East or Upper West Side. We hear Leesam's showroom also features kitchen displays and smaller setups, vanities, bathroom fixtures, shower enclosures, and more. Clients value the guidance and insight offered by the company's professional staff, saying that Leesam's unique service "enhances" the experience of designing a kitchen or bath.

Leesam's several lines of kitchen cabinetry products (including Raywal) are available at retail and to the trade.

"Whenever I had a question, they were totally accessible." "Provided superb design including recommendations for ideas we had not previously considered." "This was a hassle-free experience." "David masterminded the whole project. He sat down with me for an hour and created a computer-generated design for my kitchen, and I hired him because of this special attention. His guidance really made the project a pleasure." "Our granite countertop broke while they were moving it into the kitchen area and David replaced it—free of charge." "Their subcontractors are well-versed craftsmen."

Linda London Ltd.
200 East 62nd Street, New York, NY 10021
(212) 751 - 5011 linda@lindalondonltd.com
Comprehensive home and office organization

See Linda London Ltd.'s full report under the heading Closet Designers

	Quality 	Cost $	Value ◆	Recommend? ★

Mr. Shower Door

| | 3.5 | 3.5 | 4 | 3 |

651 Connecticut Avenue, Norwalk, CT 06854
(800) 633 - 3667 www.mrshowerdoor.com
Shower door manufacturing and installation

Supplying clients with custom shower doors and installation, Mr. Shower Door is known to deliver a quality product. Two decades of experience stand behind this reputable firm. However, we hear that service is not the firm's forte, especially with follow-through repairs. But Mr. Shower Door's high quality products can probably withstand more than a few service complaints.

"I know they are used by many of the top contractors and architects." "When my shower started leaking, Mr. Shower Door offered to send me some tubing, but did not offer to come out and fix it." "The shower door handle is now falling off—admittedly, eight years later—but they say my name is not in their files and they refuse to come to Park Avenue and take a look." "The product was delivered on time, and installation was excellent."

Nancy Mullan /
NDM Kitchens Inc. ASID, CKD

| | 5 | 3.5 | 5 | 5 |

By appointment only, New York, NY 10021
(212) 628 - 4629 www.nancymullan.com
Gourmet kitchen design, interior design, and space planning

Clients call the by-appointment-only designer Nancy D. Mullan a "traditional New York lady" who "designs rooms that people are drawn to." Kitchens and home offices are Mullan's forte, but the company also offers design and space-planning consultationfor any room in the house. From the culinary novice to the professional chef, each client completes a ten-page questionnaire and is interviewed by Mullan to assess how the client's lifestyle can best be served.

From a caterer's kitchen to complete apartment renovations, Mullan is praised for her "inventive" work. References report that Mullan oversees all aspects with strict attention to detail, and her sub-contractors and craftsmen receive stellar reports as well. We are told she manages the project with strict attention to detail. Clients laud her ability to finish on time and on budget, and say that during the project, Mullan is flexible, easily accessible, and fun to work with.

Mullan studied at Parsons School of Design and has been practicing for eighteen years. The bulk of her clientele hails from New York City, New Jersey, Connecticut, and Long Island, and is quite high-end. In addition to designing, Mullan also consults on an hourly basis. She handles projects across the United States as well, and has done some jobs as far afield as the Bahamas. ASID. KB 1992, 1995.

"Nancy is very sensitive and even intuitive about what it is that we 'truly want.'" "She took care of everything, from soup to nuts." "Nancy and I worked as a team. Planning with her made me feel as though I had my best friend's opinion on everything." "She is very eclectic in her abilities. I was most impressed with her hat changing from designer/decorator to general contractor extraordinaire."

Neff by Design Concepts International Inc.

| | 3.5 | 3.5 | 4 | 3.5 |

150 East 58th Street, 8th Floor, New York, NY 10022
(212) 308 - 9674 www.neffkitchens.com
Canadian-designed cabinetry, free-standing units and built-ins

Canadian design firm Neff has been in business for over thirty years, designing kitchens and baths and shipping their products to clients worldwide. Clients rave that Neff cabinetry is great, though some comment that dealing with its Manhattan distributor can be tough. But if you want those Neff cabinets, you may have to deal with this outfit as this retail operation is an exclusive dealer of Neff cabinetry.

Neff designs everything from country to contemporary. Customers marvel at the product's ability to adapt to a range of tastes, while still incorporating the unique space dimensions and unique "Z-cut" design. They also comment on the firm's exceptional success at creating cabinet interiors, including drawer lining and interior shelves made of glass, steel, aluminum, and exotic woods. Some say that, given its high-end pricing, Neff could improve upon customer service and be more conscientious about providing adequate project supervision.

"At first I was apprehensive about painting my kitchen, but a knowledgeable staff member guided me through the whole nerve-wracking process." "Neff has a lot of options, and seeing the showroom helped me understand just how much is available."

Nu-Facers Kitchens and Baths   3   2.5   4.5   4
1368 Lexington Avenue, New York, NY 10128
(212) 426 - 4160 www.nufacers.com
Cabinetry refacing, addition, and installation

More than twenty years in the business has taught Nate Nowygrod and his staff that sometimes a facelift is more suitable for a galley kitchen than gutting and new construction—not to mention easier on the wallet. Many clients wholeheartedly agree, and say they are pleasantly surprised by the quality of work done by Nu-Facers.

The firm offers additional services, including the installation of new countertops, sinks, faucets, appliances, floor tiles, and custom cabinet additions. The company boasts a showroom with full kitchens on display and a fabrication shop on location.

"They are honest and stand by their work." "The quality is on par with the promise— it's not a brand new kitchen, but it functions and looks like one."

Poggenpohl New York   4   4   4   4
150 East 58th Street, New York, NY 10155
(212) 355 - 3666 www.poggenpohlusa.com
Innovative German kitchen design

Industry leaders laud Poggenpohl for its slick, durable German designs. The firm has something for everyone and offers a wide selection of styles, from contemporary to traditional. In order to design kitchens that not only suit its clients' needs, but also suit their budgets, Poggenpohl separates its selection into eight different price groups.

At the forefront of high-end kitchen design and cabinetry for more than 100 years, Poggenpohl has a worldwide network of showrooms, including two in New York City. Their showrooms offer wood veneers and high-gloss lacquers along with stainless steel and glass accents. Poggenpohl also sells countertops available in teak and exotic granite and limestone.

"The process of choosing finishes, concept and design, and development was exciting and the result is a dream kitchen. My wife calls it her stress reliever." "It's not a perfect world and creating and installing a kitchen is no exception. However, the Poggenpohl kitchen experience was first rate by comparison." "I was very impressed not only with how the Poggenpohl kitchens looked, but also with the fact that they were incredibly functional."

Poliform USA
150 East 58th Street, 9th Floor, New York, NY 10155
(212) 421 - 1220 www.poliformusa.com
Closet design and installation, kitchen and door sales and installation

See Poliform USA's full report under the heading Closet Designers

	Quality +	Cost $	Value ◆	Recommend? ★

Quintessentials

| | 4 | 3 | 5 | 4.5 |

532 Amsterdam Avenue, New York, NY 10024
(212) 877 - 1919 www.qkb.com

Kitchen and bath design

Since 1988, Quintessentials has developed a loyal following of pleased customers. President David Landis uses the skills from his previous life as a general contractor specializing in high-end NYC apartment kitchen renovations to realize each design. His working knowledge of different kitchen and bath brands nicely complements the firm's talented staff of kitchen and bath designers, who offer free consultations and will recommend installers.

Both homeowners and architects recommend the company not only for the high quality of products displayed at the showroom, but also for the friendly staff of fifteen, who will walk clients through the entire project. The two-level showroom features cabinets by Wood-Mode and Brookhaven, as well as an entire floor dedicated to bath and hardware.

"Quintessentials has been exceptional in every stage of service from initial choosing of parts to installation." "They go the extra step to make sure everything is right, and then some." "Diligence and professionalism personified." "Everything was measured perfectly and designed beautifully to maximize the space." "We went to every supplier in Manhattan for the cabinets we wanted. Quintessentials won hands down." "The only problems we had occurred when we didn't follow their advice."

R.G. New York Tile

225 West 29th Street, New York, NY 10001
(212) 629 - 0712

Tile installation and marble countertop fabrication, kitchen and bath design

See R.G. New York Tile's full report under the heading Tile, Marble & Stone

SieMatic Corp.

| | 4.5 | 4 | 4.5 | 4 |

150 East 58th Street, 8th Floor, New York, NY 10155
(212) 593 - 4915 www.siematic.com

High-end German cabinetry, kitchen design

When it comes to innovation, clients say SieMatic is renowned for the unthinkable. In addition to a range of kitchen cabinetry styles, this firm has gadgets galore to ensure convenience and product durability—while maintaining the design's function and aesthetic. Sources say the showroom is spacious and features large-scale kitchen displays in a broad range of styles. The company specializes in high-end kitchen cabinetry and furniture, but also sells kitchen and bathroom fixtures, and offers some contracting services. SieMatic's reputation for quality keeps customers returning for multiple projects.

Although SieMatic is a global operation based in Germany, the Manhattan location is praised by clients for its personable customer service. They say the staff is extremely helpful, asserting that more than 30 years in the business has earned SieMatic true veteran status among industry insiders and homeowners alike.

"They've thought of everything—the workers even attached tiny soft-rollers to my drawers so they won't scratch the cabinet interiors!" "At first I disagreed with my contractor, thinking SieMatic was too contemporary for our taste, but it turns out they had exactly the traditional look we were going for on display in the showroom."

Smallbone of Devizes

| | 4.5 | 4.5 | 4 | 4 |

105/109 Fulham Road, London, UK SW3 6RL
(207) 838 - 3636 www.smallbone.co.uk

Fine hand-painted English cabinetry, custom design, and installation

Exceptional, high-quality painted cabinetry is the hallmark of Smallbone of Devizes, a London-based firm with an elite following in New York and other hubs worldwide. This firm claims to allow clients to choose "any color from the twenty or so the human eye can detect" and will paint each piece by hand, according to client-specified painting techniques. Smallbone uses a variety of woods for its cabinet construction, the most popular choices being oak, olive ash, sycamore, pine, teak, maple, and chestnut. Smallbone also designs custom furniture and wall paneling.

Smallbone operates from overseas, so choosing its services can be a big commitment. To ensure optimum client relations, the firm assigns a personal design team consisting of designers, a draftsperson, and a professional installation manager to each project. Some clients report that the quality is not quite up to the price, while others are completely satisfied, praising the designs as "free-flowing, stately, and elegant." KB, 2001.

"Stunning results, if you can deal with the wait." "There are now enough US-based Smallbone alternatives to forgo the hassle of dealing overseas with your rep." "No one compares for an extraordinary showpiece." "Better than custom, they know the kitchen business inside-out."

St. Charles of New York   4   4.5   4.5   4
150 East 58th Street, 8th Floor, New York, NY 10155
(212) 838 - 2812 www.stcharlesofnewyork.com
Complete customized kitchens

Located in the A&D building for over 30 years and Manhattan for more than 50 years, St. Charles of New York solves design issues and caters to the millworking needs of gourmand clients. For the most part, clients find the firm's performance efficient and professional, while the quality of its workmanship is consistently praised as high-end. President of St. Charles, Robert Schwartz, schedules an on-site project manager for each job. The small staff of ten has 150 years of combined kitchen-specialized design experience. Kitchens from St. Charles start at $100,000.

St. Charles works mainly in Manhattan but will also do kitchens outside the city. We've been told that the company's 3,000 square foot showroom is one of the only locations in the city where clients can find such exclusive brands as La Cornue. We also hear the showroom displays a wide range of styles, from stainless steel to the more classical and traditional Old World kitchen designs. Recent projects include kitchens for Sean Connery, Mayor Bloomberg, Martha Stewart's studio kitchen, and eleven test kitchens for *Gourmet* magazine. KB 2003.

"St. Charles has consistently demonstrated work of the highest quality and service." "Always the first place I take my clients when we begin to tackle the kitchen design." "Great suggestions." "Good follow-up." "Some installers are better than others." "A painless experience."

St. James Kitchens   3.5   3   4.5   4
102 East 19th Street, New York, NY 10003
(212) 777 - 4272 www.stjameskitchens.com
Kitchen design and installation

We hear St. James carries a broad spectrum of cabinetry styles from traditional to contemporary. This ten-year-old firm deals in a variety of fine products, such as Wood-Mode and Bentwood, all of which come with a lifetime guarantee. The showroom is praised for its quality products and prompt customer service, though some express skepticism about St. James's stable of subcontractors.

"Their creativity is exceptional. Everything flows terrifically and the set-up allows for the ultimate storage space." "On budget and approximately on time, which is a minor miracle in New York." "The style and quality of the showroom cabinetry is why I went with St. James." "The staff made really good suggestions." "The principal came to my home years later to do some repair work. I really appreciate that."

	Quality	Cost	Value	Recommend?

Thomas J. Connolly

100 West 92nd Street, Suite 27D, New York, NY 10025
(212) 787 - 2017 www.tcnyc.com

General contracting and kitchen and baths

See Thomas J. Connolly's full report under the heading Contractors & Builders

Waterworks   5   4.5   4.5   5

225 East 57th Street, New York, NY 10022
(212) 371 - 9266 www.waterworks.com

High-end bathroom design, sales, and installation referral

The very top decorators and architects depend on Waterworks for its unique and "ultimate quality" products that "last a lifetime." And sources say the level of service matches the quality of the products. Both trade and private clients tell us this is the place for someone who is serious about creating a sophisticated, elegant, albeit pricey bathroom. While qualified, truly professional Waterworks sales associates guide you through the design and spec phase, they advocate bringing in an interior designer or architect for any involved project. Tips on the process and commentary by featured designers can be found at the company's handsome, helpful website.

Waterworks works closely with contractors, providing tile and stone samples, facilitating quotes and bidding packages, and providing tech support. Products include fittings, fixtures and tubs, bath accessories, lighting, furniture, kitchen and bar, textiles, personal care, and apothecary. Waterworks does not install, but will refer clients to a stable of trusted professionals. Its service associates coordinate and track delivery of materials, and will even visit a site to trouble-shoot for proper installation. The company maintains a complete parts department and offers a lifetime warranty.

Home-owners declare that with the Waterworks line of products, it's possible to get that "high-class, decorator look," while avoiding the cost of the decorator. Waterworks also has a showroom located in Soho at 469 Broome Street, (212) 966-0605.

"What brought us to Waterworks was the high quality and excellent design of bath-room fittings. What delighted us was to find a service staff that was on the top of every detail." "Their lighting is inexpensive, quick-ship, and well made. It's so good-looking that it might just find its way into other rooms in your home." "The word 'no' is seldom in their vocabulary." "They sell one of the narrowest tubs available and it will fit in most situations—it is also nice and deep." "If ever a component is missing they are great about FedEx-ing it to you." "It is one source shopping—even down to accessories and bath linens."

Yves-Claude Design   4.5   3.5   5   4.5

199 Lafayette Street, Suite 4B, New York, NY 10012
(212) 625 - 9612 www.kanso.com

Exquisite stainless steel kitchen design and home furnishings

"Adventurous" is the word clients use to describe Yves-Claude and his profes-sional-quality stainless steel kitchens. Insiders tell us Yves-Claude coined the term "essentialism" to describe his pared-down approach, a philosophy appar-ent in his clean, sharp, and industrial-looking designs. We hear that although his work is contemporary and creative, it is far from overdone. Furthermore, Yves-Claude's designs are said to reflect his firm belief in longevity, functionality, and adaptability. Admired by his peers as well as his customers, Claude won the 1997 *Food & Wine* "Kitchen of the Year" award.

Clients rave about Yves-Claude's select designs and warm nature, calling the designer "dependable," "personable," and "inspired." In addition to kitchens, Yves-Claude now features a new line of stainless steel furniture. Sources appreciate the firm's unique direction, and his work has piqued the interest of some of the biggest interior designers in the industry.

"Can a designer be too attentive? That would be my only complaint." *"He never says 'it's impossible' and he has great manufacturers behind him."*

Hiring a Landscape Architect/Designer

Along with the hustle and bustle of living in New York City comes the need to escape the concrete and bright lights and return to nature. The ultimate refuge is your very own green space where sunlight, plants, flowers, walkways, trellises—or simply a colorful flower box in the window—create a delightful escape. The artisans who turn these dreams into reality are garden designers, horticulturists, and landscape architects. Experts in both art and science, these professionals create natural havens in any type of space. Garden and landscape designers use plants and masonry to plan, design, and construct exterior spaces in the city, the suburbs, or the countryside.

More Than Planting

Planning a garden paradise is a job for professionals, as many technical elements are involved. Garden designers create water and soil systems that are unique to city landscapes, and their craft requires a complex blend of botanical knowledge, construction expertise, and creativity. Suburban or country projects can be more or less involved, incorporating large trees and bushes, masonry and rock formations, ponds and streams. In contrast, Manhattan landscape architects and designers are faced with the everyday challenge of creating an outdoor paradise in small spaces that do not have a great deal of sunlight.

Service providers included in The Franklin Report reveal a common thread—artistry combined with a passion for creating the ultimate natural space to suit each client's unique habitat.

Where Do I Start?

The most general decision to make about your city garden or country landscape is what purpose it will serve. Are you a cook who loves using fresh ingredients and would like to build an herb, vegetable, or cutting garden? Have you discovered the joy of exotic plants and do you wish to install a greenhouse for your orchids? Or are you dreaming of a superbly designed terrace with benches and several layers of growth? With your overall purpose in mind, take stock of the space available in and around your home. If you want to create a balcony or rooftop garden, are you primarily interested in shrubs, trees, and vines-—or particular colors and species of flowers and plants? Is privacy—building a hedge to separate your yard from your neighbor's—an important issue? Do you prefer the informal charm of an English cottage garden or the elegance of a neoclassical French one? Keep in mind that the more complicated the design, the more maintenance there is. Nurture your ideas by looking through home, garden, and architecture magazines before you contact a garden designer. Foremost in a landscape designer's mind is building a setting that can be enjoyed year round. The designer will have many ideas for you, but if you have done some research and fallen in love with specific plants and flowers, you will be a step ahead in designing your perfect oasis.

On Cost

The pricing system for landscape design varies from firm to firm. Some designers charge an hourly rate—others determine a flat fee after analyzing the job. The average hourly rate in Manhattan is between $50 and $75, translating into a baseline of 3 for Cost in our book. Like other professional services, garden design companies will produce a written agreement for the client that lists what will be done and at what cost. It is not unusual for these agreements to leave room for flexibility in scheduling and pricing, should unforeseen circumstances (such as bad weather) affect the job.

WILL A DESIGNER ALSO MAINTAIN MY GARDEN?

Services provided by garden designers vary from firm to firm and depend on the scope of your project. Many companies provide a complete package of design, installation, and maintenance, and thus establish a long-term relationship with the client. Other professionals are limited to design and consulting, and subcontract for installation and maintenance. Landscape projects can vary drastically in size and detail and therefore in degrees of maintenance. Discuss these aspects with your designer and make sure you're aware of the amount of attention your yard or garden will require. Like interior designers, garden designers, horticulturists, and landscape designers work closely with clients on a one-on-one basis to bring their creative ideas to fruition.

PERMITS AND PROFESSIONAL CONSIDERATIONS

A garden-design project may require a permit from your building management if you live in a downtown city apartment. Designers are well-schooled in this process and some will even intervene with a super-strict co-op board to get your plans set in motion. No license is required to be a garden or landscape designer, and these green specialists come from a variety of educational backgrounds, including degrees in horticulture, study programs affiliated with arboretums and botanical gardens, degrees in sculpture, and other studio arts and lifetime experiences with plants and nurseries. Landscape architects, many of whom focus primarily on the hardscape aspects (hills, walls, paths, etc.) of garden design rather than on horticulture and maintenance, have degrees in the field and are licensed. There are organizations such as the Association of Professional Landscape Designers (APLD) that continually educate the landscaping field by offering classes and conferences. Although it is not necessary for the landscape architect or designer to be a member of such an organization, it certainly enhances their qualifications. All those drawn to the garden design profession, especially those devoted to the challenges of city landscapes, undoubtedly share the view of Thoreau, who wrote, "In wildness is the preservation of the world."

HERBACEOUS PLANTS FOR ALL-SEASON INTEREST

✧ **Asarum europaeum 'European Wild Ginger'** An excellent ground cover for the woodland garden. The heart-shaped leaves are glossy and dark green, and it is evergreen in most places. This is a very hardy and lovely woodland plant.

✧ **Helleborus orientalis 'Lenten Rose'** One of the finest early flowering plants in cultivation. The flowers begin in March and go through May. It also has semi-evergreen foliage and so it stays attractive during much of the winter. It needs to be cut back in early spring.

✧ **Liriope muscari 'Silvery Sunproof' 'Lily Turf'** A sturdy member of the Lily family, the Liriope also bears very attractive lavender flowers in the fall. It can grow almost anywhere and is very easy to establish.

✧ **Pennisetum alopecuroides 'Fountain Grass'** Great all-season grass. Has attractive flowers during the summer and fall. This grass has great winter interest. Very hardy, but can be slow to establish.

✧ **Sasa veitchii 'Low Bamboo'** Summer foliage is a solid green, and in the fall the leaf margins develop a tan-to-white border. The characteristic marginal stripe gives an attractive variegated appearance for outstanding winter foliage. It spreads slowly and grows well in the shade.

✧ **Vinca minor 'Ralph Shugert' 'Myrtle'** Very pretty low variegated ground cover whose purple flowers bloom in the spring.

Quality	Cost	Value	Recommend?
✚	$	◆	★

LANDSCAPE ARCHITECTS/DESIGNERS

🛍 FIRMS WITH ONLINE PORTFOLIOS* 🛍

Bonnie Billet—Horticulturists Inc. 🛍   4   4   4   4
571 8th Street, Brooklyn, NY 11215
(718) 788 - 2078
Classic urban landscape design and maintenance

Since 1981 this firm has been designing and maintaining urban gardens throughout Manhattan. Clients praise partners Bonnie Billet and Phil Schwartz for their "confidence, sensitivity, and sense of style." Billet is a graduate of the New York Botanical Garden's program. Schwartz, a former cartoonist, handles all the graphics and design of Billet's gardens, thus forming a strong and well-balanced partnership. Sources say that Billet's full-time team of three is knowledgeable, quick to respond, and a pleasure to work with.

With a flat design fee of $150 to $200 and hourly fee of $45 per hour plus materials, clients feel that the firm's prices are on par with its excellent service. We hear that Billet's hands-on attention and "exhilarating sense of color and design" keep clients coming back season after season.

"They are creative without being pretentious and seem to check their egos at the door." "As a team, Bonnie and Phil quickly assessed the challenges of the site and deftly managed to overcome its limitations with flair." "The enchanting scheme continues to thrive, as it is meticulously maintained by their well-managed, discreet, and efficient crew." "We are constantly amazed how Bonnie has influenced the evolution of our garden each year."

Canyon Antiques and Design 🛍   4   4   4   5
9 East 97th Street, Suite 6A, New York, NY 10029
(212) 722 - 5342   www.aniancientstone.com
Garden design and Turkish antiques

Fans say Canyon Antiques offers the most stunning Turkish marble stone garden containers in the city—and that principal Ani Antreasyan's love of gardening can clearly be seen in the firm's beautiful landscaped terraces. Although Antreasyan has only been in business since 1996, she has been fascinated with gardening since she was a little girl. Her love of ancient stone comes from accompanying her mother on archeological digs in Turkey.

Both satisfied customers and well-known interior decorators say Antreasyan and her team of three create "the most unusual and gorgeous" urban gardens and rooftop terraces in Manhattan. Her fees are calculated on a per-project basis and the firm designs and maintains its work. The work of Antreasyan has been published in *House & Garden, The New York Times, Hamptons Cottages & Gardens,* and *Quest.* KB 2000.

"Ani has brought her culture into our home and created a timeless style and grace that we admire every day." "Ani Antreasyan's garden design has brought the beauty and elegance of East Hampton gardens to the Upper East Side." "Ani has an incredible sense of design and she is a pleasure to work with."

	Quality	Cost	Value	Recommend?
	✚	$	◆	★

Garden Design by Dimitri

3.5   3.5   4   4

1992 Second Avenue, New York, NY 10029
(646) 672-0100   www.dimitrisgardencenter.com

Nursery and garden center, landscape design, and contracting

A family-owned and operated business for over 45 years, Garden Design by Dimitri carries a variety of products, including indoor and outdoor plants, trees, shrubs, soil, pottery, fertilizer, garden furniture, statuary, fountains, window boxes, baskets, and irrigation systems. Open seven days a week, the company also offers on-site landscape design, contracting services and ongoing maintenance. Customers say that the quality of service at Dimitri's is not affected by the fact that they are one of the largest garden centers in Manhattan. Due to the growing popularity, this firm opened a second location that is devoted entirely to the landscaping portion of its business.

The firm charges hourly anywhere from $75 and up, depending on the number of workers used for the project. Although prices are at the high end, customers rave that they always receive professional and personable customer service—and spectacular gardens—from Dimitri's.

"We have used Dimitri for three years and Dimitri and his team always give great advice regarding our rooftop garden." "My flowers always coordinate beautifully with one another. I don't know how they do it." "They showed me all of my options, and I knew exactly what to expect."

GardenWorks

4   3.5   4.5   4.5

265 Butler Street, Brooklyn, NY 11217
(212) 677 - 3920   gardenworks@gardenworksNYC.com

Landscape design, installation, and maintenance

According to industry experts, GardenWorks is a landscape design firm on the rise. The company is owned and operated by Brem Hyde, who has been designing, installing, and maintaining Manhattan landscapes for over a decade. Though Hyde and his small staff of six do it all, they especially like to work with grasses and full-flowering annuals. Hyde uses a variety of hardscape garden accessories in his creations, including rare hardwood containers and custom-designed pergolas. Clients are quick to say they discovered him first.

"Both a good person and a good gardener." "Outstanding." "Brem and his crews have been great to work with both in the downtown Manhattan area and at my homes in Oyster Bay and East Hampton."

Jane Gil Horticulture

4.5   3.5   5   5

290 Riverside Drive, Suite 15B, New York, NY 10025
(212) 316 - 6789   janeagil@aol.com

Superior landscape design, installation, and maintenance

Sources praise Jane Gil's talents as a horticulturist and designer, as well as her "top-notch" client care and attention to detail. Gil designs, creates, and maintains gardens and terraces for many illustrious residences in Riverdale and Manhattan, as well as Fairfield and Westchester counties. Clients say Gil oversees all aspects of garden creation and care, and—with her five-man crew—installs all plants, supervises tree maintenance, and takes care of irrigation and ground issues.

After working as a buyer for a prestigious Manhattan plant store, Gil began a two-year intensive horticulture program at the New York Botanical Garden. Accredited by the American Association of Botanic Garden and Arboretum, Gil recently won a grand prize from *Horticulture* magazine for one of her border designs. Thoughtful and patient, Gil is praised for readily accepting input from clients. Sources report that Gil does not limit herself to a single garden style, but rather uses her wide knowledge of plant material to create gardens specifically tailored to each individual client's tastes, while providing variety for her clients to enjoy throughout the four seasons. Prices are considered an incredible value.

"Charming personality and always listens to her clients' desires." "My terrace is radiant." "My experience with Jane has been fabulous in every way. She has worked for us responsibly, creatively, intelligently, and energetically for twenty years." "The most wonderful aspect of her work is the full, unending palette that's always changing." "Jane is great to work with and has incredible taste."

Janice Parker Landscape Design 　　4　3.5　4.5　5
52 Wakeman Hill Road, Sherman, CT 06784
(212) 929 - 6490　www.janiceparker.com
Landscape architecture and design

Janice Parker is roundly praised for being able to "read clients, then deliver a project that exceeds their expectations." Parker has been in the landscape business for over twenty years, but has kept her firm small: just three employees, including an in-house landscape architect. Devoted to her customers, Parker chooses her clientele carefully, establishing relationships that are able to evolve with her designs. We're told every project she completes "reflects the client" and is "unique, timeless, and utterly beautiful."

Educated at the Parsons School of Design and abroad in England, Parker now teaches classes at the New York Botanical Garden. Working primarily in Connecticut and Westchester, she also does a fair amount of work in New York City and as far away as Florida. The firm is also commended by peers for donating its design services to charities such as the New York Restoration Project.

"Janice Parker is a wonderful, creative, and professional designer." "Always responsive to our ideas and brought many more to us." "Incredibly knowledgeable and energetic." "I always found her bills very fair and understandable." "We've worked together twice and each time, I came away with a truly enviable project."

Judith Maniatis Garden Design 　　4　3.5　4.5　4.5
101 North 3rd Street, Brooklyn, NY 11211
(718) 782 - 5731
Terrace gardening—design, installation, and maintenance

Clients laud Judith Maniatis for pairing beautiful containers with coordinating plants in a wide range of colors and textures. Maniatis's company specializes in container gardening, particularly terrace gardening, in and around New York. Sources praise her use of exotic annuals, noting that she draws on an extremely wide plant vocabulary in creating her designs.

Maniatis and her staff of two install and maintain gardens throughout the city, providing "meticulous" maintenance with a friendly demeanor. The firm has also worked alongside top landscape architects, planting their designs. Clients describe her pricing as "a steal."

"Judith has an amazing ability to arrange the most stunning color combinations." "Tremendous sense of color." "I was impressed not only with her designs but I found her fees to be extremely reasonable." "Always cleans up afterwards." "She is a marvelous gardener. What will happen when the word gets out?" "I only hesitate to recommend her because I don't want to share her."

	Quality	Cost	Value	Recommend?
	✚	$	◆	★

KokoBo Plantscapes Ltd.

3.5 3 4.5 4

4 Fourth Avenue, Garden City Park, NY 11040
(516) 294 - 7308 www.kokobo.com

Residential and commercial landscape contracting

According to clients, Michael Madarash, owner of KokoBo Plantscapes, can do anything and everything when it comes to both interior and exterior plants. From full-size lawns in the country to small rooftop terraces, we hear that this firm is a solid choice for everyday landscape services.

Madarash worked for both his grandfather and father in the landscape industry before receiving his bachelor's degree in horticulture and turfgrass management from the University of Massachusetts. Madarash founded his firm in 2000, and now employs nine staffers, including a landscape architect. For good, consistent work that won't break the bank, clients say KokoBo is the firm to call.

"It looks great! The partners love it! Again, a real home run." "They willingly incorporated our ideas." "Nice fellow—hardworking, professional, flexible, and always calls back when I call him." "The client's satisfaction is his number-one priority." "Extremely patient with any concerns brought up by the homeowner." "They started with an incredibly overgrown 'vacant lot' that was my backyard and turned it into a beautiful, relaxing oasis." "They took real pride in their work and went beyond the original plans, making terrific changes on-site."

Mingo Design LLC

4 4 4 5

470 West End Avenue, Suite 7D, New York, NY 10024
(212) 580 - 8773 www.mingodesign.com

Landscape design, installation, and maintenance

Kari Katzander's 2004 Golden Trowel award only reinforces the client kudos she's been receiving for years. Offering brilliance on a budget, Mingo Design's Kari and Andrew Katzander (and their small team) design, install, and maintain a variety of gardens and grounds throughout the New York area. The "trustworthy" Katzander couple strives to "bring the outside in and the inside out" in their designs. Sources mention their commitment to designing with four seasons of interest and the terrific use of color.

Kari grew up working for her father's contracting company, restoring farms and farmhouses. After a confident fifteen-year run owning her own landscape maintenance and design company on Fishers Island, she brought her considerable practical construction and installation knowledge to the position of creative director at Mingo Design. Andrew's design and contracting resume includes stints at the New York Botanical Garden and the Pratt Institute. Costs are upper-end.

"Kari was able to take our firm's outside space and turn it into an extremely inviting environment for our clients to enjoy." "Whether it be the soothing sound of the water from the fountain stones, the bright color painted brick walls, or the creative use of plants in an extremely low maintenance garden, she continually surpassed our expectations." "Kari cared passionately about the design both in terms of the large concepts and the small details that make the project sing."

	Quality	Cost	Value	Recommend?
	✚	$	◆	★

Plant Fantasies Inc. ▪   3.5   3   4.5   4
224 West 29th Street, 7th Floor, New York, NY 10001
(212) 268 - 2886 www.plantfantasies.com

Interior and exterior landscape contracting and design; flowers

Plant Fantasies owner Teresa Carleo and her team of sixty have been landscaping around Manhattan since 1985. We hear Carleo handles everything from the design to the irrigation of her residential and commercial projects, including a number of penthouse and terrace landscapes. Sources report that the company does an especially fabulous job with Christmas decorations.

The self-taught Carleo began her career working for other landscape design firms. Clients say she is careful to use maintainable plants that complement the environment. The firm charges reasonable rates on a per-project basis and fair monthly maintenance fees.

"Teresa is great to work with because of her enthusiastic (but not overbearing) personality." "Not only is Teresa a gem, but everyone at the company is responsive to my needs."

Plant Specialists Inc. ▪   4   3.5   4.5   4.5
42-25 Vernon Boulevard, Long Island City, NY 11101
(718) 392 - 9404 www.plantspecialists.com

Indoor and outdoor garden design, installation, and maintenance

A large firm offering specialized attention? That's Plant Specialists, according to clients. Founded in 1973, Plant Specialists (owned by Philip Roche and Grahame Hubbard) is the only top-quality firm in New York that personally designs, implements, and maintains all aspects and areas of landscape design, from flooring and furniture to irrigation and decorative lighting systems. The team consists of over 50 talented landscape architects, designers, and horticulturists. In fact, over the years some of Manhattan's most talented gardening experts have worked for Plant Specialists before "graduating" to their own independent firms.

Though Plant Specialists provides a wide variety of services, including fresh floral contracts and firewood delivery, clients tell us a majority of the firm's work involves installation and maintenance of Manhattan rooftop gardens. We're told that decades of experience have contributed to the company's mastery in designing and implementing gardens. (New Zealand native Roche has nearly 25 years of experience in landscape design.) Projects are tailored to the location's existing conditions and the client's needs. Plant Specialists is so well-regarded that the firm regularly serves as contractor to other top-name landscape designers, installing gardens of its competitors' design. References praise the professionals at Plant Specialists for combining "ease with elegance." Most are frankly amazed by the firm's ability to do it all—and at modest rates.

"Always promptly returned my phone calls." "Amazing rooftop gardens." "With them, it's top-quality, one-stop shopping."

The Metropolitan Gardener ▪   4   3.5   4.5   4.5
344 West 23rd Street, Suite GLF, New York, NY 10011
(212) 675 - 7588

Landscape design, installation, and maintenance

Clients and peers highly recommend the knowledgeable and accommodating Karen Fausch, who studied horticulture and design at the New York Botanical Garden. As Fausch's expertise and experience grew, friends recommended her to other friends, and soon Fausch quit publishing her newsletter to concentrate on her burgeoning business. With the help of her small staff, Fausch designs, installs, and maintains gardens, primarily in Manhattan and Brooklyn.

While Fausch prefers "a little wilder style" in gardens, particularly in Manhattan, we're told she tailors her creations to suit each client's lifestyle, plant preferences, favorite colors, and home decor. We hear Fausch also serves as a general contractor on garden projects, enlisting and overseeing a small team consisting of a freelance irrigation specialist, carpenter, mason, and the like to create gardens that meet clients' specifications. References across the board are thrilled with Fausch's work and moderate pricing. Fausch is also the author of *The Window Box* Book, which is based on her teaching experiences with three- to five-year-olds at the New York Botanical Garden.

"So, so talented." "Her work is simply wonderful." "Intelligent, capable, gifted, and overall, the nicest woman."

The Window Box    **4.5   4.5   4   5**
217 East 27th Street, New York, NY 10016
(212) 686 - 5382   thewindowbox@yahoo.com
Top-notch landscape design, installation, and maintenance

Clients throughout Manhattan agree: Maggy Geiger is not only creative, but collaborative. Since 1975, Geiger has been offering clients suggestions that are "right on the mark" but "never imposing her view." Trained at the world-renowned Wave Hill gardens in the Bronx, Geiger has designed and installed gardens and greenery for a variety of elite clients, including the Carlyle Hotel and the late Richard Avedon. But prospective clients shouldn't be intimidated by Geiger's pedigree and work history; she doesn't restrict herself to big-name gardens.

As her firm's modest name indicates, Geiger will handle small projects, but her work varies in scope. She may do a set of front door planters, or an extensive rooftop or terrace garden. We're told Geiger also handles indoor plantscapes and floral arrangements. Geiger and her team take on around twenty new projects annually. The firm charges per project and is expensive, but sources say Geiger and Co. always work within budget. Geiger's designs have been featured in *The New York Times, New York* magazine, and *House & Garden.*

"Maggy is imaginative, reliable, collegial, and very service oriented." "She has turned a moderate-sized New York roof garden into an informal paradise." "Our building management has gotten calls from neighbors who can see our terrace and want to know who the landscaper is."

FIRMS WITHOUT ONLINE PORTFOLIOS

Barbara Britton   **4   3.5   4.5   5**
314 West 77th Street, New York, NY 10024
(212) 799 - 0711   bbritton212@earthlink.net
Garden design and consulting

Clients say that Barbara Britton is a real professional and a phenomenal independent garden designer. After designing, Britton will coordinate installations and maintenance. She tells us she enjoys working on ground-level and rooftop gardens for co-ops and other shared spaces "because they are, in a sense, public—even though they're private." Many comment on her considerable talent and experience, flexibility, lovely manner, and concern for clients. Britton works primarily in Manhattan.

Sources rave that Britton delivers great value and can help clients maximize a budget—if you need to keep costs down by purchasing and installing plants yourself, she will happily design and advise. Clients say that Barbara's hourly rate of $75 is a price that they would pay again and again without hesitation.

"Barbara has come through for me on a number of occasions." "She listens and then makes her suggestions. Very cooperative. I've felt as though I'm working as part

of a partnership." "Really a lady. Extremely polite." "I don't know where I would be without her. I can go away for weeks without worrying about this project." "Barbara is a true gardener's gardener."

Chelsea Garden Center Inc.   3.5   4   3.5   4

499 Tenth Avenue, New York, NY 10018
(212) 727 - 3434 www.chelseagardencenter.com

Nursery and garden center, landscape design, and contracting

In addition to offering a huge array of trees, shrubs, plants, fountains, furniture, and other accessories, clients report that Chelsea Garden Center provides a wide range of "green services," including landscape design and contracting, tree service, and general horticultural consulting. Owned and operated by David Protell, Chelsea Garden Center is one of the most widely recognized New York City nursery and gardening centers.

Though sources caution that Chelsea may be more expensive than most, we hear the garden center's agreeable staff, wide selection of unusual plants, and inside-Manhattan convenience make it worth the cost, particularly for less complicated jobs.

"They tend to be a little pricey, I think, but they have unusual plants and I have good luck with them." "Great company for smaller projects. They are happy to do just a few window boxes."

Cole Creates   5   4.5   4.5   5

41 King Street, New York, NY 10014
(212) 255 - 4797 www.colecreates.com

Superb container garden design, installation, and maintenance

Clients enthusiastically support Rebecca Cole's low-maintenance, naturalistic gardens. Drawing on her experience as a passionate gardener and antiques collector, Cole opened her much-publicized Greenwich Village store, originally named Potted Gardens, seven years ago. Cole designs, installs, and maintains rooftop and terrace container gardens around New York City; she also designs floral arrangements for festive events.

Using just about any primitive or antique container, from washtubs to watering cans, iron sinks to wooden boxes, Cole advocates an organic, wild effect. We hear that although carefully designed and planned, Cole's gardens often look as if they were planted by nature itself. Cole's services, however, cost a lot more than Mother Nature's. Cole has published two books on her carefree garden style—*Potted Gardens: A Fresh Approach to Container Gardening* and *Paradise Found: Gardening in Unlikely Places.*

"I recommend Rebecca to all of my friends. She is the greatest gardener I know." "She's a ball of energy and I envy her imagination." "Rebecca can make a beautiful garden out of a dirty rooftop."

	Quality	Cost	Value	Recommend?
	 +	$	◆	★

David Vaucher Garden Design & Care   4.5   3.5   4.5   4.5
185 West End Avenue, Suite 29P, New York, NY 10023
(212) 769 - 0724

Superior urban garden design, installation, and maintenance

Believing that it takes more than one season to have a successful garden, David Vaucher prefers working on projects where he will have long-term involvement. Sources comment that Vaucher's sensitivity and attention to detail is a combination that creates wild-looking, beautiful urban gardens. Because David Vaucher Garden Design & Care is a small company, we hear Vaucher is able to pay close attention to each client, developing ongoing relationships with his customers.

Vaucher, who hails from a family of avid gardeners, founded his company in 1992, but he has been in the landscape architecture profession since 1987. Clients say he likes to be on-site to oversee every step of the process, whether it's a city terrace or a country home. Vaucher charges a design fee that is based on the extent of the project as well as an hourly fee, but his costs are considered to be quite reasonable.

"David is serious, thoughtful, talented, and a delight to work with." "Simply the best!" "I now have the most beautiful rooftop garden in Manhattan." "I never had to worry that the project would not go well."

Deborah Nevins   5   4.5   4.5   5
270 Lafayette Street, Suite 1005, New York, NY 10012
(212) 925 - 1125

Specialized landscape design, installation, and maintenance

According to clients, Deborah Nevins's gardens are not only spectacular in the spring—they're stunning in the winter as well. The firm's close attention to the structural elements of rooftop terraces and gardens is one reason that sources call Nevins and her team "one of the best" in the industry.

Nevins's interest in gardens and horticulture began in childhood, and she founded her company in 1983. She personally visits the company's gardens, regardless of location, to oversee maintenance plans and procedures. Personalized service comes at a premium, but this small company of six is nevertheless in demand. Nevins has designed and installed gardens in New York and has been helicoptered in to work for clients in Chicago, Texas, and California. Interior designers and clients from all over the United States rank this firm at the top of the compost heap—a high honor in the world of horticulture.

"Great gardens for entertaining. She pays attention to how people actually use their gardens, as opposed to just what they look like." "Difficult to schedule, but when you get her, you're working with one of the best in the industry."

Distinctive Gardens   4.5   3   4.5   4
47 John Street, New Rochelle, NY 10805
(914) 576 - 7224   distinctivegard@optonline.net

Landscape design, installation, and maintenance

Sources say that although the talented Robert O'Keefe is "a young gardener who really knows his stuff," O'Keefe's excellent horticultural knowledge and strong design skills have already made a name for him among Manhattan landscape designers.

O'Keefe prides himself on designing, installing, and maintaining gardens that thrive in the city's harsh environment—not surprising for a man who studied Islamic courtyard gardens in Spain while pursuing his degree in horticulture. Though he admires and enjoys working in that style, he is not restricted to it in his design abilities and garden creations. "I design gardens that work within a client's space and are conducive to his or her lifestyle," O'Keefe says. Clients

	Quality	Cost	Value	Recommend?
	✚	$	◆	★

are more than satisfied with the results, praising O'Keefe and Distinctive Gardens for their careful work, attentive service, and attractive arrangements—all on a modest budget. O'Keefe sees clients by appointment only.

"Robert's vast knowledge of plants and flowers—coupled with a design eye to rival the best designers in Manhattan—makes him the best-kept secret in New York City." "Robert made the process entirely enjoyable, and the end result was magnificent." "Their work is beautiful, just beautiful." "If you have something specific in mind, Robert is willing to search the country to find the right plant or garden accent." "I recommend him without reservation."

Edmund Hollander Design   5   5   4   4.5

153 Waverly Place, 3rd Floor, New York, NY 10014
(212) 473 - 0620   www.hollanderdesign.com
Top-tier landscape architecture and environmental planning

Edmund Hollander and partner Maryanne Connelly have established one of the most prestigious landscape architecture firms in and around New York. Started in 1990, the company has offices in New York City and Sag Harbor and a staff that includes twelve landscape architects. Taking on around 40 projects at a time, the firm works in Manhattan, Greenwich, Bedford, the Hamptons, Virginia, and as far away as the Caribbean and the UK. The company specializes in residential and estate landscapes, historic landscapes, vineyard properties, swimming pool design, and horse farms.

We hear that Hollander and Connelly have an outstanding knowledge of architectural elements, and are capable of taking care of the smallest details in addition to the big picture. Hollander received a history degree from Vassar and holds a master's degree in landscape architecture from the University of Pennsylvania. Some of the finest architects in the business say that his work is unparalleled when it comes to both master planning and choosing sophisticated plants and materials. The firm's impressive projects have been published in *Architectural Digest, The New York Times,* and *House Beautiful,* to name a few. Although the company's projects start at around $250,000, architects insist that you will get a design that far exceeds your expectations.

"Ed is a great guy to work with." "They can design anything and everything." "All their projects are done with imagination and flair."

Elsa Williams   5   3.5   5   4.5

1364 Lexington Avenue, New York, NY 10128
(212) 348 - 2794   elsawill@nyc.rr.com
Premier landscape design, installation, and maintenance

Clients praise Elsa Williams for her great designs and patient personality. In her two decades of horticultural experience, Williams has earned a reputation for being thoughtful, knowledgeable, and responsible. Clients say that Williams' being a registered architect adds to her talent as a fabulous designer. Sources praise her great taste, flair with color, the way her "arrangements thrive despite the challenges of the city environment," and her extremely reasonable pricing.

Williams designs, installs, and maintains backyards, rooftop and terrace gardens, street trees, and planters throughout Manhattan. We're told that she listens well and tries to accommodate client preferences as much as possible. Sources report that Williams is very experienced and flexible regarding budgetary constraints, particularly with co-op boards. Clients say she knows "how to deal with any co-op board in a satisfactory manner, no matter how ridiculous the situation." Though some caution that Williams can be hard to reach, particularly in the busy season, they are quick to add that they highly recommend her.

"Great feel for Park Avenue—delivered the most amazing and distinguished pair of spiral cut trees for our front door." "Elsa has great taste and a flair for choosing

lovely bulbs." "Her pleasant countenance makes her easy to work with, especially in stressful situations." "Came back time after time to teach me how to properly water." "My window boxes are wonderfully color-coordinated thanks to Elsa." "She just gets it and delivers."

Estelle Irrigation Inc.　　　　4.5　3　4.5　5
262 West 26th Street, New York, NY 10001
(212) 243 - 7209
High-end garden irrigation systems and decorative garden lighting

Top Manhattan landscape designers call on the team at Estelle Irrigation to customize, install, and service irrigation systems for their clients' extensive gardens. Principal Declan Keane, a former school teacher who watered plants for other people in his spare time, launched the firm in 1990, and clients are grateful that he did.

Clients typically hire Estelle to keep their gardens watered during their escapes from the city. The vast majority of the firm's clients are in Manhattan. While Estelle is typically subcontracted by a landscape architect or designer, about one-fifth of its clients are private residents looking to purchase irrigation systems on their own. The company handles almost every kind of system, from micro-sprays and sprayheads to drip-irrigation, customizing each setup to the site requirements and the client's needs. Keane and his crew can also provide troubleshooting and regular system maintenance. Clients and other garden professionals praise the excellent and dependable service and the more-than-fair prices.

"They are clearly the best there is for irrigating your Manhattan garden." "Among landscape designers, everybody knows and uses him." "Low-key, good guy." "Due to Declan, I have the healthiest plants in Manhattan."

Glorietta Group　　　　　　4　3　4.5　4
720 Fort Washington Avenue, New York, NY 10040
(917) 202 - 1006　jjbrennan@nyc.rr.com
Landscape design, installation, and maintenance

Clients applaud J.J. Brennan's designs, noting how impressed they are with the personal attention he devotes to their gardens. Since 1996 Brennan has been designing, installing, and maintaining rooftop and terrace gardens for Glorietta Group. This designer prides himself on working with his clients to "bring their ideas to fruition."

Sources confirm that Brennan and his assistant "listen very well," "work hard to design and install beautiful, lush gardens," and "take care of everything." Despite the small size of the firm, Brennan has roughly twenty clients. Regularly praised by customers for producing high-quality work at a great price, Brennan charges a flat hourly rate of $45. We also hear Brennan will take the time to instruct clients in light garden maintenance, if they wish.

"J.J. is prompt, reasonably priced, and has an unbelievable imagination." "Gorgeous gardens." "He's really understanding." "He really takes care of the garden as if it were his own." "Very responsive to requests and pleasant to work with." "I liked his work, attitude, and service orientation so much that I hired him to service my business facility as well."

Grass Roots Garden　　　　4.5　4.5　4　4
20 Jay Street, Brooklyn, NY 11201
(718) 923 - 9069　http://homepage.mac.com/larrynathanson
Landscape design, installation, and maintenance

Larry Nathanson of Grass Roots Garden strives to create attractive gardens with plants that perform beautifully over time. It's a philosophy that comes from personal experience: In 1970, Nathanson bought a house in Brooklyn and enthusiastically began to fill the attached greenhouse with plants. His passion led him to study first at the NYU business school, then to independent research at the Brooklyn Botanic Library, and finally to open Grass Roots Garden. Today, Nathanson wins respect for his skill in designing, installing, and maintaining residential and commercial landscapes throughout the city. He has also completed major projects in the Caribbean.

Clients say Nathanson hand-selects the best plants from his growers and will sometimes avoid mapping every detail out on paper in order to leave himself "open to the possibilities" presented by the availability of unusual plants. He and his staff also maintain gardens, though not on a day-to-day basis. Sources comment on Nathanson's precision, commitment to quality, and artistic eye.

"A truly talented artist."

Halsted Welles Associates Inc.   4   3.5   4.5   4.5
287 East Houston Street, New York, NY 10002
(212) 777 - 5440
Landscape design, installation, and maintenance

Clients appreciate the way Halsted Welles Associates handles every aspect of garden design, including hardscape features like arbors and pergolas, garden lighting, irrigation systems, pools, fountains, and all plant design and installation. According to Welles, the firm's current passion is the design of gardens and garden processes that are ecologically sensitive, including water-nutrient recycling water tables to limit the need for irrigation and nontoxic pest control.

Halsted Welles is commended by customers for its ability to do it all when it comes to landscaping. The firm brings together engineering, architecture, horticulture, construction, and maintenance all under one roof. Welles, the owner and main designer, came to landscape design through a background in sculpture. Involved in "a little bit of everything," the firm also does fireplace planning, masonry, and metalwork, from ornamental iron to elaborate aluminum gazebos. The company boasts over 30 years of experience and a multi-talented crew of architects, horticulture designers, and artisans.

"Totally in-depth service—one stop shopping." "They were respectful of the fact that they were working in a co-op building and not a townhouse." "Amazing maintenance team." "I have great respect for Halsted and his company—they are extremely talented, reliable, and thorough."

Holly, Wood & Vine Ltd.   4   3.5   4.5   4.5
212 Forsyth Street, New York, NY 10002
(212) 529 - 7365 www.hollywoodandvinenyc.com
Landscape design, installation, and maintenance

Just like a Tinseltown agency, this pro firm provides excellent guidance, TLC, and plenty of client coddling. Industry leaders say that talented designers Peter Diffly and Bill Meyerson are owners of one of the hottest landscape firms in New York—designing, installing, and maintaining gardens for the city's elite. Customers rave that the firm's prices are a phenomenal deal. Diffly and Meyerson work with twelve employees, taking on thirty to forty new projects each year.

"I have used Peter and Bill for a number of years and they have never let me down." "Interesting, enaging people and interesting, engaging designs."

J. Mendoza Gardens Inc.   4   4   4   4
18 West 27th Street, 11th Floor, New York, NY 10001
(212) 686 - 6721 jmgincorp@att.net
Landscape design, installation, and maintenance

Happy customers report that Jeff Mendoza is fluent in numerous garden styles, from English to Japanese, and beyond. We're told that Mendoza draws on his sculptor's background, international travels, and extremely wide plant vocabulary to create artful manipulations of space, texture, and volume in his landscapes. Recognized as a "master" by his peers, Mendoza is known for his skillful color combinations. His solutions to the complicated problems of urban rooftop design are admired for their originality and beauty.

In business since 1987, his office designs, installs, and maintains gardens and grounds throughout New York and the Hamptons. In addition to their horticultural quality, Mendoza's designs boast custom architectural features such as arbors, fountains, screens, and trellises. References comment on Mendoza's professionalism, expertise, and calm demeanor. The firm's excellent service and unique designs make clients feel the upper-end prices are justified.

"I am in love with my galvanized metal flower boxes." "His passion for gardening is so inspiring." "A true artist."

Kevin Lambert   4.5   4   4.5   4.5
2025 Broadway, New York, NY 10023
(212) 877 - 2297

Quality terrace design, installation, and maintenance

Clients are impressed by Kevin Lambert's imaginative solutions to landscaping problems, especially when it comes to his "unbelievable" penthouse gardens. Over the years, Lambert's landscape business has narrowed its focus to terrace design and maintenance, working with a small circle of clients for years at a time. According to Lambert, the firm's designs concentrate on the seasons when his clients use their terraces most. Not surprisingly, Lambert is noted for flowery extravaganzas with vines, flowering tropical plants, and shrubs, with interesting containers.

Lambert has an extensive background in landscape architecture and has worked alongside many well-known landscape architects and floral designers. That experience comes at a premium that devotees happily pay, season after season.

"Kevin is expensive but no worse than anyone else." "He creates fabulous outside gardens, and also parties and Christmas decorations." "Imaginative solutions given with diligent care."

Landgarden Landscape Architects   4   3.5   4.5   4
215 Park Avenue South, New York, NY 10003
(212) 228 - 9500   landgarden@aol.com

Landscape architecture

We hear this firm's "fine designs" make strong use of rocks and plantings and demonstrate "true expertise." Since its founding in 1991, Landgarden, led by David Harris Engel, Dennis H. Piermont, and Michael Spitzer, has designed public and private projects throughout the United States and abroad, earning the respect of clients and peers alike. We're told the firm's design philosophy "to promote a partnership between the natural and the built environments" produces original and affordable landscapes.

"The final effect was magnificent." "Creative, innovative, and experienced designers." "They execute projects with great attention to detail and consideration for the client's desires and budget." "The projects were supervised from inception to completion." "Michael presented us with three different, complete plans. Each plan was magnificent—it was hard to choose the best one."

	Quality	Cost	Value	Recommend?
	+	**$**	**◆**	**★**

Laurel Hill Farms
4.5   4   4.5   5
2 Laurel Hill Drive, Valley Stream, NY 11581
(516) 791 - 5676   hortdiva@aol.com
Innovative landscape design, installation, and maintenance

We hear that Laurel Hill principal Sherry Santifer is consistently at the leading edge of new trends in landscape design. A specialist at forcing bulbs, Santifer uses the technique to create designs with a wide variety of textures and colors. Santifer has an impressive track record of designing, creating, and maintaining a wide variety of gardens in, around, and above the city streets. Her considerable talents and discreet service have garnered extensive recognition from the Philadelphia Flower Show and attracted a client list that includes members of the international elite.

Sources report that Santifer and her small staff of five provide the same level of excellence in customer care as they do in garden design. If clients wish to be involved in light garden maintenance, Santifer is more than happy to train them. If, however, clients want the garden oasis without the work, the Laurel Hill Farms crew will take care of absolutely everything. Clients could not be more pleased with Santifer and highly recommend her.

"Meticulous." "Great client coddling." "Very knowledgeable horticulturist and a very impressive person."

Madelyn Simon & Associates Inc.
3.5   3.5   4   4
510 West 34th Street, New York, NY 10001
(212) 629 - 7000   msaplants@aol.com
Landscape and plantscape design, installation, and maintenance

With a staff of 80-plus employees, Madelyn Simon & Associates (MS&A) provides a dizzying variety of "green services" to commercial and residential clients throughout Manhattan and beyond. MS&A offers fresh and silk flower arrangements, outdoor furniture and accessories, seasonal displays, and irrigation systems—plus complete landscape and interiorscape design, installation, and maintenance. Uniformed, experienced field personnel go to clients' homes for regularly scheduled maintenance. The firm's vaunted top-quality, ongoing garden care includes orchid and flowering plant rotations.

While references caution that they "do not have the same attachment to MS&A servicemen as close friends have with their personal landscape designers," they insist that MS&A does provide variety and interest in design, great plant and garden care, and extremely good value for the money. Clients also comment on MS&A's initiative, reporting that the staff "calls ahead to confirm regular appointments," "arrives on time," and leaves sites "neat and well-tended." The firm has received numerous awards from the Associated Landscape Contractors of America.

"They really take the initiative and call ahead to make appointments to come service my garden." "Madelyn Simon & Associates has made sure I've received a great deal of enjoyment from my garden over the years." "One tree in our garden died unexpectedly. They replaced it without charge."

Mary Riley Smith Landscape
& Garden Design
5   4.5   4.5   4.5
2211 Broadway, New York, NY 10024
(212) 496 - 2535   gardensmith@aol.com
Elite landscape design

References are "just thrilled" with Mary Riley Smith and her work. In New York City circles and beyond, Smith is considered among the best of the best in landscape design. Smith renovated and now oversees the prestigious Cooper

	Quality	Cost	Value	Recommend?
	✚	$	◆	★

Hewitt Museum garden, which is often called the best gallery garden space on Museum Mile. Smith is known for designing gardens with four seasons of interest and incorporating a wide variety of plants, from shrubs and evergreens to exotic annuals.

Smith also includes pots, urns, and trellises in her designs. While she often works in Greenwich, Bedford, and the Hamptons, approximately half of her jobs are in Manhattan. Smith's designs fall at the expensive end of the scale. She then contracts out (but oversees) all garden installation. She is happy to train her clients or their gardeners in maintenance techniques. Concerned by the number of poorly planned and underused front yards, Smith wrote *The Front Garden: New Approaches to Landscape Design* to suggest creative ways of making front gardens both decorative and functional. Her work has also been featured in *House Beautiful.*

"Mary made the beautiful planters that grace the front of my building." "Fabulous work. And she has great carpenters." "THE ONE."

Nadine C. Zamichow Inc.   4   3.5   4.5   4
205 East 69th Street, New York, NY 10021
(212) 517 - 9317
Landscape design, installation, and maintenance

Sources admire Nadine Zamichow for her flexibility, efficiency, and agreeable nature, which make it that much easier to tap into her horticultural talents. For the past 25 years she has designed, installed, and maintained gardens throughout Manhattan. If you've walked around Washington Square Park or New York University, you have probably admired Zamichow's handiwork; her largest longstanding client is NYU.

With a large base of private residences as well, Zamichow has long enjoyed designing and executing a variety of projects for a disparate client base. She does not restrict her work to big-budget projects or gardens of any particular size, but will "do anything in any style." Though Zamichow's services aren't cheap, clients rave that she is "great at sticking to a budget."

"Nadine is a good listener and is able to imagine what the client is thinking about— then plan and develop the idea into a wonderful reality." "Nadine is the only woman in the history of commerce who sticks to an estimate." "I look forward to her work every spring."

Patricia S. Ouderkirk Landscape Design   4   4   4   4.5
49 West 70th Street, Suite 3, New York, NY 10023
(212) 799 - 4870 okirk@optonline.net
Landscape garden design

Patricia Ouderkirk's clients say this established designer is detail-oriented and always listens to their needs. Ouderkirk has been designing gardens in the city and the Hamptons for over ten years. We hear her successful career took off after completing the program at the New York Botanical Garden. Now, clients and peers say that her special expertise lies in designing backyard gardens. While Ouderkirk subcontracts out the installation of projects, references say that she remains "hands-on" and involved through every stage.

"All phases of the design and installation were reviewed by me with Ms. Ouderkirk and our input was always considered." "What we got is a garden worth waiting for. She included many of our old favorites in the planting plan and also chose some new ones that we like very much but would have never thought of ourselves." "Patricia was imaginative, thoughtful, patient, and considerate of our budget." "A terrific value."

	Quality	Cost	Value	Recommend?
	✚	$	◆	★

Peter East   4   3   4.5   4.5

310 East 49th Street, Suite 11D, New York, NY 10017
(212) 832 - 2899

Terrace garden design, installation, and maintenance

Englishman Peter East has over 23 years' experience in designing and maintaining rooftop gardens and terraces throughout Manhattan. East, who caught the gardening bug while working on his own Manhattan terrace, is recognized among clients for his pleasant demeanor and congeniality. Fans say "working with him is a joy."

A graduate of Cambridge University, East holds a degree in Natural Sciences. Aside from designing and maintaining terrace gardens, East also sets up watering systems for the gardens and terraces. He works with his clients from start to finish, making weekly visits to keep the plants fresh. Customers say that by limiting his engagements to the city only, East manages to spend more time with each client. Despite the individualized attention that East offers, his prices are reported to be quite reasonable.

"Peter's arrangements on our private rooftop garden are balanced and interesting, combining privacy and openness." "Peter and his assistants are responsive, courteous, and always pleasant." "When it comes to aesthetic concept and design, Peter East is an absolute genius."

Roger Miller Gardens   4   4   4   4.5

771 West End Avenue, New York, NY 10025
(212) 662 - 6142   viburmum@interport.com

Rooftop and terrace garden design, installation, and maintenance

From shady first-floor patios to sunny rooftop container gardens, Roger Miller has been creating pleasing gardens in challenging sites for 25 years. Clients comment on Roger Miller's flexibility, attention to detail, charming personality, and strong ability to correct and respond to site problems through skilled design. With his staff of seven, he also serves as a contractor for others' designs.

Miller individualizes his designs from space to space and client to client, creating gardens that work well with their surroundings and his clients' tastes. We hear that Miller strives to design with a wide variety of plant materials from year to year so his clients can always experience something new and enjoy an assortment of greenery. Miller's clients applaud his painstaking efforts and enjoy his amusing sense of humor. Fans say his "respect for budgets" is a breath of fresh air.

"His design is wonderful. Despite the constraints of the space, he found ways to give me a lot of choice." "Roger is very willing and diligent." "I couldn't be happier. I have nothing negative to say about him." "His manner is lovely." "Very trustworthy and accessible." "He ALWAYS answers his cell phone." "Roger is terrific." "He's ethical, responsible—and he listens."

TLC Plant Care Service Inc.   3.5   3   4.5   4.5

410 East 6th Street, Suite 15H, New York, NY 10009
(212) 475 - 5399

Landscape and plantscape design, installation, and maintenance

TLC Plant Care Service is a small landscape design firm owned and operated by Peter Michael Rosenzweig, who has earned the respect of both the landscape industry and clients. A pro at both residential and commercial work, Rosenzweig designs, installs, and maintains both interior plantscapes and rooftop or terrace container gardens. He also sets up drip irrigation systems for his clients.

Rosenzweig got his start in the "green industry" in the 1970s working with various talented gardeners, including Larry Nathanson of Grass Roots Garden.

Since Rosenzweig established his own independent firm, he's never had to advertise, since all of his clients have come to him through word of mouth, impressed with the work he's done on their friends' gardens. Fees are considered moderate, especially given Rosenzweig's many years of experience.

"I trust Peter completely. He has been in the business so long and he really knows his stuff."

Tree Care Consultancy of New York Inc.   4   3   5   5
310 Park Place, Brooklyn, NY 11238
(718) 638 - 8733   treedocnyc@aol.com
Master arborist

Sources call Bruce McInnes of the Tree Care Consultancy of New York "The King of Trees." After working for a tree maintenance company in the 1970s, McInnes started his own firm in the 1980s when he grew tired of hearing "advice that was always tied to a buzzsaw." McInnes, a member of the American Society of Consulting Arborists, offers consultations on "trees and tree issues." Much of his work involves overseeing tree rescue projects.

McInnes, who is "available for any tree situation," also works with landscape architects or retail clients, advising on overall design or the installation of attractive site-appropriate trees. He will perform site analysis and set up proper tree maintenance programs for his clients. McInnes' claim, that he will "fix any tree situation," is more than backed up by satisfied clients.

"Reasonable rates, VERY reasonable, but don't tell him." "Bruce McInnes is incredibly knowledgeable. He works very hard to do the best work possible, be helpful, and act as a resource to his clients." "Goes out of his way to be excellent to people. I always recommend him." "Thumbs up. He's a fine man and certainly a qualified arborist." "Bruce is a pleasure to work with, a very easygoing man." "Nice guy. Fun to work with. Knows his stuff. Well-regarded in the business."

Urban Forest & Backyard Tree Care/
Bob Redman   4   3   5   4.5
41 West 82nd Street, New York, NY 10024
(212) 799 - 7926
Tree and shrub pruning and maintenance

Bob Redman's entry into the tree maintenance business is legendary in New York gardening circles. Defying authorities, Redman built twelve different tree houses in and around Central Park from 1978 to 1985. When police and park officials found a tree house and ripped it down, Redman would simply move on and build another in a different area of Central Park. Asked why he persisted despite threats from the law, Redman replied, "I like to be up in trees." When Redman was finally caught in his five-floor tree house in a beech tree off 78th Street, members of the Central Park Conservancy intervened to harness his unique talents.

After working with the park for several years, Redman began offering his services to private residences through his one-man firm, Urban Forest & Backyard Tree Care. Specializing in tree and shrub pruning, he serves clients exclusively in Manhattan. Sources comment favorably on Redman and his skilled work, noting his easy nature, the interest he takes in his work, and his "incredible tree talent."

"Bob is concerned about safety, aesthetics, and proper pruning techniques." "He is professional and very easy to work with." "Remarkable man."

Hiring a Millwork & Cabinetry Service Provider

In any renovation, millwork buttons up the newly pressed suit of your home. The integrity and artistry of Old World craftsmanship hasn't been lost on today's generation of woodworking professionals, who create cabinets, moldings, doors, mantels, staircases, and furniture. These service providers can tuck a plasma TV into the architectural details of a custom design/built library—or reproduce antique furniture.

Choosing a Millwork Firm

Not all millworkers are cut from the same piece of lumber. The right service provider must fit plumb with your project and personality. Some firms relish working directly with homeowners, taking an idea from concept to completion. Others are more comfortable realizing the defined plans of a designer or architect. In either case a millworker will produce detailed "shops," or working drawings for you to sign off on. Significant projects that involve the coordination of other trades (like electrical and plumbing for a serious kitchen remodel) or that involve complex structural elements (stairways) should always have a designer or contractor involved. In this case, finding a millwork firm that collaborates well with other design and construction professionals is essential.

Service providers range from individual craftsmen with a few helpers to large full-service woodworking firms with retail showrooms. Where you may get a more businesslike approach and greater capacity at a big firm, you may lose that artisan appeal and personal touch. Visit the shops of those firms you are considering. You'll not only get a good idea about the vibe of the place, but see the prod-uct being produced, whether by highly precise, computer-controlled (C&C) machines or by skillful hand and eye. Last but not least, check out the finished result and talk to references. You should be as concerned with the quality of the work—tight joints, pristine finishes, and plum doors and drawers—as with the style. Finally, consider the craftsman's style. Don't go with Mr. Euro-style sleek when you're looking for someone to hand-carve a built-in window seat at your Spanish hacienda.

Three Levels of Quality

Once you've determined the scope of your project, it is wise to determine the caliber of workmanship and quality of wood that is most appropriate for your needs. There are essentially three tiers of woodworking quality to choose from, each with its own standards for materials and craftsmanship.

Economy is the lowest grade of woodwork and may be chosen for projects that will not put a lot of demand on the structure or materials. For example, a built-in desk and shelving unit in a guest room that gets very little use could be constructed at the economy level. Although the work must be attractive, it need not be made from exotic wood or constructed with intricate joinery.

The next grade is custom woodwork, the level of craftsmanship most frequently requested. Custom woodwork ensures good quality wood and workmanship and is suitable for such popular projects as household cabinetry and moldings.

A beautiful kitchen makeover with glass-paneled cabinet doors and a new butcher-block island could be constructed using custom woodwork.

The highest grade is premium woodwork, top-of-the-line millwork that delivers the highest quality of craftsmanship, wood, and finishing. Premium jobs include outfitting an entire room with elaborately carved wall and ceiling panels made of top-grade wood, or building a grand staircase using imported wood and marble.

ON COST

Due to the specialized, diverse nature of the millwork business, there is no standard pricing structure. Most firms determine their fees based on the materials that are being used and the complexity and scope of the project, which is why it is important to collect several bids for your job. When requesting bids, it is also important to note whether or not the (often significant) cost of installation is included.

Some firms subcontract the installation process. Before you sign a contract, be sure that you know exactly who will install the work you ordered in its intended place in your home.

WHAT TO EXPECT FROM YOUR MILLWORK COMPANY

Your millworker should be as familiar with the actual installation space as he is with his client's lifestyle needs. A good millworker, like any service provider, should prove meticulous in the planning stages: asking questions, massaging the design, and triple-checking measurements—from the opening width for appliances in kitchen cabinets to the knee-height of a custom built desk for a taller client. You must also plan ahead, as lead times for fabrication and delivery are usually six to sixteen weeks.

The quality of any end product is only as good as the installation. However, not every firm installs or finishes what it fabricates. If the shop milling the pieces isn't the one assembling the puzzle, know who will be before you spill any ink on the contract, and qualify them as well. The same goes with finishing, a messy process that can effectively shut down the job site. A great deal of product comes pre-finished, however, so the dirty work is completed in a controlled environment off-site.

If the structure of your home will not be altered by your millwork project (as with replacement kitchen cabinets, for example), the job will not require a permit and can probably be done without a contractor or architect (if the millwork shop does detailed drawings). This work is very much a craft in the Old World sense, where skills are often passed down from master to apprentice. As such, there are no license or permit requirements for millwork firms, nor are there any trade associations through which millworkers are generally certified. Before you sign a work agreement, request proof of the company's insurance and warranty policies, which vary from firm to firm. If craftsmen will be working in your home, you'll want to be sure they are covered by the company's workmen's comp policy. You don't want to be held responsible for a misguided nail or toppled ladder.

MILLWORK MASTERY TIPS

✧ It's your millworker's duty to measure! If you do it yourself and give him the dimensions, you're only asking for trouble.

✧ Plan the electrical and plumbing layout meticulously or you may have to rip up fine work, send it to the scrap heap, and pay to have it redone.

✧ Don't install millwork too early in a renovation project. Your millworker should be the last person in so that other workers won't scratch your beautiful new wood finish.

✧ Hire excellent professionals for the entire renovation. Millworkers must have a level surface on which to work, and shoddy workmanship from carpenters, drywall, or plastic contractors will haunt the millwork

✧ Remember to design backing structures where necessary. You don't want a cabinet that will store heavy cookware fastened to a mere half-inch of drywall.

✧ Don't be afraid to reject a panel or piece of molding that doesn't match the quality of its brothers and sisters.

Millwork & Cabinetry

Anglo-Inscape 💼
2472 Broadway, Suite 368, New York, NY 10024
(212) 924 - 2883   www.angloinscape.com
Superior custom furniture with high-end finishes

See Anglo-Inscape's full report under the heading Furniture Repair & Refinishing

Breakfast Woodworks 💼   5   4.5   4.5   5
135 Leetes Island Road, Guilford, CT 06437
(203) 458 - 8888   www.breakfastwoodworks.com
Versatile, high-end custom millwork and cabinetry

From the sleek, cutting-edge designs of modernism to the elaborate and exquisite details of classical design, Breakfast Woodworks can make them all—and make them effortlessly, at that. With respected architect Louis Mackall and master craftsman Ken Field at the reins of Breakfast, the company produces cabinets, moldings, and doors, along with individual pieces and wall units.

The two principals met in 1976, when Mackall, an architecture graduate of Yale, who was running a flourishing cabinetry business in his free time, decided he needed a partner. Enter Ken Field, a Cornell graduate and "genius woodworker." The two formally established Breakfast Woodworks in 1978. Today the firm serves both the homeowner and the trade, with commissions in New York City, Connecticut, Long Island, and Aspen.

Combining high technology with age-old craftsmanship and a strong architectural background to boot, this duo is so good that partial clients insist they "will use no other." While the rest of the millworking world was boasting about using CNC routers and software that generates two-dimensional specs, the team at Breakfast pushed the envelope further by acquiring the German innovation Kuka—a "six-axes" robot that can maneuver its articulated arm and can carve out complex geometry in wood, plastic, or metal, thus producing amazing three-dimensional results.

This six-man firm has been commissioned to produce everything from intricate screens for a Sikh temple in Arizona to exquisite woodwork for the late John Denver in Aspen. In New York City, its commissions include sleek and seamless moldings for a Rothchild's apartment and the "railroad-style" benches at The Metropolitan Museum of Art. Projects run the gamut from $20,000 to $400,000 and everything is "absolutely custom-made" in the firm's 10,000 square foot workshop. Its work has been featured in *Architectural Digest* and *Vogue Men*. Breakfast Woodworks is a member of the American Woodworking Institute.

"Exceptional quality, beyond our wildest dreams." "Louis Mackall took a napkin sketch and turned it into a collective dream, adding value in the conceptualization and execution where we didn't know it existed." "I am an avid promoter of his work." "They solve problems with 'outside-the-box' solutions."

*We invite you to visit www.franklinreport.com to view images of their work.

Quality	Cost	Value	Recommend?
✚	$	◆	★

Cabinet Fair Inc.

241 37th Street, Brooklyn, NY 11232
(718) 369 - 1402 www.cabinetfair.com

High-end custom kitchen cabinetry, bathroom vanities, and wall units

See Cabinet Fair Inc.'s full report under the heading Kitchen & Bath Design

Chelsea Fine Custom Kitchens Inc.

325 West 16th Street, New York, NY 10011
(212) 243 - 5020 www.chelseakitchens.com

Kitchen and bathroom renovations; custom cabinetry and decks

See Chelsea Fine Custom Kitchens Inc.'s full report under the heading Kitchen & Bath Design

Crowned Woodworks   4   3.5   4.5   5

281 Greene Avenue, Brooklyn, NY 11238
(718) 636 - 4402 www.crownedwoodworks.com

Custom cabinetry, molding, and doors; bathroom renovations

Crowned Woodworks' principal, Steven DeSouza, draws rave reviews for being honest and dedicated. Clients say he really cares about customer service and is completely devoid of attitude or greed. One client reports that the job turned out to be smaller than DeSouza originally estimated, so he gave her a refund. He is unanimously reputed to be communicative, accessible, and thorough.

Insiders call DeSouza a skilled craftsman and intelligent problem solver, adding that Crowned Woodworks' excellent quality comes at a solid, competitive price. The company specializes in cabinetry, detailed molding work, and custom doors, but is also known to renovate bathrooms, including tile and marble work.

Established in 1989 by DeSouza, a third-generation contractor and carpenter from Trinidad, today the firm's five-man team works mainly in New York City and Connecticut. Sources say Crowned Woodworks typically works with decorators and architects, but will work with private clients, too. Projects run anywhere from $5,000 to $300,000, with individual pieces and units starting at $800. Crowned Woodworks' projects have been featured in *Interior Design* magazine and British *Vogue*.

"He really cares about the client—he's a gem!" "Half the cost, twice the quality." "Without hesitation, he's terrific." "Steve was a dream!" "His work is flawless." "He has a vision for the best possible look, and everything he said was absolutely true."

Culin & Colella Inc.   3.5   3   4.5   4

632 Center Avenue, Mamaroneck, NY 10543
(914) 698 - 7727 www.culincolella.com

Custom millwork and furniture

The excellent husband-wife team of Ray Culin and Janis Colella heads up this ten-person staff, keeping it small to maintain control of the firm's high standards.

	Quality	Cost	Value	Recommend?
	+	$	◆	★

Clients praise Culin and Colella's unquestionable quality and one-of-a-kind furniture designs. Insiders say the firm will work under architects and designers but prefers to work closely with the client to ensure satisfaction. We hear Culin and Colella can incorporate any kind of drawer, slide, or finish imaginable. Reliable and attentive, the firm can wow even the most demanding client with its finishes.

"They are fabulous, top quality." "Nice and decent people. Really want to do a good job." "Outstanding quality, workers, and execution." "The work they did is the highlight of our house." "Janis is an artist with her finishes." "So patient. They did a wine cellar that looks like a cave."

Eagle Custom Furniture    4   4   4   4.5
977 6th Avenue, New York, NY 10018
(212) 736 - 2394 www.eaglecustomfurniture.com
Custom millwork and furniture

For millwork fabrication and on-the-job installation, Eagle delivers dependable, committed service at a reasonable cost. This woodworker is both accommodating and flexible, and "takes the time to make improvements on the margins of design." Clients praise Eagle's employees as "real people with heart," who take responsibility for their work.

Established in 1976 by Bill Lagos, the firm works with architects, designers, and the public. The eight-man firm does whole rooms as well as free-standing furniture. Capable of handling $200,000 jobs, the company will not turn its nose up at smaller projects—even if it is just one desk—because "a small thing always leads to bigger things." This family business is now helmed by Bill's daughter Maria and her husband Vasilios. Though most of its work is in Manhattan, the team at Eagle Custom has also been commissioned to do work in New Jersey, Long Island, and Florida. The firm's work has been featured in publications like *Architectural Digest* and *Interior Design* magazine.

"As good a quality as I can discern with my own eyes." "I changed my shoe rack three times without a feather ruffled." "Great for mid-market to upscale millworking jobs." "They really worked hard to do the right thing." "Hard to reach, but excellent work."

Eisenhardt Mills   4.5   4.5   4   5
1510 Richmond Road, Easton, PA 18040
(610) 253 - 2792 dlockard@eisenhardtmills.com
Premium architectural millwork; traditional and classical revival specialists

Considered by many as "the standard" for premium millwork, Eisenhardt Mills, founded in 1937, is a third-generation family business. Eisenhardt Mills works primarily, but not exclusively, in traditional styles and classical revival themes based on architectural or interior designs. The company draws praise for its work in historic preservation, including Independence Hall in Philadelphia, and the prestigious Secretary of State and Deputy Secretary of State offices in Washington, DC, featured in *Antiques* magazine. Some of the firm's work has also been featured in *Architectural Digest*.

Clients praise principal Don Lockard's dedication to meeting their needs. Sources say that Eisenhardt's top-quality work does not include hand-rubbed finishes or ornate carvings, but that the firm collaborates with vendors who can provide those services. Insiders say that Eisenhardt's prices are comparable to other high-end firms, but the superior shop drawings, follow-through, and dependability Eisenhardt offers make it a better value. Typical rooms are in the $25,000 to $500,000 realm. Sources also compliment the firm for meeting very aggressive deadlines without a problem. Given the precious nature of its cargo and its stellar reputation, insiders call Eisenhardt an exemplary firm.

"They're totally on target." "Eisenhardt is superb, with a long tradition of exceptional service, and Don can handle very complex projects." "Lockard is personable and helpful." "We had the occasional miscommunication during installation, but still, I would definitely hire them again." "Exceptional in every way. The end result was truly amazing." "He does exactly what he sets out to do; there are no surprises."

Heights Woodworking Co. ▉   3.5   3.5   4   4
411 Third Avenue, Brooklyn, NY 11215
(718) 875 - 7497 www.heightswood.com

Custom interior millwork

Amor Villar, Jr., principal of Heights Woodworking, is a second generation woodworker. Heights was founded in 1957 by his father Amor Sr., a Spanish cabinetmaker who fought in the Spanish Civil War. This twenty-man firm keeps busy creating high-end residential moldings, doorways, entryways, windows, bookcases, and interiors. Clients say the versatile Villar will work in formica and will even make tables out of stone, and his diverse skill set allows him to work equally well in a wide variety of styles. Heights boasts a 9,000 square foot factory, a second building which houses its storage, and a third building which holds its showroom.

Villar is known for doing quality work in a timely manner. The firm works in New York City, Westchester, New Jersey, Connecticut, Boston, Chicago, Washington, and Atlanta. Typical room projects are in the $30,000 to $350,000 realm, large individual units run from $10,000, and smaller pieces start at $4,000. In addition to its bread-and-butter jobs for clients and contractors, Heights Woodworking recently participated in the Madison Avenue Presbyterian Church restoration project. The firm works with the trade as well as with homeowners.

"He always delivers with no problem—and at a great price." "Fast turnaround times with excellent results." "Although a big company, you won't get lost in the crowd."

Jacob Froehlich Cabinet Works ▉   5   4.5   4.5   5
550-560 Barry Street, Bronx, NY 10474
(718) 893 - 1300 jhanington@jfroehlich.com

Superlative millwork, staining, and varnishing

Clients speak admiringly of Jacob Froehlich Cabinet Works, noting the firm's exceptional thoroughness. The company's skills in using stains and varnishes are reputed to be top in the field. Established in 1865 by German woodworker, Jacob Froehlich, the company is now helmed by brother and sister Kristin and James Hanington, whose father bought the company in the 1980s. The firm services clients in New York and lower Westchester, but will only deal with a project if there is an architect or contractor involved.

Insiders say Jacob Froehlich Cabinet Works distinguishes itself by its excellent architectural department, which starts with a conceptual approach, provides fine shop drawings, and follows through with flawless execution and installation. Famous for their doors, this 45-man team also builds libraries, kitchens, closets, and dressing rooms—besides creating moldings, lifts, and other architectural details. Though veering towards the traditonal design aesthetic, the firm can also create woodwork to suit a modern interior. Typical projects can start at $200,000 to $1,000,000. The company has its own veneer department where any type of stain—from standard to exotic—can be achieved. It is a member of the Architectural Woodworkers Institute and the New York State Department of Economic Development.

Jacob Froehlich Cabinet Works draws accolades for its management capabilities and extremely organized team. Everything is itemized and broken down, so the budget is never an issue, nor are timetables. Professionals call the company extremely accommodating and flexible and its excellent shop drawings ensure no surprises. Its work has been featured in *Architectural Digest, Traditional Building Magazine,* and *Trends Magazine.*

"They're so communicative and articulate that there are never any problems." "We have worked with Froehlich for twenty years and have tremendous respect for the workers' ability to prioritize and coordinate work in the shop and to produce stellar quality work." "Very sophisticated and familiar with the top-end work of architects and designers." "They're excellent, top of the line—the Rolls-Royce of millworking. They can handle anything—totally unflappable."

Juliano Interior Millwork   5   4   5   4.5
223 80th Street, Suite A, Brooklyn, NY 11209
(877) 585 - 4900 www.julianomillwork.com
Superb custom cabinetry and millwork

The "fabulous" work produced by this company draws raves from all their clients. Juliano Generale specializes in coffered ceilings, libraries, raised panels, decorative architectural ornaments and mantels, and on occasion, even custom furniture. With 36 years of experience, Generale works for top architects and contractors all over the country and is particularly respected for his magnificent moldings.

Born in Egypt, Generale studied carpentry and woodworking in Alexandria at the tender age of twelve. At eighteen, he travelled to 24 European countries, working and honing his skills as a woodworker. In 1993, he came to America and established his business. Prices range from $80,000 to $300,000 for full rooms. Individual pieces run from $3,000 and up. The firm has twenty employees and serves New York, Florida, California, Connecticut, and Westchester.

Sources describe this craftsman as charming, funny—and completely honest. One trade insider reports that Generale saved a Park Avenue job from disaster after a series of contracting mistakes. We're told Generale works accurately and ably in any style, and is reliable, conscientious, timely, and accommodating.

"Juliano is more skilled than most of the architects and designers that I have met. He saved and embellished my house." "There isn't a subcontractor who can compare to the effort, timeliness, ideas, and end result." "Brilliant artisan."

Sonrise Woodcarving Studio   4.5   4   4.5   5
PO Box 12, Cottekill, NY 12419
(845) 687 - 9139 www.sonrisewoodcarving.com
Refined Old World and American woodcarving/woodworking

The self-taught Stephan Toman has been carving since 1985, creating millwork, furniture, and sculptures in both Old World and American traditions. Sources call him a kind man with a strong work ethic and high level of integrity. Insiders say Toman's respect for the craft and disregard for the bottom line means he won't rush a job if it will compromise the quality, even if that means turning down work. However, we hear Toman meets all reasonable deadlines.

Toman's decorative carving is visible on his website, and we hear he'll also do replication, repair, and restoration. Though he doesn't have formal training in historic or artistic styles, his "great eye" and brilliant craftsmanship enable him to

complete the most meticulous jobs. Toman works through architects, contractors, or directly for the client. Insiders say that while his intricate carvings are truly special, Toman also excels in interior millwork.

"Stephan's work is totally unique, all hand-done—he is truly an artist." "A guy like Stephan is one in a million—it took me forever to find someone who can do that kind of work." "There are very few people in the country who can do the intricate work that Stephan does."

Tribeca Cabinetry Corp.    4   4   4   4.5
1477 Third Avenue, Suite 2, New York, NY 10028
(212) 517 - 7023 www.tribecacabinetry.com
Custom cabinetry and millwork

Although established as an offshoot of big sister The Renovated Home, the progressive, tech-savvy Tribeca Cabinetry has now carved out its own niche in the millworking industry. The firm has been making cabinets for The Renovated Home since 1985 and was officially established as an independent company in 2000. Although frequently commissioned to create their "1930s inset kitchens," the company can produce beautiful, functional kitchens in any design aesthetic with a shorter turnaround time than most firms. At the heart of Tribeca's ability to offer fast lead times is CNC technology and its unique design software, which can design and cut pieces in as little as fifteen minutes—shaving as much as four weeks off the delivery date.

Pricipal Lee Stahl, the mastermind behind Tribeca's success, takes on about 50 to 75 projects a year. Typical projects are in the $75,000 to $200,000 realm, with commissions in New York City, Boston, Pennsylvania, Montauk, and Washington. The firm also donates 1% of a project's gross sales to any one of four charities—client's choice. To stand behind the firm's delivery guarantee, Stahl offers a $250 per week refund if not delivered on the promised date. Tribeca Cabinetry's work has been featured on Fine Living TV, Sheila Bridges Design Living, and HGTV, and in the *New York Times*.

"Beautiful kitchens and excellent turnaround times." "Stahl and his team are like a well-oiled machine. The whole process went from beginning to end without a hitch." "Visited their showroom and had the sense that they didn't want to bother with such a modest project." "Will recommend again and again."

FIRMS WITHOUT ONLINE PORTFOLIOS

Budd Woodwork Inc.   4.5   4.5   4   4.5
54 Franklin Street, Brooklyn, NY 11222
(718) 389 - 1110
Exquisite classical millwork and historic restoration; French specialists

Budd Woodwork is in the business of "providing luxury," and clients tell us they wish they could work with this masterful company "365 days a year." The firm's high-end historic restoration, replication, and preservation work includes such upscale jobs as the Louis XIV Room at the Met and the Venetian Room for the French Embassy. Insiders say Budd Woodwork Inc. specializes in a classic French style, especially Louis XV and Louis XVI, and caters to a sophisticated and exclusive clientele. The team at Budd Woodwork are dedicated to installing and replicating antique rooms—preferring to work strictly on historical and classical architecture.

Founded in 1952 by Serafin Caamano, Sr., the company is now helmed by his son, Serafin Jr., who is a fifth generation cabinetmaker. With a full-time staff of eighteen—from cabinetmakers to installers—work is "never subcontracted."

Budd Woodwork works only through architects and decorators, who describe its skilled craftsmen as "humble" and "polite." The firm takes on a limited number of jobs each year, since it only deals in the finest materials and architecture.

The company's intricate woodwork can be seen in high-end interiors in New York City, Palm Beach, and California. Pricing is per project and ranges from $200,000 to $500,000 per room. Budd Woodwork received the New York Landmarks Conservancy Award in 1998 and is a member of the Institute of Classical Architecture. The firm's work has been featured in *The New York Times* and *Architectural Digest*.

"They are impeccable, courteous, quiet, and punctual. No detail is overlooked." "Experts all the way." "Very principled about maintaining the highest level of consistent quality."

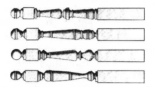

Building Block   4   3.5   4.5   4.5
80 39th Street, Brooklyn, NY 11232
(212) 714 - 9333 www.thebuildingblocknyc.com
Trade only—custom doors, paneling, and molding

Clients describe Building Block's founder, the now-retired Noah Block, as an "honorable businessman" with a "genuine love for the work." Fortunately the 22-person firm is now helmed by John Raczynski and Bob Sherman, two chips off the old Block. They uphold Building Block's reputation for quality full-service millworking and woodworking.

Well known for its custom doors, the team at Building Block is also adept at creating cabinets, lifts, bars, and moldings. Though it works only with hardwood, the company works with all types, from standard oaks and maples to the more complicated mahoganies and exotics. All work is as per shop drawing, produced by Building Block for customer approval before the start of production. Customer ideas and requirements are accommodated, and custom tooling is manufactured in-house.

Building Block's attention to detail and solid reputation have kept the firm in business for more than 36 years, with work featured in places like the Guggenheim, the Whitney, Tavern on the Green, The Frick Collection, the Bandshell in Central Park, Elaine's restaurant, the federal courthouse in Harlem, and the famous bar at The Knickerbocker Club, not to mention a number of celebrities' homes. Although most work is done through contractors, private clients are also accepted.

"Delightful to work with, just sensational." "We love these guys. Would highly recommend their excellent work." "Solid prices for excellent results." "No issues about doing smaller jobs."

Bulthaup
578 Broadway, Suite 306, New York, NY 10012
(212) 966 - 7183 www.bulthaup.com
Sleek, minimalist, contemporary German cabinetry

See Bulthaup's full report under the heading Kitchen & Bath Design

	Quality	Cost	Value	Recommend?
	✚	$	◆	★

Catskill Woodworking
4   4.5   3.5   5

11 Field Court, Kingston, NY 12401
(845) 339 - 8029 www.catskillfurniture.com

Custom millwork and furniture

Catskill's got skills, according to the loyal fans who praise Robert Allen's "excellent craftsmanship" and "attention to detail." Allen is reputed to have a pleasant personality and a talent for solving millwork problems. Trade insiders maintain an ongoing relationship with Catskill Woodworking, which they say offers high quality with relatively quick turnaround times. Sources note that Catskill works primarily with architects and contractors, not directly with the client.

The firm was established in 1991 by Robert Allen, a self-taught woodworker. With 23 employees, the firm works with all types of wood and exotics and fabricates all types of custom woodwork in their 40,000 square foot workshop. Catskill produces doors, moldings, cabinets, wall units, vanities, pool tables, and trims, while installation is subcontracted. Average projects run the gamut from $50,000 to $1,000,000 with individual pieces ranging from $15,000 to $100,000. The firm's commissions are mainly in Manhattan, with some in Connecticut and Long Island. Catskill has been featured in *Architectural Digest*.

"Not every millworker is ready to throw himself into the job when the contractor is ready. Bob is always ready with the ultimate solution." "Excellent people, excellent work."

Christopher Peacock Cabinetry

34 East Putnam Avenue, Greenwich, CT 06830
(203) 388 - 4100 www.peacockcabinetry.com

Highly detailed custom cabinetry

See Christopher Peacock Cabinetry's full report under the heading Kitchen & Bath Design

Craz Woodworking Associates
4.5   4   4.5   4.5

86 Horseblock Road, Suite A, Yaphank, NY 11980
(631) 205 - 1890 www.crazwoodworking.com

Exceptional high-end woodworking and casework

Clients go Craz-y for this Long Island-based woodworker's "great ideas and great eye." A favorite resource among top-tier trade professionals, Craz's projects range from a $2,000 side-table to $400,000 casework packages. Sources say this small firm is involved from materials selection to finish, showering its clients with attention. In turn, its Manhattan, Hamptons, and lower Westchester/Fairfield clients shower Craz Woodworking with praise.

Owner Peter Craz gained a degree in economics and studio art before teaching industrial arts in the Peace Corps in Korea. Upon his return, he embarked on his woodworking career, opening the shop in 1983. Craz plays a hand in every project, assisted by a select in-house team and longstanding network of relationships with the area's best finishers and installers. Noteworthy millwork projects include ones for the New York Yacht Club, the New York Bar Association, the Seamen's Church Institute, and the Metropolitan Museum Gift Shop, to name a few. The eleven-man crew at Craz is adept at both modern and classical architecture and will also do freestanding furniture aside from the standard moldings and panelings. The firm's work has been seen in *Architectural Digest*, *Architectural Record*, and *House & Garden Magazine*.

"I would only recommend Peter Craz because I know there will be no complaints from my very particular clients." "Peter has a good eye for design and chooses natural woods very well."

	Quality	Cost	Value	Recommend?
	✚	$	◆	★

Custom Cabinets Plus
3.5 3 4.5 4.5

34 Bergen Street, Paterson, NJ 07522
(973) 790 - 9960
Custom millwork and cabinets

Clients say this "very easy to work with" New Jersey-based mill shop delivers from concept to completion, thanks to owner Matthew Di Gioia's devotion. Custom Cabinets Plus crafts, installs, and finishes woodwork and cabinet projects of all sizes, working in high-end and exotic materials and reproducing old-fashioned finishes. Catering primarily to homeowners in Manhattan, Westchester, Fairfield, and New Jersey, the firm can also assist with design.

Di Gioia, who has a civil engineering background, established the firm in 1993. He oversees eight employees and plays point man for every job. We hear it's Di Gioia's personal attention that—as much as the well-crafted product—puts the plus in this custom shop.

"Outstanding service. You always get personal attention with any problems or concerns." "Matt is very accessible, even after the project is completed."

Danese Design
3.5 3.5 4 4

413 Sackett Street, Brooklyn, NY 11231
(718) 855 - 2311 danesedesign@gmail.com
Custom millwork design, consulting, and installation

Formerly the design guru at Elli New York Design, Carlo Danese has established an independent design consulting and supervision service for custom millwork and smaller apartment renovations. Danese combines his experience at architecture firms with his hands-on knowledge of lighting and carpentry to manage the interface between millwork and the other trades. Clients say he's "very talented," "dependable," and "easy to talk to."

Danese, who established the firm in 1989, serves New York City and has also done projects in upstate New York, Los Angeles, and Connecticut. Though the actual millworking is subcontracted, the whole process—from consultation, to designing, to the final installation—is supervised and orchestrated by Danese himself. Often called in for whole kitchen renovations, the company also does free-standing furniture and is popular for its wall units. Average room renovations are in the realm of $60,000 to $100,000, while wall units and cabinets can run anywhere from $8,000 to $30,000. The firm takes on around six to twelve projects a year.

"I highly recommend him." "Carlo absolutely came through with beautiful work." "Carlo was excellent through and through; unfortunately, one of his subcontractors wasn't up to par." "He had a high aesthetic sense and met my husband's rather stringent demands for millwork."

East End Woodstrippers Inc.
4 3.5 4.5 4.5

27 Glenmere Way, Holbrook, NY 11741
(631) 472 - 5206 www.refinishny.com
Woodwork refinishing and restoration; historical restoration specialists

This long-standing firm specializes in the stripping, refinishing, and refurbishment of old woodwork, doors, stairways, window casings, shutters, cabinets, and furniture. It also finishes new installations. Most of East End's work is performed on-site for a residential clientele concentrated in Manhattan and Brooklyn. The company teams with architects, decorators, and contractors—as well as with homeowners—on projects ranging from a fireplace mantel to larger jobs, often $20,000 to $50,000.

Owner Dean Camenares brings over twenty years' experience to this family business, established in 1959 by his father-in-law. The firm's furniture restoration roots can be seen in its mostly hand-done end product. We hear Camenares's goal is to achieve the look of old wood that has been well-cared for. Clients say his company's strength is its small size—only seven people—which gives Camenares complete oversight of the details. The only drawback can be the difficulty of scheduling projects during busier times.

Basic refinishing is $400 to $500 per door and $200 and up for basic window, shutter, casing, and sash refinishing. Recent projects include the New York Stock Exchange Lunching Club, the Old Customs House, and the Appellate Courthouse in Hartford, to name a few. Sources attest Camenares sticks to the client's budget—and his own estimate.

"Dean is thoughtful and careful to record all details." "They definitely knew what they were doing." "It wasn't cheap, but when I saw the effort and the result, I felt that the price was reasonable." "They were on time, and respectful of my belongings and of the house." "Very cooperative." "Dean is very good at what he does. A very patient man."

Englander Millwork
2369 Lorillard Place, Bronx, NY 10458
(718) 364 - 4240
Windows and doors, millwork, historical replication

See Englander Millwork's full report under the heading Windows & Doors

Enjo Architectural Millwork
16 Park Avenue, Staten Island, NY 10302
(718) 447 - 5220   www.enjo.com
Architectural millwork; restoration of windows and doors to landmark standards

See Enjo Architectural Millwork's full report under the heading Windows & Doors

European Woodworking   4 3 4.5 4.5
167 Saw Mill River Road, Yonkers, NY 10701
(914) 969 - 5724
Artisanal architectural millwork

Loyal clients applaud Joe Lo Nigro, who heads European Woodworking's small shop of three for clients in Westchester, Fairfield, and New York City. A fourth-generation millworker, Lo Nigro trained under his father, who trained under his grandfather. Sources hold Lo Nigro in esteem for his delightful personality, humility, and strong sense of responsibility. We hear that European Woodworking executes custom millwork with exactitude and abundant detail, and that Lo Nigro is obsessive about perfection.

The firm was established in 1996 and works with architects, contractors, designers, and homeowners. Typical full-room commissions are in the $15,000 to $60,000 range while freestanding furniture is in the $2,000 to $15,000 realm. The company's work has been featured in *The New York Times*.

"He's dependable, he comes through, and is a real artist. I couldn't recommend anyone more than this young man." "No one is perfect in this world, but Joe is certainly

striving for it." "Whenever I need work, I go to him, because I know I'll get the best job at the best price." "Innovative." "Very hands-on and personalized service—they make one kitchen at a time."

Fanuka Contracting
59-49 56th Avenue, Maspeth, NY 11378
(718) 353 - 4518 www.fanuka.com

Distinct gut renovations and fine custom millwork

See Fanuka Contracting's full report under the heading Contractors & Builders

Furniture Masters Inc.
81 Apollo Street, Greenpoint, NY 11222
(718) 599 - 0771 www.furnituremastersinc.com

Mostly trade—Choice upholstery, window treatments, and custom furniture

See Furniture Masters Inc.'s full report under the heading Upholstery & Window Treatments

James Schriber Furniture   4   4   4   4.5
57 West Street, PO Box 1145, New Milford, CT 06776
(860) 354 - 6452   jlschriber@charter.net

Contemporary woodworking

This studio furniture maker has run his own small shop since the 1970s and is regarded as "outstanding in every respect." James Schriber builds for designers and designs for clients in a contemporary aesthetic. Inspired by forward-looking French and Scandinavian designs of the 1930s, 1940s, and 1950s, Schriber leaves the country woodworking to others. Instead, he focuses on freestanding pieces and large-scale architectural millwork.

Schriber works most often in New York City and Westchester and Fairfield counties. There is no minimum cost, and we hear there's no limit to the understanding Schriber has with his clients. Pritham & Eames, a gallery in Easthampton, has showcased his work for the last 25 years. Full rooms range from $10,000 to $100,000 while single pieces run from $8,000 to $30,000.

Schriber has a background in furniture design and trained at Boston University. Sources describe this "meticulous" craftsman as "a good businessman." We hear his small three-man shop is patient and reliable. The firm outsources its finish work. Quality is superior and costs are consistent with those of the firm's high-end peers. Schriber's work has been featured in trade magazines like Woodwork Magazine and American Craft Magazine.

"An artist's sensibility and core. A dear to work with." "It is extraordinary to have a furniture maker with a full design vocabulary, a brilliant command of materials and details, and the willingness to apply himself to millwork and architectural installation. He is a pleasure to work with in every way." "My family and I have worked with him for years—and we would only recommend him with the highest praise and enthusiasm. His clients are fortunate indeed." "I recommend him 110%."

Jorgensen-Carr Ltd.   4   3.5   4   4.5
50 Dey Street, Jersey City, NJ 07306
(201) 792 - 2278   jorgcarr@msn.com

Custom interior millwork

Mike Jorgensen and Ken Carr, partners since 1987, earn praise for their achievements in stainless steel, wood, and leather. We hear Jorgensen-Carr finds the ultimate solutions to tricky problems. Insiders say the firm distinguishes itself with its intricate designs, moldings, finishes, and veneers. Though most commissions are in the classical aesthetic, the firm also does some modern work. Jorgenssen-Carr's work can be seen in interiors in New York City, New Jersey, Baltimore, Connecticut, and Westchester.

Clients say they admire this good-natured team and its high-quality work, though some worry that the firm is getting too popular and too busy. We're told that once on the job, Jorgensen-Carr's workers always meet deadlines, but it's sometimes hard to schedule them initially, due to filled appointment books. However customers across the board agree the end result is worth the wait. The company is a member of the Architectural Woodwork Institute and the New Jersey Woodworkers Guild.

"Mike and Ken are just the greatest guys on the face of the Earth. Working with them was such a pleasant experience." "I can't wait to do another project with them." "They were the one bright spot in my renovation."

Keats & Waugh Inc.   4.5   4   4.5   5
2293 Black River Road, Bethlehem, PA 18015
(484) 895 - 0123   www.keatsandwaugh.com
Custom cabinets and interior architectural millwork

This small but prominent firm is sought after by interior designers for more than its stunning libraries. Keats & Waugh is also coveted as a source for custom built-ins, armoires, cabinets, bookcases, furniture, children's rooms, and entertainment units. (While the firm does some paneling and a few kitchens, it does no molding or decorative carving.) We're told the firm excels at complicated jobs, a recent example being a chateau on Long Island with children's rooms, painted and stained finishes, distressed cabinetry, doors in archways, master bath vanities, and decorative painting (the last done by an associate). While the firm has worked in the Hamptons and Westchester and Fairfield areas, most of its work is in Manhattan and affluent New Jersey suburbs.

The firm is owned by Bill Keats, a "nice, chatty" guy and honest communicator. Keats stepped into millworking after studying oceanography and serving as an officer in the Merchant Marines, and is self-taught. He has clearly taught himself well, as the firm is in high demand. This means that Keats is sometimes backed up with work, but sources say he is straightforward about scheduling and reflects constraints in his initial timetables, which go off like clockwork. The firm's size allows Keats himself to keep control over the quality, which is said to be top shelf. Keats prefers to work through designers and architects, but can provide designs and drawings for smaller projects. We hear Keats' costs are competitive and the firm's satisfied customers frequently request additional work after the completion of the original project.

"Bill is meticulous and reviews each detail so there are no surprises." "If he's available we use him." "He doesn't take on more work than he can do, which means he isn't always available, but he is always true to his deadline." "Returns calls, calls with questions and suggestions, discusses detail." "Price base is excellent. He doesn't do shop drawings, which keeps costs low." "We are absolutely satisfied and continue to use him. He's one of our primary people."

Little Wolf Cabinet Shop   3   3   4   4
1583 First Avenue, New York, NY 10028
(212) 734 - 1116   www.littlewolfcabinetshop.com
Unfinished custom furniture and cabinets

No one's afraid of the Little Wolf, a reliable source for custom entertainment centers, bookshelves, and cabinets of all kinds. Its notably cost-effective process begins with the customer handing over preliminary measurements, from which the firm may conceptualize a number of possible designs and estimates.

Once the client signs off on a Little Wolf proposal, the company dispatches its own pros to take final measurements for the project. Once installed, the firm doesn't finish the piece, but rather recommends a finisher.

Principal John Wolf draws praise from clients for solving space issues and doing solid detail work. However, some clients howl that this shop could tighten up its drawings and resolve issues better. We hear prices are moderate, but be sure to get an estimate on the finishing as well.

"I feel very strongly about his work—I have total faith in him. I consider him a good friend at this point, and I can't imagine any reason to go elsewhere." "A mainstay of moderate quality work on the Upper East Side."

M&R Woodworking   3.5   3   4.5   4
49 Withers Street, Brooklyn, NY 11211
(718) 486 - 5480   buniek@msn.com

Custom cabinetry, architectural millwork, and furniture

M&R Woodworking wins accolades for precision craftsmanship and customer service savvy. Area architects and homeowners have looked to this firm for high-end cabinetry and furniture since 1983. Of particular note is this woodworker's skill in integrating stone and metal into its product.

Master woodworker Robert Wieczorkowski studies each project, obsessed with making it perfect. His can-do attitude and sense of humor elevates the experience—while prices stay grounded.

"Great value, good work." "It's a bit of a mission to get in touch with them, but they do eventually return calls."

Mead & Josipovich Inc.   4.5   4.5   4   4.5
140 58th Street, Brooklyn, NY 11220
(718) 492 - 7373

Fine specialty millwork and custom furniture

Trade insiders rely on this firm for top-quality specialty jobs on an unlimited budget. Principal Boris Josipovich has differentiated himself with the kind of creativity and attention to detail that produce "truly special" work. Insiders praise the firm's shop drawings and painstaking craftsmanship, calling Josipovich completely reliable, honest, and communicative. In addition to New York City, the firm takes commissions in Westchester and Fairfield, and has done several fashion industry jobs.

Josipovich is renowned for always meeting tight deadlines and for his unparalleled finishes and veneers. Insiders call Mead & Josipovich a perfect fit for the patron with both means and strong opinions, since the firm is said to give clients exactly what they want, rather than imposing its vision on the project.

"What differentiates Boris is that perfection is his standard." "Boris is a mensch." "I can't always afford them on my jobs—would my life be a lot easier in terms of getting the right work at the right time if I could? The answer is yes."

Michael Gordon Inc.   4.5   4   4.5   5
252 C Lake Avenue, Yonkers, NY 10701
(914) 965 - 3800   michael@mgordon.com

Custom millwork and furniture, trade only

Clients and professionals praise this father-son team for their built-in units, complete paneled rooms, and stand-alone furniture. Reported to be personable and cooperative with an imaginative flair, Michael and Eric Gordon transform private clients' conceptual designs into reality. Though most of their work is

Quality	Cost	Value	Recommend?
+	$	◆	★

with the trade, they'll also take on retail customers. With a staff of 28, the most up-to-date technology, and more than 30 years of experience, Michael Gordon Inc. is a favorite among clients for building sophisticated offices and fanciful children's rooms.

"He never just runs with the architect's plans, but always makes them better." "A pleasure. One of the best. Really fun to work with." "A most charming gentleman." "Can take longer than others but totally worth it." "Michael and my architect built a miniature St. James palace in my children's playroom. It not only looks amazing, it also houses all the latest video equipment, including a 10-foot dropdown screen."

New York Craftsmen's Collective
80 East 2nd Street, New York, NY 10003
(212) 477 - 4477   nycraftsmen@hotmail.com
Artisanal renovation, millwork, and cabinetry

See New York Craftsmen's Collective's full report under the heading Contractors, General & Job

St. John's Bridge
	3.5	3	4.5	5

25 Railroad Street, Kent, CT 06757
(860) 927 - 3315   www.stjohnsbridge.com
Custom decorative millwork

Sources say Greg St. John brings a special twist to his custom millwork by adding decorative inlays, veneers, and special finishes. We're told he will work from clients' designs or do period reproductions, but enjoys the opportunity to create his own designs. The "conscientious and personable" St. John brings a fine arts education to his love for creative expression. Insiders praise his skill with metals and exotic woods, calling his cabinetry and furniture "beautiful."

"He's talented, conscientious—and plans ahead." "If you explain what you want, he can come up with the design. He's very thorough, and a very nice person." "He uses the best materials and the cost is never a surprise."

Wohners Millworkers
	4	3.5	4.5	4

29 Bergen Street, Englewood, NJ 07631
(201) 568 - 7307   www.wohners.com
Mantelpieces and carving

Ferenc Wohner founded Wohners Millworkers in 1909 in Europe. Today, his son Robert Wohner runs the business with his three sons, all trained in the family tradition. Wohners specializes in doors, gold leaf, corbels, full rooms, carved accents, architectural pieces, mantelpieces, and carvings, mostly from the firm's own French-influenced designs. Sources say Wohners will also work from others' designs, but doesn't do much replication.

Besides its custom work, Wohners carries a retail line of imported and domestic mantels to accommodate every price range. Insiders say Wohners works mostly with private clients, and determines fees by the job's complexity. Wohners Millworkers has done rooms in the Dakota Hotel and was the subject of a chapter in John Lewman's book, *Fireplace & Mantel Ideas*.

"The Wohner touch added elegance and class to my living room." "This family-run company is incredibly reliable."

Hiring a Mover

Whether relocating downtown to a new hip apartment or moving the family and pets to the suburbs, just the thought of moving can bring the toughest New Yorkers to tears. Even more worrisome than organizing the process is the thought of placing all of one's worldly goods into the hands of a truckload of burly strangers. The less-than-sterling reputation of the moving industry doesn't help either. According to the Better Business Bureau, moving companies consistently make the list of the top-ten industries consumers complain about. Even moving companies themselves admit that three in ten moves result in a complaint against the mover. While those odds don't sound promising, there are several precautions you can take to ensure that you are one of the satisfied customers who end up providing glowing references about your moving company to your friends—and to *The Franklin Report*.

Where Do I Start?

Hundreds of moving companies are listed in the Manhattan Yellow Pages. Consider four main factors in making your choice: reputation, reliability, cost, and availability. Begin with an assessment of your needs. According to most movers, if you are a single apartment dweller, you will probably need 15 to 20 boxes for all your possessions. A family of two adults and two children will require at least five times as many. Most companies will provide an informal verbal estimate based on your description of items, number of rooms, the availability of elevators on both ends of the move, etc. If you're looking for a binding estimate, some movers will provide one after surveying your property and assessing your needs for themselves. Be forewarned that in this industry, a binding estimate is an elusive thing. Be prepared to consider any estimate a rough calculation rather than a binding agreement. In any event, be prepared with the requisite information before you call movers for estimates. Keep in mind that some movers only perform in-town moves, while others are licensed to do countrywide and international moves as well.

Most movers provide packing services in addition to transportation. Packing, of course, incurs additional cost. If you choose to have your items packed by movers, you'll need to schedule packing days. Be sure to take inventory of what gets packed into each box, making sure to make a note of any existing damage. Keep a copy of the inventory list handy as you unpack to ensure that all your items have arrived safely. While movers assume liability for damage incurred by any items they packed themselves—*they will not accept responsibility for items packed by you.* Be sure to get estimates both with and without packing services in order to ensure that you opt for the services best suited to your needs and budget.

The organization that issues licenses to moving companies in New York is the New York Department of Transportation (www.dot.state.ny.us). They have a helpful telephone line (800-786-5368) that can tell you if a company is licensed to perform moves in New York, how much business they did in the past year, and most importantly, how many complaints, if any, a company received in the current year. The DOT claims that one to two complaints in a twelve-month period is "average." While the number of complaints against a firm is definitely a good indication of their reputation, it is always a smart idea to get references and consider all information when making the final choice.

On Cost

Local moves are generally billed at an hourly rate, ranging anywhere from $80 per hour (a 1 on our Cost scale) to $200 per hour (a 5 on our Cost scale). This rate generally includes a truck and the labor of three men. Usually, moving companies will stipulate a minimum number of hours of moving time, and sometimes also a minimum amount of travel time. You should plan to factor in a gratuity of at least $5 per man per hour. Most movers will supply blankets and other padding material at no extra cost, but anything additional—rope, boxes, packing material, tape, bubble wrap, Styrofoam—will be supplied at a significant markup over retail. So you're better off buying your own packing materials ahead of time.

Weight-rated fees are usually used for long-distance moves. The charges are based on the weight of the goods and the distance they are moved. The truck is weighed before it is loaded with your household items and furniture, and then again after. The difference between the two weights will determine how you are charged. Again, get the best estimate you can before the move, but realize that the actual cost will be calculated after all the goods are loaded on the truck and weighed.

To keep the cost down, budget-minded consumers should consider packing their own books and clothes, but leave the packing of breakable items to the movers. That way the cost of moving can be contained and yet the cost of breakage and any other kind of damage can be absorbed by the moving company.

Summer is the most popular moving season. Not surprisingly, movers are generally over-extended during the summer months. The busiest time of year is generally also the most expensive. Many movers will offer up to a 30% discount on moves after Labor Day. Some will also charge less for weekday moves. However, these are options that movers don't readily mention, so make sure to ask about them when you're getting an estimate.

Contracts, Insurance, and Licenses

As with most business relationships, make sure that you negotiate a written contract before you move. Most moving companies have a standard contract form. If it doesn't include every foreseeable detail of the move, insist on adding these details. As with any contract, scrutinize it carefully before signing it. Ensure that any agreed-upon terms such as mileage, packing, standard charges, additional costs, and insurance are all included in the contract. The contract should state that the men will stay after 5:00 PM to finish the move if it takes longer than expected. If possible, attach a copy of the inventory to the contract as well. Retain a copy of the signed contract well after delivery has been completed to ensure that all of your possessions are delivered in the manner that the contract dictates. Be aware that most standard contracts require that the movers be paid before they unload their truck at your new home.

For interstate moves, basic insurance usually provides $.60 of coverage for each pound of goods transported ($.30 for local moves). While there is usually no additional cost associated with this kind of coverage, you do need to sign an additional contract to activate it. Unfortunately, the coverage itself is less than adequate: for instance, if your $500 television weighs ten pounds, you can collect only $3. Several other insurance plans are provided at additional cost, and protecting the value of the $500 television might require purchasing one of these supplemental plans. Optional plans come at varying costs and provide different degrees of coverage. The American Moving and Storage Association (www.moving.org) can provide you with greater insights about moving insurance—they also supply guidelines to follow when planning a move.

Cost-Saving Moving Tips

✧ Packing items yourself will save you a bundle. However, movers are only liable for damage resulting from their packing, so limit the do-it-yourself items to unbreakables such as books and clothes.

✧ Packing materials cost significantly more when purchased from the moving company. If you're doing your own packing, buy the materials at an office products or packing products store.

✧ Insurance may seem like an expensive frill, but it can save you a lot of money and headaches in the event of damage. There are many types of coverage, so check out all your options before choosing one.

✧ The time of year and/or week during which you move will affect the cost. Since movers are typically busiest on weekends and in the summer, many companies offer discounts on moves that take place during the week and between Labor Day and Memorial Day.

MOVERS

📁 FIRMS WITH ONLINE PORTFOLIOS* 📁

All-Star Moving and Storage 📁   4   3.5   4.5   4.5
424 Park Avenue, Brooklyn, NY 11205
(212) 254 - 2638 www.allstarnewyork.com
Residential moving and storage

Clients say the "honest," "hardworking," and "compassionate" Rich Barrale sets the tone for the team at All-Star, a full-service moving and storage company in business for over a quarter of a century. While primarily serving New York City, the firm has moved customers as far away as Chicago without the assistance of a van line (it does all moves directly). All-Star also offers storage services. References report that they were treated fairly, and that the move went smoothly and as planned. Free estimates are done onsite, and sources tell us that the prices are reasonable given the good treatment they received.

"All-Star came on time, they were far and away above the rest and everything worked out to our expectations." "There were no surprises, everything went smoothly." "Unbelievably accommodating crew, they were outstanding!" "They don't charge for boxes because they reuse them." "A great experience." "Professional, thorough, and accurate estimate." "I would not hesitate to use them again."

Liberty Moving & Storage 📁   3.5   3.5   4   4
304 East 65th Street, Suite 21C, New York, NY 10021
(212) 223 - 6440 www.libertymoving.com
Residential and commercial moving; large objects and fine art

Liberty Moving was founded on Liberty Avenue in 1939, but today the company's name could just as easily refer to the freedom it gives its clients. Liberty is an agent of the United Van Lines, a network of 600 firms across the country, making complicated cross-country relocations (either to or from New York) a relatively routine procedure. Clients also report favorably on local moves, with three locations in the metro area and in the Hamptons. They single out pricing as being particularly hassle-free: Liberty will send out an employee to provide a (printed) free estimate on the spot.

With over 200 on staff, Liberty is one of the largest moving companies in the Northeast. Principal Anthony Federico—a grandson of Liberty's founder—maintains quality control with background checks on all employees and personal involvement in bigger projects, including many for interior designers. He is also eager to invest in new technology, giving employees PDAs, which they use to make comprehensive inventory lists prior to big moves. Big moves, in fact, are a particular specialty, though clients say small jobs are also given due attention.

Liberty has a four-hour minimum charge for local work and a marginal packing cost. Sources report that the size of the company means you probably won't become best friends with your mover, but they praise the solid, dependable service that comes at reasonable rates.

"Not a scratch on anything." "They expertly pulled off a pretty complex job, one that involved picking stuff up in Los Angeles, Connecticut, and another place in Manhat-

*We invite you to visit www.franklinreport.com to view images of their work.

415

tan. Anthony loves what he does and it shows." *"The closer you can get to a princi-pal, the better."* *"Liberty was good about keeping things tidy and clean."* *"The guys that showed up were respectful and clean cut."*

Moving Ahead 🛍   5   4.5   4.5   5
101 5th Avenue, Garden City Park, NY 11040
(212) 262 - 0600   www.movingahead.com

Top-notch residential and commercial moving and storage, truck rental services

Sporting an exemplary record up and down the East Coast, Moving Ahead comes highly recommended by both private and commercial clients. Led by John Tarko, the 50-man team is described as knowledgeable and professional as well as courteous and flexible. This firm has seventeen trucks and is designated as the only official mover of Manhattan Mini Storage. Moving Ahead was established in 1983 by Tarko and can move from Southern Maine to Washington, DC. The company has its own 24,000 square foot storage facility.

From the firm's spotless trucks to the work ethic of its employees, references tell us that Moving Ahead is the only company they will use for both personal and business relocations. The firm charges by the hour, but gives estimates for really big jobs. While not the cheapest on our list, Moving Ahead is praised by its many fans, for whom a stress-free move is priceless.

"We had relationships with other movers and always had issues with customer service. Five years ago we gave Moving Ahead a shot and we've never looked back!" *"They're extremely professional and helpful—our relationship is based on trust."* *"What sets them apart is that they work with the customers to resolve the few issues that ever arise, instead of simply turning their backs and walking off, as most movers do."* *"We would never use another moving company."*

Moving Man Inc. 🛍   3.5   3   4.5   4.5
465 West 150th Street, New York, NY 10031
(212) 281 - 4300   www.movingmaninc.com

Residential and commercial moving

Moving Man Inc. has 25 people on staff, but the name of the firm refers to a specific moving man: general manager Jon Stout. Stout started this firm in 1979, when he and a handful of employees worked out of his apartment. Today the company boasts two large uptown storage warehouses, a small fleet of trucks, and two of the only certified moving consultants in Manhattan. Still, clients say it has maintained a relaxed, unintimidating attitude that alleviates stress. Moving Man Inc. earns further praise for strategic packing and planning, which clients say can make all the difference in a building with only one elevator.

An agent of the Wheaton Van Lines, Moving Man Inc. has the capability to do national and even international moves. Stout also maintains a subsidiary, the Home Storage Company, that supervises 60,000 square feet of storage space. Thus, clients hiring the firm tap into a full-service network—which comes in handy for complicated, multi-stage moving projects. Base rates are a notch lower than competitors, with travel time and gas added on top. References say that estimates are usually accurate within $100. They recommend Moving Man Inc. highly, saying that the company is easy to develop a personal relationship with, and that its moves "always go off as planned."

"I've moved with them many times, and I see the same guys over and over. Jon must treat his employees very well." *"A few things have been broken over the years, but they always offered to pay for a repair or a replacement."* *"They worked well both with us and the building management."* *"Jon is amazingly relaxed. I've never seen him yell or lose his temper."* *"The only time the estimate was significantly different than the final price, I ended up saving money."* *"They've got both brains and brawn."*

The Padded Wagon   4.5   3.5   4.5   4.5
163 Exterior Street, Bronx, NY 10451
(212) 222 - 4880   www.paddedwagon.com

Excellent residential and commercial moving; fine art and antiques moving

Judging from its high profile this large, nationwide firm has left many of the city's top decorators, auction houses, and private clients whistling "Happy Trails." The solid, well established Padded Wagon is among the city's most beloved moving companies. You cannot drive down a city street without spotting one of its many blue "padded wagons" hard at work.

In addition to residential and commercial moving services, the firm employs a mechanical crew to hang chandeliers, sconces, etc. They also have three locations in Manhattan dedicated to selling moving supplies—at prices that "won't make you cringe." Long-time customers note the company's reliability and responsiveness—especially for last-minute needs. They say Padded Wagon's crews do a professional job at a fair price.

"They have the manpower to be flexible. If I need them in an hour, they can usually pull it off." "Not only are the crews strong and professional, they are really nice and helpful." "They truly care about doing a good job." "Hardworking and a pleasure to do business with." "Padded Wagon goes beyond the call of duty—without hesitation, I'd use them again."

Yorkville Moving & Storage   4.5   4   4.5   5
1587 3rd Avenue, New York, NY 10128
(212) 722 - 3890   www.yorkvillevanandstorage.com

Upscale residential moving and storage, art and antiques

With a rock solid reputation for moving and storing the finest crystal, art, and antiques, Yorkville Moving & Storage provides a full range of top-notch services for both residential and commercial clients. Established in 1932 Yorkville's two large local warehouses are equipped to store anything from a van Gogh to modern office equipment. This third-generation family-run firm is headed by Enid Claussan, who we hear takes care of business and knows the inner workings of the premiere buildings on the Upper East Side. Fancy packing and crating is the specialty of the well-trained, polite staffers, who are up to handling the most delicate items. Yorkville's lists of notable customers reconfirm the firm's quality and reliability, and decorators often turn to Yorkville to move their clients.

Serving the New York metro area for over 70 years, the firm not only moves the rich and famous, it's happy to take on run-of-the-mill moves. We hear some students that attend Marymount College use Yorkville to store their furniture over summer break. Offering domestic and international shipping, clients say Yorkville makes moving with no worries priceless.

"I trust them with my most valuable pieces." "They take copious notes. I have over 100 items in one of their storage facilities and they have each one documented." "Enid is not your best friend, but will prove to be your best mover." "Yorkville has had the same staff for years." "The only guys I use now after a failed attempt with another mover." "Not the most expensive, but among the expensive." "I went to their storage facility to arrange for a client's things to be shipped out of town. The staff couldn't have been nicer. They even bought me lunch." "My building had a 5 PM deadline, so they called in more guys and got it done on time without a hitch."

	Quality	Cost	Value	Recommend?
	✚	$	◆	★

FIRMS WITHOUT ONLINE PORTFOLIOS

Aaron's Relocations   4   3.5   4.5   4
45-55 Pearson Street, Long Island City, NY 11101
(212) 980 - 6190   www.aaronsrelocations.com
Residential and commercial moving; fine arts and antiques

They started out as antique movers in 1996, but these days the dedicated staffers at Aaron's Relocation focus on the business of full-service moving. Clients rave about the attention they receive from this relatively small firm. Boasting specialized and personalized services, the company offers wrapping, packing, and moving for residential and commercial customers throughout the tri-state area. With fifteen full-time employees, Aaron's charges either by the hour ($30 per hour per man) or a flat fee, based on an on-site estimate—and references are pleased to report there are no hidden costs. Sources say the prices are fair, and that the level of service makes an Aaron's Relocation quite a bargain.

Once you've settled in, you can call on the firm's "alter ego," All Nite Long Party Rentals, to handle your housewarming party. This new offshoot handles "soup to nuts" event planning, including bar services and staffing for gatherings large or small.

"They are like the brothers (or husbands) you wish you had." "They did everything they promised and more." "Whether it is antiques or IKEA—they have an entire team of fabulous movers." "Their professionalism allowed me to sleep at night." "So nice to deal with—they really take the time to make sure you are happy." "For the outstanding job they did, the price is right on target."

Above and Beyond Cargo   3.5   3.5   4   4
136 West 73rd Street, New York, NY 10023
(212) 721 - 1200   www.nycmover.com
Small-load national residential moving

Above and Beyond has a unique angle: it does cross-country moves of loads too small for a van line but too large to fit into the trunk of the family car. Principal Elvis Soler has kept his firm as compact as its relocations: he and the same three employees have been around since the firm's founding in 2000. Clients praise the crew and the process, saying that each job gets the attention it deserves. The company is full-service, with crewmen packing items and shrink-wrapping them into a single pallet (a process that ensures your lamp won't end up in someone else's house). Above and Beyond then contracts out an independent carrier to weigh and transport the load. Costs are calculated by weight for national moves and by the hour for local moves, though the latter makes up only a small part of Soler's business. Clients say the prices are not always a bargain, but that the unique service is invaluable.

"Excellent personal service." "The movers were professional and courteous on both ends and breakage was minimal." "A simple process that made it easy." "Moving staff was professional, polite—and worked non-stop." "This is a unique company that provides a niche service very well." "Very straightforward and professional. Not always cheap, but never a rip-off." "The ultimate service came to more than the estimate and he billed the estimate."

AirSea Packing Group Ltd.   4.5   4.5   4   4.5
40-35 22nd Street, Long Island City, NY 11101
(718) 937 - 6800   www.airseapacking.com
State-of-the-art packing, shipping, and storage of delicate and valuable items

A family-owned company in business for more than 30 years, AirSea Packing Group Ltd. specializes in the packing and shipping of art and special items worldwide. With a client list that includes private collectors, commercial customers, and museums, this firm has operations in London, Paris, and Los Angeles, in addition to its New York location.

Consulting services include on-site advice on packing, installation, transportation, and security. The firm also assists in purchasing and project management and boasts a storage facility offering the ultimate in protection and security. Computerized temperature-controlled facilities, custom-designed storage vaults, a viewing gallery, and restoration and appraisal services round out the menu, making AirSea Packing a "one-stop-shopping" experience for fine art needs.

We hear the 80-person staff is well trained and works with integrity and discretion for the well-heeled and high-profile clients it serves. References say the services AirSea Packing offers are expensive—but then again, so is their artwork. The "door-to-door" estimates given include everything, and are said to be typically "right on the money."

"The level of experience and professionalism is high, and worth the price for my peace of mind." "Thorough and detail oriented." "Perfect for high-end jobs."

All American Van Lines Inc.   3   3   4   4
192 Quality Plaza, Hicksville, NY 11801
(888) 777 - 6683 www.cybermove.com
Residential and commercial moving

With a unique approach to pricing, All American Van Lines impresses clients with a flat-fee move and no hidden charges. In business for more than nineteen years, this company performs both commercial and residential moves locally and around the country. We hear the crews are good natured (a plus when moving day comes), willing to accommodate special treatment or storage for a particular item, and work efficiently within clearly delineated timeframes.

"I was relieved to encounter movers that were prompt, efficient, and amiable." "The crew was cheerful in spirit and meticulous in their work." "Their motto—On Time, On Budget, On Target—is exactly right." "Remarkable skill and strength."

Ann Lello & Sons Truckers   4   3   5   5
141 Troutman Street, Brooklyn, NY 11206
(917) 324 - 4464 www.annlelloandsons.com
Residential and commercial moving

Ann Lello, a lifer in the moving business, has been relocating Manhattanites since the early seventies. Though Lello's company has always had a pleasant small-business feel (her first piece of equipment was a Thomas' English Muffin truck), clients report that you can't get more professional service anywhere. They also say that Lello's knowledge of the city is unparalleled, and her staff is kind, efficient, and 100% trustworthy.

Lello specializes in local residential moves, but many of her clients in the cabinetmaking and antique businesses appreciate her knowledge of the trade; she used to operate an antique shop in the Village. All appreciate her attention to the nitpicky details, like using tissue instead of newsprint to wrap dishes ("There's a big difference!" Lello says). The firm's rates are said to be quite affordable for the highly personal service.

"New York City clients can be extremely demanding when it somes to the careful packing, moving, and unpacking of their possessions—Ann has never disappointed." "Ann cares immensely about her work, and will not let you down. You can't say the same about most movers in the city." "Not only did the final bill not contain any 'surprises,' it was almost identical to the estimate." "Ann is a character, she's a blast to work with." "The staff is extremely friendly and there was never any hesitation in having them handle my most precious personal property including fine works of art."

"They are prompt, thorough, and courteous and the fees charged are a true value in a profession where this is seldom the case."

Auer's
4.5   4.5   4   4.5

1721 Park Avenue, New York, NY 10035
(212) 427 - 7800 www.auersmoving.com

Superior rigging services; residential and commercial moving, fine art and antiques

Auer's performs the kind of stunt-like hoisting and rigging operations that draw crowds of onlookers. Top sources say it's one of the best firms in the city for dealing with oversized pieces, and Auer's has a client list (Christie's, Sotheby's) that backs up that reputation. The firm has a 30-person team, including a variety of hoisting, rigging, and installation experts that have overseen the transportation and construction of some of Manhattan's most recognizable (and biggest) public sculptures. Though not as well known for everyday moving jobs, Auer's also does local, long distance, and international household moves as an agent for Wheaton Worldwide Moving. Some references blush at the price tag, but those who rely on Auer's expertise insist they would never use another company.

"Best riggers in town." "The only people I would trust to hoist a marble table up twenty floors without damaging anything." "Their prices are high, so don't call them just to haul your couch. But if you need a grand piano brought up to the 39th floor, don't call anyone else."

Big John's Moving
4.5   4.5   4   4.5

1602 First Avenue, New York, NY 10028
(212) 734 - 3300 www.bigjohnsmoving.com

Exceptional residential and commercial moving

Clients say Big John's prides itself on the responsiveness of its staff members, who work at perfecting household moves on a local and national scale. They know that moving is a stressful experience, and we hear the crews are patient, compassionate—and come equipped with a sense of humor to usher customers through the moving day "jitters." For those in need of additional moving supplies, the company has a showroom displaying all types of boxes which they happily deliver to your door—though "at a premium," sources say. While Big John's falls near the higher end of the price scale, clients tell us they're willing to pay for the peace of mind.

"They took the monumental nightmare of moving and made it bearable." "From start to finish, an excellent experience." "Everything was handled with care and arrived in good condition."

Celebrity Moving
4.5   4   4.5   4.5

4-40 44th Drive, Long Island City, NY 11101
(212) 936 - 7171 mail@celebritymoving.com

Fine-tuned residential and commercial moving and storage, to the trade

Fans say this firm really is "good enough for celebrities." Specializing in local, high-end moving, this firm receives rave reviews from private clients as well as the trade, who say the crew at Celebrity is one of the best in the industry. Working almost exclusively through referrals from top-tier decorators, Celebrity Moving, led by Jim Gomiela, ushers merchandise through many phases of shipping for its clients. In addition to the sophisticated controlling of inventory, services include the crating of art and pianos, as well as storage. We hear Celebrity is famous for its work ethic and high level of customer care.

"Jimmy and his crew are the best!" "An exceptionally accommodating firm." "They are there for you when you are in a bind." "You spend a little bit more money and you get a lot more service." "I wouldn't think twice about leaving them alone in my home." "Their storage and inventory business is extremely well organized." "They can get there on less than 24 hours of notice." "Great for decorators." "They'll install things for us, hook up the cable, and sweep up afterwards. Really great service." "Probably one of the top three companies in the city."

Chelsea Moving & Storage   3.5   3   4.5   4
228 West 23rd Street, New York, NY 10011
(212) 243 - 8000 www.chelseamoving.com
Residential moving and storage

In business for over 22 years, clients say Chelsea is large enough to handle complex jobs but cozy enough that the owner, Alex Saidon, will do estimates himself. The firm concentrates mainly on mid-sized local moves within Manhattan, but sources also report favorably on long distance relocations. In addition to the moving business, Chelsea also has a packing supply company (The Box Depot) and large storage facility under its wing. The combination leads to a wide range of services, which clients come to take for granted after using the company multiple times (as many do). Prices vary depending on the size of the team, but clients repeatedly say this mid-level firm is quite affordable.

"I know they have celebrity clients, but they treat me like I'm their top priority." "They've pulled off pretty complicated jobs and pretty simple jobs equally well." "The final price always comes in within a couple hundred dollars of the estimate." "What sets them apart is their reliability and their intelligence. You don't have to tell them anything twice."

Collins Brothers Moving Corporation   4   4   4   4
620 5th Avenue, Larchmont, NY 10538
(914) 646 - 6316 www.collinsbros.com
Residential and commercial moving and storage

In business for over 90 years, this large, full-service moving and storage company takes pride in its dedicated staff. Three hundred strong, Collins Brothers performs local and long distance residential moves as well as international and commercial relocations. Rigorous training is said to pay off in the professionalism demonstrated on the job. All estimates are done on-site, eliminating surprises, and clients appreciate that a field supervisor monitors each move, assuring the best possible job.

"Collins Brothers made sure everything was done correctly." "Not only are they skilled packers, but gentlemen you will be happy to have in your home." "The crew was very reliable, polite, and helpful." "They got the job done with no pain." "Used repeatedly by investment banking houses' relocation departments, so they have to be reliable and good."

Cross It Off Your List   4.5   4   4.5   5
915 Broadway, 20th Floor, New York, NY 10010
(212) 725 - 0122 www.crossitoffyourlist.com
Top-notch relocation, organization, and lifestyle management services

This small and focused company offers services ranging from relocation to organization and lifestyle management. While they don't actually do the hauling, the firm will coordinate every single step of the move—right down to hiring the

mover and placing your child's favorite toy in the toy chest. Clients are thrilled at the prospect of having one conversation about a move—and then, as if by magic, arriving at a home that is completely unpacked and ready for living.

Whether it is orchestrating your entire household move or just having a few errands run, Linda Rothschild and her organized and efficient team at Cross It Off Your List are number one on our sources' list of "who to call to get it done." In business since 1990, this battalion of efficiency and organization has been assisting clients in fighting the war on chaos all around the country (and sometimes the globe) in all facets of life. Busy with committees and chauffeuring the kids to soccer practice, the firm's happy clients say they couldn't manage the details of their hectic schedules without Linda.

"I am on the road for weeks at a time and things can get a little scary in my home— mail piles up, calls go unanswered, the cable can go out. I've had to plan paint jobs and construction jobs, but I can't always be there, nor do I always have the inclination to take care of this stuff, so I call Linda—she takes care of everything." "This is the fairy godmother any fraught New Yorker is searching for." "Whether your desk is littered with your life or your closet has items from your junior high days, Linda and her team can tame it." "There is not a wasted moment and every task is tackled with the right supplies, the right priorities, and an unerring sense of the client's privacy and priorities." "I dread the thought each year of relocating to our summer home. Cross It Off Your List keeps every detail in order, and keeps me stress free and ready to enjoy the season."

Dahill Moving and Storage   3.5   3.5   4   4

5620 First Avenue, Brooklyn, NY 11220
(800) 765 - 0905   www.dahillmoving.com

Residential and commercial moving

Begun as an ice-delivering business in 1928, Dahill has undergone a number of transformations thanks to the enterprising founder Salvatore DiBattista, from refrigerator deliverer to mover of household goods. DiBattista's son, Michael Sr., bought the family business in 1956, and today his two sons, John and Michael Jr., are at the helm.

Dahill is an agent for Mayflower International and can move you locally, across the country, or across the globe. With a staff of 50, this firm handles all phases of relocation, from packing and moving to long or short term storage for jobs big and small. The company has twenty trucks and though its clientele is made up mostly of commercial clients, Dahill also accommodates some residential moves. Pricing for local moves is per hour ($130 per hour for a three-man crew). Moves outside a 60-mile radius of New York City are calculated by weight and distance based on a sliding scale.

Despite Dahill's large size, we hear that the service remains personal and attentive. Clients praise the crew for their care and flexibility and the fact that they "go the extra mile" to make sure things are done correctly. Local rates are $130 per hour for a three-man crew, which clients call "competitive."

"They provided me with more information about moving and my rights as a consumer than any company has ever given." "Dahill handled everything with great care—they even sent packing specialists along with different staff to move the boxes and furniture." "Very flexible." "Great service for a fair price."

Moishe's Moving Systems   4   4   4   4

449 West 14th Street, New York, NY 10014
(800) 266 - 8387   www.moishes.com

Residential and commercial moving and storage, art, antiques, and pianos

Started as a man-with-a-van business in 1983, Moishe's is arguably the most impressive rags-to-riches story in the Manhattan moving business: the company now boasts a staff of around 300 and proudly claims to perform more than 10,000 moves a year. Because of Moishe's size, the firm's clients have access to a large network of specialty services, including fine art and wine storage, inventory management, document storage, international relocation, and self storage.

Long-distance moves are also kept within the sphere of the company, meaning that Moishe's doesn't hand its clients' possessions over to a van agency (as many smaller companies do). References report favorably on the basic service: they say moves are fast, efficient, and careful. The word "professional" is repeated again and again, and with employees re-trained in customer service every three to four months, it makes sense. Moishe's rates are on the higher end of the scale, but during off-peak periods (any time but the beginning and end of the month), the numbers keep pace with the market average. The massive size of the company means that not all clients have an identical experience, but the vast majority report a great move with Moishe's.

"They went straight to work." "I found out at the last minute that I wasn't supposed to move out on the day I was scheduled to, so we had to rush. The guys from Moishe's were great about it. They got in, got out, and there was no damage." "Professional, and very fast." "I haven't had the same crew for every move, but the same person does my estimations. So I feel like I have a personal relationship with the company." "I've done storage with them too and it went great." "Each move is better than the last."

Morgan Manhattan Moving and Storage   5   5   4   5
434 East 91st Street, New York, NY 10128
(212) 633 - 7800   www.morganmanhattan.com
Superior residential, fine art, and antiques moving; wine storage

In business since 1851, Morgan Manhattan is literally the oldest moving company in the United States. Started as a horse-and-wagon operation, current president (and fifth-generation descendant of the founding Morgan) Jeff Morgan oversees a fleet of vans, roughly 700,000 square feet of storage, and a sophisticated web-based tracking and inventory system. Still, what clients highlight most is the service, which they say is impeccable. Crews are described as friendly, on-time, and well-dressed. And considering the fact that Morgan's training process involves a mock apartment setup (which potential employees are required to navigate while lifting delicate, heavy objects), it's perhaps no surprise that its movers are also frequently called "uber-professional." In case of damage, the company has an in-house cabinet shop, meaning that even the slightest scratch can be repaired immediately.

Morgan has a wide range of services available, including storage and inventory control of fine wine collections. Clients tell us they can view their collections online and make notations as to vintage, price, and "best drinking date." Other collections (records, documents, van Goghs) can be similarly catalogued and viewed online, and a growing decorator/designer division allows professionals to search their inventory of furnishings. Morgan handles all local moves directly, with all estimates done in person. For long-distance relocations, the company uses the United Van Lines. The one drawback, sources report, is top-of-the-market pricing. However, those who insist on spotless service continually report that Morgan's white-glove professionalism is well worth the cost.

"Very careful, very seamless, very professional." "An icon in the industry." "I wouldn't trust my valuables to anyone else." "Very personal attention." "I demand the best, and I got white-glove treatment from this company." "I was amazed at the technology used to track my wine collection. My husband is in the computer industry, and even he was completely impressed."

Personal Touch
65-02 Otto Road, Glendale, NY 11385
(718) 417 - 6740

Quality	Cost	Value	Recommend?
4.5	4.5	4	5

Superb residential moving, packing, and storage

Working exclusively through referrals, Sal DiPiazza and the team at Personal Touch have developed a reputation for being one of the finest moving companies in New York. Working almost exclusively in Manhattan, this company takes the name Personal Touch to new levels—by meeting with each client to estimate the individual needs of the job and establish a flat fee to cover the entire move. Happy patrons remark that there are no hidden costs—the price estimated is the price paid.

Personal Touch is expensive, but sources happily pay the bill for the level of service and a "job extremely well done." Moreover, sources appreciate the fact that DiPiazza never "rakes you over the coals" by overcharging for moving supplies (a practice all too common in the industry). Instead, his prices for supplies are just above cost.

Customers report that DiPiazza brings far more men (each one reported nicer and more helpful than the next) to each job than most firms—and more than they ever expected. All involved seem to benefit from this unique "high manpower policy"—clients get a speedy move and the crew gets in and out in a reasonable time. Loyal fans couldn't be happier with DiPiazza and his "amazing" staff, and they add that the value and service at Personal Touch is truly exemplary.

"Their attention to detail went beyond what I ever thought possible." "Best mover I have ever used!" "There is no reason to consider another company." "The entire experience was pleasant from the time they arrived until the time they left." "Efficient, courteous, careful— and anxious to please." "Not only is Sal one of the hardest working men I have ever met, his staff is equally motivated and enthusiastic." "Unbelievably organized, pleasant, and fast." "Not that anyone enjoys moving, but these guys were so great I was almost sad when the day was over." "I had absolutely NO worries." "They packed, moved, and unpacked me, and I was pretty much removed from the entire process. I almost fell over when I moved into my new home and it looked like I had been there for years, everything perfectly in its place—these guys are fabulous."

The Velvet Touch
780 East 133rd Street, Bronx, NY 10454
(718) 742 - 5320   www.tvtmovers.com

Quality	Cost	Value	Recommend?
4	3.5	4.5	4

Residential and commercial moving and storage; art and antiques

This relatively young company has taken the New York City moving industry by storm, developing a client list of top decorators and antique dealers in record time. Sources praise The Velvet Touch for being professional, trustworthy, and—most importantly—careful.

With a team that's been in the moving business for seventeen years, the firm handles residential and commercial jobs, and specializes in art and antiques. Clients say crews at The Velvet Touch handle their delicate and expensive items

with the utmost care, as if they were their own possessions. Others nod to the personalized service, applauding owner Kimon Thermos for personally doing on-site estimates and stopping by the job to assure things are going as planned.

"They are always willing to work with clients to agree on fair pricing." "I have confidence in them." "They are very reliable and very careful." "Working with The Velvet Touch was a pleasure. They have moved millions of dollars worth of antiques for us and I can confidently say they are one of the best truckers in New York." "They treated my property as if it was their own."

William B. Meyer Inc.   4   4   4   4.5
181 Route 117 Bypass, Bedford Hills, CT 10507
(800) 873 - 6393   www.williambmeyer.com
Residential and commercial moving

Clients praise William B. Meyer for the TLC it gives to moves large and small. The company is known to be United Van Lines' largest and oldest agent. In business since 1915, we are told the firm's drivers and crew are still rolling out on time, and with very good results. Clients applaud the staff, saying "the guys on board couldn't be more careful and caring." Combining the efficiency of a well-oiled machine with the old-fashioned honesty and integrity of a family business, Meyer Inc. impresses both residential and commercial clients.

Whether moving from the tri-state area to anywhere in the country—or the world—we hear this 91-year-old company has the manpower, facilities, and experience to get the job done right. In addition, the firm handles rigging, courier services, and off-site data protection for businesses. The added muscle, however, comes at extra expense.

"First class operation." "Would never use another mover." "They changed my opinion about moving to a positive one." "Our furniture was big, but not a scratch, bang, or peep." "They moved my elderly mother from one floor to another, and treated her like a queen." "Price was much less than my mother thought it would be, but more than the figure my husband came up with." "Fantastic." "We were moving to Florida and needless to say we were very anxious. The crew made us feel that we were in good hands." "They suggested ways we could save money on our move by packing ourselves—they even showed us how to do it."

Hiring Painters & Wallpaperers

Walk into a room smoothly painted in a beautiful celadon green and immediately your mood changes—you become calmer, more relaxed. A pristine paint job can produce a feeling of drama or tranquility in a space. Designers know that painting is one of the quickest, most versatile and cost-effective things you can do to transform a room. A professional painter masks imperfections, creating a surface as smooth as an eggshell, or one as perfectly swirled as the most beautifully frosted cake.

Paint contractors with a wide range of abilities and services abound in the New York City area. Choices range from small start-ups to large established firms, from straight painters to custom muralists (described in detail in the "Decorative Painting" section of this book). Depending upon the size of the job and the quality and complexity of the work, there is a paint contractor out there for you.

Where to Look for a Professional

Finding the right paint contractor for your job requires some research. It is critical to check references and ask to see a certificate of insurance. Each contractor should have worker's compensation and general liability insurance to protect you from jobsite-related liabilities. Several trade organizations, such as the Painting and Decorating Contractors of America (www.pdca.org), list paint contractors in your area. And of course, The Franklin Report offers a range of client-tested choices.

Contracts

Reputable contractors will encourage using a written contract. Your contract should clearly explain the scope of the work to be performed and include a list of the surfaces to be painted, a time schedule for the project, payment procedures, and any warranty or guarantee the contractor might offer.

Pricing Systems

When considering the price for painting it is important to know that the cost structure for straight painting is much different than that of decorative work. While some firms do both types of work, your bill for each job will be determined using different factors.

The cost for straight painting in residential homes varies based on such factors as the cost of the materials and the company's overhead costs. You should invite at least three paint contractors to bid on your paint job, and ask each to submit a detailed written proposal. Painting contractors charge on a per person per day basis, which generally runs in the $425 to $475 range for nonunion jobs (this equates to approximately a 2.5 to 3 on our Cost scale). Union jobs start at about $500 per person per day. The contractor should provide you with an overall cost estimate for the job that is broken down by room. Also ask for a step-by-step plan outlining how the job will be spackled, skimmed, and painted. If colors are being matched, ask the painter to apply 24-inch-square samples on the walls before going full-steam ahead.

When considering the "bottom line" for any painting job, ask for client references. They can provide valuable insight into not only the quality of work and timing, but cost as well.

How Many Painters Will Be in My House?

The size of the crew largely depends upon the scope of the job involved. Some painters listed in this guide are sole proprietors who work on small jobs themselves and subcontract larger jobs. Others are larger companies with complete crews. Ask how many men will be working on your job and whether there will be a supervisor or principal on site.

The Elements of a Professional Paint Job

Flat-painting a room involves preparing the walls, trim, and ceiling surfaces for the paint, as well as executing the paint job itself. To prepare walls, paint crews will do all the taping, plastering, plaster restoration (if needed), and skim coating. This prep work is considered one of the most important elements of a paint job as it provides the foundation for the paint. A primer coat, which prepares the walls for the paint, should be applied to dry walls. Finally, two coats of high-quality paint should be applied to the wall surfaces.

Which Paint?

The quality of the paint is crucial in determining its longevity. Fine quality paint, properly applied, should last for six to seven years. If you or your contractor skimp on the quality of the paint, you may be facing a new paint job a lot sooner than you would like.

The two most common types of paints are latex and oil-based paints. Latex paint is water-based and dries quickly, which allows for more than one coat to be applied in a day. Latex paint is better at resisting mildew, easier to clean, and lasts longer than alkyd paints, which are oil-based. Alkyd paints are preferred by many painters because they are durable and long-lived; however, they take longer to dry, have a significant odor, and can yellow over time. Most experts agree that oil-based paints are best suited for the doors and trim, while latex paints are preferred for the walls and ceilings.

Lead Paint Hazards

The presence of lead paint presents health hazards in many homes. The federal government banned the use of lead paints in 1978, so if you live in an older home or apartment building, your walls may conceal an ancient layer of lead paint. When sanding is done in advance of painting, it may cause lead dust to enter the air in your home.

Your contractor should provide you with a pamphlet that discusses lead paint issues in your home. Ask your contractor what measures he takes to ensure that lead particles are eliminated. If you need to have your home inspected or have lead removed, the Environmental Protection Agency (www.epa.gov) issues licenses for companies and professionals who work with lead control, including removal, inspection, and risk assessment. Other good resources for information about lead and asbestos include the American Lung Association (www.lungusa.org), the US Consumer Product Safety Commission (www.cpsc.gov), the American Industrial Hygiene Association (www.aiha.org), the Department of Housing and Urban Development (www.hud.gov), and the Occupational Safety and Health Administration (www.osha.gov).

Wallpaper

Wallpaper can add depth, texture, and visual interest to a room. Floral or striped wallpaper can make even small, windowless rooms cheerful. It can also be a costly investment, so it is important to find a qualified, competent professional to install your paper. Finding a wallpaper hanger can be as easy as talking to your paint contractor, as most also provide this service. Depending upon the complexity of the job, it may be appropriate to contact a professional who specializes in wallpaper hanging. One source is the National Guild of Professional Paperhangers (NGPP). To reach a local chapter, call (516) 433-5701 or visit www.ngpp.org.

Cost for wallpapering is based on a per-roll basis, with rates averaging about $50 per roll. Most wallpaper is sold in double-roll units, which measure approximately 60 square feet. The price quoted should include trimming the sides of the paper if necessary. Professionals will strip your walls of existing paper and prep it for the new paper for an additional fee. Your wallpaper hanger should calculate the quantity of paper you will need for the room, based on the room size as well as the "repeat" pattern on your paper. The larger the repeat, the more paper you will need. The newer vinyl wallpaper comes pre-pasted, while traditional and costlier papers need to be trimmed and pasted with freshly-mixed wheat paste.

Paint-Choosing Tips

✧ Use oil-based paint for metals and trim; latex for wood and drywall.

✧ High-traffic areas need a durable, easy-to-clean paint job. Use delicate paint applications in light-traffic areas only.

✧ Use flat paint for base coats; gloss to set off trim and doors.

✧ Be alert to the number of coats required. Eggshell paints, for example, take at least one extra coat.

PAINTERS & WALLPAPERERS

🛍 FIRMS WITH ONLINE PORTFOLIOS* 🛍

Audra Frank Painting 🛍   4.5   4   4.5   5
1118-A North Avenue, Plainfield, NJ 07062
(800) 293 - 2212 www.audrafrankpainting.com

Exceptional straight and decorative painting, wallpapering, and color and product consulting

Audra Frank has provided "tip-top" painting, plastering, and wallpapering services in New York City and surrounding areas for two decades and counting. Employed in some of the most prestigious apartment buildings and by top contractors, the firm works for residential and commercial clients. Whether tackling a straight painting or wallpaper project or using her expertise in special finishes like glazing and color plastering, principal Audra Frank is said to be helpful, versatile, and—given the high quality of work—competitively priced.

Audra runs the firm she and late husband David started in 1981, with a staff of twelve who are said to be as "meticulous" as Audra herself. The multi-talented and busy principal is available for product and color consultation, and has been featured on HGTV's "Do It Yourself." She has also been elected president of The Mid-Atlantic Council of the PDCA, and involves herself in many charitible organizations.

"Audra runs a tight ship, and goes out of her way to accommodate your schedule. When things go wrong, she is very good about taking care of the situation." "She and her team are very reliable—they handled the job quickly and professionally." "They will try to accommodate clients' needs and correct issues." "Their work is exceptional, their results are incredibly reliable, and I have never been disappointed with their work, professionalism, or follow-through." "They have been in the business for years, and their experience really shows."

Bernard Garvey Painting 🛍   4   3   5   5
63-62 78th Street, Middle Village, NY 11379
(718) 894 - 8272 bgarvey@nyc.rr.com

Straight painting, plastering, and decorative finishes

Described as "clever, with a good eye," Bernard Garvey offers meticulous painting and plastering services to Upper East Side clients who claim he's one of the nicest, most accommodating people you could ever have working in your home. When a customer sought to freshen up her apartment for her baby's imminent arrival, Garvey arrived the next day with three workmen and transformed her home with "the most amazing" paint job. Others rave about the staff, noting the universal positive attitude, good character, and professional work ethic.

Garvey came to the US from Ireland in the early 1980s, founding the business in 1989. In addition to straight paint work, he has been known to take on decorative painting and plaster restoration projects, which are said to be very nice for the money. Patrons note that this company's evenhanded prices, coupled with its hand-holding service, provide a phenomenal value.

*We invite you to visit www.franklinreport.com to view images of their work.

429

"All you have to do is take one look at Bernie's work bag, and you know you're in for a very precise and tidy job." "His crew worked fast in order to finish the job before moving day, and my apartment was left immaculate." "I recommend him to all my friends—the quality is excellent!" "Very organized, kind, and helpful." "It is a pleasure doing business with Mr. Garvey." "One of the best!" "The entire team is honest, ethical, and professional." "Anyone looking for a fantastic paint job without any B.S., call Bernie."

BK Wallcovering

4.5   4   4.5   4.5

500 West 42nd Street, Suite 6B, New York, NY 10036
(212) 629 - 3040 www.bfkinc.com

Exacting wallpapering

Described as "superlative" by top decorators, Brian Kehoe of BK Wallcovering is strictly a wallcovering specialist. We're told the firm handles both large and small projects on Manhattan's Upper East Side with care, and has been entrusted with the hanging of a mural at the Guggenheim and the wallpapering of designer showrooms.

The "wonderfully intuitive" Kehoe and his small staff are said to be "so good" that professionals want to keep them all to themselves. Clients say the team is a pleasure to work with, and while the expert services are costly, they are said to be even with similarly tiered professionals. Kehoe also offers wallpaper removal services with a safe solution.

"Brian makes every job run smoothly—that's why I call him again and again." "Would like to say bad things so no one else will use him but me!" "Their work is outstanding." "Willing to be flexible and accommodate our schedule." "Brian has always provided the highest level of professional, reliable service." "Small workforce, but they get it accomplished." "I find his prices competitive and his work excellent." "I would recommend Mr. Kehoe and his staff with complete confidence."

Deco NY

4.5   3.5   5   4.5

56-52 64th Street, Maspeth, NY 11378
(631) 266 - 1808 decony@earthlink.net

Skilled wallpapering, plastering, and painting

Clients love John "Jack" Fallon for his strong work ethic, his willingness to go above and beyond, and his creative skills and talent. Known for his ability to get the job done flawlessly, Fallon is solicited by decorators, contractors, and home-owners for painting, plastering, wallpapering, and any renovations they might need.

A graduate of the Culinary Institute, Fallon apprenticed himself to a European paperhanger before venturing off on his own in 1982. Like the work of a five-star chef, Fallon's painting and wallpapering are said to be "very exact," but this feast for the eyes comes at a reasonable price.

"So great to work with." "I needed a painter and wallpaperer and he took care of it all! Without one problem." "Really down to earth and professional in every way." "Honest and careful." "Always willing to go the extra mile."

DFB Sales Inc.

21-07 Borden Avenue, Long Island City, NY 11101
(718) 729 - 8310 www.vitruv.com

Trade only—Custom wall upholstery, wall surfaces, and window treatments

See DFB Sales Inc.'s full report under the heading Upholstery & Window Treatments

	Quality	Cost	Value	Recommend?
	+	$	◆	★

Ira Smolin Painting

	4	3	5	4.5

1435 Lexington Avenue, New York, NY 10128
(212) 831 - 0205 www.smolinpainting.com

Straight and decorative painting, wallpapering, and color consultation

Engaging, straightforward, and easy to work with—that's how clients describe Ira Smolin, who has been providing decorative and straight painting and wallpapering to New York City residents since 1975. The firm's decorative specialties, handled by partner Jenny Blackburn, include marbling, gold leaf, and trompe l'oeil. Sources describe the work as "beautiful."

Smolin personally supervises every member of his "excellent and efficient" crew, and has the work ethic to complete any painting project "seamlessly," no matter how demanding the client may be. We are told the team is so skilled "they can't help but pay microscopic attention to the details of wall quality that matter so much." Customers appreciate the company's neatness and pleasant approach, praising Ira Smolin's promptness and habit of coming in, on, or under budget (written estimates are always provided). We're told the brilliant quality produces a value that far exceeds expectations.

"Ira and crew bring 50 plus years of experience and the energy of ten-year-olds to uncover and transform even the worst spaces." "The quality and value of the work they did withstood two floods that ruined the apartments above and below mine." "Ira came up with a clever solution for a wallpapered bathroom while steering me clear of a few expensive procedures." "Ira's team spent a lot of time prepping the ceilings and walls, so by the time the paint went on, everything looked fantastic." "They actually painted while the movers were moving boxes and furniture and seemed unintimidated by the challenging work environment—very professional!" "These people are delightful; true craftsmen in the most down-to-earth way possible."

John A. Weidl Inc.

	5	4.5	4.5	5

379 Huguenot Street, New Rochelle, NY 10801
(914) 636 - 5067

First-rate straight and decorative painting

Working primarily through decorators, John A. Weidl Inc. is considered by many to be one of the best painting outfits in New York. Sources say they are "as professional as it gets," noting the fact that crews work diligently to build a relationship with the homeowner. John A. Weidl is known for its extraordinary attention to detail, and clients concur, raving that every single brushstroke is handled with care. Freelancers are brought in for mural work, which is noted as quite good.

This large firm, established in 1935, performs decorative painting (including glazing, faux finishing, and trompe l'oeil) in addition to its straight painting, which we hear is exquisite. Scott and Thomas Salzberger now lead the firm their dad owned for years, delivering five-star results at somewhat less-than-expected prices. KB 2001.

"The BEST painters in NYC, they do all finishes, and did glazing and trompe l'oeil for us." "Not only is Weidl's work incredible, their work ethic is wonderful. Each and every worker was clean, polite, and very reliable." "The very best in every way." "The care

and attention that they gave was truly impressive, even when I changed my daughter's bedroom wall color three times." "They were pickier than I was, and I am a stickler for detail." "No more expensive than the next guy with an amazing result." "The only painter in New York I can trust to go to a client without upsetting a household." "Their in-house colorist was there to consult with us at the drop of a hat." "They took the initiative to touch up marks that were not even on my punch list." "When I was desperate to get my kids into their bedrooms before school started, they brought in double crews to make sure that happened." "Did my house while I was in Provence—I couldn't believe they got the colors just right."

John Gregoras Paper Hanging & Painting LLC 🛍

4.5	3.5	5	5

76 Kisco Avenue, Mt. Kisco, NY 10549
(914) 241 - 6959 www.johngregoras.com
Skilled interior and exterior painting and wallpapering

Portrayed as extremely professional and easy to work with, John Gregoras and his crew handle wallpaper projects as well as interior and exterior painting assignments with finesse and skill. Since 1986, whether working for a high-profile client or "your average Joe," sources say Gregoras has treated each project with personalized care and genuine interest. We hear Gregoras is a detail fanatic, but also a "no-nonsense and easygoing guy" who is not merely knowledgeable and experienced, but "a real sweetheart." Whatever a customer needs, insiders say Gregoras is there every step of the way—at a price that won't break the bank.

"John's mission is to be the very best, and we see this in his work." "Reasonably priced for the exemplary caliber of his work." "Super job on all counts—high quality, fast and pleasant." "John and his crew are great—they are respectful, talented, neat as a pin." "I heard that John works for some celebrity types so I was a little intimidated—when I met him that feeling immediately vanished. He was so down to earth—he took as much interest in my project as I did."

P.J. McGoldrick Co. Inc. 🛍

4.5	4	4.5	5

34 Young Avenue, Pelham, NY 10803
(914) 712 - 1280 pjmcgoldrick@optonline.net
Excellent interior and exterior painting and wallpapering

New Yorkers paint Paul McGoldrick as upfront, easily accessible, and extremely good at what he does. McGoldrick's been mixing colors since 1998, and has a reputation for superior quality. All together, it's a talented team of 22, and we're told the crew does its best to make the customer comfortable, with each member of the staff more courteous than the last. The firm has done work for some "notable names" who appreciate the crew's professional demeanor and dignified approach. We're told a McGoldrick paint job is "money well spent."

"Paul and crew are AMAZING—feels like we had a complete makeover." "Expensive but worth it." "I did not even know they were there—so respectful of my home and my time." "Paul returns calls immediately and all issues are resolved without delay." "His crew is extremely good, well trained, and knowledgeable." "My clients expect the best and Paul delivers—and then some."

Robert Star Painting 🛍

4.5	3.5	5	4.5

178 East 80th Street, New York, NY 10021
(212) 737 - 8855 robert@robertstar.com
Fine painting, decorative finishes, and wallpapering

The witty Robert Star and his professional team of 22 artfully orchestrate all types of projects—from wallpapering to flat painting to gilding, glazing, wood graining, and Venetian plaster. Star's family boasts a century-long history of painting in England, where he was born. He started his own business in 1982.

In high demand from an elite list of architects, interior designers, and private clients—who praise the firm's extraordinary results and ordinary prices—Robert Star Painting has been published in *Town & Country, Architectural Digest,* and *New York* magazine.

"I would hire him again and again—he made the process enjoyable." "An absolute joy to work with." "Robert is a cut above the rest." "I couldn't dream of better service." "Not only is Robert fun to work with, he and his team are true professionals and produced results that I am proud to show off."

Sheridan & Sugrue   4   3   5   5

165 Christopher Street, Suite 3L, New York, NY 10014
(917) 549 - 1530   www.paintplaster.com
Straight residential painting, plastering, and carpentry

Clients praise Michael Sheridan and Cliff Sugrue for their creativity and professionalism, and for the "great" way they have about them. Partners since 1998, these two handle straight painting, plastering, and carpentry projects. Specializing in prewar restorations, Sheridan and Sugrue strive to create "work that will outlive them." In addition to the firm's evident talent and experience, sources say Sheridan and Sugrue bring great ideas to a job, pay close attention to detail, and go the extra mile to make sure everything is as it should be. Given the quality and care rendered, clients consider the firm to be quite a bargain.

"A dream team—no egos." "Fantastic, imaginative, respectful—not enough great adjectives to describe Michael and Cliff." "I'd recommend them in a New York minute." "When faced with unexpected problems along the way, they met them with creativity and expertise." "They actually made the process—dare I say it—fun."

SilverLining Interiors

2091 Broadway, 3rd Floor, New York, NY 10023
(212) 496 - 7800   www.silverlininginteriors.com
Considerable interior renovation and decorative finish specialists

See SilverLining Interiors' full report under the heading Contractors & Builders

Skinner Interiors   4.5   3.5   4.5   5

71 First Place, Brooklyn, NY 11231
(718) 243 - 1378   www.skinnerinteriors.com
Straight and decorative painting, wallpapering, and plasterwork

A favorite of hot young designers looking for exceptional craftsmanship at decent prices as well as old-guard designers who have been pleased with its work for years, Skinner Interiors does straight and decorative painting, plastering, and wallpapering for some of New York's most demanding clients. Known for its attention to detail and professionalism, the firm is frequently cited by showroom dealers in the D&D building for its expertise. Principal Mark Skinner and his team are aces at wallpapering, faux bois, faux stone, glazing, and plaster finishes. We hear they're great with traditional paints and wallpapers, but their talent really shines when dealing with fine European paints (such as Schreuder Hascolac or Farrow & Ball) and high-end wallpapers (such as foils or paperback silks).

In business since 1989, Skinner has a reputation for being hands-on. In addition to supervising all of the painstaking prep work required to achieve a fine finish, he is said to nurture close relationships with clients during the process, keeping them updated on progress and staying sensitive to their needs and budgets.

"Wizards! They miraculously transformed our place." "Mark is always on site, working with the client. He cleans up every day." "Great employees with a great attitude." "A true full-service painting, paper, plaster contractor." "From the first day of preparation to the completion of the job, we knew we had made the right choice." "They understand quality and were sensitive to our needs." "Skinner Interiors is highly creative and professional." "A real artist." "Truly worth every penny for the most meticulous work."

Walter Shostak Painting   3   3   4   4.5
262 Clinton B. Fiske Avenue, Staten Island, NY 10314
(917) 312 - 5810   wshostak@verizon.net
Straight residential painting and plastering and wallpaper removal

Considered an excellent (if lesser-known) source among decorators and private clients, Walter Shostak has been painting and plastering Manhattan homes since 1987. In addition, Shostak offers wallpaper removal services. His down-to-earth style, good quality, and extremely modest prices have earned him numerous fans who value his opinions and recommendations and appreciate his keen interest in the project at hand. Shostak is such a find, clients often ask him to do their second homes outside of the city.

"Walter is a delight to work with, he is always polite, prompt, reliable, and totally ethical. He does additional small painting repairs at no extra cost." "Walter is very careful with fabrics and furniture." "He transformed our apartment from average into a place we are just dying to live in." "Walter gives great advice." "He is honest, efficient and ethical." "High-quality work at reasonable fees." "I found him to be quite accommodating about scheduling." "Walter gave our home so much attention, but didn't break us with the price."

FIRMS WITHOUT ONLINE PORTFOLIOS

Alton Inc.
40-19 35th Avenue, Long Island City, NY 11101
(718) 784 - 4230   tom@altonpainting.com
Straight and decorative painting and wallpapering

See Alton Inc.'s full report under the heading Decorative Painters & Colorists

Carl Masi Painting   4   3.5   4.5   4.5
321 East 12th Street, New York, NY 10003
(212) 475 - 1789
Straight painting and plastering

Carl Masi, a one-man operation, has been performing interior residential painting and plastering in New York City since 1978. Clients love the fact that Masi has a passion for what he does—which is probably why he gets so much repeat business. Sources tell us that his repair work is "built to last," since Masi takes great care in making sure every step is done correctly.

The son of a painter, Masi has left his mark on Manhattan's elite residences, and clients appreciate his many years of experience and his expert opinion. The meticulous, professional, and "wonderful to work with" Masi is said to offer high-end finish at an honest price.

"Carl is a perfectionist! Going out of his way to make sure he was achieving the highest-possible standards of finish." "When it came time to start the work, he was

reliable, organized, and meticulous. He ordered all the materials in advance, and on each day of the six-day project, he worked very hard." *"Mr. Masi is not only a great painter—he was also a terrific advocate for my children and a provider of sage advice. I told my nine-year-old twins they could pick their own colors, and when I got nervous about their choices, he reassured us that it would look great, and reminded us about the importance of respecting the children's choices. He was right on both counts—the rooms look great and the kids are thrilled—and empowered."* *"Carl always does excellent work, and is a pleasure to work with."* *"Honest and reliable—I totally trust him."*

Creative Wall Decor & Decorating Inc.   4   4   4   4.5
4 Mallard Drive, West Nyack, NY 10994
(203) 509 - 8256
Wallpapering

Not only do Peter Milmore and the team at Creative Wall Decor work with the best decorators in the area, they are often called upon to consult for some of the most prestigious wallpaper houses in the industry. Milmore, who represents the third generation in a family of fine craftsmen, was taught by his father and grandfather, and ventured out on his own in 1977. Customers say when he does a job, the results are flawless. Fans say they keep coming back because of Milmore's attention to detail and "vast experience." Prices fall at the higher end, but the perfect seams are said to be "worth every penny."

"He is an absolute perfectionist." *"We can't say enough GREAT things about his work—the best."* *"Really down-to-earth and a popular guy."*

Donald Smith Design Services Inc.   4   4   4   4
555 Main Street, Suite 1007, New York, NY 10044
(212) 688 - 4537
Straight painting and wallpapering

On the scene since 1983, Donald Smith performs high-end straight painting and wallpapering for residences in New York City and the Hamptons. We hear Smith and his staff of four do all the prep work, including plastering, plaster restoration, and skim coating, which clients characterize as phenomenal. They tell us the firm is a pleasure to work with and the quality results justify the significant dollars spent.

"With the upmost sincerity, he wants to make your home beautiful." *"Donald is a very charming man to deal with."* *"High-end and definitely worth the expense."* *"Absolutely fantastic, I think they are great!"*

Edward Micca Decorative Painting
312 Bayport Avenue, Bayport, NY 11705
(631) 472 - 3559   edmicca@yahoo.com
Distinctive decorative and straight painting and wallpapering

See Edward Micca Decorative Painting's full report under the heading Decorative Painters & Colorists

Gotham Painting   4.5   3.5   5   5
123 East 90th Street, New York, NY 10128
(212) 427 - 5752   dgoldstein@gothampainting.com
Impeccable straight and decorative painting, plastering, and wallpapering

For top-quality workmanship and exceptional service, notable designers, contractors, and private clients highly recommend this leading full-service firm. Crews are said to be attentive and neat, and Gotham's customers are impressed with their skill in straight painting, decorative finishes, restorative plastering, and wallpapering. In addition, the company handles period restorations, plus some decorative work.

David Goldstein's team of 65 fans out all over Manhattan, and clients say the foremen are the "best in town." Goldstein, who ran someone else's company for many years, brings big-league experience to the firm he started in 1990. We are told that for this level of impeccable service, you can't beat Gotham's price.

"Gotham painting is perfection." "Very responsive and professional." "I've contracted numerous painters over the years—Gotham was prompt, friendly, neat. Also, they were in and out on time." "Their price is a bargain for the high-end work—not a speck of spackle dust to be found." "The foremen are clear, polite, and run a smooth job site." "If you are a particular person who expects full service and amazing results, this is the firm for you!"

Old Vienna Painting   4.5   3.5   5   5

24316 Thornhill Avenue, Douglaston, NY 11362
(718) 428 - 5457   oldvienna@verizon.net

Choice decorative and straight painting and wallpapering

Old Vienna Painting specializes in straight and decorative painting and wallpapering in New York City residences. Principal Hans Pavlacka has been painting all his life. Trained in apprenticeships throughout Europe, this artisan handles glazing, faux finishes, plastering, and restoration of moldings. Clients report the small team at Old Vienna restores old apartments back to their original glory through meticulous prep work and a great sense of color. Many insist that Pavlacka is the only person they'll allow near their walls with a paintbrush. In business since 1966, Old Vienna is known to maintain excellent relationships with clients, and has thrived largely on referrals, thanks to its superior work and its popular prices.

"Over fifteen years of working with numerous painters, one stands out as the best. Hans has painted some of the finest Fifth and Park Avenue apartments and lobbies for us and our clients." "Reliable, consistent, and top quality." "Great eye for color when doing decorative painting." "Consider yourself fortunate if Hans paints your apartment." "His painting is beautiful, his prep work is first rate." "Old Vienna is the absolute top end of what a great painter should be." "Such a wonderful experience—Hans is a gem."

Painting by Picker   3.5   3   4.5   4.5

219 East 85th Street, New York, NY 10028
(212) 535 - 6380

Straight and decorative painting and wallpapering

A good pick since 1980, Robert Picker and his small and charming crew are as popular with private clients as they are with the trade. The firm offers straight and decorative painting (specializing in faux finishes such as sponging and ragging) as well as wallpapering services. Upper East Side references love Picker's helpful, funny, and easygoing manner, and tell us his crew is fastidiously neat, very prompt, and attentive to the furnishings. Clients rave that Picker does high-quality work at fair and reasonable prices.

"Managed the crew very well, kept them laughing. They love working for him, always on time." "The apartment was cleaner after he left than it was before he came." "He is an artist—I loved working with him." "Robert is flexible and able to work with different budgets—while he did my mother's apartment to the highest standards, he did a terrific but less detailed, less expensive job for me." "The crew is extraordinarily helpful."

	Quality	Cost	Value	Recommend?
	➕	💲	◆	★

Penna Inc.

4 4 4 4

405 East 51st Street, Suite 6F, New York, NY 10022
(212) 935 - 5747 www.pennainc.com

Straight and decorative painting, custom glazes, wallcovering and leather installation

Described by A-list clients as professional and hardworking, owner Dean Penna and his team of 40 have a reputation for being polite, friendly, and an "absolute pleasure" to deal with. Whether a straight painting job or an elaborate decorative project, we hear the boss is a perfectionist and the finished product is marvelous—and that throughout the process, crews are known for being meticulously neat.

In business since 1989, Penna's talents go beyond the paintbrush. Often working with decorators, the company handles more complicated tasks such as fabric wallcovering and "masterful" leather installations. Sources say prices are on the higher side, while praising Penna's clear and up-front job descriptions, proper staffing, immaculate upkeep during the project, and timely execution. Fans say, "Expect exceptional results."

"Excellent teams. They are discreet, careful, conscientious, hard working and accommodating." "They always have a big smile, and create a smile on the client and designer." "Dean has a 'can do' personality that actually delivers." "A no-fuss painting contractor who understands the service business." "I've known Dean for years, and he keeps getting better with each job." "Dean's mantra is 'no sweat.'" "All of Penna's tradespeople are highly skilled, efficient, and a pleasure to work with." "I wish all my experiences with contractors could be this rewarding. They may be a bit pricey, but it is well worth it."

Pennington Painting & Restoration LLC

5 4 4.5 5

800 Hoydens Hill Road, Fairfield, CT 06824
(203) 319 - 1800 fpball@yahoo.com

High-end interior and exterior painting, decorative finishing, cabinet glazing, and wallpapering

Glancing at the list of posh clients and decorators on Pennington's "to-do" list, you would think you were reading a who's who in construction and interior design. Industry leaders and homeowners alike praise Frank Ball and his multitalented staff for their skill—and their solid business practices. Equally comfortable with a designer, on a construction site, or in the home of a well-to-do homeowner, the team at Pennington could never be called "prima donnas." In fact, quite the opposite is true. The crew has been described as flexible, accommodating, and "professional—a real group of team players."

A former art teacher, Ball not only inspires his staff of 22, but likes to educate his clients. Truly a full-service firm since 1986, Pennington handles interior and exterior painting, an endless list of decorative finishes, and wallpapering at hefty prices.

"In my book, he gets the gold medal." "A higher class of painting contractor." "Their personal touch (along with the highest level of detail that I have seen in the industry), separates them from the pack." "The decorative finishes are so good that people often think it's wallpaper." "Frank encourages the homeowner to learn more about the process—I felt a great sense of ownership with respect to our project. I even joined the crew in sanding the edges of knot holes in antique floor boards before they were stained."

Simonson & Baric

5 4 5 4.5

847 Lexington Avenue, Suite 3F, New York, NY 10021
(212) 570 - 1996 simonsonandbaric@aol.com

Tip-top straight residential painting and wallpapering

Knowing that you are only as good as your last job, the large team at Simonson & Baric put customer service at the head of the table when serving up residential painting and wallpapering. "Charming" partners Arthur Simonson and John Baric met on the job and formed a business in 1981. In-the-know insiders say the firm can handle anything, and that the "over-the-top" attention exhibited on each job translates into exceptional quality. Of course, all this comes at a premium, but sources tell us the superb work is well worth it.

"Maestros of straight painting—capable of really big jobs." "Old World, but can do new." "They like to be pushed and get it." "Always does a meticulous job. A real treat." "Simonson is the best of the best." "Expensive, but you get what you pay for." "Painstaking attention to detail."

Thomas Lent Painting   3.5   3   4.5   5
414 East 89th Street, New York, NY 10128
(212) 722 - 7312
Straight and decorative painting and wallpapering

Thomas Lent Painting came on the straight and decorative painting scene in 1972. Since then, its painting and wallpapering services have made many Upper East Side decorators look good. Sources tell us Lent himself (who has been painting since his high school days) and the small staff are hardworking, knowledgeable, and committed to excellence. Despite the care dedicated to each and every task, we hear prices haven't changed much in years.

"A reliable painting company that always delivers." "Takes every job seriously, and we have used him for years." "They are helpful in choosing color and finish." "Wonderful and caring." "From beginning to end, a top-rate job." "No detail is overlooked—I'm thrilled."

UK Fabric & Wallcovering   4.5   4   4.5   4.5
56 Soundview Avenue, Norwalk, CT 06854
(203) 979 - 1960   dhukusa@yahoo.com
Choice fabric and English wallpaper installation, decorative painting

Upper East Side clients thank their lucky stars that they've found David Haith and his twenty-two-year-old company, UK Fabric & Wallcovering. Specializing in fabric and English wallpaper, the charming and personable Haith began training at the age of sixteen in his native England. There he learned Old-World techniques and graduated from Her Majesty's School of Professional Paperhanging. Working primarily through decorators, Haith has developed a reputation of excellence in the industry—so much so that he has been called upon to conduct instructional seminars for the likes of Osbourne & Little and other high-end paper houses.

Haith handles all of the wallpapering himself, but has a meticulous crew that takes care of all the prep work. In addition, Haith also has a decorative painter on staff to round out the company's offerings. UK's prices are not inexpensive, but sources insist "it costs money to get a master."

"David is a lovely man whose realized work is admired. I was fortunate to have the opportunity to engage his services." "Highly professional, and delivers impeccable work on a consistent basis." "There is no one else that I would trust to work with our high-end wallcoverings and fabric." "Beautiful work—the only one I'd trust to hang English 'paper-paper'."

Hiring a Pest Control Service Provider

Roaches, mice, rats, termites, carpenter ants, ants, fleas, ticks, spiders, and silver fish. These are the ten most common household pests, and according to the National Pest Management Association (NPMA), every house in America has been visited by at least one of them in the past year. Even though do-it-yourself pest-control kits are readily available, they are not as effective as the services offered by professionals. The application of pesticides is just one part of a total pesticide management program, which typically includes safety considerations, prevention methods, and structural modifications. Whereas untrained homeowners may be able to apply pesticides with varying degrees of success, professionals rely on training, expertise, and sophisticated techniques to control pesticide infestations in an efficient, economical, and safe manner—protecting the long-term interests of the homeowner's family and the environment. Not all pest control service providers are alike. While most work to eliminate a wide range of infestations, termite abatement requires a different kind of training and licensing and, therefore, a different kind of exterminator. In addition to eliminating bugs from your living space, a lot of these professionals also specialize in removing birds and rodents, persuading squirrels to nest elsewhere, etc. Generally, exterminators advocate that home owners practice prevention to the greatest extent possible to minimize disease and damage to property. In fact, most reputable firms will happily provide training on standards of cleanliness in order to prevent infestations and mating, as well as counsel on cleanup of eggs and droppings.

Where Do I Start?

The first step involved in seeking the services of a pest control expert is to perform a preliminary inspection of your home yourself. Beware of exterminators who arrive at your doorstep unsolicited and offer free inspections. They tend to prey on homeowners' general ignorance about pests by intimidating them into authorizing immediate and expensive treatments. It has been rumored that some such service providers will bring bug specimens with them and release them into the premises of unsuspecting homeowners (a clever variation on the "fly-in-my-soup" routine). When seeking an exterminator, be sure to have ready a list of the kind of infestation you have or suspect you have, the number of pets, children, and adults that inhabit your home, any allergies these inhabitants have, and the number of rooms in your home. These factors will determine the kind of exterminator you need to hire and the processes that will ultimately be used to eliminate infestations.

A Variety of Pest Control Methods

Pest control is a highly specialized industry and its jargon can be confusing. Be sure to ask the service provider for a description of each project and a success-rate estimate for each procedure. If, for instance, an exterminator advises fumigating your home with toxic gas to get rid of termites, ask for a detailed description of the method and its possible hazards. Not every extermination, however, requires you to leave the premises for a few hours and subsequently air out your home. New technology, such as microwave and electro-gun systems, may be safer for families with children (and pets). Work with the professional to choose which option best suits your needs.

ON COST

Once you've conducted a preliminary inspection and suspect the presence of a residential freeloader, contact a licensed pest control service provider. Since large projects are often costly and require skill, expertise, and knowledge, it is generally suggested that you get several bids from multiple vendors for large projects. Different firms charge varying rates, depending on 1) the scale and nature of the project, 2) the complexity of the infestation, and 3) the potential need to remove walls and other structures. While there are no standard hourly or per-room charges, most exterminators are usually happy to give free estimates when they perform preliminary inspections.

CONTRACTS AND GUARANTEES

Once you decide on a firm, negotiate a contract and get it in writing. In the contract, specify the nature of the infestation, the extent of the infestation and the resulting damage, the exact services to be provided, description of guarantees, the desired end result (abatement only or continuing control), and how long the treatment is expected to last. Some exterminators do offer guarantees with their contracts. Be realistic about guarantee provisions that promise a one-time total solution! Cockroach abatement, for instance, needs to be renewed every six months in order to be completely effective. While this may seem a little excessive, remember that roaches can survive a nuclear explosion—one electronic or chemical application will merely amuse them.

IMPORTANT ISSUES ABOUT THIS HIGHLY REGULATED INDUSTRY

Because exterminators handle highly toxic products, they should undergo rigorous training to practice their profession. A pest control specialist's membership in a national or regional professional association is usually a good indicator that the service provider has access to the most cutting-edge technical information and is committed to ongoing education. Inquire about a service provider's affiliations and follow up by verifying membership with the professional organization. The NPMA is one of the largest and best-known national organizations in the field and can be reached online (www.pestworld.org) or by calling (703) 573-8330. State organizations include the New York State Pest Management Association (www.nyspma.com) which can be contacted at (877) 521-7378 for more local information.

INSURANCE

Permits and licensing are not the only business issues to verify before hiring an exterminator. It is crucial to find out whether or not the exterminator carries liability insurance to cover potential damage to property and/or to people in the course of the exterminator's work. If the exterminator doesn't carry such insurance, check your homeowner's policy for coverage. In the absence of both, consider buying insurance to protect your belongings and yourself from liability.

WHAT'S BUGGING YOU?

A few precautions to help prevent pest-nesting in your home:

✧ **Termites:** Wet wood is every termite's favorite meal. Get rid of old tree stumps, foam boards, and wood debris around your house and rid your home of excess moisture, making sure gutters are unclogged and all pipe leaks are promptly fixed.

✧ **Rodents:** Take out the trash. Daily! Garbage is a rat's favorite nesting ground, and they begin to mate at the tender age of five weeks to produce up to 48 spawn a year. Also, be vigilant about keeping all the entry points into your home clean and clear, including ducts, vents, and chimneys.

✧ **Cockroaches:** While it is very hard to combat a cockroach infestation without professional help, a few tactics will go a long way toward keeping them at bay: proper ventilation, fitting all holes with screens, sealing around pipes where they come through the floor and ceiling, and storing and/or covering all food (yours and your pets'!).

PEST CONTROL

A All Borough Exterminating Co.
139 Finlay Street, Staten Island, NY 10307
(718) 356 - 1100   billybugs@aol.com
Pest control

4   3   5   4

We're told that A All Borough Exterminating completes major jobs in just a few house calls—saving many customers the hassle of a series of visits. William Macri and his five employees handle anything—including birds. But most regulars say that it's the firm's awareness of the environment that attracts them, noting the shop uses fewer chemicals. The firm's "animal-friendly" policy ensures that birds, skunks, or squirrels are returned to their natural habitat. Clients commend Macri and his staff for their "cheerful attitude" and concern for the health and safety of all parties involved—both animal and human.

In business since 1975, the shop services the five boroughs in addition to Long Island, Westchester, and New Jersey. The company also performs home and building inspection for both buyers and sellers. Rates and the number of check-ups depend on the client and the job, but A All Borough also offers weekly, monthly, or yearly maintenance plans at very sane prices.

"Bill frequently calls and will come by to check everything out." "Right away he realized our rodent problem was coming from our next door neighbor." "Quickly got rid of my pest problem." "Honest and reliable!" "He's a great guy who does an excellent job." "Bill seems to really care about what he does. He showed up on time, and stayed to talk about preventive measures we could take."

A.C.E. Inc.
717 East 52nd Street, Brooklyn, NY 11203
(718) 629 - 6660   a23pest@aol.com
Environmentally sensitive pest control

4   2.5   5   4.5

An environmentally sensitive choice for pest control, A.C.E. stresses the importance of using "nontoxic," long-term methods. Principal Donovan Glave and his employees are known to use creative techniques when dealing with insects, rodents, birds, and any other animals that may invade the home or business. Sources say this small firm prides itself on its training program, which helps establish consistency throughout the company. Many tell us A.C.E. carefully screens customers to ensure that the firm associates with people who share its vision of long-term toxin-free abatement and eradication. Its loyal customers are pleased when A.C.E educates them on procedures, even when it requires that they become active participants in the elimination of pests.

A.C.E. has been coming to the aid of clients in the five boroughs, Long Island, Westchester, and northern New Jersey since 1990. We hear Glave will go above and beyond for a customer, climbing the ladder himself to reach a ceiling infested with mice. Patrons say the continual communication between customer and vendor is strengthened with quality evaluation surveys and independent quality assurance teams, which inspect recent projects. Although A.C.E.'s methods may seem too hands-on for some, those willing to take matters seriously say the techniques produce a safe and pest-free environment. Costs are low, especially considering the emergency service available Sunday through Thursday.

"Donovan is one of the most personable people I've met." "He always finds a solution and explains everything to me." "Just amazing at finding areas I would have never thought to plug up." "I call him my beloved exterminator—we haven't seen a mouse in two years." "A guy who is very capable and knows what he's doing." "We like the fact that he uses natural products." "Keeps his appointments and always on time." "Our 100-year-old townhouse in the West Village was infested with rats. Donovan saved the day." "Not cheap but I'm not complaining." "I felt very comfortable giving him the run of the house." "Donovan's an ace."

Broadway Exterminating Company Inc.   4   2.5   5   4.5
782 Amsterdam Avenue, New York, NY 10025
(212) 663 - 2100 www.broadwayexterminating.com

Quick, effective pest control

New Yorkers bugged by household irritants say Broadway Exterminating Company corners the problem with a "safer" solution using smaller amounts of pesticides to combat the problem. Most references are happy with Broadway's swift results and describe its work as "top quality." They also praise the firm for its "reliability." Not surprisingly, a large share of Broadway's revenues come from the repeat business of satisfied customers, many of whom remark that the crew go in like detectives to clear up the mess right away.

A family-owned operation, Richard Miller oversees the company he founded in 1971. Service is available to all New York City boroughs and the storefront shop in Manhattan offers do-it-yourself products said to be well worth the affordable prices.

"After four visits the bed bugs were gone." "A good company I have relied on for years." "They are quick and get the job done." "Worked in my townhouse for the past six years and are very efficient." "I can only say the results were excellent for the price and the follow-ups were less expensive than the initial visit." "You can tell it's a family-run business, they were incredibly thorough."

Exterminare Pest Control Service   4   4   4   4.5
430 East 6th Street, New York, NY 10009
(212) 254 - 4444 www.exterminare.com

Top-notch, multi-faceted pest control; bird control specialists

Exterminare Pest Control Service "thoroughly wipes out" pest problems and comes up with "smart solutions" to put customers at ease. Although its specialty is rodent proofing and removal, Exterminare also provides insect, bird, and animal eradication as well. Clients tell us owner Herb Schneider takes charge of the situation "swiftly" and with "positive results." The small company is known to handle several high-profile commercial and residential clients who say Exterminare Pest Control Service's child-friendly methods allow for safety and convenience.

Schneider's firm (which he runs with his wife, daughter, and son) has been around since 1973. He is said to have extensive knowledge of the field and serves on the board of directors of the Professional Pest Control Association of NYC. All Schneider's technicians are licensed and trained in bird control—another one of its specialties. Schneider and his team offer friendly service to the five boroughs, Mt. Vernon, New Rochelle, and parts of Nassau County, accompanied by ample follow-up with competent (if slightly pricey) service.

"We use Exterminare for our residential buildings with real pest problems because I know they will do a better job than most." "I found them through one of my unit owners, and Herb has proven to be an expert." "A knowledgeable and thorough shop." "We had a terrible rodent problem and they showed up right away and relieved our anxiety." "They are well worth the expense." "I have never had a complaint from any of my residents." "Caring and efficient."

	Quality	Cost	Value	Recommend?

Knockout Pest Control — 3.5 3 4.5 4.5
1009 Front Street, Uniondale, NY 11553
(800) 244 - 7378 www.knockoutpest.com

Knowledgeable, reliable pest control

Knockout Pest Control KO's household pests. We're told it's one of the first companies in the New York City area to offer the Sentricon Termite Colony Elimination System—a specific noninvasive termite prevention and eradication method. This 30-year-old firm offers helpful services for ridding the home of rodents, birds, animals, and insects. Although this company prefers bait technology for its value and efficiency, they are open to other methods. Sources highly recommend Knockout Pest Control for being "very respectful" while in a home and praise its "knowledgeable" technicians.

Founder Arthur Katz and his 27 employees do residential, commercial, and industrial work in all five boroughs as well as Suffolk and Nassau counties. As certified home inspectors they will examine all areas of a house for prospective homebuyers. Insiders note Katz's commitment to the industry—he has served on the Board of Directors of the Long Island Pest Control Association and has been a past president of the New York State Pest Control Association. Continual up-to-date employee training is mandated and clients are educated in all areas of pest control. Free estimates are available, and Knockout offers an excellent one-year protection plan at reasonable prices.

"I called three services, and Knockout Pest Control was the only one that was able to help me immediately by having a representative answer my questions when I called." "They are always on time." "Knockout's technicians are very professional and polite." "Everyone is very patient and friendly with my 'bug phobia' and I appreciate it."

Magic Exterminating Company — 3.5 3 4.5 4
59-01 Kassena Boulevard, Flushing, NY 11355
(212) 645 - 6191 www.suburbanexterminating.com

Pest control

Magic Exterminating Company makes insects and rodents disappear in buildings and apartments throughout the five boroughs of New York. Founded by Hal Byer, this family-owned and operated shop eliminates infestations using fewer pesticides. Clients applaud this "dependable" and "efficient" firm and commend Byer for his genuine concern for their environment.

In business since 1961, the shop has a large staff of technicians and quality control experts that are fully qualified in their respective fields. Big and small jobs are taken for residential, commercial, and institutional pest problems with prices that are said to be mid-range. While Magic's service area is limited to the five boroughs, its sister company, Suburban Pest Control, handles jobs on Long Island.

"They always respond quickly when I have any bug problem in my home." "I trust them in my apartment all the time." "They performed magic—the pests were gone."

Metro Pest Control — 4.5 4 4.5 4.5
70-09 73rd Place, Glendale, NY 11385
(212) 545 - 0888 www.metropest.com

Expert all-around pest control; non-chemical specialists

Metro Pest Control has been in the rat race since 1977 and knows how to handle "big city" infestations. Offering all standard services, Metro is also equipped to hunt down mosquitoes, rodents, and bed bugs, and to capture birds, squirrels, and bats. Sources tell us Metro uses a non-chemical natural botanical pesticide, a less toxic way to eliminate pests. Customers who are sensitive and prefer an environmentally friendly solution appreciate Metro's commitment to providing a "safe" alternative.

Owner Ben Weisel leads this large firm of 65 employees, whose technicians are background-screened. The company serves all five boroughs, mainly working for residential clients but also handling commercial and institutional customers. We hear this well-established shop prides itself on its "friendly relationships" and that if you leave a message after hours, someone will get back to you quickly. Prices are described as a little higher than expected, but fans say the service is definitely well worth the cost.

"Metro has been servicing our residential buildings for ten years without a complaint." "We tried out twelve other pest control companies before we found Metro—they are the very best." "Our firm has 35 buildings in the New York area and we use them for all our pest problems." "They are very knowledgeable and always know what they're doing." "Metro gets the job done." "The employees are polite and courteous." "Has done the building for over five years, comes every two weeks." "Reliable, many buildings on my street use them."

Positive Pest Management   3.5   3   4.5   4
154-52 Tenth Avenue, Whitestone, NY 11357
(800) 294 - 3130 www.positivepest.com

Pest control

With "indisputable determination" we hear Positive Pest Management sweeps away the infestation fears of apartment dwellers and homeowners alike. Sources tell us owner Benett Pearlman has a "driven" personality and his staff is known to "get down to the nitty gritty of the problem." Positive prefers to use fewer chemicals and has a specialist on board to handle all wildlife problems with sensitivity.

The well-respected Pearlman was elected by his peers to the position of regional director of the New York State Pest Management Association. Founded in 1999, his firm has done business in all five boroughs, Long Island, and lower Westchester. We hear Pearlman's small staff is eager to take on even the most challenging jobs—like ridding an infested job site of thousands of water bugs. Prices are more than reasonable considering the good work and 24/7 service.

"Even though he's a new guy on the block, Benett is performing as well as some that have been in business for years." "Benett handles all our residential buildings with very satisfactory results." "Good prices—eager to please." "I have to say he is very reliable and knows what he's doing."

Terminate Control   4.5   3.5   4.5   5
441 East 12th Street, New York, NY 10009
(212) 995 - 0668 terminatecontrol@aol.com

Time-tested, multiple-method pest control

With over 50 years' experience stamping out household nuisances, Terminate Control is used to playing the part of Terminator. Clients and insiders appreciate the "personal service" and "lasting relationships" developed by this family-run firm. Principal Gary Packer has clocked many hours in protecting homes from insects, rodents, birds, and animals. Sources say the shop's traditional methods of exterminating are complemented by newly developed, more environmentally friendly techniques that use fewer chemicals.

Quality	Cost	Value	Recommend?
✚	$	◆	★

Aiding generations of customers from Wall Street to Harlem to the outer boroughs, Terminate has a large and devoted following. Packer took over the reins in 1985 from his great-uncle, who started the business in 1945. Working with residential and commercial clients, Packer and his five employees are reputedly happy to answer any questions 24/7, and we hear Packer recently saved a damsel in distress when a scorpion trespassed in her Upper East Side apartment. Depending upon the job, we hear prices can run from reasonable to high end.

"A walking encyclopedia—they know everything." "We have used his services forever with excellent results." "Gary is very trustworthy." "They come to my house like clockwork, even when it's an emergency." "We have a great relationship with him, really nothing bad to say." "He is always on time, and his fees are reasonable for what he does." "They're really on top of things."

Hiring a Plumber

Whether it's trimming out a kitchen and bath remodel, installing an entire system for a new home, a routine repair or maintenance call, or an absolute emergency, you need a plumber you can count on. Although most plumbers are available for a simple service call, some high-end service providers prefer to limit such calls, especially 24-hour emergency service, to existing customers. This practice ensures that the firm's established clientele will receive the highest level of service and quality with a prompt response.

Where Do I Start?

Hold on to that plumbing contractor who has proven himself over the course of a major project. Handpicked by your trusty general contractor (GC), he knows the guts of your home better than anyone. Even if you aren't planning a renovation and just need someone to handle more mundane problems like leaky faucets, it's worth putting in the effort to build a relationship with a plumber who can offer quality and service, so he'll be there before you're sunk. If you are starting from scratch, remember that some plumbers focus only on larger-scale contract installations and remodels, while others devote their efforts entirely to service and repair. Marry your job to the right plumber. The best first sign is someone answering the phone—not just an answering service—but a live company employee in an actual office. If you can't get hold of someone during business hours, the chances you'll get a response on a Saturday night when your bathroom looks like Niagara Falls are slim.

A decent high-end plumber shouldn't be spooked by foreign or custom fixtures, nor should he force his standard ones down your throat. With product he is unfamiliar with he should do his homework, consulting with the manufacturer to ensure proper installation. While plumbing basics haven't changed much in 100 years, the firm should also be up on the latest technology—like energy-efficient tankless water heaters and sound suppression systems—and be able to deliver options at different price points.

Calling references is your last line of defense. For larger jobs like kitchen remodels that require coordination between trades, contractors are the best assessors of a firm's performance. For smaller service and maintenance jobs, clients are your best bet. To both you'll want to ask the usual questions about quality of work and whether the project was finished on schedule and on budget. However, because plumbing can be a messy business, respect for surroundings and cleanliness are equally important.

A Job for Professionals

You should only consider a full-time licensed professional for your plumbing needs. Though a license is not required in New York to perform basic plumbing maintenance work, your service provider must be licensed for any jobs that require the filing of a permit. As always, ask about insurance, including worker's compensation and liability insurance. Your plumbing professional should always be responsible for obtaining all permits necessary for your job.

ON COST

For larger projects, each plumbing contractor will submit its bid to the GC, who will then incorporate it into the overall bid submitted to the client. Often the GC for your project will bring in a trusted plumber for the job, but you are free to ask your GC to include another plumber in the bidding process, which ensures that bids are competitive. If your renovation is relatively small and a GC is not involved, get several estimates for the proposed work.

For smaller jobs and service calls, which include repair and maintenance, most companies charge an hourly rate, usually $100 for a single plumber, $150 for a dispatched two-man team. A 3 Cost rating in *The Franklin Report* approximately reflects these standards. However, please remember, a company's standards in relation to product and safety, the depth of its resources, and the demand of its customer base can all affect cost on top of hourly rates, and are factored into the rating.

Some companies charge a set one-time diagnostic fee to produce an estimate even for smaller jobs, while others will send troubleshooters or technicians to assess the work and come up with a price free of charge. All will work up fixed estimates for larger jobs to be executed in a contract. Fees for contract renovation work are typically higher than fees for new construction per hour and per square foot. In the end, it should come down to the company with the best reputation for quality and service, not just the low bidder.

GUARANTEES AND SERVICE AGREEMENTS

When your equipment is installed, it should come with both a warranty from the manufacturer and a guarantee from the service provider. Be sure to ask about service agreements. Many plumbing professionals will provide regular "checkups" and inspections. It may seem like wasted money at first, but over time these measures can prevent an emergency.

SAVE MONEY BY SAVING TIME

If you inventory the state of your plumbing and think ahead about work that will need to be done, your plumber will be able to work more effectively. Check faucets, drains, radiators, and fixtures throughout the house and compile a list. Present this list to the plumber upon arrival so he can prioritize the various tasks and work simultaneously if possible. This way, you won't have to call him in again for another minor repair in a few weeks.

If the plumber will need access to the pipes under your kitchen sink, clear out the area to save billable time. Also put away or protect anything vulnerable to damage. Your plumber will appreciate being able to get to work without having to wade through piles of children's toys or rummage around in a cabinet full of cleaning supplies.

Don't wait until your bathroom is flooded with four inches of water. Develop a good relationship with a plumber now, and you'll never have to page frantically through a phone book and throw yourself at the mercy of whatever plumber happens to be free.

<u>MORE THAN PIPES</u>

Your plumber is trained to do much more than fix clogged drains. A full-service plumber can:

✧ Provide condensation drains for air-conditioning units.

✧ Install the boiler, lines, and radiators necessary for household heat.

✧ Install hot water recirculation and water pressure booster pumps.

✧ Hook up major appliances (gas stoves, washing machines).

✧ Make a gas-meter connection, install gas lines, and provide gas shutoff valves.

✧ Install storm/slop drains for the kitchen, patio, garage, and laundry rooms.

PLUMBERS

AC Klem Plumbing & Heating   4   3.5   4.5   4
37-24 33rd Street, Long Island City, NY 11101
(718) 433 - 2400

Plumbing installation; pipe and drain cleaning specialists

With a history reaching back over 50 years, over 50 people on staff, and a booming uptown business, AC Klem is widely recognized as one of the city's premier plumbers. The firm mainly does large renovations and new construction to the trade, but keeps its existing clients happy with 24-hour emergency service and radio-dispatched trucks. AC Klem also installs and repairs radiant heating systems and condensation pipes for AC units. Clients say the firm provides highly skilled and friendly service, delivering "top, top" quality to both residential and commercial clients in New York. References report that the staff is reliable and trustworthy, and that the company's response times are hard to beat. Above-average costs are reflected in above-average quality.

"Everyone says best of the best." "Great guys. Great company." "Call them for big projects."

Anchor Plumbing   4   3   5   4.5
449 Graham Avenue, Brooklyn, NY 11211
(718) 383 - 5100 anchorplbg@aol.com

Plumbing installation; renovation specialists

In business since 1977, this small shop is recognized for its solid workmanship and affordable prices. The firm's strong suit is renovation, and principal Steve Einhorn, the dependable anchor of the firm, has worked in Manhattan's finer townhouses, apartments, and brownstones. Sources say he and his team have the know-how to work with high-end residential contractors, from the design stage to cleanup. We also hear that the company excels at radiant heating jobs.

Though Anchor has a dedicated truck for service calls, it will only work on existing clients' pipes. Some sources have experienced service back-ups, prompting them to wish Anchor was a larger outfit. However, the same sources are quick to point out that the firm's small size allows Einhorn to put his invaluable personal stamp on all of the company's work.

"Incredibly well-priced." "Good man with a good company. Timely, knowledgeable, and effective." "Steve is a whiz-kid. Calling him is like calling a plumbing encyclopedia." "Anchor gets involved at the design stage in a meaningful way."

Demar Plumbing & Heating Corp.   3.5   3   4   4
147 Attorney Street, New York, NY 10002
(212) 614 - 9717

Plumbing installation and service; gas boiler specialists

Principal Alex Demarines has run Demar plumbing for eleven years—and his father ran it for 25 years before him. The succinct and efficient Demarines says the company is named "Demar" because "Demarines" is too long. Sources say this firm is quick and extremely reliable, both for full-scale renovations and smaller repairs. Its 30-person staff works primarily with downtown building management companies, but they'll send out a two-man team for service jobs to anyone in Manhattan. Rates are reasonable for the quality, with a standard one-hour minimum charge. The firm specializes in gas boiler installation/repair and sprinkler maintenance, but we're told they'll take on whatever's necessary, day or night.

"They handle emergencies well." "I've worked with them for fifteen years, and they've never showed up late once."

Efficient Plumbing & Heating   3.5   3.5   4   4
580 Sackett Street, Brooklyn, NY 11217
(718) 237 - 4114   efficientplumb@aol.com
Commercially focused plumbing installation

Having recently scaled back in size to a ten-person team, Efficient lives up to its name. The firm is well respected by both residential and commercial contractors, and with over twenty-five years and two generations in the plumbing and heating business, these plumbers have earned their stripes over time.

Efficient does have a commercial bent, which reduces the amount of energy the firm has to expend on residential clients. However, the firm's big-job focus means it can bring big-job expertise to your home. We're told that Efficient especially excels at working in high-rise co-ops or townhouses, on jobs like combining two apartments into one or splitting a single brownstone into two duplexes—in other words, the complicated stuff. The firm is also licensed to install and maintain sprinkler systems. It will only service existing clients.

"Great for those interesting jobs that you don't see every day."

Fred Smith Plumbing & Heating Co.   5   3   5   5
1674 First Avenue, New York, NY 10128
(212) 744 - 1300
Top-notch plumbing installation and service

The professionals at Fred Smith—known informally as the "rocket scientists" of plumbing—lend their NASA-level expertise to both small and large jobs at all phases of the plumbing process. The company brings 85 years of experience and one of its nine field supervisors to troubleshoot and assess each job, free of charge, before sending the mechanic. Led by principal Phillip Kraus, the firm reportedly can "adjust to anything" and consistently delivers efficient, top-quality work. Based right in the heart of the city, we're told Fred Smith keeps service technicians in reserve to ensure a quick response time.

While references tell us the firm has "A" and "B" crews, clients describe all of Fred Smith's men as consummate professionals—courteous of clients, respectful of space, and highly skilled. Managers of prestigious co-ops and flagship general contractors all recommend Fred Smith without exception. Interestingly, as a result of economies of scale and the firm's meticulous troubleshooting, Fred Smith's prices are competitive with anyone in the city. And considering the fact that about 60% of the firm's repair jobs are done with one man and charged accordingly, the firm may be not only the city's best overall plumbing contractor, but one of its best values as well.

| | Quality | Cost | Value | Recommend? |

"They are fabulous. Fred is tremendous!" "The best of the best—no question." "Has the best response time in town because of the large staff. Does great work." "Clean, efficient, friendly." "No job is too tough." "Came in under their estimate. What more could I ask for?"

Henry Myers Plumbing & Heating   4   3   4.5   5
68-10 Eighth Avenue, Brooklyn, NY 11220
(718) 836 - 1324
Plumbing installation and service

Word is this mid-sized, family-run business "does great work" serving both residential and commercial clients, and is ranked among the city's finest afford-able plumbers. The firm operates with four crews: two focused on working with contractors on major renovations, the other two attending to service calls. Most jobs are either in Manhattan or Brooklyn, but if you have a serious undertaking, they'll make the trek. References report Henry Myers is at its best in smaller jobs, which the owner takes as seriously as major overhauls. Free estimates precede most jobs, which clients find valuable. Hourly rates are slightly below standard, another perk.

"The kind of guy that you call to come in and fix what some other plumber messed up." "Owner does work himself, which says a lot!" "Even though I'm way out in Queens, they came up to do a small job because we got along well."

John Sideris Plumbing   3.5   3   4   4
123 West 79th Street, New York, NY 10024
(212) 501 - 0971
Plumbing installation and service

A company comprised entirely of master plumbers, John Sideris Plumbing spe-cializes in large residential projects, particularly complete installations, renova-tions, and specialty jobs, such as relocating chimneys or boilers. Its service department also performs 24-hour emergency calls for both residential and com-mercial customers. Whatever the task, the firm charges at a fixed flat rate, alleviating the stress of hourly costs. There is, however, a standard minimum service charge, so think twice before calling Sideris for a mere loose washer.

Clients laud this Manhattan firm's commitment to proper safety practices, and note that it is often called in to fix dangerously faulty installations.

"He's never gone over budget with me." "He's got great political connections. Know-ing the right city employees can help more than you'd think it would."

Kapnag Heating & Plumbing Corp.   3   3   4   4
150 West 28th Street, Suite 501, New York, NY 10001
(212) 929 - 7111
Plumbing installation and service

Kapnag, an octogenarian firm that will renovate, install, and service plumbing systems, carries endorsements from blue-chip city realty companies. However, individual Manhattan homeowners can also call on this twenty-person team for help when the bathroom sink gives out. We hear Kapnag stays as active in smaller repair and maintenance tasks as it does on larger installations and reno-vations, though references tell us the firm's response times could be snappier. However, all agree that one can expect very competent service for a standard price.

"Polite and considerate."

	Quality	Cost	Value	Recommend?
	+	$	◆	★

Mac Felder Plumbing

4   3.5   4.5   4.5

610 Eleventh Avenue, New York, NY 10036
(212) 877 - 8450   mickey@macfelderplumbing.com

Plumbing installation and service

This veteran plumbing contractor keeps both clients—and their pipes—gushing. In business since 1936, the firm takes on jobs of all sizes, almost exclusively in Manhattan. Its speciality is large residential renovations, but it also has a number of service contracts with some very prestigious Upper East Side buildings. Felder fields a "friendly and helpful staff" of 30, reputed to be "very neat," which is no small feat when working with water. The firm repairs heating systems on occasion. Securing this company's services is a notch more expensive than average, but fans are happy to pay for the "outstanding" service.

"Incredible. They never make a mess." "I work with them whenever I can."

McManus Mechanical Maintenance
Plumbing & Heating Inc.

3   3.5   3.5   4

429 Beach 135th Street, Belle Harbor, NY 11694
(718) 945 - 3966   bmcma5@aol.com

Plumbing installation and service; in-floor heating specialists

We hear this plumber provides lightning-quick service to clients both old and new in four of the city's five boroughs (sorry, Staten Island). Cheerful owner Robert McManus brings over two decades' experience to this firm, which performs both small and large installations and repair of plumbing, heating, and fire suppression systems for residential, commercial, institutional, and industrial clients. It's also installed a number of in-floor heating systems recently. Clients tell us McManus's thirteen-person staff is always honest, keeping them 100% informed about the status of their job, along with its pitfalls and hurdles. Rates aren't rock bottom, but they're mid-range for this level of service. Prices drop for jobs outside Manhattan.

N. Pagano Heating & Plumbing
Contractors Ltd.

4   4   4   4.5

370 East 134th Street, Bronx, NY 10451
(718) 993 - 7337

Plumbing installation and service

This small Bronx-based company is run by master plumber Maurizio Taormina, who sources tell us is "a real character" who can "fix everything except broken hearts." The firm's bread and butter is repair and maintenance, but N. Pagano also does full-scale installations and renovations on select residential projects. Clients rave about the "courteous professionals" on staff, whom they describe as thorough, patient, and always quick to respond to calls.

We hear the company fosters a familial atmosphere and delivers consistent high-quality work and excellent service. This may be why Taormina and company are called on by some of the top contractors in the city, one of whom noted that N. Pagano provides "outstanding service at very busy times." The price tag is top-tier, but sources report that you always get what you pay for, if not a little extra, with this personable company.

"Keep up the good work!" "Every mechanic has a certain area of expertise, so the work goes together without much trouble through the job." "You can get the owner on the phone as late as 7:00 PM." "Good company, good men, very responsible." "Good follow-up—I would not hesitate to use them again." "Friendly, funny people."

	Quality	Cost	Value	Recommend?
	+	$	◆	★

New York Plumbing, Heating & Cooling Corp.

3.5   3.5   4   4

87-71 Lefferts Boulevard, Richmond Hill, NY 11418
(718) 441 - 6800   www.nyplumbing.com

Plumbing installation and service; repair specialists

With a military-scale fleet of trucks, 130+ employees, and offices in four boroughs, New York Plumbing, Heating & Cooling is as large as a local plumbing company can get. Twenty-four-hour, seven-day service is their promise, on anything from a dripping pipe to a burst water main. Admittedly, you may not want to call them in to service your imported Belgian fixtures, but we hear their employees are skilled generalists. New York Plumbing charges by the job, not the hour, which many clients prefer.

"Straightforward about prices."

Ozery Plumbing & Heating Inc.

5   4   5   5

206 East 119th Street, New York, NY 10035
(212) 410 - 6800   eddeo@aol.com

High-end plumbing installation and service; heating and fire suppression specialists

If Manhattan plumbers can be called "rough," Ed Ozery is the diamond among them. His small, select, and highly skilled team has been pleasing residential and commercial clients in Manhattan for 27 years on larger installation and renovation projects. We hear the hands-on Ozery offers "simple explanations to complex problems" and a "serious can-do attitude." Top contractors, architects, and designers all look to this firm, citing his planning and supervisory capabilities.

Ozery specializes in high-end residential and commercial plumbing, heating, fire suppression, gas boilers, hydronics, and radiant floor heating. He's also been getting into construction and design on townhouses and co-ops. With a teaching degree in art education, Ozery's aesthetic sense goes beyond bathtubs and sinks. Plumbing-wise, we are told that maintaining and servicing his existing clients (a rather star-studded list) is his top priority, so he tends to stay away from all other basic service calls. Recently, his firm adopted a somewhat pricey minimum service charge, but if it's something small and the talkative Ozery is in your neighborhood, he might fix it for free. Though prices are clearly not for the faint of heart, his loyal clientele would not think of hiring another.

"I've used Ed Ozery for two years now and other than the occupational hazard of over-chattiness, he's just great. You can consider yourself lucky if he works for you." "You may pay a lot, but you only pay once and it's fixed. That says a lot."

Pro-Tech Heating & Plumbing Corp.

4   3.5   4   4

11-12 Clintonville Street, Whitestone, NY 11357
(718) 767 - 9067   www.protech-plbg.com

Plumbing installation and service

One of the better mid-sized, full-service operations in the city, the accurately named Pro-Tech is said to have "knowledgeable, good mechanics" who carry themselves professionally. In addition to all-encompassing plumbing, hot-water and steam heating, sewer, and gas work, the firm also offers HVAC service and repair. Top-tier contractors and architects, as well as managers of high-end buildings in New York, repeatedly call on this firm for large projects and small service.

Most appreciate the high priority the firm puts on speed and customer service, with teams "on-call" 24 hours a day. The medium-sized firm has the manpower to deal effectively with emergencies but still offers the personal attention of a smaller firm. Clients' "only complaint" is that the firm always dispatches two men, even when the job doesn't demand it, "so you tend to pay more for tiny jobs."

"They know what they are doing. Definitely among the top three in the city." "Very knowledgeable."

R&R Plumbing & Heating   3   3   4   4
By appointment, (718) 981 - 3808   www.rrsc.com
Plumbing installation and service; emergency specialists

R&R is part of the Roto-Rooter corporation, the Starbucks of plumbing services. While emergency service is this company's speciality, the firm's ever-expanding residential services also include the installation, repair, and replacement of whole plumbing systems. As with other large organizations, sometimes quality varies from office to office, but most clients report that on emergencies and small-scope jobs, the company does solid work. Roto-Rooter offers free estimates and charges on a flat-fee basis. Appointments and service calls can be scheduled online.

Ranger Plumbing   3.5   3.5   4   4.5
10-15 48th Avenue, Long Island City, NY 11101
(718) 392 - 6607   rangerinc@aol.com
Plumbing installation; renovation specialists

Clients tell us Ranger isn't afraid to explore new ground in high-end residential renovation. Principal Tony Ruggi and VP Gary Kromer go deep to deliver not just quality behind the walls, but a finely buttoned-up finish. We hear they and their small staff have the patience and experience to incorporate imported, handcrafted, or vintage fixtures into their installations. We also hear they've lent their particular talents to a number of bathtubs clogged with celebrity hair. However, clients insist that Ranger's crews offer the same level of service to all their clients, famous or not.

The firm typically takes on everything from small bath fit-outs to apartment guts with heating and gas work. When tackling something outside its expertise, Ranger will subcontract the job out to a seasoned pro. Clients report that the firm is good on follow-through. Prices are just above average for the high-end market.

S. Hoffman Plumbing   3   2.5   3.5   3.5
1775 Broadway, New York, NY 10019
(212) 664 - 0770
Plumbing installation and service

Sources say this competent mid-sized firm cares about getting your pipes in order. S. Hoffman does both smaller repairs and maintenance as well as larger installations for residential clients in Manhattan. While we hear S. Hoffman can get backlogged during busy periods, the crewmen are said to be nice, the work solid, and the rates reasonable, especially for repeat clients.

"Decent guys, fine work—they send me a Christmas card every year." "Always polite, even when things go wrong."

	Quality +	Cost $	Value ◆	Recommend? ★

Sandy's Plumbing

	3.5	3.5	4	4

410 West 48th Street, New York, NY 10036
(212) 475 - 6510

Plumbing installation and service

When we spoke to the principal of Sandy's, he was in the midst of a nine-bathroom installation for a TV star, but his technicians were out fixing leaky faucets. This old-fashioned (they don't even own a computer) father-and-son company has built its reputation on taking both large and small jobs alike. The outfit serves commercial and residential clients throughout Manhattan, including some of the city's finest restaurants and management agencies. We hear the staff at Sandy's is friendly and informative. While they "definitely know what they are doing," some sources report late crewmen. Free estimates are given for major jobs, while minor ones are handed to a two-man team and charged by the hour.

Sanitary Plumbing & Heating Corp.

	3	3.5	3.5	3

211 East 117th Street, New York, NY 10035
(212) 534 - 8186

Plumbing installation

Sanitary Plumbing has been keeping Manhattan pipes clean since 1946. With the benefit of a large staff, this professional firm serves residential and commercial customers on both large and small plumbing and heating jobs. References report that the firm is known mainly for alterations and renovations, so don't call if you only need a washer replaced. Sanitary has an excellent reputation in the business, but some clients balk at its high hourly charges.

Hiring a Rug Cleaning, Installation & Repair Service Provider

Does your heirloom Oriental retain an impression of your adorable yet hard-to- house-train puppy? Did Uncle Mike spill a Bloody Mary on your Persian? Did your cat sharpen his claws on that carefully-hidden corner of your needlepoint? Or is your rug just overdue for its regular cleaning (every two to four years, according to The Oriental Rug Importers of America)? Not to worry: rug cleaners and restorers can address every kind of need on every type of rug, from museum-quality handmade rugs to inexpensive carpeting.

Gathering Information

When choosing cleaners or restorers, there are many factors to consider. Ask if they perform free, written estimates. If they make house calls, do they charge a travel fee, and do they have free pickup, delivery, and reinstallation? Before they quote you a price, you may wish to inquire how they set their rate: by the job, the hour, or the size of the rug? Do they require a deposit? Will they arrange a payment plan if you need one? Do they offer discounts for multiple rugs or rooms? It's a good sign if they honor their estimate, even if the job overwhelms their expectations. It's an even better sign if they guarantee perfection, and don't consider the job finished until you are satisfied. Such an assurance (especially in writing) may be more valuable than letters of reference or membership in one of the professional associations, though both of these would add further reassurance of competence.

If your rug is handmade and you think it may be valuable, you may want to get it appraised by a rug care service before having it cleaned or repaired. If it is valuable, you'll need to consider more expert (and expensive) services. On the other hand, you may also discover that the rug isn't worth nearly as much as you believed, and hence may not warrant lavish attention. Either way, a professional appraisal certifies the value of your belongings in case of mishaps—you may want to inquire beforehand whether liability falls in your court or whether the cleaner/restorer's insurance covers any mishaps. Many rug cleaning and re-weaving establishments appraise rugs for insurance, estate sale, tax, and charitable donation purposes. Watching appraisers evaluate your rug also allows you to preview their professionalism. If their work instills confidence, hire them for the whole job—if not, you can still use their appraisal (and estimate, if they perform one simultaneously) as a first opinion in approaching another establishment. For complicated (expensive) repair or restoration jobs, ask how long it will take. Often the expert restorers have other jobs they must finish before they can get to yours. If your rug is valuable, it is worth waiting for the best.

If the rug needs repair before cleaning, confirm that the restorer knows the techniques of the tradition in which the rug was made: Navajo yarn-dying and rug-weaving methods differ vastly from those of Iran. Ask to see a portfolio of their previous repair work, which will often feature "before" and "after" pictures. Inspect how well they match colors, recreate designs, and blend repairs into existing weaves. If your rug is valuable, inquire whether an expert or an apprentice will perform the repair work. Also, see to it that all repair work is included in the estimate, whether it be reweaving holes, remapping worn areas, repairing moth damage, rewrapping seams, re-fringing, re-blocking your rug to its original shape. Particularly thorough rug conservationists will even unravel strands and overcast weaving to blend repairs into the rug's existing texture and design.

Cleaning and Drying Techniques

There are many different cleaning methods, each of which addresses different situations with varying degrees of efficacy and expense. Carpet cleaners typically have mobile operations, and will clean rugs and wall-to-wall carpets in your home with hot "carbonating" systems, steam-cleaning, or dry-cleaning. Will they move the furniture to clean under it or do they expect the room to be ready when they arrive? Make sure to find out beforehand. Rug cleaners, on the other hand, usually perform the cleaning at their site. They may expect the rug to be rolled up and waiting for their pick-up. Silk rugs, fragile tapestries, and textiles with "fugitive" (short-lived) dyes, or bright colors that might "bleed" (run), should be hand-washed—the most delicate and expensive method. Luster cleaning immerses the entire rug in cleaning solutions, and thus achieves a deep clean while minimizing wear on the fabric. Soap washing involves running a vacuum-like machine over the rug; this vigorous method is only for particularly rugged or less-valuable rugs. Discuss in advance what problems the cleaner can and can't fix. For example, excessive wear on a hallway rug will still be there after a cleaning, though it will be much less noticeable. If you are health or environmentally conscious, ask whether the company offers nontoxic cleaners.

Any rug that's washed must also be dried properly to avoid mildew and dry rot. Be sure to ask about the time and drying technique for in-home jobs—you should know beforehand if you need to reroute traffic through the patio for three days. For in-plant jobs, bigger outfits have dry rooms where they control temperature and humidity levels. In the home, drying basically involves not walking on the rug until it is dry, which depends on humidity and other factors. Some businesses also offer stain protectants, which they apply directly to the rug to shield it from future accidents (should the tipsy uncle return). Other companies may take a purist approach, preferring periodic cleaning to chemical protectants.

Carpet and Rug Installation

Before the carpet or rug is put down, padding should always be laid first. Padding gives more cushioning for your feet and keeps the rug from sliding, which helps prevent slips, falls, and spills. Ask what kind of padding the installer will use, as there are generally different quality and price options.

For wall-to-wall carpeting installation, the most common method is to lay wooden tack strips around the perimeter of the room. The tack strips have pins sticking up that grab the carpet and hold it in place. The tack strips are attached to the floor using small nails, which leave holes in the floor when the carpet is removed. The padding also is usually either nailed or stapled to the floor. If you must cover your nice wood floors (for the kids, maybe), you should discuss with the installer how to minimize the floor damage. Unfortunately, there is not that much that can be done if you want wall-to-wall. Some installers may suggest attaching the carpet with double-faced tape, but most say that this doesn't hold well and the carpet shifts and buckles. If your floor contributes to the value of your apartment, it is simply better to stick with area rugs. Remember to ask whether or not there are any potential extra charges, such as for ripping up existing wall-to-wall carpeting before installing the new one or for disposing of the old carpeting and pads if you don't want to keep them. Some rug cleaners focus on just stain and odor removal services to meet the needs of pet owners, smokers, and families with small children (or just klutzes). Many providers offer stain protection for future spills, which, depending on your lifestyle, may be a sound investment. Other companies specialize in emergency services in case of fire, smoke, or water damage, and may even be available round-the-clock. If you're moving, remodeling, or otherwise in need of storage, look to the larger outfits for mothproofing and storage services. After storage or in-plant services, many companies will reinstall your rug over appropriate padding.

Rug cleaners and restorers also offer many other services for rugs and other furnishings. Many rug cleaners also clean curtains and upholstered furniture.

Some businesses prefer to remove the draperies from the home and wash them at their facilities. In-home carpet cleaners are more likely to clean curtains in the house.

Since curtains, upholstered furniture, and rugs dominate most of the space (not to mention the attention) in a room, rug cleaners and restorers emphasize the importance of maintaining these items. Their colors will be clearer, they'll last longer, you'll be inhaling less dust, and your home will look more beautiful.

On Cost

Prices among rug companies vary immensely because each has its own specialties and services. Some rug firms perform only standard cleaning and can work on wall-to-wall broadlooms, upholstery, and drapery. For this type of cleaning, some charge by the square foot, which could start at $.25 (a 2.5 for cost in *The Franklin Report*) per square foot and could go up to $1 to $1.25 per square foot. Most companies charge $.30 to $.60 per square foot. Then again, some give a flat rate after inspecting the carpet and seeing how much cleaning needs to be done. This usually conforms to their minimum rate, which most companies have. Minimum rates start at $50 and go up to $150 for standard wall-to-wall broadloom cleaning.

Area rugs are a different terrain altogether. New York has numerous experts and "specialized" firms that only deal with area rug cleaning, repair and restoration—those that work mostly with the rare, the old, the valuable and in most cases, only the handmade ones. Most companies who do standard wall-to-wall cleaning also clean area rugs, but the older and rarer the rug is, the more specialized the cleaning, repair, and attention it needs. Pricing for area rug cleaning starts as low as $1 (a 2.5 for cost in *The Franklin Report*) per square foot and could go as high as $3 to $5 per square foot, depending on the amount of cleaning needed and the value of the rug. These firms also have minimum rates, and fees start at $100 minimum up to $700. Then again, if your area rug is not a hundred years old and requires only regular cleaning or minimal repairs, you could end up paying a standard $50 to $100 per job or $1.25 to $2 per square foot.

Don't Let the Rug Be Pulled Out From Under You!

◇ Get several bids. Prices among competent cleaners can vary quite a bit.

◇ When you have an estimate, ask if it's binding. Also ask what factors may cause it to become higher (or lower) when the job is actually done.

◇ Is there a minimum charge for a house call? If the cost of cleaning your rug is below the minimum, you might want to have them perform another service (such as clean or stain-proof another rug, piece of furniture, or curtains) at the same time.

◇ Once they are in your house, the rug cleaner will often do another rug for much less money, especially if paid in cash.

◇ Some of the larger more commercial cleaners have regular "sales." Get on their mailing list to receive updates. If you're not in a hurry, wait for a sale.

RUGS—CLEANING, INSTALLATION & REPAIR

💼 FIRMS WITH ONLINE PORTFOLIOS* 💼

800 Rug Wash 💼   4   3.5   4.5   4.5
20 Enterprise Avenue, Secaucus, NJ 07094
(800) 784 - 9274   rugwash@aol.com

Rug, carpet, upholstery cleaning and repair; flooring installation and maintenance

There is an excited buzz around this "do-it-all" company. Aside from selling handmade area rugs, 800 Rug Wash also cleans and repairs rugs and wall-to-wall carpets. The firm cleans upholstery, fabric walls, drapery, and fabric blinds—and the company's flooring division handles installation, sanding, and finishing of all types of floors.

Even before establishing the company in 1980, owner Benjamin Hatooka, a chemist by trade, had a number of rug dealers come to him asking him to change the colors of rugs to make them look old. Antiquing is still one of the firm's strong points. Serving residential and commercial interiors mostly in Manhattan, as well as in some parts of Los Angeles, Florida, Boston, Virginia, and Canada, 800 Rug Wash is an upstanding member of the Oriental Rug Importers Association and The National Wood Flooring Association. The team at 800 Rug Wash has recently scored some major accounts, including Best Buy, Modell's, Applebee's, and the New York Design Center. Due to the upsurge in business, the company opened a second plant in January 2005. Pricing is generally per square foot and sources describe the firm's prices as moderate. Minimums for area rug cleaning start at $50, carpet cleaning start at $150 per project and $500 for flooring installation and refinishing. Clients like the firm's reliable, prompt service and delivery, and appreciate Hatooka's good work ethic.

"Gets the job done." "Knows his business." "Prompt. Very good work." "Fair prices for efficient service." "I can always count on them. Benjamin will personally drive and deliver the rugs—even on a weekend." "Very professional staff." "Always reachable—his calls are forwarded to his cellphone after-hours!" "Does very religious work on each of my rugs."

All Clean Carpet & Upholstery Cleaning 💼   4.5   4   4.5   4.5
10 Hilltop Place, Albertson, NY 11507
(516) 621 - 0524   www.allcleancarpetinc.com

Rug, upholstery, furniture, and drapery cleaning

A secret source for industry insiders, rug retailers, celebrities, and well-heeled residential clients, All Clean Carpet has been satisfying customers since 1986. The company cleans rugs, furniture, upholstery, drapery, and wall fabrics. Helmed by John Mauser, the firm specializes in protection systems, which they apply to newly cleaned or purchased carpets and upholstery. All Clean also does some minor repairs. All technicians are IICRC-certified. From wall-to-wall carpets to the finest antique rugs, drapery, leather, and wall fabrics, we hear this firm can clean them all. Mauser and his team do only on-site residential work and are also experts in estate and brownstone cleaning.

*We invite you to visit www.franklinreport.com to view images of their work.

	Quality	Cost	Value	Recommend?
	✚	$	◆	★

Pricing is per square foot with minimums in the realm of $150. Clients say they are thrilled with the skill and knowledge that All Clean brings to the job. Customers also appreciate that the crew moves furniture and puts it back, rather than just cleaning around it. Those in the know tell us that All Clean's prices are "upper-end" but insist they're "an excellent value" because the service is unquestionably "top-notch."

"Fabulous, very high standards." "He takes time to find out what stains there are and breaks them down properly." "Very professional." "Neat and responsive. They know what they are doing." "Excellent customer service—punctual, conscientious and accommodating." "Saved me from buying new carpets!" "Gave recommendations on what I should do for future spills. Very helpful." "Rectified shoddy work done by another rug company." "I was having guests and had a spill on my rug. As they couldn't work in my home that night, they picked up the piece, worked on it overnight, and had it spic-and-span in time for my party."

Cohen Carpet, Upholstery and Drapery Cleaning

4   4   4   4.5

2565 Broadway, New York, NY 10025
(212) 663 - 6902   davidddsj@aol.com
Rug and upholstery cleaning

"Offbeat" and "laid-back," David Cohen nonetheless attacks stains with "amazing" results, sources say. Cohen does most of the work at his firm himself, so he gets the credit for the high level of customer service the company has maintained since its establishment in 1983. Cohen cleans area rugs, wall-to-wall carpets, upholstery, fabric blinds, fabric walls, and draperies both on- and off-site, mostly for residential customers. While Cohen doesn't do restoration work, he will do minor repairs. Pricing is by the square foot with a minimum of $190 per project. Celebrity clients like Michael Moore, Kate Spade, and Ann Bass join some of the city's top designers and furnituremakers in calling on Cohen for repeat business. References praise the quality of the work and the excellence of Cohen's professional conduct, saying he is always pleasant, prompt, straightforward about pricing, and trustworthy.

"Easy to work with." "Really great with tough stains—nail polish, cranberry juice, etc." "The rugs look like new." "Not cheap, but very fair." "Great at troubleshooting." "We were ready to get new carpeting, but he somehow managed to repair our old one." "Performed miracles on our carpet."

Costikyan Carpets Inc. ▮

4.5   4   4.5   4.5

28-13 14th Street, Astoria, NY 11102
(718) 726 - 1090   www.costikyan.com
Fine rug dealer; rug, fabric, and upholstery cleaning and restoration

Known for its exceptional cleaning and restoration work, we hear Costikyan Carpets has been satisfying discriminating clients since its founding in 1886 by Kent Costikyan. The company is now managed by his great-grandson Philip. Costikyan buys, sells, cleans, repairs, restores, manufactures, and imports fine antique, semi-antique, and modern rugs. The firm also cleans fabric upholstery and fabric walls. Prices are high-end, but for valuable pieces, clients say they will trust no other.

Costikyan works mostly in Manhattan, in some parts of the tri-state area, the Hamptons, and Westchester. This mostly residential company also works with designers, dealers, private collectors, and museums. The firm works on-site and off, and in most cases provides free pickup and delivery. The highly skilled workmen at Costikyan are described as professional, reliable, and trustworthy, and a number of the area's top designers and elite homeowners entrust Costikyan with their most expensive and rare rugs.

	Quality	Cost	Value	Recommend?
		$	◆	★

"Highly skilled." "Great." "Easy to work with—will go the extra mile." "One of the best in the business. Impeccable credentials." "My carpets were beautifully cleaned." "Courteous, conscientious, efficient, and on time."

Fabra Cleen Carpet and Fabric Specialists Inc.

	4	3	5	4.5

PO Box 280471, Queens Village, NY 11428
(212) 777 - 4040 www.fabracleen.com

Carpet, upholstery, and fabric cleaning and repair

"Some of the nicest people around," is what many clients say about the staff at Fabra Cleen, who repair and clean area rugs, carpets, upholstery, leather furniture, fabric headboards, fabric walls, and drapery. The company also sells and installs wall-to-wall carpets, does post-construction cleanup, and has been known to handle some minor repairs on carpets and rugs. The firm also does marble and stone polishing and ceramic tile and grout cleaning.

Established in 1949 by Samuel Kornet, the firm is now managed by his son Brian, and Brian's wife, Wendy. Fabra Cleen serves both residential and commercial clients in Manhattan, parts of the tri-state area, the Hamptons, and Westchester County. Cleaning is done on location or at the company's facilities, in which case, pickup and delivery is free. Sources tell us Fabra Cleen prides itself on meticulous attention to detail and will move furniture for free in order to clean under it and not just around it. Pricing is per square foot. Minimums for area rugs start at $60, carpet and upholstery at $80, and marble, tile, and stone range from $150 to $350.

Honest, trustworthy, reliable, responsive, and punctual are some of the superlatives used to describe this company. Sources say they appreciate the efficient service and the moderate prices.

"Excellent." "When I need them they are here at the drop of a hat." "They have my keys and my security codes—they are completely trustworthy." "Courteous."

Hayko Restoration and Conservation

	5	4.5	4.5	5

857 Lexington Avenue, 2nd Floor, New York, NY 10021
(212) 717 - 5400 www.hayko.com

Museum-quality antique carpet, tapestry, and needlepoint cleaning, retail, and restoration

"Hayko's work cannot be seen. That's the point, quality restoration is invisible," proclaims Hayk Oltaci of Hayko Restoration and Conservation. Oltaci's loyal clientele tell us he's a man who understands that rugs are not only decorative and functional pieces, but historic artifacts as well.

Hayk Oltaci's interest in rugs began in Istanbul at the age of 16 when his grandfather gave him an old Turkish rug in need of repair. Oltaci worked in France prior to founding his New York firm twelve years ago. The company boasts a top-notch atelier where staffers custom mix the dyes that make their needlework invisible. Impeccable credentials and an industrious nature make Oltaci a favorite of top designers, upscale private collectors, homeowners, museums, dealers, and auction houses. High-end clients from around the globe can't say enough about Hayko's delicate and painstaking work, which can take over a year on a complicated restoration.

Reportedly, Oltaci is a "pleasure to work with" and a "true artisan." Christie's regularly refers its clients to this firm to care for antique rugs. Prices may be higher than most, but clients say this "amazing craftsman" is worth every penny.

"The most honest man I know." "There's nobody else as good as Hayko." "A wonderful craftsman. I've been using him for at least ten years now." "He goes out of his way for his clients. He came to my aid in an emergency—came to my home in the evening

and repaired my rug right there." "Major museums know his work is nothing short of perfect." "Produces results in a timely manner."

Rug Renovating Co. 🛍   3.5   3.5   4   4.5
532 North Grove Street, East Orange, NJ 07017
(212) 924 - 0189 www.rugrenovating.com
Rug, carpet, and upholstery cleaning, repair, and restoration

A trusted name in the business, Rug Renovating has been satisfying clients in the tri-state area since its establishment in 1896 (yes, really). Four generations later, this family business is now helmed by Paul Iskyan, who ensures that the level of excellence his great-great grandfather mandated is still maintained. From wall-to-wall broadlooms to the finest antique area rugs to delicate wall fabrics, Rug Renovating "can clean them all." The company can clean on-site or in their 70,000 square foot plant.

A mainstay in the rolodexes of some of the most prominent interior designers, rug dealers, and celebrity homeowners, the firm has a team of twelve technicians who are all IICRC-certified. Three of these are considered Master Technicians. Sources tell us the firm is also "superb" at doing repairs, from minor stitching and reweaving to binding and refringing. Pricing is by the square foot, with minimums for rug cleaning starting at $75. Clients laud the firm's excellent service and knowledgeable team and though some say it's "hard to get through," all claim "they will always return your call." The company was chosen as one of the "Best of New York" by *New York* magazine in 2003.

"One of the top choices for unique repairs." "I love these guys." "Great (but not incredible) job for on-site spot removal, but always helpful and professional." "Expensive but nice quality work." "Great staff and team is super knowledgeable."

FIRMS WITHOUT ONLINE PORTFOLIOS

ABC Carpet & Home
888 Broadway, New York, NY 10003
(212) 473 - 3000 www.abchome.com
Retail—Reupholstery, window treatments, rug cleaning, and installation

See ABC Carpet & Home's full report under the heading Upholstery & Window Treatments

Abraham Moheban & Son Antique Carpets   4.5   4.5   4   4.5
33 East 33rd Street, Suite 708, New York, NY 10016
(212) 758 - 3900 www.moheban.com
Superb fine rug dealers; expert cleaning and restoration

One of the city's best dealers, Abraham Moheban & Son specializes in fine antique European and Oriental rugs. The company also cleans, restores, repairs, and appraises antique and semi-antique decorative rugs and carpets. All cleaning is done in-house and is heavily supervised. This family-run business is now being managed by a fourth-generation Moheban, David, and services clients mainly in Manhattan, with a few jobs in the Hamptons and Westchester County.

The firm was established in 1961 by Abraham Moheban, a Persian-born craftman who is considered one of the pioneers of the rug trade here in America. The company works mostly with designers and architects and boasts an impressive roster of well-heeled residential and celebrity clients. The firm is a member of the Oriental Rugs Importers Association and ASID. Aside from the Aubussons and Orientals, the impressive inventory includes Oushaks from Turkey, Agras from India, and Tabriz from Persia.

Enthusiastic clients rave about this firm's wide array of high-quality rugs and the exquisite repair and restoration work it does. Though prices may be expensive, references agree that the exquisite quality is definitely worth the cost. Indeed, sources say, this firm's impeccable taste, knowledge of the industry, and meticulous attention to detail make them one of a select handful of masters of the rug business in New York.

"Beautiful repair and restoration job." "Their inventories are just exquisite." "Wouldn't hesitate to go back." "They understand and appreciate the history of the rugs." "Great eye for quality."

Action Carpet Cleaners   3.5   3   4.5   4
676A Ninth Avenue, Suite 248, New York, NY 10036
(212) 757 - 2554

Rug, upholstery, and floor cleaning and retail; water damage specialists

Action Carpet Cleaners has won over a solid group of happy clients since opening its doors in 1980. The firm's principal, Joe Carilli, has developed a reputation for honesty and reliability—as well as for delivering top-quality service at reasonable prices. The company serves both residential and commercial clients mostly in Manhattan. The business mainly cleans, installs, repairs, and sells rugs and wall-to-wall carpets. Action also provides some flooring services, as well as drapery, fabric walls, furniture, and upholstery cleaning. The company is also one of the few in the city that specializes in water damage restoration and offers a 24-hour emergency service.

Pricing is usually per square foot with a minimum of $85. There is a moderate minimum per project and the workmen will move furniture within reason. There is no extra charge for spot cleaning. Described as "easygoing," "friendly," and "genial," Carilli is a firm believer in personalized service and does most of the work himself. We hear the firm recently acquired a bigger and better high-pressure steam cleaner which gives "far superior" results. Clients praise the firm's efficient and reliable service and the fair prices that go along with it.

"Used them for five years. I am thrilled with them." "Trustworthy, reliable, and on time." "Bottom line—he satisfies his customers." "Excellent work with my water-damaged basement but was so-so with my furniture." "I tested him against a few other vendors—Action delivered higher quality and lower cost."

Apple Window Cleaning
121 West 25th Street, Suite 303, New York, NY 10001
(212) 620 - 0708

Commercial and residential window cleaning, post-construction cleanup

See Apple Window Cleaning's full report under the heading Window Washers

Beauvais Carpets   4.5   4.5   4   4
595 Madison Avenue, 3rd Floor, New York, NY 10022
(212) 688 - 2265   www.beauvaiscarpets.com

Exquisite fine rugs and tapestries dealer; superior cleaning and restoration

Beauvais Carpets is primarily a dealer with a "preeminent collection of fine antique rugs and tapestries." But Beauvais also provides high-quality restoration, appraisal, and cleaning services for fine antique, semi-antique, and contemporary rugs. Insiders tell us that their gallery is a haven for rug collectors and dealers, with an outstanding selection of rugs and tapestries from 16th through

19th century Europe and Asia, as well as custom broadloom carpets that allow custom size and design specifications. The team at Beauvais also sells and installs wall-to-wall carpets.

Established in 1966 by David Amini, the firm will clean and repair only hand-made area rugs. Pricing is generally by the job with minimums in the $200 to $300 range. Pick-up and delivery are available, but at extra cost. Though the firm deals mostly with designers and architects, it also serves several distinguished residential clients. Amini and his twelve-man team also work with museums and auction houses. With regard to spot cleaning, we hear that Beauvais pre-tests stains and informs the client of the expected results. All repairs and cleaning are done in the company's Brooklyn and Manhattan workshops. Sources say Beauvais' staff members are thorough, polite, and knowledgeable.

"The definitive source for fine antique rugs." "Exceeded my expectations." "Impeccable taste." "Excellent inventory and great with repairs, too."

Beyond the Bosphorus   5   4.5   4.5   4.5
79 Sullivan Street, New York, NY 10012
(212) 219 - 8257

Expert antique rug cleaning, retail, and restoration

It's not just the eye-catching name—with its impressive credentials, knowledge, and resources on Turkish and Oriental flatwoven rugs, Beyond the Bosphorous stands out from the crowd. The company is owned and managed by Istanbul native Ismail Basbag, who had ten years of training and experience working in the Grand Bazaar of Istanbul before he founded the firm in 1985.

This firm cleans, repairs, sells, and restores antique and semi-antique Turkish flatwoven rugs (kilims), Turkish cylindrical pillows (bolster pillows), trunks upholstered with kilims, and other types of Oriental area rugs. Work is done in or out of Basbag's workshop, depending on the type of project. His sophisticated clientele appreciates Basbag's fine taste and shares his knowledge of antique rugs. The firm has clients at some of the city's most elite addresses as well as in California, New Jersey, Connecticut, and Texas. Beyond the Bosphorous was also mentioned in *New York* magazine's spring issue of Manhattan's 1,000 Best Shops. Sources describe Basbag as a nice, quiet, and polite man who does a splendid job with a pleasant demeanor and excellent work philosophy. Though prices are high-end, clients say the service is worth every penny.

"Reliable—excellent at following up." "Did what he should. Excellent work ethic." "Knowledgeable about his work." "Entering his shop is like entering another time and place." "One of the few remaining Old World craftsmen."

Cleantech/Clean Bright Process Co.   3.5   3.5   4   4
450 Westbury Avenue, Carl Place, NY 11514
(212) 619 - 7600   cleantech@cleantech-newyork.com

Rug and upholstery cleaning and other cleaning services

Cleantech provides on- and off-site carpet and rug cleaning services to high-end residential and commercial clients in the New York metro area, and has been doing so since 1964. The firm also cleans draperies, blinds, fabric walls, and acoustical ceilings, and waxes floors. The firm has been known to do terrific work with sisal rugs, which many companies decline to address. We also hear that top designers call on the firm for post-construction cleanup work. Owned and managed by Robert Kleber, Cleantech has a sister company, Clean Bright Process Co., which also cleans and repairs carpet, upholstery, and window treatments.

"Great rug cleaner—will get out most spots." "Couldn't get over the great job Cleantech did with the nasty stains in my rugs." "Great for mid-priced and standard cleaning jobs."

	Quality +	Cost $	Value ◆	Recommend? ★
Cleantex Process Co.	3.5	3.5	4	4.5

2335 Twelfth Avenue, New York, NY 10027
(212) 283 - 1200   cleantex@lycos.com
Cleaning and repair of rugs, upholstery, and draperies

For all-around good rug, upholstery, and drapery cleaning, Cleantex is a well-liked, good-value option. Established in 1929 by Paul Eurow, Cleantex is now helmed by John Molla who, along with his brother Tony, bought the company seventeen years ago. The firm cleans wall-to-wall broadlooms, fine antique Orientals and Aubussons, drapery, fabric walls, and upholstery. One of the few in the city to specialize in flameproofing fabrics, this fifteen-man firm serves residential and commercial clients in Manhattan, all the outer boroughs, New Jersey, Connecticut, Long Island, the Hamptons, and Wetschester.

Pricing is per square foot with minimums for on-site cleaning starting at $150 and pickups at $50. The firm is capable of cleaning both on-site and in their 20,000 square foot plant. There is an extra charge for roll-up and spreading carpets.

Molla and his team use Stodart Solution for cleaning—a mineral solvent which is much milder and does less harm on fabrics and draperies than conventional methods. Cleantex's notable clients include Radio City Music Hall, Alice Tully Hall at Lincoln Center, Sony Recording Studios, Blue Water Grill, Atlantic Grill, Ruby Foo's, and The Supper Club. The firm is a member of the Neighborhood Cleaning Association.

"Wonderful, cooperative, no-nonsense people." "We know it will be done professionally." "Everything always goes smoothly." "They are getting up there with some of the best in the city."

Delmont Carpet and Upholstery Cleaning	3	3	4	4

217 East 86th Street, New York, NY 10028
(212) 513 - 7500   www.delmontcleanny.com
Rug and upholstery cleaning

A top choice of numerous references in the city, Delmont has been cleaning carpets, rugs, upholstery, and draperies since 1973. Sources describe this company's workmen as prompt, courteous, and efficient. The firm is also known for its attentive and personalized service.

The company serves residential and commercial clients around Manhattan, Brooklyn, Long Island, the Hamptons, and Westchester County. Pricing is usually per rug with a minimum of $97. We hear the workmen will move furniture at no extra cost, as long as it is nonbreakable and not unreasonably heavy. Appreciative clients applaud the firm's reasonable rates.

"Fastidious job." "The only company in the city I will use." "I couldn't have imagined a better job. On time and so reliable." "Not fabulous, but generally good all around." "Great seasonal discounts."

Fiber-Seal of New York	4	4	4	4.5

214 East 52nd Street, New York, NY 10022
(212) 888 - 1070
Upholstery fabric sealing

A force-field against stains? One could call it that. Clients tell us that Fiber-Seal provides an invaluable service to protect upholstery from staining. These professionals spray an invisible and odor-free stain-repellent coating on any home fabric, including upholstery, draperies, lampshades, and bedspreads.

Fiber-Seal's service comes with a solid eighteen-month warranty. If the fabric becomes stained and the cleaning products the firm provides won't get it out,

	Quality	Cost	Value	Recommend?
	+	$	◆	★

Fiber-Seal will return to your home and remove the stain at no additional cost. The cost of the seal is not insubstantial, but customers say the service is well worth it to protect their original upholstery investment.

"They must be doing something right, as there was a one-month wait for an appointment." "Quick and painless, but expensive."

Irwin Cohen   4.5   3   4.5   4.5

16-10 212th Street, Bayside, NY 11360
(718) 224 - 9885

Carpet, area rug, and upholstery spot cleaning and repair

When other cleaners give up on a stain, sources say, they call on Irwin Cohen. We hear that Cohen has yet to be truly stumped by a stain—despite being faced with some very stubborn ones. Clients say he will personally come out to tend stains on short notice and always does so with a smile, using little potions from his briefcase.

Cohen, whose grandfather and father were also in the business, has been serving clients around Manhattan, New Jersey, Long Island, Connecticut, Westchester County, and the Hamptons for 36 years. The firm does spot cleaning only (no whole rugs) and will work on area rugs, wall-to-wall broadlooms, fabric walls, and upholstery. The company also demonstrates a talent for reweaving and minor repairs. Pricing is by the job (with minimums in the $95 to $130 range) and all work is done on-site.

"Couldn't live without him." "Excellent! Takes out spots that baffle other carpet cleaners." "Works on stains that other cleaners can't get out." "Pleasant and easy to work with."

Kalust Barin   4.5   4.5   4   4.5

1334 York Avenue, New York, NY 10021
(212) 606 - 7896   kalust@msn.com

Discriminating antique rug and tapestry restoration and repair

"A man of many talents" is what people are saying about Kalust Barin. Clearly, Sotheby's thinks so too, since he holds fort in their building, where Barin does a number of jobs for some of the auction house's famous and distinguished clients. The firm repairs, restores, and cleans antique rugs, with a specialty in Caucasian, European, and Middle Eastern pieces. Barin also conserves tapestries and needlepoint. While most of his work is done at Sotheby's, he occasionally works on-site and has several clients whose rugs he checks on a regular basis. His showroom in Sotheby's is open to the public and the trade.

Barin has been in the rug business his entire life, starting with his family's business in Turkey, where he worked in the Grand Bazaar. This soft-spoken man serves mostly residential clients in Manhattan and some areas of New Jersey. Sources tell us that this gentleman is a hard worker who is dedicated to his craft. Prices are definitely "expensive," but clients agree, "you get what you pay for."

"An extremely nice and honest man." "Worked for us for fifteen years now." "Extremely skilled. Knows his business." "Best man for the job." "Has such a discriminating eye for repairing and restoring fine pieces."

Kermanshah Oriental Rugs Inc.   4.5   4.5   4.5   4

57 Fifth Avenue, New York, NY 10003
(212) 627 - 7077   kborugs@aol.com

Fine rug and tapestry cleaning, repair, restoration, retail and wholesale

Now in its second century, the Kermanshah family rug business started in 1880. Kermanshah has locations in New York, Saudi Arabia, Iran, and other parts of the Middle East. Sources tell us the firm's impeccable credentials and rich legacy make it one of the foremost authorities in the rug industry. The New

York establishment was founded in 1960 and has a growing list of clients that includes private collectors, decorators, dealers, museums, and homeowners. The firm cleans, repairs, restores, buys, and sells fine antique, semi-antique, and contemporary handmade area rugs and tapestries. Its showroom is open to the public and the trade.

Sources rave about the efficiency of this firm's services. These tapestry experts are described as extremely trustworthy, reliable, and responsive. All cleaning and restoration is done in the firm's workshop, and prices include pick-up and delivery. Customers appreciate the fact that the firm is knowledgeable about the product, its history, and the business. Though prices fall at the upper end of the range, clients across the board agree the service and the product quality are worth the expense.

"Wide inventory. Exquisite pieces." "Worked with them for years. Never had a problem with them." "Miracle workers. Took out a stain that proved to be difficult for others."

Marvin Kagan Gallery   4.5   4   4.5   5
115 East 57th Street, New York, NY 10022
(212) 535 - 9000 www.marvinkagan.com

Impeccable fine rugs and tapestries; cleaning and restoration

Sources simply rave about the high-quality and excellent workmanship of this upscale gallery. Established 45 years ago, we hear the employees at Marvin Kagan are specialists at restoring, cleaning, conserving, and repairing antique and semi-antique area rugs. They also do appraisals and retail. The firm's clients range from museums, designers, and dealers to affluent owners and private collectors.

The professionals at this company are described by references in superlatives—honest, personable, respectful, and knowledgeable about the business. Clients tell us Kagan's primary interest is in establishing and maintaining strong customer relationships based on trust and an impeccable reputation in the field. Most clients agree that the high quality of Marvin Kagan's work makes it an excellent value, despite the expensive price tag.

"Astoundingly pleased with the job." "Expensive, though." "Best men for the job." "Gives honest advice." "Difficult to reach but worth the wait."

Nemati Collection   4   4   4   4.5
1059 Third Avenue, New York, NY 10021
(212) 486 - 6900 www.nematicollection.com

Dealer; fine rug and tapestry repair and conservation

A dealer in antique Oriental rugs and European tapestries, Nemati also has a full-service restoration department. Clients marvel at its expertise in working with vegetable dyes and in matching yarns. The firm cleans, repairs, restores, conserves, buys, and sells antique area rugs, tapestries, and needlepoint. All cleaning is done by hand to put minimal stress on the piece.

Parviz Nemati, who founded the firm in 1963, is now the company's acquisitions consultant. Nemati's son, Darius, directs the gallery. The showroom is open to the public and the trade. Nemati's distinguished clientele hails from all over the world, turning to the company to procure and restore its rare and antique treasures. A knowledgeable staff with low turnover have contributed to Nemati's excellent reputation. This high-end company is a member of the Oriental Rug Retailers of America and has been featured in prominent publications such as *Town & Country* magazine.

"They look at a rug as a piece of art, not just a rug." "All the workmen are terrific."

	Quality	Cost	Value	Recommend?
	✚	$	◆	★

Pasargad Carpets   4   4   4   4

180 Madison Avenue, New York, NY 10016
(212) 684 - 4477 www.pasargadcarpets.com

Dealer of fine antique rugs; rug cleaning and restoration

In business in Iran since 1904, Pasargad Carpets has been serving New York for 25 years. The company buys, sells, cleans, repairs, and restores antique, semi-antique, and modern handmade area rugs. The firm's 4,500 square foot showroom in Manhattan (and another showroom in Washington, DC) are open to the public and the trade.

The company boasts of a wide selection of rugs, from scatter to oversized—as well as mansion-sized—rugs. The Pasargad website also allows customers to fill out a form with information on size, color, and design. They, in turn, will send back a digital photo that most closely matches the request.

This firm's sophisticated clientele varies from decorators to dealers, homeowners, and distinguished private collectors who come from Manhattan, Washington, New Jersey, the West Coast, and Canada. Cleaning and restoration are done in-house and are carefully supervised.

"Widest selection of rugs." "Excellent restoration and repair." "Responsive and cooperative. Nice fellows—easy to work with."

Ronnee Barnett Textile Restoration   5   4.5   4.5   5

182 Cherry Hill Road, Accord, NY 12404
(212) 966 - 3520 ronneebarnett@hvc.rr.com

Artisanal fine antique rug, tapestry, needlepoint, and textile restoration, repair, and cleaning

References agree that Ronnee Barnett is a woman dedicated to her craft and passionate about her work. Barnett started her own textile restoration business in 1978 after pursuing a career in psychology because she "had an intense desire to weave." She restores, conserves, cleans, re-weaves, and repairs rare antique area rugs, needlepoints, tapestries, and textiles. She also works part time for the Metropolitan Museum of Art, where she restores and mounts medieval textiles.

The firm does business mostly in Manhattan, but has clients from all over the US. This one-woman company works with museums, decorators, dealers, private collectors, and homeowners. We are told Barnett believes in in-depth client interviews to discuss the project in advance to understand her customers' specifications. Barnett also educates clients in the proper way to care for their priceless treasures. Sources consider her work museum-quality and find her incredibly professional, trustworthy, and communicative. Her many fans say she takes her time, does the job right, and treats each piece like a work of art.

"She is the best. Such a find." "Artistic, capable, and businesslike." "Can't tell it was repaired. Great workmanship." "Fair, honest, professional." "A joy to work with." "She examines the problem with intelligence and insight."

Safavieh Carpets   4   3.5   4.5   4

902 Broadway, New York, NY 10010
(212) 477 - 1234 www.safavieh.com

Dealer and restorer of antique and contemporary rugs, needlepoints, and tapestries

One of New York's prominent retailers, appraisers, and restorers of fine antique, semi-antique, and contemporary rugs, Safavieh Carpets has been serving affluent clients since its establishment in 1914 by Hamil Yaraghi. Now managed by his grandson Arash, the firm continues to provide the same top-notch service to its discriminating modern-day clientele. Safavieh's wide selection of rugs includes Orientals, Aubussons, Persian, Pakistani, Indian, and Tibetan, plus tapestries and needlepoints. With three showrooms located in Manhattan—one of them exclusively open to the trade—Safavieh also maintains seven more locations around Long Island, Connecticut, Westchester, and New Jersey.

Safavieh takes pride in its restoration department, where workmen meticulously do all the work by hand and in the same method that the original weaver used. The firm also does some restoration and conservation for museums. All cleaning and repair is done in-house and is heavily supervised.

"Fabulous. Wouldn't think of going to anyone else." "Meticulous and thorough."

Sutton Carpet Ltd.   3.5   3.5   4   4
417 East 57th Street, 8th Floor, New York, NY 10022
(212) 980 - 5967 www.suttoncarpetltd.com

Rug and upholstery cleaning, repair, and restoration; wood, tile, and carpet flooring retail and installation

Sutton Carpet cleans, repairs, sells, restores, and installs wall-to-wall carpets and all types of area rugs. The company is managed by husband-and-wife team Ray and Diane Martine. This residential and commercial company also cleans leather, chenille, upholstery, fabric walls, and window treatments in their own cleaning plant in Mt. Vernon. The company has three cleaning crews who are all licensed by the New York Rug Cleaners Institute and by the Association of Cleaning and Restoration Specialists. Cost is determined by the square foot, with minimums starting at $195. Their showroom on 57th Street is by appointment only.

The firm accomplished projects for Cushman & Wakefield, The Joyce Theater, Henry Mancini, Park Avenue Tennis & Racquet Club, UN Plaza, and Scalamandre, to name a few. Sutton Carpet also does some projects in parts of New Jersey, Connecticut, the Hamptons, and Long Island.

"Excellent source." "Fast, efficient, and reliable." "Great for standard wall-to-wall cleaning. Always gets the job done." "Someone will always pick up the phone to help you. Diane is on top of things."

The Durotone Company   3.5   3.5   4   4
510 Ogden Avenue, Mamaroneck, NY 10543
(914) 381 - 1167 hasklar@earthlink.net

Cleaning and repair: rugs, upholstery, drapery, and fabric walls

"Excellent," "efficient," and "professional" are some of the words clients use to describe The Durotone Company. In business since 1944, the firm was established by Irving Mermer and is now headed by grandson-in-law Howard Sklar. Durotone is a specialist in cleaning and repairing area rugs, wall-to-wall carpets, drapery, upholstery, and fabric walls. A well-kept secret among decorators and rug dealers, the firm is lauded for its exceptional cleaning of woven goods and often receives rugs from all over the country to be cleaned and repaired. It is also one of the few companies that can clean natural-fibered rugs like seagrass, jute, sisal, and hemp. The firm recently established a divison specializing in cleaning, sealing, and maintaining stone, marble, and tile.

With seven full-time workers who are all certified by the IICRC, the company charges by the square foot for cleaning wall-to-wall carpets, per rug for area rugs, and by the piece for upholstery. Minimums are in the $175 to $225 range. Durotone serves a mostly high-end residential clientele in all the five boroughs, Westchester, the Hamptons, New Jersey, and even as far away as Martha's Vineyard and Chicago.

Clients laud this firm's professional demeanor and efficient service. The high-end prices are considered a good value for the excellent service.

"Clients laud this firm's professional demeanor and efficient service." "The high-end prices are considered a good value for the excellent service." "Fabulous." "If they can't do it, no one can." "Courteous and reliable." "The best in the business."

Hiring a Security Service Provider

Some of us turn on the TV set when leaving the house and consider it a security measure. Others won't settle for less than motion sensors and barbed wire. Luckily, thanks to the ongoing integration of security and entertainment systems, you can split the difference. If you really think "Three's Company" reruns will frighten potential burglars (and you may have a point), you can program your TV's routine—along with your security system's more effective functions—over your cell phone or the Internet while vacationing halfway around the world. Now, if only you could get the vacuum cleaner to pick up your mail.

Like their A/V brethren, security system service providers are marketing themselves as one-stop shops for your home's central nervous system. No one company may be best at everything yet, but security is a safe place to start smartening up your home.

A Host of High-Tech Options

Options once reserved for technophiles, super-villains, museums, and celebrities have become available to anyone. Closed circuit television (CCTV) can now be fed through your TV or computer and can be monitored online, allowing you to check on your home from virtually anywhere. Card Access Control is another viable option on pricier security systems. This feature lets you arm or disable security settings with the simple swipe of a magnetic card key about the size of a driver's license. Sensors can be installed that detect motion, temperature change, smoke and carbon monoxide, fluctuation of sound waves, broken glass, or breached barriers. When tripped, they transmit the disruption to a central control panel, which in turn relays the home location and the point of alarm to the monitoring company. The monitoring company immediately attempts to contact the homeowner (unless specifically instructed to call authorities right away) to verify that a break-in has occurred. If there is no response, or if the respondent fails to give the proper secret password, the police or fire department is notified. In addition, some monitoring companies will dispatch their own personnel to check out the situation, either from the street or, if keys are provided, inside the home itself.

The explosion of cellular and wireless technology promises further protection options and convenience to homeowners. Teamed with battery packs in the event of power failure, these state-of-the-art communication systems are fully safeguarded. Wireless modular components (touch-pads) can be placed in convenient locations by homeowners themselves. (This is great for renters, too, who can take the wireless system with them when they move). Alarm warnings range from the sound of a voice calmly repeating "fire" or the crazed, vicious barks of a pack of Rottweilers, to sudden illumination of all the lights in your home. All of these functions are managed through a central control panel, traditionally a keypad and display. But as this industry charges toward the home-automation front, touch screens or PC platforms are increasingly becoming the way to go, which makes it much easier to program and manage your systems. You can keep tabs on alarm history and security status or play back the sequence of lights you turn on and off while driving home from work—and do it all remotely, via computer or cell phone.

For the celebrity glitterati crowd there are high-end options like safe rooms and bodyguard services. For the right price, you can be as safe as a Saudi Prince or an American senator. However, cost and inconvenience are so prohibitive as to limit these services to the unlucky celebrities who really need them.

Choosing the right system is as much about the logistical characteristics of your location (i.e. apartment vs. house, rural vs. urban) and budget as it is about the degree of system integration you want in your home. Options range from an "I'm Protected" warning sticker on a window to a virtual HAL 5000. How sophisticated do you want to get? How intrusive? A homeowner's personal circumstances and susceptibility must also be considered.

ON COST

The cost of any security system depends upon the number of devices, the sophistication of the control unit, the degree of integration, the term and service of the monitoring contract, and whether or not the technology is wireless. Basically, cost reflects the time and material for installation plus the monitoring agreement. For the equipment and installation itself, the range is quite large, anywhere from $200 up to the tens of thousands. The important thing to consider is not the level of sophistication but the reliability. Don't skimp, but don't automatically opt for the most newfangled, expensive choice. Monitoring agreements vary from month-to-month contracts to long-term commitments of up to five years. At the end of the term, the monitoring agreement should be automatically renewable, with a ceiling for rate hikes spelled out in the contract. Payment can be made on a monthly, quarterly, or annual basis. If you break your contract, you may be held responsible for as much as 90% of the unexpired term, but most high-end security firms will let it go to avoid ill will or tarnishing their reputation. If you sell your home, however, you should be able to transfer your monitoring agreement over to the new owners.

It is important to know the parameters of your monitoring agreement before you sign it. Many people are involved in your security, and awkward mistakes will cost you time and could cause system malfunction. Usually security providers allow a familiarization period in which no signal is acted upon. Use this time wisely. Once you're up and running, you may be charged by both the monitoring company and the city for false alarms that waste their time. They will also charge you to reprogram controls. Be absolutely sure you're comfortable with the system setup and its use before signing the agreement. Warranties should cover parts and labor for one year, and you can opt for a maintenance agreement that covers such extras as emergency service. After you invest in a security system, check with your homeowner's insurance company. You may be able to get a reduction in your insurance rate.

GETTING PLUGGED IN

Finally, your security system provider may need an installation permit, and certain components and installation methods may need to comply with local regulations. As the homeowner, you must provide permanent electrical access and a permanent telephone connection.

WHAT TO CONSIDER WHEN CHOOSING A SECURITY SYSTEM

- ✧ Do you own or rent?
- ✧ Is it a house or an apartment?
- ✧ Are there children or pets in the home?
- ✧ How often are you around?

Security Systems Design & Installation

All-Time Detection Inc. 🛍   5   4   5   5
28 Willett Avenue, Port Chester, NY 10573
(914) 937 - 2600 www.alltimedetection.com

Superior integrated home security systems and central monitoring; fire detection

With 200 employees and a reputation across New York and Connecticut for providing some of the best service around, All-Time Detection is a popular choice. This local security design and installation firm is said to be "one of the last of the local guys that can compete with the big national companies." Principal Michael Backer runs this 45-year-old firm, which was established in 1960 by his now-retired business partner. Most of the company's work comes by way of trade referrals from architects, but All-Time welcomes inquiries from homeowners as well.

True to its name, All-Time offers 24-hour service from its own monitoring facility. From home CCTV surveillance and fire detection to electronic parking control systems for commercial establishments, this company handles it all with its service fleet of 40 trucks and scores of certified installers. And when it comes to on-site training, Backer has a separate staff whose sole job is to make sure clients know how to use their system. Monitoring rates are competitive, while service costs fall at the high end of the range.

"Really professional security that takes care of you as a person, not just your property." "Expensive, high-end, great." "The staff is incredibly helpful, even if they have to explain something to you a million times."

ADT Security Services Inc.   3.5   3   4.5   3
47-40 21st Street, 10th Floor, Long Island City, NY 11101
(718) 392 - 9335 www.adt.com

Home security systems and monitoring

This national company is something of a household name in New York, where customers have been slapping ADT stickers on their front windows for over 125 years. The behemoth ADT installs and maintains home systems covering burglary, fire, flood, and carbon monoxide detection. But lest you think the size of the company adversely affects quality, clients describe ADT as "serious security." The efficiency and quality of its services are roundly praised. Sources say the systems are reasonably priced, as are the ongoing monthly fees.

"If the baby sets off the alarm, there will be two fire trucks at your door, even if you call ADT to try and stop it!" "Even though they're a large national company, I still felt like I got personalized, attentive service."

*We invite you to visit www.franklinreport.com to view images of their work.

474

	Quality	Cost	Value	Recommend?
	+	$	◆	★

American Security Systems Inc.   4.5   4   4.5   4
5-44 50th Avenue, Long Island City, NY 11101
(718) 784-2880 www.americansecuritysys.com

Home security systems with central monitoring, fire detection

Since 1979, American Security Systems has provided bread-and-butter services like burglar alarms, locks, and fire alarms. The tech-savvy firm also offers video intercoms, card access systems, telephone entry systems, and closed-circuit televisions. We hear American stays on top of developments in security technology, like DVR cameras that record easily searchable color surveillance. And after its recent acquisition of another security firm specializing in fire alarms, American became one of the few New York City Fire Department-certified security companies in the tri-state area.

Clients give the firm high marks for the quality systems it installs, praising American's skill with detail-oriented specialty systems. Customers rave about the fact that American has its own central monitoring station for alarm systems, which they say makes a huge difference. The reliable staff gets high marks for providing efficient, timely customer service.

"You can always get a guy on the phone." "They did an excellent job on a system that had both hard-wired and wireless parts." "Any problems I had were addressed expediently." "They installed a security system with video so I can watch my kids play while I'm traveling."

CJT Inc.   3.5   3.5   4   5
35 Tulip Drive, Kings Park, NY 11754
(631) 366 - 4236 cjtinc@optonline.net

Home security and telephone systems

A small, personalized security firm, CJT specializes in designing alarm and telephone systems, primarily for clients living above 59th Street. The firm also handles computer wiring, biometric door controls, heat detectors, and a variety of other security devices.

Clients appreciate the creative, intelligent security solutions that CJT offers, as well as its solid systems, reliable, prompt service, and trustworthy personnel. We're told that projected costs are close to actual ones, so there are few surprises when the bill comes. CJT does subcontract its monitoring work, but to a reputable firm, Alarmtech.

"Very creative in assessing your security needs." "Wouldn't trade them for anyone else." "Prompt, attentive service."

Intelli-Tec Security Services LLC   4   4   4   5
2000 Shames Drive, Westbury, NY 11590
(516) 876 - 2000 www.intelli-tec.net

Top-notch home security systems, telephone systems, and home automation

Many of New York's leading museums and banks trust Intelli-Tec to handle their security. Since 1977, the firm has served some of the Northeast's most prestigious residences and businesses in the city and on Long Island's East End and North Shore. Principal Marty McMillan and his staff of 51 garner high praise for their superior workmanship and professional service.

Services offered by this prestigious firm include integrated security systems, central station monitoring, access control systems, closed-circuit television, engineered fire systems, intercoms, satellite dish and CATV, data cabling, telephone systems, lighting control, sound and A/V systems, and home theaters. The company also offers specialized 24-hour protection for valuable paintings and artwork. Intelli-Tec comes recommended by many of New York's high-end contractors, as well as top security consultants and executive protection firms. Considering the quality of the work, clients say, the costs are more than reasonable.

"Great service! Available 24/7." "Marty's incredible—my walls were open and another company let me down. Marty had workers at my house that same day so my construction could continue." "I have worked with Marty McMillan for more than ten years, and find him and his company to be of the highest caliber." "Makes the most complex challenges seem simple."

L.J. Loeffler Intercom

95 Center Avenue, Secaucus, NJ 07094
(212) 924 - 7597

Intercom systems

	Quality	Cost	Value	Recommend?
	4	4	4	5

In business for over a hundred years, this small firm keeps Manhattan buildings safe by providing security intercoms. L.J. Loeffler's clients and peers are enthusiastic about its expertise. Because the firm's technicians have been in the business so long, sometimes they're the only ones qualified to repair more ancient intercom systems. But the company also installs new CCTV cameras and roof alarms. Fans say the years of experience shine through in L.J. Loeffler's work.

"I won't use anyone else in the city." "Not on the cutting edge, but very sincere."

P.D. Security Systems

336 Warwick Avenue, Teaneck, NY 07666
(718) 680 - 6216   patrick.donofrio@pdsystemsinc.com

Home security, telephone, and A/V systems

	Quality	Cost	Value	Recommend?
	4	3.5	4.5	5

A jack of all trades in the home electronics business, P.D. Security Systems' principal Patrick D'Onofrio has been designing, installing, and servicing residential alarm, entertainment, and communication systems in New York and northern New Jersey for twenty years. An electrical engineer by degree, D'Onofrio is a human one-stop shop for all low-voltage systems.

Clients describe D'Onofrio and his staff as "wonderful to work with," citing their dependable and responsive service as well as excellent follow-up practices. We hear this small firm's employees are straightforward, hardworking types who keep the space tidy. The company sells the top brands in all areas of home electronics at competitive prices.

"They follow up with everything." "Tremendous effort." "Even referred them to my in-laws, who don't like anyone. They love him." "Always available and calls back." "They were very patient showing me how to use the system."

Protection One

125 East Bethpage Road, Bethpage, NY 11803
(800) 438 - 4357   www.protectionone.com

Home security systems and monitoring

	Quality	Cost	Value	Recommend?
	3	3	4	4

With over one million North American customers served, Protection One has found a following with its solid, simple systems, tried and tested by years of experience. The firm's mammoth size (over 2,300 employees) allows it to monitor its alarm systems carefully. Then again, it's easy to imagine why some sources say personalized service is not the company's strong suit. Protection One has a branch office in Waterbury, Connecticut, where potential clients are invited to stop in for a consultation about its modestly priced services.

"A painless way to get the job done." "They've seen it all."

	Quality 	Cost $	Value ◆	Recommend? ★

Scarsdale Security Systems

4.5   4   4.5   5

132 Montgomery Avenue, Scarsdale, NY 10583
(914) 722 - 2222   www.scarsdalesecurity.com

Expert home security systems and monitoring

The name may imply a local company, but the protective arms of Scarsdale Security extend nationwide. Since 1982, residential, commercial, and industrial clients have put their trust in this 75-person company. From monitored burglar and fire systems to closed-circuit TV and access control system installations, this firm has a proven record of "exceptional" quality, particularly in high-end residential work. Happy clients say Scarsdale stacks up to some of the best out there. The pleasant and accommodating technicians are singled out for special praise. Scarsdale's own monitoring station, with thirty technicians keeping a close eye on alarms in the field, gives the firm a leg up on most of the competition.

"They are exceptional and do incredible work. I use them for all my large, high-end jobs." "They go out of their way to do extra things." "Really accommodating people."

Scott Security Systems Inc.

3.5   3   4.5   4

236 West 30th Street, 10th Floor, New York, NY 10001
(212) 594 - 2121   www.scottsecurity.net

Home and commercial security systems

Started 22 years ago as a private investigation and polygraph firm, Scott Security had so many clients asking for security advice that it decided to get into the business itself. Today Scott Security offers a full range of services, from DVR surveillance to card access and beyond, to complement its gumshoe division. With a dozen employees, this small-to-mid-sized company is described as a good fit for those who want individualized attention. The firm's focus is on commercial work, where its roster includes impressive clients like the New York Public Library and Trinity Church, but Scott Security will take on elite residential jobs in New York, Long Island, and New Jersey.

"You can always get the owner on the phone." "Pleasant to work with."

Sonitrol

3   3   4   3

20 Murray Hill Parkway, Suite 110, East Rutherford, NJ 07073
(212) 967 - 9828   www.sonitrol.com

Home security systems

Sonitrol, a large international company, has been protecting homes since 1977. With local offices throughout New York State, Sonitrol "comes when you need them," clients say. Local dealers are responsible for sales, installation, and service of monitored systems. While sources caution that personal attention isn't the firm's forte, clients do receive solid home protection at a reasonable cost.

"Not the best, not the worst. A solid value."

Speakeasy Intercom & Electric Service Inc.

2.5   2.5   4   3

43-44 162nd Street, Flushing, NY 11358
(718) 939 - 6461

Intercom systems and security surveys

Clients say the security is tight at this Speakeasy. Since 1977, the Queens firm has been serving residential and commercial clients around New York City, focusing on intercom installation and relocation, card access systems, and audio/video security. Alarm systems are not part of the firm's repertoire, but the company will perform site surveys to assess the security of a client's home.

Speakeasy gets mixed reviews for responsiveness and tidiness, but clients report that the service staff is knowledgeable. The firm is frequently hired by management companies.

"Competent...completed the job to my satisfaction." "Can be hard to get in touch with, but the work is satisfactory." "We use them on all our jobs."

The SecureCom Group   3.5   3   4.5   4
22-26 College Point Boulevard, College Point, NY 11356
(718) 353 - 3355

Home security systems

Some of the top management companies in the city use SecureCom to protect their residents against theft and fire. The firm will also work with homeowners on large projects. SecureCom's services include wire or wireless security and fire alarm systems, CCTV surveillance systems, card access control, and 24-hour service. Follow-up training on each system is said to be thorough and clear, and clients say the company's technicians are helpful and responsive—although it may be difficult to get in touch with a higher-up. We're told that its moderate pricing makes SecureCom a very good deal.

"Their central monitoring facility doesn't charge for false alarms, which was certainly a help to my family when we first got the system." "All of the employees I dealt with were really helpful and pleasant—a plus in my book."

Hiring a Telephone Service Provider

It all used to be so simple. One phone. Black. If you weren't around it just rang. If you were on a call, it droned busy. Now, local telephone companies offer a wide array of services: voice mail, call forwarding, three-way calling, and caller ID (with or without ID block). The wealth of options combined with the rise of the Internet and the home office has changed the playing field for telephone system service providers. But for systems that integrate multiple phone lines, intercoms, and door buzzers to a networked and net-savvy home office, these are still the people to call. Don't be daunted by the NASA-level complexity of modern phone systems. It's not really rocket science, as long as you know the basics and hire a great service provider.

Plan Ahead and Allow for Expansion

Before calling a service provider, think, plan, discuss—and think again. Figure out what you want and where. If you're putting in a home office, know how many lines you will need, where the fax and printers are going to be located, which computers will be networked and online, and where you're going to sit. If you like to rearrange the furniture from time to time, consider putting phone jacks on both sides of the room. And always run more cable and reserve more lines than you need: today's bedroom is tomorrow's office. Running an empty conduit gives you enormous flexibility to change with the times down the road. When you run phone, cable, and other lines, the wires are usually buried in the walls or hidden behind moldings. This involves messy, disruptive and expensive construction, not to mention the need to redo your decorating touches. Avoid these problems by planning ahead and allowing for expansion. Also, don't overlook unusual spaces in your planning. You can hide a bulky fax or copy machine in a closet—just don't forget to install a phone jack and electrical outlet.

Check the Brand

Most telephone system service providers have licensing agreements with certain manufacturers and will only deal with those systems. If you're keen on a particular product, it's a good idea to contact the manufacturer for preferred service providers in your area. On the whole, all the systems perform the same functions (automated directories, voicemail boxes, multiple lines/extensions, on-hold music, interoffice paging, caller ID) and offer the same accessories (headsets, holsters). It's the brand, sophistication, complexity of integration with other systems, and convenience of use that affect the cost. Systems can either be purchased outright, leased, or financed.

It's All About Service

What really sets telephone system service providers apart is the quality of their follow-up service and support. If you're running a business from home, you can't afford to be cut off from the rest of the world for days or even hours. If you're just trying to live your life, non-responsive service is still a supreme annoyance. Find service providers with guaranteed response times and emergency service. Know that you'll be able to reach them in a phone-meltdown emergency. A good service provider will suggest and make additions and modifications to your system as times and technologies change. Warranties typically last six months to one year after installation.

TELEPHONE SYSTEM TIPS

✧ An installer is only as good as his service.

✧ Plan and pre-wire for the future.

✧ Bear in mind that a typical phone system lasts five to ten years. Build in excess capacity.

✧ Explore the new variety of telephone ring options— your life may change with a serene, low-key incoming call signal.

✧ Consider sending a request for proposal (RFP) to a number of vendors; having written proposals helps you compare features, service, and price.

TELEPHONE SYSTEMS

Ahl Tone
3.5 3 4.5 4

6749 Fifth Avenue, Brooklyn, NY 11220
(212) 684 - 5959

Residential phone systems—Panasonic

Ahl Tone, which operates a retail center in Brooklyn and a sales office in Manhattan, provides soup-to-nuts service for residential phone systems, from sales and installation to maintenance and repairs. We hear the firm is involved in every step of the project, monitoring the process to ensure the quality of the end result. Panasonic systems are Ahl Tone's specialty. Insiders report that the firm is prepared to take on even the most complex phone systems—like the recent installation of a complete multi-line phone system for a four-story Upper East Side brownstone.

Clients applaud the Ahl Tone guarantee of one-day response time on normal service calls and two-hour response to emergency calls—seven days a week, twenty-four hours a day. We hear the "friendly," "polite" technicians are helpful, knowledgeable, and accessible.

"Good honest guys."

Audio by James Inc.

571 Knollwood Road, Ridgewood, NJ 07450
(201) 493 - 7282   abyj@msn.com

A/V and telephone system installation and service; audio specialist

See Audio by James Inc.'s full report under the heading Audio/Video Design & Installation

Automated Answering Systems Inc.
3 3 4 3.5

875 Avenue of the Americas, New York, NY 10001
(212) 947 - 4155

Residential phone systems—Avaya

This Manhattan company has been providing telecommunication services to clients in the city since 1962. The firm currently sells, installs, and services Avaya systems, usually recommending the Partner Advanced Communication System (ACS) for residential needs. Sources say the twenty-person staff handles everything from start to finish, and each client is assigned to a technician who programs the system at setup and continues to work with the account on an ongoing basis. One year of maintenance is included free with installation. Clients praise the staff's professionalism and efficiency.

Birns Telecommunications Inc.
3 3 4 3.5

233 West 17th Steet, New York, NY 10011
(212) 633 - 8600   www.birns.net

Residential and small business phone systems—NEX, Sprint, and Tadiran

Since 1973, Birns Telecommunications Inc. (BTI) has been answering to clients in the New York metro and northern New Jersey areas. BTI sells, installs, and services NEX, Sprint, and Tadiran systems which clients say are simple and easy to use. We're told the company's service is consistent, with certified technicians being routed on a "call-out basis." With over 100,000 clients served, there can be "occasional bureaucratic snags," but references say the technicians are friendly and good about cleaning up after themselves.

"Great spare part availability—called customer service and received a spare part that same day."

CJT Inc.

35 Tulip Drive, Kings Park, NY 11754
(631) 366 - 4236   cjtinc@optonline.net

Home security and telephone systems

See CJT Inc.'s full report under the heading Security Systems

Compushine

30 East 60th Street, New York, NY 10021
(212) 371 - 1525   www.compushine.com

Computer networking and support, A/V systems, telephone systems

See Compushine's full report under the heading Computer Installation & Maintenance

Electronic Environments

247 West 37th Street, Suite 704, New York, NY 10018
(212) 997 - 1110

A/V and telephone system installation and service

See Electronic Environments' full report under the heading Audio/Video Design & Installation

Fone Booth   4   3.5   4.5   5

330 Seventh Avenue, New York, NY 10001
(212) 564 - 0900   harveystuart@att.net

Residential phone systems—Panasonic

In the business since 1977, Fone Booth covers all five boroughs, concentrating primarily on the Upper East Side of Manhattan. Panasonic systems are its specialty, and the company offers full installation, training, and maintenance services. Clients say you'll never get a busy signal when you call on principal Harvey Stuart for service. An industry veteran, Stuart is said to be quick to come in an emergency. Stuart and his staff of four are praised for their ability to get the job done with minimal disruption.

"Very informative, helpful, and accommodating—great service." *"Installation was done with no disruption to our business."*

Intelli-Tec Security Services LLC

2000 Shames Drive, Westbury, NY 11590
(516) 876 - 2000   www.intelli-tec.net

Top-notch home security systems, telephone systems, and home automation

See Intelli-Tec Security Services LLC's full report under the heading Security Systems

Lorna/PSI Communications Inc.   3.5   3.5   4   3

148 West 37th Street, New York, NY 10018
(212) 695 - 6300

Residential and business phone systems—Nitsuko, Panasonic

Founded in 1956, Lorna/PSI Communications Inc. is a full-service telecommunications company. This 25-person firm uses Panasonic, NEC, Samsung, and

Quality   Cost   Value   Recommend?

Nitsiko systems to meet the communication needs of Manhattan clients. The company offers training and follow-up help, and keeps a group of technicians on staff to handle repairs and maintenance calls on a "next available" basis.

Reliable Voice & Data Systems   3   3   4   4
366 East Meadow Avenue, East Meadow, NY 11554
(212) 319 - 6109   www.reliablevoice.com
Residential phone systems—Avaya, Toshiba

Featuring Toshiba and Avaya systems, Reliable has been providing residents and small businesses with end-to-end services since 1972. The firm sells, installs, and maintains phone systems. A group of twenty technicians is dedicated to Manhattan clients, though none are assigned to specific accounts. Reliable provides remote maintenance and service 24 hours a day, 7 days a week.

"Prompt response." "They were extremely professional throughout the installation, and have followed up quickly when I've run into problems with my system."

S&S Interconnect   4.5   4   4.5   5
308 West 40th Street, 2nd Floor, New York, NY 10018
(212) 465 - 0505   info@ssinterconnect.com
Residential phone systems—Panasonic

Clients, contractors, and architects alike say Stu Shulman and his seven-person team do outstanding work with residential and small business phone systems, from the very simple to the complex. Shulman gives the same enthusiastic effort for small home systems as he does for large corporate clients. With all those pluses it's "no wonder his phones are ringing off the hook," but nevertheless, clients say Shulman is quick to return calls, even if an assistant has to page him on another job site. Sources agree that Shulman is a pleasure to work with, making note of his reliability, honesty, and likable character.

"In an emergency, he's extremely reliable." "Even a Verizon tech said how impressed he was with Stu. He said he never sees people as committed to quality service as Stu is." "Not only does Stu know his stuff, but the fact that he stays on site to test everything is impressive." "Stu strides in, solves the problem, tells a few jokes, and leaves. He's great." "Stu always seems very busy, but he does a great job squeezing you in. However, I still think he could use a bigger staff." "Stu is very knowledgeable and a pleasure to deal with." "Really knows his stuff—I wish I could say the same about my contractor."

Tele-Dynamics   3.5   3.5   4   4
330 Seventh Avenue, 21st Floor, New York, NY 10001
(212) 594 - 7333   www.tele-dynamics.com
Residential phone systems—Avaya, Toshiba

Robert Pullman and his 30-person team have been helping New Yorkers get the hook-up since 1977. As a full-service telecommunications company, Tele-Dynamics installs and maintains Avaya and Toshiba phone systems for residents and small to mid-size businesses in Manhattan. The company also installs and maintains web-based phone systems, an increasingly popular technology. The Tele-Dynamics technicians are all union-certified and factory-trained and "friendly" and "courteous" to boot. Service calls are handled in the "next available" fashion, which clients characterize as "timely."

"The technician knew what he was doing, and did his work quickly and efficiently. He was also polite—a bonus in my book." "They can rig it to divert phone calls from your office to your swimming pool in the Hamptons, while keeping it a local charge. It's neat stuff."

Telephone Traders

	Quality	Cost	Value	Recommend?
	3	3	4	3

545 Eighth Avenue, Suite 1502, New York, NY 10018
(212) 643 - 0950 www.telephonetraders.com

Residential phone systems—Avaya

Telephone Traders relies upon Avaya Technologies to meet the communications needs of residential clients. We're told the products offered and serviced by the Traders include the Partner Advanced Communication System (ACS) as well as other Avaya products like Merlin. The company's services include installation, training, and follow-up technical help. Repairs and maintenance calls are handled on a "next-available" basis by a group of Avaya-certified on-staff technicians.

Ultimate Sound & Installation Inc.

36-16 29th Street, Long Island City, NY 11106
(718) 729 - 2111 www.ultimateinstallations.com

A/V, automation, and lighting system design and installation

See Ultimate Sound & Installation Inc.'s full report under the heading Audio/ Video Design & Installation

Hiring a Tile, Marble & Stone Service Provider

Tile, marble, and stone can transform a room. Granite kitchen counters make beautiful surfaces on which to work. Marble brings a dramatic flair to the bathroom, and what could be more elegant than a travertine fireplace at the heart of your home? Colorful, artistic tiles can brightly define the style of a kitchen—Spanish, French, Scandinavian. These materials come in a staggering range of types, qualities, shapes, and colors. Tiles, for example, range in size from five-eighths of an inch square to one square foot and up. Marble can come in tile form or in slabs that can be as small or as large as you need. Slabs—pieces of stone larger than 24 inches square—can be cut in various sizes and shapes to fit the area.

Where Do I Start?

The kind of tile that you choose will depend on your specific needs. For example, if you are selecting tiles for a high-traffic area like an entryway or kitchen, you'll want durable tiles that will not show wear and tear. If you are tiling your kitchen, you might consider a durable stone such as granite or a ceramic tile that is easy to clean and maintain. Smaller tiles tend to be used for decorative purposes because they are more laborious to install and harder to clean, while larger tiles are used for more practical purposes such as covering a floor.

Remember, each kind of tile has its advantages and drawbacks. The installer that you choose should be able to help you explore what kind of tile will work best for you. Tiles, either man-made or natural, can be as plain as classic bathroom-white ceramic or as intricate as hand-painted/embossed pieces from Portugal. Man-made tiles are generally porcelain or ceramic and are durable and resistant to stains. Some manufacturers rate ceramic tile on a scale from 1 to 4+, from least to most durable. Porcelain is considered more durable than ceramic because porcelain is not glazed. Note that porcelain is actually a form of ceramic, but is fired at such high temperatures that it is denser than the material labeled ceramic. Porcelain is vitreous, or glass-like, meaning that water cannot penetrate it—and this is one reason why porcelain is stronger than ceramic.

Because of the firing process that ceramic tile undergoes, the color as well as the shape of the tile is permanent.

Natural Tile and Stone

Most natural tiles—such as marble, granite, limestone and slate—will last forever. But that doesn't mean they will look like new forever. Marble is one of the most classic, desired, and expensive stones, and because it scratches and stains easily, it must be sealed after installation. Even after the marble is sealed, it will still be more vulnerable to scratching than other stone, such as granite, so be prepared to care for and maintain a marble installation. There are many types of seals to choose from: a matte seal preserves the stone's natural color or texture, a glossy seal makes the stone appear shiny and smooth and gives it a more formal appearance, and a color enhancement sealer brings out the stone's colors and beauty. Like marble, granite is a natural stone that comes in both tiles and slabs.

Granite is one of the strongest stones, although it also needs to be sealed after professional installation. Granite is more impervious to stains than marble, and also less expensive.

In general, marble and granite slabs are more expensive than tile because the slabs are customized and take more of the installer's time. Slabs are commonly used for areas such as countertops and around fireplaces. Installing slabs requires different skills than installing tile; therefore, you should ask a potential installer if he normally installs tile or slab.

On Cost

With the exception of hand-painted tiles, tile is generally priced per square foot. This simplifies price comparisons of tiles that differ greatly in size or shape: once you know how many square feet you need for your area, it's easy to calculate the difference in total cost between tile choices. Basic ceramic and porcelain tiles range from $2 to $20 per square foot. Hand-painted tiles can cost anywhere from $8 to $150 each.

On the whole, stone tiles like marble and granite are more expensive than their ceramic counterparts. The price of marble and granite depends on color and type. Natural stone is quarried all over the world, and a particularly desirable origin can make it more expensive. Some stone is easier to find and is not considered as rare as other types of stone. Like ceramic tiles, natural stone tiles are priced per square foot. Marble and granite slab, however, is priced per project because there are so many variables in slab work. The price depends on the edges, the customization, and the amount of work that goes into the actual installation. Slabs also have to be cut to fit the area precisely. The pricing of slab work depends on how difficult the stone was to get and how large the slab is. The larger the slab, the more expensive it is going to be to transport.

Tile and stone installers generally charge per project. The more custom work they have to do, such as edges and corners, the more expensive the project. Also, note that more artistic tile installation, such as creating mosaics, is much more expensive. Hiring a larger company can be cheaper because much work can be done in house, and the company can buy in bulk to save on materials. Also, installers will not have to be subcontracted and the materials will often be in stock. If you order from a smaller company and they do not keep a particular, expensive tile in stock, the price could be higher than from a larger company. With any installer, tile or marble that has to be ordered can significantly delay your project.

Who Installs the Tile, Marble, and Stone?

Some of the service providers in this guide use their own installers and some subcontract the work out. If you choose a company that uses installers that are not in house, make sure that the company has used them before and ask for references. Some companies also keep a list of installers that they use on a regular basis.

Qualifications

No professional certification is required to install tile, marble, and stone, but there are other ways of screening potential installers. For example, they should have a business license and, ideally, a general contractor's license. An excellent way to evaluate potential installers is to ask for references, speak to them, and look at photographs of previous installations. Membership in professional organizations may also confer credibility on a service provider. These associations can offer general information as well as answer some of your simple questions about tile and marble installation.

The main professional associations to contact for information are:

The Marble Institute of America (440) 250-9222 www.marble-institute.com
Ceramic Tiles Distributors Association (800) 938-2832 www.ctda-home.org
The Tile Council of America (864) 646-8453 www.tileusa.com
The Ceramic Tile Institute of America (805) 371-TILE www.ctioa.com

Whether you decide to install simple ceramic tile in your shower or rare marble in your living room, the entire process will go more smoothly with a basic understanding of the special materials described above.

DECORATIVE IDEAS

⬥ For tile in the kitchen or high-traffic areas, consider a darker grout for easier up-keep and a more formal appearance.

⬥ Install tile mosaics around kitchen windows and add a tile inlay to your floors and walls, or scatter tiles with a thematic print (herbs for a kitchen or shells for the shower).

⬥ Use a stone or tile molding to crown your master bathroom, or mix marble counter tops with a ceramic tile backsplash.

⬥ For the children's bathroom, use hand-painted tiles in favorite colors to make washing more fun, or give the playroom some pizzazz with a bright tile chair rail or "homemade" mosaic.

⬥ Too traditional? Exotic stones such as quartzite, slate, and alabaster can offer a unique alternative to other natural surfaces, and are just as functional!

⬥ Don't overlook the nouveau! Some of the latest metallic and glass tiles are made to refract light, giving a glimmer to the dullest spaces.

	Quality	Cost	Value	Recommend?
	+	$	◆	★

TILE, MARBLE & STONE

🛍 FIRMS WITH ONLINE PORTFOLIOS* 🛍

A&G Marble Inc. 🛍   3.5   3.5   4   4.5
132-19 34th Avenue, Flushing, NY 11354
(718) 353 - 9415 www.agmarble.com
Marble and granite installation and fabrication

A&G Marble fabricates and distributes marble, limestone, granite, onyx, travertine, and slate throughout the United States. Established in 1968, this family-owned and -operated company, founded by Charles Gambino, is now run by son Anthony. We hear that A&G provides individualized customer service to both residential and commercial clients from its vast New York showroom. Considered "the source" for stone by its dedicated clients, A&G's Tepeaca, Mexico plant manufactures and quarries plenty of product.

A&G takes on projects that range from exterior jobs to public spaces to vanity and kitchen countertops, offering its clients a large selection of stones imported from around the world. Recent projects include hotels like The Mark, The Belvedere, The Warwick, and The Carlyle, as well as the Neue Gallerie and the private retreats of some very prominent homeowners. Clients say these "Old World artisans" are efficient and affordable.

"A&G's treasure trove of stone makes it the first and only stop for me." "No question, a firm that takes great pride in their work." "Extremely satisfied." "They are quite knowledgeable about their materials." "We were happy with the work they did in our kitchen—beautiful craftsmanship and very professional." "It was a difficult installation, with a lot of on-site cutting and adjusting, but I would hire this company again." "With A&G Marble we never have to worry about problems; they anticipate and communicate potential problems before it is too late." "A&G Marble's dedication to quality and service is unmatched by other marble companies we have worked with."

D.M.S. Studios 🛍   4   3.5   4.5   4.5
5-50 51st Avenue, Long Island City, NY 11101
(718) 937 - 5648 www.dms-studios.com
Superb traditional marble and stone fabrication; carving and sculpting

Highly regarded for its custom fireplaces, D.M.S. has been creating and carving customized stonework since 1984. Owner Daniel Sinclair has earned a reputation for "making the most beautiful stone more beautiful." We are told Sinclair creates unique fireplaces and mantels by combining traditional methods of handcraftsmanship with genuine marble and limestone from its quarries in Europe and America.

The firm works in all areas of stone carving, fabricating, and sculpting, and insiders say D.M.S. is now taking on more complicated and elaborate jobs such as artistic and architectural detailing. Because fireplaces and mantels are handmade, it may take longer than average for a project to be completed, but according to D.M.S.'s many satisfied clients, that's the price you pay for a "true work of art."

*We invite you to visit www.franklinreport.com to view images of their work.

488

"A master craftsman and a cut above the rest." "Not just a fireplace, it's art." "Daniel is an Old World technician—all he uses is a hammer and chisel." "Amazing detail work." "I'd say his only shortcoming is his lack of technology. Not having the proper machinery can slow him down." "Very bright and well-spoken."

Estia Tiles by Dionysus ■   3.5   3.5   4   4.5

1189 Lexington Avenue, New York, NY 10028
(212) 861 - 5616   www.dionysusmarble.com
Marble and tile sales, installation, maintenance, and repair

Estia Tiles by Dionysus displays a wide selection of marble, tile, and stone out of its NYC showroom. The firm gets solid reviews from clients who appreciate its personalized service. Mike Giordas and his wife, Joanna, have been in the business since 1989—and still possess "infinite patience." The crew at Dionysus takes care of everything from design to installation of ceramic, marble, limestone, and mosaic. Other services include restoration of marble and ceramic vases, as well as fabrication of custom fireplaces. Maintenance and repair work is available to all customers and although the firm's services are limited to the city, Estia will sell and ship materials to any location.

"Mike loves what he does, a real perfectionist." "I have never had an easier task to complete while living in New York." "He figured out how to use one singular piece of granite that went from our counter to window sill." "Mike and Joanna were a pleasure to work with." "He could have charged more, but didn't." "Mike is not just a salesman—he's incredibly talented." "Very involved in helping you find what you're looking for." "They give you the attention that larger companies can't offer."

Gurri Installation Inc. ■   4   3   5   4.5

PO Box 2327, New York, NY 10021
(212) 734 - 2300   gurri_inc@usa.com
Marble, tile, and mosaic installation and repair; apartment remodeling

Considered a specialist in the installation of tiles, marbles, and mosaics, Gurri will also take on small repair jobs in any of the five boroughs. For larger kitchen and bath projects, the company limits itself to Manhattan and Long Island. We hear the brothers Gurri operate their decade-old firm with availability and honesty, and are "truly a pleasure to work with." Respectful of deadlines and budgets, the firm can satisfy the most demanding of clients, staying on the job until every last issue is taken care of. In addition to its excellent reputation in tile, marble, and stone, clients also feel "Gurri understands the challenges of remodeling a Manhattan co-op." The firm does not have a showroom but will recommend a tile and marble supplier.

"Easy to work with and flexible about adjusting course mid-project. I would hire Gurri again in a heartbeat and recommend them to friends considering renovations." "The original bathroom was gutted and all-new plumbing and electrical systems were installed, as were pocket doors and new fixtures. We are very happy with his work and would definitely work with him again." "When subcontractors did not deliver according to specs, Sami had it corrected immediately—he is very well-suited as a contractor." "Very responsive in every possible way." "I use them repeatedly." "We lived in the apartment during the majority of the remodeling process, and they were always very polite and tidy."

	Quality	Cost	Value	Recommend?
	✚	$	◆	★

HartzStone 🛍

	4	3.5	4.5	5

PO Box 3265, Newtown, CT 06470
(866) 710 - 6688 www.hartzstone.com
Stone maintenance, cleaning, and restoration

Clients say HartzStone is among the best in the business for stone and tile restoration. Sources praise the "expert" owner Ed Hartz for never offering a cookie cutter approach to any task, making each job special since 1996. We hear Hartz and his team of six can restore any natural stones, including limestone, slate, marble and even Mexican saltillo tiles. Services range from removing scratches and stains to stone fireplace restoration. Clients say Hartz patiently talks clients through the technical and aesthetic aspects of the process. Hartz works with both retail and trade customers. The high quality of service keeps HartzStone's clients returning year after year. Although most of the company's projects are in the Westchester-Fairfield area, its Manhattan clientele-base continues to increase.

"Ed's focus was on doing the very best job possible. The results demonstrated his expertise and professionalism in getting the job done right." "Besides his fine work, Ed was very personable and willing to accommodate the family's schedule and nuances." "He made a big effort to find the right products and applied them as many times as was necessary to get the surfaces clean and looking wonderful." "The terra-cotta floor looks brand new. It is hard to believe that this is the same floor that was covered with years of embedded dirt and wax build-up."

FIRMS WITHOUT ONLINE PORTFOLIOS

Andy's Marble and Granite Shop

	4	3.5	4.5	4

55 Caven Point Avenue, Jersey City, NJ 07305
(201) 451 - 9383 amg2014519383@aol.com
Marble and tile installation

The team at Andy's Marble receives glowing reviews for its commitment to the job, reliability, and performance. Established in 1987, this small group of professionals reportedly goes above and beyond the call of duty. Industry insiders report that these artisans have a reputation for completing jobs with impressive speed and tinkering until everything is perfect.

Since there is minimal stock in the showroom, the staff actually escorts clients to the stoneyards to purchase project materials. Andy's Marble generally works through contractors and designers, accepting residential projects on occasion. References agree the company produces high-quality work at a good value, which may explain why prices have climbed a bit recently.

"Andy's works hard and fast." "Truly excellent." "I just completed a brownstone with Andy. Of course there were some headaches, but they came through." "Even if it's the architect's fault, they will fix it." "I call his workmen 'magic elves'—they had everything fixed almost overnight!"

Ann Sacks Tile and Stone

	5	5	4	4.5

37 East 18th Street, New York, NY 10003
(212) 529 - 2800 www.annsackstile.com
Deluxe handcrafted tiles and luxury bathroom fixtures

Home design professionals and clients hail Ann Sacks as an industry leader in tile and stone that stays at the head of the pack by being "creative" and "adventurous." In 1981 Sacks opened her first shop, and the rest, as they say, is history. Stores can be found in prime locations across the continental United

States, including Manhattan, Atlanta, Boston, Chicago, Denver, Dallas, Detroit, Los Angeles, Miami, Portland, San Francisco, Seattle, Greenwich, and Kohler, Wisconsin.

Specializing in handcrafted tile, limestone slab, antiquated stone and terracotta custom mosaics, the firm displays an ever-changing palette of products in its showroom. Its new collection of leather, glass, concrete, and metal is said to be inventive and stylish. Sacks's unique offerings now extend to luxury plumbing products, bathroom fixtures, and exclusive tile collections by the likes of Barbara Barry, Angela Adams, Michael S. Smith, and Clodagh. They do not install, however they do have a list of recommended intallers.

"One of the most fashionable and innovative collections around today." "Every time I set foot in the showroom I'm like a kid in a candy store because there is just so much to marvel at." "The new leather collection is scrumptious." "My clients are always pleased with their tile collection." "Amazing showroom selection, disappointing staff assistance—basically, they didn't want to speak with me unless I was a definite buyer or with an architect or designer." "I worked with them on numerous occasions..they were very helpful...even faxed things to clients in Paris."

Bisazza Mosaico   4   4   4   4.5
43 Greene Street, New York, NY 10013
(212) 334 - 7130 www.bisazzausa.com
Artistic mosaic, glass, and terrazzo tiles

Top designers and retail clients frequent Bisazza for its high quality craftsmanship and consistently superior glass products. Launching its New York showroom in 1998, the firm was established in 1956 in Alte, in the northern Italian province of Vicenza, and has become a world leader in its field. With the artistic work done in Miami, we hear that the turnaround for tile orders is quick and painless. Using the latest computer technology and graphics, Bisazza has developed products in a wide array of colors. The firm's tiles are UV-stable and frostproof, allowing the tiles to be used both indoors and out.

Bisazza's traditional glass mosaic tiles are sold by the carton and are priced by the square foot ($8.70 to $40). The company also makes terrazzo tiles that we hear are phenomenal for residential and commercial floors, counters, and walls. The firm does not install, but will recommend a professional.

"Brilliant color selection and fantastic combination possibilities in glass mosaics." "It's never boring—I can spend hours at their Soho location." "I love the terrazzo tiles because they require no maintenance at all." "We use the small glass tiles in almost every project." "We would use Bisazza on all our projects if budget permitted." "Staff could not be more accommodating to expedite sampling." "They stand behind their product—even to the point of replacement after it has been installed." "I have never had a problem with delivery or product." "Excellent correspondence."

Ceramica Arnon Inc.   4.5   3.5   4.5   4.5
134 West 20th Street, New York, NY 10011
(212) 807 - 0876 www.ceramicaarnon.com
Specialty tiles, custom tile murals and fabrication

Third-generation ceramic tile and stone artisan Arnon Zadok has been wowing clients for over three decades. Starting his own firm in 1991, Zadok continues to impress some of the city's more notable designers and homeowners with his unique selection of tiles. Industry insiders note that Ceramica Arnon keeps up with trends and is "always looking for the next big thing." Zadok can also handle all the components of a traditional project, recently recreating a hundred-year-old stone floor with perfect authenticity.

Sources say Zadok imports products from Italy two to three years ahead of everyone else. Ceramica's latest item, "Cementi" (a 24" x 48" porcelain tile) has caught the eye of people in the know for its modern and minimalist appeal in residential and commercial spaces. We hear the firm has moved away from installations, focusing most of its energy on the sale of products. Ceramica's showroom features an array of products, from ceramic and glass tiles to metallic tile mosaics.

"Arnon is a genius when it comes to tile." "The fact that we called him back for another project speaks volumes." "We were blown away by his creativity and great solutions." "He was able to research and come up with all the pieces to remake a design to perfection. Customers didn't realize the floor was new." "He was able to interpet the past flawlessly." "Able to deliver within our tight construction schedule." "I wish someone would come over and take pictures, we are so happy with the outcome of our bathrooms." "Arnon takes great pride in his work. He has a good eye for product." "I guess you could call Arnon a temperamental artist, but that's overlooked. He is just so focused on perfecting everything." "Very honest, meticulous craftsmen." "If there were any problems, Arnon would physically correct everything himself." "Since the completion of the project and the full payment of the balance, Arnon has come back to make corrections on the plaster job...his dedication is amazing." "Low-key but extremely intelligent, his input really made a difference."

Certified Tile   3.5   3   4.5   4
54 Walnut Drive, Upper Saddle River, NJ 07458
(201) 978 - 6774   certifiedtile2003@yahoo.com
Tile and marble installation

Certified's Joe Del Biondo guarantees quality work, at times surpassing client expectations. Established in 1985, Del Biondo's shop offers installation, maintenance, and repair services, working with homeowners and the trade. With over twenty years in the business, Del Biondo is hired most often through referrals. Customers say Del Biondo shows up at a job "well equipped with great ideas." References trust Biondo with a range of projects, from placing a simple backsplash to completing a highly detailed installation of century-old tile.

"Certified's a tremendous value." "Joe is pleasant to work with, and did not cause any extra headaches." "He was very neat and clean. I went to work and when I returned, everything was in order." "I always recommend him and I'll continue to do so." "Joe is honest and explained all of my options, taking into consideration certain aspects of my lifestyle." "I wish I had a son like him. He has a great sense of humor." "I'm comfortable working with him because he's so down-to-earth."

Corcoran Marble & Monument Co. Inc.   4.5   3.5   4.5   5
50 West Hills Road, Huntington Station, NY 11746
(631) 423 - 8737   joe@corcoranmarble.com
Expert marble, tile, and stone sales and installation

Corcoran shines for being incredibly service-oriented, with some industry professionals using the firm for most of its tile work. Since 1984, Joseph Corcoran has serviced clients in the New York City area, providing installation from countertops to flooring. The company also does work in Westchester and Fairfield counties. Corcoran gets high marks from top builders who note that the owner-to-owner relationship they get results in first-class finishes. The Huntington Station showroom displays a selection of high-quality limestone, slate, granite, marble, travertine, and tile. Those who have worked with Corcoran and his staff are quick to praise its high-quality work at lower-than-market prices.

	Quality	Cost	Value	Recommend?
	✚	$	◆	★

"We give him 70% of our work, that should tell you something about their quality and performance." "They work well under pressure." "Corcoran is incredibly accommodating. When I need five extra men, they're on site right away." "I work directly with Joseph's son, Robert and he's terrific." "Joseph is knowledgeable and the work is exquisite." "Beautiful work...and everything fell right within my budget."

Country Floors Inc.   4.5   4.5   4   4
15 East 16th Street, New York, NY 10003
(212) 627 - 8300 www.countryfloors.com
Handmade and imported tile sales

Manhattanites call Country Floors a precious source for hard-to-find tiles, and a great stop for any flooring needs. The NYC shop opened in 1969 and carries a wide variety of handmade and imported tiles, from rustic to sleek, including several lines of its own—such as its popular Mediterranean and French floral tiles. Customers say the showroom staff is reliable and efficient, and overall, we hear the experience of working with Country Floors is a pleasurable one. Although the firm does not do installations, references report that its outsourced installers are dedicated and exacting. Country Floors has other locations in Greenwich, Los Angeles, San Francisco, and Florida.

"Inspiring selection of tiles." "Their attention to detail assisted in securing matching materials that we weren't even thinking about—but added to the beauty of the finished rooms." "We were on a very tight schedule and they always went the extra mile to help us." "Some sales people are not really knowledgeable, while others are great. Switch quickly rather than get bogged down." "Much higher level of service to the trade—use your architect or contractor to secure the product." "We were particularly struck by Country Floors' unique combination of professionalism and affability." "I can tell you that our experience with Country Floors was excellent." "The installers they recommended were excellent—they were right on the ball with everything from start to finish." "Surprisingly, there were no time issues or delays."

David Garbo Artisan Tile Work LLC   4   3   5   4
5 Tudor City Place, Suite 737, New York, NY 10017
(212) 856 - 9481 finetilework@aol.com
Highly detailed tile installation; stone and glass mosaics

David Garbo's tile work is reminiscent of old European styles, especially Portuguese and Italian traditions. In business since 1990, Garbo is known primarily for his work with handmade and stone tiles, but has recently taken on more projects involving glass mosaics. Garbo learned his craft in San Francisco and has been practicing for more than twenty years. Clients describe him as detail-oriented, trustworthy, and personable. Many consider David Garbo the man to call for extraordinary tile work, some of which has been featured in *Architectural Digest*.

"David's work is so unique—and of high caliber." "A specialist and attentive to detail. Good sense of design, maintains a tidy jobsite, and is easy to work with." "Not only does he work well with everyone, but there is a definite exchange of trust between David and his clients." "Painstakingly detailed." "Very hands-on, he does most of the installation himself." "I am the pickiest person at my firm, and I think David is the best of the best."

Fordham Marble   5   4   4.5   4.5
421 Fairfield Avenue, Stamford, CT 06902
(203) 348 - 5088 www.fordhammarble.com
Superior marble sales and installation

For its many devoted fans, Fordham is the only choice. With over 100 years in the business, Fordham Marble has a "dazzling" reputation for high-quality work and an even more sparkling reputation for its customer service. Founded in 1905, Fordham has expanded from its original Bronx-based fabrication plant to a second location in Stamford, Connecticut. With a century of satisfied clients standing behind it, the Fordham team now covers the territory from Manhattan to Fairfield County—and everything in between. A wide variety of marble, granite and limestone slabs are displayed in its Stamford showroom. This service-minded firm will outfit clients with the appropriate materials to fit the individual project, offering personalized guidance to architects, designers, and homeowners. The company offers a one-year guarantee on its services.

"Basically, there is no one better." "With this many years in business—I expected high results, and that's exactly what I got." "Beautiful work, good customer relationships. If I ever needed stone, I would only deal with Fordham Marble." "Very accommodating when we need to change gears—unusual in this business."

Formia Marble & Stone Inc.   3   3   4   4
44-36 21st Street, Long Island City, NY 11101
(718) 482 - 0606 formiamarble@msn.com
Granite and stone slab sales and installation

Formia sells and installs a wide range of products including tiles, countertops and customized fittings. In business since 1981, the firm has a showroom located in Long Island City. Patrons report Formia is a good place to get marble and granite, either by the slab or for a particular installation, but forewarn potential customers that the company does not provide repair or maintenance services. Stone or marble tile is manufactured and customized right in Formia's warehouse—where the firm also has a limited supply of ceramics. Formia services both homeowners and the trade, and the company offers a guarantee on all of its installations. Excellent pricing is of great appeal to the client base.

"A good choice for stone, and reasonably priced." "They have a great set-up and a reliable team of workers at the showroom and the warehouse." "I'm pleased with the work but a little disappointed by knowing that they won't repair." "Product and service was worth the trip to Long Island City."

K&K Marble Importers   4   3   5   4.5
17 Seaman Avenue, Bethpage, NY 11714
(516) 932 - 5630 www.kkmarble.com
Imported marble sales, fabrication, and installation

Sources say K&K Marble goes to great lengths to meet each client's specific and sometimes unusual requirements. With its sister branch in Greece, K&K has been importing fine marble from its Greek quarries since it opened the shop here in 1985. Both residential and commercial clients report that the Long Island showroom is well appointed, with up to 72 colors of marble in stock. A polite and professional staff—along with the company's 100% guarantee—has earned this hard-working firm a lot of fans in its first two decades.

"An exceptional selection to choose from—not your run-of-the-mill supplier." "The quality is self-explanatory, just visit the showroom." "They stand behind their product and deal well with clients." "Manager installed top himself. Very professionally done, polite and accomodating." "Altered the slabs to fit my color and size specifications."

Lodestar Statements In Stone   4.5   4.5   4   4.5
231 East 58th Street, New York, NY 10022
(212) 755 - 1818 mrlodestar@aol.com
Exquisite semi-precious stone and tile mosaics, design, and installation

For those searching for a true master in the art of Byzantine and Florentine mosaic work, references say the search ends with Stewart Ritwo and his select staff of artisans at Lodestar Statements in Stone. What makes this firm unique, according to clients, is the incorporation of semi-precious stones such as onyx, malachite, sodalite, and quartzite into its famous tabletops, decorative floors, and murals. Insiders say Lodestar's commissions can be found in some of the world's most elegant homes, hotels, and restaurants, and that a visit to Lodestar's showroom and gallery is well worth the trip.

Prices are based on three variables—the stones used, intricacy of the design, and size of the panel. While Lodestar's work is not within everyone's budget, clients who have seen this star have been known to stretch in its direction.

"Not only is their work exquisite but Stewart has a great sense of humor." "Stewart works with the precision of a jeweler." "They are always timely, even on large-scale jobs."

Marble, Tile & Terrazzo 3 2.5 4.5 4
305-311 Douglass Street, Brooklyn, NY 11217
(718) 802 - 1512

Terrazzo flooring, marble, and tile installation and maintenance

This fabricator has a solid reputation among clients who applaud its quality work and reasonable pricing. Typical projects include custom-made marble tables, marble mosaics, countertops, bathrooms, kitchens, lobbies—plus terrazzo floors and tables. In addition to fabrication, we hear that the firm's talented craftsmen install, polish, clean, and maintain tile and marble surfaces. Samples of marble and granite can be found at the firm's Brooklyn showroom. Consultations are available by appointment only.

"Custom at a good price." "He seems to be very busy and rightfully so." "Carlo and his staff have a great service and they really deliver on quality. I have already recommended them several times."

R.G. New York Tile 3.5 3.5 4 4.5
225 West 29th Street, New York, NY 10001
(212) 629 - 0712   rgnytile@gmail.com

Tile and marble sales, installation, and fabrication; kitchen and bath design

Called upon by professionals, R.G. New York Tile earns praise for its speedy service and friendly staff. In business since 1987, the firm installs ceramic and stone tile, fabricates kitchen countertops, and sells tile and marble. All of these products are on display in the company's showroom. Further services include kitchen and bath design and installation. We hear that while the firm frequently works on large jobs, it has been known to take on something as simple as replacing a single tile. Clients say the high-end work comes at a reasonable price, and the staff is remarkably efficient.

"Rafael is a great guy, and will do whatever it takes to get the job done." "R.G. does over 80% of our work because their craftsmanship is beautiful." "Quality exceeds price." "They had to retile a ceramic kitchen floor that was not laid properly the first time around a year and a half ago. Very nice, patient, and professional." "They always come back if something needs fixing." "Excellent! Fast."

Stone Source 4 4 4 4.5
215 Park Avenue South, Suite 700, New York, NY 10003
(212) 979 - 6400   www.stonesource.com

Natural stone, ceramic, and glass tile sales, fabrication, and installation

Stone Source carries a large selection of alternative stones and tile materials, including award-winning Veneto Glass Tiles. In business since 1981, the company has locations in New York, Chicago, Massachusetts, Philadelphia, and Washington, DC. Long reputed to be a primary source of natural stone for top designers and architects in the Northeast, this firm is a favorite of industry professionals.

The firm will also do slab work. Stone Source is said to be the largest importer of limestone in the eastern United States and has its own warehouse and fabrication shop in Brooklyn, where it receives frequent deliveries of natural stone and ceramic tile from Italy. The firm deals mainly with the trade—much of its work is for architects—but will service some high-end residential clients. References assess the firm's staff as knowledgeable and helpful.

"Professionals and proud of their work, and that shows." "Generous with showroom samples." "Very honest in educating about true quality and the best uses for different stones." "The showroom itself is a veritable tool for gathering ideas and researching the options." "Trustworthy—which is more than I can say about most." "My one reservation was not receiving enough follow-up calls, but then again, it's New York, and everyone's busy." "They always call to check up on the finished project, and make sure everyone is satisfied."

Vladimir Obrevko Stoneworks Inc.   4.5   3.5   5   4.5
79 Putnam Park Road, Bethel, CT 06801
(203) 798 - 7713

Artisanal custom stone fabrication and installation; fireplace and sculpture restoration

Amiable is not a word heard everyday in descriptions of craftsmen, but it is one used time and again by clients in describing Vladimir Obrevko of Stoneworks. For several years before coming to the US, Obrevko worked restoring cathedrals in historic St. Petersburg, Russia, a trade he learned from his father.

Now Obrevko's architectural stonework can be seen in elaborate homes and commercial locations throughout New York City, Long Island, and Westchester and Fairfield counties. Obrevko's onyx wall is prominently displayed at Metrazur, a restaurant in Grand Central Station. Clients laud his pleasant demeanor and dedicated work ethic, calling him personable and true to his craft.

Stoneworks offers fabrication and installation services in marble, granite, limestone and slate. It also does specialty work such as fireplace and sculpture restoration.

"A very driven artisan." "We hire Vlad about every six weeks to two months...very pleased with the work. Fabulous on price, on time, and no problems. He does a good job." "I always refer him. His work is flawless and his templates are true to size." "Our clients use him all the time." "We don't hire anyone else for our countertops, he does a magnificent job."

Waterworks
225 East 57th Street, New York, NY 10022
(212) 371 - 9266   www.waterworks.com

High-end bathroom design, sales, and installation referral

See Waterworks' full report under the heading Kitchen & Bath Designers

Wholesale Marble and Granite   3.5   3.5   4   4
150 East 58th Street, New York, NY 10155
(212) 223 - 4068   www.wholesalemarbleandgranite.com

Granite and marble sales, fabrication, and installation

Don't be fooled by the name. Although Wholesale Marble & Granite deals mostly with the trade, it does offer fabrication and installation services to residential clients all over New York City. We hear Wholesale stocks a terrific selection of natural stone from around the world, which includes marble, granite, limestone, travertine, crystallized glass, and onyx. In addition to its Manhattan showroom, Wholesale Marble encourages clients to visit its massive 20,000 square foot outdoor showroom and gallery at 31 Cobek Court in Brooklyn.

"An emporium, a stone source unlike anyone else's." "Their ability to fabricate complicated edge detail is outstanding due to their onsite waterjet machine." "It's a trip to Brooklyn, and well worth it." "They are dedicated to producing a quality product and stand behind their work 100%."

Hiring an Upholstery & Window Treatment Service Provider

Did you inherit a gorgeous set of French 1940s chairs that need reupholstering? Would you like to transform your aging—yet amazingly comfortable—armchair into a spectacular piece that matches your sofa and decor? Or are you ready to buy a brand-new complete set of custom-upholstered furniture for your living room? Whether you are thinking about the design and construction of a piece or which fabric to choose, upholstery and window treatment experts are the professionals to call.

Before you begin your research, you should know that many high-end upholsterers and drapers who do specialized work deal exclusively with the trade (decorators and architects), and not the public at large, which is noted in our reviews. Also, many of these service providers focus on custom work—creating a piece from scratch rather than from a line of showroom choices. Usually the decorators provide sketches or pictures to point the artisans in the right direction, and fabrics are provided by the customer.

What Type of Upholstery Service Do I Need?

Your three basic choices are custom upholstery fabrication, reupholstery, and custom slipcovers. You may not need a completely new piece of furniture. Depending on the condition of your frame and webbing, you may choose to reupholster or have custom-made slipcovers as a less-expensive alternative. A favorite decorator trick is to use a Crate & Barrel frame and upgrade the fillings to create a well-priced custom piece.

To help narrow down the service you need, determine how the furniture will be used. Is it a seating piece that is frequently used by the family and guests (and pets), or a more stylized piece that is located in a less frequently used space? If it will receive heavy use, you'll choose springs and cushioning that will stand up to this treatment, as well as a fabric that is durable and easy to clean.

Know Your Upholstery Construction

Frames: The frame is the skeleton of your piece, determining the sturdiness as well as overall appearance of the object. The best frames are made of kiln-dried hardwood, preferably premium alder maple. Oak and ash are less expensive, but decent options. Pine will fall apart very quickly. Kiln drying removes moisture and sap from the wood, which could cause the frame to warp or bend. When assembling the frame, the ideal method involves using dowels and corner-blocks. This is more costly than using nails and glue but will greatly increase the quality and add years to the life of your piece. Tacks are the preferred method for attaching fabric to the frame, although staple guns are sometimes used. Staple guns should never be used in constructing a quality frame, however.

Springs: The main function of springs is to support the furniture's cushioning. The two basic spring systems for upholstered furniture are round coil springs (like a slinky) and flat, continuous S-shaped, "no-sag" coils. Most fine, traditional pieces use hand-tied steel spring coils, in which coils are tied by hand in eight places around the diameter of the spring ("8-way, hand-tied").

S-shaped continuous or zig-zag coils are sometimes used in contemporary pieces for a flatter look, but do not provide the same support as spring coils. S-shaped springs can become lumpy or uneven over time, and put much more pressure on the frame since they are attached directly to it. Therefore, if you are using S-coils, the frame must be built very sturdily, so it won't break apart over time.

In very high-quality cushion construction, the springs are then individually wrapped, encased in foam, and covered in a down and feather mixture (see below for details). This is all encased in a muslin bag to contain the fluff before being covered with fabric. This combination provides firmness and helps the cushion to hold its shape. The ultimate upholstery houses also put down in the arms and backs of their pieces, but this generally adds about 30% to the price.

CUSHIONS: These come in two types—attached and loose. In attached construction, fiber or down and feather are wrapped around a foam core and placed over the spring system, which is then covered with fabric. Loose cushions resemble big pillows that are easily fluffed, moved, or turned over to prevent signs of wear. Both types of cushions can be stuffed with a wide variety of fillings, from luxurious pure goose down and down blends to synthetic foam.

Down is the ultimate cushion filling and comes at a premium price. The typical down-feather blend consists of 50% goose down and 50% duck feathers, and is used for very high-end custom upholstery. The ultimate puff look is 100% goose down, which offers almost no support and must be fluffed by the housekeeper once a day to look right and remain comfortable. Because of the high level of maintenance and much higher cost required for goose down, many consumers prefer to go with a combination of 50/50 down and feather over a foam core. Upon request, however, most of the houses reviewed below can deliver whatever the customer prefers. A lesser-quality cushion is 25% goose down and 75% duck feathers, which is harder and should cost less. All Dacron foam is the least costly alternative, and is not generally found in high quality work.

FABRICS: The possibilities are endless when choosing upholstery fabric. With so many options, you can narrow your search by exploring a few basic issues. Prices vary widely, from $10 to well over $400 per yard. The most important issue is how the piece will be used. Do you need a super durable fabric that can withstand daily use? Or is it a not-to-be-touched showpiece? Some fabrics are simply stronger than others. Ease of cleaning should also be considered. Pieces in the family room or children's bedroom may attract more dirt. Darker, more durable fabric that withstands frequent cleaning would be appropriate for this furniture. Upholsterers handle the issue of fabric in a variety of ways. Some have catalogs and swatches from which you can choose—but most ask you to bring in your own fabric, better known as COM (customer's own material).

Keep in mind that the ease or difficulty of working with a particular fabric will affect the price of the job. Thicker fabrics, velvets, and horsehairs can be more difficult to edge properly. Also, you will need more yards of fabric with a large repeat or pattern, so the upholsterer can match the design perfectly at the seams—a key factor in separating fine quality pieces from ordinary ones.

WHAT TO LOOK FOR IN QUALITY WORK

When viewing the work of an upholstery professional in the workroom or at someone's home, keep the following points in mind:

✧ Check all the seams for pattern matching and a perfectly centered and balanced design on any cushions or surfaces. This can be particularly important with more intricate patterns.

✧ Are the sofa skirts lined? Is the cushion of the slipper chair invisibly secured with clips, as it should be? Is the welt or trim tightly stitched?

✧ Ask what percentage of the seams are hand-sewn. In the finest workrooms, all the curtain trims, leading edges, and hems are completely hand-done. Some even do the curtain basting and sofa seams entirely by hand.

✧ Check to see if any of the seams pucker, such as those along the arm of a sofa or on the back of a club chair. Seams and welts should be perfectly smooth, unless you are looking for that Old World, hand-sewn look. Slight needle marks on the edges are fine if the pieces are actually done by hand (and the ultimate look for the sofa connoisseur), but wavy edges are unacceptable.

ON COST

As with any specialized custom work, upholstery prices vary significantly based upon the quality aspects discussed above. To choose the appropriate expense level, you should assess the application. A chair in your four-year-old's room will probably not require the same quality of fabric or workmanship as a sofa in your living room where you entertain regularly. Most decorators separate the "public" (living room, dining room) vs. "private" (bedrooms, playrooms) with two different price points.

For the high-quality work reviewed above, sofas are generally $700 to $900 per foot for attached cushion, and an additional $25 per foot for loose cushions. This means a high-quality, eight-foot sofa is $5,500 to $7,000 net, before the cost of the fabric, and receives a 4 cost rating in the reviews of The Franklin Report. Of course, you can get a complete sofa for $2,000 at a retail store, and this may be very appropriate for many circumstances, but is not of the same genus.

WINDOW TREATMENTS

From a simple minimalist panel to a layer-upon-layer, elaborate design, many elements come together to make a window treatment. Carefully selected shades, sheers, curtains, and valances may be held together with various trims, chords, brackets, and hardware—and possibly finished off with decorative finials. Some upholstery and window treatment professionals also do hard window treatments, which include all types of shades, laminated shades (roller shades, covered in your choice of fabric), and blinds, custom-made in your choice of materials to coordinate with your curtains.

WHERE DO I START?

To help you decide on the perfect window treatment for your room, many shops can work miracles with photos and magazine clippings. Once you've settled on a basic design (perhaps with the help of your decorator or examples from your upholsterer), measurements are taken. Most high-quality service providers will come to your home and measure as part of the cost. Less expensive workrooms or retail stores will charge a fee to take measurements, which may or may not be applied to the order. Ask about the costs before asking for a home visit.

It is highly recommended that you do not take the measurements yourself—lest you be held responsible when they are an inch off. Most window treatments, for example, take up wall space as well as cover your window—which is not obvious. Will you have finials that may add extra yardage on each side of the window? Will your drapes actually open and close or just be decorative? All of these factors will need to be considered when measuring and drawing up the plans.

WINDOW TREATMENT FABRIC AND CONSTRUCTION

As with custom furniture upholstery, fabric choices for window treatments are endless. As with upholsterers, retail window treatment shops will provide you with a choice of fabrics and custom workrooms will require you to provide your own (COM). Some retail stores will charge you extra if you provide your own fabric. In addition to selecting a fabric for color, texture, and print, consider how easy it will be to clean. Curtains and window sills in the city are vulnerable to dust, dirt, grime, and soot, whereas the elements are a bit more forgiving in the suburbs.

Most window treatments require more than one layer of fabric. For the most luxurious look, with excellent volume, curtains have a three-layer construction: fabric, a lining of silk or Dacron, and interlining. The interlining is commonly made of flannel, which not only provides heft and a bit of structure, but also a measure of soundproofing. The ultimate interlining is bump—a special, hard-to-get, super-thick flannel from England. If you're looking for a lighter, airy look, a lining will be sufficient.

On Cost

High-quality, mostly hand-sewn curtains are expensive. A three-layer construction, with lining and interlining, will be significantly more expensive to produce than a single or two-layer construction. For an eight-foot window with a double fabric panel trim on each side and a box-pleat valance, the fabrication can cost about $1,100 to $1,400, before fabric and trim costs (considered a 4 cost in *The Franklin Report*). This includes lining and interlining provided by the

workroom, home measuring, and installation.

Tips on Caring for Upholstered Furniture

General Care

◇ Ask your upholsterer or fabric supplier exactly how to care for your new fabric.

◇ Vacuum often to get rid of dirt particles that cause abrasion and wear.

◇ Don't allow pets on fine fabrics—their body oils rub off onto the fabric and are tough to remove.

◇ Protect fabric-covered pieces from the sun—if not in use—to avoid fading and deterioration.

◇ Turn over loose cushions every week for even wear.

◇ Beware of sitting on upholstered furniture while wearing blue jeans or other fabric-dyed clothing—the color may "bleed" onto the fabric.

◇ Do not set newspapers or magazines onto upholstered furniture, as the ink may also bleed onto the fabric.

◇ Regular professional cleaning is ideal.

Spills

✧ Immediately after the spill, blot (don't rub) the area with a clean cloth. Dried spills are more difficult to remove.

✧ Carefully follow the instructions on the cleaning product (don't wing it).

✧ If you use water for cleaning, be sure it is distilled.

✧ Choose a hidden area on the fabric to pretest the cleaner for color fastness before applying to the spill.

✧ Avoid making a small spill larger by working lightly, blotting out from the center. To avoid rings, 'feather' the edges by dampening the edge of the spill irregularly and blotting quickly.

✧ Using a small fan or blow-dryer (on low setting), quickly dry the cleaned area.

UPHOLSTERY & WINDOW TREATMENTS

🛍 FIRMS WITH ONLINE PORTFOLIOS* 🛍

A. Schneller Sons Inc. 🛍   5   4.5   4.5   5

129 West 29th Street, 9th Floor, New York, NY 10001
(212) 695 - 9440   aschnellersons@msn.com

Trade only—Exquisite custom upholstery and window treatments

The provenance of this 124-year-old firm is equally as impressive as its top-of-the-line custom-built, all hand-done, upholstery and draperies. Today, A. Schneller Sons is led by third-generation principal John Schneller, whose great-uncle started the business in 1881. While many New York decorators turn to this prestigious shop, we hear A. Schneller Sons is selective and careful not to overextend itself. Many commend its responsiveness, excellent craftsmen, and "incredibly" gracious service, which some say is the best there is.

Clients report that each piece is built by hand with "amazing attention to detail," marveling that "even the frames are beautiful." New models are added to the extensive showroom frequently, and many are named for former clients: the "Astor sofa," the "Vanderbilt sofa," the "Whitney sofa." The firm works only with the trade, with prices that reflect its five-star quality.

"Upholstery that is truly a work of art. The firm appreciates and understands elaborate designs." "Unquestionably one of the top companies around and very respected." "John is a gentleman." "Old-World style—it's hard to get better than this." "Only for the customer who appreciates the finest and can pay for it." "It will cost you a pretty penny." "Absolute top-of-the-line custom built, all hand done." "The proof, as they say, is in the pudding."

Albert Menin Interiors Ltd.   4   3.5   4.5   4

345 East 104th Street, 4th Floor, New York, NY 10029
(212) 876 - 3041   www.albertmenin.com

Mostly trade—Window treatments, upholstery, wall upholstery, and lampshades

Producing quality window treatments and upholstery since 1939, Albert Menin Interiors is highly recommended by the trade for the trade. We hear this firm comes up with great ideas, and delivers high quality on time, and with friendly service. Russian-born owner Emil Shikh—who took over the company in 1985—has 25 exacting craftsmen on board. Though some mention communication snags, customers tell us the firm always comes through, providing service and product at a price "less expensive" than other respected firms.

"Menin doesn't take his work lightly, and makes sure you come away happy with a good quality finished product." "Emil has an engaging personality and comes with a pile of experience." "These guys are the most professional that I have ever dealt with. I have recommended them to several people in my building and they are in love with them also." "Great work, but not worth the roller coaster." "I give strong marks for the quality of his work." "Reliable and delivered exactly what I wanted."

*We invite you to visit www.franklinreport.com to view images of their work.

502

	Quality	Cost	Value	Recommend?
	✚	$	◆	★

Casanova Home Corp. 🛍   3.5   2.5   4.5   4.5
355-7 East 78th Street, Suite 1B, New York, NY 10021
(212) 639 - 9486   www.casanovahome.net

Retail and trade—Custom window treatments and upholstery

With just one look clients fall head over heels for Casanova, crooning over the firm's "great taste" and "great service." Since 1996, the shop has been creating "beautiful" custom window treatments from shades to curtains and doing upholstery work for retail clients in New York and the surrounding areas. Principal Ana Rosa McGinnis's "calm and pleasant nature" adds to the appeal.

Open by appointment only, Casanova's retail showroom offers a wide selection of fabrics at a wide variety of prices, and many unique window treatments. Clients may bring in their own fabrics if they prefer. Casanova works in the chosen style of the client or decorator, and we hear that it is typical for each job to begin with a consultation in the home. Given the quality of work and service, prices are surprisingly moderate.

"I am meticulous and Casanova is the best in my opinion." "Ana is a dream to work with." "Exquisite workmanship." "Prices are right there in the mid-range and quality is up there in the high-range." "Custom finishes on hardware are truly unique and complement the beauty of the overall design." "Every good job takes time." "Ana has gorgeous taste and I respect her input."

Custom Design Studio 🛍   3   2   5   4.5
49 Bruckner Boulevard, Bronx, NY 10454
(718) 665 - 0777   www.customdesignny.com

Retail and trade—Custom upholstery and furniture, slipcovers, furniture restoration, and some window treatments

This "friendly, helpful, and attentive" shop works with several area decorators on a regular basis, as well as directly with clients. Manhattan designers insist that the great prices and "lovely workmanship" are worth the trek up to the Bronx. The firm produces custom upholstery and furniture, and will also do antique and furniture restoration, repair, and window treatments upon request.

Since 1989, Denise Cruz has been building her firm on quality work and "loyalty to her customers." A small group of seamstresses and hand finishers produce pieces for both commercial and residential customers, keeping the shop busy and eager to please. Custom Design Studio has been praised in print from *New York* magazine to the *Antiques Newsletter*.

"Denise has integrity and always delivers." "Can-do firm, determined to please." "I have been working with Denise for fifteen years and am always satisfied." "Her prices are a good deal for the work she produces." "If I tell a client her sofa will be delivered on January 15th, Denise makes it happen." "I can get to her shop quicker than traveling to other upholsterers in Manhattan." "Very rarely is there ever a problem—and if there is they fix it right away." "Very nice people."

DFB Sales Inc. 🛍   3   3   4   4
21-07 Borden Avenue, Long Island City, NY 11101
(718) 729 - 8310   www.vitruv.com

Trade only—Custom wall upholstery, wall surfaces, and window treatments

This large, long-established firm manufactures and installs an impressive array of window shades and wall upholstery. We hear its product Vitruv (a durable tinted plaster wall surface, which comes in a variety of colors), is getting great reviews from industry insiders.

Harvey and Elliott Fine run the business their father started in 1946, and 2006 will mark their 60th year in business. Measurements and installations are performed by the firm's own people, who are roundly praised for timely service and good project management by its corporate clients. We understand one of DFB's areas of expertise is its motorized shades. The firm services notable commercial and high-end residential clients all over Manhattan. References have found its window shades to be especially high quality, and a good value for the price.

"We recently remodeled a lobby with Vitruv wallcovering and the client couldn't be happier." "They get the job done, but have a commercial viewpoint." "Very satisfied, terrific." "Even if someone in their category gives me a lower bid for window treatments, I go with DFB because I know the job will be excellent." "Unless there is a holdup in fabric, timing is right on."

Furniture Masters Inc.   4.5   3.5   5   4.5
81 Apollo Street, Greenpoint, NY 11222
(718) 599 - 0771   www.furnituremastersinc.com

Mostly trade—Choice upholstery, window treatments, and custom furniture

Furniture Masters distinguishes itself with a fully integrated workroom, excellent service, and reasonable costs. Building a following since 1971, father-son team Jeremy and Alan Skow have been working with top decorators and architects for many years, ably serving the residential and commercial/hospitality market. Clients have included the Metropolitan Museum of Art, Escada, Coach Leather, Bergdorf Goodman, and Burberry. There is an 8,000 square foot showroom that features 200 upholstered pieces and a dozen drapery treatments. People in the know say its custom furniture shop (where the firm builds cabinets, armoires, built-in wall units, and more) produces lovely pieces.

A "one-stop shop," this firm of 45 manufactures frames, applies fine finishes, fabricates metal piecework, and creates drapery hardware. Clients say FM's hand carving and specialty finishes are at the top end of the quality scale. Sources say this cross-referencing of knowledge cultivates a greater insight that results in a more integrated product. The location and the volume allow for more competitive pricing.

"Very high-end, highly capable custom upholstery and cabinet shop." "Jeremy goes to bat for the designer." "Furniture Masters' inlay floors are especially wonderful." "Fantastic custom finishes." "Very pleasant staff—always a pleasure to work with." "Pricing is tremendous for residential work but not so happy with commercial pricing." "Really professional. So much better than the smaller shops I have dealt with in the past." "Given a strong design and some direction, they can produce anything." "Their tented ceilings are especially impressive." "With everything under one roof, the timing is appreciably improved." "Their service and follow-up is what makes me come back.

La Regence   5   4.5   4.5   5
129 West 29th Street, 12th Floor, New York, NY 10001
(212) 736 - 2548   nylaregence@msn.com

Trade only—Very high-end curtains, custom shades, and some upholstery

Clients say La Regence treats each project like a couture dress; each piece is designed to achieve the perfect balance of length, lining, and fullness. It's no surprise that La Regence owners Kathy Jones and Jay Perlstein come highly recommended by some of the top decorators for curtains and shades. The firm only offers limited upholstery as a courtesy to its loyal clients, most of whom would not consider straying insisting that "nothing else compares."

"Draperies are exquisitely made and my clients so appreciate the details." "You might spend a lot of money but you will never be sorry afterward." "Glamorous and sophisticated for the client who appreciates great design." "I've used other well-respected firms and La Regence is clearly better. I really love their fabulous curtains." "It is the best investment in town." "Cost is over the top, but worth every penny." "I have never had a dissatisfied client with their curtains." "People deserve the highest quality if they buy the highest-quality fabric. La Regence gets it just right."

Ray Murray Inc. 🛍️

| 4.5 | 4 | 4.5 | 5 |

143 West 29th Street, New York, NY 10001
(212) 838 - 3752   raymurrinc@aol.com

Trade only—Well-crafted upholstery and curtains

Established in 1913, this shop does "fabulous work," with "meticulous attention to details" creating an array of both traditional and modern custom upholstery, wall upholstery, headboards, and other window treatments. Current principal Rita Blake took over in 1996 and she carries on the firm's long-running tradition of high-quality results. Sources in the trade note that Blake is a "real professional" with a "warm personality." Clients find the firm to be highly service-oriented and extraordinarily dependable.

Blake (who has a background in art, design, and renovation) helms a staff of fifteen out of the firm's large workroom. Blake explains what can be achieved within a client's budget, and if the shop cannot do the job, she will recommend another workroom. While some mention prices are "a bit high," sources tell us the firm's modern pieces can be less expensive to produce. Designers have often selected Murray for their own personal furnishings.

"One of the few women in a male-dominated field that can run with the big boys." "We've had a business relationship for years, and she does most of my upholstery with first-rate results." "Rita's not only professional, she has a warm and fuzzy personality." "I worked with the original owners and Rita maintains the high standards." "Its drapery workroom is impressive." "Murray is great about expediting your goods on time—never a wait." "The modern pieces are right up there with the traditional work."

Soft Touch Interiors 🛍️

| 4 | 2 | 5 | 5 |

115 Labau Avenue, Staten Island, NY 10301
(718) 448 - 1028   sthb@msn.com

Retail and trade—Slipcovers, window treatments, and bedding

After 30 years, Harvey and Maureen Berkowitz of Soft Touch Interiors still have the exuberance and patience to deal with a varied clientele. Specializing in slipcovers, Harvey arrives in your home, fabric in hand, knees padded, pins on magnet, and very large scissors in his back pocket, ready to work his magic. (He will cover just about anything.) We hear that ideas and concepts are thoroughly discussed and approved before even one stitch is sewn. Maureen oversees her husband's endeavors, as well as designing draperies, bedspreads and other soft treatments such as lampshades. In one project she draped an outdoor gazebo that appeared on HGTV.

Decorators look to Soft Touch mainly for reupholstery and slipcovers, describing this team as "efficient, brilliant, and a joy to work with"—a real bargain. We hear the staff of twelve provides the perfect complement to Berkowitz's fabulous design concepts and eye for color. KB 2000.

"Harvey and Maureen are easy to work with and try very hard to please." "The two of them installed the curtains together." "His patience, knowledge, and professionalism are without equal!" "They take pride in their work and the finished product shows it." "It's refreshing to work with such honest people." "Working with Mr. Berkowitz was indeed a pleasurable experience."

	Quality	Cost	Value	Recommend?
	+	$	◆	★

The Ruffled Window

4   3.5   4.5   4.5

8B South Washington Avenue, Bergenfield, NJ 07621
(201) 439 - 9799 www.theruffledwindow.com

Trade only—Window treatments and some upholstery

Not only a unique talent but a nice person, Robin Feuer of The Ruffled Window delights clients around town with her luxurious drapery and lovely personality. Designers swear "you won't find a wrinkle in her work," and affirm that Feuer "can follow and execute detailed drawings and specs to a 'T.'" We're told TRW tackles hard-to-treat windows with ease. The firm also creates upholstery for bedding, headboards, pillows, and walls.

A third-generation designer, Feuer graduated from the Fashion Institute of Technology, transferring to interior design after she thrilled a family member with couture curtains. Feuer now accomplishes projects for high-end residential and commercial clients. Everything is hand finished by a small staff of craftspeople. We hear the firm will give free estimates, but charges for measurements. Customers say Feuer's work is a tremendous value given its quality, charging prices that won't ruffle your feathers.

"Robin genuinely cares about her client and the end product." "Understands and knows how to engineer elaborate designs." "She takes great pride in her work and made sure our client as well as our firm was 100% satisfied every step of the way." "Robin has a keen eye for understanding the glamour sought after by our clients." "As an out of town designer, I was referred to Robin—this was one of the best referrals I have ever had!" "Not as well known, but is getting her name out there." "Very professional, reliable, and knowledgeable." "Excellent work, excellent service."

Varadi Decorator & Upholstery Inc.

4   4   4   4.5

807 Middle Neck Road, Great Neck, NY 11024
(516) 487 - 0778 tvaradi@optonline.net

Mostly trade—Custom upholstery, furniture and window treatments

It's no surprise that Tamas Varadi's family was famous in Hungary for its upholstery creations—the work speaks for itself. Varadi Decorator & Upholstery builds custom upholstered furniture in the European tradition, French and English drawing room style. To the delight of its high-end residential and commercial clients in Manhattan, Varadi's other forte is French pleated drapes, along with Roman, Austrian, and balloon shades. Trade professionals note that "Varadi works well to make the vision a reality."

Considered an "upholstery master" by some clients, Varadi has 54 years of experience in the business, learning the trade at age six. After arriving in the US, Varadi worked at the renowned upholstery firm Baron, before striking out on his own in 1992. Celebrities and institutions such as the Union Club turn to Varadi for a beautifully realized finished product. The eight-way tied coil springs, and exquisite hand finishes in its custom-built sofas justify the upper-tier prices.

"I trust his judgment and he often surpasses expectations." "Varadi's upholstery work is outstanding, and it's hard to find someone better than him." "No question about it, knows upholstery inside and out." "Very prompt and easy to work with." "He works hard to please his customer." "Lovely work and a nice guy."

	Quality	Cost	Value	Recommend?
	+	$	◆	★

FIRMS WITHOUT ONLINE PORTFOLIOS

ABC Carpet & Home
888 Broadway, New York, NY 10003
(212) 473 - 3000 www.abchome.com

| | 3 | 3 | 4 | 3 |

Retail—Reupholstery, window treatments, rug cleaning, and installation

An emporium for the home, this retailer offers a range of services, including reupholstery, refabrication of window treatments, carpet cleaning, and reinstallation of the rugs it sells. ABC offers reupholstery customers a selection of over 3,500 fabrics to choose from, or you may order from the store's extensive lending library.

ABC Carpet & Home services the New York metropolitan area, and deliveries average six to eight weeks for sofas and chairs. We're told ABC charges $45 to survey your sofa, while pick-up and delivery fees depend on weight. Though ABC has its loyal fans among New Yorkers, some report "less than thrilling" service but all are seduced by the rich variety of fabrics.

"The array of fabrics to choose from is a big plus." "They did what I asked of them, but no more, and without a nod of goodwill." "Workmen could be more careful, particularly on rug installation." "The premium prices don't come with premium service." "ABC provides an option for the client who can't go to a trade-only upholsterer."

Aldo Di Roma
327 East 94th Street, New York, NY 10128
(212) 688 - 3564 babygrlc@aol.com

| | 4.5 | 3.5 | 5 | 4.5 |

Trade only—High-end custom upholstery and window treatments

New York designers note that Aldo Di Roma has an "especially strong gift" for starting from ground zero with a picture or concept of an upholstered piece and getting it just right. Clients note this reliable shop is also a find for non-upholstered custom furniture and drapery. Fans say "it's a pleasure" to visit this family-run business.

Established in 1975, Di Roma is easy to work with and straightforward about money, and is noted for its reliability and helpfulness. With a group of fourteen craftspeople working on a manageable number of jobs at any one time, customers say their pieces get "first-class attention."

"Upholstery that inspires." "You'll find it to be tops where quality is concerned, and the staff is incredibly nice." "I started using them ten years ago and today I call on them exclusively for everything." "Craftsmanship is the best in my opinion." "Big workshop, high price points but worth it." "I know people out there that are less in price, but I'd rather pay more and not worry about it."

Alexander Upholstery
334 East 78th Street, New York, NY 10021
(212) 472 - 0340 cajejoem@aol.com

| | 3.5 | 3.5 | 4 | 5 |

Retail—Custom upholstery and window treatments

This small, unimposing shop comes highly recommended for its service, quality, and promptness. While Alexander's "does not operate at the very top," some of the most discerning homeowners in New York recommend the firm. Czech-born principal Ervin Alexander started the company in 1967, and runs it today with son Jeff. We're told these professionals are particularly responsive under tight deadlines, handling problems with ease. Conveniently located for designers and decorators, Alexander's second shop is at 410 East 64th Street. With prices that won't break the bank, Alexander's is also a find for window treatments and draperies.

	Quality	Cost	Value	Recommend?
	✚	$	◆	★

"Ervin and Jeff have a lot of happy clients." "Impeccable. I was so blown away." "I had an upholstery emergency and they were right there to solve my problem in no time flat with surprisingly good work. I was amazed." "You can't beat the quality for the price." "Prompt, courteous service." "Everything was aligned correctly and it was done in three days."

Anthony Lawrence - Belfair   4.5   4.5   4   4.5

53 West 23rd Street, 5th Floor, New York, NY 10010
(212) 206 - 8820   www.anthonylawrence.com

Trade only—Very high-end custom upholstery and window treatments

Anthony Lawrence and Belfair Draperies joined forces years ago to provide decorators both custom upholstery and window treatments from one workroom. Some of the greatest brand names in decorating who have depended on these two companies for generations, consider the merger "a godsend," turning to the firm for "exquisitely crafted" custom upholstery and draperies.

Insiders say owner Joseph Lawrence is "professional with an easygoing manner." Extraordinary quality and outstanding showroom selection (with over 200 floor models) are the strengths Belfair brings to the table. Together they create draperies that are among the most perfect—and extravagant—in the business.

"Draperies that are unmatched." "We have been going to them for years—the workmanship is consistently high." "Phenomenal quality at not-completely-insane prices." "Even if we made the mistake—they will fix and quickly." "There was an obvious defect and I cannot imagine why it was not caught and addressed. In short—not a good job." "Fantastic shop. Does hard goods and soft goods." "The costs can be very high." "Can't say enough nice things about Joseph and his staff." "They make us look good."

Baron Upholsterers   5   4.5   4.5   5

545 West 45th Street, 3rd Floor, New York, NY 10036
(212) 664 - 0800   www.barononline.net

Trade only—Top-tier custom upholstery, wall upholstery, and window treatments

Fit for a baronial mansion, Baron's trade-only product is said to be "the Rolls-Royce of our industry." Designers enjoy working with Baron Upholsterers and its owners Steve and Paul Urban, thanks to their creative selection of fabrics and styles, superior skill, and "honest and reliable" manner.

This family-owned business has been around since 1980, but has a new location offering over 4,000 square feet of showroom samples. The firm's staff of 30 includes several very talented craftsmen, who reportedly adhere strictly to deadline. Complicated purchase orders are no problem and are always tracked. Besides being "a joy to deal with," Baron is considered among the very best workrooms in New York by its long-standing, well-satisfied decorator clientele.

"Majestic upholsterers." "I love using these guys for the amazing workmanship." "We have worked with this family-owned company for 25 years with great satisfaction." "Way up there in terms of quality, reliability, and style." "I love the large offering in their catalog and their flexibility." "Pricey but worth it." "I can always count on Baron to be honest and fair, which is the bottom line for me." "Delivers a quality product at good prices." "Their work is perfect." "The two brothers, Steve and Paul, are simply the best!" "I couldn't speak more highly of Baron Upholsterers."

Beckenstein Fabric & Interiors   3   3   4   3.5

4 West 20th Street, New York, NY 10011
(212) 366 - 5142   www.beckensteinfabric.com

Custom upholstery and window treatments

For less-demanding jobs, Beckenstein Fabric & Interiors delivers patient, professional installation and good workmanship. Clients recommend the firm for upholstered headboards, and all items for the maid's room, children's rooms, and the kitchen. While some sources also recommend Beckenstein for straightforward shades or simple inexpensive draperies, we hear the firm is not terrific with proportion or installation. Services are quite inexpensive, and rendered in a timely, amiable fashion. The firm has recently added a collection of accessories from India.

"The workmanship is good. It's the kind of shop you go to for basic pieces." "Very Old World, no e-mail, and notes are scattered on pieces of paper." "Pleasant salesmanship, no bull, helpful suggestions." "Beckenstein's just needs a project manager." "Not the most organized shop—you have to be very specific." "Costs are moderate to high, not the cheapest around." "I still mourn my former chair, but fortunately they didn't charge for the disaster." "Good follow-up on minor problems."

Berthold's Upholstery   4.5   4   4.5   4.5
119 West 25th Street, 4th Floor, New York, NY 10001
(212) 633 - 0071
Trade only—High-end custom upholstery

All projects are hand-hewn at this spin-off helmed by a former De Angelis manager. Since opening the trade-only Berthold's Upholstery in 1993, Berthold Goldenberg has wooed his fair share of decorators to his showroom.

Clients say Berthold, who started working as an upholsterer in his native Romania when he was thirteen years old, is an "amazing craftsman with a wealth of knowledge." While small, working on only ten to fifteen pieces at a time, the boys at Berthold's can create anything of quality if you provide a sketch.

"Exceptional talent, and I applaud Berthold's work ethic." "You can tell he's been doing this forever." "Bert is a pro. He knows everything about custom furniture." "I've worked with him for almost twenty years, and he takes extraordinary pride in his work." "Very special upholsterer—details of Old-World craftsmanship."

Cappa Upholstery Company Inc.   3   2.5   4.5   5
118-04 149th Avenue, South Ozone Park, NY 11420
(718) 847 - 6030   robertjcappa@yahoo.com
Mostly retail—Custom upholstery and window treatments

Clients tell us Cappa's operation is as professional as they come—with owner Robert Cappa computerizing his shop and owning his building and delivery and service fleet. All one needs is a simple sketch or drawing and this third-generation upholsterer and his staff of seven can bring that idea to life. We hear Cappa will even make house calls to take measurements, and bring his pleasing demeanor with him. Others say Cappa can get "animated" when things don't go as planned. Most of Cappa's work is retail—evenly distributed between custom upholstery and window treatments. Clients appreciate the reliable quality and the low price point.

"Cappa will jump through hoops for you." "Beautiful end product and the delivery was on time." "They made a special trip for me." "You need to be very specific about what you want." "A helpful and organized company." "They listen, but are not long on patience." "I hope he doesn't get too big—I want him to be available for my jobs."

Classic Sofa Ltd.   3.5   3   4.5   3.5
5 West 22nd Street, New York, NY 10010
(212) 620 - 0485   www.classicsofa.com
Retail and trade—Custom-made, down-filled furniture

While we hear clients can expect excellent service and customer-vendor communications, this firm is not a "hand-holder." In business since 1986, Classic Sofa offers a wide selection of down-filled furniture and fabrics in its New York City showroom. Clients appreciate the speed with which you can choose a piece from the floor and get it in your home, but they are less impressed with the "uniqueness of the choices." However we do hear decorators remark on "its ability to interpret their sketches with very good results." The firm is a "quick and reliable" resource when needed, particularly on a basic bedroom. We are told that Classic produces "decent quality at low prices." The firm sells both to the trade and at retail, with a client list that includes celebrities and top decorators.

"I can draw them a picture of a sofa and they do it." "I use them solely for custom furniture. My other upholsterer is 40% more in price and Classic is just as good!" "They even traveled to my client's home to clean a sofa they didn't stain." "I use them for high-end clients but not in their high-end rooms." "What you see is what you get, with fast service but limited choices." "If there is an issue they are really good about fixing it." "Expedient and responsive to quote requests." "Pleasant about changes to the standard fare. Great product."

Daniel's Custom Upholstery   3   2.5   5   4
2935 Boston Road, Bronx, NY 10469
(212) 249 - 5015
Retail and trade—Slipcovers, recaning, and antique furniture restoration

While fundamentally a retail store, Daniel's is also a "secret source" for a number of very high-end decorators who use it primarily for slipcovers and recaning. While decorators reportedly get excellent treatment, some retail clients say the staff at Daniel's can get frustrated with those who don't know the inner workings of the trade. Still, clients seek out Daniel's for antique furniture restoration and fabric wall covering. Patrons may choose from a variety of frames and fabrics (books and samples available in the shop), or may bring their own fabric and ideas.

"Delivers excellent product, but you should know what you want before entering the shop." "Madge, who manages the place, doesn't suffer fools gladly." "A mom and pop organization." "Incredibly priced. Can't get better for the money." "Client service is not their specialty—especially to the retail customer." "We rely on them and they have never disappointed us."

David Haag   4.5   4.5   4   5
114 Horatio Street, Suite 110, New York, NY 10014
(212) 741 - 8557   dhaag@nyc.rr.com
Trade only—Elegant curtains and slipcovers

The jury is in, and clients declare Haag guilty of consistently pleasing them with the comfortable, casual elegance of his work. Known as an excellent collaborator, and communicator extraordinaire, David Haag started his business in 1987, and comes highly recommended for his skills in creating window treatments and slipcovers. He is called on regularly by top designers for his "masterful" knack for executing curtain details; many say they rarely use anyone else. Some go as far as to say Haag "is the only one left in New York" who knows how to cut fabric properly. The beautiful draping of the fabric, pleating, and trimming make it very apparent that Haag has a background in fashion design.

Haag only does soft goods—curtains of all styles and levels of detail, slipcovers, tablecloths, and decorative bench cushions. However, we hear he offers Venetian blinds as an added service. It's Haag's vivid attention to detail that keeps clients wowed. Insiders say Haag is also realistic about deadlines, and "lets you know if he's not going to make it." They enjoy working with Haag, a reliable and responsible professional whose services are considered "well worth the expense."

"His quality is magic and most definitely unmatched." "David is a fabulous resource, and really has a way with fabric." "Really knows how to bring a dressmaker's quality to your every detail." "David's work has a certain style to it. His curtains are not static and contrived looking." "He has always come through for me, fulfilling unrealistic deadlines and installations." "David has a lot of integrity and returns phone calls." "He has great ideas, and I know the end result is going to be chic."

Diamint Upholstery Inc.   3.5   3.5   4   4.5
336 East 59th Street, New York, NY 10022
(212) 715 - 0903 www.diamintupholstery.com
Retail and trade—Custom upholstery

Located near the D&D building, Diamint is known to work closely in providing custom upholstery to a number of high-end interior designers. Husband and wife team Silvia and Michael Gonzalez opened the firm in 1962. Their ten employees perform exceptionally under tight deadlines, producing "excellent results" on slipcovers and headboards as well. For new custom furniture, Diamint provides a selection of different frames, or the client may bring in a picture of his or her own. Customers are as pleased with the firm's product as with its ability to stick to schedules.

"Diamint and our company have grown up together—we have a very good relationship with them." "Have used other companies over time and always return to Diamint because they offer such personalized service." "No matter how much you plan there are always hiccups and Diamint are the people to have on your team when changes are needed." "Well-crafted, no nonsense, you get what you ask for and more in terms of quality." "Great service, thorough, and good follow-up."

Doreen Interiors Ltd.   4   4   4   5
221 West 17th Street, New York, NY 10011
(212) 255 - 9008
Trade only—Custom upholstery and window treatments

With a decorator's eye and an engineer's precision, principal Boaz Sharoni takes his time to create excellently priced masterpieces. The ethos of this small, respected firm is to listen carefully and get it right. Hand-holding is big here; Doreen Interiors is lauded as one of the few firms that is willing to be creative and accommodating "no matter how wild and impossible" the client's request may be. And Sharoni has been known to drop everything to get to a job site before a client takes off for a long overseas trip, or jump on an airplane to a client's residence to solve a problem or make repairs.

Doreen has a variety of pieces on display, and likes to start with pictures and sketches to better define ideas for custom work, which usually takes about twelve weeks. Excellent patterns are made for both the curtains and the upholstery, so there are few surprises in the finished product. Doreen is used by many a top-tier decorator for a wonderful alternative, causing some of the smaller designers to worry that the firm may become overcommitted—though despite their concerns, they keep coming back for more.

"We have built a relationship over the years and now he speaks my language—couldn't be happier." "Even if we go to them with a crazy idea, they are pro-active to see if it works." "He asks all the right questons." "He is so attentive and will pick up the phone and call me to make sure nothing goes wrong." "All of my clients enjoy

having them at the job site because they exude confidence in their work and people feel comfortable with them." "Minor things are resolved without issue. I have never been disappointed." "Timing can be an issue, but they are always friendly and helpful." "Very knowledgeable, and they are good about taking the customer's lead even when asked to go back to the proverbial drawing board several times." "Excellent in every regard, even their installation guy is a gem. He rebuilt the support mechanism on the convertible day bed that was not even part of the Doreen job, and at no cost." "Boaz is terrific about understanding the design the customer seeks, even if they cannot quite define it themselves."

E. Polarolo & Sons

		4	**3**	**5**	**4.5**

213 East 120th Street, New York, NY 10035
(212) 255 - 6260

Retail and trade—Remarkable reupholstery work and furniture restoration

Clients tell us this high-end reupholsterer and furniture restorer is as much of "a gem" as the pieces it restores. E. Polarolo & Sons opened its doors during the roaring twenties. Today third-generation Richard Polarolo comes highly praised by clients for his "attention to detail and excellent service orientation." Clients say Richard learned well from his dad, of whom they still speak fondly.

Polarolo not only specializes in the restoration and reupholstery of antique pieces but performs all variants of reupholstery work. Clients include some of the most notable antiques collectors. Mr. Polarolo accommodates both the trade and retail customers and will try to help anyone out with a quote over the phone. Pickup and delivery services are available for those who choose not to brave Polarolo's shop.

"Reupholstery master." "Richard worked on my American Gothic secretary and brought it back to its original splendor." "Would never consider going to anyone else. Meticulous craftsman in the old tradition." "Prices are so reasonable for the skill he puts into each piece." "Mr. Polarolo is a pleasure to deal with. He knows antiques and takes no short cuts—unlike many other upholsterers." "Amazing at matching fabrics." "Richard's an artist—the best restorer in town."

Fine Upholstery by Pizzillo

		5	**4.5**	**4.5**	**5**

515 West 29th Street, 3rd Floor, New York, NY 10001
(212) 889 - 7070   pizzillostyle@aol.com

Trade only—High-end custom upholstery

This family-run business has been wowing New York clients for three generations with its top-of-the-line upholstery work, characterized by hand stitching, hand-tied springs, and hair construction. Frequently partnered with the absolute best decorators in town, Pizzillo also impresses customers with its "singular focus on customer satisfaction" and the outstanding quality of the custom pieces it creates. Many sources mention their amazement at the speed at which this firm will come to the house and immediately resolve any outstanding issues.

Principal Madeline Mione is now running the company her father built and grandfather started in 1939. Trade experts say the firm is still pleasing customers today with its superior finishes, remarking that "Pizzillo is so easy to work with because they are such artisans." Though most of its work is done with the trade, Pizzillo will take on larger retail projects. Prices are known to be big, but all are willing to pay the tariff for the chance to own a Pizzillo piece.

"Upholstery genius." "They understand a designer's concept like no one else." "All I can say is they do high-end upholstery, and you will want to work with them." "Used by the highest-quality decorators." "Expect to pay top dollar for work this good." "They are wonderful, absolute TOP-quality work." "Deliveries are strong." "Of unequalled quality."

French Needle   4.5   4.5   4   4.5

152 West 25th Street, 4th Floor, New York, NY 10001
(212) 647 - 0848

Trade only—Top-tier custom curtains and wall upholstery

With an eye for detail that would make Gustave Eiffel blush, the French Needle serves a clan of elite decorators at its custom workroom. The firm is used primarily for curtains and wall upholstery by designers looking to elevate the overall quality of a room. Sources agree the firm is best at working with complicated designs, demonstrated in both elaborate, historic Louis XIV styles and cutting-edge contemporary.

"Fringe upon fringe, layer upon layer, they really know what they are doing." "Exquisite workmanship." "Only for the customer who appreciates the very best and can pay for it." "Highly recommend."

Guido De Angelis Inc.   5   5   4   5

312 East 95th Street, New York, NY 10128
(212) 348 - 8225

Trade only—High-end custom upholstery

Clients rhapsodize about the fabulous work of De Angelis while critics are left speechless by the even more fabulous prices. The craftsmen at De Angelis specialize in hand-done work, and clients say its pieces last forever. The service level also receives very high marks, as does the selection of fabrics and trim. Some note that this firm has an impressive showroom with hundreds of pieces to help in your selection, and that it will adjust anything. While several references suggest that comparable quality could be found elsewhere for less, many decorators think De Angelis is in a class by itself, ranking it among the top two in the city.

"Upholsterers on a much higher plane." "Bottom line: it's very prestigious to have a De Angelis sofa." "Truly extraordinary furniture at outrageous prices." "Nothing else will do for your top, top-of-the-line client." "If you have the money, do it." "Out-of-this-world quality with sky high prices." "The quality of service is amazing." "It takes forever and a day." "They can do it with no direction. Timing can be an issue though."

Henry Chan Upholstery Inc.   4.5   3.5   5   4.5

247 West 37th Street, 5th Floor, New York, NY 10018
(212) 689 - 1845

Trade only—Impressive custom upholstery

Henry Chan's stellar reputation among the city's elite designers is as much a guarded secret as the "reasonable price" he charges in comparison to his talented competition. Chan established the business in 1995 after lending his skills to other firms for many years. All work is custom and includes furniture upholstery, wall upholstery, and window treatments with clients describing Chan's work as "couture." The showroom includes over 100 pieces for clients to review, and we hear that Chan will create anything the client wants in any size and does so with an eye to real value. Customers also mention their appreciation of the highly skilled and reliable installers.

"Unheralded master." "He is the top upholsterer in New York." "I don't give out praises unless they are well deserved and Henry gets many from me." "Henry is highly talented and the details are amazing." "Never anything less than perfect." "Can copy whatever you want."

	Quality	Cost	Value	Recommend?
	➕	$	◆	★

Houston Upholstery Co. Inc.

Quality	Cost	Value	Recommend?
4	3.5	4.5	4.5

39 West 19th Street, Suite 4, New York, NY 10011
(212) 645 - 4032   pde47@aol.com

Trade only—Custom upholstered furniture

Houston never has a problem. This high-end family-run upholstery firm works exclusively with the trade, creating custom pieces for marqueed decorators and architects, many of whom have clients whose names really are on the marquee. Houston prefers to do larger jobs with new pieces and steers clear of restoration.

In business since 1947, owner Paul Deutch has the know-how to sew up a full range of upholstery assignments—from traditional to hard-edged contemporary—"with style and grace." Clients say Deutch is extremely loyal to his long-time customers who have been giving him work for almost 30 years. An excellent value at purchase, Houston's upholstery only becomes a better and better investment over its long lifespan.

"When you visit the shop everyone walks around with nails in their mouth." "Paul is eager to please, caters to his customers." "I have been working with Houston for over twenty years. In the beginning I didn't think Paul was as good as his father-in-law but today he is even better." "Creates a piece you can live with forever." "You don't find shops like this anymore, it's a dying breed." "The owner makes sure that you always leave happy and completely satisfied."

Innovative Touch in Design Inc.

Quality	Cost	Value	Recommend?
4	3	5	4.5

15 Liberty Street, Little Ferry, NJ 07643
(201) 931 - 0500   www.innovativetouch.com

Custom upholstery and window treatments

We hear this trade-only firm has the right touch, with everything running "as smooth as silk." Started by Alyne Schwartz in 1993, Innovative Touch provides custom upholstery, window treatments, soft goods, and custom furniture to a wide range of top quality decorators. Clients are very pleased with the quality and workmanship put into the projects, and report plenty of direct involvement at all stages.

Innovative Touch is truly innovative in its ability to offer a wide range of economic flexibility while still ensuring good-to-extraordinary quality with stellar service. Though the firm does not have a showroom, this fifteen-year-old business has a huge workroom. The staff and installers are reportedly extremely knowledgeable and take significant pride in their work.

"Alyne comes to a job with portfolio in hand, ready to do business." "Clients are always 100% satisfied." "One of their talented craftsmen, Frank, does absolutely lovely wall upholstery." "Responsible, creative staff—it is a pleasure working with the people at Innovative Touch in Design." "So good with fabrication, they are producing my high-end line of shower curtains." "The attention paid to every detail is incredible! Their workmanship is beautiful!" "Prices are up there, not cheap, but that's not a bad thing." "Alyne treats her employees with respect and they love her for that." "We have used their services for years and rely upon them for beautiful window treatments, bed covers, etc., as well as upholstered goods that continually make us look great!"

Interiors by Royale

Quality	Cost	Value	Recommend?
3	3.5	4	3

964 Third Avenue, Suite 2, New York, NY 10022
(212) 753 - 4600   www.interiorsbyroyale.com

Mostly trade—Custom upholstery, window treatments, and bedding

Housed in this firm's shop near the D&D building, clients have discovered a good selection of fabrics and a sometimes helpful staff. Interiors by Royale does upholstery work at its workshop on Long Island, and specializes in window treatments and bedding, all created custom to the client's specification. Many of the top designers drop by this shop for draperies.

Carl Romanowski opened the firm in 1963 and has eighteen on staff. We hear the product is of good quality but pricey with a typical turnaround of six weeks.

"Carl flies to Tokyo and all over the world for my clients." "We have a fifteen-year relationship with Interiors and can say they offer excellent service with the highest quality." "Carl has a great sense of humor." "I have another upholsterer who does the same work and is three times higher in price." "Carl comes with me to the client's home, and does all the measuring with a smile on his face." "Just did a big job and my clients are delighted."

Jonas Upholstery   5   5   4   4
44 West 18th Street, Suite 10, New York, NY 10011
(212) 691 - 2777
Trade only—High-end upholstery and curtains

Jonas Upholstery is unquestionably recognized as one of the very top upholstery workrooms in the city (many say the best), although the astronomical pricing seems to be affecting the appeal. While top decorators agree this high-end practitioner is definitely one of their favorites, more clients are balking at the cost and suggesting that their decorators go elsewhere. Additionally, several West Coast designers are finding that their own local workrooms have vastly improved requiring fewer calls back East.

Others continue to find the sophisticated approach, reliable timing, and phenomenal quality "worth any price," knowing that each piece is made with the highest-quality ingredients and crafted with superior care. Many decorators enjoy treating their clients to a visit to Jonas's workroom to see their pieces being made by friendly, informative craftsmen from exquisite raw material—"even the naked frames are beautiful."

"One of the top three upholsterers in the city." "Can work in different styles to each individual taste of a client." "The most comfortable piece of furniture I have ever sat in." "While we used to use Jonas all the time, now my clients demand lower-cost alternatives." "They say, 'A good upholsterer makes a good decorator.' I believe that." "I continue to come back because they inherently know what I want with little guidance." "We find them less flexible than others." "When I called a few years later for the reupholstery of my living room sofa, and it came back with the innards ripping the expensive fabric, they refused to deal with the situation." "Most of my clients cannot afford Jonas, and we only use them for the big public pieces." "If one does very high-end design and quality, this is the only place to go."

Joseph Biunno Ltd.
129 West 29th Street, New York, NY 10001
(212) 629 - 5630 www.antiquefurnitureusa.com
Furniture restoration and custom drapery hardware

See Joseph Biunno Ltd.'s full report under the heading Furniture Repair & Refinishing

K. Flam Associates Inc.   4.5   4   4.5   5
805 East 134th Street, Bronx, NY 10454
(718) 665 - 3140
Trade only—Exceptional contemporary custom upholstery

A staple (or tack in this case) in the cupboard of New York's most-celebrated interior designers with modern inclinations, K. Flam Associates sets the mark for contemporary custom upholstery and window treatments. Clients praise Kenny Flam for the attention he lavishes on customers and the job, and for his expertly

	Quality	Cost	Value	Recommend?
	✚	$	◆	★

tailored product. Flam has a staff of thirteen including a "terrific" installer. It's a sign of Flam's quality that after starting his own firm in 1964, he worked almost exclusively with John Saladino for over twenty years. Clients say Flam is as sweet as sugar and "once you start working with him, you'll be hooked."

"Takes the prize!" "They do what they say they will do and more." "Kenny and his wife Eileen make a great team." "Delivers the same quality as all of the best upholsterers, but with a modern story." "There's always lots of energy in the shop." "If you want quality, you have to pay for it." "He is the best in his field." "Incredible workmanship and top-of-the-line service. Would not use anyone else."

Langsam & Breuer Custom Upholsterers   4   3.5   5   4.5

13 Adams Lane, Spring Valley, NY 10977
(212) 362 - 8600   upholster@gmail.com
Retail—Custom upholstery

A primarily retail-based clientele delights in the professionalism exhibited by this firm. They recommend Langsam & Breuer for solid quality, reasonable prices, and on-time delivery of reupholstering and custom upholstery. The firm is reputedly organized and reliable. We hear company skipper Leon Breuer provides clients plenty of personal attention and is backed by a good crew—friendly, hardworking, and loyal. Clients tell us they have seen the same faces working at his shop "all these past years." While the firm does not discount for decorators, its upstanding service keeps them coming back.

"An expert choice for the retail client." "Leon seems to be on the go, constantly staying on top of all projects." "Leon Breuer is charming, honest, and flexible. He works with me directly, never through an assistant." "Very pleasant people to deal with—cooperative and dependable on all counts." "I have sent many friends to Langsam & Breuer and they are just as enthusiastic and pleased as I am." "A pleasure to work with." "The fact that we've gone to him three times attests to our confidence in Leon's work." "Leon Breuer has upholstered and reupholstered my entire brownstone. He has gone out of his way to deliver on time and made necessary alterations."

Le Decor Francais   4.5   3.5   5   4.5

1006 Lexington Avenue, New York, NY 10021
(212) 734 - 0032   www.ledecorfrancais.com
Retail and trade—Elegant custom upholstery, window treatments, and fabrics

The beauty and unusual quality of Jacqueline Coumans' Continentally styled work has clients cooing, "ooh-la-la." Since 1989 this high-end custom upholsterer, with a workroom staff of nine trained in Paris, has been creating custom projects for retail clients and the trade at the same prices. Products include furniture, window treatments, pillows, and lampshades.

Le Decor Francais also offers its own collection, with a wide selection of uniquely Continental fabrics and trimmings. We are told Coumans has a good eye for color, and sometimes takes interior design projects. While she is known to shower clients with attention, turnaround can leave a pressed-for-time project a bit high and dry. Still, fans tell us Coumans' talent is beaucoup worth the wait with excellent prices (and rough estimates given over the phone).

"Fabulous, Jacqueline's curtains resemble ball gowns." "A collection of special fabrics you won't see at the D&D building." "Slow, but truly beautiful." "Oddly enough I know companies with simpler styles that charge the same if not more." "You can't imagine how incredible the linings are." "Always satisfied with her work—she is one of the best." "If you want spectacular draperies, this is the place to go."

Lore Upholstery Shop   3.5   2.5   4.5   4.5
2201 Third Avenue, New York, NY 10035
(212) 534 - 2170   www.lore.qpg.com

Retail and trade—Custom window treatments, upholstery, and restoration

"Competent, highly creative, and a joy to work with," clients will recommend Lore to anyone. This family business boasts over 40 years' experience providing custom window treatments, along with reupholstery, custom upholstery, and antique furniture restoration services. Lore's "extremely helpful and time-efficient" service and the "beautiful" finished product keeps the customer satisfied.

Service is a strength, with principal Florence Cangelosi dropping by a client's home to discuss fabrics, and coordinating pick-up and delivery of pieces in the time frame promised. Workers too are "friendly and on time." We hear Cangelosi and crew make a point of following up with clients. Lore does a substantial amount of its work with some of the top interior designers and architects in the city.

"Lore provided top-notch service from top to bottom, from the selling process to manufacturing to installation. I would not ordinarily respond to surveys such as this, but I would like anyone else looking for upholstery work or window treatments to have the benefit of my experience with Lore." "They kept to their word." "Lore is a very professional and dependable company. The quality of work is at a very high standard." "They even came to our apartment to pick up the fabric." "Florence was VERY helpful in helping me choose a fabric for my chairs. We went through many different swatches of colors, textures, and prints, and I think I now sit on the best!!!"

Luther Quintana Upholstery   4.5   4   4.5   5
151 West 26th Street, 4th Floor, New York, NY 10001
(212) 462 - 2033   www.lqupholstery.com

Trade only—Choice custom upholstery and draperies

Sources brag that Luther Quintana's performance in the highest-quality custom upholstery camp beats the best of the bunch for excellent service with less maintenance. Quintana, who launched his firm in 1987, trained in his homeland of Guatemala and comes highly recommended by top decorators, who also use him for wood carving and creating reproductions to match a client's existing pieces.

Located in a spacious industrial loft, Quintana Upholstery's showroom displays a huge array of choices. Clients are quite happy that Quintana is now doing curtains, too. The firm's professionalism, capacity to "do anything you want" and diligent follow through—not to mention Quintana's incredibly personable nature—have won him a loyal following.

"Luther is a prince of a guy." "We have a long-standing relationship and when I'm in a crunch for time, he always comes through." "Luther is open to new ideas, so he's great with different styles of furniture." "His work is definitely worth every penny." "Less expensive answer to De Angelis." "Can make any frame—as good as anyone else's." "Why go anywhere else?" "Their customer service is amazing—they will bring a piece downstairs to the street as I drive by if I am running late." "They strive to be inventive. Not doing the same old thing as everyone else."

Manhattan Shade & Glass Co. Inc.   4.5   4.5   4   4.5
1297 Third Avenue, New York, NY 10021
(212) 288 - 5616   sales@manhattanshade.com

Retail and trade—Window treatments

Extraordinary service is the mantra of Manhattan Glass & Shade, a firm that sees being the best at what they do as the only acceptable result. After a recent top-to-bottom reconfiguration of the now-computerized workflow system, clients happily report that the company has met its goal. Each step of the process including initial consultations, all appointments, estimates, drawings, notes, digital images, technical visits, sales orders, invoices, and shop orders—is now tracked and easily accessible by the sales associates. Follow-up with all clients has become the rule. E-mail has become an integral part of communication with the client and additional staff have been hired and trained to handle the workflow.

Manhattan is a third-generation family business that has been serving clients for over 75 years. Traditionally, the firm has sold, fabricated, installed, and serviced a wide variety of window treatments, glass, and mirror products. In 2000, they also began to fabricate custom furniture and to offer a full range of upholstery and drapery services. Their motorized window systems continue to be a source of pride, which are often outsourced to other drapery firms of the highest quality.

The firm is often used (sometimes exclusively) by Manhattan's most esteemed designers, and also by many retail clients in the neighborhood and beyond. While there are over 44 employees, the staff in the front office are reportedly helpful, courteous, and informed. Repeat customers have learned to rely on Manhattan Shade & Glass and to feel its results are well worth the cost.

"Excellent work, very efficient. If there is a problem they are honest and always fix it." "I have worked with Manhattan my entire career and my mother, who was also a designer, worked with them before me." "The prices may not be the lowest around, but they are worth it." "Generally, the staff is excellent." "Less room than other providers for a decorator markup, but clearly better client service." "Response time is not a strong point. They came two weeks ago and I still do not have a quote." "They volunteered to replace the blind cords for free when the cats chewed them off a week after they were installed." "They do the impossible and they do it well."

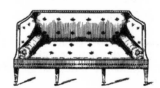

Martin Albert Interiors   3.5   3   4.5   3.5
9 East 19th Street, New York, NY 10003
(212) 673 - 8000   mail@martinalbert.com
Mostly trade—Custom upholstery and window treatments

Clients report Martin Albert Interiors transforms traditional furniture into contemporary elegance. Principal Martin Zeliger, an organized guy with a terrific staff, has been taking specs since he opened the company in 1980. Clients say Zeliger's not phoney about delivery dates and is known to get projects done quickly. Most of the firm's work is with the trade, primarily custom reupholstery and custom covered furniture, slipcovers, and both hard and soft window treatments. Several projects have been successfully completed at large New York hotels.

"Reupholstered a man-size heart-shaped back chair beautifully and in six days!" "We require quick turnarounds and we don't have a problem paying for this kind of service. Martin has never disappointed us." "We have worked with dozens, Martin Albert is one of two we only work with now." "Great at interpretation." "We depend on them quite often." "Best suited for kids' rooms." "We have had a few tricky projects so naturally it took longer than we expected." "Going to Martin Albert for over six years. They stand behind their work."

	Quality	Cost	Value	Recommend?
	+	$	◆	★

Mary Bright Inc.

4.5   4.5   4   4.5

636 Broadway, Suite 620, New York, NY 10012
(212) 677 - 1970 www.marybright.com

Retail and trade—Architectural custom window treatments

Mary Bright Inc. is said to be "the ultimate for exceptional contemporary lines with flair," according to many very high-end architects. Working with both retail clients and the trade, head designer Erik Bruce carries on Mary Bright's amazing legacy with all his creativity and innovative utilization of fabrics in the design and fabrication of draperies. Clients say Bruce is incredibly talented and an excellent collaborator whose creations are really "sculpture for the window." Bright Inc.'s superior service isn't forgotten in the final bill.

"Erik has a great eye." "Only firm that takes windows to art form." "Sleek, modern, and minimalist." "Bright Inc. are the only ones that do this kind of work." "Not your average window guy." "Amazing at fabrications." "Figured out a track system to support our installation." "Very high-end and equally expensive." "Contemporary designs. No swags. No chintz." "Works hard to achieve the client's wishes."

Penn & Fletcher Inc.

5   5   4   5

21-07 41st Avenue, 5th Floor, Long Island City, NY 11101
(212) 239 - 6868 www.pennandfletcher.com

Trade only—Embroidery artisans and designers

Penn & Fletcher stands in a league of its own. No one else even attempts to do what this firm accomplishes on a regular basis. Using patterns and techniques long forgotten by all except a few scholars of 18th century decorative arts, the company recreates and/or uniquely composes embroidery motifs too large and too complicated for others. Their scope is limited only by the imagination—and they stretch that too. The showroom includes an endless variety of house patterns (more cost effective), embroidery samples, picture albums, a research library, and thread stocks. Top-tier decorators say embroidery work "doesn't get better than this."

Since 1986, the firm's custom embroidery has been commissioned by many of New York's most elite decorators for drapery borders, valances, chair seats and backs, headboards, canopies and bed curtains, bed covers, table covers, sofas, wall coverings, fabric screens, and pillows. Once a concept is confirmed, the firm creates an estimate, a sketch, and a swatch for the designer's approval. Usually, a muslin pattern of the curtains or the upholstery fabric is required to custom fit the pattern to the shape. Close collaboration between all parties is necessary, and it can be time-consuming to create the ultimate result.

All of the work is done in Penn & Fletcher's Long Island City workroom, across from the Queensboro Bridge. Owner Ernie Smith, who is the designing inspiration, has legendary and contagious enthusiasm. The staff is equally professional. Projects can take anywhere from four to twelve weeks.

"I go in with an idea and scout their fabulous library of books. Meticulous results are what follows." "Ernie really makes each project so special. We try to use Penn & Fletcher whenever we can." "Once you have seen the work that can be produced, you are hooked." "They not only can be faithful to past but are very much on top of today's trends, pushing the edge of the design envelope." "While some of the projects can get beyond pricey, they are also good about scaling back to get a certain look for a contained cost." "They will not think about executing until the design is exactly perfect." "Could not be nicer or better at what they do."

	Quality	Cost	Value	Recommend?

Peter J. Rizzotto Co. Inc.   4.5   4   4.5   5
30 West 24th Street, 5th Floor, New York, NY 10011
(212) 645 - 1578 www.peterjrizzottoco.com

Trade only—High-end custom upholstery and window treatments

Decorators say that the old-fashioned craftsmanship that comes out of this shop is "hard to find anywhere else." Peter Rizzotto has been running his own shop since 1992 and is known for his handcrafted custom upholstered furniture and window treatments. Everything is created with incredible care, with no shortcuts taken along the way. The shop invites both designers and architects and their clients to visit each of its showrooms so that they may examine the process for themselves. Rizzotto takes pride in the fact that whether he does one room or an entire residence, furniture and draperies are always completed on time. We hear that though his work is "quite expensive," the quality makes it worth every penny.

"Rizzotto's custom furniture is superb." "Works like guys did in the old days—builds with the best materials." "Expect all the bells and whistles with this shop." "Makes our job so easy." "He's not very expensive but expensive." "Pete can interpret any style of furniture."

Phoenix Custom Furniture Ltd.   4   3.5   4.5   4
119 West 25th Street, 8th Floor, New York, NY 10001
(212) 727 - 2273

Trade only—Custom upholstery

We understand Phoenix did all of the upholstery work for the late Renny Saltzman, and many decorators of note value this firm for its reliable service and ability to do work "one-half step down" from the very best at quite reasonable prices. Designers who have worked with Jack Clarke's firm say that "no detail is ever overlooked."

The firm creates custom upholstered furniture for the trade in a variety of styles, providing samples from its showroom or using concepts from the client. Most find the company and its staff of fourteen very "skillful," "consistent," and "easy to work with." The frames it uses are all kiln-dried maple, doweled and corner-blocked. It offers two lines of products: one regular line and one very high-end that includes horsehair fill and other top features. All custom work takes about eight to ten weeks to complete.

"Jack is one of the nicest people I know." "I can go in with a sketch or choose from their selection of floor samples. Jack is great with suggestions—and has very good taste." "I used to use Jonas but find the personalized client service here much easier." "If you need something quick they will try to accommodate you." "Prices are a little above reasonable mark." "The fact that they have two levels of quality makes my life so easy—I can go here for everything." "They are calm and considerate in a world of hectic design."

Sandringham Ltd.   4.5   3.5   4.5   5
224 West 29th Street, 3th Floor, New York, NY 10001
(212) 594 - 9210 sandringham@nyct.net

Trade only—Custom upholstery and window treatments

We hear principal Erik Dahl's agreeable and professional manner complements his firm's flexibility, follow-up, and exceptional skill. Sandringham Ltd. opened its doors in 1996 and is described as a company that "always meets deadlines" and is "very dependable." The firm is a popular choice with many high-end designers for custom upholstery and window treatments. Insiders cite the workmanship as "outstanding" and the upholstery "of the highest quality." Due to Sandringham's popularity, the company can be quite busy juggling many different projects. Nevertheless, clients report that this shop is very conscientious and has exceptional customer service, possessing the ability to come through on short notice without sacrificing the quality of the work.

"Eye-catching quality." "The highest integrity and a pleasure to work with." "One step below super excellent." "Especially ready and willing to make the last-minute changes that clients inevitably request." "Deliveries quicker than most of the other upholsterers I work with." "Especially nice ceiling-height headboards." "Quality service from estimates to installation." "Window treatments are gorgeous." "Erik's just a dear. Nice ideas." "Very personable, helpful, and easy to work with." "Very competitive with excellent capacity to produce anything I sketch."

The Silk Trading Co.   3.5   3.5   4   4.5
888 Broadway, New York, NY 10003
(212) 966 - 5464   www.silktrading.com

Sophisticated, modern, and luxurious fabrics, drapery, and upholstery

"Affordable, accessible luxury" is how The Silk Trading Co. bills itself, and clients agree. Known by many as a purveyor of fine silk and textiles by the yard, the company has moved into custom upholstery, custom drapery, and a highly successful ready-to-wear drapery line called "Drapery Out-of-a-Box." The firm's signature style—luxurious, classically derived, and consistently well crafted—is reflected in these products. Of course, the key differentiating factor here is cost (much less since you do it yourself) and availability (immediate gratification). Clients include both homeowners and decorators looking for that perfect shade of silk dupioni.

Owners Andie and Warren Kay started Silk Trading in the early 1990s after international careers in opera singing and fashion, respectively. Coming from London to LA, they opened a 600 square foot shop in Santa Monica. Today, they boast 8,000 square feet on La Brea and five additional, substantially sized showrooms throughout the United States, including a very large showroom in the basement of ABC Carpet at the address above. The firm's reputation gains momentum every year due to its ever-widening array of quality products and, now, services. About 30 pieces are available for upholstery in the furniture line, which may be covered in either Silk Trading fabrics (done 80% of the time) or your own choice of materials (COM). Drapery and reupholstery services may be done only with the company's fabrics. Orders may take from four to ten weeks.

Prices vary, but approximate wholesale—a welcome concept for homeowners. There is also a relatively small but growing interior design service. For a modest $500 fee, a well-trained staff decorator will visit your home or help you choose among the resources of the entire ABC store at a 10% discount.

"Quality is excellent for the price—we use them for clients with lower budgets." "Fashionable, but not trendy." "Their silks are regularly used interchangeably with the best available in the D&D and are about 30% less expensive." "The sales staff in the basement of ABC could not be nicer and they really know the product line." "It was so easy—they came, they measured, they installed. No muss, no fuss." "The reupholstery service was very well managed. Once I chose one of their fabrics, they came the next day, took away my sofa, and it reappeared five weeks later looking brand-new."

Trade France   4   4   4   4.5
135 West 29th Street, Suite 1103, New York, NY 10001
(212) 758 - 8330   www.tradefranceusa.com

Retail and trade—Custom upholstery and window treatments

This firm earns compliments for its ability to stitch and summon exactly what a client envisions, at a level some top-end decorators say almost rivals the best quality in the city. Designers and homeowners alike turn to Trade France for curtains, upholstery, and reupholstery. Clients describe this firm as creative with a French flair, noting that it provides "unique and interesting frames" and a wide range of fabric choices.

With all work done on-site in midtown, Trade France has also been commended for its promptness in delivery, excellent follow-up, and highly skilled workroom, which we hear has an incredibly knowledgeable personnel and is able to provide the "ultimate in quality." Sources also add that working with Trade France could not have been easier, describing the firm's practice of home consultations and willingness to fax sketches back and forth with the client until it turns out "just right." "Not at all snobby" with retail customers, the firm happily educates non-professionals along the way.

"Depends on situation, but finished a job for me in three weeks." "They make house calls." "The highest quality and creativity makes for a perfect product." "Costly but not insane." "Developed relationship with workman. When I was desperate, they came through for me." "Ultimate pleasure at all times." "Very efficient people. Very helpful, creative, competent."

TriBeCa Upholstery & Draperies Inc. 3.5 3.5 4 4
103 Reade Street, New York, NY 10013
(212) 349 - 3010

Trade only—Custom upholstery, slipcovers, and window treatments

For those in the trade looking for a more intimate experience and a little better price, we hear look no further: all paths lead to TriBeCa. Owner Deborah Miller has been taking in work since 1989, and reputedly runs her business in the Old-World style, always showing up personally at installations. With a small work-room downtown, this tiny shop focuses on reupholstery work, as well as custom furniture, draperies, and pillows. We are told it is especially good with mid-20th century furniture. Clients say it's the little things TriBeCa does that set it apart, such as always asking a lot of questions to get it right.

"Stands behind everything she does." "Deborah's shop accomplishes good work for fair prices." "I like the fact Deborah goes to each project—very involved in all steps." "Has done everything from custom furniture to draperies, and my pieces all turn out better than expected." "Prices are good but not cheap." "Orders written out by hand—doesn't seem to be computer savvy." "Great and reliable."

Upholstery Unlimited 4.5 4 4.5 5
138 West 25th Street, New York, NY 10001
(212) 924 - 1230 www.upholsteryunlimitedinc.com

Retail and trade—Custom upholstery and curtains

The people at this shop are "very kind and nice" and their highly dependable approach to clients and superb product have garnered consistent compliments. A circle of the most discriminating decorators and showrooms in New York, in-cluding Brunschwig & Fils, rate the firm among the trade's best. Its large work-room provides an opportunity for clients to acquire a sense of the workmanship and style on which Upholstery Unlimited has built its reputation. Clients say that the work is quite expensive but well worth it.

"Not the cheapest, but the best." "Every issue is taken care of immediately." "Client service beyond great." "Fairly priced, but not cheap." "They saved our lives for a client's Christmas party. The eight-foot sofa could not fit in the door, so they cut it in pieces and reconstructed it on the spot." "My clients can absolutely see the quality, so they are happy to pay the price."

	Quality	Cost	Value	Recommend?
	✚	$	◆	★

Versailles Drapery & Upholstery

| | 4.5 | 4 | 4.5 | 4.5 |

37 East 18th Street, New York, NY 10003
(212) 533 - 2059

Trade only—Fine custom curtains and upholstery

Like fine wine, this posh firm seems to just get better with age. Versailles' all-hand-stitched work keeps it a major destination for many decorators, who praise this custom workroom for its "absolutely remarkable quality" in creating custom draperies and upholstery. Simon Fischer runs the company he and his brothers started back in 1962. An experienced and attentive staff of twelve deliver expert service and a top-notch foreman keeps the work rolling.

"Simon is so smart, he has it all figured out—knows everything about upholstery." "Their reupholstered antique furniture work is beautiful." "The shop has a nice steady work force—not a lot of turnover, which is a good sign." "Simon's a jewel, he will travel to my out-of-town clients." "When you walk into the shop it's full of good energy—lots happening." "I've been going to Versailles for over twenty years. If you're a regular client, and you need a piece right away, Simon will do his best to get it done."

White Workroom

| | 4.5 | 4 | 4.5 | 5 |

62 White Street, Suite 5, New York, NY 10013
(212) 941 - 5910

Retail and trade—Meticulous custom window treatments

Top-flight New York designers say it "doesn't get any better than this" when it comes to curtains, White Workroom's specialty. Insiders say owners Gary Weisner and Vivian White just "get it." Vivian "inherently understands the drape and flow of fabric," and Gary, an architect by training, "understands design and is incredibly meticulous." In business since 1980, the firm offers the ultimate in service and we hear its installer, Fred, is among the best in town. Even Connecticut and Westchester designers go the extra distance to use White for their most creative projects and all agree the expense is justified.

"Vivian and Gary are the dream team." "They are extraordinary." "It's such a pleasure to work with someone like Gary—his knowledge and great suggestions are so appreciated." "Expensive, but my clients are so happy to pay for a piece of White's work." "Vivian has a dressmaker's sensibility." "When we meet—its always a collaborative effort." "You think you can cut corners and expense by going somewhere else, but you are always wrong." "White creates works of art that the clients are pleased with forever. While a true capital investment, the annual depreciated value is a bargain."

Windows Walls & More

| | 4 | 3.5 | 4.5 | 4.5 |

1592 Second Avenue, New York, NY 10028
(212) 472 - 4800

Custom upholstery

Top designers describe Victoria Gorelik of Windows, Walls & More as "a goddess." Gorelik, who will go to great lengths for her clients, runs a "solid, helpful, reasonable, and reachable" firm. It's no wonder that the trade flocks to this small shop for upholstered walls, window seats, custom window treatments, and its reupholstery service.

Fans say owner Gorelik has a can-do attitude, asks all the right questions, and knows her business. The shop provides an abundant selection of fabrics, from basic to Ralph Lauren and some other "top" lines. Its work for luxury retail establishments and Manhattan high-end residential customers is considered to be of high-end quality without the super-high prices, and designers note the staff is as "sweet and friendly" as they come.

"Fantastic! I use them solely for all my curtains." "They can work around a whole construction team which is not the easiest thing to do." "I give her 75% of my work and I use her in my own home." "The word NO is seldom used in Victoria's vocabulary."

	Quality	Cost	Value	Recommend?
	+	$	◆	★

"Make sure you write everything out clearly so there's no misunderstanding with her workers." "She is not a nickel-and-dime person." "Installation goes off without a hitch." "I was recommended to them by a client of mine who has extremely high standards and I was blown away." "Gorelik drove three hours to fix someone else's mistake." "They return your call immediately." "The bottom line, they do beautiful work."

Zelaya Interiors   3.5   3   4.5   4.5

6220 Park Avenue, West New York, NJ 07093
(201) 868 - 3818   zel718@aol.com

Retail and trade—Custom upholstery, window treatments, and decorative hardware

Trade and retail clients say Zelaya Interiors delivers just the quality one expects of a high-end service professional. Ivan Zelaya started out in the trade 26 years ago in Honduras, opening his shop here in 1989. Today his firm specializes in custom upholstery and a full range of window treatments, including some custom work in a private line of shades and high-end wood and metal hardware. Sources say Zelaya, always quite busy, is "great if you are not in a rush." However, we hear that a real effort is made to come through on shorter time frames for long-standing customers. The incredibly honest Zelaya is known to return extra fabric to the client, and to produce a tasteful end result at a palatable price.

"Ivan is a breath of fresh air, opposite of other upholsterers I have worked with in the past." "Zelaya developed a hardware collection that is beautifully crafted." "Overall a very good experience." "Great upholstery." "I had been working with a less expensive guy who was a big headache; Ivan is a joy and worth every dime." "I needed to show my client a specific sofa and he threw one in the truck and brought it up to her apartment so she could test it out before making a decision." "His shop may be in New Jersey but he's always in town." "Sent me oodles of my fabric back!" "My designer wanted to charge me $7,000 more for the same job that Zelaya charged me." "Above average work. Great upholstery. Not cheap, not expensive."

Hiring a Window Washer

Everyone just adores a magnificent view, but without upkeep from a professional window cleaning firm, it's near-impossible to keep your windows crystal-clear in sooty New York. On the other hand, with regular cleanings, you can make sure that on a clear day, you can see forever.

Though window washing may seem like a straightforward project, it's not. Because city buildings come in a variety of shapes, sizes, and conditions, there are many variables for your service provider to deal with. You'll want to go over the particulars of your job by phone before anyone shows up to do the actual washing.

Do Your Homework

Before you contact any window washers, take stock of your windows. How many do you have? Are they storm windows, dormer windows, or French doors? Do you have window guards or grates? How many? Do the windows open in, slide up and down, or tip out? Are they old or new? Are they dirty enough that they'll need to be power-washed or scraped? If you live in a high-rise condo or loft building, are there hooks outside the windows to which the washer can connect himself and his equipment? If so, are they all secure? Taking these factors into consideration, the service provider should be able to give you a rough "guesstimate" over the phone. But beware: If you omit any information, the work may end up costing more than the original quote once someone arrives in person to give you a formal estimate.

It's customary for window washers to provide a free estimate, but you may want to confirm this on the phone with the service provider too. Once your windows are inspected, you should receive a written estimate. Getting the estimate in writing will help prevent unexpected charges later. For example, a service provider could claim that the job was more involved than expected, and try to charge a higher fee after the work is done.

What Should I Expect?

You'll want to ask the service provider a few questions before signing any contracts. Inquire about the length of time the company has been in business (the longer, the better), where most of its customers are located, and whether the firm can provide references. The references will help you get an idea of how reliable the provider is: how long it takes to schedule an appointment, if it gets the work done on time and thoroughly, and if its workers clean up after themselves. The window washers listed in this section don't vary enormously—you might have to wait longer for an appointment with one company than another, but all have received good reviews from customers.

Be sure that your service provider is fully insured and can show proof of workmen's compensation and liability insurance. If it does not have this coverage, you may be responsible for any accidents that happen on your property. There is no specific license or certification for window cleaning companies other than filing to operate as a business with the Department of Labor.

On Cost

There are three general methods of pricing: per window, per job, or per hour, with an estimate of the time necessary to complete the job. In addition, some companies have minimums and/or charge for estimates. The most common method of pricing is a basic rate per window, taking window size into account.

It is a good idea to inquire about a discount if you have a large job (20 or more windows). Many vendors will negotiate a better price if there is a substantial amount of work to be done. For a basic 6-over-6 window (a window that has two frames that slide up or down, each with six separate panes) with no window guards, paint, or unusual amounts of dirt, you can expect a price range from $7 to $15 per window, with the majority of vendors charging $8 to $10. However, factors like location, type of window (Do you have thermal panes, storm windows, etc.?), accessibility (Are the windows hard to reach? Do you have hooks or crevices for the window washer to secure himself to?), and amount of dirt should be considered and discussed, since these might affect the final estimate.

PREPARING FOR WINDOW-WASHING DAY

Once you have set up an appointment, clear a path to the windows to prevent mishaps. Move that antique table with the priceless lamp. Remove objects that may obstruct access to sills and benches. Draw back your curtains and window treatments. A service provider should show the utmost respect for your home and protect your carpets and walls from drips and spills. If it makes you more comfortable, schedule free time for yourself on window-washing day so you can keep an eye on the process.

CLEANING CALENDAR

A professional window cleaning twice a year is usually sufficient, but if your residence is especially exposed to the elements of city life, you may need more frequent cleanings. Spring and fall are generally the busiest times of the year for this industry: An early spring cleaning will remove any dirt and grime left by winter rains, snow, and frost, and a scrub in the fall will wash away spring and summer's pollen, bugs, and dirt. Be sure to call well in advance if you want your windows cleaned at peak times.

SOMETHING EXTRA

Window cleaners often offer a variety of other services, from cleaning screens and blinds to waxing and sanding floors. They might pressure-wash canopies, awnings, sidewalks, garages, and greenhouses—or do heavy-duty cleaning of gutters, carpets, upholstery, and appliances. Some also offer basic handyman services, house painting, and clean-up after renovations. If you are pleased with the company, consider using it for other household projects. Now that you can see through your windows again, you might notice all kinds of things.

TIPS FOR WASHING WINDOWS BETWEEN PROFESSIONAL SERVICE CALLS

✧ Never wash windows in the bright sunlight. They'll dry too fast and carry a streaky residue.

✧ Use a squeegee instead of paper towels.

✧ For best results, skip the store-bought spray cleaner and use a mixture of one cup white vinegar diluted with a gallon of warm water.

✧ Sponge the cleaning solution onto the window then drag the squeegee across the glass. Wipe the squeegee blade with a damp cloth after each swipe.

✧ For extra shine, rub window glass with a clean blackboard eraser after cleaning.

✧ If you absolutely don't do windows, share these tips with your housekeeper.

WINDOW WASHERS

AAA Window Cleaning   3   3   4   4
223 East 85th Street, New York, NY 10028
(212) 249 - 7186
Residential window cleaning

Talk about standing the test of time. This family business has been brightening New Yorkers' windows since its founding in 1930. AAA (whose sister company is Red Ball Window Cleaning) serves mainly residential clients and only works in Manhattan (below 111th Street on the East Side and 110th Street on the West Side). Pricing is per window, with factors such as size and location considered in the final estimate.

Known as a pleasant and professional outfit, this firm has served clients all over Manhattan for 71 years. Customers say they are extremely satisfied with AAA's work and continue to use the company year after year—and the moderate prices don't hurt, either.

"Personable, nice, and courteous." "Extremely professional people."

Apple Window Cleaning   3.5   3   4.5   4
121 West 25th Street, Suite 303, New York, NY 10001
(212) 620 - 0708
Commercial and residential window cleaning, post-construction cleanup

Apple Window Cleaning has been brightening views in the Big Apple since its establishment in 1983. Helmed by founder Mitch Bulaw, Apple Window serves residential and commercial clients throughout Manhattan and the surrounding boroughs. This twenty-man company also does post-construction cleanup, carpet cleaning, and floor waxing—and holds a rigger's license for scaffold and awning cleanups.

Prices start at $11 per window and the minimum charge is in the $55 to $65 range. From high-end residences in the city's exclusive neighborhoods, to hotels and high-rise office buildings, Apple's repeat customers rave about the superb service and the straightforward, reasonable prices.

"Responsive, professional, and neat." "No fuss. Gets the job done." "Personable staff and great follow-ups." "No hidden fees."

Belnord Window Cleaning Co.   4   3   4.5   4.5
322 Eighth Avenue, Suite 1401, New York, NY 10001
(212) 787 - 4969   cleaningny@yahoo.com
Commercial and residential window cleaning

"Solid" and "reliable" are two of the adjectives customers use to describe this window cleaner to the stars. Belnord has a loyal following of both residential and commercial clients in the Manhattan area, where the company conducts most of its business.

Established in 1948, the venerable firm is now helmed by owner Joseph Roitblat, who took over the reins in 1991. Aside from its high-end residential patrons, Belnord includes jeweller Harry Winston among its faithful commercial clientele, and has been cleaning away window-shoppers' prints on the store's plate glass for the past thirteen years. Roitblat and his 30-man team also do general clean-

	Quality	Cost	Value	Recommend?
	✚	$	◆	★

ing and post-construction cleanup. Pricing is per window, with prices starting at $8 per window, and minimums are in the $36 to $50 range. Sources appreciate the firm's moderate prices and efficient service.

"Sense of humor, yet professional." "Helpful and pleasant." "Finished on time and no hidden fees."

Careful Cleaning Contractors   3   3   4   4.5
153 Lincoln Avenue, Bronx, NY 10454
(718) 863 - 2727
Commercial and residential window cleaning; exterminating services

Since opening its doors in the 1930s, Careful Cleaning Contractors has been satisfying residential and commercial clients throughout Manhattan. Unlike other window washing companies where prices for windows vary according to size, location, or type, this firm charges one flat rate per window of any type or size ($10). In addition to window washing, the company also provides exterminating services.Clients appreciate this company's thorough work and professional attitude, and the fact that they can take care of two problems with one phone call.

"Polite and thorough." "Did a good job." "Hard to reach but will return phone calls." "Reasonable and prompt."

Clear View Window Cleaning Co.   4   3.5   4.5   4.5
450 East 81st Street, New York, NY 10028
(212) 737 - 2913
Residential window cleaning

True to its name, Clear View has been giving Manhattanites a better and cleaner view since opening its doors (and windows) in 1940. Mainly serving commercial and residential clients in the Yorkville and Upper East Side area, the firm's workmen will occassionally accommodate customers in other areas of New York City. The company, which was acquired by Frank's Window Cleaning in 1975, also provides floor waxing, carpet cleaning, and general cleaning services.

Insiders tell us they love this firm's reasonable and flat-rate pricing (one rate for any size or type of window) as well as its thorough, no-nonsense work. Customers also appreciate the company's diligent follow-ups and organized routine during jobs.

"Quiet. Low key. They do their work and leave." "Very professional. Someone always answers the phones." "Neat and punctual. They get the job done."

Crystal Globe Windows Inc.   4   3.5   4.5   4.5
3 West 46th Street, Suite 311, New York, NY 10036
(212) 533 - 6712
Commercial and residential window cleaning

Everyone loves a beautiful view, and Crystal Globe has been providing just that to its clients by giving them crystal clear windows since 1993. Owner Igor Tshem exclusively serves Manhattan residential and commercial clients, including high-rise buildings. Aside from window washing, Crystal Globe also cleans screens, blinds, and awnings, and restores glass.

Most of this licensed, bonded, and insured company's work is on the Upper East Side. Pricing is per window (starting at $10) and there is a moderate minimum required amount. Clients like the firm's reasonable prices and efficient and prompt service.

"Gets the job done with a small amount of fuss." "Reasonable prices." "Would recommend to friends."

Frank's Window Cleaning Co.   4   3.5   4.5   4.5

450 East 81st Street, New York, NY 10028
(212) 288 - 4631

Residential window cleaning

Talk about a family legacy. Frank's Window Cleaning was established by Frank Kulzer in 1929. After he passed away, his wife took over from 1961 to 1970 and the firm is now being helmed by their son, Richard.

Described as relaxed, but professional and knowledgeable, this family-owned firm has been winning over fans in Manhattan for decades. In 1975, Frank's acquired a sister company, Clear View Window Cleaning. While the team at Frank's mainly serves residential customers on the Upper East Side, its servicemen will occasionally work in other areas of the city as well (the West Side and some areas downtown). The firm provides bonus services like floor waxing, carpet shampooing, wall washing, upholstery cleaning, and post-construction cleanup. Clients say they love the quality of Frank's work and consider its prices to be fair.

"Quick, helpful, and very reasonable." "Once you hook up with these guys, you will never think again about using someone else." "Neat. Punctual."

Johnny's Window Cleaning Inc.   3   3   4   4

4459 Broadway, New York, NY 10040
(212) 942 - 0464

Residential window cleaning

With more than sixteen years of service, this Manhattan firm is known for its high-quality work. Although Johnny's serves mostly high-end residential clients, the company also has a number of commercial accounts, which keep the company under contract for months. While much of Johnny's work is on the Upper East Side, the firm does serve clients in other neighborhoods throughout the city. One index of the firm's reputation is the large number of prestigious buildings along Fifth Avenue that have relied on Johnny's work for more than a decade.

"Minimal fuss. In-and-out service." "Gets it done in a jiffy." "Quite satisfied with their service."

Prestige Window Cleaning Co.   4   4   4   4

408 Woolley Avenue, Staten Island, NY 10314
(212) 517 - 0873

Residential window cleaning

Prestige Window Cleaning has been a favorite among Manhattanites since 1987. Now under new management, this small firm is helmed by Paul Benalcazar, who does most of the work himself, sometimes with an assistant in tow.

This family business serves mostly residential clients, including those in highrises. Pricing starts at $8 per window with a minimum of $55. The company works only in Manhattan, a locale noted for its picky consumers, but still gets high marks from clients for being prompt, responsive, and thorough.

"Fantastic—tidy and quick." "A real people person." "Special. Cool." "Easy to work with." "Very fair and reasonable. Returned my call within hours."

	Quality	Cost	Value	Recommend?
	✚	$	◆	★

Shields Window Cleaning
31 Bedford Street, New York, NY 10014
(212) 929 - 5396

Quality	Cost	Value	Recommend?
3	3	4	4

Residential window cleaning

Shields Window shields its customers' windows from the dirt and dust that can block a beautiful city view. In business for more than fifteen years, the company serves mainly residential clients in Manhattan, as well as in the outer boroughs in New York. Generally considered to be reliable, prompt, and thorough, the company has built a strong following of loyal clients. Recently, some references have noticed a decline in the firm's efficiency and easygoing demeanor, but loyal customers report that they are still very pleased with Shields' work, and recommend it without reservation.

"High quality of work. I recommend them highly." "Efficient. Worked out issues well." "Used to be easygoing and pleasant." "Does the work quickly and without fuss." "Used them for years."

Steven Windows Co.
342 West 71st Street, New York, NY 10023
(212) 595 - 6620

Quality	Cost	Value	Recommend?
4.5	3.5	4.5	5

Commercial and residential window cleaning

This window cleaning company has accumulated some very devoted celebrity clients, including one who flies the principal out to Beverly Hills periodically to take care of his West Coast panes. We hear Steven Windows will cheerfully clean windows for all clients near and far, from Manhattan to Queens to New Jersey to the West Coast. Though the firm is available for service six days a week, insiders advise potential clients to call this busy company about two weeks in advance to set a date.

The firm is owned and run by Steven Trobish, a native of Ukraine, who did "top-secret" work in the Navy before retiring and becoming an expert window washer. Trobish established his business in 1993. Today his crew of three also installs and removes air-conditioners, repairs glassworks, does general housecleaning, and post-construction cleanup. Prices start at $10 per window, with a minimum amount ranging from $40 to $55.

Clients laud Trobish's professional and pleasant demeanor with more than a few exclaiming that his prices are "ridiculously cheap" when coupled with service that is "extremely thorough."

"Dependable, trustworthy, and hardworking." "Simply charming." "Very professional." "Good people." "Used him for several years. Would not consider using anyone else." "Really nice guy. Respectful of my home and furnishings." "Would trust him with my keys."

Window Cleaning Services
3224 Grand Concourse, Suite F22, Bronx, NY 10458
(917) 701 - 0306   thomcastro2@yahoo.com

Quality	Cost	Value	Recommend?
5	3.5	5	5

Residential and commercial window cleaning

Customers heap praise upon Window Cleaning Services and highly recommend its owner, Thom Castro, whose "wonderful smile and pleasant demeanor" have been winning over residential and commercial clients since 1981. Clients across the board agree that Castro is not only extremely professional, thorough, and efficient, but also polite, courteous, and pleasant. Castro is said to always arrive on time and work quickly with the greatest respect for the home's interior.

The firm works mostly in Manhattan, but also in some areas of the Bronx, Brooklyn, and will even travel to the Hamptons. Sources say clients with larger projects will find Window Cleaning Services a great value as the company tends to provide a substantial discount for volume. Pricing starts at $10 per window and (yes, it's true) the company has no minimum amount required to do a project. Due to Castro's rising popularity, we hear it's best to call two weeks in advance.

"The most reliable window cleaning service I have ever used. Clean, efficient, and most agreeable." "A real find!" "Thom's a professional—an excellent window cleaner and such a nice person!" "Flexible in adjusting to my schedule." "Very good at what he does." "He is so trustworthy, you can leave your keys with Thom and forget about it." "I didn't know my windows could get so clean." "A rare find in a world of mediocrity."

WK Window Cleaning Company   4.5   3   4.5   4.5
163 East 87th Street, New York, NY 10128
(212) 860 - 3454
Residential and commercial window cleaning

In business for more than sixteen years, this family firm serves many high-end residential and commercial clients around Manhattan. Sources say the company has built a solid reputation on careful and thorough work. References, many of whom have used WK for ten years or longer, report that the service is excellent.

Prices start at $7 per window, with a minimum amount of $40 per project, and we're told that WK Window Cleaning is willing to negotiate rates for clients with large numbers of windows.

"Nice guys." "Very helpful. They want to do a good job." "Excellent service." "Love the personalized service from this family business." "Hard to reach but will always return phone calls."

Yorkville Window Cleaning/
M&E Window Cleaning   4.5   3.5   4.5   5
163 East 89th Street, New York, NY 10128
(212) 534 - 3551   york2468@aol.com
Commercial and residential window cleaning

Small, medium, or large—French, regular, or storm—Yorkville cleans all types of windows. Described as friendly, helpful, and attentive, sources say this firm has brightened windows in Manhattan since its establishment in 1975 by Mel Landsman. Now managed by Landsman's son, Darren, Yorkville specializes in store fronts (The Gap, Banana Republic, Nine West, Van Cleave and Arpels, Warner Brothers, and Swatch) and handles some residential jobs.

We hear that many of New York's finest buildings have established ongoing maintenance contracts with Yorkville. Prices start at $8 per window with minimums per project ranging from $25 to $35. Aside from window washing, this company also provides janitorial services, power washing, awning cleaning, painting, sign cleaning, and metal cleaning.

"Great work ethic. Timely." "Personable. Reliable." "I wouldn't trust our windows to anyone else." "Our windows look like new!"

Hiring a Window & Door Service Provider

A brisk autumn breeze can be a wonderful thing, as long as it's not blowing through your living room. Are your doors and windows to blame? Perhaps everything is nice and toasty, but noise is still getting through—do you crave a quiet room where you can close a door and leave the world behind? Or do you simply wish that the appearance of your windows matched the great views they hold? Whether you're looking for better insulation, soundproofing, or a new style, there are some things you'll need to know before you call a service provider.

A Matter of Form and Function

Oddly enough, purchasing windows and doors can be similar to purchasing a car. Once you've selected a style (which should match the architectural style of the house), the next step is to decide what amenities to include in the package.

If you'd like to limit the sound of your child's piano practice to one room, or if you feel cold air coming through your windows even with the heater on, you're likely looking for special doors or windows equipped with soundproofing and extra insulation. There are numerous grades of soundproofing (usually measured in percentages), and the cost, naturally, depends upon the extent of silence you'd like. The complexity of the installation can also factor in: putting in a floor-to-ceiling window on the fortieth floor is going to be more expensive than a standard job. Keep in mind that as with cars, the more amenities and specifications, the higher the cost. Most vendors will charge a fixed fee for the window or door, with the greatest cost variables being the installation and amenities.

Is Money Flying Out Your Windows?

Windows and doors, on average, are responsible for approximately 30 to 40% of your heating and air-conditioning bill, so a good product properly installed can make a big difference. However, keep in mind that there's another 60 to 70% to consider. If your energy bill resembles the national debt, make sure you know where the money is going before you splurge on new windows and doors. Heat could be escaping through poorly insulated walls, through a faulty roof, or even the floor. Overuse of appliances also plays a part. Bottom line—before you talk to a service provider, think hard about your energy use. Even a simple spot check can help: try holding a lit candle (carefully) up to the edges of your windows and doors. If the flame bends or wavers, a breeze could well be sneaking into your home.

Door Insulation Basics

Insulating an outside entrance door is relatively simple. Before holding your current door responsible for the unwanted breeze, make sure that the problem is not concentrated in the weatherstripping, doorframe, or threshold. Nature's elements may be sneaking in around the door, not through it. If everything is secure, you may want to purchase a heavy mass door or a door that has insulation built into its core.

When looking for a quality door, keep in mind that there is no significant difference between a seven-ply and a five-ply door. There are either two or three layers of ply on each side of a door, with the outermost ply being the veneer and the innermost ply being the core. When all is said and done, the total thickness of ply is the same for seven- or five-ply doors. The most important distinguishing factors in a door are the quality of ply used and the framing and joining.

If you're looking for internal doors to connect one room to another, your major concerns will be style and soundproofing. Depending on your needs and preferences, there are many interior doors to choose from—pocket doors, louvered doors, French doors, etc. The complexity of the installation and whether you choose a custom-designed door or a manufactured door will determine the price. Be strategic about interior doors. Think about the rooms that will be noisiest, or, conversely, the rooms that you'd like to be the quietest. Spend the money where it counts.

WINDOW INSULATION BASICS

If your back alley is getting more heat than your bedroom, you might need better insulation and a better window. First, get a window contractor to determine the extent of the problem: sometimes one line of caulk will do the trick. If you truly do need new windows, one simple method for better insulation is to replace single-pane with double-pane windows. The dead-air space between the panes provides additional insulation. To maximize the use of dead-air space, you can choose to inject it with either argon or krypton—both gases are denser than air, with krypton being denser and more expensive. Argon is the more economical and popular choice for this type of insulation. Some firms in New York also will install triple-pane windows, which offer another layer of protection. "Interior windows" (see below) have a similar function.

The best way to compare windows is to check for a rating from The National Fen-estration Rating Council (NFRC). Most major brands of windows have a sticker onthem that lists their NFRC rating—the lower the number, the better the insulation.

GLARE AND UV PROTECTION

All New Yorkers know that summer in the city is an excruciating battle with heat and humidity, so protecting your home's interior from too much sun (and ultraviolet rays) is another factor to consider when purchasing windows. To keep out the ultraviolet rays, Low-E (low-emittance) glass is essential. Low-E glass is coated with a clear material that blocks ultraviolet rays. Thus, Low-E glass improves the thermal efficiency of a window, cuts glare, and helps prevent damage that ultraviolet rays might cause to furnishings. Also, a window with good Low-E can help lower your energy bill since it reflects sunlight in the summer and absorbs it in the winter. If you need UV protection but don't want to replace the whole window, some companies manufacture and install transparent films that are cut to fit your windows. These films are often as efficient as Low-E coating, and can also prevent glass from shattering.

REPAIRING AND REPLACING

If your antique door looks like a dog tried to dig an escape route through it or your landmark windows have seen better years, you'll need a specialized repair or reproduction job. Don't worry—the right professional is just a few pages away. Before calling a professional, however, you should know what type of window or door you're working with. Do you have operable or non-operable windows? Are they single hung (upper portion is fixed) or double hung (both portions open and close)? Is it a steel casement window (unit is hinged at the side, opening vertically) or a landmark building window with its own special configuration? Is it a steel door or a wood door? If a screen door, is it retractable or not? It is also important to note the architectural type of the house so that the windows and doors will match. All of these factors will affect the cost, so be sure to get an estimate for the cost of the window or door, as well as for the installation and labor.

Once you've updated, renovated, or added the ultimate window and door treatments for your home, you'll enjoy rooms that are cozier in the winter and brighter in the summer. Windows are your portals to the sights of New York, and the professionals in this guide are ready and able to keep the sights in view while keeping the weather and noise at bay.

NOISY NEIGHBOR?
SOME WINDOW AND DOOR SOUNDPROOFING METHODS

✧ **Interior Windows**—Made to fit inside the frames of your existing windows, these create a large airspace between the two windows and dramatically   reduce noise from the outside. Since interior windows don't require new construction, they don't require a permit either.

✧ **Window Plugs**—Removable sections of matting material or matting-over-board that can be placed snugly over a window to cut noise and light—put them up at night and take them down in the morning. For large windows, plugs can be custom made with handles for easy insert and removal.

✧ **Acoustical Curtains**—Usually made of polyester with a heavy plastic lining, these curtains are installed on two sets of rods to create a dead air-space between the first set of curtains and the second, which blocks sound. Weighing in at about eighteen pounds a panel, these heavy curtains require sturdy rods and expert installation.

✧ **Acoustical Doors**—To lessen the noise inside your home, consider replacing ordinary, hollow doors with acoustical doors that reduce escaping noise by about 50 percent. These doors are made of soundproofing layers and special sealing components.

WINDOWS & DOORS

🧰 FIRMS WITH ONLINE PORTFOLIOS* 🧰

Panorama Windows   4.5   3.5   5   5
767 East 132nd Street, Bronx, NY 10454
(718) 292 - 9882 www.panoramawindows.com

Installation and repair of steel, wooden, aluminum, and fiberglass casement windows; landmark work

President Peter Folsom entered the business as a dissatisfied customer during his own home renovation, determined to bring high quality and service to an underserved market. And indeed, Panorama is known for its customer service. Folsom's outfit sells, installs, and repairs aluminum, wood, and steel windows, as well as restoring windows and doors in many of Manhattan's landmark buildings. Folsom's personally developed fiberglass case windows allow for replacing historic steel casements. This improves insulation and provides weatherproofing without compromising landmark standards.

Clients compliment Panorama's crew for being neat, tidy, and efficient. Folsom and his partner, Doug Simpson, reportedly return calls promptly. They work only in Manhattan in order to assure quality installation and follow-up services to all clients. (In 2002, the company acquired another company, Panorama Windows Service Corp.) The quality of Panorama's work is undisputed among architects, decorators, elite residential superintendents, and homeowners.

"One of the most pleasant experiences in New York. Doug is a perfect gentleman and a nice and smart guy." "Doug Simpson is the best in the business. So neat you don't even know that they were there, except that you have a new window—like Santa's elves." "Peter was amazingly nice and generous with his time and knowledge."

FIRMS WITHOUT ONLINE PORTFOLIOS

CitiQuiet   4   4   4   5
11-11 43rd Road, Long Island City, NY 11101
(212) 874 - 5362 www.citiquiet.com

Custom interior noise reduction windows

CitiQuiet indeed. Specializing in custom interior windows, CitiQuiet offers almost 100% noise elimination—satisfaction guaranteed. This 21-person firm's custom-manufactured and custom-installed windows fit inside original windows, meaning no construction or permits are required. Besides noise reduction, CitiQuiet windows eliminate most drafts and dirt, according to clients. Customers can barely contain their enthusiasm for CitiQuiet—like the Upper West Side resident who raves that his apartment is now "silent as a tomb." The company will take on both one-window jobs and massive undertakings, like outfitting the Mercer Hotel or the Supreme Court in Washington D.C. Sources describe the installation process as efficient and praise the full customer service.

"I don't hear a thing." "Not cheap, but absolutely worth it." "Great service, and a lot of options, so you don't have to spend more than you need to." "A growing business,

*We invite you to visit www.franklinreport.com to view images of their work.

535

with new clients every day." "I totally and utterly would recommend CitiQuiet. It was done beautifully." "They came with the highest recommendations. No one else came close."

Cityproof Corporation   4.5   4   4.5   5

10-11 43rd Avenue, Long Island City, NY 11101
(718) 786 - 1600   www.cityproof.com
Custom interior windows for soundproofing and thermal control

We hear bountiful praise for Cityproof's custom interior window systems, which provide soundproofing, energy conservation, and protection against drafts and dust, as well as thermal insulation. Cityproof has been operating since 1960, and there are plenty of clients who have enjoyed their Cityproof windows for twenty years without a single problem. Rather than replacing or modifying existing windows, Cityproof customizes interior windows to fit inside the original exterior window, preserving its original appearance and minimizing complications with landmark regulations. We're told the firm's technicians are extremely professional, neat, and polite, earning praise from buidling managers for their quick, no-fuss, no-damage installations. Cityproof has been featured in *New York* magazine and *The New York Times*, and is used by the Peninsula and Regency Hotels, as well as several hospitals.

"The windows did the job they were promised to do." "The workmen were very polite, and they were always on time." "What sets them apart is their overall quality and professionalism. There was no abuse to the building, and no complaints from the tenants. I would absolutely recommend them." "Their product is good and their installations are always on time. There's nothing more you can ask for." "The crew left our apartment cleaner than when they started."

East End Woodstrippers Inc.

27 Glenmere Way, Holbrook, NY 11741
(631) 472 - 5206   www.refinishny.com
Woodwork refinishing and restoration; historical restoration specialists

See East End Woodstrippers Inc.'s full report under the heading Millwork & Cabinetry

Ekcer Window & Home Improvement   3.5   3.5   4   4

305 Madison Avenue, 11th Floor, New York, NY 10165
(212) 472 - 4666
Window sales and installation

Ekcer has been selling and installing windows for New Yorkers for almost 50 years. This fourteen-person, family-run business offers windows in all price ranges and styles, including double-hung, triple-layered, soundproofed, and arched. Ekcer been known to order rarer windows from Canada and Europe. In addition to its residential work on the Upper East and Upper West Sides of Manhattan, we hear the firm is qualified for landmark work. It prides itself on having no minimum charge and taking on one-window jobs (though you might have to wait until there's a break between bigger projects). Ekcer also does some general contracting work, which, clients say, can come in handy when dealing with more complicated window issues.

"A small company that works hard to compete with the bigger guys." "They have an answering service, so you don't have to leave a ton of machine messages." "The windows are great, but the communication can be stressful." "The owner is very talkative and informal, you get the feeling he really likes his work."

Englander Millwork   4   3.5   4.5   4.5
2369 Lorrilard Place, Bronx, NY 10458
(718) 364 - 4240

Windows and doors, millwork, historic replication

Clients say they've had a jolly good time with Englander Millwork. Principal Jay Winston runs the company that his grandfather started in the 1920s. Specializing in custom doors, windows, and moldings, Englander also excels in replication and installation, sources say. Offering mortise and tenon construction, soundproofing, glass and paneled wood doors, solid oak, and the restoration of antique doors and old glass, Englander has a reputation for effectively executing curvework and other tricky millwork.

Winston typically works for contractors as well as for commercial and institutional clients, such as Columbia University, but some private clients name him as the only man capable of doing their work. References describe Winston as a "kind and supportive man" and his staff of six as a "team of reliable craftsmen."

"A workshop of talented, committed artisans." "They have pulled me through some tight deadlines." "Others had looked at the cracked wood, threw up their hands and said it was not possible to repair—that I should replace the pre-war door with something from Home Depot. Not only did Jay repair the original door, I cannot even tell where the wood splintered."

Enjo Architectural Millwork   3.5   3.5   4   4.5
16 Park Avenue, Staten Island, NY 10302
(718) 447 - 5220   www.enjo.com

Architectural millwork; restoration of windows and doors to landmark standards

Founded in 1962, this large, third-generation family company specializes in custom door manufacturing for landmark buildings. Enjo also manufactures wood and glass partitions, wainscoting, wood storefronts, trimmed openings, and moldings for both commercial and residential properties. Recently, they added fireproofing to an already long list of options on new doors. We hear principals Joseph and John Autovino and their team of qualified professionals utilize a state-of-the-art facility to achieve extraordinary levels of detail. Sources report occasional difficulty in getting in touch with a principal, but no one doubts the quality of the product.

Heights Woodworking Co.
411 Third Avenue, Brooklyn, NY 11215
(718) 875 - 7497   www.heightswood.com

Custom interior millwork

See Heights Woodworking Co.'s full report under the heading Millwork & Cabinetry

Mr. Shower Door
651 Connecticut Avenue, Norwalk, CT 06854
(800) 633 - 3667   www.mrshowerdoor.com

Shower door manufacturing and installation

See Mr. Shower Door's full report under the heading Kitchen & Bath Design

	Quality	Cost	Value	Recommend?
	✚	$	◆	★

New York Window Film

| | 4 | 3 | 5 | 4.5 |

131 Florida Street, Farmingdale , NY 11735
(631) 420 - 4101 www.nywindowfilm.com

Glass coating and tinting

Established in 1990, New York Window Film offers over 70 varieties of window coatings to protect homes against everything from ultraviolet rays to hurled bricks. Most common in the city are the UV-blocking variety, which prevent furniture from fading while conserving energy, reducing glare, and increasing privacy. But the company also sells and installs decorative films (which can tint the color of light, or make transparent glass look papered), security films (which prevent glass from shattering), and storm protection films. Clients praise both the top-quality products and the peace of mind they gain from having from one of the largest liability insurances policies in the business.

With twelve full-time workers, the company serves all five boroughs of New York, most of Long Island, Westchester, and northern New Jersey. The firm can usually provide an estimate over the phone, and most projects are completed within a couple of days. New York Window Film boasts a long list of high-profile clients and jobs, including NBC Studio's "Today" show site, the Theodore Roosevelt National Historic Site, and Walt Whitman's Birthplace. Recent clients include the International Center for Photography, Goldman Sachs, the Asia Society, and SUNY Stonybrook. Clients praise the professional, friendly service.

"Fabulous service. Very professional." "They have one of the widest selections in the country." "They've got pretty much every kind of coating you'd need." "Did a great job, and my apartment is on the 44th floor." "An expert in a very specialized trade."

Panorama Window Service Corp.

| | 3.5 | 3 | 4 | 4.5 |

767 East 132nd Street, Bronx, NY 10454
(718) 993 - 0607 www.panoramawindows.com

Aluminum window replacement and repair; custom screens

The new "Mr. Fix-It" for aluminum windows, this firm (previously known as RE: Views) was recently acquired by its parent company, Panorama Windows Ltd. The company repairs, replaces and soundproofs aluminum windows. All work is done on-site by its own highly trained workmen.

Clients say the company is a pleasure to work with and we hear that the personalized service is a strength. Insiders say the firm is preferred by some of the top apartment buildings on the Upper East Side.

"Very reliable, helpful and nice." "Marvelous!" "Installing those screens was the best thing I've done to this apartment." "Polite, quick, efficient—and leaves no mess behind."

Seekircher Steel Window Repair Corp.

| | 4.5 | 4.5 | 4 | 5 |

423 Central Avenue, Peekskill, NY 10566
(914) 734 - 8004 www.traditional-building.com/brochure/seekir.htm

Historic window restoration and repair

John Seekircher, the "traveling chiropractor" of the historic window business, has restored antique frames in 36 states. Specializing in English Tudor, leaded windows, and steel casements, Seekircher uses his considerable stock of vintage window, door, and hardware materials to replace period pieces. He will clean rust, install new steel casements, and restore brass hardware to operable condition, all while maintaining the building's historic integrity. Since opening this family-owned (his son, brother, wife, and nephew are all involved) shop in 1977, Seekircher has seen his work grace some of New York's most prestigious residences and historic buildings, as well as landmarks across the country—most famously, Frank Lloyd Wright's Fallingwater. Clients praise Seekircher, saying he and his crew of six are amenable, reliable, and timely.

"The greatest recommendation is that we hired him back." "John was very easy to get in touch with, very responsive, conversant, friendly, easy-to-work with, and an all-around nice guy." "I would hire him for any historical work." "He treats windows like works of art." "He is very reliable, always finishes early, charges reasonably, and the crew works long hours to get the job done in a timely fashion."

Skyline Windows   4.5   4   4.5   4

625 West 130th Street, New York, NY 10027
(212) 491 - 3000 www.skylinewindows.com

Custom window manufacturing, installation, and service

Skyline Windows has been manufacturing, installing, and repairing high-end custom windows since 1921. A third-generation family-owned business, Skyline has established a reputation as a go-to firm for landmark buildings and luxury high-rises. Comparison shoppers report that Skyline stands out for doing the most research on building codes and architectural requirements.

The company's size (over 100 installers) means that it can take on one-window jobs easily. Many clients say Skyline is committed to customer service, which has earned them a high-profile clientele. However, some sources report that the large staff results in occasional instances of sloppy installation. Overall, though, customers speak of an improved quality of life due to their Skyline windows, and add that matching landmark specifications is not an issue.

"They're the best company I've ever used." "I cannot tell you how whole-heartedly I recommend Skyline Windows for the security, insulation, look and sound. I plan to use them again." "When I needed a window serviced, it was hard to get in touch with the right person." "Window installation in my high-rise was a big job, but Skyline was willing to go through with it 100%"

N

O

P

THE FRANKLIN REPORT.
The Insider's Guide to Home Services

FILL-IN REFERENCE REPORT FORM

Client Name:

Client E-mail: Client Phone:

Service Provider Company Name:

Company Contact: Company Phone:

Service (i.e. plumbing):

Company Address:

PLEASE RATE THE PROVIDER ON EACH OF THE FOLLOWING:

QUALITY OF WORK: ❏ Highest Imaginable   ❏ Outstanding   ❏ Strong
❏ Moderate   ❏ Adequate   ❏ Poor

COST: ❏ Over the Top   ❏ Expensive   ❏ Reasonable   ❏ Moderate
❏ Inexpensive   ❏ Bargain

VALUE: ❏ Extraordinary Value, Worth Every Penny   ❏ Good Value
❏ Mediocre Value   ❏ Poor Value   ❏ Horrible Value   ❏ Unconscionable

RECOMMENDATION: ❏ My First and Only Choice   ❏ On My Short List, Would Recommend to a Friend   ❏ Very Satisfied, Might Hire Again   ❏ Have Reservations
❏ Not Pleased, Would Not Hire Again   ❏ Will Never Talk to Again

COMMENTS:

THE FRANKLIN REPORT.
The Insider's Guide to Home Services

INSTRUCTIONS: To contribute to a service provider's review, fill out the form below and **fax** it back to us at **212-744-3546** or mail to 201 East 69th Street, Suite 14J, New York, NY 10021. Or you may complete a reference on our website, www.franklinreport.com. Please make sure that you give us a contact e-mail address and a phone number. While all information will remain anonymous, our editorial staff may need to reach you to confirm the information.

Thank you.

FILL-IN REFERENCE REPORT FORM

Client Name: _____

Client E-mail: _____ Client Phone: _____

Service Provider Company Name: _____

Company Contact: _____ Company Phone: _____

Service (i.e. plumbing): _____

Company Address: _____

PLEASE RATE THE PROVIDER ON EACH OF THE FOLLOWING:

QUALITY OF WORK: ❏ Highest Imaginable ❏ Outstanding ❏ Strong ❏ Moderate ❏ Adequate ❏ Poor

COST: ❏ Over the Top ❏ Expensive ❏ Reasonable ❏ Moderate ❏ Inexpensive ❏ Bargain

VALUE: ❏ Extraordinary Value, Worth Every Penny ❏ Good Value ❏ Mediocre Value ❏ Poor Value ❏ Horrible Value ❏ Unconscionable

RECOMMENDATION: ❏ My First and Only Choice ❏ On My Short List, Would Recommend to a Friend ❏ Very Satisfied, Might Hire Again ❏ Have Reservations ❏ Not Pleased, Would Not Hire Again ❏ Will Never Talk to Again

COMMENTS: _____
_____
_____
_____
_____
_____
_____
_____

www.franklinreport.com   1-866-990-9100